# THE DEVELOPMENT OF A PREHISTORIC REGIONAL CENTER IN LOWLAND SUSIANA, SOUTHWESTERN IRAN

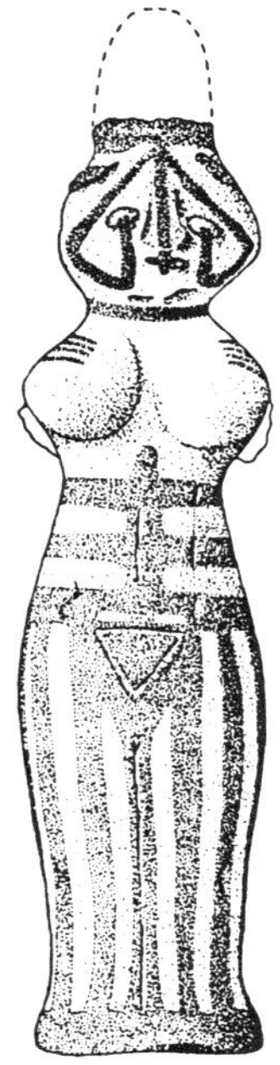

Possible Reconstruction of Female Figurine Composed from Several Fragments: *Chogha Mish* I, pl. 236:A; herein pls. 27:A, 28:A, C

# CHOGHA MISH II

## THE DEVELOPMENT OF A PREHISTORIC REGIONAL CENTER IN LOWLAND SUSIANA, SOUTHWESTERN IRAN

### FINAL REPORT ON THE LAST SIX SEASONS OF EXCAVATIONS, 1972–1978

ABBAS ALIZADEH

THE ORIENTAL INSTITUTE OF THE UNIVERSITY OF CHICAGO
ORIENTAL INSTITUTE PUBLICATIONS • VOLUME 130
CHICAGO • ILLINOIS

Library of Congress Control Number: 95072170
ISBN-10: 1-885923-52-X
ISBN-13: 978-1-885923-52-3
ISSN: 0069-3367


Published 2008. Printed in the United States of America.

*The Oriental Institute, Chicago*

Oriental Institute Publications

Volume 130

*Series Editors*

Leslie Schramer

*and*

Thomas G. Urban

*Series Editors' Acknowledgments*

The assistance of Lindsay DeCarlo and Katie L. Johnson is acknowledged in the production of this volume.

*Spine Illustration*

Reconstruction of decoration on Middle Susiana pottery vessel. Figure 42:F (B 1074)

*Title Page Illustration*

Sealing. *Chogha Mish* I: plate 155:A.

*Printed by Edwards Brothers, Ann Arbor, Michigan*

The paper used in this publication meets the minimum requirements of American National Standard for Information Services — Permanence of Paper for Printed Library Materials, ANSI Z39.48-1984.

∞

This book is dedicated to the settled **Zalaghi Tribe** of the **Bakhtiyari**, for their unwavering hospitality and their contribution in the eleven seasons of excavations in Khuzestan

این کتاب به طایفه‌ی زَلَقی از بختیاری در خوزستان تقدیم می‌شود.

# TABLE OF CONTENTS

# LIST OF ABBREVIATIONS

| | |
|---|---|
| Ach. | Achaemenid |
| AMS | accelerator mass spectrometry |
| AS | Archaic Susiana |
| B | Chogha Bonut, seasons 1976/77, 1977/78 |
| BF | Boneh Fazl Ali |
| B.P. | before present |
| BRB(s) | beveled-rim bowl(s) |
| B.S. | below surface (measured in meters unless otherwise noted) |
| ca. | circa |
| cf. | *confer*, compare |
| Ch.M. | Chogha Mish |
| *Chogha Mish* I | *Chogha Mish*, Volume I: *The First Five Seasons of Excavations, 1961–1971*. By Pinhas Delougaz and Helene J. Kantor. Edited by Abbas Alizadeh. Oriental Institute Publications 101. Chicago: The Oriental Institute, 1996. |
| cm | centimeter(s) |
| E | east |
| e.g. | *exempli gratia*, for example |
| EMS | early Middle Susiana |
| ES | Early Susiana |
| et al. | *et alii*, and others |
| etc. | *et cetera*, and so forth |
| fig(s). | figure(s) |
| f(f). | *fecerunt*, and following |
| ha | hectare(s) |
| ICHTO | Iranian Cultural Heritage and Tourism Organization |
| i.e. | *id est*, that is |
| INAA | instrumental neutron activation analysis |
| km | kilometer(s) |
| KS | Khuzestan Site |
| LMS | late Middle Susiana |
| LS | Late Susiana |
| M | middle |
| m | meter(s) |
| misc. | miscellaneous |
| mm | millimeter(s) |
| MS | Middle Susiana |
| N | north |
| N/A | not available |
| N.B. | *nota bene*, note carefully |
| no(s). | number(s) |
| NSF | National Science Foundation |
| PCA | Principle Components Analysis |
| PL | Protoliterate |
| pl(s). | plate(s) |
| p(p). | page(s) |
| ppm | parts per million |
| prob. | probably |
| reg. | registration |
| S | south |
| Sdg. | sounding |
| sq. | square |
| st. | stone |
| Tr. | trench |
| trans. | transitional |
| UTM | Universal Transverse Mercator |
| W | west |

# LIST OF FIGURES

# LIST OF PLATES

# LIST OF TABLES

# PREFACE

The present publication is the second and final volume on the eleven seasons of excavations at Chogha Mish, in lowland Susiana, Iran. Excavations at the site were co-directed by Helene J. Kantor and Pinhas Delougaz from 1961 to 1975, the year Delougaz died. Helene Kantor directed the expedition for three more seasons from 1976 to 1978. Although both scholars worked for years to prepare the results of the first five seasons of excavations, they died before they could bring the results of their immense work to fruition. Based on the available evidence and on Kantor's and Delougaz's copious notes, the results of the first five seasons were published in 1996. In preparing the manuscript for that volume, I had greatly benefited from working for many years with Helene Kantor.

As is common with publications of this nature, there are inevitably gaps in the available date — information that only the original excavators could have possessed. In the course of preparing the results of the remaining six seasons of excavations, I realized that this problem is aggravated by the fact that several field notebooks, and even registration books of the objects found in the tenth through eleventh seasons, were destroyed along with the dig house nearly two decades ago. Although I have been able to present a number of objects from the last two seasons, notebooks on two trenches with Archaic and Middle Susiana occupation were not available and are perhaps lost forever. In addition, all the section drawings from the sixth through the eleventh seasons were lost in the dig house at the village of Qaleh Khalil, near Chogha Mish. The only one available in Chicago belongs to the Gully Cut, which, unfortunately, lacks the necessary stratigraphic data to link it to the top plans of the area.

A major problem that I could not solve with the available data relates to the assignment of the Protoliterate pottery types to the two major architectural phases of this period. Based on the pottery types found at the site, Chogha Mish seems to have been re-occupied in the second half of the fourth millennium B.C. It is nevertheless possible that the site was re-occupied even earlier, ca. 3600 B.C.; but in the absence of the necessary statistics for the various stratified ceramic types I am prevented us from establishing a more percise chronological position for the initial phase of the re-occupation of Chogha Mish.

In addition to the problems just cited, the reader will notice that analyses of the fauna and chipped stone objects are also absent from this volume. As explained in the first volume, James Phillips analyzed the flints and was to write a chapter on his results. That chapter was never produced and the lithic collection has since been lost. Furthermore, the available records do not allow for quantitative information regarding the finds and their spatial distribution in various contexts. The interpretion of the information gathered from all the available fauna and flora (from the eleven seasons of excavation) is limited to what was published in the first volume. This information has been culled from the first volume and used in the body of the text in *Chapter 1*.

During the first five seasons, Jane Wheeler Pires-Ferreira was the resident zooarchaeologist at Chogha Mish. Mrs. Wheeler Pires-Ferreira worked on the specimens both in the field and in Chicago. She then transferred her immense body of data onto computer punch cards. These cards included Mrs. Wheeler Pires-Ferreira's analysis and identification of some 40,000 bones representing various species with stratigraphic information. Under the supervision of Helene Kantor and occasionally Mrs. Wheeler Pires-Ferreira, Mr. James Lichtenstein, now the Director of Production Technology at the University of Chicago Networking Services and Information Technologies (NSIT), converted the data into a readable English database. On behalf of Helene Kantor, I would like to thank Mr. Lichtenstein for his aid and genuine interest in processing the Wheeler Pires-Ferreira records and for creating a comprehensive list of all the bones recovered from Chogha Mish.

Since a chapter on the fauna was not forthcoming, I decided to make the raw data available to the interested specialist. The detailed, comprehensive list of all the identified species from all the excavated loci can be found on the Internet by logging on to: http://oi.uchicago.edu/research/pubs/catalog/oip/oip130.html; see also *Appendix 3*.

The following is a short introduction to the Chogha Mish numbering system that was used to organize pottery, other objects, and excavated loci. When available, all illustrated objects are accompanied by their provenances, elevation (always above sea level), field registration, and Oriental Institute Museum numbers. In the object numbers, whether written as arabic or roman numerals, the first digit shows the season in which the item was found. The roman numeral prefix is usually reserved for whole objects, while the arabic numeral prefix indicates that the item is a sherd or an incomplete object. For example, VI-1 is the first complete object registered in the sixth season, and 6.001 the first sherd or fragmentary object cataloged in that season.

Findspot allocations consist of a letter followed by one or two digits, a colon, and three more digits. The letter and the first one or two digits indicate the specific square; the last three digits refer to the number of the locus in that square. Again, the first number in the three digits that follow the colon indicates the season in which that locus was opened. Therefore, P26:601 indicates that it is the first locus opened in the sixth season in Square P26. Sometimes locus numbers are accompanied by the suffixes "W," "E," "N," "S," and "M," respectively representing west, east, north, south, and middle, indicating that the object or any feature was found west, east, etc., of that specific locus. Normally the first digit of the object number is the same as the first digit of the loci where they were found. Occasionally, when objects were found in an area opened in a previous season, the first digit of the field number differs from the first digit indicating the season.

A few words should also be mentioned on the terminology we have used in this and the first volume. This basic chronological terminology was developed in the 1970s by Delougaz and Kantor. The Susiana sequence as proposed by Le Breton is, in general, confirmed by the large quantities of stratified material from Chogha Mish and other sites. We think it both practical and fair, therefore, to retain Le Breton's term "Susiana" as the general name for all the prehistoric periods. In order to avoid any terminological confusion between the Susiana regional sequence and the phases at Susa itself (e.g., Susiana *e* = Susa A = Susa 1) and also to indicate which of Le Breton's divisions we consider to be subphases within a larger cultural period, Le Breton's lower-case letter designations are abandoned in favor of "Early," "Middle," and "Late," to which "Aceramic," "Formative," and "Archaic" phases are added. Our main deviation from Le Breton's classification involves his three middle phases, namely Susiana *b*, *c*, and *d*; these phases are considered here as subdivisions of the long Middle Susiana period. Our Early Susiana period and Late Susiana 2 phase correspond to Le Breton's Susiana *a* and *e* respectively. Here, as in the first volume, we have added another phase to Le Breton's sequence by subdividing his Susiana *d* into two separate phases. Le Breton's phase d (Le Breton 1957, fig. 7:8–10) includes some late Middle Susiana types (e.g. his fig. 7:8) that stratigraphically do not occur with the types he assigned to his phase d. Therefore without these earlier types, Le Breton's phase d equals our Late Susiana 1 phase (Farukh phase in Deh Luran). We thus consider any prehistoric archaeological deposits in southwestern Iran whose pottery assemblage includes "dot motif" as belonging to the Late Susiana 1 phase.

In addition, we have chosen Delougaz's terminology "Protoliterate" instead of the popular term "Late Uruk" to apply to the archaeological phase in Susiana dating to the second half of the fourth millennium B.C., even though Susiana and southern Mesopotamia share an almost identical repertoire of material culture. This choice of terminology is intended to make a crucial distinction between the two contemporary, but structually and socially different cultures in southwest Asia.

A number of scholars consider two earlier phases for the first half of the fourth millennium B.C., that is, Early and Middle Uruk. As we discuss in *Chapter 1*, at Chogha Mish we do not have any convincing evidence for this division of fourth-millennium archaeological materials. Nevertheless, it is obvious that the Protoliterate period followed an earlier phase in Susiana with related material that represents an early evolutionary stage of urban development in the region. But referring to the archaeological phases in Susiana prior to the second half of the fourth millennium B.C. as "Early and Middle Uruk" requires explanations of the role of southern Mesopotamia in the evolution of Susiana society in that period that have yet to be formulated. Therefore, to be consistent with our characterization of the Susiana internal development vis-à-vis that of southern Mesopotamia, we refer to the first half of the fourth millennium as the Early Susa 2 phase (Gregory Johnson's Early Uruk), identified but poorly known from Susa Acropole level 22. Our Middle Susa 2 phase (Johnson's Middle Uruk) corresponds to Susa Acropole levels 21–19.

The Protoliterate period at Chogha Mish is represented by two phases of architecture, Protoliterate 1 and 2. These phases represent the temporal dimension of the settlement, but changes in the material culture, especially pottery, do not seem to be present. The archaeological sequences from Chogha Bonut and Chogha Mish are delimited and defined primarily on the basis of specific classes of pottery that are characteristic of the major periods discussed in this study; that is, Archaic, Middle, and Late Susiana periods. The subdivision of these major periods (e.g., Early and Late Middle Susiana, Late Susiana 1 and 2) are based on the presence/absence of certain pottery shapes and decorative motifs within each period, as well as stratigraphy. When the available information permited, other artifacts such as spindle whorls, stone tools, and architectural components and features were also used as criteria for defining the various periods and phases, but inconsistently, as the available records for each period vary considerably. While we have not been able to quantify our ceramic diagnostics for each period/phase, we believe the resulting information can be used as a basis for assessing periodization of the surveyed sites in the region.

The contour map of Chogha Mish (fig. 6) extends only over those parts of the ancient site that are clearly discernible on the surface, but not over those presumably covered by wash from higher parts and now lying under cultivated fields. When I resurveyed the site in 1995, it became clear that the occupational deposit at Chogha Mish extends farther to the east and west than the map indicates. Therefore the adjusted 75 m contour map of 18.6 ha in table 3 seems an underestimation of the total area of occupation at Chogha Mish. This inference, of course, will have to be confirmed by test trenches at the site.

The High Mound, measuring about 200 × 150 m, is steepest toward the north and northwest, where it slopes about 23 m in 60 m, that is, an incline of nearly 1 in 3 m. Its western edge is fairly regular, but on its northeast, east, and southeast sides it has four irregularly shaped lobes separated by deeply eroded gullies. The terrace, about 400 × 300 m, has four less prominent peaks in Squares H14 (elevation 82–83 m), R16 (elevation 84–85 m), O25 (elevation 84–85 m), and H27 (elevation 82–83 m).

The summit of the High Mound is at elevation 100.54 m above sea level. It is about 27 m above the surrounding plain (at 73.50) and over 30 m above the riverbed of the Shur, to the east (elevation 70.30 m). The lowest elevation at Chogha Mish was reached at 71.70 m (Archaic 1 phase) in S22, putting the virgin soil here at 71.60 m. In other areas, the virgin soil was reached at higher elevations, about 72.00 m and even 73.50 m, indicating that in the seventh millennium B.C. and perhaps much later the plain looked very different than it does now. Approximately 5 km to the west, at Chogha Bonut, the present plain is at about 74 m above sea level, just 1.0 to 0.5 m higher than the area around Chogha Mish. The virgin soil at Chogha Bonut, however, was reached at 73.10 to 73.00 m, just 1 m below the present surface of the plain. In this part of the plain the pattern of alluvial deposition must have been very different from elsewhere in the region, indicating that the region around Chogha Mish was less susceptible to flooding. This observation should partly explain the high concentration of settlements, particularly those of the early Neolithic period, in this region.

Figure 88 (kindly produced by Nick Kouchoukos) is a computer-generated image that shows both the surface features and a cross section of this part of the plain. The image, as Kouchoukos noted, indicates that this area may have been the remnant of a bluff or even a ridge and thus higher than the lands on either side of the Shur and Sia Mansur rivers. As just noted, this is the area in Khuzestan where almost all the Archaic period sites, namely Chogha Mish, Chogha Bonut, and Boneh Fazl Ali are located. At the level of our present understanding of the geomorphology of the plain, it is facile to think that when the first farmers colonized the land they chose this higher part of the plain, away from the marshes and the parts of the plain that flood. One can further speculate that as the climate became gradually drier and the rivers started to cut down their beds, it became possible to occupy the regions on the west of Sia Mansur and east of the Shur. Whether or not the Shur started cutting its bed down to the present elevation, perhaps around the second millennium B.C., remains speculative until geomorphological analysis is conducted in that area.

To avoid repetition and to make this volume more manageable to use, only summaries of lengthy descriptions of pottery and objects are provided here. Therefore, the reader is invited to consult the first volume for detailed information not included here. In addition, we have included data obtained from the earlier site of Chogha Bonut, as well as from other sites in both Susiana and the nearby Deh Luran to fill in the missing data from Chogha Mish itself.

*Chapter 1* is a rather lengthy summary of prehistoric cultural development in lowland Susiana, with Chogha Mish as the main source of information. We feel that by presenting this summary first, the reader is provided with a general landscape against which numerous technical data and analyses offered in the following chapters may be placed. This chapter mostly consists of a narrative, the fabric of which is woven from the available archaeological data. The narrative, however, is embellished with a certain number of assumptions, inferences, and even imagination. Nevertheless, we hope we have been able to lay out the facts clearly enough so that the reader can sift through what is fact and what is speculation. As a regional center for over two thousand years, Chogha Mish offers a unique opportunity to study prehistoric socioeconomic and crafts development at a single site. Since Chogha Mish did not develop in isolation, in *Chapter 1* we use the site as a focal point to discuss numerous lines of evidence that pertain to the cultural development in the region.

*Chapter 2* deals with the architectural evidence from the Archaic to the Iron III/Achaemenid periods. It describes all the relevant excavation areas individually, namely the Gully Cut, Trench XXI, the High Mound, etc. When appropriate and possible, contemporary architectural remains in the various excavation areas are linked to provide a larger picture.

The pottery assemblages of all prehistoric and historical phases are described in *Chapter 3*. A much more detailed description of the various classes of pottery was offered in the first volume by Helene Kantor; in some respects *Chapter 3* is therefore an abbreviated version. For more information and a lengthier treatment of the pottery, the reader must consult the first volume.

*Chapter 4* is a survey of the stylistic trends and mannerisms used by ancient potters to decorate various classes of prehistoric pottery. One of the objectives of this survey is to present a general picture of some aspects of the "grammar" governing the designs and compositions of Susiana prehistoric painted pottery. From the early Neolithic period, southwestern Iran was in close contact with Mesopotamia; so the first part of the chapter is devoted to a summary of the development and evolution of some components of material culture, especially pottery in that region. In our opinion, this was particularly necessary because the question of the origins of the Archaic 3 close-line ware and its contemporary Chogha Mami Transitional pottery and the el-Oueili ware cannot be addressed without reference to the Samarran pottery and its characteristics. In addition, a general survey of the potteries of the early phases of Ubaid (Ubaid 1–2), possessing many shared features with those of the Early and Middle Susiana periods, is also provided in the same section to demonstrate change and continuity throughout the prehistoric sequence, as well as interregional stylistic trends.

The general description of Mesopotamian prehistoric pottery in the first part of *Chapter 4* provides a background for the second part, which deals primarily with the evolution of designs and shapes of the Susiana prehistoric painted pottery. It is in this section that the arguments for the special characters of the crucial Late Susiana 1 pottery assemblage and its highland connection are formulated.

A foundation of knowledge on the ecology of crafts in prehistoric Susiana is essential in making theoretical inferences on the evolution of pottery production in the region. But at present that knowledge is slim. I hope the analyses in *Chapters 1–4* make it clear that increasing sophistication of the Susiana prehistoric pottery form, decoration, and manufacture technique roughly corresponds with the growth of Chogha Mish as a regional center. The development of Chogha Mish as a regional center did not, of course, occur in isolation. The steady rise in regional population in the Archaic period and the sharp population rise of the Early and Middle Susiana periods seems to be associated with the fertility of the land, ample water supplies, improved agricultural practices and tools, and perhaps the reduction of the aggrading regime of the region's main water courses as well as population donation from the intermontane valleys of the Zagros.

*Chapter 5* is devoted to the evidence of administrative technology throughout the prehistoric sequence and the Protoliterate period. In the first volume, Helene Kantor offered an extensive and detailed treatment of the Protoliterate glyptic art. Here we limited ourselves to the description and evaluation of some new types of sealings and some glyptic designs not addressed in the first volume.

Clay and stone figurines of all phases are presented and discussed in *Chapter 6*. *Chapter 7* deals with small objects, including metal and bone objects, as well as stone tools and stone vessels. The evidence of basketry is discussed at the end of this chapter. The similarities of the types of objects discussed in this chapter to those published in the first volume are the reason for the brevity of *Chapter 7*. The reader, therefore, is advised to consult the first volume for more details.

*Appendix 1* deals with instrumental neutron activation analysis (INAA) of some Susiana sherds, which was provided by Royal Ghazal and Nick Kouchoukos of the University of Chicago's Department of Anthropology and their colleagues at the University of Missouri Research Reactor (MURR). The reader should bear in mind that the results of Ghazal's INAA and his present contribution must be considered a work in progress, since the final analysis and detailed discussions will appear in his doctoral thesis. The rationale for Ghazal's INAA of certain classes of pottery from the Late Susiana 2 and Protoliterate phases — in the course of which state organizations presumably developed in the region — is ultimately to test the validity of Johnson's (1973) and Wright and Johnson's (1975) hypothesis that sociopolitical and economic evolution affected the production of crafts, especially pottery. Judith Berman performed a similar analysis (1986, 1989) by dividing her samples of 1,021 sherds from 104 Susiana sites into compositionally similar groups, but her results were inconclusive (Berman 1989: 262). In his contribution, Ghazal discusses improved INAA techniques and argues that his initial analysis is promising in establishing a link between compositionally similar ceramic groups and hypothetical archaeological groups. The most interesting conclusion of this analysis was the possibility that, despite Johnson's hypothesis (Johnson 1973), Chogha Mish, Susa, and Abu Fandoweh were not the only centers of pottery manufacture.

*Appendix 2* consists of a master list of all the available information on the excavated areas, various loci within these areas, their elevations, and the type of archaeological contexts that defined the loci or were found associated with them. The data provided in this list pertain primarily to the loci not depicted on the top plans, though some are included. Information about the loci missing from the list can easily be found on the top plans and in *Chapter 2*.

*Appendix 3* presents the faunal information.

The text concludes with two indices, an *Index of Loci and Illustrated Finds* and an *Index of Geographical Names*.

# ACKNOWLEDGMENTS

The research and completion of the manuscript for this final publication were made possible through a generous grant from The Shelby White-Leon Levy Program for Archaeological Publications. Thanks to the unique opportunity the White-Levy program has provided, scholars around the world are enabled to publish important archaeological materials which would otherwise remanin in the basements of museums.

* * * * *

I owe a debt of gratitude to Frank Hole, Barbara Helwing, Nick Kouchoukos, and Tony Wilkinson, who read the entire or parts of an early draft of the manuscript and made valuable suggestions and criticisms. One fact should not be forgotten: this book is the fruition of decades of hard work by Helene J. Kantor, my primary mentor. She would, however, be the most vociferous critic of this work. Had Helene lived long enough to write Chogha Mish II, she would certainly have acknowledged the gigantic efforts of Guillermo Algaze. In the years that Guillermo and I worked closely with Helene, it was Guillermo who was primarily responsible for checking the excavation records, collecting the pertinent data, organizing, collating, and classifying the records for presentation and interpretation. Without Guillermo's meticulous efforts this publication would not have been possible.

Finally, some of the results of our archaeological excavations at Chogha Do Sar (KS-04) and KS-108 discussed in *Chapter 1* were obtained during our Joint ICHTO-Oriental Institute 2004/05 expedition to Khuzestan. The expedition was made possible by a grant from the National Science Foundation (B.C.S-0345988). We are grateful to Dr. John Yellen for his help and favorable consideration of our grant application. The National Science Foundation grant was supplemented by additional funds from the Oriental Institute. We thank Professor Gil Stein, Director of the Oriental Institute, for his encouragement and valuable assistance.

# BIBLIOGRAPHY


Adams, Robert McCormick

1962 "Agriculture and Urban Life in Early Southwestern Iran." *Science* 136: 109–22.

1974 "The Mesopotamian Social Landscape: A View from the Frontier." In *The Reconstruction of Complex Societies*, edited by Charlotte B. Moore, pp. 1–20. Supplement to the Bulletin of the American School of Oriental Research 20. Philadelphia: American Schools of Oriental Research.

1981 *Heartland of Cities: Surveys of Ancient Settlement and Land Use in the Central Floodplain of the Euphrates*. Chicago: University of Chicago Press.

1983 "The Jarmo Stone and Pottery Vessel Industries." In *Prehistoric Archaeology Along the Zagros Flanks*, edited by Robert J. Braidwood, Linda S. Braidwood, Bruce Howe, Charles Reed, and Patty Jo Watson, pp. 209–32. Oriental Institute Publications 105. Chicago: The Oriental Institute.

Adams, Robert McCormick, and Hans J. Nissen

1972 *The Uruk Countryside: The Natural Setting of Urban Societies*. Chicago: University of Chicago Press.

Alberti, A.

1985 "A Reconstruction of the Abu Salabikh God-list." *Studi Epigraphici e Linguistici sul Vicino Oriente* 2: 3–23.

Alden, John R.

1979 Regional Economic Organization in Banesh Period Iran. Ph.D. dissertation, Department of Anthropology, University of Michigan.

1987 "The Susa III Period." In *The Archaeology of Western Iran: Settlement and Society from Prehistory to the Islamic Conquest,* edited by F. Hole, pp. 157–70. Smithsonian Series in Archaeological Inquiry. Washington, D.C.: Smithsonian Institution Press.

Algaze, Guillermo

1989 "The Uruk Expansion: Cross-Cultural Exchange in Early Mesopotamian Civilization." *Current Anthropology* 30: 571–608.

1993 *The Uruk World System: The Dynamics of Expansion of Early Mesopotamian Civilization*. Chicago: University of Chicago Press.

2001 "The Prehistory of Imperialism: The Case of Uruk Period Mesopotamia." In *Uruk Mesopotamia and Its Neighbors*, edited by Mitchell S. Rothman, pp. 27–84. School of American Research Advanced Seminar Series. Santa Fe: School of American Research.

Alizadeh, Abbas

1985 "A Protoliterate Kiln from Chogha Mish." *Iran* 23: 39–50.

1988a Mobile Pastoralism and the Development of Complex Societies in Highland Iran: The Evidence from Tall-e Bakun A. Ph.D. dissertation, Department of Near Eastern Languages and Civilizations, University of Chicago.

1988b "Socio-economic Complexity in Southwestern Iran during the Fifth and Fourth Millennia B.C.: The Evidence from Tall-e Bakun A." *Iran* 26:17–34.

1992 *Prehistoric Settlement Patterns and Cultures in Susiana, Southwestern Iran: The Analysis of the F. G. L. Gremliza Survey Collection*. Technical Report, No. 24. Ann Arbor: The Museum of Anthropology, University of Michigan.

1996 "Editor's Preface." In *Chogha Mish,* Volume I: *The First Five Seasons of Excavations, 1961–1971*, by Pinhas Delougaz and Helene J. Kantor, edited by Abbas Alizadeh, pp. xxiii–xxv. Oriental Institute Publications 101. Chicago: The Oriental Institute.

1996/97 "Iranian Prehistoric Project." In *Oriental Institute Annual Report 1996/97*, edited by William M. Sumner, pp. 49–56. Chicago: The Oriental Institute.

1997 "Excavations at Chogha Bonut, an Aceramic Neolithic Site in Lowland Susiana, Southwestern Iran." *Neo-Lithics* 1: 6–7.

2003a *Excavations at the Prehistoric Mound of Chogha Bonut, Khuzestan, Iran: Seasons 1976/77, 1977/78, and 1996*. Oriental Institute Publications 120. Chicago: The Oriental Institute.

2003b "Report on the Joint Archaeological and Geomorphological Research Expedition in Lowland Susiana, Iran." *Oriental Institute News & Notes* 177: 1–8.

2004 "Wanderhirten: Ihre Bedeutung für die Kulturgeschichte Irans in geschichtlicher und vorgeschichtlicher Zeit." In *Persiens Antike Pracht: Bergbau, Handwerk, Archäologie; Katalog der Ausstellung des Deutschen Bergbau-Museums Bochum vom 28. November 2004 bis 29. Mai 2005,* Volume 1, edited by Thomas Stöllner, Rainer Slotta, and Abdolrasool Vatandoust, pp. 76–91. Bochum: Deutsches Bergbau-Museum.

2005 "New Challenges and Perspective in Iran." *Oriental Institute News & Notes* 187: 1, 4–8.

2006 *Tall-e Bakun A: The Origins of State Organizations in Prehistoric Highland Fars, Southern Iran*. Oriental Institute Publications 125. Chicago: The Oriental Institute.

Alizadeh, Abbas, and Ali Mahfroozi

2005 "Joint Archaeological Excavations at KS-04 and 108 in Khuzestan." *Oriental Institute Annual Report 2004/2005*, edited by Gil J. Stein, pp. 56–68. Chicago: The Oriental Institute.

Alizadeh, Abbas; Nicholas Kouchoukos; Tony Wilkinson; Andrew Bauer; and Marjan Mashkour

2004 "Human-Environment Interactions on the Upper Khuzestan Plains, Southwest Iran, Recent Investigations." *Paléorient* 30: 69–88.

Alizadeh, Abbas; Shapour Malek-Shahmirzadi; and Yousef Majidzadeh

1999 *The Iranian World: Essays on Iranian Art and Archaeology Presented to Ezat O. Negahban*. Tehran: Iran University Press.

Amiet, Pierre

1957 "Glyptique susienne archaïque." *Revue d'assyriologie et d'archéologie orientale* 51: 121–29.

1961 *La glyptique mésopotamienne archaïque*. Paris: Centre National de la Recherche Scientifique.

1966 *Elam*. Auvers-sur-Oise: Archée Éditeur.

1972 *Glyptique susienne des origines à l'époque des perses achéménides: Cachets, sceaux-cylindres et empreintes antiques découverts à Suse de 1913 à 1967*. Mémoires de la délégation archéologique en Iran, Mission de Susiane 43. Paris: Paul Geuthner.

1979a "Alternance et dualité: Essai d'interprétation de l'histoire élamite." *Akkadica* 15: 2–22.

1979b "Archaeological Discontinuity and Ethnic Duality in Elam." *Antiquity* 53: 195–204.

1986 "L'usage des sceaux à l'époque initiale de l'histoire de Suse." In *Fragmenta Historiae Aelamicae: Mélanges offerts à M.-J. Steve*, edited by L. de Meyer, H. Gasche, and F. Vallat, pp. 17–24. Paris: Éditions Recherche sur les Civilisations.

1992 "Sur l'histoire Élamite." *Iranica Antiqua* 27: 75–94.

Arnold, E. Dean

1985 *Ceramic Theory and Cultural Process*. Cambridge: Cambridge University Press.

Azarpay, Guitty

1999 "Elamite Terracotta Figurines." In *The Iranian World: Essays on Iranian Art and Archaeology Presented to Ezat O. Negahban*, edited by Abbas Alizadah, Shapour Malek-Shahmirzadi, Yousef Majidzadeh, pp. 131–36. Tehran: Iran University Press.

Bader, Nicolai O.

1993 "Tell Maghzaliyah: An Early Neolithic Site in Northern Iraq." In *Early Stages in the Evolution of Mesopotamian Civilization: Soviet Excavations in Northern Iraq*, edited by Norman Yoffee and Jeffery J. Clark, pp. 7–40. Tucson: University of Arizona.

Bader, Nicolai O.; N. Ya. Merpert; and R. M. Munchaev

1981 "Soviet Expedition's Surveys in the Sinjar Valley." *Sumer* 37: 55–95.

Baines, John, and Norman Yoffee

1998 "Order, Legitimacy, and Wealth in Ancient Egypt and Mesopotamia." In *Archaic States*, edited by Gary M. Feinman and Joyce Marcus, pp. 199–260. School of American Research Advanced Seminar Series. Santa Fe: The School of American Research.

Baxter, Michael J.

1992 "Archaeological Uses of the Biplot – A Neglected Technique?" In *Computer Applications and Quantitative Methods in Archaeology 1991*, edited by G. Lock and J. Moffett, pp. 141–48. British Archaeological Reports International Series 577. Oxford: British Archaeological Reports.

1993 "Principal Component Analysis in Archaeometry." Department of Mathematics, Statistics, and Operational Research, pp. 2–23. Nottingham, U.K.: Nottingham Trent University.

Baykal-Seeher, Ayse, and Julia Obladen-Kauder

1996 *Demircihüyük: Die Ergebnisse der Ausgrabungen 1975–1978*. Volume 4: *Die Kleinfunde*. Mainz am Rhein: Philipp von Zabern.

Beale, Thomas W.

1978 "Bevelled Rim Bowls and Their Implications for Change and Economic Organization in the Later Fourth Millennium B.C." *Journal of Near Eastern Studies* 37: 289–313.

1986 *Excavations at Tepe Yahya, Iran 1967–1975: The Early Periods*. American School of Prehistoric Research 38. Cambridge: Harvard University Press.

Berman, Judith C.

1986 Ceramic Production and the Development of Complex Polities in Late Prehistoric Southwest Iran. Ph.D. dissertation, City University of New York.

1987 "Ceramic Production and Its Implications for the Sociopolitical Organization of the Suse Phase Susiana." *Paléorient* 13: 47–60.

1989 "Ceramic Production and Its Implications for the Sociopolitical Organization of the Susiana Plain During the Late 'Ubaid." In *Upon This Foundation: The 'Ubaid Reconsidered*, edited by Elizabeth F. Henrickson and Ingolf Theusen, pp. 257–80. Copenhagen: Museum Tusculanum Press.

Bernbeck, Reinhard

1992 "Migratory Patterns in Early Nomadism." *Paléorient* 18: 77–88.

Blackman, Michael

1992 "The Effects of Natural and Human Size Sorting on the Mineralogy and Chemistry of Ceramic Clays." In *Chemical Characterization of Ceramic Pastes in Archaeology*, edited by Hector Neff, pp. 113–24. Monographs in World Archaeology 7. Madison: Prehistory Press.

1999 "Chemical Characterization of Local Anatolian and Uruk Style Sealing Clays from Hacınebi." *Paléorient* 25: 51–56.

Boehmer, Rainer Michael

1972 "Die Keramikfunde im Bereich des Steingebäudes." In *XXVI. und XXVII. vorläufiger Bericht über die von dem Deutschen Archäologischen Institut und der Deutschen Orient-Gesellschaft aus Mitteln der Deutschen Forschungsgemeinschaft unternommenen Ausgrabungen in Uruk-Warka*, by J. Schmidt, pp. 31–42. Berlin: Gebrüder Mann.

1999 *Uruk: Früheste Siegelabrollungen*. Ausgrabungen in Uruk-Warka Endberichte 24. Mainz am Rhein: Philipp von Zabern.

Boucharlat, Rémy, and Audran Labrousse

1979 "Le palais d'Artaxerxès II sur la rive droite du Chaour à Suse." *Cahiers de la délégation archéologique française en Iran* 10: 19–136.

Braidwood, Robert J.

1960a "Preliminary Investigations Concerning the Origins of Food-Production in Iranian Kurdistan." *British Association for Advancement of Science* 17: 214–18.

1960b "Seeking the World's First Farmers in Persian Kurdistan." *The Illustrated London News*, October 22, pp. 695–97.

1961 "The Iranian Prehistoric Project." *Iranica Antiqua* 1: 3–7.

Braidwood, Robert J.; Linda S. Braidwood; Bruce Howe; Charles Reed; and Patty Jo Watson

1983 *Prehistoric Archaeology Along the Zagros Flanks*. Oriental Institute Publications 105. Chicago: The Oriental Institute.

Braidwood, Robert J., and Bruce Howe

1960 *Prehistoric Investigations in Iraqi Kurdistan*. Studies in Ancient Oriental Civilization 31. Chicago: University of Chicago Press.

Brandes, Mark A.

1979 *Siegelabrollungen aus dem archäischen Bauschichten in Uruk-Warka*, 1–2. Freiburger altorientalishe Studien 3. Wiesbaden: Franz Steiner.

Broman Morales, Vivian

1990 *Figurines and Other Clay Objects from Sarab and Çayönü*. Oriental Institute Communications 25. Chicago: The Oriental Institute.

Brumfiel, Elizabeth M., and Timothy K. Earle, editors

1987 *Specialization, Exchange, and Complex Societies*. Cambridge: Cambridge University Press.

Burkholder, Grace

1972 "Ubaid Sites and Pottery in Saudi Arabia." *Archaeology* 25: 264–75.

Burkholder, Grace, and Marny Golding

1971 *Surface Survey of al-'Ubaid Sites in the Eastern Province: Contribution to the Anthropology of Saudi Arabia*. Coconut Grove: Field Research Projects.

Caldwell, Joseph R.

1967 *Investigations at Tal-i-Iblis*. Illinois State Museum Preliminary Reports 9. Springfield: Illinois State Museum Society.

1968 "Tell-i Ghazir." *Reallexikon der Assyriologie und verderasiatischen Archäologie* 3: 348–55.

Calvet, Yves

1983 "Le sondage profond en Y. 27 (1981)." In *Larsa et 'Oueili: Travaux de 1978–1981*, edited by J.-L. Huot, pp. 15–70. Recherche sur les Civilisations, Mémoire 26. Paris: Éditions Recherche sur les Civilisations.

1985/86 "The New Deep Sounding X 36 at Tell el-'Oueili." *Sumer* 44: 67–87.

1986 "Le niveau Obeid 1 de Tell el-'Oueili." In *Préhistoire de la Mésopotamie*: *La Mésopotamie préhistorique et l'exploration récente du Djebel Hamrin*, edited by J.-L. Huot, pp. 129–39. Colloque international du Centre National de la Recherche Scientifique. Paris: Éditions du Centre National de la Recherche Scientifique.

Canal, Daniel

1978 "La haute terrasse de l'Acropole de Suse." *Paléorient* 4: 169–76.

Carter, Elizabeth

1978 "Suse "Ville Royal." *Paléorient* 4: 197-211

1979 "Elamite Pottery, ca. 2000–1000 B.C." *Journal of Near Eastern Studies* 38: 111–28.

1980 "Excavations in Ville Royale I at Susa: The Third Millennium B.C. Occupation." *Cahiers de la délégation archéologique française en Iran* 11: 11–134.

Carter, Elizabeth, and Matthew W. Stolper

1984 *Elam: Survey of Political History and Archaeology*. University of California Publications in Near Eastern Studies 25. Los Angeles: University of California Press.

Childe, V. Gordon

1936 *Man Makes Himself*. The Library of Science and Culture 5. London: Watts & Co.

1951 *Social Evolution*. London: Watts.

Contenau, George, and Roman Ghirshman

1935 *Fouilles du Tépé Giyan près de Néhavand 1931 et 1932*. Paris: Paul Geuthner.

Costin, Cathy L., and Melissa B. Hagstrum

1995 "Standardization, Labor Investment, Skill, and the Organization of Ceramic Production in Late Prehispanic Highland Peru." *American Antiquity* 60: 619–39.

Coursey, Cheryl L.

1997 Shaping, Stewing, Serving, and Brewing: Uruk Period Pottery Production and Consumption in Alluvial Mesopotamia. Ph.D. dissertation, Department of Anthropology, State University of New York at Binghamton.

Cribb, Roger

1991 *Nomads in Archaeology*. Cambridge: Cambridge University Press.

D'Altroy, Terence, and Timothy Earle

1985 "Staple Finance, Wealth Finance, and Storage in the Inca Political Economy." *Current Anthropology* 26: 187–206.

Damerow, Peter, and Robert Englund

1985 "Die Zahlzeichensysteme der archäischen Texte aus Uruk." In *Zeichenliste der archäischen Texte aus Uruk*, edited by M. W. Green and Hans Nissen, pp. 117–56. Berlin: Gebrüder Mann.

1989 *The Proto-Elamite Texts from Tepe Yahya*. American School of Prehistoric Research Bulletin 39. Cambridge: Harvard University Press.

de Genouillac, Henri

1934 *Fouilles de Telloh*. Vol. 1: *Époques présargoniques*. Paris: Paul Geuthner.

Delougaz, Pinhas

1952 *Pottery from the Diyala Region*. Oriental Institute Publications 63. Chicago: University of Chicago Press.

Delougaz, Pinhas, and Helene J. Kantor

1996 *Chogha Mish*. Volume 1: *The First Five Seasons of Excavations, 1961–1971*. Edited by Abbas Alizadeh. Oriental Institute Publications 101. Chicago: The Oriental Institute.

Delougaz, Pinhas, and Seton Lloyd

1942 *Pre-Sargonid Temples in the Diyala Region*. Oriental Institute Publications 58. Chicago: University of Chicago Press.

de Mecquenem, Roland

1912 "Catalogue de la céramique peinte susienne conservée au Musée du Louvre." In *Céramique peinte de Suse et petits monuments de l'époque archaïque*, edited by J. de Morgan, pp. 105–58. Mémoires de la mission archéologique en Perse, Cinquième série 13. Paris: Ernest Leroux.

1934 "Fouilles de Suse 1929–1933." In *Archéologie, métrologie et numismatique susienne,* edited by M. F. Allotte de la Fuÿe, N. T. Belaiew, R. de Mecquenem, and J.-M. Unvala, pp. 177–237. Mémoires de la mission archéologique de Perse, Mission en Susiane 25. Paris: Ernest Leroux.

de Mecquenem, Roland; G. Contenau; R. Pfister; and N. T. Belaiew

1943 "Fouilles de Suse, 1933–1939. " In *Archéologie susienne*, edited by R. de Mecquenem and G. Contenau, pp. 3–161. Mémoires de la mission archéologique en Iran, Mission de Susiane 29. Paris: Presses Universitaires de France.

de Miroschedji, Pierre

1978 "Stratigraphie de la période néo-élamite Suse (c. 1110 – c. 540)." *Paléorient* 4: 213–28.

de Morgan, Jacques

1905 *Recherches archéologiques*. Mémoires de la mission archéologique de Perse, Troisième série 8. Paris: Ernest Leroux.

Diakonoff, Igor M.

1974 *Structure of Ancient Society and State in Early Dynastic Sumer*. Monographs of the Ancient Near East 1(3). Malibu: Undena Publishers.

Dietler, Michael, and Ingrid Herbich

1998 "Habitus, Techniques, Style: An Integrated Approach to the Social Understanding of Material Culture and Boundaries." In *Archaeology of Social Boundaries,* edited by Miriam T. Stark, pp. 232–63. Smithsonian Series in Archaeological Inquiry. Washington, D.C.: Smithsonian Institution Press.

Dittmann, Reinhard

1984 *Eine Randebene des Zagros in der Frühzeit: Ergebnisse des Behbehan-Zuhreh Surveys*. Berliner Beiträge zum Vorderen Orient 3. Berlin: Dietrich Reimer.

1986 "Seals, Sealings, and Tablets: Thoughts on the Changing Pattern of Administrative Control from the Late-Uruk to the Proto-Elamite Period at Susa." In *Ǧamdat Naṣr: Period or Regional Style?* (Papers given at a symposium held in Tübingen, November 1993), edited by U. Finkbeiner and W. Röllig, pp. 332–66. Beihefte zum Tübinger Atlas des Vorderen Orients, Reihe B 62. Wiesbaden: Ludwig Reichert.

Dollfus, Geneviève

1971 "Les Fouilles: Djaffarabad de 1969 à 1971." *Cahiers de la délégation archéologique française en Iran* 1: 17–161.

1975 "Les Fouilles: Djaffarabad de 1972 à 1974, Djaffarabad, périodes I et II." *Cahiers de la délégation archéologique française en Iran* 5: 11–222.

1978 "Djaffarabad, Djowi, Bandebal: Contribution à l'étude de la Susiane au début V^e^ millénaire et au début du IV^e^ millénaire." *Paléorient* 4: 141–67.

1983 "Djowi et Bandebal: Deux villages de la plaine centrale du Khuzistan, Iran, V^e^ millénaire avant J.-C., Travaux de 1975, 1977, 1978." *Cahiers de la délégation archéologique française en Iran* 13: 17–284.

1985 "Le peuplement de la Susiane au cours de V^e^ millénaire." *Paléorient* 11: 11–20.

Dollfus, Geneviève, and P. Encrevé

1982 "Marques sur poteries dans la Susiane du V^e^ millénaire: Réflexions et comparaisons." *Paléorient* 8: 107–15.

Dyson, Robert H., Jr.

1966 Excavations on the Acropolis at Susa and Problems of Susa A, B, and C. Ph.D. dissertation, Harvard University.

Earle, Timothy

1997 *How Chiefs Come to Power*. Stanford: Stanford University Press.

Eerkens, Jelmer W.

2003 "Residential Mobility and Pottery Use in the Western Great Basin." *Current Anthropology* 44: 728–38.

Eerkens, Jelmer W., and Robert L. Bettinger

2001 "Techniques for Assessing Standardization in Artifact Assemblages: Can We Scale Material Variability?" *American Antiquity* 66: 493–504.

Eerkens, Jelmer W.; Hector Neff; and Michael D. Glascock

2002 "Ceramic Production Among Small-Scale and Mobile Hunters and Gatherers: A Case Study from the Southwestern Great Basin." *Journal of Anthropological Archaeology* 21: 200–29.

Egami, Namio, and Seiichi Masuda

1962 *Marv-Dasht*. Volume 1: *The Excavation at Tall-i-Bakun 1956*. The Tokyo University Iraq-Iran Archaeological Expedition, Report 2. Tokyo: Yamakawa Publishing.

Egami, Namio, and Toshihiko Sono

1962 *Marv-Dasht* 2: *The Excavation at Tall-i-Gap 1959*. The Tokyo University Iraq-Iran Archaeological Expedition, Report 3. Tokyo: Yamakawa Publishing.

El-Wailly, Faisal, and Behnam Abu es-Soof

1965 "Excavations at Tell es-Sawwan, First Preliminary Report (1964)." *Sumer* 21: 17–32.

Emberling, Geoff, and Norman Yoffee

1999 "Thinking about Ethnicity in Mesopotamian Archaeology and History." In *Fluchtpunkt Uruk: Archäologische Einheit aus Methodischer Vielfalt: Schriften für Hans Jörg Nissen*, edited by Hartmut Kühne, Reinhard Bernbeck and Karin Bartl, pp. 272–81. Internationale Archäologie Studia Honoraria 6. Rahden/Westf.: Marie Leidorf.

Englund, Robert K.

1993 Review of *Before Writing*, by D. Schmandt-Besserat. *Science* 260: 1670–71.

1998 "Texts from the Late Uruk Period." In *Mesopotamien: Späturuk-Zeit und Frühdynastische Zeit*, edited by Josef Bower, Robert K. Englund, and Manfred Krebernik, pp. 15–217. Orbis Biblicus et Orientalis 160. Freiburg: Universitätsverlag; Göttingen: Vandenhoeck & Ruprecht.

Englund, Robert K., and Hans Nissen

1993 *Die lexikalischen Listen der archäischen Texte aus Uruk*. Archäische Texte aus Uruk 3. Berlin: Gebrüder Mann.

Falkenstein, Adam

1936 *Archäische Texte aus Uruk*. Ausgrabungen der Deutschen Forschungsgemeinschaft in Uruk-Warka 2. Leipzig: Harrassowitz.

Feinman, Gary M.

1998 "Scale and Social Organization: Perspectives on the Archaic State." In *Archaic States*, edited by G. Feinman and Joyce Marcus, pp. 95–134. School of American Research Advanced Seminar Series. Santa Fe: School of American Research.

Fiandra, Enrica

1981 "The Connection Between Clay Sealings and Tablets in Administration." In *South Asian Archaeology 1979*, edited by H. Härtel, pp. 29–43. Berlin: Dietrich Reimer.

Fiorina, Paolo

1984 "Excavations at Tell Hassan, Preliminary Report." *Sumer* 40: 277–89.

1987 "Tell Hassan: Les couches halafiennes et obeidiennes et les relations entre les deux cultures." In *Préhistoire de la Mésopotamie*, edited by Jean-Louis Huot, pp. 243–56. Paris: Centre National de la Recherche Scientifique.

Flannery, Kent V.

1972 "The Origins of the Village as a Settlement Type in Mesoamerica and the Near East: A Comparative Study." In *Man, Settlement and Urbanism*, edited by Peter J. Ucko, R. Tringhaus, and G. W. Dimbleby, pp. 23–53. London: Duckworth.

1998 "The Ground Plans of Archaic States." In *Archaic States*, edited by Gary M. Feinman and Joyce Marcus, pp. 15–57. School of American Research Advanced Seminar Series. Santa Fe: The School of American Research.

1999 "Chiefdoms in the Early Near East: Why It's so Hard to Identify Them." In *The Iranian World: Essays on Iranian Art and Archaeology Presented to Ezat O. Negahban*, edited by Abbas Alizadeh, Shapour Malek-Shahmirzadi, and Yousef Majidzadeh, pp. 44–63. Tehran: Iran University Press.

Forbes, Robert J.

1964 *Studies in Ancient Technology*. Second edition. Leiden: Brill.

Friberg, Jöran

1978 *The Third Millennium Roots of Babylonian Mathematics: A Method for the Decipherment, through Mathematical and Metrological Analysis, of Proto-Sumerian and Proto-Elamite Semi-Pictographic Inscriptions*. Department of Mathematics, Chalmers University of Technology Report 1978/79. Götenborg: Department of Mathematics, Chalmers University of Technology.

1984 "Numbers and Measures in the Earliest Written Records." *Scientific American* 1984: 110–18.

1994 "Preliterate Counting and Accounting in the Middle East: A Constructively Critical Review of Schmandt-Besserat's 'Before Writing.'" *Orientalische Literaturzeitung* 89: 477–502.

Friedrich, M. H.

1970 "Design Structure and Social Interaction: Archaeological Implications of an Ethnographic Analysis." *American Antiquity* 35: 332–43.

Fukaii, Shiniji; Kiyoharu Horiuchi; and Toshio Matsutani

1970 *Telul eth-Thalathat: The Excavation of Tell II: The Third Season (1964)*. Tokyo: Yamakawa Publishing.

Garfinkel, Yosef

2003 *Dancing at the Dawn of Agriculture*. Austin: University of Texas Press.

Gasche, Hermann

1973 *La poterie élamite du deuxième millénaire a.C.* Mémoires de la délégation archéologique en Iran, Mission de Susiane 47. Leiden: Brill.

Geddes, David S.

1983 "Neolithic Transhumance in the Mediterranean Pyrenees." *World Archaeology* 15: 51–66.

Ghirshman, Roman

1938 *Fouilles de Sialk près de Kashan.* Volume 1: *1933, 1934, 1937.* Musée du Louvre, Département des antiquités orientales, Série archéologique 4. Paris: Paul Geuthner.

1954 *Village perse-achéménide.* Mémoires de la mission archéologique en Iran, Mission de Susiane 36. Paris: Presses Universitaires de France.

Gilbert, Allan S.

1975 "Modern Nomads and Prehistoric Pastoralism: The Limits of Analogy." *Journal of Ancient Near Eastern Societies of Columbia University* 7: 53–71.

1983 "On the Origins of Specialized Nomadic Pastoralism in Western Iran." *World Archaeology* 15: 105–19.

Glascock, Michael D.

1992 "Characterization of Archaeological Ceramics at MURR by Neutron Activation Analysis and Multivariate Statistics." In *Chemical Characterization of Ceramic Pastes in Archaeology*, edited by Hector Neff, pp. 11–26. Madison: Prehistory Press.

Goff, Clare L.

1970 "Excavations at Baba Jan, 1968: Third Preliminary Report." *Iran* 8: 141–56.

1971 "Luristan Before the Iron Age." *Iran* 9: 131–52.

Goodarzi-Tabrizi, Shoki

1999 "Elamite Terracotta Figurines in the Rosicrucian Egyptian Museum." In *The Iranian World: Essays on Iranian Art and Archaeology Presented to Ezat O. Negahban*, edited by Abbas Alizadeh, Shapour Malek-Shahmirzadi, and Yousef Majidzadeh, pp. 137–45. Tehran: Iran University Press.

Haerinck, Ernie, and B. Overlaet

1996 *The Chalcolithic Period Parchinah and Hakalān: Belgian Archaeological Mission in Iran, the Excavations in Luristan, Pusht-i Kuh (1965–1979).* Brussels: Royal Museum of Art and History.

Haiman, Mordechai, and Yuval Goren

1992 "'Negbite' Pottery: New Aspects and Interpretations and the Role of Pastoralism in Designating Ceramic Technology." In *Pastoralism in the Levant: Archaeological Materials in Anthropological Perspectives*, edited by Ofer Bar-Yosef and Anatoly M. Khazanov, pp. 143–52. Madison: Prehistory Press.

Hansen, Donald P.

1965 "The Relative Chronology of Mesopotamia, Part 2: The Pottery Sequence at Nippur from the Middle Uruk to the End of the Old Babylonia Period." In *Chronologies in Old World Archaeology*, edited by Robert W. Ehrich, pp. 201–13. Chicago: University of Chicago Press.

Harner, M.

1970 "Population Pressure and Social Evolution of Agriculturalists." *Southwest Journal of Anthropology* 26: 67–86.

Heinrich, Ernst

1932 "Die Schichten und ihre Bauten." In *Vierter vorläufiger Bericht über die von der Notgemeinschaft der Deutschen Wissenschaft in Uruk unternommenen Ausgrabungen*, by A. Nöldeke, pp. 6–24. Abhandlungen der Preussichen Akademie du Wissenschaften, Jahrgang 1932; Philosophische-historische Klasse 6. Berlin: Verlag der Akademie der Wissenschaften.

1937 "Die Grabung im Planquadrat K XVII." In *Achter vorläufiger Bericht über die von der Deutschen Forschungsgemeinschaft in Uruk-Warka unternommenen Ausgrabungen*, by A. Nöldeke, pp. 27–55. Abhandlungen der Preussichen Akademie du Wissenschaften, Jahrgang 1936; Philosophische-historische Klasse 13. Berlin: Verlag der Akademie der Wissenschaften.

Helbaek, Hans

1969 "Plant Collecting, Dry-farming, and Irrigation Agriculture in Prehistoric Deh Luran." In *Prehistory and Human Ecology of the Deh Luran Plain: An Early Village Sequence from Khuzistan, Iran*, by F. Hole, K. V. Flannery, and J. A. Neely, pp. 383–426. Memoirs of the Museum of Anthropology 1. Ann Arbor: University of Michigan.

Helwing, Barbara

2000 "Regional Variations in the Composition of Late Chalcolithic Pottery Assemblages." In *Chronologies des pays du Caucase et de l'Euphrate aux IV^e^–III^e^ millénaires*, edited by Catherine Marro and Harald Hauptmann, pp. 145–64. Paris: De Boccard.

Henrickson, Elizabeth

1985 "An Updated Chronology of the Early and Middle Chalcolithic of the Central Zagros Highlands, Western Iran." *Iran* 23: 63–108.

Herzfeld, Ernst

1930 *Die Ausgrabungen von Samarra: Die vorgeschichtlichen Töpfereien von Samarra*. Berlin: Dietrich Reimer.

Hijjara, Ismail

1997 *The Halaf Period in Northern Mesopotamia*. Edubba 6. London: Nabu Publications.

Hinz, Walther

1973 *The Lost World of Elam: Re-creation of a Vanished Civilization*. New York: New York University.

Hoffman, Marta

1964 *The Warp-weighted Loom: Studies in the History and Technology of an Ancient Implement*. Studia Norvegica 14. Oslo: Universitetsforlaget.

Hole, Frank

1974 "Tepe Tula'i: An Early Campsite in Khuzistan, Iran." *Paléorient* 2: 219–42.

1975 "The Sondage at Tappeh Tula'i." *Proceedings of the Third Annual Symposium on Archaeological Research in Iran*, pp. 63–76. Tehran: Iranian Center for Archaeological Research.

1977 *Studies in the Archaeological History of the Deh Luran Plain: The Excavation of Chagha Sefid*. Memoirs of the Museum of Anthropology 9. Ann Arbor: University of Michigan.

1987 *The Archaeology of Western Iran: Settlement and Society from Prehistory to the Islamic Conquest*. Smithsonian Series in Archaeological Inquiry. Washington, D.C.: Smithsonian Institution Press.

1990 "Cemetery or Mass Grave? Reflections on Susa I." In *Contribution à l'Histoire de l'Iran: Mélanges offerts à Jean Perrot*, edited by François Vallat, pp. 1–14. Paris: Éditions Recherche sur les Civilisations.

Hole, Frank; Kent V. Flannery; and James A. Neely

1969 *Prehistory and Human Ecology of the Deh Luran Plain: An Early Village Sequence from Khuzistan, Iran*. Memoirs of the Museum of Anthropology 1. Ann Arbor: University of Michigan.

Huot, Jean-Louis; L. Bachelot; J. P. Braun; Yves Calvet; Serge Cleuziou; J. D. Forest; and J. Seigne

1980 "Larsa: Preliminary Report of the Seventh Campaign at Larsa and the First Campaign at Tell el-'Oueili (1976)." *Sumer* 36: 99–127.

Jéquier, G.

1900 "Travaux de l'hiver 1898–1899." In *Fouilles à Suse en 1897–1898 et 1898–1899*, by J. de Morgan, G. Jéquier, and G. Lampre, pp. 111–38. Mission archéologique en Perse 1. Paris: Ernest Leroux.

Johnson, Gregory Allan

1973 *Local Exchange and Early State Development in Southwestern Iran*. Anthropological Papers, Museum of Anthropology 51. Ann Arbor: University of Michigan.

1987 "Nine Thousand Years of Social Change in Western Iran." In *The Archaeology of Western Iran: Settlement and Society from Prehistory to the Islamic Conquest,* edited by Frank Hole, pp. 286–91. Smithsonian Series in Archaeological Inquiry. Washington, D.C.: Smithsonian Institution Press.

1988/89 "Late Uruk in Greater Mesopotamia: Expansion or Collapse?" *Origini* 14: 595–611.

Jordan, Julius

1932 *Dritter vorläufiger Bericht über die von der Notgemeinschaft der Deutschen Wissenschaft in Uruk unternommenen Ausgrabungen*. Berlin: Verlag der Akademie der Wissenschaften.

Kaboli, Mir Abedin

2000 *Archaeological Survey at Qomrud*. Tehran: Iranian Cultural Heritage Organization.

Kantor, Helene J.

1970/71 "Excavations at Chogha Mish and Boneh Fazili in Khuzestan, Iran." In *The Oriental Institute Annual Report 1970/71*, edited by J. A. Brinkman, pp. 23–30. Chicago: The Oriental Institute.

1972/73 "Excavations at Chogha Mish." *The Oriental Institute Annual Report 1972/73*, edited by J. A. Brinkman, pp. 10–17. Chicago: The Oriental Institute.

1974/75a "Excavations at Chogha Mish." *The Oriental Institute Annual Report 1974/75*, edited by J. A. Brinkman, pp. 17–26. Chicago: The Oriental Institute.

1974/75b "Excavations at Chogha Mish: 1974–75." *Second Annual Report to the Shancellor and to the Fellows of the Institute 1974/75*. Los Angeles: Institute of Archaeology, University of California Press.

1976 "The Prehistoric Cultures of Chogha Mish and Boneh Fazili." In *The Memorial Volume of the Sixth International Congress of Iranian Art and Archaeology, Oxford, September 11–16, 1972*, edited by M. Y. Kiani, pp. 177–93. Tehran: Iranian Center for Archaeological Research.

1976/77 "Excavations at Chogha Mish and Chogha Bonut." *The Oriental Institute Annual Report 1976/77*, edited by J. A. Brinkman, pp. 15–24. Chicago: The Oriental Institute.

1977 "The Elamite Cup from Chogha Mish." *Iran* 15: 11–14.

1989/90 "Chogha Mish." *The Oriental Institute Annual Report 1989/90*, edited by William M. Sumner, pp. 29–37. Chicago: The Oriental Institute.

Kirkbride, Diana

1972 "Umm Dabaghiyah 1971: A Preliminary Report." *Iraq* 34: 3–19.

1973a "Umm Dabaghiyah 1973: A Second Preliminary Report." *Iraq* 35: 1–7.

1973b "Umm Dabaghiyah 1973: A Third Preliminary Report." *Iraq* 35: 205–09.

1975 "Umm Dabaghiyah 1974: A Fourth Preliminary Report." *Iraq* 37: 3–10.

Kirkby, Michael J.

1977 "Land and Water Resources of the Deh Luran and Khuzestan Plains." In *Studies in the Archaeological History of the Deh Luran Plain*, edited by Frank Hole, pp. 251–88. Memoirs of the Museum of Anthropology 9. Ann Arbor: The University of Michigan Press.

Kohl, Phillip L.

1996 "The Ancient Economy, Transferable Technologies and the Bronze Age World-system: A View from the Northeastern Frontier of the Ancient Near East." In *Contemporary Archaeology in Theory: A Reader*, edited by Robert W. Preucel and Ian Hodder, pp. 143–64. Oxford: Blackwell.

Kouchoukos, Nicholas

1998 Landscape and Social Change in Late Prehistoric Mesopotamia. Ph.D. dissertation, Yale University.

Kramer, Carol

1985 "Ceramic Production and Specialization."*Paléorient* 11: 117–19.

Labrousse, Audran, and Rémy Boucharlat

1974 "La fouille du palais du Chaour à Suse en 1970 et 1971." *Cahiers de la délégation archéologique française en Iran* 2: 61–167.

Lamberg-Karlovsky, Carl C.

1970 *Excavations at Tepe Yahya, Iran, 1967–1969: Progress Report No. 1*. American School of Prehistoric Research 27. Cambridge: Harvard University Press.

1971 "The Proto-Elamite Settlement at Tepe Yahya." *Iran* 9: 87–95.

Lamberg-Karlovsky, Carl C., and Jeremy A. Sabloff

1979 *Ancient Civilizations: The Near East and Mesoamerica*. Menlo Park, CA: The Benjamin/Cummings Publishing Co.

Langsdorff, Alexander, and Donald E. McCown

1942 *Tall-i-Bakun A: Season of 1932*. Oriental Institute Publications 59. Chicago: University of Chicago Press.

Layard, Austin Henry

1846 "Description of the Province of Khuzistan." *Journal of the Royal Asiatic Society of London* 16: 1–105.

Le Breton, Louis

1947 "Note sur la céramique peinte aux environs de Suse et à Suse." In *Archéologique susienne*, by R. de Mecquenem, L. Le Breton, and M. Ruten, pp. 120–219. Mémoires de la mission archéologique en Iran, Mission de Susiane 30. Paris: Presses Universitaires de France.

1957 "The Early Periods at Susa, Mesopotamian Relations." *Iraq* 19: 79–124.

Le Brun, Alain

1971 "Recherches stratigraphiques: L'acropole de Suse 1969–1971." *Cahiers de la délégation archéologique française en Iran* 1: 163–216.

1978 "Suse, chantier "Acropole 1." *Paléorient* 4: 177-92

1980 "Les 'écuelles grossières': État de la question." In *L'archéologie de l'Iraq du d'époque néolithique à 333 avant notre ére*, edited by M.-T. Barrelet, pp. 59–70. Colloques internationaux du Centre National de la Recherche Scientifique 580. Paris: Éditions du Centre National de la Recherche Scientifique.

Lenzen, Heinrich

1964 "Die Siegelabrollungen." In *XX. vorläufiger Bericht über die von dem Deutschen Archäologischen Institut und der Deutschen Orient-Gesellschaft aus Mitteln der Deutschen Forschungsgemeinschaft unternommenen Ausgrabungen in Uruk-Warka*, edited by H. Lenzen, pp. 22–23. Berlin: Gebrüder Mann.

1974 "Terrakotten." In *XXV. vorläufiger Bericht über die von dem Deutschen Archäologischen Institut und der Deutschen Orient-Gesellschaft aus Mitteln der Deutschen Forschungsgemeinschaft unternommenen Ausgrabungen in Uruk-Warka*, edited by H. Lenzen, pp. 27–30. Berlin: Gebrüder Mann.

Levine, Louis, and T. Cuyler Young

1987 "A Summary of the Ceramic Assemblages of the Central Western Zagros from the Middle Neolithic to the Late Third Millennium B.C." In *Préhistoire de la Mésopotamie: La Mésopotamie préhistorique et l'exploration récente du Djebel Hamrin*, edited by J.-L. Huot, pp. 15–53. Colloque international du Centre National de la Recherche Scientifique. Paris: Éditions du Centre National de la Recherche Scientifique.

Levy, Thomas Evan

1983 "The Emergence of Specialized Pastoralism in the Southern Levant." *World Archaeology* 15: 15–36.

Lieberman, Stephen J.

1980 "Of Clay Pebbles, Hollow Clay Balls and Writing: A Sumerian View." *American Journal of Archaeology* 84: 339–58.

Lloyd, Seton

1978 *The Archaeology of Mesopotamia from the Old Stone Age to the Persian Conquest.* London: Thames & Hudson.

Lloyd, Seton, and Fuad Safar

1943 "Tell Uqair: Excavations by the Iraq Government Directorate of Antiquities in 1940 and 1941." *Journal of Near Eastern Studies* 2: 131–58.

1945 "Tell Hassuna: Excavations of the Iraq Government Directorate General of Antiquities in 1943 and 1944." *Journal of Near Eastern Studies* 4: 255–84.

1948 "Eridu: A Preliminary Communication on the Second Season's Excavations, 1947–1948." *Sumer* 4: 115–27.

Loftus, William Kennett

1857 *Travels and Researches in Chaldaea and Susiana.* London: James Nisbet.

Lupton, Alan

1996 *Stabilty and Change: Socio-political Development in North Mesopotamia and South-East Anatolia 4000–2700 B.C.* British Archaeological Reports International Series 627. Oxford: British Archaeological Reports.

Mackay, Ernest

1931 *Report on Excavations at Jemdet Nasr, Iraq.* Field Museum of Natural History, Anthropology Memoirs 1(3). Chicago: Field Museum Press.

Malek-Shahmirzadi, Sadegh

1977 "The Excavation of Sagzabad Mound, Qazvin Plain, Iran, 1970–71." *Marlik* 2: 67–79.

1979 "A Specialized Housebuilder in an Iranian Village of the VIth Millennium B.C." 5: 183–92.

1980 "Tepe Zagheh and the Problem of the Fugitive Painted Pottery." *Survey and Excavations* 3: 13–21.

Mallowan, Max E. L., and J. Cruikshank Rose

1935 "Excavations at Tell Arpachiyah, 1933." *Iraq* 2: 1–178.

Mander, Pietro

1986 *Il Pantheon di Abū-Ṣalābīkh.* Series Minor, Istituto Universitario Orientale Dipartimento di Studi Asiatici 26. Naples: Istituto Orientale.

Marro, Catherine, and Harald Hauptmann, editors

2000 *Chronologies des pays du Caucase et de l'Euphrate aux IV$^{e}$–III$^{e}$ millénaires.* Paris: De Boccard.

Marshack, Alexander

1972a *The Roots of Civilization: The Cognitive Beginnings of Man's First Art, Symbol and Notation.* New York: McGraw-Hill Book Company.

1972b "Upper Paleolithic Notation and Symbol." *Science* 178: 817–28.

Masson, V. M., and Victor I. Sarianidi

1972 *Central Asia: Turkmenia Before the Achaemenids.* Ancient Peoples and Places 79. London: Thames & Hudson.

Masuda, Seiichi

1972 "Excavations at Tappeh Sang-e Čaxmāq." In *Proceedings of the First Annual Symposium on Archaeological Research in Iran*, edited by F. Bagherzadeh, pp. 1–5. Tehran: Iranian Center for Archaeological Research.

1974 "Excavations at Tappeh Sang-e Čaxmāq." In *Proceedings of the Second Annual Symposium on Archaeological Research in Iran*, edited by F. Bagherzadeh. pp. 23–33. Tehran: Iranian Center for Archaeological Research.

Michalowski, Piotr

1993 Review of *Before Writing*, by D. Schmandt-Besserat. *American Anthropologist* 95: 996–99.

Miller, Daniel

1985 *Artefacts as Categories: A Study of Ceramic Variability in Central India.* Cambridge: Cambridge University Press.

Miller, Naomi F.

1996 "Seed-eaters of the Ancient Near East: Humans or Herbivore?" *Current Anthropology* 37: 521–28.

2003a "Archaeobotany in Iran, Past and Present." In *Yeki Bud, Yeki Nabud: Essays on the Archaeology of Iran in Honor of William M. Sumner,* edited by Naomi F. Miller and Kamyar Abdi, pp. 9–16. Cotsen Institute of Archaeology Monograph 48. Los Angeles: University of California, Los Angeles.

2003b "Plant Remains from the 1996 Excavation." In *Excavations at the Prehistoric Mound of Chogha Bonut, Khuzestan, Iran: Seasons 1976/77, 1977/78, and 1996*, by Abbas Alizadeh, pp. 123–28. Oriental Institute Publications 120. Chicago: The Oriental Institue.

Mortensen, Peder

1964 "Additional Remarks on the Chronology of Early Village Farming Communities in the Zagros Area." *Sumer* 20: 28–36.

1976 "Chalcolithic Settlements in the Holailan Valley." In *Proceedings of the Fourth Annual Symposium on Archaeological Research in Iran,* edited by F. Bagherzadeh, pp. 42–62. Tehran: Iranian Center for Archaeological Research.

Munchaev, R. M., and N. Ya. Merpert

1981 *Earliest Agricultural Settlements of Northern Mesopotamia: The Investigations of the Soviet Expedition in Iran.* In Russian with English summary. Moscow: Nauka.

Munchaev, R. M.; N. Ya. Merpert; and N. O. Bader

1984 "Archaeological Studies in the Sinjar Valley, 1980." *Sumer* 43: 32–53.

Neff, Hector

1993 "Theory, Sampling, and Analytical Techniques in the Archaeological Study of Prehistoric Ceramics." *American Antiquity* 58: 23–44.

1994 "RQ-mode Principal Components Analysis of Ceramic Compositional Data." *Archaeometry* 36: 115–30.

2000 "Neutron Activation Analysis for Provenance Determination in Archaeology." In *Modern Analytical Methods in Art and Archaeology,* edited by E. Ciliberto and G. Spoto, pp. 81–134. Chemical Analysis Series 155. New York: Wiley-Interscience.

Neff, Hector, and Michael D. Glascock

1997 Compositional Analysis of Early Third Millennium Mesopotamian Painted Ceramics. Unpublished report prepared for Geoff Emberling, Oriental Institute, the University of Chicago. University of Missouri Research Reactor, Columbia, Missouri.

Negahban, Ezat O.

1973 "Preliminary Report of the Excavation of Sagzabad." *Marlik* 1: 1–9.

1977 "Preliminary Report of Qazvin Expedition: Excavations of Zaghe, Qabrestan, and Sagzabad 1971–72." *Marlik* 2: 26–44.

Nicklin, Keith

1981 "Pottery Production and Distribution in Southeast Nigeria." In *Production and Distribution: A Ceramic Viewpoint*, edited by H. Howard and E. Morris, pp. 169–86. British Archaeological Report International Series 120. Oxford: British Archaeological Reports.

Nissen, Hans J.

1970 "Grabung in den Quadraten K/L XII in Uruk-Warka." *Baghdader Mitteilungen* 5: 101–91.

1986 "The Development of Writing and Glyptic Art." In *Ǧamdat Naṣr: Period or Regional Style?*, Papers given at a symposium held in Tübingen, November 1993, edited by Uwe Finkbeiner and Wolfgang Röllig, pp. 316–31. Beihefte zum Tübinger Atlas des Vorderen Orients, Reihe B, Geisteswissenschaften 62. Wiesbaden: Reichert.

1988 *The Early History of the Ancient Near East 9000–2000 B.C.* Chicago: University of Chicago Press.

2001 "Cultural and Political Networks in the Ancient Near East during the Fourth and Third Millennia B.C." In *Uruk Mesopotamia and Its Neighbors*, edited by Mitchell Rothman, pp. 149–80. The School of American Research Advanced Seminar Series. Santa Fe: School of American Research.

Nissen, Hans J.; Peter Damerow; and Robert K. Englund

1991 *Frühe Schrift und Techniken der Wirtschaftsverwaltung im alten Vorderen Orient: Informationsspeicherung und -verarbeitung vor 5000 Jahren*. Bad Salzdetfurth: Franzbecker.

Oates, Joan

1959 "Late Assyrian Pottery from Fort Shalmaneser." *Iraq* 21: 130–46.

1960 "Ur and Eridu: The Prehistory." *Iraq* 22: 32–50.

1968 "Prehistoric Investigations Near Mandali, Iraq." *Iraq* 30: 1–20.

1969 "Chogha Mami 1967–68: A Preliminary Report." *Iraq* 31: 115–52.

1993 "Trade and Power in the 5th and 4th Millennia B.C.: New Evidence from Northern Mesopotamia." *World Archaeology* 24: 403–22.

Oates, Joan; T. E. Davidson; D. Kamilli; and E. McKerrell

1977 "Seafaring Merchants of Ur?" *Antiquity* 60: 221–34.

Oppenheim, A. Leo

1959 "On an Operational Device in Mesopotamian Bureaucracy." *Journal of Near Eastern Studies* 18: 121–28.

Pollard, A. M.

1986 "Data Analysis." In *Greek and Cypriot Pottery: A Review of Scientific Studies*, edited by R. E. Jones, pp. 56–83. Fitch Laboratory, Occasional Paper 1. Athens: British School at Athens.

Pollock, Susan

1989 "Power and Politics in the Susa A Period." In *Upon This Foundation: The 'Ubaid Reconstructed*, edited by Elizabeth F. Henrickson and Ingolf Thuesen, pp. 281–92. Copenhagen: Universty of Copenhagen Press.

2001 "The Uruk Period in Southern Mesopotamia." In *Uruk Mesopotamia and Its Neighbors*, edited by Mitchell S. Rothman, pp. 181–232. The School of American Research Advanced Seminar Series. Santa Fe: School of American Research.

Porada, Edith

1969 "Iranian Art and Achaeology: A Report of the Fifth International Congress, 1968." *Archaeology* 22: 54–71.

Possehl, Gregory L.

1998 "Sociocultural Complexity Without the State: The Indus Civilization." In *Archaic States*, edited by Gary M. Feinman and Joyce Marcus, pp. 261–93. The School of American Research Advanced Seminar Series. Santa Fe: The School of American Research.

Pottier, Edmond

1923 *Corpus Vasorum Antiquorum: France, Musée du Louvre,* Fascicule 1. Paris: Librairie Ancienne Edouard Champion.

Potts, Daniel T.

1999 *The Archaeology of Elam: Formation and Transformation of an Ancient Iranian State.* Cambridge: Cambridge University Press.

Powell, Marvin Adell, Jr.

1981 "Three Problems in the History of Cuneifom Writing: Origins, Direction of Script, Literacy." *Visible Language* 15: 419–40.

Redding, Richard

1981 Decision Making and Subsistence Herding of Sheep and Goats in the Middle East. Ph.D. dissertation, University of Michigan.

1993 "Subsistence Security as a Selective Pressure Favoring Increased Cultural Complexity." *Bulletin of Sumerian Agriculture* 7: 77–98.

2003 "First Report on Faunal Remains." In *Excavations at the Prehistoric Mound of Chogha Bonut, Khuzestan, Iran: Seasons 1976/77, 1977/78, and 1996,* by Abbas Alizadeh, pp. 137–47. Oriental Institute Publications 120. Chicago: The Oriental Institute.

Rezvani, Hasan

1999 "Prehistoric Settlement Patterns and Cultures in Semnan Province, Central Plateau, Iran." In *The Iranian World: Essays on Iranian Art and Archaeology Presented to Ezat O. Negahban,* edited by Abbas Alizadeh, Shapour Malek-Shahmizadi, and Yousef Majidzadeh, pp. 7–20 (English summary, pp. 220–21). Tehran: Iran University Press.

Rice, Prudence

1987 *Pottery Analysis.* Chicago: University of Chicago Press.

Rosen Miller, Arlene

2003 "Preliminary Phytolith Analyses." In *Excavations at the Prehistoric Mound of Chogha Bonut, Khuzestan, Iran: Season 1976/77, 1977/78, and 1996,* by Abbas Alizadeh, pp. 129–35. Oriental Institute Publications 120. Chicago: The Oriental Institute.

Rothman, Mitchell S., editor

2001 *Uruk Mesopotamia and Its Neighbors*. School of American Research Advanced Seminar Series. Santa Fe: School of American Research.

Safar, Fuad; Muhammed Ali Mustafa; and Seton Lloyd

1981 *Eridu*. Baghdad: Republic of Iraq, Ministry of Culture and Information, and the State Organization of Antiquities and Heritage.

Scheil, Vincent

1923 *Textes de comptabilié proto-élamites (nouvelle série)*. Mémoires de la Mission archéologique de Perse 17. Paris: Ernest Leroux.

Schmandt-Besserat, Denise

1974 "The Use of Clay Before Pottery in the Zagros." *Expedition* 16: 11–17.

1977a "An Archaic Recording System and the Origin of Writing." *Syro-Mesopotamian Studies* 1: 1–32.

1977b "The Beginnings of the Use of Clay in Turkey." *Anatolian Studies* 27: 133–50.

1978 "The Earliest Precursor of Writing." *Scientific American* 238: 50–59.

1992 *Before Writing*. Volume 1: *From Counting to Cuneiform*. Austin: University of Texas Press.

Schmidt, Erich F.

1932 *Researches in Anatolia*. Volume 4: *The Alishar Hüyük Seasons of 1928 and 1929,* Part 1. Oriental Institute Publications 19. Chicago: University of Chicago Press.

1957 *Persepolis*. Volume 2: *Contents of the Treasury and Other Discoveries*. Oriental Institute Publications 69. Chicago: University of Chicago Press.

Schwartz, Glen

1988 "Excavations at Karatut Mevkii and Perspectives on the Uruk/Jemdet Nasr Expansion." *Akkadica* 56: 1–41.

Senior, Loise

1998 Time and Technological Change: Ceramic Production, Labor, and Economic Transformation in a Third Millennium Complex Society (Tell Leilan, Syria). Ph.D. dissertation, Department of Anthropology, University of Arizona.

Sheffer, Avigail

1981 "The Use of Perforated Clay Balls on the Warp-Weighted Loom." *Journal of the Tel Aviv University Institute of Archaeology* 8: 81–83.

Sherratt, Andrew

1983 "The Secondary Exploitation of Animals in the Old World." *Paléorient World Archaeology* 15(1): 90–108.

Sinopoli, Carla

1988 "The Organization of Craft Production at Vijayanagara, South India." *American Anthropologist* 90: 580–97.

1991 *Approaches to Archaeological Ceramics*. New York: Plenum.

Smith, Andrew B.

1983 "Prehistoric Pastoralism in the Southwestern Cape, South Africa." *World Archaeology* 15: 79–89.

Smith, Philip E. L.

1976 "Reflections on Four Seasons of Excavations at Tappeh Ganj Dareh." In *Proceedings of the Fourth Annual Symposium on Archaeological Research in Iran*, edited by F. Bagherzadeh, pp. 11–22. Tehran: Iranian Center for Archaeological Research.

Speiser, Ephraim A.

1935 *Excavations at Tepe Gawra*. Volume 1. Joint Expedition of the Baghdad School, the University Museum, and Dropsie College to Mesopotamia. Philadelphia: University of Pennsylvania Press.

Spycket, Agnès

1992 *Les figurines de Suse*. Volume 1: *Les figurines humaines des IV$^{e}$–II$^{e}$ millénaires avant J.-C*. Mémoires de la délégation archéologique en Iran 52. Paris: Gabalda.

1995 "Kassite and Middle Elamite Sculptures." In *Later Mesopotamia and Iran: Tribes and Empries 1600–539 B.C.*, edited by John Curtis, pp. 25–32. London: British Museum Press.

Stark, Freya

1934 *The Valleys of the Assassins and Other Persian Travels.* London: John Murray.

Stein, Gil

1994 "Economy, Ritual, and Power in 'Ubaid Mesopotamia." In *Chiefdoms and Early States in the Near East: The Organizational Dynamics of Complexity*, edited by Gil Stein and Mitchell S. Rothman, pp. 35–46. Monographs in World Archaeology 18. Madison: Prehistory Press.

1999 *Rethinking World-Systems: Diasporas, Colonies, and Interaction in Uruk Mesopotamia.* Tucson: University of Arizona Press.

Stein, Sir Mark Aurel

1936 "An Archaeological Tour in the Ancient Persis." *Iraq* 3: 112–225.

Steinkeller, Piotr

1993 "Early Political Developments in Mesopotamia and the Origins of the Sargonic Empire." In *Akkad, The First World Empire: Structure, Ideology, Traditions*, edited by M. Liverani, pp. 107–30. History of the Ancient Near East 5. Padova: Sargon.

Stève, Marie-Joseph, and Hermann Gasche

1971 *L'Acropole de Suse: Nouvelles fouilles (rapport préliminaire).* Mémoires de la délégation archéologique en Iran, Mission de Susiane 46. Leiden: Brill.

1990 "Le tell de l'Apadana avant les Achéménides: Contribution à la topographie de Suse." In *Contribution à l'histoire d'Iran: Mélanges offerts à Jean Perrot,* edited by F. Vallat, pp. 15–60. Paris: Éditions Recherche sur les Civilisations.

Stommenger, Eva

1980 *Habuba Kabira: Eine Stadt vor 5000 Jahren: Ausgrabungen der Deutschen Orient-Gesellschaft am Euphrat in Habuba Kabira, Syrien.* Mainz am Rhein: Philipp von Zabern.

Strommenger, Eva, and Dietrich Sürenhagen

1970 "Die Grabung in Habuba Kabira-Süd." *Mitteilungen der Deutschen Orient-Gesellschaft zu Berlin* 102: 59–71.

Stronach, David

1961 "The Excavations at Ras al-ʿAmiya." *Iraq* 23: 95–137.

1978 *Pasargadae: A Report on the Excavations Conducted by the British Institute of Persian Studies from 1961 to 1963.* Oxford: Oxford University Press.

Stronach, David, and Michael Roaf

1978 "Excavations at Tepe Nush-i Jan, Part 1: A Third Interim Report." *Iran* 16: 1–28.

Sürenhagen, Dietrich

1974/75 "Untersuchungen zur Keramikproduktion innerhalb der Spät-Urukzeitlichen Siedlung Habuba Kabira-Süd in Nordsyrien." *Acta Praehistorica et Archaeologica* 5/6: 43–164.

1986 "Archäische Keramik aus Uruk-Warka, Erster Teil: Die Keramik der Schichten XVI–VI aus den Sondagen 'Tiefschnitt' und 'Sägengraben' in Eanna." *Baghdader Mitteilungen* 17: 7–95.

1987 "Archäische Keramik aus Uruk-Warka, Zweiter Teil: Keramik der Schicht V aus dem 'Sägengraben'; 'Keramik der schichten VII bis II' in Eanna; die registrierte Keramik aus den Sondagen O XI–XII und K–L XII–XIII; Keramik von der Anu-Zikkurat in K XVII." *Baghdader Mitteilungen* 18: 1–92.

Theusen, Ingolf, and Kaj Heydorn

1991 "Instrumental Neutron Activation Analysis of EDI–II Pottery from the Diyala Region and Farukhabad." In *Uch Tepe* 2: *Technical Reports*, edited by McGuire Gibson, pp. 65–89. Hamrin Report 11. Chicago: The Oriental Institute.

Tobler, Arthur J.

1950 *Excavations at Tepe Gawra.* Volume 2: *Levels IX–XX.* American School of Oriental Research in Baghdad, Publications of the Baghdad School 2. Philadelphia: University of Pennsylvania Press.

Vallat, François

1971 "Les documents épigraphique de l'acropole (1969–1971)." *Cahiers de la délégation archéologique française en Iran* 1: 235–45.

Vallet, Régis

1996 "L'architecture des phases Obeid 0 et 1: Travaux de 1989." In *Oueili: Travaux de 1987 et 1989*, edited by Jean-Louis Huot, pp. 103–40. Paris: Centre National de la Recherche Scientifique.

Vanden Berghe, Louis

1970 "La nécropole de Kalleh Nisar." *Archéologia* 32: 64–73.

1973a "Le Luristan avant l'âge du Bronze: La nécropole de Hakalān." *Archéologia* 57: 49–58.

1973b "Le Luristan avant l'âge du Bronze: La nécropole de Hakalān." In *Proceedings of the Second Annual Symposium on Archaeological Research in Iran*, edited by F. Bagherzadeh, pp. 66–79. Tehran: Iranian Center for Archaeological Research.

1975 "Luristan: La nécropole de Dum-Gar-Parchinah." *Archéology* 79: 46–61.

1987 "Luristan: Pusht-i-Kuh au chalcolithique moyen (les nécropoles de Parchinah et Hakalān)." In *Préhistoire de la Mésopotamie*: *La Mésopotamie préhistorique et l'exploration récente du Djebel Hamrin*, by Jean-Louis Huot, pp. 91–106. Colloque international du Centre National de la Recherche Scientifique. Paris: Éditions du Centre National de la Recherche Scientifique.

Veenenbos, J.

1958 *Unified Report on the Soil and Land Classification Survey of Dezful Project, Khuzestan, Iran.* Tehran: Khuzestan Development Project.

Voigt, Mary

1983 *Hajji Firuz Tepe, Iran: The Neolithic Settlement.* University Museum Monograph 50. Philadelphia: The University Museum, University of Pennsylvania.

von Haller, Arndt

1932 "Die Keramik der archäischen Schichten von Uruk." In *Vierter vorläufiger Bericht über die von der Notgemeinschaft der Deutschen Wissenschaft in Uruk unternommenen Ausgrabungen*, edited by A. Nöldeke, pp. 31–47. Berlin: Verlag der Akademie der Wissenschaften.

Warren, Peter

1972 *Myrtos: An Early Bronze Age Settlement in Crete.* Oxford: Alden Press.

Weiss, Harvey

1976 Ceramics for Chronology: Discriminant and Cluster Analyses of Fifth Millennium Ceramic Assemblages from Qabr Sheykheyn, Khuzistan. Ph.D. dissertation, University of Pennsylvania.

1977 "Periodization, Population and Early State Formation in Khuzistan." In *Mountains and Lowlands: Essays in the Archaeology of Greater Mesopotamia*, edited by Lou Levine and T. Cuyler Young, Jr., pp. 347–69. Bibliotheca Mesopotamica 7. Malibu: Udena Publications.

Weiss, Harvey, and T. Cuyler Young, Jr.

1975 "The Merchants of Susa: Godin V and Plateau-Lowland Relations in the Late Fourth Millennium B.C." *Iran* 13: 1–17.

Wenke, Robert J.

1975/76 "Imperial Investments and Agricultural Developments in Parthian and Sasanian Khuzestan, 150 B.C. to A.D. 640." *Mesopotamia* 10–11: 31–221.

Wheeler Pires-Ferreira, Jane

1976/77 "Tepe Tula'i: Faunal Remains from an Early Camp Site in Khuzestan, Iran." *Paléorient* 3: 275–80.

Woolley, C. Leonard

1955 *Ur Excavations.* Volume 4: *The Early Periods.* Philadelphia: Allen, Lane & Scott.

Woosley, Anne I.

1996 "Early Agriculture at Chogha Mish." In *Chogha Mish,* Volume 1: *The First Five Seasons of Excavations,* by Pinhas Delougaz and Helene J. Kantor, pp. 307–18. Edited by Abbas Alizadeh. Chicago: The Oriental Institute.

Woosley, Anne I. and Frank Hole
1978 "Pollen Evidence of Subsistence and Environment in Ancient Iran." *Paléorient* 4: 59–70.

Wright, Henry T.
1981a *An Early Town on the Deh Luran Plain: Excavations at Tepe Farukhabad.* Memoirs of the Museum of Anthropology 13. Ann Arbor: University of Michigan.
1981b "The Southern Margins of Sumer: Archaeological Survey of the Area of Eridu and Ur." In *Heartland of Cities: Surveys of Ancient Settlement and Land Use in the Central Floodplain of the Euphrates*, by Robert McCormick Adams, pp. 295–345. Chicago: University of Chicago Press.
1998 "Uruk States in Southwestern Iran." In *Archaic States*, edited by Gary M. Feinman and Joyce Marcus, pp. 173–98. School of American Research Advanced Seminar Series. Santa Fe: The School of American Research.
2001 "Cultural Action in the Uruk World." In *Uruk Mesopotamia and Its Neighbors*, edited by Mitchell S. Rothman, pp. 123–48. School of American Research Advanced Seminar Series. Santa Fe: School of American Research.

Wright, Henry T., and Gregory A. Johnson
1975 "Population, Exchange, and Early State Formation in Southwestern Iran." *American Anthropologist* 77: 267–89.
1985 "Regional Perspectives on Southwest Iranian State Development." *Paléorient* 11: 25–30.

Wright, Henry T.; James A. Neely; Gregory A. Johnson; and J. Speth
1975 "Early Fourth Millennium Developments in Southwestern Iran." *Iran* 13: 129–48.

Wright, Henry T., and E. S. A. Rupley
2001 "Calibrated Radiocarbon Age Determinations of Uruk-Related Assemblages." In *Uruk Mesopotamia and Its Neighbors*, edited by Mitchell S. Rothman, pp. 85–122. School of American Research Advanced Seminar Series. Santa Fe: School of American Research.

Yoffee, Norman
1995 "Political Economy in Early Mesopotamian States." *Annual Review of Anthropology* 24: 281–311.

Young, T. Cuyler, Jr.
1965 "A Comparative Ceramic Chronology for Western Iran, 1500–500 B.C." *Iran* 3: 53–83.
1969 *Excavations at Godin Tepe: First Progress Report.* Royal Ontario Museum, Art and Archaeology, Occasional Paper 17. Toronto: The Royal Ontario Museum.

Young, T. Cuyler, Jr., and Louis D. Levine
1974 *Excavations of the Godin Project: Second Progress Report.* Royal Ontario Museum, Art and Archaeology, Occasional Paper 26. Toronto: The Royal Ontario Museum.

Zeder, Melinda A.
1999 "Animal Domestication in the Zagros: A Review of Past and Current Research." *Paléorient* 25: 11–26.

Zeder, Melinda A., and Brian Hesse
2000 "The Initial Domestication of Goats (*Capra hircus*) in the Zagros Mountains 10,000 Years Ago." *Science* 287: 2254–57.

Ziegler, Charlotte
1953 *Die Keramik von der Qal'a des Ḥağği Moḥammed.* Ausgrabungen der Deutschen Forschungsgemeinschaft in Uruk-Warka 5. Berlin: Gebrüder Mann.

Zimansky, Paul
1993 Review of *Before Writing*, by D. Schmandt-Besserat. *Journal of Field Archaeology* 20: 513–17.

# CHAPTER ONE

# THE STORY OF CHOGHA MISH AND ITS WIDER CONTEXT

## INTRODUCTION

Chogha Mish (KS-01), 32°13′ north, 48°33′ east (3567887 N/269677 E, UTM 39N), in lowland Susiana (in modern-day Khuzestan province), is the largest pre-Sasanian settlement in northeastern Susiana. The site is located between the outlets of the large perennial rivers of Dez and Karun. Closer to the site are two important tributaries of the Dez River, the Sia Mansur River, about 8 km to the west, just west of Jundi Shapur; and the Shur River, slightly less than 1 km to the east of Chogha Mish (figs. 1–2, pls. 1:A, 31). As in most areas in northern Khuzestan, dry farming is possible but involves some risk. However, the seepage from the Karkheh, Shaur, Dez as well as the Sia Mansur, the Lure, and the Shur rivers considerably reduces the risk. It was perhaps this environmental feature that encouraged the early settlements (Chogha Bonut, Chogha Mish, and Boneh Fazl Ali [Boneh Fazili in the literature]) to be established in this part of Khuzestan. Moreover, this area is much closer to the mountains (see pl. 1:A) and one can reach the nearby hill without having to cross major water courses (for more details, see Adams 1962:109–10; Layard 1846; Lees and Falcon 1952).

Lowland Susiana is often referred to by archaeologists and historians as an extension of the Mesopotamian plain. This is, of course, true geologically and to some extent ecologically; both regions consist of flat alluvial fertile land with major rivers. Nevertheless, there are some fundamental differences between the two regions that must have contributed to their specific long-term trajectories of cultural development. Lowland Susiana is much closer to the mountains and the entire width of the plain can be crossed on foot in less than a day. This proximity provides easy access to stone and wood. Additional sources of stone are provided by the Dez and, especially, the Karkheh rivers that deposit on their banks in upper Susiana large to small size pebbles of many types of rocks. The banks of the rivers and major water channels have thick stands of reeds that are used for fuel and in a number of utilitarian objects.

Before the introduction of modern canal irrigation technology, the center of the plain was crisscrossed by many small natural streams that could be easily tapped for small-scale irrigation (Adams 1962). The difficulty involved in crossing numerous water channels for sheep and goats perhaps can account for the historical spatial distribution of the pastoralist tribes in the region, with the Dez as the borderline between the Bakhtiyari tribes who descend on the plain from the east and northeast and the Lurs and Arab-speaking tribes who come from the northeast.

In the upper Susiana plain, the pebbly soil is fed by underground springs and high water table from the seepage of the Karkheh and the Dez rivers that make the area ideal for both pasture and dry farming (Adams 1962: 110) — in fact the Shaur River originates some 20 km north of Susa from many small and large springs on the east bank of the Karkheh. In the eastern sector of the plain, before the area was cut by numerous wadis that today mark the landscape, seasonal floodwaters were distributed widely across the area, making the practice of recessional, or décrue, farming possible (Alizadeh et al. 2004). This is the heart of the winter pasture land of the Bakhtiyari tribes, and compared with the lands on the west bank of the Karun River, ancient villages here are rare, especially before the second millennium B.C., as are modern-day villages today. In 1961, when archaeological and geomorphological evidence from Khuzestan was much more limited, Adams (1962: 115) observed that "...Elamite military prowess did not derive from a large, densely settled peasantry occupying irrigated lowlands in what is often loosely considered the heart of Elam. Instead, the enclave around Susa must have been merely one component in a more heterogeneous and loosely structured grouping of forces."

Unlike southern Mesopotamia, dry farming is much less risky and major canal irrigation does not seem to have been practiced until the middle of the second millennium B.C. at the earliest (Alizadeh et al. 2004). If this was the case, then in lowland Susiana, unlike southern Mesopotamia, there could not have been a fierce competition between upstream and downstream irrigators, which Adams (1974) considers as a major source of conflict and perhaps a practical reason for the development of urban life and fortified cities as an adaptive measure against the uncertain conditions of farming.

The gradient in upper Susiana is much steeper than in lower Mesopotamia and therefore salinization, especially in the central and western part of the region, is not and may not have been a problem. No permanent or seasonal marshes exist in upper Susiana; but in the lower part, south of the Haft Tappeh anticline, vast areas become seasonally inundated and when dried in summer, a layer of salt covers the dried bottoms of these marshes.

Eleven seasons of excavations at the site have provided a long, almost uninterrupted prehistoric sequence of cultural development in southwest Asia.[1] Thus, Chogha Mish is uniquely qualified to demonstrate in a single location a series of major developments that took place during the entire prehistoric period in southwestern Asia. These developments include the gradual appearance of central places, increasing specialization and improvement in the production of material culture, changes in subsistence economy, integrated interaction in material culture and ideas, and the development of social complexity that resulted in the emergence of state society.

It was, nevertheless, at the small nearby site of Chogha Bonut (KS-428, 3567695 N/264950 E, UTM 39N) where the earliest episode of human colonization of lowland Susiana occurred (fig. 2). Therefore a better understanding of the prehistoric initial sociocultural development in the region must include the archaeological results obtained from this aceramic site (Alizadeh 2003a–b). The purpose of this chapter is to provide a narrative backdrop against which the reader may follow the myriad of archaeological data presented and discussed in this and the previous volumes.

The earliest cultural phase discovered at Chogha Mish, the Archaic Susiana 1 phase, dates to ca. 6800 B.C. Cultural phases much earlier than the basal levels of Chogha Mish were accidentally discovered in the nearby mound of Chogha Bonut in 1977.[2] Helene Kantor first investigated the mound, but her work at the site was postponed indefinitely in 1978. Eighteen years later I was able to secure a permit and resume Kantor's work at the site. To date, Chogha Bonut stands as the oldest lowland village in Susiana. It is a small mound; in its truncated and artificially rounded state, it has a diameter of about 50 m and is about 5 m high. The calibrated radiocarbon dates indicate that Chogha Bonut was first occupied sometime in the second half of the eighth millennium B.C., in the aceramic period. The site continued to be occupied until the beginning of the Archaic Susiana 1 phase (the earliest phase attested at Chogha Mish, some 6 km to the east) when it was deserted for at least one millennium. Then, sometime in the early fifth millennium B.C. (late Middle Susiana phase),[3] Chogha Bonut was re-occupied and remained inhabited for perhaps several generations. It was deserted once again sometime before the end of the beginning of the Late Susiana 1 phase (see tables 1–2).

The discovery of an early, aceramic phase of occupation at Chogha Bonut not only provided a wider context for the evolution of the Archaic period, but also indicated that farmers colonized the lowlands much earlier than we had anticipated. Except for Tappeh Ali Kosh, located in the Deh Luran plain north of Susiana, all aceramic Neolithic sites in Iran are situated in the highlands of the Zagros Mountains. These early Neolithic sites with a mixed economy of farming and hunting-gathering are informative about the beginning of village life in western Iran. Unlike Chogha Bonut and Ali Kosh, these early villages were located in the natural habitats of the early domesticates during the transitional period from hunting animals to herding and managing them (Zeder and Hesse 2000).

Before the 1996 investigations of the basal aceramic levels of Chogha Bonut, the Bus Mordeh phase at Tappeh Ali Kosh was the earliest lowland village thought to have been established at or soon after the initial phase of animal and plant domestication (Hole, Flannery, and Neely 1969). The location of Ali Kosh was considered special because it lay outside of the presumed natural realm of the major domesticated species of wheat, barley, sheep, and goats. Therefore, scholars interpreted the case of Ali Kosh as evidence for the early Holocene Agricultural Revolution. After initial steps toward domestication in the highlands, it is assumed that increases in population forced some communities to split and move to more marginal areas where their survival depended on an economic strategy of farming and herding animals mixed with hunting and gathering.

As we argue elsewhere (Alizadeh 2003a), radiocarbon dates reported from the early highland sites put all the early Neolithic aceramic sites in western Iran within the 8000–7000 B.C. brackets. However, considering the problems with radiocarbon dating, these dates alone are not sufficient as a definite criterion to establish chronological priority of any of these early sites. Some sites (e.g., Tappeh Asiab[4] and Tappeh Ganj Dareh[5]) yielded morphologi-

1. The only exception is the short interval during the Late Susiana 1 phase when Chogha Mish appears to have been temporarily abandoned. For more details on this phase, see *Chapter 3*.
2. See Alizadeh 1997, 2003a.
3. For a detailed discussion on the subdivision of the Middle and Late Susiana periods into Early Middle Susiana, Late Middle Susiana, Late Susiana 1, and Late Susiana 2 phases, see *Chapter 4*; Alizadeh 1992: 22–26; idem 1996; and *Chogha Mish* I, pp. 280–84, 298–300.
4. Braidwood 1960a, 1960b.
5. Smith 1976.

cally wild species of the plants and animals that at Tappeh Ali Kosh and Chogha Bonut are considered morphologically domesticated. Based on these remains, Ali Kosh and Chogha Bonut can be assigned a later date than Asiab and Ganj Dareh. Zeder's AMS analysis of bones also shows that Asiab and Ganj Dareh are earlier than Tappeh Guran and Ali Kosh (Zeder 1999; see also below).

The chronological position of the Chogha Bonut aceramic phase vis-à-vis the Bus Mordeh phase in Deh Luran has theoretical implications in terms of the occupation of the lowlands on the eve of domestication. However, the paucity of excavated materials dating to the initial phases of the Neolithic prevents us from proposing a chronological framework without the use of radiocarbon dates. Nevertheless, comparative analyses of the pottery sequences from the early villages in Susiana and Deh Luran indicate that, at least in southwestern Iran, pottery manufacture began earlier in Susiana than it did in Deh Luran and continued to influence Deh Luran for several millennia (Alizadeh 2003a: 43–48). Moreover, the T-shaped figurines, so characteristic of the early Neolithic sites in western and southwestern Iran (e.g., Tappeh Sarab,[6] Chogha Bonut,[7] Chogha Mish,[8] and Tappeh Ali Kosh[9]) and northeastern Iraq (e.g., Jarmo), occurred from the beginning of the occupation at Chogha Bonut but seem to have appeared later in the Ali Kosh and Mohammad Jafar phases in Deh Luran.[10] Admittedly, this observation is based on uncertain grounds and it is perfectly possible that the aceramic deposits at Chogha Bonut and Ali Kosh were contemporary.

New approaches and analyses shed more light on this problem. As mentioned above, using AMS technique, Zeder and Hesse (2000) dated four samples of charred barley and twelve bone collagen samples from all five levels at Tappeh Ganj Dareh and concluded that the site had a short period of occupation (100–200 years) sometime around 10,000 B.P. The same authors also provided some new AMS dates from Tappeh Ali Kosh that indicate a much shorter occupation there than previously thought, lasting some 500 years. These new dates put the initial occupation at Ali Kosh (Bus Mordeh phase) at about 8,900 B.P. and thus at least 500 years later than that of Ganj Dareh. The authors conclude that the initial domestication of goats must have taken place in the highlands, the natural habitat of the species. These new AMS dates support our claim that Chogha Bonut may have been occupied earlier than Ali Kosh. Samples from the basal levels at Chogha Bonut provided a date of 7505–7025 B.C. (Beta-104552), suggesting that Chogha Bonut was occupied at least 100 years before Ali Kosh.

An understanding of the environmental conditions suitable for practicing agriculture and animal husbandry is, of course, of great importance in interpreting the early stages of the development of domestication in the Near East. Unfortunately, comparatively little research in terms of post-Pleistocene/early Holocene climates has been conducted in Iran; prior to the 1996 excavations at Chogha Bonut, the environmental and climatic conditions of the early Neolithic period in lowland Susiana were extrapolated from the data pertinent to the Deh Luran region. Important evidence for the environmental conditions of lowland Susiana in the beginning of the early Neolithic period is provided by the results of the analysis of the flora, phytoliths, and fauna from Chogha Bonut. The results of these analyses indicated that in the eighth millennium B.C. Susiana was a wet grassland and perhaps contained a number of marshes with attending characteristic fauna and flora.[11]

In the *Preface* we briefly discuss the evidence indicating that the region between the Shur and Sia Mansur rivers, where most of the Archaic sites are located, is today higher than the surrounding areas (fig. 88). The shallow bases of both Chogha Mish and Chogha Bonut (only between 1.0 and 2.5 m below the level of the plain) also indicate that perhaps in the early Neolithic period vast stretches of marshes dotted the upper Susiana plain. The early inhabitants of the plain seem to have chosen to settle on higher ground away from marshes and from areas susceptible to flooding by the rivers and natural streams before they had started to cut down their beds much later. If further research supports this settlement pattern, then it is not surprising that, with the exception of Tappeh Tuleii, presumably a pastoral nomadic camp (see below), all the known Archaic period sites are located in the triangular region between the Sia Mansur and Shur rivers. Furthermore, this evidence also explains why site preservation is much higher here than elsewhere on the plain.[12]

6. Braidwood 1960a, 1960b, 1961.
7. Alizadeh 1997, 2003a.
8. *Chogha Mish* I.
9. Hole, Flannery, and Neely 1969.
10. At Tappeh Ali Kosh the earliest aceramic phase of Bus Mordeh did not produce any T-shaped figurines. The following phases of Ali Kosh and Mohammad Jafar produced respectively two and ten examples (Hole, Flannery, and Neely 1969: 226, fig. 98).
11. See Redding 2003 and Miller 2003b.
12. In our 2004–2005 research in central Khuzestan, we found on the east bank of Nahr-e Khalaf (an artificial irrigation canal issuing from the Ojirub River) remnants of an unreported small Early Susiana site some 100 m northwest of Chogha Do Sar (KS-04) that had been bulldozed, according to the local farmers, in the last two decades. Our test trench, located at what we thought to be the center of the mound, reached virgin soil 50 cm below the present level of the plain. The project was supported by NSF grant B.C. S-0345988.

# INITIAL COLONIZATION OF LOWLAND SUSIANA (ACERAMIC PHASE)

The combined archaeological evidence from Chogha Bonut and Chogha Mish is now sufficient to revise the chronological sequence originally suggested by Kantor. Thus the earliest basal levels at Chogha Bonut that did not produce any ceramic vessels comprise the initial aceramic phase. In this phase, the early settlers of the Susiana plain chose to settle on top of a low natural hill surrounded by shallow marshes at an elevation where dry farming was possible — presumably Ali Kosh in the Deh Luran plain, too, was established on the edge of a swamp (Woosley and Hole 1978:64). Even today, when the region is much drier than it was in early Neolithic times, some farmers practice dry agriculture as a supplement. The early farmers of lowland Susiana cultivated wheat, barley, and lentils and kept domesticated sheep, goats, pigs, and dogs. Hunting and gathering supplemented this mixed subsistence economy.

During the initial aceramic phase, the chipped stone industry and the manufacture of stone vessels were highly developed. In the limited exposure of the 1996 excavations at Chogha Bonut, no traces of solid architecture were found, but fragmentary pieces of straw-tempered mudbricks suggest the existence of solid architecture. We assume that the inhabitants of this early site came from the highlands, for there is a great similarity of the Chogha Bonut chipped stone industry, clay and stone figurines, and tokens to those found at the early sites in the highlands.

# FORMATIVE SUSIANA PHASE

Soon after the initial aceramic phase at Chogha Bonut, plain, crude pottery vessels of simple shapes appeared, marking the beginning of the Formative phase of the Archaic period. During this phase several classes of simple decorated pottery vessels, some with fugitive paint, appeared. The crude pottery of the Formative phase evolved into several outstanding classes of painted pottery, but the following Archaic Susiana 0 straw-tempered ware continued almost unchanged during the entire Archaic sequence.

The architectural evidence of the Formative phase consists of small rectangular houses with two or three rooms. Often, an open court with fire pits containing fire-cracked rocks accompanied these rooms. These simple nuclear-family residences were built with the characteristic long, cigar-shaped mudbricks that continued in use until the end of the Archaic period and even into the Early Susiana period. These architecturally awkward bricks have a surprisingly wide geographic distribution, from the Susiana plain to southern and central Mesopotamia (at Tell el-Oueili and Chogha Mami) and Central Asia.[13] In addition to these peculiar bricks, stone and T-shaped clay figurines and a simple coarse ware were alo shared by a number of early Neolithic cultures in southwest Asia. Exotic materials not native to the region consisted solely of obsidian blades and shells from the Persian Gulf. These non-local items were possibly procured by a trickle-down interregional exchange system, rather than any direct exchange mechanism.

Neither Chogha Mish nor Chogha Bonut yielded any evidence of burial until the Archaic 3 phase; it is thus difficult to assess social status solely on the basis of the distribution of other artifacts, which seem homogeneous in all the excavated areas. The evidence of architecture, however, points to some type of communal activities at this early stage of social development, though these social practices are not yet understood. Two partially preserved buildings are all that were excavated from this phase. As mentioned above, both buildings were made of long, cigar-shaped mudbricks mixed with bricks of smaller size. The better-preserved building may have had a non-domestic as well as domestic function.[14] The plan of the buildings and the presence of numerous fire pits suggest non-domestic character or special status of these buildings as well, the nature of which can only be speculated. The possibility that an extended family resided in this building cannot be ruled out, however.

13. Similar mudbricks (with and without finger impressions) seem to have been typical in various regions in the early Neolithic period; they are not, however, all of identical type or as similar to the Susiana examples as those found in Deh Luran. For examples, see Smith 1976: 14–15 (Tappeh Ganj Dareh, Level D, in the Zagros Mountains); Masuda 1974: 25 (Tappeh Sang-e Chakhmaq, Iranian Central Plateau); Malek-Shahmirzadi 1979: 184, fig. 3 (Tappeh Zagheh, Iranian Central Plateau); Oates 1969: 116, pl. 22:C (Chogha Mami, central Mesopotamia); el-Wailly and Abu es-Soof 1965: 21, fig. 56 (Tell es-Sawwan, central Mesopotamia); Lloyd and Safar 1948: 121 (Eridu, southern Mesopotamia); Vallet 1996: 113–15, figs. 2–5 (Tell el-Oueili, southern Mesopotamia); Masson and Sarianidi 1972 (Central Asia).

14. See Alizadeh 2003a.

## ARCHAIC SUSIANA 0 PHASE

The appearance of the painted-burnished variant ware, a new class of painted pottery that provides an antecedent for the entire Archaic Susiana ceramic sequence, marks the transition from the Formative phase to the Archaic period. Another site, Tappeh Tuleii,[15] northwest of Chogha Bonut near the provincial town of Andimeshk (fig. 2), is the only other known site that was occupied during this phase. The fact that neither of these two early sites in lowland Susiana was located close to any detectable canal or source of water is another indication of sufficient precipitation for dry farming. Faunal, floral, and phytolith evidence from Chogha Bonut indicate the presence of marshes in upper Susiana during this phase.[16]

Evidence of gazelles, onagers, some unidentified large mammals, domesticated sheep, goats, and dogs, as well as that of wheat and barley shows that the mixed economy of farming, herding, and hunting continued in this phase. In addition to these species, the presence of bones of the giant Indian gerbil and of bears at Chogha Bonut also indicates the wetter climate in this region during the initial phases of the Archaic period.

The painted-burnished variant ware is well represented at Tappeh Tuleii but is rare in the nearby Deh Luran plain to the north. In contrast to this distinct class of early Neolithic Susiana pottery, the stone tools, chipped stone industry, and small objects such as T-shaped human figurines and animal figurines are almost indistinguishable among the two Susiana sites and the contemporary sites of Chogha Sefid and Tappeh Ali Kosh in the Deh Luran plain. The great similarity in the objects other than pottery suggests that, while the stone industry and the manufacture of small clay and stone objects found at these sites may have had a shared origin, the painted-burnished variant ware was developed in Susiana proper.

The excavated architecture of the Archaic Susiana 0 phase at Chogha Bonut consists of two separate buildings, the complete plan of which cannot be restored (Alizadeh 2003a: 33–40). A rather large rectangular structure is all that was left of one building that, based on its rather comparatively large size, must have been a hall or courtyard of a much larger structure. The three surviving walls are neatly made of long, cigar-shaped mudbricks laid as stretchers. Two platforms or buttresses made of the same construction material were built against the outer face of its southern wall. The western portion of this building, where presumably the living quarters were located, was entirely destroyed, but the presence of two rows of headers, one slightly higher than the other, suggests a doorway that may have provided access to the rooms on this side. The other, smaller building was better preserved. The building material was the same as that used for the larger structure, but the neat division of space and straightness of the walls indicates a degree of architectural sophistication, if not specialization, even in this early phase of architecture in Susiana.

No solid architecture was found at the contemporary site of Tappeh Tuleii. One interpretation of the archaeological evidence from Tuleii argues that the site might have been a mobile pastoralist camp (Hole 1974; Bernbeck 1992),[17] though this is by no means certain.[18] Bernbeck (1992) considers the evidence from Tuleii as indicative of the existence of village-based herders who moved seasonally between Susiana and Deh Luran, presumably in an effort to keep the herds away from cultivated fields. This speculation is not tenable given the extremely low population density of the plain during this phase.

Nevertheless, it is difficult — if not impossible — to assess the size of the initial settled farming population in lowland Susiana. Erosion, later occupation, and alluviation could cover or obliterate earlier deposits, complicating the interpretation of the remains of early Neolithic sites and their antecedents. Susiana's landscape and topographic features have changed from the early Holocene to such a dramatic degree that almost all surface surveys failed to reveal early Neolithic sites in Khuzestan. Even the three well-preserved sites of Chogha Bonut, Chogha Mish, and Boneh Fazl Ali did not reveal their earliest cultural components before they were excavated. At Boneh Fazl Ali, a porcupine digging deep into the base of the mound was responsible for the few early Archaic potsherds found in the heap of dirt next to its burrow. Early deposits at Tuleii and Chogha Bonut were also discovered accidentally.

Thus it is perfectly possible that there exist, or existed, other contemporary sites not yet discovered, or never to be discovered, for the reasons just cited. With this problem in mind, we have identified at least five sites with a total of perhaps 3–4 ha of occupation area that belong to the early phase of the Neolithic in the region. They include

15. Hole 1974, 1975 (Tuleii, pronounced *to-**le**-ee*, and spelled Tula'i in the original report, is the name of an edible tuber similar to truffles in northern Khuzestan and in Fars).
16. See Redding 2003 and Rosen Miller 2003.
17. See also Hole 1975, 1987: 39.
18. See Wheeler Pires-Ferreira 1976/77: 279, who considers Tappeh Tuleii to be "a village based fallow herd camp site."

Chogha Bonut, Tappeh Tuleii, Boneh Fazl Ali (KS-02, 3570599 N/269194 E, UTM 39N), Chogha Mish, and Boneh Rahimeh (KS-120, 3550616 N/270425 E, UTM 39N).[19]

## ARCHAIC SUSIANA 1 PHASE

For unknown reasons, Chogha Bonut, Tuleii, and the other sites just mentioned were deserted during the Archaic 0 phase. Since these early sites in upper Susiana are close to one another, it is unlikely that environmental or climatic reasons were responsible for their abandonment, in which case, Chogha Mish, too, should have been abandoned. While admittedly we have no evidence for this early settlement development, it is possible that safety could be a tenable reason for scattered population to aggregate at a single site. If this were the case, we still cannot offer the source of insecurity in the region at this early stage of social development, but the possibility of tension between the early farmers and pastoralists cannot be ruled out. The continuation of the Archaic period thus will have to be sought at Chogha Mish and possibly at Boneh Fazl Ali (Kantor 1970/71), a small site just north of Chogha Mish on the eastern part of the plain (fig. 2).[20] The initial occupation of Chogha Mish is marked by the presence of the earlier painted-burnished variant of the Archaic 0 phase and its developed version, the standard painted-burnished ware. This phase, therefore, is primarily defined by its distinctive pottery style. Sometime during the Archaic Susiana 1 phase, the painted-burnished variant completely disappeared. The standard painted-burnished ware was associated with other artifacts, such as the tiny T-shaped figurines, which occur both in Susiana and Deh Luran to the north. As mentioned above, during this phase striking parallels can be found in the pottery and figurines from distant sites in the Iranian Central Plateau.[21] The T-shaped figurines are frequently interpreted as belonging to a Zagros complex,[22] but very similar material far to the northeast of Iran (Masuda 1972, 1974) may represent a wider sphere of cultural interaction.

The earliest inhabitants of Chogha Mish subsisted on domesticated goats and sheep and hunted gazelles, onagers, and aurochs. It was during the Archaic 3 phase and the Early Susiana period that cattle and pigs became important, comprising almost half of the assemblages at Chogha Mish and Jafarabad levels 6–4, while sheep and goats made up 40% of the total.

The question of the transition from the Archaic 0 to the Archaic 1 phase is difficult to address on the basis of the available material. While the flint industry and clay figurines of the previous phase continued into this phase with little change, the pottery had developed into a distinct style. Unfortunately, we have no intervening phase for the evolution of the standard painted-burnished ware from the earlier painted-burnished variant ware. In Susiana proper, Chogha Mish is the only site that yielded standard painted-burnished ware; to date, no intervening or overlapping style that can be considered transitional has been found. In any case, Chogha Mish and Boneh Fazl Ali seem today to be the only sites that were occupied during the Archaic Susiana 1 phase, though they were perhaps the only sites that existed on the plain.

Architectural remains of this phase at Chogha Mish (just above virgin soil at an elevation of 72.33 m above sea level) were inconclusive. They consist of poorly preserved pisé and mudbrick wall fragments, beaten earth surfaces, and several cooking installations. The use of long bricks (usually about 95/80 × 12 × 10 cm) continued into this phase. As in the earlier and later phases, the floors of the cooking installations were covered with fire-cracked rocks, but no change in the subsistence economy from the previous phase was noted.

We believe that the close parallels cited for certain types of artifacts from widely separated sites in southern Turkmenistan (Jeitun),[23] the Zagros Mountains (Jarmo),[24] and Susiana can be interpreted as a regional variety of a single incipient cultural horizon, which can be taken as common ancestors of many later regional traditions in Iran. It should be noted, however, that the great problem in accepting such a proposal is that we do not have any representative of an analogous cultural phase in any of the intervening sites. For example, at Tappeh Sialk, the early straw-tempered pottery of levels 1 and 2 is quite different from the contemporary sites in southwestern Iran. At Tappeh

19. Boneh Rahimeh was identified from the Gremliza survey collection. See Alizadeh 1992.
20. Evidence from the limited excavation at this site was kept at the Chogha Mish dig house and was destroyed in 1978.
21. For examples, see Tappeh Sang-e Chakhmaq (Masuda 1972, 1974), Deh Kheir, Elikahi, and Tappeh Siah (Rezvani 1999).
22. Braidwood et al. 1983: 369–424; Broman Morales 1990.
23. For Jeitun, see Masson and Sarianidi 1972.
24. Braidwood et al. 1983.

Zagheh, northwest of Sialk, nothing has been published that antedates the Zagheh phase.[25] Recent surveys around Qazvin and Abyek (near Tehran) have identified a crude reddish straw-tempered pottery (Mehranabad) that seems to be earlier than both the basal levels at Sialk and Zagheh.[26] In the northwest, the Neolithic site of Haji Firuz has nothing similar, although it has produced a primitive pottery (Voigt 1983).

## ARCHAIC SUSIANA 2 PHASE

The size of the small initial settlement of Chogha Mish increased in this phase, as is suggested by the presence of Archaic Susiana 2 sherds in the Trench XXI area and in Trench XXXVIII, some 15 m to the south (fig. 6).[27] Thus, a settlement of approximately 90 × 100 m can be established for the Archaic Susiana 2 village, but it may well have been larger, if we take as evidence a mixture of Archaic 2 and 3 sherds found in higher levels in Trenches XI and XIII. Thus, Trench XIII, about 90 m west of Trench XXXVIII, may quite possibly have been part of the continuous Archaic Susiana 2–3 settlement.[28] Taken together, the Archaic Susiana village at Chogha Mish may have been some 2 ha with about 200 to 300 inhabitants.

As with the preceding phase, the Archaic Susiana 2 phase at Chogha Mish is also poorly known. Based on the fragmentary architectural evidence, building materials and the general plan of the earlier Archaic Susiana 1 phase continued. Long, cigar-shaped mudbricks, bound together with an ashy mortar, continued to be used. A single incomplete building dates to this phase,[29] but enough was preserved to indicate the general plan of the building. The excavated portion measures 25 × 5 m, but the structure must have been larger. The building consists of at least three rectangular rooms with a storage bin. No hearth or kiln was found in the excavated area, but the presence of ashy patches protruding from under the unexcavated portion suggests cooking activities. Here we have clear evidence of mud plaster that covered the long bricks of the walls. Stone foundations for mudbrick walls were found in this phase. At Chogha Mish, mudbrick platforms of uncertain nature were also introduced during this phase and continued to be used throughout the sequence. Contact with the Hassuna/Samarran tradition of northern Iraq was perhaps established during this phase.

The chipped stone industry continued from the preceding phase without much change. Other artifacts, such as T-shaped figurines, bone tools, and stone tools also continued into this phase. A new class of highly stylized clay figurines appeared in this phase and were designated by Kantor as "chessman figurines" (*Chogha Mish* I, pl. 237:G, I–K). They are generally cylindrical in shape and were decorated with punctate and incised marks. This phase is further defined by the replacement of the standard painted-burnished ware with the distinct red-banded/line ware. Other types of plain wares continued into this phase.

Excavations at Chogha Sefid, in nearby Deh Luran, provided more information on this phase. Domesticated species, such as sheep, goats, wheat, and barley, were now morphologically fully developed and the emphasis on hunted animals decreased.

## ARCHAIC SUSIANA 3 PHASE

Major changes took place in the Archaic Susiana 3 phase. A new class of pottery, the close-line ware, appeared; stone pavement in front of rooms and doorways was first used; cattle were introduced; non-domestic architecture appeared; and the settlement expanded to a minimum of about 2.5–3.0 ha. In addition, the group of regions that shared similarities in material culture now included southern Mesopotamia.

In Deh Luran, this final phase of the Archaic period is considered to have coincided with the introduction of canal irrigation agriculture. If this is in fact the case, there is no reason to think that this technique did not reach Susiana. This conclusion is based, however, not on geomorphology, but on the evidence of plant morphology de-

25. Negahban 1973, 1977; Malek-Shahmirzadi 1977, 1980. Recent investigations by Hasan Fazeli (pers. comm.) have indicated that Tappeh Zagheh was dated too early. The entire Zagheh sequence must date from the late sixth to the late fifth millennia B.C., ca. 4300 B.C., when Zagheh was deserted and Ghabrestan was occupied.

26. Malek-Shahmirzadi, personal communication.

27. Top plan and exact location of this trench on the contour map are missing.

28. At Chogha Mish, Archaic Susiana levels are below the present plain level and are not to be found weathered out on the surface. Although the Archaic Susiana levels at the small site of Boneh Fazl Ali, some 3 km northwest of Chogha Mish, are also below the present surface, sherds of all three phases of the period were found in the spoil heap of a deeply dug porcupine burrow. This suggests that small Archaic villages may have been more numerous than can be established on the basis of survey data.

29. See *Chogha Mish* I, pl. 271.

rived from measurements of flax seeds, which presumably grow larger when irrigated (Helbaek 1969). Hole (1977: 35–36) uses this indirect evidence to suggest that irrigation technology and the development of new crops allowed rapid expansion of population into marginal areas. Kouchoukos (1998: 67), arguing from geomorphic conditions and paleoclimatic evidence, suggests that the early inhabitants of the plain may have taken advantage of seasonally flooded fields along the major watercourses in the plain. It should be noted that in Susiana there is no physical evidence of large irrigation canals like in southern Mesopotamia. The earliest evidence for large-scale canal irrigation seems to date to the Elamite period in the second half of the second millennium B.C. (see Alizadeh et al. 2004). It is important to note that it was in the second millennium B.C. that southern Susiana (south of the Haft Tappeh anticline) was settled, most probably as the result of the adoption of large-scale canal irrigation technique.

If the new pottery represents an innovation brought to southwestern Iran as a result of outside cultural or technological influence or migration, the new immigrants did not replace the indigenous population. The interface between the Archaic Susiana 2 and 3 levels at Chogha Mish indicates no violence or sharp break. Except for the introduction of the new pottery, the close-line ware, other material objects of the Archaic Susiana 2 phase continued into the new phase and continued to develop. The close-line ware also occurred in Deh Luran and the Mandali region of central Mesopotamia, where it is known as Chogha Mami Transitional after the type site. Although the close-line ware, Chogha Mami Transitional, and Ubaid 0 pottery have close affinities with pottery of the Samarra period, they also exhibit considerable differences in style and the grammar of design (see *Chapter 4*).

No complete architectural plan of Archaic Susiana 3 domestic residences was discovered at Chogha Mish. Nevertheless, the remnants of the buildings dated to the Archaic Susiana 3 phase indicate no substantial change in layout from the preceding residential houses. People lived in multi-room houses with shared open yards in between. Some walls, presumably those exposed to the elements, had stone foundations. Long, cigar-shaped mudbricks were still in use. The walls of at least one building in Trench XXV[30] were thick enough to suggest an upper level, but this is by no means certain.

A large building excavated in the eighth and ninth seasons provides evidence for a possible non-domestic architecture in this early phase (fig. 13), though, as Dietler and Herbich (1998) caution, inferring organization and structure of an archaeological society requires much more successive evidence than has been found in the early phases at Chogha Mish. The preserved and excavated parts consist of at least two long halls with no traces of domestic installations such as hearths, fireplaces, and bins on its beaten earth floor. Similarly, no burials were found associated with this building, unlike other domestic buildings of this phase. The southern wall of this building has four buttresses made of headers and the wall itself is made of stretchers using long bricks, a building technique remarkably close to that found at Tell el-Oueili in southern Mesopotamia.[31] The unusually thick western wing of the building suggests an upper level, a landing area, or a foundation for a staircase. The huge horseshoe kiln/oven located in the open court next to the long hall may have been used for food preparation, for the only material remains found within it consist of some animal bones, bits and pieces of flint blades, and ash. The general layout of this structure was already anticipated in the Archaic Susiana 0 phase architecture at Chogha Bonut.[32]

The dead were buried under the floors of the houses and possibly in the adjacent open areas. Most graves were devoid of funerary gifts, even though they were found undisturbed. The possibility that perishable gifts had accompanied them should not be ruled out, however. The graves, as preserved here, are simple pits with no special features. Similar graves at Tappeh Ali Kosh in the Deh Luran plain indicate that some of the skeletons were wrapped in over-two, under-two twilled mat and were accompanied with simple stone beads and worked stone implements. Both extended and flexed positions were common (Hole, Flannery, and Neely 1969: 248–53). Similar burials were also found at Chogha Sefid, near Ali Kosh (Hole 1977: 91–94). Bones of the skeletons at both sites were covered with red ochre. Some of the skeletons had artificially elongated skulls, a tradition that continued until the Middle Susiana period in lowland Susiana (*Chogha Mish* I, pl. 69). However, the practice was by no means common, suggesting that it was limited to certain members — possibly the elite — of the society. If, as in Mesoamerica (Flannery 1998: 45), intentional deformation of the skull was an elite practice, then the last phase of the Archaic Susiana period may be considered a phase of social differentiation. Such elongated skulls that are represented in the Samarran clay figurines from Chogha Mami (Oates 1969, pls. 25–27) could be considered as precursors of the famous Ubaid figurines and perhaps of the Early Dynastic statuettes from Eridu (Safar, Mustafa, and Lloyd 1981, fig. 150).

30. See *Chogha Mish* I, pl. 272.
31. See Vallet 1996, figs. 2–4, pl. 2.
32. See Alizadeh 2003a.

The floral evidence from Chogha Mish is discussed extensively in the first volume.[33] It therefore suffices here to present an overview of the evidence. Carbonized remains of cereals and legumes collected from all the Archaic levels at Chogha Mish indicate a developing farming community.

Cereal remains include barley (*Hordeum*), bread wheat (*Triticum aestivum*), and oat (*Avena*). In addition, some species of wild grasses such as goat face grass (*Aegilops*), rye grass (*Lolium*), canary grass (*Phalaris*), and fescue (*Festuca*) also occurred with the domestic varieties. Wild and domestic legume species account for the majority of seeds recovered from the site, indicating that such plants were more cultivated/exploited by Chogha Mish farmers. The recovered seeds include *Alhagi*, milk vetch (*Astragalus*), medick (*Medicago*), clover (*Trifolium*), as well as screw beans (*Prosopis*), vetch (*Vicica*), pea (*Pisium*), and lentil (*Lens*); the latter two show morphological signs of domestication. Other carbonized seeds besides legumes, grasses, and flax were also present in the Archaic levels. The most frequent were rye grass, goat face grass, and plantain (*Plantago*). Less frequent seeds include rush (*Scripus*), bed straw (*Galium*), sea blite (*Suaeda*), caper (*Capparis*), members of the mint family (*Lamiaceace*), shepherd's purse (*Capsella-bursa-pastoris*), as well as seeds from the borage family (*Boraginaceace*), goosefoot family (*Chenopodiaceace*), lily family (*Liliaxeace*), mallow family (*Malvaceace*), poppy family (*Papaveraceace*), and nettle family (*Urticaceace*).

Based on the available carbonized seeds from the Archaic levels at Chogha Mish, Ann Woosley (1996: 316) tentatively concludes that the evidence from the site does not support the importance of cereals (primarily emmer, einkorn wheat, and barley) in the early stages of domestication. Rather, during the entire Archaic period, legume crops (namely, *Pisium*, *Lens*, and *Vicica*) seem to have been more significant in the subsistence economy. In fact, legumes comprise the largest portion of total seeds counted from Archaic through the end of the Susiana sequence. This picture changes in the Protoliterate phase, when cereals become dominant in the record. Nevertheless, since carbonized seeds come from animal-dung fuel, Woosley's results may be more of a reflection of the diet of domesticated animals than those of humans (see Miller 1996 and 2003a).

## EARLY SUSIANA PERIOD

The cultural contact among several regions in southwest Asia, which was suggested above on the basis of the appearance of the Samarran-related pottery during the Archaic Susiana 3 phase, increased in the Early Susiana period in southwestern Iran and the Ubaid 1/Eridu phase in southern Mesopotamia. Although the ceramics of each region exhibit local characteristics, on the whole the pottery repertoires and other utilitarian objects in both regions share many common features. The one significant difference, however, is the total absence in Iran of any structure that can be considered a temple, while in Mesopotamia such buildings become the focal point at a number of sites. This trend continues in Iran until the Late Susiana 2 (Susa 1) phase, when presumably a substantial temple was erected on a huge platform surrounded by a communal cemetery at Susa.[34]

A number of small test areas between the west side and the southern part of the terrace at Chogha Mish show that the size of the settlement almost doubled in this period. It was at about 3.5 to 4.0 ha during the Early Susiana period, but it could have been much larger. The Early Susiana remains were found primarily on the southern and western sectors of the mound. If we assume that the unexcavated space between these areas also contains Early Susiana remains, then the size of the settlement can amount to about 5 ha, an assumption that is also supported by the presence of Early Susiana pottery on the southern part of the mound.

The analysis of the pottery from the Gremliza survey collection (Alizadeh 1992) indicates that the number of settlements increased to seven in the Early Susiana period, including Jafarabad, the earliest settlement on the western part of the plain.[35] Our examination of the survey materials collected by Robert Wenke, now in the National Museum in Tehran, indicates that to this list we can add Tappeh Washkara (KS-12, 358275 N/243257 E, UTM 39N), Tappeh Sharafabad (KS-36), and KS-277. Adams, however, reports that thirty-four villages were established during the Early Susiana period (Adams 1962: 112). While this huge increase in the population from the Archaic to the Early Susiana period is a strong possibility, Adams' estimate cannot be corroborated by the results of other surveys, as Adams did not publish examples of the pottery of the various phases he detected in his survey. The strong possibility that small, low mounds of the Archaic period are buried or have simply eroded can comparatively inflate the size of population for the Early Susiana period. A number of degenerate Archaic Susiana close-line ware sherds

33. For detailed analysis of the plant remains, see Woosley 1996.

34. See Hole 1990 for a detailed discussion of this cemetery.

35. See Alizadeh 1992, tables 4–9.

decorated on the outside with a series of connected Xs suggests that Jafarabad may have been occupied during a transitional phase between the Archaic 3 phase and Early Susiana period. The inhabitants of early Jafarabad, therefore, can be considered as the first colonizers of western Khuzestan.

In the absence of evidence of canal irrigation, one can safely assume that the development of the Dez into many small streams in central Khuzestan may have encouraged settlements away from marshes and immediate sources of water, a development that was paralleled in neighboring Deh Luran (Hole, Flannery, and Neely 1969: 354–55; Hole 1977: 7). Adams (1962: 110–12) notes, however, that not all Early Susiana settlements in Khuzestan practiced irrigation agriculture, suggesting that the new technology was initially adopted as an insurance against drought. Bread wheat, emmer, and six-row barley became the main staples, along with cattle, sheep, and goats. As a supplement to their diet, the inhabitants of Susiana in this period continued hunting, gathering, and fishing.

In our 2004/05 archaeological investigations in Susiana, we not only discovered Early Susiana sherds from Chogha Do Sar (KS-04), we also found a bulldozed site that was located next to Nahr-e Khalaf, an irrigation canal, 100 m northwest of Chogha Do Sar (Alizadeh 2005; Alizadeh and Mahfroozi 2005). We discovered the site (temporarily named KS-04b) because of the huge number of Early Susiana sherds scattered in an area about 1.0–1.5 ha. The bulldozed area of the site was under cultivation. However, in our test trench where we thought to be the center of the site, we reached virgin soil some 50 cm below the surface. The owner of the land confessed that the mound had been bulldozed two decades ago. Nevertheless, this Early Susiana site has never been reported even though the nearby site of Chogha Do Sar had been surveyed at least twice. One can only speculate that the site may have been very low or covered with dense vegetation, but the fact remains that the population of this early period is underestimated.

The Early Susiana pottery tradition was a direct continuation of the preceding phase; in both technology and decorative style, Susiana was in a lockstep development with southern Mesopotamia. In fact, the close similarities between the cultural assemblages of the two regions prefigure the shared interregional development in the second half of the fourth millennium B.C. While in the preceding Archaic Susiana 3 phase the pottery of southern Mesopotamia and Susiana show general similarities, the two traditions show closer and specific parallels during the succeeding Early Susiana period. It is difficult to determine whether the regional — as well as interregional — homogeneous character of the pottery of this period is an indication of socioeconomic transformations in pottery production, especially in times of specialization and close contact among the prehistoric potters. It should be noted, however, that no pottery kilns were found in this period. The development of agriculture and possibly irrigation technique, and population growth can be considered factors affecting the transition of pottery production from a cottage industry to a full-time activity (see Arnold 1985 for example).

A distinct class of Early Susiana pottery vessels (the so-called "flanged vessels" [fig. 64]) bears scratched and excised signs on their bases that are considered "potter's marks" (Dollfus and Encrevé 1982). Since only this class of pottery bears such marks, the following explanation may be valid. These highly specialized vessels, not reported from Mesopotamia, are undecorated and as such it is perfectly conceivable that the potters marked their vessels to distinguish their own in a bonfire, if that was indeed how they baked their vessels in the Early Susiana period. Nevertheless, the large number of individual signs (over 200 at Chogha Mish alone) argues against this interpretation. It is, however, possible that these marks indicated household or corporate groups[36] who either had their vessels baked in a common fire, or else identified their vessels in common storage facilities, of which there is no evidence.

A clear change both in the quality and technique of flint tools and stone industry occurred in the Early Susiana period. Flint blades were less carefully shaped and the fine bladelets of the Archaic period were no longer produced. A new type of stone tool, considered to be a hoe, appeared in this period both in Susiana and Deh Luran and continued throughout the prehistoric sequence and even into the Protoliterate phase.[37] Such hoes have a sharp crescent-shaped tip with an elongated narrow handle usually smeared with bitumen; in a few specimens the rope wrapped around the handle for a better grip was still preserved. Whether such tools were used to break the ground or to cut weeds, the task must have been a backbreaking job. Saddle-shaped stone mills continued from the previous phase.

If the Early Susiana period was a time of the development of local khans, the architecture provides the best evidence (fig. 12).[38] The most coherent architectural plan of the Early Susiana period was found in Trench XXI. Here,

36. See Kramer 1985 for a number of characteristics in ceramic production.

37. In Deh Luran they are reported from the earlier Ali Kosh-Mohammad Jafar phase, but the illustrated examples are dated to the later Sabz (Early Susiana) phase (Hole, Flannery, and Neely 1969: 189, fig. 81; Hole 1977: 209, pl. 49:h–j). In northern Mesopotamia they first appeared in Tell Hassuna level Ia (Lloyd and Safar 1945, figs. 19–20) and, as in Susiana, continued throughout the entire prehistoric sequence (see Stronach 1961).

38. See Flannery 1998 for a detailed discussion and comparison of chiefly residences.

a series of comparatively large multi-room structures was excavated during the sixth through eighth seasons of excavations (fig. 14). The ubiquitous long mudbricks continued to be used along with smaller rectangular bricks. The technique of paving the open spaces in front of rooms and entrances with cobbles also continued from the Archaic Susiana 3 phase.

At least two structures seem to have been residences of extended or chiefly families, while a third, with a series of long, parallel chambers with an open area in front, may have been used both as a residence and a warehouse. The large mudbrick platform in the southwestern part of the open court in front of architectural units 7 and 8 (fig. 14) is difficult to interpret, particularly in the absence of detailed information on the materials found there. The platform measures 7 × 5 m and is only one course high. Walls surround it on the south and east sides. Thus, it may have been another residential unit with paved floors. Though not common, such floors are found in two rooms in architectural unit 8 as well. No traces of walls were found that would have stood on the west and north sides of this platform, arguing against its reconstruction as an enclosed unit. Taken together with the other architectural features, this platform may have served as a preparation area or a "loading dock." The Early Susiana architectural layout consisting of an open central area and perhaps a warehouse surrounded by residential units provides an antecedent for the much later administrative quarters in Iran, particularly in Fars (Tall-e Bakun A)[39] and Sistan (Shahr-e Sokhteh).[40]

## MIDDLE SUSIANA PERIOD

The transition from the Early to the Middle Susiana period was smooth and gradual. At Chogha Mish the areas of the village that were occupied during the preceding phase continued to be occupied in this period as well. Based on detailed analysis of pottery shapes and decorations, as well as changes in other components of the material culture and settlement patterns, this long period is divided into two phases, early and late. This is a pivotal phase in southwestern Iran. Primarily based on stylistic and formal analysis of the pottery and partially on stratigraphy, Middle Susiana is divided into early Middle and late Middle Susiana phases. In the early part of the period, contact with southern Mesopotamia (Ubaid 2 phase) is still strong. In the later phase this contact seems to be much reduced and Susiana shares many aspects of material culture with the highlands. Thus, the Middle Susiana period also marks the first major stage of social, economic, and demographic transformation in prehistoric Susiana; it also anticipates Susiana's long and presumably complex relationship with the highlands.

A detailed analysis by Kouchoukos (1998: 105ff.) of all the available survey data has shown that, of the sample of 264 prehistoric sites surveyed in lowland Susiana, only half can be dated with some certainty to the specific archaeological phases known from excavations. Kouchoukos further argues that this number represents less than half of the total sites founded on the plain in the prehistoric phases (Kouchoukos 1998: 105). Using various statistical and analytical techniques in reconstructing the survey data, Kouchoukos (1998: 20–57) suggests a rapid population growth during the Middle Susiana period. According to the same analysis (Kouchoukos 1998: 109), during the early phase of the Middle Susiana period, the estimated population in Susiana reached 8,700 people, a population threshold much higher than is necessary to develop and sustain a complex chiefdom.[41] In neighboring Deh Luran the population in this period was just over 2,000. Even though the population decrease in Deh Luran corresponds to the increase of population in lowland Susiana, Kouchoukos argues against migration, noting that the calculated rate of population growth of 0.0022% for the Middle Susiana period does not exceed that expected for the pre-industrial societies.[42]

The Middle Susiana period was a time of population increase in southwestern Iran, as indicated by a number of surveys (Adams 1962; Hole 1987; Dittmann 1984; Alizadeh 1992). By the second phase of the period, the number of sites in Susiana reached a maximum. Chogha Mish grew to be the largest settlement, a development paralleled in Deh Luran where at least two sites grew to more than 3 ha (Hole 1987: 37, 40). Although Middle Susiana settlements do not exhibit any particular pattern of clustering, sites in the eastern part of the plain seem to be much closer to one another. If the region's security was threatened by the contemporary pastoral nomads, loss of village independence to a regional khan, or a combination of these factors influenced the clustering of the northern and northeastern sites, they were not important in western and south-central Khuzestan.

39. Alizadeh 1988a, 1988b, 2005.
40. Fiandra 1981.
41. See Feinman 1998 for a detailed discussion of the demographic issues in the development of complex chiefdoms and early states.
42. See Johnson 1988/89: 597–600 for a discussion of this population estimate for his Uruk period; and Weiss 1977 for the problems associated with such estimates. See also Pollock 2001.

Diet did not change much from the previous phase. Wheat, six-row barley, lentils, vetch, and flax were the main cereals. Sheep and goats were common; cattle were also present. This diet was supplemented by fishing and hunting of onager and gazelle, though hunting was not as important as it was in the preceding phase. The pattern of spatial distribution of the bones of the hunted animals would have been helpful in speculating on the type of residence and associated objects, but that information is not available.

The dead, as before, were buried under the floors of residential units and in open spaces. Similarly, the orientation of the body seems to have depended on the availability of space rather than on any fixed spatial and ritual considerations. As in the previous periods, most of the graves were devoid of funerary objects. All the burials belong to the earlier phase of this period; no burial was found dating to the late Middle Susiana phase. Except for four burials dating to the Late Susiana 2 and, possibly, the Protoliterate phases, it seems that the practice of burying the dead within the residential areas was abandoned by the end of the early Middle Susiana phase.[43] That this situation may be an accident of discovery is suggested by the intramural graves found at other Middle Susiana sites in the region.

Houses were still made of mudbricks with occasional stone foundations. The Archaic long bricks were no longer used in this period. House floors were either of beaten earth or covered with a layer of twilled mat; pierced stones were used as door sockets. In Trench XXI, the architectural plan of the preceding Early Susiana period seems to have been preserved. The only Middle Susiana building that was excavated in this area is similar in plan to the Early Susiana architecture with rectangular multiple rooms, long storage magazines, and evidence of both domestic and industrial activities.

Microlithic and obsidian blades were absent in this period and the types of ground stone tools were limited, presumably because of the naked grain varieties that had been developed.[44] The prominent Early Susiana star-shaped spindle whorls continued into the early Middle Susiana phase along with a variety of new painted shapes; they disappeared in the following late Middle Susiana phase.

If pottery is any indication, contact (emulation, imitation, or movement of potters) between lowland Mesopotamia and Susiana reached its maximum during the early phase of the Middle Susiana period. As mentioned before, during the early Middle Susiana phase a strong shared interregional pottery tradition existed, as indicated by the close parallels between the ceramics of Susiana, Deh Luran ("Khazineh phase"), and southern Mesopotamia (Ubaid 2/Haji Mohammed and Eridu XII–IX).

The following late Middle Susiana phase is pivotal in the socioeconomic life of lowland Susiana. This phase corresponds to the Ubaid 3 phase and possibly the early stages of Ubaid 4. Whereas in the early Middle Susiana phase the pottery closely resembles that of Haji Mohammed/Ubaid 2, the ceramics of the late Middle Susiana diverge and share a number of features with the contemporary cultures of Tall-e Bakun B2 and Tall-e Gap in highland Fars and Tappeh Giyan V in the central Zagros Mountains, a dramatic shift of attention from lowland Mesopotamia to highland Iran, a trend that continued until the end of the Terminal Susa phase in the beginning of the fourth millennium B.C. The late Middle Susiana phase, therefore, represents the first phase of highland-lowland integration. Since the late Middle Susiana pottery forms and decorations are rooted in millennia-old tradition, and since there is hardly any antecedent to the Bakun B2 pottery in Fars, we have to conclude that the latter was inspired by the former. Whether this inspiration involved movement of people is difficult to say with the present knowledge of prehistoric Fars, but economic exchange and itinerant potters may have played a major role. A parallel development occurred in Mesopotamia when by the beginning of the Ubaid 3 phase the similarity between the material cultures of southern and northern Mesopotamia became strongest in the sequence.

The late Middle Susiana at Chogha Mish is also the most extensive occupation of the prehistoric period. Almost the entire 17 ha of the mound shows signs of occupation, though it is not absolutely certain whether the whole mound had been occupied at the same time. Chogha Mish was the largest settlement in the region, followed by Chogha Do Sar, about 8 km to the southeast. The rest of the sites ranged in sizes between 3 and 1 ha. After Chogha Mish was deserted in the beginning of the Late Susiana 1 phase, Chogha Do Sar remained the largest site east of the Dez River (see below for more details of our 2004/05 excavations at the site).

The archaeological materials and architectural remains from Chogha Mish that are dated to this phase may be taken as a reflection of the changing organization of the society. A major difference in the architecture from the previous phases is marked by the appearance of a large monumental building. Almost in the middle of the settlement,

---

43. See Flannery 1972 for an analysis of inter- and intramural burial practices.

44. *Chogha Mish* I, chapter 11; see also Hole, Flannery, and Neely 1969: 359.

toward the eastern edge of the mound, a substantial building was found in the ninth season (fig. 15). The excavated portion consists of four large parallel halls. The outer walls are furnished with buttresses. The substantial walls of this building, about 1.5 m thick, its plan of regularly aligned rooms, and the facade with symmetrical buttresses indicate its monumental and formal character. A back room on the north side of the building still contained numerous storage jars; another room had a stack of eighteen complete thin-walled bowls typical of the late Middle Susiana phase. Found on the floors of this building were numerous flint nodules for the manufacture of flint blades, some of which were also found in the rooms. The presence of this building indicates that a level of social differentiation was achieved by the late Middle Susiana phase. At the same time in the nearby site of Chogha Bonut, a comparatively large building in the middle of the site dominated the settlement.[45]

The destruction by fire of this monumental building marks the end of the Middle Susiana period at Chogha Mish. Whether the destruction was a sign of hostile contact or was accidental is impossible to say. Whatever the case may be, Chogha Mish and a number of its satellites were deserted. The desertion of Chogha Mish and some of its satellites may be an indication of hostile contact with the developing highland mobile pastoralist population. Or these sites may have been deserted as the result of a course change of the Dez River, which Veenenbos (1958) suggests had flowed much closer to Chogha Mish in this phase.[46] Although geomorphologic evidence is needed to further investigate this hypothesis, it need not be exclusive and a combination of social and environmental factors may have caused the abandonment of Chogha Mish and a number of other sites by the end of the late Middle Susiana.

The large size of the settlement and population of Chogha Mish around 5000 B.C., the presence of at least one monumental building, the evidence of craft and architectural specialization, a three-tiered settlement pattern on the plain, and possible competition with the highland pastoralists can be taken as indicative of the type of socioeconomic complexity that is necessary for the development of state organizations. In an article devoted to the discussion of the physical characteristics of Near Eastern chiefdom societies, Flannery (1998) uses ethnographic analogies of modern-day chiefly societies to argue that the White Room of Gawra level XII may have belonged to high-ranking chiefs and their retinue and as such was the specific target of hostilities, and that such buildings and not necessarily the whole settlement were routinely targeted for violence by the competing chiefs. The Burnt Building at Chogha Mish can be considered one of these chiefly residences. If that was the case by the end of the late Middle Susiana phase, the likeliest candidate for the aggression against Chogha Mish would have been the developing highland mobile pastoralist communities who may have been vying with the Chogha Mish elite to control the eastern Susiana plain.

Before we continue our discussion of the characteristics of the various archaeological phases discovered at Chogha Mish, we feel it is absolutely necessary to provide a wider context that includes ancient mobile pastoralists of the region for a better understanding of the developments that took place in the course of the fifth and fourth millennia B.C.

## QUESTION OF REGIONAL SECURITY AND GROWTH OF CHOGHA MISH

The location of Chogha Mish in eastern Susiana is not of any particular strategic importance, nor has Chogha Mish yielded any physical evidence pertaining to its importance in the region as a religious center in prehistoric times, two important characteristics that can give rise to an increase in size and population. In the apparent absence of these two important criteria for growth, we are forced to look for other possibilities for the site's rapid growth.

While specific research design is needed to address the environmental and demographic imperatives that shaped different systems of settlement and growth of regional population centers in prehistoric Susiana, given our hypothetical Susiana demographic dichotomy (i.e., settled farmers and mobile pastoralists) it should not be too farfetched to consider the principle of safety in numbers as a major imperative for the growth of Chogha Mish into one of the largest prehistoric sites in southwest Asia.

The size of the settlement at Chogha Mish at least tripled by the beginning of the fifth millennium B.C., reaching ca. 17 ha. This unprecedented growth occurred at roughly the same time when we have strong archaeological evidence of hierarchically organized highland mobile pastoralists at the isolated cemeteries of Hakalān and Parchineh. Concern for safety, therefore, seems to have created the pressure against wide dispersal and the impetus for aggregation. Despite these security measures, Chogha Mish seems to have been invaded and its monumental building burned sometime in the first half of the fifth millennium B.C.

45. See Alizadeh 2003a.

46. See Kouchoukos 1998 for a detailed analysis.

The available archaeological evidence indicates that the violence at Chogha Mish was focused on the seat of its ranking population on the eastern sector of the settlement (see below for details). But it must have had profound impact on the entire community, for the entire settlement was deserted subsequent to the attack. Though we do not have solid evidence, we argue that the Chogha Mish diaspora chose the westernmost part of the plain and resettled at Susa. While this may not be the case, this simple model could explain the wholesale desertion of Chogha Mish and the meteoric rise of Susa on the opposite side of the plain, where mobile pastoralist presence was minimal and the area therefore safer.

# LATE SUSIANA 1 PHASE

## MOBILE PASTORALIST PRELUDE IN SUSIANA

The presence of mobile pastoralism as a parallel subsistence economy and way of life is assumed to have existed from the beginning of village life in southwest Asia (particularly in highland Iran) and elsewhere.[47] However, the evidence for interactions between the mobile pastoralist highlands and settled, agricultural lowlands in preliterate times has been elusive. There are now a few lines of evidence and clues available that can shed more light on this problem.

In the first volume of Chogha Mish and elsewhere,[48] we suggest a chronological gap between the time Chogha Mish and a number of its satellites were deserted and the time when Susa was founded, though the available data make it difficult to estimate the time lag. We propose the terms "Late Susiana 1" for the phase when Chogha Mish remained abandoned and "Late Susiana 2" for the phase known as Susa 1 (Acropole levels 27–25), during which Chogha Mish was re-occupied. The evidence for this proposal is presented in detail in *Chapter 4*.

Chogha Mish enjoyed a central status in the entire Susiana plain from the Archaic Susiana through the end of the Middle Susiana period, when, sometime around the beginning of the fifth millennium B.C.,[49] its monumental building (the Burnt Building) was destroyed by fire and the site, along with a number of its satellites, was subsequently deserted. As mentioned above, it is not at all certain whether hostile forces destroyed the monumental building or whether the fire was accidental, although a settlement as large as Chogha Mish could not have been abandoned because of a localized fire, intentional or accidental. However, this event coincided with others that, taken together, suggest a changing organization in the settlement pattern during the first half of the fifth millennium B.C. The destruction of the monumental Burnt Building coincided not only with the abandonment of Chogha Mish, but also with the abandonment of a number of sites in the eastern part of the plain and the appearance of rich communal cemeteries in the highlands with no associated settlement (Vanden Berghe 1973a, 1973b, 1975, 1987). A number of pottery shapes and decorative motifs we have considered specific to the Late Susiana 1 phase (see *Chapter 4*) are characteristic of the pottery found in these cemeteries.[50] What is more, the pottery assemblage from the graves is an amalgam of motifs and shapes specific to the contemporary cultures in Susiana and highland Fars (Tall-e Bakun B2 and Tall-e Gap) in Iran and in Mesopotamia (Ubaid 3/4), a collection that suggests the nomadic, interregional characteristics of the builders of the cemeteries.

On the basis of detailed reanalysis of all the survey materials, Kouchoukos (1998: 114–15) discerns little change in the distribution of settlements from the previous phase. According to the same analysis, there was a slight population increase in the regions south of Susa that clustered around Tappeh Abu Fanduweh (KS-59, 3553852 N/246852 E, UTM 39N). Based on our joint 2006/07 ICHTO-Oriental Institute excavations, the earliest levels at the site date back to the late Middle Susiana phase.

The shift in settlement pattern and the desertion of some Middle Susiana sites, however, seem to have been caused by interregional factors. Similar developments occurred in Deh Luran. Helbaek used botanical analysis to look for environmental factors in the termination of the Bayat phase (late Middle Susiana) in Deh Luran (Hole, Flannery, and Neely 1969: 364). He postulates that millennia of land-use in the area caused salinization, which forced the population to search for new lands.[51] Conversely, Kirkby (1977: 255) argues that the plain is not subject to drastic

47. For examples, see Adams 1974; Bernbeck 1992; Cribb 1991; Geddes 1983; Gilbert 1975, 1983; Levy 1983; and Smith 1983.
48. See Alizadeh 1996: xxiii–xxvii; *Chogha Mish* I: 155; Alizadeh 1992: 22–26.
49. For radiocarbon dates of this phase (mostly overlapping with Le Breton's Susiana *d*) and their analysis, see Weiss 1977.
50. Vanden Berghe 1975, fig. 5:6, fig. 6:7–8, 17, 20 (Late Ubaid style); fig. 5:13–15, 18, fig. 6:9, 13, 16, 18 (Late Susiana 1 style); fig. 6:11 (Central Plateau style); fig. 5:2, 12 (Fars style).
51. Salinization is not a problem in Susiana. Today, the region is heavily farmed and irrigated, thanks to the introduction of a modern canal system in the early 1960s. Yet, there is no sign of salinization in Khuzestan. In the areas primarily east of the Karun

salinization. Whatever the local causes for the desertion of some sites in eastern Susiana and Deh Luran may turn out to be, the possibility that such drastic interregional development could be attributed to some degree to the rise and development of the highland mobile pastoralist groups must be considered.

With Chogha Mish lying deserted during the Late Susiana 1 phase, it appears that no single site attained a central status in terms of size and population. Nevertheless, the results of our 2004/05 block survey and excavations at Chogha Do Sar ("two-headed mound," 3561127 N/263535 E, UTM 39N) indicate that the site, only about 8 km southwest of Chogha Mish, had an area of occupation of about 5–6 ha during the Late Susiana 1 phase (Alizadeh and Mahfroozi 2005). Our investigations also showed that the site was first occupied during the Early Susiana period and continued to be occupied until the end of Late Susiana 2, or just prior to the end of that phase, for we found no pottery at the site datable to the Terminal Susa phase (ca. 4000 B.C.).

In our stratigraphic trench at Chogha Do Sar, we found a slight erosion layer that separated a massive mudbrick work of Late Susiana 1 date from the late Middle Susiana deposits. While there must have been a hiatus between the two phases of occupation, the time between the abandonment of the site, perhaps linked to the events that led to the demise of Chogha Mish, could not have been long. Moreover, the presence of a mudbrick platform, about 50 × 50 m, suggests the importance of the site in this sector. Further, this platform was superimposed by another, larger mudbrick platform some 60 × 60 m dating to the following Late Susiana 2 phase, contemporary with the famous mudbrick platform of Susa Acropolis. While it is too early to make a definitive statement about our findings and their theoretical implications, it seems warranted to assume that Chogha Do Sar, previously ranking second in size to Chogha Mish, may have replaced Chogha Mish as the regional center in eastern Susiana; Susa was not the only large population center with evidence of social complexity in the late fifth millennium B.C. The apparent absence of materials datable to the Terminal Susa phase at Chogha Do Sar and the fact that there was evidence of fire-destroyed buildings, presumably located on the platform, may be linked to the violence at Susa (Acropole levels 26/25), thought to be the rival settlement in western Khuzestan. The abandonment of Chogha Do Sar and the destruction of Susa's high terrace may therefore be considered part of a much larger and more complex regional development that possibly involved the settled farmers and mobile pastoralists. Hole (1990) suggested several possibilities responsible for the destruction of Susa that include nomadic invasion, accidental fire, famine, and epidemics. While Hole entertains the possibility of a hostile rival in the region, the then available data precluded this conclusion. If the hostilities involved a regional rival, then Chogha Do Sar is a promising site to explore the idea.

Leaving the results from Chogha Do Sar aside, the settlement size for the Late Susiana 1 phase in the region is estimated to have been 94 ha (Weiss 1977). Data on the internal structure of the Susiana society during this phase primarily come from Tappeh Bandebal and Qabr-e Sheikheyn (in Susiana), and Farrukhabad (in the Deh Luran plain).[52] The observed westward movement of the settlements around 4800 B.C. and the appearance of the highland communal cemeteries provide a relevant context for the observation made by Hole (1987: 42), that "sites were often occupied for only short periods, then abandoned for a time and re-occupied. About half the sites changed status from occupied to unoccupied or vice versa, implying that settlements were unstable and that land was not particularly scarce and therefore not valuable." While Hole does not offer the details of how this observation was made in the field or what the cause of the assumed instability was, the westward movement continued until the region east of the Shur River became almost deserted until the mid-fourth millennium B.C. Even during the second half of the fourth millennium B.C., only six sites are reported from the area. We have attributed this development to the increasing presence of the highland mobile pastoralist in eastern Khuzestan.

The presumed correlation between the increased activities of the highland pastoralists and the westward shift of Susiana settlements at the end of the Middle Susiana period becomes more tenable when we note that the eastern part of the Susiana plain has traditionally been, and still is, the locus of the winter pasture for the mobile pastoralists of the region (pl. 31). Northeastern Khuzestan is ideal winter pasture for the highland pastoralists. The tribes can enter the plain either directly from the east or from the northeast without having to cross the Karun River. If this environmental niche was also used in antiquity, as one might expect, then the westward shift of the settled communities may also be taken as an indication of an increase in the population and activities of such mobile pastoralist groups in the area, and as an indication of the initial conflict of interest between the settled and mobile populations of the region, a dichotomy that remained the leitmotif of Iranian history throughout the ages.

---

River, where salt crystal can be formed, farmers solve this problem in less than six months by digging ditches along their farmed land to drain the salt with rainwater or even water from irrigation canals.

52. Dollfus 1983; Weiss 1976; Wright 1981a.

As noted above, Chogha Mish may have remained deserted for most of the Late Susiana 1 phase, though this may be an accident of discovery, even though I have searched the surface of the site several times since 1995 for any Late Susiana 1 diagnostic sherds, with no positive result.[53] The archaeological records pertaining to the Late Susiana 1 phase are found in other sites in Susiana and Deh Luran, however. The small exposure at Tappeh Bandebal, north of Susa, revealed an incomplete plan of domestic architecture with small rectangular rooms. The dead were still buried in residential areas; the chipped stone industry continued from the previous phase without much change; sheep, goats, and cattle, as well as wheat and barley, constituted the diet with some hunting and gathering as dietary supplement. Among the most interesting aspects of this phase are the architectural remains discovered at Qabr-e Sheikheyn (KS-168, 282337 N/3560949 E, UTM 39N), southeast of Chogha Mish, and Farrukhabad (in the Deh Luran plain). During this phase, a series of large mudbrick houses built on top of mudbrick platforms presumably dominated some settlements, including the newly discovered mudbrick platform at Chogha Do Sar.[54] Such single structures crowning the settlement are consistent with the residential patterns of the modern-day tribal headquarters in southwestern and southern Iran.[55] The relative abundance of gazelle bones in and around the monumental building at Farrukhabad is taken as a sign of ranking status of its residents (Wright 1981a: 64). The evidence of sealings and tokens also points to the administrative technology at Farrukhabad, a technology apparently developed to process information on bitumen exchange, most probably with southern Mesopotamia.

Sometime during or by the end of the Late Susiana 1 phase (ca. second half of the fifth millennium B.C.), Susa was founded and presumably replaced Chogha Mish as the largest site on the plain;[56] Susa retained this status for several millennia, save for a short interval during the Protoliterate phase when the settled area was estimated to have been about 9 ha (Johnson 1973: 21), while the entire 17 ha of Chogha Mish were re-occupied. A massive mudbrick platform, the *haute terrasse*, was constructed at Susa probably after the smaller platform, the *massif funéraire*, was destroyed or abandoned after a few generations.[57] The *haute terrasse* was presumably topped by a monumental building, but we remain uncertain of its nature. Whether this project was completed in the course of several generations or in one attempt is not known, but such an undertaking would have required a tremendous amount of labor and the attending organizations and ideology — a level of social complexity that could not have evolved so rapidly at Susa itself shortly after it was founded. The social complexity and regional status of Chogha Mish before it was deserted warrant the assumption that Chogha Mish could have been the early context for social development in western Susiana. Since we argue that Susa was founded earlier than what is generally accepted (see *Chapter 4*), the possibility that the site may have been settled by a diaspora from Chogha Mish is not too farfetched.

## ISOLATED CEMETERIES OF PARCHINEH AND HAKALĀN

Not only are Parchineh and Hakalān the earliest tangible evidence of the existence of ancient mobile pastoralists, these two cemeteries also provide clues to the changing social environment of lowland Susiana in the first half of the fifth millennium B.C. The oldest nomadic cemeteries in Iran, and in fact in the entire ancient Near East, are found at these two neighboring sites. The cemeteries are located along the Meimeh River (also known as Mehmeh) in the Pusht-e Kuh region of Luristan in the southwestern piedmont of the Zagros Mountains. At an elevation of 930 m above sea level, Parchineh, the richer and better-preserved site, is situated on the east bank of the river, about 50 km north of the provincial town of Deh Luran and nearly 60 km east of the frontier town of Mehran, on the Iraqi border. About 20 km north of Parchineh, and at the higher elevation of 1,370 m above sea level, the second cemetery, Hakalān, is located on the west bank of the river. Both cemeteries have easy access to lowland Susiana through Deh Luran and to Mesopotamia and the inner Zagros Mountains through the Mehran plain.

---

53. When I was preparing a pottery workshop at the Oriental Institute in the fall of 2003, I found a few pieces of painted pot sherds from Chogha Mish decorated with the specific dot motif. This accidental discovery shows that the Late Susiana 1 phase did exist at Chogha Mish. Because the pottery is extremely rare and could have belonged to the ancient mobile pastoralists who (as today) may have used the site as a camp, the picture we have drawn of the fifth-millennium B.C. development remains the same.
54. In her commentary on Pollock's paper (Pollock 1989: 290), Dollfus rejects the idea of platforms crowning some sites in the region in mid-fifth millennium B.C.
55. See Flannery 1999 for a full discussion.
56. Weiss (1977) argues that Susa during the Late Susiana 2 phase was as large as 17 ha, but this is by no means clear and in fact the available evidence suggests that it might have been much smaller during its earlier phase of occupation and grew in size gradually (see Dollfus 1985: 18–19 and comments on Pollock's 1989 paper, p. 289; Stève and Gasche 1990).
57. See Le Brun 1971; Canal 1978; Hole 1990.

The sites are considered nomadic cemeteries because they are not associated with any known settlements. Moreover, the tombs are similar in location and construction to tombs of nomads of the later Bronze and Iron Age in the same region. Finally, the region is unsuitable for grain agriculture and is almost devoid of permanent villages — ancient as well as modern — with agriculture as the subsistence base.[58] Vanden Berghe (1973a, 1973b, 1975) led excavations at both cemeteries from 1971 to 1973, and Haerinck and Overlaet (1996) superbly published the final report.

## Parchineh

Three excavation areas (A–C) were opened at this site. In Area A, sixty-four tombs were excavated; in Area B, ninety-eight; and in Area C, only three. The site had contained many more, but these have now been almost completely looted (my own observation). The tombs are rectangular in plan with varying width; they were lined on four sides with vertically set stone slabs, most of which were then covered by large, locally available fieldstones; this basic construction was used as the blueprint for the subsequent nomadic tombs in the region. Of the total 165 tombs excavated at Parchineh, only twenty-eight contained skeletal remains. Of these, only Tomb 72 in Area B contained an almost complete skeleton. No skeletal remains from either site seem to have been collected; it is possible that skeletal remains were lost subsequent to their excavation, but there are no records to validate this assumption. This is unfortunate because when, in the summer of 2001, I was permitted to study the collection at the National Museum of Iran, I was hoping to find enough bones to have them analyzed for age and sex determination.[59]

Many of the tombs, particularly the larger ones, were reused for multiple burials. Judging by the illustrated extant bones, it seems that only adults were buried in these cemeteries. The possibility remains that some of the tombs with no bones belonged to children, whose fragile bones had deteriorated entirely. The total lack of funerary deposits in some of the undisturbed tombs, together with the evidence of the varying quality and quantity of the deposits, indicates social differentiation. In Area B, for example, forty-six tombs contained no artifacts; nineteen had only one; two had two; ten had three; and eleven had three or more.

Because the pottery vessels found in the tombs of both cemeteries consist of several distinct regional styles (i.e., those of Mesopotamia, Susiana, and the inner Zagros valleys), the hypothesis (aside from the possibility of exchange in material goods) that such vessels found their way into these tombs as dowries through interregional marriages, so common among the ethnographic present, could be tested.

## Hakalān

Thirty-six tombs were excavated in two areas at Hakalān. No plans of the excavated areas (designated A and B) are available. According to the final report (Haerinck and Overlaet 1996: 12), the orientation of the tombs varied from east–west to northeast–southwest, the latter similar to those from Parchineh Area B. Similar methods and materials as those used at Parchineh were used in the construction of the Hakalān tombs. Almost all the tombs here contained objects; six tombs had no objects; fourteen had only one; six had two; one had three; three had four; two had five; two had six; one had eight; and one had eleven objects. Of these, only eleven had some poorly preserved skeletal remains consisting mostly of skulls, long bones, and teeth.

The apparent absence of child burials at these cemeteries prevents us from speculating on the acquired versus hereditary status in the society. But the obvious continuum of the material richness of the tombs at both cemeteries is an indication of at least a level of socioeconomic differentiation. At this level of social evolution and military superiority over the settled farming communities by virtue of their mobility, it is not difficult to assume the mobile pastoralists' motivation to control lowland Susiana, for more pasture and arable land.[60]

In both cemeteries, pottery vessels were the most abundant funerary objects. Other funerary objects consisted of stone (34) and copper (1) mace-heads, stone vessels (7), stone hammers and axes, some stone beads, stamp

58. When I visited the sites in the summer of 2001, some small villages had been established in their vicinity, thanks to modern roads and technology.

59. I would like to thank Mr. Kargar, the Director of the National Museum, for giving me permission to see the collection; and Ms. Zahra Jafar-Mohammadi, Keeper of the Prehistoric Collection, for kindly and painstakingly locating and preparing the collection for my viewing.

60. See Flannery 1999 for a comparative study of the modern-day mobile pastoralist confederacy of Khamseh and chiefdom societies in the Middle East.

seals (17), clay figurines (2), and a number of flint blades, including one made of obsidian. In general, the tombs at Parchineh, particularly in Area B, seem to be richer than those excavated at Hakalān.

Based on a general comparison to the ceramics of the fifth millennium B.C. in the central Zagros Mountains (Henrickson 1985), Haerinck and Overlaet (1996) date the cemeteries in Area A at Parchineh to 4600–4200 B.C. Area B at Parchineh and all the tombs at Hakalān are dated to 4200–3600 B.C. (Haerinck and Overlaet 1996: 27). While the earlier date of the second half of the fifth millennium B.C. is supported by parallels, there is no reason to consider a later date for the entire assemblage at these two cemeteries.

Pottery vessels from both cemeteries show strong affinities with the pottery of the Ubaid 3 phase in Mesopotamia and Late Susiana 1 phase in lowland Susiana, with some very close parallels to the typical straight-sided Late Susiana 1 bowls decorated with thick bands and bold designs, as well as bowls with sinuous walls decorated with embellished concentric circles.[61] Vessels decorated with the typical Late Susiana 1 dot motif also occur in both cemeteries.[62] Others (especially simple bowls with wide zigzags bordered by two wide bands) have close parallels in Gawra levels XVII–XV.[63] Small jars decorated with the same motifs have exact parallels at Ras al-ʾAmiya.[64] In addition to the pottery vessels, some stone objects also have close and exact parallels from the same phase in Mesopotamia. Polished stone celts/adzes have exact parallels from Ur and Ur-Ubaid levels,[65] while close parallels for the Parchineh/Hakalān stone hammers are found at Gawra XV.[66]

The most interesting characteristic of the artifacts from the cemeteries, particularly the pottery vessels, is the specific regional styles they exhibit, representing Mesopotamia, lowland Susiana, and highland Iran. For example, while a number of shapes and painted decorations are specific to the Late Susiana 1 phase in lowland Susiana, others betray unmistakable Mesopotamian style. The style of pottery decoration of the mid-fifth-millennium B.C. highland Iran is reflected in the tall beakers decorated with stylized sheep/goat and upper bodies of horned animals rising from the baseline.[67] A combination of this design with the typical Mesopotamian motif of a series of chevrons bordered by narrow and wide horizontal bands also occurs.[68] The Mesopotamian component of the artifacts makes much more sense when we consider the intricate relationship Layard observed (1846: 46–47)[69] between the Iranian mobile pastoralist tribes of this region with those in the Diyala region of Iraq:

> During the summer the [Arab] tribes congregate near that river and on the borders of the vast inland marshes formed by its waters. In the winter and spring they usually encamp in the sandstone and gypsum hills running parallel to the great range [of the Zagros Mountains], or in the plains at the foot of the mountains. They mix with the [Luri] Feili tribes of the Pusht-i-Kuh, and pasture their flocks on their lands for which they yearly pay a small sum to the Wali Ali Khan [Luri chief]. They are usually on good terms with the inhabitants of the mountains, whose chiefs continually take refuge in their tents when opposed by the government, or expelled by their own tribes. The Arab Sheikhs at the same time frequently seek asylum among the I'hiyats [*sic*, Illiat = tribes] of the hills. Thus it is for their mutual interest to be on friendly terms.

If these cemeteries belonged to highland mobile pastoralist communities of the fifth millennium B.C. — and there is no compelling reason to believe otherwise — it is not unwarranted to assume that their mode of subsistence economy put them in a position of intermediary between lowland Susiana, Mesopotamia, and highland Iran. The question as to how the various types of non-perishable objects found at these cemeteries were acquired may involve several mechanisms. Exchange is an obvious mechanism that comes to mind; such objects (at least some of them) may have been part of the "dowries" acquired through interregional marriages, an important factor in forging interregional alliances through kinship. The hybrid style of some painted pottery vessels, not found elsewhere, may not only be attributed to the practice of interregional marriages; assuming women were active in pottery production, it also fits nicely with the mobile characteristic of the migratory tribes.

61. For examples, see Haerinck and Overlaet 1996, figs. 11:A37 (2–3); 14:A17 (1); 15:A23 (2), A36 (1); 42; and 19:6.
62. Haerinck and Overlaet 1996, figs. 50–51; 78; 82–83.
63. Compare Haerinck and Overlaet 1996, fig. 42:1–3, with Tobler 1950, fig. 125:137.
64. Compare Haerinck and Overlaet 1996, fig. 47:5, with Safar, Mustafa, and Lloyd 1981, pl. 18:3.
65. Compare Haerinck and Overlaet 1996, fig. 87:1–7, with Woolley 1955, pl. 14.
66. Compare Haerinck and Overlaet 1996, fig. 58:3–5, with Tobler 1950, fig. 178:38–39.
67. Haerinck and Overlaet 1996, figs. 19:9–11; 21:5–6; 23:1, and passim.
68. Compare Haerinck and Overlaet 1996, fig. 25:3–4, with Woolley 1955, pl. 15:2070.
69. See also Stark 1934: 1–175 for a similar relationship among the Luri and Laki tribes of what is now Ilam province and those in the Iraqi Mandali area.

Admittedly, a portion of the materials found at these cemeteries do not have good and convincing parallels in other regions. But, given their proximity to the archaeologically almost unknown region of the Mehran plain, it is possible that future research in this region may shed more light on this problem. The Mehran plain, some 100 km north of Susiana on the modern-day Iran-Iraq border, is the most northerly lowland region in western Iran and for millennia was the major thoroughfare between Mesopotamia, lowland Susiana, and highland Iran. As such, the control of this territory would have been a strategic goal for the polities based in each of these regions.[70]

By the late Middle Susiana phase sheep and goats were dominant in Susiana, accounting for about 65% of faunal remains at Jafarabad, with sheep becoming more dominant in the later phases (Kouchoukos 1998: 68). If this development is an indication of the increasing importance of wool in Susiana, as well as in southern Mesopotamia,[71] then the concomitant appearance of large cemeteries may not be coincidental. Thus, the manifest development of highland mobile pastoralism by the end of the late Middle Susiana phase may have been in part related to the importance of wool in the economies of both Susiana and southern Mesopotamia. In an approach that favors ratios of NISP (number of identified specimens) values among taxa, Richard Redding (1981, 1993) has shown that, with the exception of Hassunan and Halafian sites in northern Mesopotamia and Syria, sheep/goat ratios were more or less uniformly low (> 0.5%) prior to 5500 B.C. By 4500 B.C. the ratios changed to 1.5–4.5%, indicating a changing trend in herding strategy from a subsistence economy to an economy where animal by-products were becoming important.[72] Analysis of the faunal remains from Qabr-e Sheykhein and Sharafabad also indicates low occurrence of cattle and the highest sheep/goat ratios (Redding 1985).

A number of positive-feedback mechanisms would have been involved in the assumed rapid development of the highland mobile pastoralist communities. One may envision that, as the population of the later urban centers in both lowland Susiana and southern Mesopotamia increased, the demand for pastoral productions such as meat, dairy products, and wool may also have increased (Sherratt 1983). The wetter climate during the sixth and fifth millennia and the increase in canal irrigation agriculture in southern Mesopotamia, according to Kouchoukos (1998), may have changed the landscape of southern Mesopotamia in such a way that it created a shortage of suitable pasture for sheep and goats in this region. Kouchoukos (1998) has argued that the demand for wool in such an environment may have led to an increasing investment in pastoralism by moving the herds seasonally to the Zagros piedmonts and northern Mesopotamia during the Uruk period. Prior to this period, such demand may have been met directly by the highland mobile pastoralist communities who, as a result, developed their own economic and social cohesion and strength, so much so that such communities may have become a force in the sociopolitical and economic life of southwestern Asia as early as the fifth millennium B.C. As the populations of both southern Mesopotamia and Susiana increased, more land was brought under cultivation. On the other hand, as demands for pastoral production increased, the size of herds increased and by extension the demands for more pasture. At one point, presumably by the beginning of the fifth millennium B.C., the equilibrium was upset and a conflict of interests between the pastoralists and farmers may have resulted in hostilities and violence that forced the abandonment of many settlements in eastern Khuzestan.

Further and more tangible information on the nature of some of the Late Susiana sites in eastern Khuzestan was provided during our 2001 joint ICHTO-Oriental Institute archaeological and geomorphological expedition in eastern Khuzestan. Here, some 30 km southeast of the provincial town of Shushtar, we chose the mound of Dar Khazineh (KS-1626) for investigation.[73] The mound dates to the entire course of the fifth millennium B.C. with both Late Susiana 1 and 2 phases represented.

In this part of the Susiana plain, both prehistoric and historical sites are buried under some 2 m of alluvial deposits; our geomorphological investigations hinted that the digging of the huge irrigation canal (now the Gargar River/irrigation canal) presumably during the Parthian/Sasanian period may have been responsible for this situation in the area. As a result, sites here are only visible in the exposed sections of the wadis. The wadi at Dar Khazineh had sliced the mound in such a way that an extensive section was exposed on its western part. This gave us an excellent opportunity to study its stratigraphy and collect archaeological, botanical, and faunal samples without having to excavate it for several seasons.

---

70. For some later historical references to strategically located Der, see Carter and Stolper 1984: 23, 38–39, 43–46, passim.
71. For the detailed study of the importance of wool in southern Mesopotamian economy during the Uruk period, see Kouchoukos 1998.
72. See Kouchoukos (1998: 294–301) for an extensive treatment of this subject.
73. See Alizadeh 2003b for a preliminary report; see also Alizadeh et al. 2004.

From the exposed sections, we could see that under the thick layers of alluvium the cultural layers continued down to the bed of the wadi. When we eventually cleared the sections to the wadi bed we realized that the depth of the mound ranged only from 30 cm to about 180 cm. In some parts of the mound there was no cultural deposit at all. Excavations in our main trench revealed a peculiar depositional pattern not reported before. Clayish and sandy sediments ranging from 5 to 10 cm thick were superimposed on thin lenses of cultural deposits. No solid architecture was found except for extremely badly preserved pisé partition walls whose faces were usually burnt; we also found postholes, traces of ash, and fireplaces. In fact, the "floors" on which these activities took place consisted of alluvial deposits. Thus, in the main area of excavation, when we factored out the alluvial levels from the cultural lenses, we were left with just over 30 cm of deposit for perhaps the entire duration of the fifth millennium B.C.

Marjan Mashkour of the Centre National de la Recherche Scientifique, Paris, analyzed the faunal samples. Although we collected every piece of bone, recovered faunal remains number some 400 fragmentary bones, of which only 45% could be identified. Sheep and goat bones dominate the assemblage but are more numerous in the Late Susiana 2 levels, the latest phase at the site (ca. 4350–4100 B.C.). Significantly, many of the caprine bones are from juvenile or newborn animals, possibly indicating occupation of Dar Khazineh (KS-1626) in February to April. Other fauna present include domestic cattle, pigs(?), onager (*Equus hemionus onager*), fallow deer (*Dama dama mesopotamica*), rodents, and marine mollusks. According to Mashkour, the high percentage of the bones of young animals also suggests butchering patterns of the mobile pastoralists (see tables 3–4).

Naomi Miller of the University of Pennsylvania Museum Applied Science Center for Archaeology (MASCA) analyzed the floral samples. Only a small volume of seeds was recovered, despite the fact that we wet-sieved huge quantities of dirt, especially from the fire pits. Of the exceedingly few (< 30) identifiable charred seeds recovered at Dar Khazineh, most are from wild grasses (*Poaceae*) and legumes (*Fabaceae*). Barley (*Hordeum*), the only cultivated plant in the assemblage, is present only as a few fragmentary seeds.

Based on these observations, we concluded that KS-1626 was occupied seasonally by the prehistoric mobile pastoralists of the region, a pattern that is still evident in eastern Khuzestan (pl. 31). The analyses of the fauna and flora samples from the site also does not rule out the strong possibility that Dar Khazineh was a mobile pastoralist camp. It is important to bear in mind that the primary occupation at Dar Khazineh coincides with the Late Susiana 1 phase, a period we consider the crystallization of mobile pastoralist mode of production in western and south-central Iran.

Another line of evidence is now available from the Central Plateau. This remarkable evidence for contact between lowland Susiana, highland Fars, and the Central Plateau comes from a series of surveys conducted by Mir Abedin Kaboli (2000) of Tehran ICHTO. The survey region is located northeast of the city of Qom, some 100 km south of Tehran. The unmistakable characteristic ceramics of the Late Susiana 1 phase were found on at least six mounds.[74] Although I have not had the opportunity to examine the actual pottery, the illustrations and descriptions of the ware leave no doubt that the published pieces represent genuine Susiana ceramics of the early fifth millennium B.C. Other surveys near the Qazvin plain also produced three pieces of the typical dot motif painted pattern both on typical Susiana cream-buff ware and on the typical late Cheshmeh Ali red ware.[75] Without excavations at these sites, it is difficult to draw tenable conclusions based on circumstances that led to the introduction of Susiana ceramics in the Central Plateau. Nevertheless, when one bears in mind that the fifth millennium B.C. ushered in a period of increasing occurrence of exotic material such as turquoise, lapis, and copper, all native to the Central Plateau and points east, then it is not unwarranted to assume that this specific style of pottery appeared in the Central Plateau as a result of exchange in raw material conducted by mobile pastoralists, the ideal medium of interregional exchange.

Although the socioeconomic spheres of the Susiana plain must certainly have been dominated by its sedentary population during the Late Susiana period, I have argued that control of socioeconomic affairs in Fars during the same period may have been exercised by its mobile pastoralist population, possibly with Tall-e Bakun A as its center.[76] If the isolated highland cemeteries of Parchineh and Hakalān are evidence of developed, organized mobile pastoralist groups in southwestern Iran, one can reasonably assume that the regional centers maintained their "contact" through these mobile groups who were well suited for long-distance trade as intermediaries as well as meeting the increasing demand for wool and other animal by-products. As mentioned above, this suggestion is helpful in describing the mechanism through which certain ceramic traits became widespread and common in Fars, Susiana, Deh

74. For examples, see Kaboli 2000, pls. 19:1; 29:1–3; 33:15–16; 36:10; 37:1–5; 39:11.
75. These surveys were conducted by Miss Lili Niakan of the ICHTO and Mr. Alireza Asgari of the Modares University in Tehran, as part of their masters and doctoral theses, to which I have been an advisor. I thank both of them for showing me their materials.
76. Alizadeh 1988a, 1988b, 2006.

Luran, Behbahan, and the central and eastern Zagros Mountains. The subsequent appearance of semiprecious stones and copper objects in Fars, Susiana, and the Zagros Mountains may also be linked to this mechanism and to the rise of sumptuary behavior.[77]

### MOBILE PASTORALISM AND PRODUCTION OF POTTERY

Before we leave the question of ancient highland mobile pastoralist tribes as a major factor in the cultural development of lowland Susiana in the late fifth millennium B.C., a few words must be offered to describe the connection between the vast geographic distribution of certain classes of pottery and the prehistoric highland mobile pastoralism. While suggesting that less than 30% of mobile societies make and use pottery, Arnold (1985) argues that a number of practical, logistical, and economic (economies of scale) problems are involved in the production of pottery by groups with high residential mobility. However, in a series of articles, Jelmer Eerkens (2003) and her colleagues (Eerkens and Bettinger 2001; Eerkens, Neff, and Glascock 2002) discuss a number of strategies through which such obstacles were overcome by the highly mobile tribes of Paiute and Shoshone of the southwest Great Basin in North America. The pottery manufactured by these Native American tribes is basically simple, crude, and limited in shape and accessories (Eerkens, Neff, and Glascock 2002: 203–05). The same is true of the Negbite pottery of the Negev, which has been attributed to the nomadic groups of the region (Haiman and Goren 1992). These observations suggest that, even when mobile groups do manufacture pottery, their product is technologically and aesthetically inferior to those produced by sedentary peoples.

In the case of the vertical mobile pastoralists of the Zagros Mountains, this distinction need not be made. First, despite their mobile way of life, the Zagros pastoralists spend only a fraction of the year moving from their summer to winter pastures and vice versa. While in their summer pastures they occupy regions not suitable for grain agriculture and thus are lightly populated, in their winter pastures of Fars and lowland Khuzestan they stayed for several months in heavily populated and agriculturally rich areas. Some tribes even own villages with solid architecture or a mixture of tents and mudbrick or stone houses. If this situation was obtained in the fifth millennium B.C. and thereafter, to some extent attributing to the mobile pastoralist groups the manufacture and thus the spread of the very specific class of the fifth-millennium B.C. pottery in southwestern, south-central, and the Central Plateau of Iran is theoretically not farfetched (see Alizadeh 2004). Interregional and inter-tribal marriages, an important factor in forging interregional alliances through kinship, could also be considered as a contributing factor in the spread of some classes of pottery.

These and other examples suggest increasing contact between the lowland and the highland at the end of the Middle Susiana period. Based on an analysis of materials from Fars, I have attributed this unprecedented contact between the lowland and the highland to the development of mobile pastoralism in southwestern and southern Iran (Alizadeh 1988a, 1988b, 2006), a factor that may also have contributed to the gradual desertion and shifting of sites from the eastern part of the Susiana plain, traditionally the winter pasture of the mobile pastoralist groups, to the western sector of the plain.

## LATE SUSIANA 2 PHASE

The Late Susiana 2 phase is poorly known at Chogha Mish. It is a phase when Susa had replaced Chogha Mish as the paramount settlement in the entire plain. Our 2005 investigation in central Khuzestan, however, indicates the possibility that Susa may have had to contend with at least one rival (Chogha Do Sar) situated between Susa and Chogha Mish on the east bank of the Ojirub River, an eastern branch of the Dez (see above). Next to Susa, with some 6–8 ha of occupation, Chogha Do Sar was the largest Late Susiana 2 phase site east of the Dez and a potential rival for the newly founded Susa.

77. The appearance in the central Zagros region (Tappeh Giyan, Tappeh Godin, and Se Gabi) of the unmistakable Central Plateau (Tappeh Sialk III) type of decorated pottery vessels by the end of the fifth millennium B.C. may also have been due to a similar desire and necessity for interregional alliances to facilitate the movement of goods. For examples, see Contenau and Ghirshman 1935, pls. 9:2; 58: top row, second from right in third row from top; Levine and Young 1987, figs. 17:1, 4; Young 1969, fig. 7:1–2. It is extremely puzzling why Young considered the genuine Central Plateau pottery of Sialk III:6–7 of Godin Period Vi as "Ubaid."

According to MASCA-corrected weighted average (Weiss 1977: 357) this phase spans from 4350 to 4190 B.C. The following phase, Terminal Susa, not attested at Chogha Mish or at Chogha Do Sar, lasted for 100 to 150 years. If we accept the 150-year estimate for this phase as suggested by Wright (2001, table 4.1), given the thin archaeological deposits dated to the Terminal Susa at Susa (Dyson 1966; Le Brun 1971), then the entire prehistoric sequence at Susa spans from 4350 to ca. 4000 B.C. The absence of the type of pottery known from Acropole 1, levels 24–23 (Terminal Susa) at Chogha Mish and possibly Jafarabad suggests that both sites were abandoned earlier.

The origins of the fourth-millennium B.C. societal transformations in Susiana, therefore, must be traced to yet another earlier period. During the Late Susiana 1 phase, a decrease in the size of the population in the eastern part of Susiana was balanced by an increased population in the western part of the plain, with Susa as the largest regional center. On the whole, however, there seems to have been a decrease from the previous phase in the size of the population on the entire plain (Wright et al. 1975: 137). In the Dimcheh region, just south of Chogha Mish, only four out of twenty-seven sites remained occupied. Although Veenenbos' hypothesis relating to major watercourse change in the region may have been a factor in the distribution and density of population centers in this region, geology is not sufficient to account for such major trends. This evidence, when taken together with the assumed increasing activities of the highland mobile pastoralist tribes in this part of the plain and the ensuing conflict of interest, provide a more balanced interpretation of the data. The westward movement of the population centers in eastern Susiana could lead to more available land for pasture and consequently to the increasing nomadic presence here, creating even more tension between the settled farmers and mobile herders of the region.

The available data from Chogha Mish are not sufficient to suggest an absolute date for the re-occupation of Chogha Mish during this phase. Unlike Susa, where examples of the dot motif were found in the basal levels of the Acropole, the almost total absence at Chogha Mish of any ceramic carryovers from the preceding phase in the excavated areas of the mound suggests that the site may have been re-occupied sometime during the Late Susiana 2 phase. The architectural remains of the Late Susiana 2 phase at Chogha Mish were fragmentary and are limited to the High Mound. Nevertheless, the presence in Trench XXI of sherds dating to this phase suggests that this area, too, may have either contained Late Susiana 2 architecture or was used to manufacture pottery. No direct evidence is available to support this inference, however.

Prior to the sixth season of excavations, a series of kilns and ashy floors mixed with stone blades, potsherds, and wasters were found in Square N10 of Trench XXIII on the High Mound. When excavations in the tenth season continued in the area, two superimposed architectural levels were found (see *Chapter 2* for details). The Late Susiana 2 architecture in Square N10 reveals only a partial plan of the building. The surviving and excavated portions exhibit multi-room structures with rectangular and square rooms. The open areas surrounding the rooms were filled with ashy and clayish layers. The millennia-old practice of paving open areas with cobbles continued into this phase.

The limited area of Late Susiana 2 occupation at Chogha Mish and the abundance of associated kilns and ashy deposits suggest that, as at Jafarabad, Chogha Mish may have been re-occupied during this phase as a small industrial center rather than a strictly residential one. Nevertheless, one should bear in mind the degree of destruction and leveling that Protoliterate and Old Elamite building activities caused the Late Susiana 2 remains on the High Mound.

Johnson (1973: 21) suggests that, toward the end of the Late Susiana period, known as the Terminal Susa phase, Susa shrank in size to about 5 ha, though this estimate is by no means certain. It has been suggested that the disappearance of the long tradition of Susiana painted pottery, marking a new era, should be explained by as-yet "unresolved problems of social organization rather than strictly economic or subsistence affairs."[78] Parallel transformations in Mesopotamia and Fars suggest interregional dynamic and causes that underlie these transformations by the early fourth millennium B.C. Any attempt to explain these transformations must take into account regional and interregional contributing factors. At present, insufficient archaeological evidence from the first half of the fourth millennium B.C. in Susiana prevents us from reaching an understanding of the dynamics of these changes.

As mentioned above, the founding of Susa, according to the pottery analysis presented in *Chapter 4*, occurred sometime during the latter part of the Late Susiana 1 phase, when contacts between the lowland and the highland increased rapidly and Chogha Mish lay deserted. This proposition is based partly on the similarities among regional ceramic traditions. These similarities may have been the result of an increased interaction between the lowlands and

78. Johnson 1987: 286. See also Nissen's (1988) functionalist approach, where he argues that a change in pottery technology — use of the wheel — is behind all the stylistic changes and the shift toward the use of unpainted and band-painted vessels that occurs toward the end of the Ubaid period.

highlands, which probably developed out of increasing demand for various local commodities and resources of both regions, as well as through forging interregional alliances in a much larger sphere of interaction. We may attribute this development to the growth of a regional elite in both the lowlands and the highlands, an elite who resided in the nascent urban centers and competed for supremacy through interregional kin alliances and perhaps through warfare, as suggested by the Burnt Building at Chogha Mish and the presumed burning of the buildings on the high terrace at Susa, as well as the burning of Chogha Do Sar sometime during the Late Susiana 2 phase. Nevertheless, Susa may have started off as a cluster of small population centers that became integrated and grew after its first phase of occupation.[79] That the much-discussed high terrace was constructed on over a meter of residential refuse is another indication that Susa attained its regional status sometime after its initial occupation, perhaps during Acropole levels 26–25.

## PROTOLITERATE (LATE URUK) PHASE

Sometime before the end of the Late Susiana 2 phase, Chogha Mish was deserted again for at least half a millennium.[80] The paucity of information on the Late Susiana 2 occupation at Chogha Mish prevents us from speculating on the resurgence of the site and the high status it regained in the Protoliterate phase as the largest town in lowland Susiana. Susa, on the other hand, remained occupied after the Late Susiana 2 phase, but apparently went through substantial changes in settlement size and socioeconomic structure (Johnson 1973; Weiss 1977). Nevertheless, despite the limited nature of the materials from Susa Acropole levels 22–19, the change does not seem to have been either violent or abrupt, roughly paralleling similar artifactual changes in southern Mesopotamia.

It is speculated that during the poorly known Terminal Susa phase, Susa was reduced to only 5 ha (Johnson 1973). The settlement then presumably expanded to cover some 12 and 25 ha during the Early and Middle Susa 2 phases in the first half of the fourth millennium B.C., i.e., Early and Middle Uruk according to Johnson (1973: 71, table 18). Susa shrank in size again in the second half of the millennium to about 9 ha, and Tappeh Abu Fanduweh (KS-59) shrank from 9.56 to 8.16 ha, though it is by no means certain how the latter estimate was calculated. In our own 2006/07 joint ICHTO-Oriental Institute season at Abu Fanduweh we could not isolate a "Middle Uruk" phase as Johnson defines it. Nor did we find a substantial occupation of the site during the "Early Uruk" phase. The most extensive occupation (ca. 12 ha) belonged to the second half of the fourth millennium B.C., that is, the Protoliterate phase (Late Uruk). Surveys and excavations at Chogha Mish indicated that the entire 17–18 ha of the site were re-occupied at the beginning of Susa Acropole level 18, if not slightly earlier, contemporary with what we call the Protoliterate phase at Chogha Mish.

Prior to the excavations at Chogha Mish in 1961, the pottery of the earlier part of the Protoliterate phase (Late Uruk/Protoliterate a–b), as suggested by Delougaz (Delougaz and Lloyd 1942), was primarily known from Warka.[81] The latter part of the Protoliterate phase (c–d/Jemdet Nasr) was best known from the Diyala sites as well as from Jemdet Nasr, Kish, and Tell Uqair. Susa had also produced a considerable number of Protoliterate pottery types, which, on the basis of Mesopotamian comparisons, Le Breton attributed to phases termed Susa B (Susa 3) and C (Susa 4),[82] or the Protoliterate and proto-Elamite phases.

The pottery types of the Jemdet Nasr phase are well known from the Diyala region and other central Mesopotamian sites (Delougaz 1952). Despite extensive excavations at Chogha Mish, no pottery definitely datable to this phase has been found. The most noticeable include the total absence of the typical polychrome wares, the monochrome four-lugged jars, the slender red-washed spouted vessels, and the solid pottery stands. Thus, Chogha Mish

79. See Dollfus 1985 and Pollock 1989: 283.

80. According to Weiss (1977), this span of time corresponds with the Early Uruk (3700–3450 B.C.) and Middle Uruk (3450–3200 B.C.) phases. Based on the Syrian and Anatolian evidence and using the OxCal program in a Bayesian framework (Wright and Rupley 2001), Wright (2001: 130, table 4.1) suggests ca. 4150–3800 B.C., 3800–3350 B.C., and ca. 3350–3100 B.C., respectively, for the Early, Middle, and Late Uruk phases. In his table 4.1, Wright (2001: 130) assigns 150-, 300-, 350-, and 200-year estimates for the duration of the Terminal Susa, Early, Middle, and Late Uruk phases, respectively. These estimates are puzzling to me since they do not correspond to the OxCal dates for the three phases of the Uruk period suggested. For example, if we add all the estimated years beginning with the Late Uruk phase, we reach a date of ca. 4150 B.C. for the beginning of the Early Uruk phase in Susiana, clearly too early, given the calibrated date of the beginning of Late Susiana 2 (Susa 1) phase at 4350 B.C.

81. Von Haller 1932; for later pottery from Nippur, see the discussion in Hansen 1965.

82. Le Breton 1957, figs. 10–13.

does not seem to have been occupied during the latter part of the Protoliterate phase and lay deserted again until the Old Elamite (Sukkalmah) period.

Previously, the relative chronological position of the Protoliterate deposits at Chogha Mish was based on a comparative analysis of the materials from Nippur and the Eanna deep sounding at Uruk.[83] In using the data from the pit, the inevitable incompleteness of materials from a limited area is still a handicap.[84] At Warka, the final Ubaid level (level XIV) is superimposed by deposits with primarily unpainted pottery types, including long, slender, straight spouts with either rounded or cut-away tips (von Haller 1932, pl. 17 D:p–q [level XIII]), and narrow vessels with bodies sharply tapering toward the base (von Haller 1932, pl. 17 D:r [level XIII]). These types thus appear as diagnostic for the Uruk period, as Nissen (1986, 2001) defined it (Warka Deep Sounding XII–IX).

The most detailed periodization of fourth-millennium B.C. Susiana was suggested by Johnson (1973). Based on the poorly known and controversial sequences from Warka, Nippur, Tall-e Geser (Ghazir), and Susa (Acropole levels 22–17), as well as a detailed seriation of surface pottery, Johnson proposed three distinct phases for the fourth-millennium B.C. Susiana, namely, the Early, Middle, and Late Uruk phases. Johnson assigns sixteen types of pottery to his Early Uruk phase. Of these, only Types 13, 18 (impressed strip bowls), 44 (heavy lugs), and 45 (straight [upright] spouts) do not occur at Chogha Mish. Presumably, these three distinct types are primarily limited to level 22 of Susa Acropole 1. Perhaps these three types continued through the later levels 21–19 of Susa Acropole 1, but these levels are poorly known and not reliable references for establishing temporal distribution of the first half of the fourth-millennium B.C. ceramic types in Khuzestan. The rest of Johnson's Early Uruk types occur at Chogha Mish with no apparent spatial or temporal distribution. Johnson's Middle Uruk phase in Susiana is characterized by the appearance of nine new pottery types (Johnson 1973: 56–57), all of which occur at Chogha Mish with the characteristic types of the later phase, namely band-rim bottles, jars with drooping spouts, complex incised crosshatched decoration, and twisted handles. All these types are also known from Eanna levels VIII–IV, that is, Nissen's Late Uruk.

At Chogha Mish, for instance, specimens of distinctive types with rocker decoration, the miniature handled jars (fig. 32:D), and the slender ovoid jars (*Chogha Mish* I, pl. 121:A) occur both in pits and in primary deposits. The rather numerous representatives of another distinctive type, the trough-spouted bowl, appear in the East and West Areas in deposits of both higher and lower architectural levels.[85] The concentration of certain types may be taken as a chronological indication. For example, the "flowerpots" (Nissen 1970: 132–36), restricted to the Late Uruk phase in Mesopotamia and at Susa's Acropole to level 17, abound in Trench VI and in the northeasternmost part of the East Area but are very rare elsewhere. In both areas, however, these pots are associated with the types that are standard everywhere and thus cannot serve as chronological indicators for the dates of the two areas where they are so common. The uneven patterns of distribution seem to be correlated with variations in the activities carried out in different areas, rather than temporal distribution patterns.[86] Again, at Tappeh Abu Fanduweh (KS-59), we observed the same mixture of types in all the levels we excavated.

So far, the Protoliterate types from Acropole levels 18 and 17, Eanna VII–IV, and from Habuba Kabira South provide the closest parallels for the types discovered at Chogha Mish.[87] It should be noted, however, that most of the parallels from Warka come from Eanna VI and earlier, rather than from Eanna V or IV. On the other hand, tables 1–8 in *Chogha Mish* I (pp. 37–93) indicate that out of 130 Chogha Mish Protoliterate vessel types, over 25%, do not occur (or remain to be discovered) at Susa Acropole. It is therefore absolutely necessary that detailed analyses of form and style of the entire fourth-millennium pottery assemblages in Susiana will have to await more reliable and larger stratigraphic exposures than what is now available from Chogha Mish and Susa — we hope the results of our excavations of Tappeh Abu Fanduweh (KS-59) provide the framework. Without indisputable stratified sherds, the archaeologist remains handicapped in the interpretation of regional social, economic, and political changes that took place in the fourth millennium B.C.

---

83. Von Haller 1932. As Nissen (2001) clearly states, however, the pottery types from Levels XIII–IX of the deep sounding are not reliable comparative material. Materials from the more secure Levels VIII to VI may be relied on for comparative analysis.

84. The original Eanna pit in square Pc-XVI4 has since been supplemented by another stratigraphic test pit in K/L XII (Nissen 1970); see also Sürenhagen (1987, 1988) for additional new Late Uruk material and reanalysis of the published pottery from the deep sounding.

85. This type is the most distinct in Eanna VIII–VII; it appears at Chogha Mish with diagnostic shapes of the Protoliterate phase.

86. For a comprehensive list of the types attested at Chogha Mish and their parallels elsewhere, see *Chogha Mish* I, tables 1–9.

87. Most of Chogha Mish Protoliterate parallels seem to be with Susa 18, suggesting the maximum size for Chogha Mish during Susa level 18 and probably level 19. Both Algaze (1993: 129) and Dittmann (1986) believe that Chogha Mish had contracted by the time of Susa 17.

On the basis of the above types, Chogha Mish was re-occupied perhaps around 3600 B.C. But the available evidence of the pottery types and their stratigraphic distributions at Chogha Mish does not lend itself to be broken down into a middle and a late phase with two distinct classes of pottery forms and decorations, even though at least three architectural phases are recorded at Chogha Mish, indicating a long duration of the Protoliterate phase there. The architectural remains at Chogha Mish can be assigned to early and later phases, with a possibility of a third phase (see *Chapter 2*). If one agrees with Nissen (1986, 2001: 153) that the real break in the Uruk sequence at Warka is evident only between Levels IX and VIII, then the Chogha Mish Protoliterate pottery assemblage represents a long, uninterrupted period, assuming that both southern Mesopotamia and lowland Susiana had parallel temporal development in pottery types, an assumption that may not be valid. Almost 6 m of Protoliterate phase deposit at the northern complex of Tappeh Abu Fanduweh (KS-59) lends support to our assumption that the Late Uruk may have been much longer than thought.

## SETTLEMENT PATTERNS AND POPULATION DENSITY

According to the results of Johnson's survey (1973: 87), only eighteen sites totaling 30 ha[88] were occupied during the Terminal Susa 1 phase. Most of the sites are located in the southwest and central part of the upper plain, with only two, widely dispersed sites — KS-182 and KS-190 — on the eastern sector. In the following Early Susa 2 phase (Early Uruk), the number of sites increased to forty-nine (a total of 95 ha),[89] but the spatial pattern remained the same. A three-level settlement hierarchy is detected in this phase (Johnson 1973: 90), with Susa (KS-00) and Tappeh Abu Fanduweh (KS-59) as the major centers of population. As in southern Mesopotamia,[90] in the following Middle Susa 2 phase (Middle Uruk), the number of settlements in lowland Susiana continued to increase from forty-nine to fifty-two sites, with a total of 127 ha of occupation. As in the previous two phases, sites are primarily located in the western and central sectors of the plain. According to Johnson (1973: 110), Chogha Mish was re-occupied in this phase and had a size of about 10 ha.[91] By this time, three major population centers co-existed in lowland Susiana: Susa, Chogha Mish, and Abu Fanduweh.

The Protoliterate (Late Uruk) phase was a period of a major change in settlement patterns in Susiana. During this phase, only thirteen sites totaling about 100 ha were occupied, with Chogha Mish the largest population center on the plain. The spatial distribution of sites is the same as the earlier phase, but this time only one site (KS-171; Johnson 1973: 143–47, fig. 14) remained occupied in the far side of the eastern portion of the plain. Whether the demographic trends of the Protoliterate phase were a continuation of the assumed similar trends that started after the Middle Susiana period is impossible to say. But if, as Wright and Johnson (1975) suggest, the demographic and social development of highland mobile pastoralist communities resulted in their interest in eastern Susiana (the traditional winter pasture of the modern-day Bakhtiyari tribes), then one might speculate that their renewed increasing presence in this part of the plain created tension and thus insecurity, hence the almost complete depopulation of this part of the lowlands by the late fourth millennium B.C. and well into the third.

The circumstances that resulted in the abandonment of Chogha Mish must have been operating at regional, if not interregional level, for by the end of the fourth and early third millennia B.C., the settled population of Susiana reached a minimum. Susa apparently was the sole large site in the region with more than half the settled population of the entire plain residing there (see, e.g., Alden 1987). It is true that the pottery of the early third millennium B.C. is difficult to recognize in Khuzestan, but this difficulty alone cannot possibly account for the low population estimate of the region in this period. Besides, our 2006/07 excavations at Tappeh Abu Fanduweh (KS-59) indicated at least 5–6 ha of occupation during the early Susa 3 phase. My study of the Geser (Ghazir in the literature) material at the Oriental Institute indicates that this early third-millennium B.C. pottery gradually replaced the typical Late Uruk ceramic repertoire. This specific ceramic that occurred at Abu Fanduweh, Geser and Susa (LeBrun 1978) preserved most of the major forms of the preceding phase, but it was tempered primarily with chaff and the vessels usually bear red, brown, and gray wash and are often decorated with horizontal bands of different colors. This early type is not reported from Deh Luran. Rare examples of the very scarce highland type of painted four-lugged vessel (figs. 29:G;

88. Compare Wright 2001, table 4.1, where using Dewar's model he estimates the total area of the occupation on the plain to be 21.5 ha, with a population of 2,150–4,300 for 100 and 200 people per hectare respectively.
89. See also Wright 2001 for different estimates.
90. See Adams and Nissen 1972; Adams 1981; Englund 1998: 43.
91. This is an arbitrary estimate by Johnson (1973: 73). In our opinion, the entire area of Chogha Mish was occupied during this phase.

33:D) seem to anticipate the following proto-Elamite phase. The same type of vessel also occurred in Susa Acropole level 17 (Le Brun 1971, fig. 53:17) and elsewhere.[92] Specific pottery stands/rings from Chogha Mish (*Chogha Mish* I, pl. 81:U–W) can also be considered as harbingers of the changes to come in the early third millennium B.C. These stands are rare at Chogha Mish and their closest parallels come from Susa Ville royale I (Carter 1980, fig. 33:9), from Tall-e Malyan Banesh (proto-Elamite) phase (Alden 1979, fig. 54:1–24), and from the contemporary Habuba Kabira South (Sürenhagen 1974/75, pls. 19:157, 32:1).

The archaeological phase that is characterized with this pottery and administrative tablets with pictographic signs is widely known as proto-Elamite with connection to Fars, Kerman, Sistan, the western Zagros Mountains, and the Central Plateau. During the early proto-Elamite phase most of the upper Susiana, especially the eastern part, the hypothetical winter pastures of the ancient mobile pastoralists, became completely devoid of any settlement, suggesting that the takeover of eastern Khuzestan by the mobile population had now been completed.

## CHOGHA MISH URBAN DEVELOPMENT

With this brief account of Chogha Mish's regional position in lowland Susiana, we can now turn our attention to the structure of the urban center at the site. Eleven seasons of excavations at Chogha Mish have revealed a planned Protoliterate town with streets, side alleys, sewer and irrigation drains, water wells and cesspools, workshops, and public and private buildings. From the beginning, the town was divided into upper and lower quarters; the upper town was located on the High Mound and the lower town on the Terrace.

At least two distinct architectural phases are documented for this period: Protoliterate 1 and 2. Occupational remains of periods later than the Protoliterate (particularly the Old Elamite) had substantially damaged the remains of the upper town; nevertheless, enough survived to provide hints of its bygone glory. Most of the architectural remains of the period have been either destroyed or covered by the massive Old Elamite fortification walls and other buildings. What remains shows an incomplete plan of a large structure with rectangular rooms, cisterns, and a substantial drainage system (fig. 8). The presence of several pottery kilns, huge amounts of broken sherds and wasters, layers of ash, as well as mosaic cones, clay tokens, and sealings suggests that this area was the locus of administration and industrial activities. No fortification wall was found associated with the town or any other settlement in lowland Susiana in this period, but the substantial rectangular structure in front of this quarter may have served as a watch tower (see *Chapter 2*).

The lower town on the Terrace was much better preserved. Baked bricks were used almost exclusively for pavements, drains, wells, and cesspools. Riemchen mudbricks were used in domestic and public buildings. The residential units usually have mudbrick walls 30–50 cm thick. The mudbricks contained ash and sherds of earlier periods and thus the clay may have been taken from the numerous pits (some dug to Archaic levels) that dot the settlement. Frequently, stumps of earlier walls (primarily of Middle Susiana date) were used as foundations for the Protoliterate Phase 1 walls.[93] Rooms vary greatly in size and shape, from square to rather oblong rectangle. Sometimes, the shape of the available space and the position and orientation of earlier or contemporary walls may have been the reason for some trapezoidal rooms or storage bins. On the whole, the entire town has a general northeast–southwest orientation that it retained throughout the two main phases of occupation.

Some residential buildings have relatively large rectangular areas that can be interpreted as courtyards based on the fragmentary cobble pavements found in them. It is difficult to say with certainty if all residential buildings had their own open courts. The evidence suggests that several buildings shared the available open spaces. Some rooms were provided with a fireplace and a bench on which were placed (some still in situ) a number of beveled-rim bowls and small spouted jars. In contrast to the Diyala region, no burials were found under house floors, with the sole exception of a simple burial in the East Area (see *Chapter 2*, Q16:1101 in fig. 16), which may well be intrusive. Numerous kilns and fireplaces were found throughout the settlement. During the Protoliterate phase, as in the earlier phases, Chogha Mish was a major center for manufacturing pottery, as the numerous simple and complex pottery

92. This ware is also found at Tappeh Godin V (Weiss and Young 1975, fig. 3:2) and Warka, K/L XII Sounding, layer 42 (Nissen 1970, pl. 103:15).

93. A detailed record of the exact location of these early foundations would have allowed further reconstruction of the Middle Susiana settlement that no longer exists. But that information is not available.

kilns found on the Terrace attest.[94] Large numbers of clay sealings, impressed tablets, clay balls, clay bullae, and tokens indicate administrative activities at Chogha Mish during this phase as well.

The entire Protoliterate town at Chogha Mish was crisscrossed by both open and covered water and sewage channels. Such drains were made of both baked bricks and baked pottery pipes that fitted nicely together. Another indication of the planned architecture throughout the phase is the perpendicular angle at which buildings and drains cross one another. Subsidiary drains from narrow side alleys and even from some individual houses joined the main drains at right angles.

The available evidence does not allow us to make a distinction between the drains that were used to supply the town with freshwater and those that were used to lead sewage and wastewater to cesspools or out of the settlement. The closest freshwater source to Chogha Mish is the Shur River, about 1 km to the east. Today, this stream runs below the level of the plain. Based on his geomorphological observations, Kouchoukos (pers. comm.) believes that in the past the Shur River ran much higher, a view supported by the remnants of the river's ancient levies. Though it is feasible that an artificial canal brought water to the site, the problem of getting the water to the top of the mound would remain unresolved. However, a number of deep brick-lined wells that were often connected to the drainage system are more likely candidates for the source of freshwater at Chogha Mish. It must be noted, however, that none of these features was completely excavated. In addition, if some of the wells were actually dug to reach water, it is very odd that they had to be dug from some 20 meters above the plain. This can only make sense if siege warfare was practiced at the time, an unlikely event given the absence of fortification walls, the suggestion of some of the contemporary glyptic scenes notwithstanding.

Despite the presence of numerous mosaic cones, presumably typical of monumental buildings in southern Mesopotamia, no building was found in the first five seasons that can reasonably be called monumental. We have good evidence that the Protoliterate settlement at Chogha Mish was established as an administrative and production center with a number of secular and possibly religious monumental buildings, or a combination of both. In the course of the eighth to eleventh seasons, a large complex of buildings was partially excavated in the East Area. To the west of this major complex, in the West Area, a substantial polygonal mudbrick platform was erected, the function of which is not known.[95] Measuring about 350 sq. m, this platform was surrounded and abutted by subsidiary structures. If the platform supported a building, no traces of it remain. The surface of the platform, however, was littered — even imbedded — with potsherds of the Parthian period.

The tripartite monumental building that was found in the East Area dominated the settlement. It consists of a central court with recessed niches, and square and rectangular chambers surrounding it on two sides (fig. 16). The main entrance to the building leads to a long, mudbrick-paved antechamber, at one end of which a heap of gazelle bones was found (pl. 13:B). There is not a shred of evidence to indicate this central building was a temple, though its plan has general resemblance to temples at Uruk. All the evidence of early administrative technology in Susiana comes not from monumental or religious buildings, but from small to medium size domestic architectural units.

The relative dearth of objects in the various chambers of the monumental building and its subsidiaries suggests the possibility that at the end of the Protoliterate phase, Chogha Mish was deserted peacefully and left exposed to the elements for over 1,500 years. Subsequent occupations were concentrated on the High Mound, though parts of Squares P17–18 and Q17–18 were used during the Achaemenid period.

## QUESTION OF "URUK EXPANSION" IN LOWLAND SUSIANA

As mentioned in the *Preface*, throughout this chapter we outline the evidence pertaining to the origins of fourth-millennium B.C. social complexity in Susiana. While this is a relatively easy task for the prehistoric sequence, it is less clear whether the development of state organizations in fourth-millennium Susiana was fundamentally affected and influenced by its southern Mesopotamian neighbors. The following is intended to briefly address this widely and intensely discussed issue.

State organizations developed regionally within geographic boundaries amid myriad socioeconomic interactions. Within these boundaries, sociopolitical and economic powers (polities) and their attendant institutions were concentrated in a particular center, usually the largest and presumably most populated. In periods with historical records, it is possible to reconstruct the boundaries of states with some certainty. In the absence of historical documents, either

94. For a detailed analysis of Chogha Mish Protoliterate pottery kilns, see *Chogha Mish* I: 29–30 and Alizadeh 1985.

95. See *Chogha Mish* I, pl. 265.

in prehistoric times or when records are mere numbers, tallies, and lists of professions and commodities,[96] spatial distribution of artifacts is used to determine the boundaries of prehistoric cultures, chiefdoms, and pristine states. Moreover, when materials attributed to a specific culture are found in regions outside the deemed boundaries of a given polity, that evidence is taken as indicative of cultural, political, and economic influence in that region.

While several prehistoric phases in Susiana exhibit material culture, primarily pottery, similar to contemporary phases in southern Mesopotamia, the material culture of fourth-millennium Susiana is almost entirely Mesopotamian in character, technique, and, presumably, function. This strong similarity in the material culture between the two regions has been the source of numerous speculations, ranging from "ethnic duality" to "colonialism" to inspired yet indigenous development. Moreover, the similarity of the archaeological materials from Susiana with definite geographical boundaries, as well as of those discovered in some Syrian and southeastern Anatolian sites, to the archaeological assemblage of the second half of the fourth-millennium southern Mesopotamia, is one factor many scholars have used the term "Greater Mesopotamia" to include not only lowland Susiana, but also the highland region of western Iran, eastern Syria, southeastern Anatolia, and even highland Fars as part of the integrated sphere of southern Mesopotamian political and economic influence. While this high degree of similarity between southern Mesopotamia and lowland Susiana's archaeological assemblages can safely be attributed to a sphere of socioeconomic and cultural interactions, there have been numerous efforts to interpret this development in terms of political and economic hegemony of one population center (Uruk) over others.

Sometime in the second half of the fourth millennium B.C., a number of sites in Syria, Anatolia, and one (Tappeh Godin) in the central Zagros Mountains exhibit a mixture of local tradition and a limited repertoire of the late fourth-millennium pottery vessels and artifacts related to administrative technology. This picture clearly shows that local communities/polities were not replaced by a wave of foreign entrepreneurs from the lowlands.[97] Some special sites, like Habuba Kabira South,[98] yielded nothing but genuine Uruk pottery and other artifacts.[99] But the majority of the so-called colonies outside of southern Mesopotamia exhibit a limited range of Uruk-related materials mixed with predominantly local artifacts.

The distribution of these "colonies" in the Near East offers a mosaic of sites in northern Mesopotamia, Syria, Anatolia, and highland Iran separated from Uruk, presumably the core, by vast stretches of land.[100] Lowland Susiana presents an entirely different problem. When Uruk materials appear on the Susiana plain, they cover the entire region and are hardly limited in space or type of materials.

There are, nevertheless, some differences. Detailed analysis of the glyptic art of the second half of the fourth millennium B.C. reveals both strong similarities in the basic iconography of southern Mesopotamia and lowland Susiana and major differences in the execution techniques and subject matters of the regions. While the glyptic art in both regions exhibits a general standard in the modeling and spacing of the figures, there are major differences in the subject matter and in the way details are rendered. The majority of the figures depicted on sealings from southern Mesopotamia show facial details (such as eyes, ears, and mouths); figures (both animals and humans) on sealings from lowland Susiana almost always lack such details. Amiet (1957: 126; 1972: 76) pointed out the rare occurrence in Mesopotamia (Lenzen 1964, pls. 26:g, 28:c) of the horizontal-winged griffin, popular both at Susa and Chogha Mish.

While a large number of glyptic scenes from Susa and Chogha Mish exactly parallel each other, they only show general similarities with those found at Uruk. The glyptic alone shows that the exchange of portable goods must have been within the confines of lowland Susiana rather than between this region and southern Mesopotamia. Absent from the Mesopotamian glyptic corpus are the scenes of men squatting in a row with animals. In general, scenes in which people are engaged in various activities are rare in southern Mesopotamia. Completely absent in Mesopotamia are men and women shown sitting with their legs crossed, just as many people still do in the Middle East.

The absence in Susiana of a number of scenes and individual elements so common in southern Mesopotamia is equally important. The popular Mesopotamian serpent-necked "panther" (Boehmer 1999, pl. 60) occurs only once

96. Falkenstein 1936; Englund 1998; Englund and Nissen 1993.
97. See Marro and Hauptmann 2000 and Rothman 2001 for the most recent analyses.
98. Strommenger and Sürenhagen 1970; Strommenger 1980.
99. Helwing (2000) notes about 10% of the pottery is of local material relating to the chaff-faced ware known from Arslan Tappeh and other sites in northern Syria.
100. See Marro and Hauptmann 2000 and Wright 2001 for a number of criticisms and re-evaluations of the nature of the late fourth-/early third-millennium north Syrian and southeastern Anatolian sites.

at Susa (Amiet 1972, nos. 475–76) but is completely absent from Chogha Mish. Scenes depicting animals emerging from a hut (Boehmer 1999, pl. 89:A–E; Brandes 1979, pl. 32) are completely unknown from Susiana;[101] extremely rare are scenes depicting the Inana symbol/standard with or without the associated animals (Boehmer 1999, pls. 10, 89:A–E), as well as the scenes depicting presumably the ruler/priest with animals and/or vegetation. Also rare are the scenes with the typical southern Mesopotamian high-prow boats (Boehmer 1999, pl. 91). The southern Mesopotamian hybrid creature, the "frog-headed" human, always depicted frontally (Boehmer 1999, pl. 66), as well as flying "eagles" spaced in a network of twisted cables (Boehmer 1999, pls. 67–68), are completely absent from lowland Susiana. While some of the scenes and motif elements may have been related to varying practical issues and style/convention in both regions, others (such as the Inana symbol, calves emerging from the hut, and ruler/priest engaged in feeding animals) are culture specific and underlie the differences in religious and ideological issues between the two regions, a difference that should not exist if southern Mesopotamians actually lived in Khuzestan and were responsible for the creation of the administrative technology there directly.

Algaze (1989, 1993) sees the similarity between the material cultures in several regions during the fourth millennium B.C. as an indication of Uruk centralized character and its political hegemony over its neighbors. Algaze used world-system theory as a model to explain the events of the fourth millennium B.C. in southwest Asia.[102] There is no question that during this period Susiana was heavily under the influence of its Mesopotamian neighbors. The question that remains to be addressed is whether there was any migration from southern Mesopotamia to lowland Susiana.

To address this question we need to consider Susiana in the fourth millennium in a much wider context. We know that by the mid-fifth millennium B.C. Susiana had already achieved a hierarchical society with monumental buildings and an advanced administrative technology that included door sealings. This was not a society that could easily be conquered by outside forces of presumably equal strength and social complexity without leaving any physical traces. Yet the archaeology of the region leaves no doubt that Susiana was indeed colonized by people from southern Mesopotamia. This contradiction will resolve once we consider the fact that by the end of the fifth millennium B.C. the society in Susiana had already collapsed and the region lost most of its settled population prior to the appearance of Uruk material culture there.

We have already proposed that the highlands and lowlands established close contact by the end of the late Middle Susiana phase around 5000 B.C. We also hypothesized about the causes of Chogha Mish's abandonment and the westward migration of the prehistoric settlements on the plain. Further, we attributed these events to the presumed conflict of interest between the highlanders and lowlanders and that the collapse of Susa by the end of the Late Susiana 2 phase (ca. 4000 B.C.) and the regions depopulation were taken as indicative of this presumed tension.

It is in this vacuum that farmers and entrepreneurs from southern Mesopotamia appeared on the scene to take advantage of the new opportunity in farming and trade. There is no question that some of the indigenous population remained in the region and most probably cooperated or peacefully co-existed with the new comers. If our assumptions about the highlanders are valid, then the affairs in the early fourth-millennium B.C. Susiana could not have taken place without their consent. As a primarily pastoral society, the highlanders would have welcomed the opportunity to tax the new farmers and traders in their newly acquired territories.

The new immigrants, however, grew in size and complexity and if the glyptic scenes are to be taken as representing some aspects of that society, competition seems to have resulted in intra-regional warfare. The insecure environment coupled with the growth of settlements in northern, and especially in northeastern Susiana, the primary winter territories of the highland pastoralists, may have rekindled the old conflict of interest with the colonizers and the outcome was once more a severe depopulation of the region. Just as previously during the first half of the fourth millennium B.C., one would expect that after some time the region would recover its lost population and bounce back. This did not happen. Until about 2700 B.C. Susiana seems to be an almost empty landscape that consisted of a much reduced Susa and a few small villages. Yet, it is precisely during this period (proto-Elamite) that we see the

101. One type of tapering pole with a single half-loop attached to its summit occurs both at Susa and Chogha Mish, though it is not common (Amiet 1972, nos. 456, 694; *Chogha Mish* I, pl. 154:A). This symbol, representing perhaps a temple or a deity (Englund 1998: 69), should not be confused with the specific Inana symbol.

102. For a criticism of the application of this model, see Stein 1999: 108–16; see also Kohl 1996.

continuation of the fourth-millennium B.C. administration and the establishment of a truly international trade network connecting Susiana to points in the Zagros, the Central Plateau, Kerman, Sistan, and Fars.

## OLD ELAMITE PERIOD

During the second half of the fourth millennium B.C. Susa and Chogha Mish may have been competing for regional economic and political supremacy (Johnson 1973). By about 3100 B.C., Chogha Mish seems to have lost its millennia-old status to Susa permanently. The demise of Chogha Mish cannot be based solely on its loss to a rival regional center, for such rivalry was common among southern Mesopotamian polities without the disappearance of any major center. Although the available evidence from Chogha Mish does not allow speculation on the total demise of the site after the Protoliterate phase, the ever-present insecurity of the frontier northeastern part of Susiana may have been a contributing factor.

From ca. 3100 B.C. until the re-occupation by the Elamites in ca. 1800 B.C., Chogha Mish lay deserted. The occupation of Chogha Mish during the Sukkalmah period (ca. 1900–1600 B.C.) was part of the expansion of settlement pattern that started in the earlier Shimashki period (ca. 2100–1900 B.C.). The size of the settlement at Susa reached some 85 ha and twenty new villages were established on the plain during this phase (Carter and Stolper 1984: 150).

Sometime during the Old Elamite period, the High Mound was occupied again. A massive fortification wall was built on the highest point of the mound, roughly corresponding to the circumference of the High Mound. Within this enclosure wall, a number of individual buildings were erected, but none was preserved well enough to reveal a complete plan. From what remains one may speculate on the existence of at least one monumental, perhaps religious, building whose enclosure wall and gate are parallel to the massive enclosure wall of the complex. The inner and outer faces of this building's enclosure wall were plastered and decorated with alternate bands of red and white.

During the Old Elamite period, Chogha Mish may have served as a military post guarding the eastern flank of the Elamites' territory in Susiana. The archaeological records from Chogha Mish do not indicate exactly when the site was once again deserted, but it must have been sometime close to the end of the Old Elamite period. Again, whatever contributed to the abandonment of Chogha Mish around the seventh century B.C., it must have been deserted peacefully, as in the earlier Protoliterate phase, for no traces of fire or any other violence was discovered in the Old Elamite remains.

## LATER HISTORICAL PERIODS

Chogha Mish was next occupied sometime during the final stages of the Iron III phase, and settlement continued into the Achaemenid period. The only solid architectural remains from this period consist of a circular mudbrick "silo" and a few fragmentary walls that were reported in *Chogha Mish* I. Even less is preserved from the next, Parthian, phase of occupation, from which nothing except some huge pits, some burials, hearths, and a kiln survived. The Parthian period was the last time Chogha Mish was used as a settlement. During the rest of its history, the site was used as a cemetery and a Bakhtiyari winter-spring camp.

Table 1. Relative Chronology of Prehistoric Sites in Iran and Mesopotamia

| Date B.C. | Susiana | | Deh Luran | Zagros Mountains | Fars | | Central Plateau | | Mesopotamia | Site | |
|---|---|---|---|---|---|---|---|---|---|---|---|
| | Period | Site | | | Period | Site | Period | Site | Period | North | South |
| 3500 | ↑ Protoliterate | Chogha Mish (Terrace)<br>Susa Acropole 21–19 | | | | | Late Plateau | Ghabrestan III | Early Uruk | Tepe Gawra XII | Eridu V–IV |
| 4000 | Terminal Susa | | Zargarab | Godin VI | | Lapui | | | Terminal Ubaid<br>Ubaid 4 | Tepe Gawra XIV–XIV | |
| 4200 | | Jafarabad 1–3<br>Susa Acropole 25–26<br>Bandebal II | | | Late Fars | | | Ghabrestan I (Levels 13–11) | | | Eridu VII–VI |
| 4400 | Late Susiana 2 | (Level 10)<br>Susa Acropole<br>27(?)<br>Bandebal II | | | | Tall-e Bakun A | | Hessar I–A | | | |
| 4600 | Late Susiana 1 | (Levels 11–17)<br>Qabr Sheikeyn | Farrukhabad A23–31, B32–47 | Godin VII | Middle Fars 2 | Tall-e Gap | Middle Plateau | Ghabrestan I (Levels 19–17) | Ubaid 3 | | al-Ubaid |
| 4800 | | Jafarabad 3m–n<br>Chogha Mish | Bayat Phase | | Middle Fars | | | | | | |
| 5000 | Late Middle Susiana | Jawi I<br>Bandebal II | Mehmeh Phase | Godin VIII | | | | Tappeh Zagheh | | | |
| 5200 | Early Middle Susiana | Chogha Mish | Khazineh Phase | Godin IX | Middle Fars 1 | Tall-e Bakun B2 | | | Ubaid 2 | Arpachiyah H3–H4 | Haji Mohammad |
| 5400 | | | | | | | Early Plateau | Cheshmeh Ali Upper | | | |
| 5600 | Early Susiana | Jafarabad 6–4<br>Chogha Mish | Sabz Phase | | Early Fars | Tall-e Bakun B1/ Jari A | | | Ubaid 1 | Arpachiyah H1 | Eridu XIX |
| 5800 | | | | Godin X | | | | | | | |
| 5900 | Archaic Susiana 3 | Chogha Mish | CMT | | Archaic Fars 2 | Jari B | | Cheshmeh Ali Lower/Sialk I | | | |
| 6100 | Archaic Susiana 2 | Chogha Mish | Surkh Phase | | Archaic Fars 1 | Mushki | Archaic Plateau | | Ubaid 0 | Samarra es-Sawwan I | Tell el-Oueile 11–19 |
| 6300 | | | | Haji Firuz | | | | | Hassuna | Hassuna Ia | |
| 6500 | Archaic Susiana 1 | Chogha Mish | Sefid Phase | | | | | Tappeh Deh Kheir<br>Tappeh Sang-e Chakhmaq | | Um Dabaghieh IV | ? |
| 6700 | Archaic Susiana 0 | Chogha Bonut (Zone F)<br>Tuleii | Mohammad Jafar Phase | Abdul Husein/ Guron | | | | | Jarmo | | |
| 6900 | Formative Susiana | Chogha Bonut (Zones B–E) | Ali Kosh Phase | | Aceramic Fars | ? | Aceramic Plateau | ? | | Late Jarmo<br>Early Jarmo | |
| 7200 | Aceramic Susiana | Chogha Bonut (Zone A) | Buz Murdeh Phase | | | | | | | Maghzalieh | |
| | | | | Asiab<br>Ganj Dareh E | | | | | | | |

Table 2. Cultural Phases Attested at the Sites Excavated in Susiana by the Oriental Institute

| *Period* | *Sites* |
|---|---|
| Parthian | Chogha Mish High Mound, Terrace |
| Achaemenid | Chogha Mish Terrace |
| Neo-Elamite | Absent |
| Middle Elamite | Absent |
| Old Elamite (Sukkalmah) | Chogha Mish High Mound |
| Shimashki | Absent |
| Awan | Absent |
| Protoliterate (Late Uruk) | Chogha Mish High Mound, Terrace |
| Susa 2, levels 21–19 | Chogha Mish Terrace(?) |
| Susa 2, level 22 | Absent |
| Terminal Susa 1 | Absent |
| Late Susiana 2 (Susa 1) | Chogha Mish High Mound |
| Late Susiana 1 | Chogha Mish Terrace(?) (few sherds) |
| Late Middle Susiana | Chogha Mish High Mound, Terrace, Boneh Fazl Ali, and Chogha Bonut |
| Early Middle Susiana | Chogha Mish High Mound, Terrace, and Boneh Fazl Ali(?) |
| Early Susiana | Chogha Mish Terrace and Boneh Fazl Ali |
| Archaic Susiana 3 | Chogha Mish Terrace and Boneh Fazl Ali |
| Archaic Susiana 2 | Chogha Mish Terrace and Boneh Fazl Ali |
| Archaic Susiana 1 | Chogha Mish Terrace, Boneh Fazl Ali, and Chogha Bonut(?) |
| Archaic Susiana 0 | Chogha Bonut |
| Formative Susiana | Chogha Bonut |
| Aceramic Susiana | Chogha Bonut |

# CHAPTER TWO
# ARCHITECTURE

## HIGH MOUND

### TRENCH XXIII, LATE SUSIANA 2 ARCHITECTURE, PHASE 2
(Figs. 6, 7)

The Late Susiana 2 phase on the High Mound has two phases of architecture. During the first five seasons, excavations in Trench XXIII revealed fragmentary walls and floors of the Protoliterate phase, which were heavily damaged by late (Achaemenid and Parthian) burials and building and possibly pitting activities. In the ninth and tenth seasons, the area of Trench XXIII was expanded to the west and north to clarify the nature of a few features that appeared to be tops of walls (fig. 6). After excavating a series of beaten earth floors at various depths, Late Susiana 2 deposits were reached and continued to a depth of 81.50 m above sea level, 6.0 m below the surface of the High Mound, where late Middle Susiana remains appeared. Here, about 10 m of Middle Susiana deposits lay on virgin soil.[103]

In the tenth season, the western extension of Trench XXIII revealed at least two architectural levels of the Late Susiana 2 phase — no traces of walls, floors, or any other features datable to the Late Susiana 1 have been encountered at Chogha Mish (fig. 7). The topmost layer on the southern part of the trench (N10:1001S) consisted of a large Parthian pit dug deep into a Middle Susiana deposit. On the north part of the trench, in N10:1002, the uppermost layer had a series of ashy layers (3–5 cm thick) alternating with a hard, clayish deposit. This deposit must be associated with two kilns. The walls of these kilns had been destroyed, but their burnt, reddish floors, which were covered with vitrified sherds and soot, had been preserved. A heap of ash had also been dumped against the northern wall of room N10:1003. Both the interior and exterior faces of this wall had several layers of mud plaster. Room N10:1005 also had mud-plastered walls and floors and a small hearth in its northwest corner. Apart from scattered sherds of Late Susiana 2 date, some bones and a stone pestle were also found here. Room N10:1004/1011 of Building 2 may have been part of Building 1, but there is no evidence for this reconstruction, therefore we consider it to be a room of a separate building. Except for a heap of round, clay "sling shots" in the northwest corner of the room, no special feature was found here.

In N10:1002, below the level of the kilns, was found a single grave. The burial pit was roughly rectangular, measuring 90 × 180 cm. The skeleton was oriented east–west, with the head turned toward the east; a single vessel had been placed at the feet.

### TRENCH XXIII, LATE SUSIANA 2 ARCHITECTURE, PHASE 1
(Figs. 6, 7)

Below the walls of rooms N10:1003, 1004, and 1005 was found another structure. This structure had a similar floor plan and consisted of at least two rectangular rooms (fig. 7). Judging from the existing walls, rooms N10:1008/1009/1012/1014 and 1010 may have belonged to a much larger building, the rest of which remains unexcavated under the baulk of the trench. Building 1 (N10:1008/1009/1012/1014) consists of a small room with a mudbrick bench built against its walls. An ashy deposit mixed with flint blades and small sherds was scattered on the floor of this room. Building 2, to the south of this chamber, has a long room (N10:1010) that shares a common wall with Building 1. The walls of room N10:1010 were thinner than those of Building 1 but were plastered with mud as in the latter. No special features or objects are reported from this area or from the presumably open space to its north and south. An oval pit found next to the southern wall of room N10:1010 might have been a burial pit, but

103. No information as to the nature of the Middle Susiana deposit in the trench has been found in the records. The missing information, which may have been recorded separately, must have been lost in the dig house after 1979.

it had been damaged and only a few badly preserved bones, a stone hoe, and a complete vessel were found associated with it. A fragmentary wall projecting outward from the southern wall of room N10:1010 may have been the southern extension of this building, but this whole area was badly damaged by a huge Parthian pit.

## TRENCH XXIV, PROTOLITERATE AND ELAMITE STRUCTURES AND FORT

(Figs. 8–10, Pls. 1:B–5)

The second major desertion of Chogha Mish occurred at the end of the Protoliterate phase around 3100 B.C. The site remained unoccupied until the Old Elamite (Sukkalmah, ca. 1900–1500 B.C.) period. Sometime during that period, Chogha Mish was re-occupied, apparently not as a residential place but as a military post, presumably to guard the eastern flank of lowland Susiana. No intermediate layers of debris or construction separated the earliest Old Elamite structures from the underlying Protoliterate ones. Rather, millennia of erosion had leveled the Protoliterate buildings here to such a degree that the Elamite construction was erected directly on their mudbrick detritus and occupational debris.

During the Old Elamite period, only the High Mound seems to have been occupied. Here, a polygonal brick structure, illustrated in *Chogha Mish* I, figures 1–2, was erected with a number of inner rooms and chambers. The baked-brick enclosure wall ranges in thickness from 8 to 11 m (fig. 8, pls. 1:B, 2:A–B). Along the western enclosure wall, remains of towers and buttresses, some bonded to the wall and some built against the wall's mud plaster, suggest a multi-phase construction. The outer face of the massive enclosure wall was fire blackened in several areas. No fire or cooking installations were found associated with these dark spots, but slight accumulations of ash and soot at the base of the wall were found.

## TRENCH XXIV, OLD ELAMITE FORT

A major fortification system marks the beginning of Old Elamite occupation at Chogha Mish. The preserved tops of a massive brick wall running northwest–southeast were revealed in Squares N7, N8, N9, and O9. Excavation of the massive wall did not penetrate below the associated floors, so we cannot elaborate on the nature of the foundation of this wall. In places where the associated floors and surfaces were eroded or destroyed by later pitting and burials, the massive wall seems to rest on the mudbrick detritus of the architectural remains of the Protoliterate phase. No architectural remains outside the fortification wall could be assigned to this phase, but fragmentary patches of hard, mud-plastered surface, some running up to the exterior face of the wall, kilns, jar burials, and what appear to have been deep wells and cisterns were discovered.

An elaborate H-shaped gate found in Squares N9 and O8–9 gave access to the interior of the fort (figs. 8, 10). The gate room O8:1001 had a hard, plastered floor. The walls of the inner gate entrance, too, were mud plastered. A stepped niche in the northern wall of this inner gate chamber may have led either to a staircase leading to the top of the fortification wall, or to a higher chamber not preserved.

Just inside the fort, in Squares N8, O8–9, another fragmentary but substantial wall, about 1.5 m thick and with the same orientation as the massive fortification wall, was discovered. Bits and pieces of mud plaster on the wall and on the pavement bore vertical strips of paint of alternating red and white (see the diagram on the plan in fig. 8). In O8:1006 a partial pavement of square baked bricks leading to another structure, now destroyed, was found (fig. 8, pl. 5:A). The pavement itself consists of only one layer of bricks, but the threshold has two layers and is thus higher than the pavement.

About 10 m northeast of this brick pavement in Square O7 was found a 1.5 m thick wall with the same orientation as the massive fortification and the wall in O8. This baked-brick wall was preserved to only a few courses and the rest had been destroyed either by erosion, later pits, foundation trenches, or burials. A doorway about 2.5 m wide gave access to the interior of the building, of which nothing is preserved.

## TRENCH XXIV, LATER ELAMITE OCCUPATION

If the fate of this fortification had any connection with the end of the Sukkalmah dynasty, or if hostile contact with Mesopotamia brought an end to this structure, there is no evidence of it. The fort must have laid in ruins for some time during the Old Elamite period before it was re-occupied as either a pottery manufacturing center, a small-scale settlement, or both. The evidence of occupation — the scattered fragmentary walls and hard surfaces, adult burial pits, child burials in large jars, pottery kilns, and a large pottery trough found in N9:1009 (but marked as

N8:1003) (fig. 8, pl. 3:A) — cannot be attributed to either the beginning or the terminal phase of Old Elamite occupation. It is possible that these scattered features mark the initial occupation of the Old Elamite period at Chogha Mish. No coherent plan can be reconstructed because later, particularly Parthian, activities and erosion had destroyed much of the area.

Two Old Elamite features, probably of a later phase of occupation, are the well-constructed water wells or cisterns made entirely of baked bricks and dug into the Protoliterate remains. One, N9:1003 (figs. 8, 9; pl. 4), was found outside the fortification wall in the northwest corner of the Protoliterate room N9:1002. This cistern has a corbeled oval mouth and widens as it descends. The shaft was filled with debris of Old Elamite and later periods; the bottom was not reached. The second well or cistern (fig. 8, N9:1002) was located in another Protoliterate room southeast of the first one. The construction of this cistern was almost the same as that of N9:1003, but it had a more regular oval rim. As in the other cistern, the shaft widens as it goes down. It too was filled with potsherds and wasters, presumably a by-product of the nearby kilns. In addition, a series of vertically stacked pottery pipes (a well?) was found in the same general area, but it was erroniously marked N9:1002 (pl. 3:B).

## TRENCH XXIV, PROTOLITERATE REMAINS

As noted above, Old Elamite buildings were directly constructed on the remains of the Protoliterate phase in this area. A partial plan of one building was all that could be salvaged. The preserved building consists of several well-built rooms on a northeast–southwest axis. Features that belong to this building include: a circular hearth in O9:1004; two similarly constructed pottery kilns in O9:301 and O9:302, one under the Elamite fortification wall, and one just outside, to the southwest; a cistern made of baked bricks (25 × 12 × 8 cm) under the fortification wall in O9:1008; another pottery kiln made of square baked bricks in N9:1003W; and several clusters of beveled-rim bowls in room O9:1006/1007. In addition, a nicely built drain made of baked bricks and sloping from northeast to southwest, using gravity by following the slope of the mound, was also found in this area (fig. 8, pl. 5:B). A nicely constructed well lined with stone slabs was found associated with the drain to its southeast. Immediately north of this well the drain branches to the south and north to join other drains that are now completely destroyed.

The presence of this drain and, more importantly, what appears to have been a watch tower straddling the junction of Squares N9, N10, M9, and M10 suggests that this area was the locus of a monumental building during the Protoliterate phase. No doorway to the small inner chamber of the tower has been found. A carefully constructed pavement of baked bricks abutting the tower to its northeast may have provided a landing if the tower had a staircase. Southeast of the tower, remains of what may have been an enclosure wall to the complex were found. The base of the tower was not explored beyond the level of the brick pavement. The assignment of this and the pavement to the Protoliterate phase rests solely on the size of the bricks, which differed from those of the Old Elamite period. The bricks used in constructing the pavement, the tower, and the walls of the preserved rooms measured 28 × 12 × 8 cm. Those used in the architectural remains of the Old Elamite period varied, measuring 33 × 33 × 15 cm, 35 × 19 × 16 cm, and 26 × 12 × 7 cm in the fortification wall, 20 × 20 × 7 cm in the pavement in Square O8, and occasionally 50 × 30 × 12 cm.

The Protoliterate remains in this area are not contiguous with those on the Terrace and therefore it is impossible to determine to which architectural phases they belong. Specific pottery types found in this area could have been of some service, but the present data preclude a comparative analysis.

# GULLY CUT

(Figs. 6, 11–13)

About 140 sq. m of this area were excavated during the first five seasons. The top strata consist of erosion layers deposited during the millennia between the Protoliterate and Achaemenid periods (ca. 3400–450 B.C.). Below this, pits and depositional layers dating to the Protoliterate phase were excavated. An erosion layer and the Protoliterate deposit had badly damaged the layers just below. Pits 802, 803/808, and 904 penetrated deep into even the Archaic levels (fig. 11). About 40 cm below the Protoliterate deposit, mudbricks measuring 40 × 12 × 10 cm with a central groove and six to eight finger imprints on a slightly convex surface were found (pl. 6:C). Although the surrounding debris was filled with Archaic 2–3 sherds, it cannot be used to date the bricks, especially the long, cigar-shaped mudbricks that were consistently used during the Archaic period and in combination with rectangular bricks during the Early Susiana period (pl. 16:C, E). Based on the general similarities of these bricks to those found at Tappeh

Sialk in Period 2 and at Eridu Level 15,[104] these bricks may date to the early Middle Susiana phase, though this is by no means certain. During the eighth and ninth seasons of excavations, the area of the Gully Cut was expanded northeast to Square S22 in the hope of finding stratified architecture of the earliest phases of occupation at Chogha Mish. Here, a series of buildings dating from the Archaic to the end of the Middle Susiana period were found.

## PROTOLITERATE REMAINS

No architecture of this phase was found in the Gully Cut. The only Protoliterate deposit here consists of several pits (S22:802, 803/808, 904, and one unassigned in room S22:918) and a concentration of sherds in S22:801S (fig. 11). A mass of Protoliterate potsherds was found almost directly under the erosion layer at the elevation of 77.13 m. Some slabs of baked bricks were found among the sherds but do not appear to be part of a construction that once existed in the same area. The sherds were also mixed with numerous rocks and flint blades. Judging by the contents of the two Protoliterate pits in the area, this concentration may also have been part of a large pit adjacent to S22:803, the edge of which may not have been detected at the time of excavation. In the northwest corner of the Gully Cut, a cluster of stones was found. Some of these stones were clearly tools, others were broken rocks and pebbles in what turned out to be a partially preserved room of the early Middle Susiana phase (fig. 11, S22:918). Associated with these, a broken club-rim jar of the same phase was found leaning on the north face of the southwestern wall of room 918.

## MIDDLE SUSIANA PERIOD LEVELS

No occupational or other types of debris from the Late Susiana period was found in the Gully Cut. The interface between the Protoliterate and Middle Susiana deposits is composed of a sloping layer of sandy mudbrick detritus. The preserved architecture below the Protoliterate deposit dates to the early and late Middle Susiana phase, as indicated by the stratigraphy, the pottery, and other objects. At least three architectural phases can be reconstructed on the stratigraphic positions of walls and floors. The top plan of the construction, in figure 11, seems somewhat confusing for two reasons. First, the area is heavily damaged by pitting activities of the Protoliterate phase. Moreover, the room designated as S22:811 could be dated to the Protoliterate phase, but the available data preclude the possibility of further investigation. If S22:811 does in fact belong to the late Middle Susiana period, as the pottery found in it indicates, then two architectural phases can be attributed to this period.

## EARLY MIDDLE SUSIANA PHASE
(Fig. 11)

The first and earliest architectural phase of the Middle Susiana period in the Gully Cut consists of a series of rectangular rooms of possibly three separate units. The unit that consists of rooms S22:814, 815, 816, and 818 may have had an open court, S22:810. A circular hearth filled with small to medium fire-cracked rocks was found in S22:814. A doorway leads from room 814 to the open court 810, where the only feature preserved is a circular kiln with a thick burnt floor. A bin-like structure links room 814 to the rectangular room 818, which has no special features. To the southeast of room 818, a larger area, perhaps another room of this unit, contains a circular hearth with a thick burnt floor at an elevation of 76.71 m above sea level.

The second architectural unit consists of a single rectangular room, S22:918. A cluster of rocks mixed with flint blades and some pounders, mostly dating to the Protoliterate phase, was found in the southwest of this room. Northeast of this cluster, a Protoliterate pit (S22:804) was found; its lowest point was at 75.93 m above sea level.

A possible third architectural unit was excavated at the northwest extremity of the trench, in S22:819. It consists of an east–west wall and a partition wall that separates an area paved with pebbles and a partially preserved pottery kiln.

104. See Ghirshman 1938, pl. 10:4; Lloyd and Safar 1948: 121; Safar, Mustafa, and Lloyd 1981: 88–90, fig. 42:B.

## LATE MIDDLE SUSIANA ARCHITECTURE, PHASE 1
(Fig. 11)

The only architectural unit that survived from this phase consists of two rectangular rooms, S22:806E and 809. Room 806E has only three rather thick walls, with a recess in the southwestern wall. A fireplace with a thick burnt floor was located in the southeastern corner. From the available plan, the room seems to have been open to a courtyard (S22:806) immediately in front. A large slab of stone surrounded by chipped stone debris as well as a large piece of kiln grate were found imbedded in the ashy layer of the court. The second room (S22:809) also has a fireplace filled with fire-cracked rocks on the floor. A partially preserved thick wall runs along the northwest–southeast axis. This wall may have been an enclosure wall of the unit. A small cubicle (S22:807) filled with ash and pottery wasters was constructed between a kiln and room 806E. Judging by the relatively thick size of the walls, this unit may have been much bigger than shown on the plan and possibly served as an industrial area during this phase.

## LATE MIDDLE SUSIANA ARCHITECTURE, PHASE 2
(Fig. 11)

If this area was used in the late Middle Susiana, Phase 1, to manufacture pottery, stone tools, and perhaps other objects, it retained this function during the latter part of the late Middle Susiana. An irregularly shaped room (S22:811) with thick walls was constructed on the stumps of the walls of the earlier room 809 (fig. 11). As with the earlier room 806E, one side of the room is open to what seems to have been an open area. Here, an oval-shaped pottery kiln, an L-shaped partition wall, and a partially preserved mudbrick pavement were discovered surrounded by layers of ash and soot in S22:812 and 813. A partially preserved pavement made of potsherds was found immediately under the mudbrick pavement and the L-shaped partition wall.

The large amount of ash, potsherds, stone flakes, kilns, and fireplaces in the open areas that surround all the architectural units in this area suggest that this part of the mound may have been used as an industrial quarter from the beginning of the Middle Susiana period until the site, or this particular area, was abandoned.

## EARLY SUSIANA ARCHITECTURAL PHASE
(Fig. 12, Pl. 6:A–B, D)

During the eighth and ninth excavation seasons, the northern part of the Gully Cut was extended to reveal the architectural remains of the Early Susiana period. Unlike those of the Middle Susiana period in this area, the architectural remains of this period are much better preserved. The whole complex consists of at least three architectural units, separated from one another by a narrow space and a large open area.

The largest unit consists of a long room (S22:825) with a southeast–northwest axis. Attached to the northwest wall of this room, a rectangular room (813) leads through a doorway to a narrow alley and another rectangular room (819) of which only the southern and eastern walls are preserved (see also pl. 16:A). No special features were found in rooms 819 and 825. Room 813, however, is furnished with a low rectangular bench and a small bin. An L-shaped wall marks the western extent of this unit. A partially preserved cobble floor in this area indicates that it was an open court.

Immediately south of the L-shaped structure and attached to its wall, a platform was found made of the typical long cigar-shaped mudbricks (fig. 12, pl. 6:B). The southwestern edge of this platform is marked by a low partition wall of rectangular mudbricks, joining what appears to be a pottery kiln, of which only the burnt floor is preserved. The base of this structure is built against a U-shaped enclosure of unknown function.

Immediately south of this U-shaped structure, a round feature (808), heavily damaged by the Protoliterate pit (803), was found with its base resting on a blackish dirt layer. The rectangular room 818 — the only room found of the second architectural unit — was excavated immediately south and almost adjacent to this round structure. A mudbrick bench was constructed on its northern corner. Clustered immediately to the southeast of this bench were a number of stone implements, finger-shaped clay tokens, rubbing stones, querns, pestles, pounders, and ten stone "balls," suggesting that this area may have been used as a workshop. A partially preserved hearth with fire-cracked rocks on its floor was also found in S22:823.

Only part of the third architectural unit was excavated in the southeastern part of the trench. It seems to have the same axis as the northern unit, but what appears to be the main room (822) is much larger than the rest. A narrow hall, perhaps a long bin, is constructed in the southern part of the main room. A hearth outside this structure, built against the southwestern part of this long bin, may have belonged to either the second unit or to yet another architectural unit not yet uncovered.

An interesting feature of the Early Susiana architecture in the Gully Cut is the combined use of long, cigar-shaped, and rectangular mudbricks. Long mudbricks are typical of the Archaic period at both Chogha Mish and Chogha Bonut. They are also found in the Bus Mordeh and Tappeh Ali Kosh phases in Deh Luran, as well as in Ubaid 0 and Ubaid 1 deposits at Tell el-Oueili in southern Mesopotamia. The intermittent use of both types of mudbricks suggests a transitional phase during which both types of bricks were used simultaneously.

### ARCHAIC SUSIANA 3 PHASE ARCHITECTURE
(Fig. 13)

A large, unusually constructed building is the only architecture dating to the Archaic 3 phase in the Gully Cut. Other features associated with this structure are a large burnt area (S22:831S), a partially preserved horseshoe-shaped hearth in 901, and a simple grave between 914 and 824 (fig. 18:T). The building consists of a rectangular "central hall" (S22:923/828/813/929) with four buttresses built into its southeastern wall. The northeastern flank of this hall leads directly to what was presumably an open space. A rectangular room northwest of and not connected to the central hall leads to perhaps another unit that remains unexcavated. The diagonal southwestern wall of this room has a similar construction to that of the southeastern wall of the central hall; one buttress is exposed. The northwestern corner of the central hall is constructed twice as thick as the rest, suggesting the existence of a bench or platform here.

The relatively large scale of the building, the carefully constructed walls, and the presence of buttresses suggest that this building may not have been a regular residential unit. But no other special feature in the excavated rooms exists to corroborate this assumption, nor do any artifacts other than the usual debris point to its assumed non-residential character. Similar and contemporary buildings have also been reported from Tell el-Oueili and later examples come from Tell Abada.

## TRENCH XXI
(Fig. 14, Pls. 7–9)

During the third and fifth seasons of excavations at Chogha Mish, two building complexes and a substantial structure made of long mudbricks were discovered in Trench XXI and presented in *Chogha Mish* I (pp. 162–63, pl. 275). During the sixth through eighth seasons, the exposure was expanded to the north into Squares P22 and Q22, toward Trench XII, and to the east and south in Squares Q22–23, toward Trench XXXII, to reveal a more complete plan of the Early Susiana architectural complex. The new areas revealed a complex of large Early Susiana buildings, as well as traces of Archaic Susiana 3 architecture. These buildings are numbered and presented on a single plan in figure 14.

### MIDDLE SUSIANA COMPLEX

Building 1 is the only Middle Susiana structure preserved in Trench XXI. Prior to the sixth season, only the southern part of the building had been excavated (see *Chogha Mish* I, pl. 275). We now have a complete plan of Building 1, which consists of at least five rooms (fig. 14, P22:602E, 603, 604; P23:504 and 505). Immediately east of room 504, a trapezoidal hearth/kiln was found encased within a square enclosure. The two southern rooms in P23:504–05 and the kiln are surrounded by a relatively thick east–west enclosure wall. The amount of scattered Early Susiana sherds found within the rectangular mudbricks of the walls of this building and the early Middle Susiana occupational deposits at the base of its walls form our basis for dating this building to the early Middle Susiana phase. Except for a dense layer of ash in P23:502, beaten earth was the norm for all the floors in this building. A small square bin in P23:505 and two long rectangular bins south of rooms 504 and 505 may have been used as storage facilities.

Two simple burials were found under the floors of rooms P22:604 and P22:603 (see plan, fig. 14). The bodies in both graves were deposited in simple oval pits dug into the remains of the Early Susiana period. The burial in room 603 may actually date to the Early Susiana period because part of the skeleton was found under the wall separating rooms 602E and 603. The orientation of the skeleton in 603 is north–south with the head turned toward the west.

The skeleton in 604 was oriented east–west with the head facing north. One simple vessel was found associated with the latter burial. Other burials, in P23:605 and P23:607 (figs. 14, 18:M, S), were found in what were presumably open areas.

## EARLY SUSIANA COMPLEX, PHASE 1

At least two architectural phases can be assigned to the Early Susiana period. Of the earlier phase, Phase 1, we have almost complete plans of Buildings 2 and 3, at the north of the trench, and a partial plan of Building 4, straddling Squares P22 and 23 at the west of Trench XXI. Building 4 was heavily damaged by the construction of Buildings 1 and 5 of the later phase of the Early Susiana; the western part of Building 4 remains unexcavated. Although Early Susiana potsherds were found scattered around the various features of this building, none come from a primary context. The assignment of Building 4 to the Early Susiana period therefore rests on stratigraphic observations and the similarity of its plan to the rest of the Early Susiana buildings with long narrow magazines, presumably for storing goods. The trapezoidal kiln/oven in P22:601 and its rectangular enclosure are remarkably similar to the kiln discovered in the early Middle Susiana Building 1 (P23:502). On the other hand, the horseshoe-shaped kiln/oven built at the corner of a partially preserved room in P23:603 is similar to the one found in another Early Susiana room in Q23:508/819.

Building 2 is the best-preserved structure of this phase. This building is divided into eastern and western sections by a long narrow magazine (P22:610), much the same as the narrow magazine separating the northern and southern parts of Building 3. The eastern part of Building 2 consists of a small rectangular room (P22:612N) with a circular hearth built in its northwest corner. P22:612S, a relatively large rectangular area, may have been the courtyard of this architectural unit. Two short partition walls are built against the exterior of the southern wall of room 612N. The function of these partition walls is not clear, but scattered ashy layers, bits and pieces of chipped stone found there, and the presence of a hard brown surface between the partition walls suggest that this area accommodated a workshop. The western portion of Building 2 consists of a central court (P22:608M) surrounded on three sides by four small rectangular chambers. An open area may have been located in front of Buildings 2, 3, and 4, where the Early Susiana, Phase 2, Building 5 was excavated. This assumption is based on the fact that about a meter of occupational debris was encountered under the floors of the later houses with no architectural remains.

Two thin partition walls link Building 2 to Building 3, the third structure of the first architectural phase of the Early Susiana period. Building 3 of this phase is also well preserved. It is an elongated structure with two somewhat square back rooms (Q22:605N, 608W) and a large hall (606) leading to two small rectangular rooms (605, 606N). In this "central hall" were found two hearths filled with fire-cracked rocks (pls. 7:B, 15:B). No doorway was found leading from this hall to the southern part of the building, presumably a courtyard (602/607W). A long narrow bin separates this courtyard from the central hall. The eastern part of the building consists of two long chambers that seem to have been suitable only for storage, though no direct archaeological evidence can support this reconstruction (fig. 14, pl. 7:D). The entire building may have been enclosed by a relatively thick outer wall, of which only the eastern part has been preserved. It is also possible that Building 3 originally consisted of two separate units, built back to back. The two fragmentary walls straddling the junction of Squares Q22 and 23 originally may have belonged to a southern unit. Nevertheless, based on the plan of the adjacent Building 2, it is a stronger possibility that this building was one single unit.

A simple burial pit was found at the corner of the fragmentary T-shaped wall in P23:608 (fig. 18:I). On the basis of pottery, this burial is dated to the Early Susiana period, phase 1. The body is in stretched position, its head facing north.

## EARLY SUSIANA COMPLEX, PHASE 2

At least four separate structures (Buildings 5–8) can be attributed to Phase 2 of the Early Susiana period on stratigraphic evidence. Building 6 has been published (*Chogha Mish* I: 162–63) and needs no introduction. Buildings 5, 7, and 8 were found during the sixth to eighth seasons of excavations. The end of Phase 1 architecture is marked by the leveling of the entire area of occupation in Trench XXI and Building 5 was erected in the presumed empty space between the buildings of Phase 1 (Buildings 2–4). In comparison with known sixth-millennium B.C. examples from Iran, Building 5 is a monumental structure with thick walls, numerous rooms, and long magazines (pl. 7:A). It is possible that Building 5 is actually composed of two separate structures erected side by side. However, the nice alignment of the walls and the bond between the walls of the western and eastern flanks of the building suggest a single structure. The only suitable candidate for a courtyard, based on the difference in the debris, is the space P22:609/615/620.[105] This presumed courtyard and six rectangular rooms are located on the north of the building, while all the long, narrow magazines are located on the south, in front of which we envision the existence of an open area prior to the erection of the Middle Susiana Building 1. This makes sense if the long narrow chambers were indeed storage rooms used for depositing and withdrawing goods. The only entrance to the building was found in the well-preserved southern wall of P22:621E/801, but the available data do not permit a reconstruction of the communication system between the various units.

The vestibule P22:621E/801 must have had some significant character, as five burial pits were found within it. The two burials found at the northwest corner of the room belong to adults, while the other four seem to be those of children (fig. 18:G–H, L). The graves consist of simple pits dug into Archaic Susiana levels; except for some scattered stone blades, which may or may not have belonged to the burials, no funerary objects were found. All the skeletons were found in a stretched position with the exception of the burial next to the western wall of the vestibule, which was oriented north–south, facing up.

Building 7, which may in fact be the eastern flank of Building 6, consists of a large central courtyard with a low partition wall projecting from its western wall (Q23:504/703). Its northern wing consists of a square room with a low partition wall (Q23:511/806) and a trapezoidal enclosure (Q23:515/705, Q23:801), while on the south a relatively large rectangular room (Q23:501/805) shares a wall with Building 8 to the south. Immediately east of this room, another trapezoidal room (Q23:807) with a recess in its northern wall and a horseshoe-shaped hearth filled with fire-cracked stones forms the eastern flank of the building. It is possible that this latter enclosure actually belonged to Building 8, because the northern part of Building 8 was not preserved; the northern extension of the wall between Q23:821 and 824 might have enclosed the trapezoidal unit. Of all the courtyards assigned to various buildings in this area, Q23:504/703/818, is the most certain because the interpretation of these units as courtyards rests on the observation that throughout the Susiana sequence, open spaces were usually paved with pebbles.

Only the northern part of Building 8 has been excavated. This building also matches Buildings 6 and 7 in both orientation and floor plan. A partially excavated courtyard lies on the southwestern part of the building in Q23:820. Some of the relatively thick outer and inner walls suggest that Building 8, as Building 5, may have had an upper floor, particularly between rooms 827 and 828. Unlike other buildings of the same period in Trench XXI, two different sizes of mudbricks (51 × 51 × 10 cm and 41 × 15 × 8 cm) were used to erect the walls of Building 8 (pl. 9:B).

Whereas beaten earth floors are the norm in all the buildings of this and the previous phase of architecture, room 803/813 on the northwest flank of Building 8 is provided with a partially preserved brick floor made of long, cigar-shaped mudbricks (fig. 14, pls. 8:B, 9:A). Immediately to the northeast of this room, two more areas have partially preserved brick floors that were made of the same type of long mudbricks. The only burial in this building was found in room 802. The body was found in a simple oval pit, lying on its back, facing south.

Immediately to the west of this building, a large "platform" made of long mudbricks was excavated (fig. 14, pl. 8:A). The west part of the platform is damaged, but there is no question that a corridor existed between it and the southwestern part of Building 6. This platform may have been enclosed on the west by a wall and a long magazine (P23:601). As was common in the Early Susiana buildings in the Gully Cut (see above), both rectangular and long bricks were used in the construction of this platform. The available evidence precludes functional reconstruction of this feature. However, taken together with the evidence of large buildings with storage facilities it may have served as some kind of drop-off zone for the distribution of agricultural products, or it might have been a threshing ground, though admittedly none of these hypothetical reconstructions can be supported by archaeological evidence. Several earlier but similar mudbrick platforms were found at Chogha Sefid in the Deh Luran plain, dated to the Surkh Phase (Hole 1977: 73, fig. 24). One (Hole 1977: 69) in Zone C was constructed of long mudbricks and another (Hole 1977, fig. 24) in Zone F was made of rectangular mudbricks.

## ARCHAIC PERIOD REMAINS

All the structural features dating to the Archaic period belong to its final phase, Archaic 3. The best-preserved Archaic building comes from the southeast extension of the trench. Here, only a partial plan of Building 9 could be

105. Good parallels for Building 5 are reported from the Ubaid phase at Telul al-Thalathat (Fukaii, Horiuchi, and Matsutani 1970).

reconstructed. Within this building, a number of Archaic graves with various orientations were found (fig. 18). The eastern extension of Early Susiana building activity seems to have deliberately stopped at the edge of the eastern enclosure wall of Building 7, as if its inhabitants had stopped at the edge of a still-remembered cemetery of their ancestors.

The partial plan of the Archaic 3 Building indicates a structure with at least three rectangular rooms (Q23:808, 810N, and 810S) and a possible courtyard (Q23:807). Whether the cross walls between 803 and 814 at the eastern edge of the trench served as an enclosure wall to this building is not clear. A horseshoe-shaped kiln under the stump of the wall of room Q22:801 of Early Susiana Building 7, the circular hearth in Q23:804 (pl. 9:D) filled with fire-cracked rocks, a pebble pavement partially preserved in Q23:801N, and a fragmentary floor with mat impression at the northwest intersection of the cross wall are other features preserved from the Archaic 3 phase. A curious feature consisting of a line of rocks imbedded against the western face of the southern part of the cross wall may have been used to prevent the mudbrick wall from eroding.

# EAST AREA

(Figs. 15–17)

## HISTORICAL REMAINS

The East Area was the highest part of the Terrace south of the High Mound (see fig. 6) until the end of the Middle Susiana period and thus it is not surprising to find major Middle Susiana building complexes here. The latest archaeological remains and structures, reported in the first volume (*Chogha Mish* I: 10–11), belonged to the Achaemenid period. Except for a round brick structure (the Circular Structure) dug deep into the Protoliterate remains and a simple grave with some funerary objects from Trench XIII in the West Area (*Chogha Mish* I: 10–11, pl. 263), Achaemenid remains consist only of small objects. When the trenches in East Area were expanded in later seasons, no other structures datable to this period were uncovered, save for a fragmentary wall in Q17:807.

Extensive architectural remains of the Protoliterate phase were reported in the first volume (*Chogha Mish* I: 30–32, pl. 264) with a number of houses clustered around what seems to have been an open space.[106] The residential units in both East and West Areas had a northeast–southwest orientation. The extensive drainage system that crisscrossed the settlement in northeast–southwest and northwest–southeast directions (*Chogha Mish* I, pls. 264–65) suggests a planned settlement. Three meters of Protoliterate deposit (from an elevation of 84.50 m to 81.50 m above sea level) in this area consisted of at least three architectural phases (see *Chogha Mish* I: 30–32). With the exception of the High Mound, Protoliterate deposits here rest directly on the mudbrick detritus and occupational debris of the late Middle Susiana phase. No monumental building of the Protoliterate phase was discovered during the first five seasons of excavations at Chogha Mish. However, the huge, 20 × 20 m polygonal mudbrick platform found in the West Area (*Chogha Mish* I: 32–33, pl. 265) may have served as a foundation for such a building, though admittedly no direct evidence supports this reconstruction. During the seventh to ninth seasons, however, a huge Protoliterate architectural complex with unquestionably monumental character was discovered in the East Area.

## THE LATE MIDDLE SUSIANA PHASE (THE BURNT BUILDING)

The earliest prehistoric monumental architecture in Iran is thought to have existed on the huge mudbrick platform that was discovered at Susa (KS-00), dated to the late fifth millennium B.C. The putative monumental buildings on top of Susa's mudbrick platform were destroyed, presumably as a result of hostile contact, accidental fire, or earthquake, thus, no coherent plan of Susa's prehistoric monumental buildings is available. Therefore, the discovery at Chogha Mish of a series of much earlier monumental buildings dating from the Early Susiana to the end of the Protoliterate phase provides an antecedent for later formal buildings, as well as evidence of increasing socioeconomic and political development in lowland Susiana, providing a historical context within which sociopolitical and cultural achievements at Susa could be addressed (see *Chapter 1*).

106. To visualize the layout of the complex better, some of the architectural units excavated during the first five seasons (not blackened) and published in the first volume are included on the plan in figure 17.

We have already discussed several such buildings, found in Trench XXI, dating back to the Early Susiana period. The level of Early Susiana socioeconomic and political complexity continued uninterruptedly during the following Middle Susiana period. A late Middle Susiana monumental building was found in Squares R17–18 and S18 during the ninth season of excavations. Although this area was heavily damaged by later Protoliterate construction and numerous pits dug deep into Middle Susiana and earlier architecture, enough had remained to allow the reconstruction of a complete plan.

The walls of the preserved parts of the building appeared just under the modern surface of the mound during the ninth season of excavations. The mudbrick walls, which were plastered and fire-hardened, were preserved to a height of 1.5 m (pls. 10–11). The fire that had destroyed the building also helped preserve imprints of reeds and beams of the building's ceiling. Mixed with burnt lumps of clay bearing reeds and beam impressions were fragments of charred wood and chunks of charcoal.

Only half the monumental building was excavated; the northern and western parts remain unexcavated. Based on the available evidence, the original plan of this building must have measured at least 20 × 20 m. This formal building, much larger and entirely different from the residential buildings of the same period, is made of mudbricks measuring 20 × 10 × 8 cm, with several layers of mud plaster applied to both interior and exterior surfaces of the walls. The building is oriented northwest–southeast and consists of a series of rectangular, elongated chambers. Four entrances with recessed doorways have been found on the southern and eastern sections of the building. Based on the available plan, the main entrance may have been located on the southeastern part of the building in S18:901. There is no direct evidence for this assumption except for the fact that this entrance is wider than the rest and leads to a wide rectangular antechamber. Nevertheless, any of the preserved entrances could lead to the entire complex. Several square meters of pebble pavement in front of the southern entrances indicate that this was an outdoor space. This is in sharp contrast with the northeast flank of the building where part of a mudbrick platform — only a small section of which was excavated — was built against the eastern wall of the building.

In general, almost all the rooms in the building contained abundant pottery vessels, tools, and intact small objects. Specifically, a number of typical late Middle Susiana jars with painted decoration on the shoulder were found stacked in the back room S18:905W (figs. 15, 46:E–F, 47:A–D). In the western recess of antechamber S18:902 four complete vessels, three intact pottery horns, over twenty flint blades, and a large quantity of flint cores were discovered. The large quantity of flint chips found in S18:902 indicates that the manufacture of flint blades may have taken place in this area. The only door socket found inside the building was located on the corner of the threshold between rooms S18:905W and S18:904. In the latter, two dozen clay "sling shots," flint blades and cores, and several intact vessels were also found.

The original, complete plan of the building, particularly its outer enclosure walls, may have been different from what we have suggested here. The doorway in S18:907, as the one in S18:901, leads to an antechamber (S18:902) with a niche in the east wall (fig. 15). This room itself leads to another rectangular room (S18:904), which in turn leads to the back rooms S18:905E and 905W. Two long halls, R18:915/916 and 921 represent the western flank of the building. One (R18:901) has a square mudbrick platform and the other only a recessed doorway. The northern and parts of the western flanks of the building remain unexcavated; most of the eastern flank has been destroyed by later building activities. There is little doubt that the western wall of the long room R18:921 cannot be the western enclosure wall of the building. Thus we may imagine a much thicker wall on the west side paralleling the eastern wall. Although this reconstruction solves the problem of the missing western enclosure wall, it raises the question of whether the thick eastern wall was indeed an enclosure wall to the whole complex. The problem with this reconstruction rests in the observation that a partially excavated 4 × 5 m area immediately outside rooms S18:902 and 903 (in S18:901N and 906) consists of a mudbrick pavement, or possibly platform, only one course high. It is possible that this feature was a foundation for a much more massive enclosure wall of the Burnt Building. Or it may have been a room with a mudbrick floor, known from other Early and Middle Susiana architectural examples. Thus, the reconstruction of the original plan of the building as shown here must remain tentative.

## LATE MIDDLE SUSIANA DOMESTIC ARCHITECTURE

Fragmentary walls and rooms just south of the Burnt Building are the only evidence of what may have been domestic or auxiliary buildings in the East Area. As shown in figure 15, this area was heavily pitted during the Protoliterate phase. In Square R19, a partially preserved plan indicates two rectangular rooms built back to back with a partition wall projecting from the common wall to the south. The orientation of this and what remains in Square S19 is the same as the Burnt Building. A southwest–northeast wall with buttresses on both sides, an east–west wall perpendicular to the latter, and a fragment of a wall to the east (S19:901) are all that are preserved of the architecture of this area. The shared alignment of these fragmentary walls suggests that they all belonged to a single, much larger building. Two more fragmentary walls on the east side of Square S19 may also belong to the same phase of architecture, but the presence of Early Susiana and Archaic sherds on the base of these walls and the difference in the size of mudbricks used to erect them raise the possibility that they belong to the Early Susiana period or Archaic 3 phase.

## PROTOLITERATE ARCHITECTURAL PHASE 1: MONUMENTAL BUILDING COMPLEX

Chogha Mish and Susa were the largest population centers in Susiana during the Protoliterate phase. But it was only during the ninth through eleventh seasons when major architecture of the period, commensurate with Chogha Mish's status as a regional center, was discovered. Excavations during the ninth–eleventh seasons provided the first substantial evidence of the presence of a monumental, formal building of the Protoliterate phase at Chogha Mish.

In the course of post-fifth season excavations, the East Area was expanded on all sides and the levels that had been reached in the fifth season were taken down to reveal earlier architectural phases. In the expanded northern, eastern, and western areas, under the remains of the Protoliterate buildings that were revealed during the first five seasons, a large complex of monumental buildings was discovered.

The largest building, unique in Iran, was found in Squares P16, Q16, R16, and Q17 (fig. 16). Only the southern half of this well-preserved building was excavated; the northern flank remains unexcavated under the northwestern baulk of the trench — the proposed reconstruction as indicated on the plan is based on the principle of symmetry. The thick walls of the building were made of bricks measuring 20 × 10 × 8 cm and laid with a combined techniques of *stack* and *English*, as shown on the plan (fig. 16). This monumental building consists of a wide vestibule, the access to which is provided by a niched entrance from a wide alley paved with pebbles. Two niched entrances lead from this vestibule to a large courtyard. From here, other niched entrances lead to various chambers clustered around the courtyard.

It is unknown whether the area around which various chambers are built (Q16:1104 and 1105) was an open courtyard or a roofed central hall. The width of the area is 8.5 m. Even if timbers long enough for this purpose were available to the builders, several columns may have been required to bear the weight of the roof. No evidence for such architectural features has been reported. It is possible that such features originally existed and were later destroyed by Protoliterate building and pitting activities.

A row of ceramic pipes found under the floor of room Q16:1101 probably drained the courtyard. This and another pipe drain in the alley in front of the building, Q17:1106, may have led the excess water to the well/cistern in Q17:1109. The pipes average 16–17 cm wide × 39–41 cm long with the narrowest opening about 10 cm in diameter.

The only burial found in this building is a simple oval pit in Q16:1101. The body is laid on its side, facing southwest. The lower jaw and the lower legs of the skeleton are missing. No objects were found associated with this burial and its odd location suggests that it may have been dug into this room from a later, higher deposit. The available data do not allow further comment on the stratigraphic position of the burial pit, but it might be intrusive.

With the exception of the vestibule, all other floors in the building consist of beaten earth with no special treatment. The southwestern part of the vestibule's floor was paved with baked bricks measuring 25 × 10 × 8 cm; the rest of the vestibule floor consisted of beaten earth. On this, more than thirty-five pieces of gazelle femurs were found with the concentration near the base of the southeastern wall of the building (pl. 13:B). Large patches of clay with wickerwork mat impressions were found on the floor of Q16:1106.

A wide alley (Q17:1108/1107/1106) that ran northeast–southwest gave access to the building (fig. 16, pls. 13:A, 14:A). The alley itself was paved with pebbles, a millennia-old tradition at Chogha Mish to prevent mud in rainy seasons. A rectangular trough of baked brick was found in the alley near the southwestern corner of the building. A large vat was embedded next to the pipeline, but there does not seem to exist any relation with the piping system and, in fact, the vat may belong to the upper, later phase of the Protoliterate phase. The partially preserved pipeline in the alley may have continued to the northeast, joining another fragmentary piece of the drainage system found in R16:1101. In this long room, two water sinks, linked together on the bottom by two holes (see the diagram in fig. 16), and a rectangular area paved with baked brick, may have been used for processing food or simply for washing. A large open spout, about 48 cm long × 9 cm wide at the narrow opening, was set next to the last row of the bricks, presumably to guide the water. Thus, the entire drainage system in the alley may have been originally connected to this area.

A second entrance to the monumental building was provided through a simple opening in Q16:1008, in front of which three intact vessels were found on the ground. From this entrance, a narrow corridor leads to a long hall with a recess on the southwest wall (1004/1108) and eventually to room 1106. Northeast of this entrance, another narrow corridor (1007) leads to a large chamber with a buttress built against its northern wall. The wall here is by far thicker than any other places in the building and it is possible that it served as a landing for a set of staircases leading to an upper floor; however, there is no direct evidence for this. Rooms Q16:1005 and R16:1103 might have led to the eastern flank of the building complex, but that part remains unexcavated.

South of alley 1008 and leading to the main building, fragments of straight, thick walls with clean corners were found. Later construction and pitting in this area (see *Chogha Mish* I, pl. 264) had destroyed much of this architectural feature, so it is impossible to integrate it functionally with the rest of the complex. Another long but much narrower chamber has been reconstructed immediately south of this unit. A well-preserved niched entrance with a raised doorway was found in the middle of the wall leading to a third long hall in R17:1111/1115. The southwestern extension of this hall is not preserved, but on the northeast it leads to a set of three communicating rectangular chambers. The first one, in R16:1107, is furnished with two circular hearths. The middle chamber, R16:1106, has no special features, but the last one (R16:1104) contained a number of copper/bronze pins in its western corner.

### Subsidiary Buildings

The southeastern wall of room R16:1107 connects this part of the main complex to another, perhaps subsidiary, building to the east (fig. 16). The main entrance to this building must have been through the open alley 802, paved with the usual cobblestones. Only the southern part of this building has been excavated. Here, the only entrance seems to be the opening that links a long hall (R16:802) to an elongated narrow chamber R16:801. No special features were found here. The walls were plastered with mud and the floors consisted of beaten earth.

The third architectural unit of this complex straddles Squares P16, P17, and Q17. Again, this unit is badly damaged by construction and pitting activities of the later Protoliterate phase, as well as by those of the Achaemenid and Parthian periods. A narrow space in Q17 separates the southwestern enclosure wall of the monumental building from the northeastern wall of this unit. Judging by the surviving fragments of the thick enclosure wall of this smaller unit, it must have been larger than shown on the plan. This unit consists of a long rectangular central hall (P17:1103) with a niche built into its northwestern wall. This central hall is surrounded on three sides by long communicating chambers. Two narrow and, presumably, long magazines form the southwestern flank of this central hall (1101). The presence of a number of intact vessels on what seems to be the floors of these magazines suggests that the middle partition wall separating the two chambers may have only extended part way into the space.

A curious circular baked-brick construction (P17:1109) was found south of the building in perfect alignment with the pipe drains in the alley of the main building. It does not penetrate below the surface level here and most probably belongs to the later phase of Protoliterate occupation (pl. 6:B). The similarity of this brick-lined construction to those that were found in the later phase makes this assignment even more certain.

## PROTOLITERATE ARCHITECTURAL PHASE 2: DOMESTIC BUILDINGS
(Pls. 12, 14, and 16:B)

Sometime during the Protoliterate phase all the monumental buildings in the East Area were abandoned. A thin layer of mudbrick detritus and occupational debris separates the remains of the monumental complex from the next architectural phase. The available data do not allow speculation about whether Chogha Mish was entirely abandoned for a short time or whether only this part of the settlement went out of use. Whatever the case may be, a new complex of what seem to be residential buildings and workshops was erected in the area. To facilitate the visualization of the entire plan, I have included in figure 17 some of the architectural units (shown in outline) that were published in the first volume (*Chogha Mish* I, pl. 264). If the outline is a continuation of a solid, blackened wall, then that outline represents reconstruction, as in House 5 in Squares S17 and S18.

A cluster of at least four separate buildings was found in Squares P17, Q17, and R17. Building 1 straddles Squares Q17 and R17.[107] The plan of the building and all the buildings of this later phase are similar to those found earlier. The entrance to Building 1, Q17:824, leads in from an open space, which is surrounded on three sides by

107. Numbered squares on figure 17 indicate building numbers.

buildings. The entrance is relatively wide and leads to what seems to be an antechamber (Q17:807) with a circular hearth and a row of intact vessels set against the southwestern enclosure wall of the building. Nicely built doorways between the various rooms of this unit help visualize communication between the rooms. Not all walls are preserved high enough to see how various rooms communicated, though some of the long, narrow magazines may have had short partition walls and no need for a doorway to access them.

Two large rectangular rooms with thin walls (most probably partition walls) were attached to the southern flank of this building. In R17:812 a low bench made of mudbricks and a circular pottery kiln are the only features. The room was filled with soft ash mixed with potsherds and some flint blades. Just to the right, the room R17:808 has only a circular hearth or kiln, but with similar floor composition as R17:812. Another pottery kiln was found just outside the southern wall (R17:702) and was published in *Chogha Mish* I (pl. 264). The concentration of hearths, kilns, and layers of ash and soot in this area suggests a workshop.

Building 2 is located just opposite Building 1 in Square Q17. It is a smaller unit; its northwestern part was destroyed by later activities. A long rectangular central hall (Q17:806/811/813) divides the unit into two separate wings. The southern wing consists of two long parallel chambers (Q17:819 and 820) and a square room 823 just northeast of 820. No doorways were found between these chambers. The northern wing of Building 2 consists of at least two square communicating rooms with a pivot stone located just next to the doorjamb of 808. The central hall is provided with a circular hearth and a thick burnt floor. Along the southern wall of this hall was found a row of several vessels in situ (pl. 14:C). Building 3 forms the northwestern border of this building complex. The only existing feature of this unit is a partially preserved rectangular room paved meticulously with bricks. The eastern and northern parts of this building, if preserved, remain unexcavated.

Building 4 (Q17:817) is also heavily damaged, but the preserved part consists of a square room with thick, nicely built walls. The only preserved feature in this room is a circular hearth built directly on the beaten earth floor. A large pottery kiln (Q17:822) may or may not have belonged to this building; a portion of a similarly constructed thick wall with a nice corner may have been part of the southeastern extension of this building.

The open area flanked by Buildings 1–3 has several features consistent with the industrial activities presumed to have been conducted here. The central feature (feature 1) consists of a baked-brick cistern and a similarly constructed square bin (feature 2) and a low platform built against its western wall. The available data preclude any speculation on the function of this assemblage. The fact that feature 1 is nicely aligned with the drain system in Square R18 (919) and that two rows of baked bricks form a channel leading to the cistern suggest that feature 1 was part of the drainage system or water supply of the settlement here. A third feature seems to be a water well made of baked bricks, but the bottom of the feature remains unexcavated. However, the fact that lower levels of this feature did not seem to have penetrated earlier levels suggests that it was not very deep. Features 4 and 5 are circular kilns or ovens, while feature 6 is a fragment of a wall dated to the Achaemenid period on the basis of sherds found at its base. This wall may have been part of an Achaemenid installation built around the circular structure, shown here in outline only. The Achaemenid circular structure and its attendant features cut into and destroyed a number of Protoliterate buildings here, of which only a combination of cobble and baked-brick pavement and a wall fragment survived.

The rest of the surviving architecture of the later Protoliterate phase of occupation is found in the eastern portion of the East Area in Squares R17, S17, R18, and S18. An almost complete plan of a relatively large building, Building 5, consists of a courtyard (S18:910) with partially preserved cobble pavement. A wide doorway leads to a rather large rectangular room (R18:904), which had no special features. A small, square magazine (R18:905), built against the southwestern corner of room 904, forms the southwestern corner of Building 5. The northern part of the building consists of three parallel rectangular rooms with beaten earth floors and no special features.

The final building of the Protoliterate phase in this area is Building 6, the entire plan of which cannot be projected on the basis of the surviving walls. The two buttresses built into the southwestern wall of this unit, in R18:919, suggest that this wall was an outer wall of this unit, but this is by no means certain. Although the baked-brick drain just to the northeast of Building 6 (published in *Chogha Mish* I, pl. 264) certainly belongs to this later phase of occupation, the drain just to the south seems out of phase and may have belonged to another, poorly understood phase. The same is probably true about the pottery kiln just to the south of this drain, for if the northeastern wall of Building 6 were projected, it would cover the kiln and hence not be contemporary with it. Just below the southwestern enclosure wall of Building 6, a large cluster of beveled-rim bowls was carefully stacked against a low partition wall made of baked bricks (R18:923), which is surrounded by a number of pottery kilns (R18:925, 921, 916, 902, and 906). Farther down, more pottery kilns and pits were discovered in R19:909 and R18:908 and 909.

The above-ground baked-brick drain running northeast–southwest in Squares S17 and R17 was discovered in the first five seasons and published in *Chogha Mish* I (pl. 264). Two fragments of the same type of drain were found, one between Buildings 5 and 6 and the other southwest of Building 6, in R18:919. Although the latter may have been part of the larger drainage system in this phase, originally linked with the straight drain in S17 and R17, the former, as mentioned above, may have belonged to a different drainage system now destroyed.

## PREHISTORIC BURIALS

A number of graves were discovered in the course of the eleven seasons of excavations at Chogha Mish. Except for a large number of Islamic graves, as well as one Achaemenid and a few Parthian jar burials that were published in the first volume, no graves dating to the historical periods were found during the sixth–eleventh seasons. Burials were dated by either funerary objects or, in the absence of burial objects, by context.

The majority of prehistoric graves date to the Archaic and Early Susiana periods. Most of the graves that were discovered in the sixth–eleventh seasons and that contained more or less articulated skeletons are represented in figure 18. Of these twenty graves, ten date to the Archaic Susiana 3 phase (fig. 18:A, C, F, J, N–R, and T; pls. 17:A–D, 18:A–B and D), seven to the Early Susiana period (fig. 18:B, E, G–I, and K–L; pl. 17:E), and three to the Middle Susiana period (fig. 18:D, M, and S; pl. 18:C). No graves were found dating to the Archaic Susiana 1–2 phases. The two single burials that might belong to the Late Susiana 2 and the Protoliterate phases appear only on the architecture plans in figures 7 and 16.

Most of the Archaic burials were found in Trench XXI in an open space between the architectural remains of Early and Archaic Susiana 3; some burials were found under the floor of residential units in the area. Even though most of the burials represent single interments and were thus undisturbed, only a few contained funerary gifts (fig. 18:A, F, O, and R). No child burial was found in the area. A few of the skeletons found in the prehistoric burials were covered with red ochre (e.g., see fig. 18:A, D, L, and O).

# CHAPTER THREE
# POTTERY

## INTRODUCTION

A detailed analysis of the pottery of all periods attested at Chogha Mish was published in the first volume. This chapter is therefore devoted to brief descriptions of various types of pottery in each assemblage. To avoid repetition and constant cross-referencing between this and the first volume, this chapter consists of a synopsis of the descriptions of all the known pottery wares and their characteristics. The following chapter deals with a synopsis of pottery stylistic development in southwest Asia, which in turn is followed by a discussion on specific stylistic change and continuity from one period to the next in lowland Susiana.

## PARTHIAN PERIOD

(Fig. 19)

The Parthian period seems to be the latest occupation at Chogha Mish. Except for a number of torpedo-jar burials from the West Area, Trench XIII, and Sounding E, and a well-preserved pottery kiln in J15:301 (*Chogha Mish* I: 8–9, pl. 265), no architectural units from this period are preserved. Nevertheless, the Terrace may have been the locus of some residential units judging by the presence of some hearths and pebble pavements associated with Parthian pottery (*Chogha Mish* I: 8–9). Although the available data preclude any estimate of the size of the Parthian occupation at Chogha Mish, the original Parthian occupation at the site may have been scattered and confined to the High Mound and the western part of the Terrace.

The date of the occupation of Chogha Mish during the long Parthian period is equally uncertain. However, a large number of Parthian pottery vessels from Chogha Mish have good parallels from Level 2 of the Artaxerxes II palace on the Shaur River at Susa, dated to the late Parthian and Sasanian period (Boucharlat and Labrousse 1979; Labrousse and Boucharlat 1974).[108]

The examples of the Parthian pottery discussed and illustrated here come exclusively from secondary and tertiary contexts, primarily large pits. The pottery commonly has a buff paste mixed with both sand and grits (fig. 19). In finer examples (fig. 19:M), no inclusions are visible. The plain examples are sometimes buff slipped and the surface may vary from light to dark buff with occasionally a reddish tinge. One specific type of buff ware has a paste mixed with both grits and white particles, presumably crushed shells or some other type of calciferous rocks (fig. 19:L, O). The colors of the glazed specimens vary from green to greenish gray, greenish blue, and light grayish blue; the glaze is often cracked and somewhat thicker on the lower body and inner surface of the vessel.

Accessories are limited to simple loop handles, disc or ring bases, and sometimes complex, channeled rims. Surface decoration is usually limited to excised channels, molding, or scoring on the upper part of the vessel (fig. 19:A–B, D, and M). One example (fig. 19:D) seems to have a plastic or impressed decoration. It may belong to the latest stage of the Parthian period and is thus related to the later Sasanian stamped decoration. Another example (fig. 19:L) is reconstructed as a funnel on the basis of a more complete example found in the fourth season (*Chogha Mish* I, pl. 70:O). The dating of this specimen is based on the context and on the ware. The possibility exists that this particular shape may have belonged to the Achaemenid period or even late Iron Age because examples of the general shape have been reported from the Late Assyrian context at Nimrud (Oates 1959, pl. 39:109).

---

108. For a list of parallels, see *Chogha Mish* I: 10, n. 10.

# IRON AGE III (NEO-ELAMITE)/ACHAEMENID PERIOD

(Figs. 20–24)

In the first volume of *Chogha Mish*, a group of pottery vessels and sherds associated with the circular building (*Chogha Mish* I: 10–16) and some graves were attributed to the Achaemenid period. Although some specimens, such as the tall pointed base jar in figure 22:A and most examples of the large open vessels in figure 20, are typical shapes of Achaemenid pottery from Susa, Persepolis, and Pasargadae,[109] the majority of the specimens and their wares have their closest parallels in the late Iron Age[110] and Neo-Elamite period. Therefore, in this volume the "Achaemenid" pottery is treated as a reflection of an Iron III/Neo-Elamite (mostly illustrated in fig. 21) presence at Chogha Mish and its continuance into the Achaemenid period.

The use of "Achaemenid" in this context does not mean that Chogha Mish was actually inhabited by the Persians themselves. If we are correct in our assumption that the Persian Achaemenids did not bury their dead directly in the ground in accordance with their religion, then the three graves found during the fourth and fifth seasons at Chogha Mish may well have belonged to a late Iron Age tribe. Settling in eastern Susiana perhaps in the late seventh and sixth centuries B.C., the late Iron Age tribes would have observed different burial practices from those of the Persian Achaemenids.

The pottery assemblage dated to this presumably transitional phase has been described in detail in *Chogha Mish* I (pp. 13–16). The following is a description of the major characteristics of the wares and surface treatment of the illustrated examples (figs. 20–24). As with most late Iron Age pottery assemblages in western and southwestern Iran, the quality and composition of the ware and surface treatments of the Chogha Mish assemblage have a wide range. The colors of the wares range from light to warm buff to grayish buff and gray. Sherds belonging to large vessels have multi-color grits, sometimes mixed with fine sand. Sherds that belong to medium and small vessels, particularly open vessels, have a much denser fabric mixed with sand; sometimes finer sherds do not show any sign of inclusions.

The surfaces of both common and fine wares are covered with either a creamy buff slip or a monochrome red wash. Thinner and finer sherds (usually of open bowls with sharp carination just below the rim) have highly polished surfaces, while the surface of some specimens of the common ware is smoothed and exhibits burnishing strokes.

Shapes range from open bowls with sharp carination, bowls with a sinuous curve and flat base, convex-sided bowls, bell-shaped bowls with thin walls, to cylindrical jars with usually ribbing just below the rim, and various types of closed forms with club or everted rims. Such examples may have one or two handles and sometimes are provided with open or trefoil spouts. Bowls with a single horizontal handle, typical of the Iron Age period, also occur. The only examples with painted decoration are a rim sherd and a complete cylindrical jar. The rim sherd (fig. 22:D) is a closed form decorated with a series of straight and wavy horizontal lines; the cylindrical jar (fig. 22:E) is decorated with four horizontal bands painted in black. The shape and ware of these decorated examples are typical of the period. The closest parallels are reported from Pasargadae (Stronach 1978).

Although most of the examples dated to the Achaemenid period include a number of long-lived types, three types are specific to the late Iron Age period. Two examples of the typical Iron Age gray ware with a channeled rim (fig. 20:G and I) have close parallels found at Ziwiye and Tappeh Godin.[111] Vessels with a bridged spout (fig. 22:M) are the second type. Similar vessels have been found at Susa in both Level 7 of the Ville royale II and Level I of the village perse-achemenide.[112] The third type, illustrated in *Chogha Mish* I (pl. 74:A), is a ring-based open bowl that was commonly found in late Assyrian context at Nimrud.[113] Numerous examples of a similar, related type were also found (fig. 24:H, J, and M–N).

---

109. See Ghirshman 1954; Stronach 1978; de Miroschedji 1978; and Schmidt 1957.
110. For examples, see Young and Levine 1974 (Tappeh Godin period II); Goff 1970 (Baba Jan, period 1); Stronach 1978 (Nushi Jan, Median).
111. For Ziwiye, see Young 1965: 58, fig. 3:4; for Tappeh Godin, see Young 1969: 119, fig. 43:11, fig. 44:12; Young and Levine 1974: 127, fig. 45:19.
112. Ghirshman 1954, pl. 29:G. S. 2242; de Miroschedji 1978: 223, fig. 54:7.
113. Oates 1959: 132, 141, pl. 36:31.

# OLD ELAMITE (SUKKALMAH) PERIOD

(Fig. 25)

Excavations subsequent to the fifth season did not reveal any new Old Elamite pottery types or wares. As in the first five seasons, no specimens of true gray ware nor the so-called "Elamite flask" were discovered at Chogha Mish. A thick-walled shallow "plate" with three feet (fig. 25:C) is an exception. This object is dated to the earlier Shimashki phase (Carter and Stolper 1984, fig. 10:4), but at Chogha Mish it was found in a secure Old Elamite context.

The following is a short description of the illustrated examples. The Old Elamite pottery assemblage at Chogha Mish has a buff color fabric with a varying tinge of orange-yellow to brown-gray buff. The paste is usually tempered with grits and straw. In small vessels, grit is the main tempering agent, while in larger vessels straw is predominant. Some pieces exhibit an extremely thin, light buff layer on the exterior and interior, which may be interpreted as slip. Such an effect could also result from wet smoothing of the surface. The surface of most vessels is coarse and shows fast wheel striations, particularly on the interior.

Low ring-based bowls with an almost vertical upper body and a slight carination near the base are the most common (fig. 25:E).[114] Shouldered jars (fig. 25:Q–T) are the most dominant among the closed forms. Such jars are characterized by a relatively flaring high neck, narrow shoulder, sharp carination just below the shoulder, a low disc base or foot, and strong striation marks, particularly on the interior.[115] Less common are the globular jars without shoulder (fig. 25:H, M), while large vats with heavy rims and often a prominent ledge near the lip are more common at Chogha Mish (fig. 25:L, U). The two most common shapes at Chogha Mish include the storage jars with incurving walls and recumbent rim (fig. 25:L, U). The second type (fig. 25:P) includes large vats with almost vertical walls and pronounced overhanging rims.

# PROTOLITERATE PHASE

(Figs. 26–34)

As discussed in detail in *Chogha Mish* I (pp. 37–102), the Protoliterate pottery assemblage found at Chogha Mish can be divided into six major groups on the basis of ware, tempering agent, and surface treatment: (1) coarse ware, (2) standard ware, (3) fine ware, (4) brittle ware, (5) gray ware, and (6) red ware. Detailed discussion of the major and minor characteristics of each ware is provided in the first volume. The following is a brief definition of each distinct group of the assemblage.

## COARSE WARE

The predominant tempering agent of this group of pottery is straw, but in some cases grit and/or sand is also present. The clay is rough and does not seem to have been levigated. The color of the paste ranges from brownish buff to grayish brown to orange and red buff. Several classes of prominent Protoliterate pottery are made with this ware, namely, beveled-rim bowls, "flowerpots," some convex- and straight-sided bowls, trays, and pipes (figs. 26:D, G, K; 33:I, K–L). The low-neck jars with a painted base, illustrated in figure 28:E–F, are the only examples of jars made of coarse ware. Both handmade and wheel-made specimens are included in this group. The surface is usually untreated, but in some cases wet smoothing produced the appearance of a slip. In almost all the examples of this group, the core is darker than the surface.

## STANDARD WARE

As with many pottery classifications, there is an overlap of the coarse and standard wares, the latter having a better quality of clay. The major difference between the two wares is the absence of vegetal tempering in the standard ware, which is primarily grit tempered, but in some cases fine sand and crumbled shell or some type of calcite particles are also present. The size and concentration of grits vary from small to large particles and from dense to

114. See Gasche 1973, pl. 3:10, 15, pl. 24:23.

115. For parallels from Susa, see Gasche 1973: 40–41, pl. 24:23; Carter 1979: 119; Carter 1980, figs. 45:79, 46:1–8, 47:1–3; Carter and Stolper 1984, fig. 10.

sporadic (see figs. 26–33). Vessels in this group are primarily buff in color, but shades of yellowish buff, pinkish buff, and reddish buff also occur. Some examples are fired to a greenish buff or greenish gray. In general, vessels were not baked at high temperatures and the reduced atmosphere in the kiln is apparently responsible for occasional gray cores.

While in most cases wheel striations are visible on the interior of the vessels, the exterior is usually smoothed, scraped, pared, or scratched in such a manner that all traces of striations are obliterated. The application of slip, usually creamy buff, is apparent in some examples, but whether all vessels in this group were slipped is not clear, as a false slip can be created by wet smoothing. A true slip can be seen on the vessels whose wet-smoothed surface is scraped with a blunt tool (reserved slip). This type of surface treatment is usually limited to some open forms and some spoutless closed forms. Reserved slip does not seem to occur on jars with handles, spouts, or on four-lugged vessels. The surface of the latter exhibits various forms of incision, excision, punctuation, rocker, imprints, as well as plastic decoration.

## FINE WARE

The clay of fine wares at Chogha Mish seems to have been levigated and primarily tempered with fine sand; occasionally grains of grits are included, but they are rare enough to be considered accidental. The color of the clay ranges from creamy to pinkish and yellowish buff. In cases when the vessel was overheated, both the core and the surface display a greenish buff color.

Unlike standard wares, vessels of fine clay tend to be relatively small and exhibit a uniform, oxidized core. The entire surface is evenly smoothed and is usually covered with a creamy buff or yellowish buff slip. Although the upper body of the vessel is much smoother than that of the standard ware, the lower body, close to the base, remains comparatively rough.

The corpus of vessel shapes in this group is limited, as this type is obviously neither suitable nor economic for ordinary or cooking vessels. But rare specimens of strap-handled ovoid jars are made of fine clay. In addition, examples of four-lugged jars and bowls with pouring lips (usually made of standard ware) made of fine clay also occur.

## BRITTLE WARE

Known also as "shatter ware" in *Chogha Mish* I (p. 38), the paste of brittle ware either has no visible inclusions or is tempered with sand so fine that cannot be seen with the naked eye. Whole brittle ware vessels are difficult to distinguish from those made of fine clay. Sherds of this group produce a clinky sound when gently hit against a solid surface and tend to shatter into small pieces under slight pressure. The color of the ware tends to be red or tan. Some small and miniature vessels are made from this ware, but they are rare.

## GRAY WARE

Of all the types of Protoliterate ware, gray ware is the rarest at Chogha Mish. Vessels made of this ware have a dense, dark to light gray clay tempered with fine sand, occasionally mixed with some grit and even straw. The shapes of gray ware vessels are almost the same as those made of the standard buff ware. This, and the rarity of the type, suggests that perhaps the gray ware vessels were imitations of stone vessels.

## RED WARE

Equally rare are vessels made of red clay (fig. 29:E). Although some examples have red-washed surface, it is not the red wash that defines this group, for such washes occur on standard buff and fine wares as well. In true red ware vessels, the paste of the ware itself is red and tempered with sand and occasional grits. Sometimes a bright red wash is applied to the surface, which may or may not be burnished. In burnished examples, burnishing strokes may be visible or the entire surface of the vessel is evenly polished.

# LATE SUSIANA PERIOD

(Fig. 35)

In the first volume (*Chogha Mish* I: 284, 302–505) and elsewhere,[116] we argue for the existence of an intermediate phase between the Middle and Late Susiana periods. To be consistent with the terminology we adopted for the Susiana prehistoric sequence, we designated this phase "Late Susiana 1," to be followed by Late Susiana 2, best represented at Susa. Two major events mark the beginning of this period in lowland Susiana: (1) the abandonment of Chogha Mish and some of its satellite sites in eastern Susiana, and (2) the appearance of a new class of painted pottery.

After a hiatus of perhaps several hundred years (the Late Susiana 1 phase), Chogha Mish was re-occupied during the Late Susiana 2 phase. Unlike the preceding Middle Susiana, the Late Susiana 2 occupation of Chogha Mish seems to have been limited to the High Mound. The presence, however, of sherds typical of this phase on the Terrace, particularly in the East Area, suggests that Late Susiana 2 occupation must have been more extensive than previously thought, even though none of the sherds found outside the High Mound came from a primary context. This should not be surprising because during the following Protoliterate phase extensive leveling of the surface of the mound must have destroyed any architectural remains of this period on the Terrace.

The pottery assemblage of the Late Susiana 2 phase (fig. 35, pl. 19) can be divided into two major groups: (1) standard buff ware, and (2) red ware. In addition to these major wares, small quantities of gray ware and black-on-red ware also occur.

## STANDARD BUFF WARE

Standard buff ware comes primarily in two varieties, common standard buff ware and fine buff ware; each class includes a number of sub-varieties. The clay of the fine ware is dense and often tempered with fine sand that is invisible to the naked eye. In examples of common ware, sand and occasional grits, as well as traces of chaff, are clearly visible. The color of the ware varies considerably, ranging from warm buff to yellow/cream buff to brownish buff to apricot or pink buff. Some over-fired pieces exhibit a greenish buff surface. The core of the buff ware is monochrome and completely oxidized. The vessels in this class are made on a slow wheel, and some irregular striations are visible. Horizontal wheel striations are often visible on the surface, particularly on the interior and on jar necks. The decorated specimens are painted with black, purple-black, or reddish brown paint. Both matte and glossy paint occur.

## RED WARE

The manufacture of red ware continues from the Middle Susiana into the Late Susiana 2 phase. There is a wide range in the surface color from deep red to pinkish buff. The clay is dense and often has a metallic tone, due perhaps to high temperatures in the kiln. As with the fine buff ware, the clay of the red ware is tempered with fine sand, usually undetectable with the naked eye; sometimes scattered small grits and air pockets do occur.

The examples of the red ware at Chogha Mish can be divided into two categories depending on the color of the core. The first category has a monochrome core the same color as the surface (sometimes paler). The second category has a dark core that does not seem to have been the result of low firing, for even some examples of this category produce a metallic clink when struck. The dark core does not gradually turn red toward the surface; rather, two thick layers of red clay sandwich the black core.

The red ware can occur with or without a red wash, which is applied to the vessel either densely or in uneven smears. the color of the wash is sometimes plum or reddish brown. The surface may be matte or burnished with visible burnishing strokes.

Much less common is the red ware with an off-white surface wash, sometimes thick and dense and sometimes applied as a film so thin that the original red surface is visible under the white coating. The coarser variety of red ware comes with or without a surface wash. It has either a plain matte surface or is burnished.

116. See Alizadeh 1992: 21–25.

## GRAY WARE

Compared with other classes of pottery, gray ware is extremely rare at Chogha Mish. The ware is dense and has no visible inclusions; horizontal burnishing strokes are often visible on both surfaces. Both open and closed vessels were made of this ware. Its rarity may indicate a desire to produce the appearance of stone vessels.

## BLACK-ON-RED WARE

Black-on-red ware is the least common ware at Chogha Mish and is represented by only one example (*Chogha Mish* I: 170, fig. 21). Other examples, however, are reported from contemporary Jafarabad and Susa.[117] The Chogha Mish example, as well as those from Susa and Jafarabad, have their closest parallels in Luristan[118] and are most certainly foreign to the Susiana prehistoric pottery tradition. A finer version of this particular type is illustrated in figure 35:E. It is a handmade, painted, four-lug jar with a low neck. The clay is pink and both the interior and exterior surface have a pinkish buff slip; highly irregular striations are visible only on the interior. The decorative lines are carelessly applied to the overall design. The painted color changes from dark gray-brown to reddish brown as the lines extend away from the start of the brush strokes. This vessel and the one depicted in figure 21 in *Chogha Mish* I do not fit the Late Susiana 2 pottery assemblage of lowland Susiana and may well have come from the highlands.[119]

# MIDDLE SUSIANA PERIOD

(Figs. 36–54)

The Middle Susiana pottery assemblage is characterized primarily by two major wares, buff and red, and their variations (figs. 36–52, pls. 19–20). In addition to these two wares, a specific type of gray ware appears during the second phase of the period, the late Middle Susiana phase. Examples of gray ware have the same shapes as the buff ware (e.g., fig. 45:J). Identical ware and shapes were also found in our 2004/05 joint ICHTO-Oriental Institute excavations at Chogha Do Sar, some 15 km southwest of Chogha Mish (Alizadeh 2005; Alizadeh and Mahfroozi 2005).

## STANDARD BUFF WARE

As with most prehistoric pottery, Middle Susiana standard buff ware varies in color from brownish buff through creamy buff to a greenish or grayish buff. The clay is usually tempered to varying densities with sand and grits. Although the vessels are not as gritty as those of the Early Susiana period, those dating to the first phase of the Middle Susiana period still show a gritty face. As a result, the vessels made with a paste with high concentration of grits are coarser.

The entire pottery assemblage is handmade and the vessel surfaces often show shaping and scraping marks, particularly on the lower part, close to the base. In the latter phase of the period, the vessels' surface is comparatively smoother, but scoring marks are still seen on larger specimens. In some examples it is easy to see a thin buff slip, but since the majority of the vessels were wet smoothed, the dense surface often creates an illusion of a separate slip.

Dark paint, ranging from black to dark brown to (very rarely) dark maroon, was used for decoration. When the vessel was overheated, both the surface and the paint exhibit a greenish tinge. When the paint is thick, it is granular and tends to flake off, leaving a perfect impression. Due perhaps to the chemical components of the paint, the paint sometimes has eaten into the surface and is slightly sunken. This characteristic is more common during the second half of the period, a situation similar to the pottery of the Ubaid 3 and 4 periods.

## FINE BUFF WARE

The fine version of buff ware has a comparatively dense, but thin (6 mm or less) paste and is tempered with fine sand; no grits were used as tempering agent. As a rule, the fine ware was used for small vessels, but sometimes larger vessels were made of this ware as well, particularly the plain, bell-shaped bowls. During the second phase of

117. Dollfus 1971: 47, fig. 12:16–24; de Mecquenem 1912, pl. 19:10, 25:2; Le Breton 1947: 212, fig. 52:10.
118. Vanden Berghe 1973a: 51–53, 58; Mortensen 1976: 56, fig. 5:b–c; Goff 1971: 141, fig. 5:3–5, 8–11, 51.
119. A very similar, perhaps identical, vessel fragment was found in Trench IV during the first season, but it was not published (registration number 1.236).

the Middle Susiana period, there was an increase in the proportion of the vessels made of fine ware, a development that continued into the Late Susiana 1 phase and tapered off in the succeeding Late Susiana 2 phase.

## GRITTY BUFF WARE

A group of large buff ware vessels with thick walls has a comparatively larger amount of grit than others. Such vessels have a gritty face and are by far more abundant in the first phase of the Middle Susiana period, an Early Susiana tradition that continued into the Middle Susiana period. Large, deep, bell-shaped bowls, a continuation of the flanged vessels of the Early Susiana, are good examples of this ware. The surface treatment is limited to a very thin matte buff slip under which individual grits are visible.

## STRAW-TEMPERED BUFF WARE

A very small group of utilitarian and domestic vessels are made with a buff and granular paste tempered with chaff and straw. Some grits occasionally occur, but they may be accidental. Other than wet smoothing and scraping, no special surface treatment is visible.

## PLAIN RED WARE
(Fig. 53:B, C, L, N)

A limited number of varieties of plain red ware occur at Chogha Mish, primarily in the second phase of the Middle Susiana period. The paste is the same in all varieties; only the surface treatment differs from one variety to the other. The red ware has a dense granular paste tempered with fine sand and is often fired at such high temperatures that the sherds, when hit against a solid surface, produce a metallic sound. In some examples, the sand is mixed with mica and calcite particles. Because mica-bearing sand is not native to lowland Susiana but is very common in the highlands, it is highly possible that the increasing connection with the highlands in the Middle Susiana period led to the appearance of this type of inclusion in the lowlands. It is equally possible that such mica-bearing vessels are imports or an indication of movement of artisans.

The color of the paste of plain red ware is basically brick red with shades of reddish brown, light orange, or pink-red. In some rare examples, the reddish tone of one surface grades into orange-buff toward the other. Dark cores are uncommon but do occasionally occur; they certainly were not as common as in the succeeding Late Susiana period. Based on the surface treatment, the Middle Susiana red ware can be divided into three sub-groups of red-washed red ware, white film ware, and buff-slipped red ware.

### *Red-washed Red Ware*

Red-washed ware is the most common variety of red ware. Vessels are distinguished by a thick wash, usually darker than the color of the paste. Open vessels in this group are covered with wash on both the interior and exterior.

### *White Film Ware*

Infrequently, a plain red ware vessel was covered with a very thin, almost transparent, white wash. When moistened, the white film disappears and the actual color of the ware shows through, albeit darker. Whether this thin white coating was actually a separate layer of wash or the effect is produced through some chemical reaction in the clay or in the red wash underneath can only be determined through laboratory analysis.

### *Buff-slipped Red Ware*

The surfaces of a small group of red ware vessels are covered with a buff slip. The color of the slip is so uniform and applied so evenly that in most complete examples it is difficult to distinguish between this ware and the buff ware.

### GRAY WARE

During the second phase of the Middle Susiana period, some vessels appeared with a fine gray paste, tempered with sand and occasional grits. The surface is usually burnished and is used almost exclusively on simple convex bowls. This rare Middle Susiana ware has a relatively wide spatial distribution in lowland Susiana.[120]

## EARLY SUSIANA PERIOD

(Figs. 55–65, Pl. 21:A–D, F–H)

The standardization of pottery manufacture that began with the Archaic Susiana 3 phase became established in the Early Susiana period. The overwhelming majority of Early Susiana pottery vessels are made of a buff ware tempered with multi-colored grits of various sizes and mixed with straw, chaff, sand, or a combination of these. Some of the decorated open forms have neither straw nor chaff mixed with grits. The color ranges from warm buff to brownish buff and sometimes to very pale pinkish buff. Among the various classes of the prehistoric Susiana pottery, the Early Susiana vessels have the grittiest face. Vessels are handmade but exquisitely formed. On larger vessels, scoring marks are sometimes visible on the lower body, near the base. Although the application of a slip is evident on some pieces, particularly the plain flanged vessels and open bowls with flaring rim, it is not always easy to detect a slip.

There is no difference in the manufacture and surface treatment between the decorated and plain vessels. The paint is predominantly black, but sometimes brown, olive-black, or reddish brown can be seen. A number of vessels (particularly those with heavy walls, such as the pedestaled bowls) are overheated, exhibiting a greenish black or greenish brown paint and greenish buff surface.

## ARCHAIC SUSIANA PERIOD

(Figs. 66–75, Pls. 20:D–F, 21:E, I–K)

A number of prominent wares and various styles of decoration and manufacture mark the pottery assemblages of the Archaic Susiana phases. Some wares and surface treatments are specific to a phase and others continue along side new classes. Based on surface treatment and the type of tempering agents, Archaic Susiana pottery can be divided into a number of distinct wares.

### STRAW-TEMPERED SMOOTHED WARE

The paste of straw-tempered smoothed ware ranges from warm buff to yellowish buff to reddish orange often with a gray core. Large amounts of straw in the clay make it porous. Thus, many pieces made of this paste were smeared with bitumen on the interior to decrease porosity.

The surface of the vessels made of this ware is usually mottled but carefully smoothed and feels soft to the touch. Some vessels were polished and exhibit a considerable sheen. A few examples have a thick white wash and were smoothed. Most of the vessels were manufactured by superimposing several layers (usually 3 mm) of clay (see *Chogha Mish* I: 227–28 for more details). This ware continued to be manufactured throughout the entire Archaic sequence. A coarser variety of this ware, designated as straw-tempered coarse ware, was considered in *Chogha Mish* I as a separate ware. But, except for a coarser surface, no other characteristic warrants a division between the two wares.

### STRAW-TEMPERED STANDARD AND FINE RED-WASHED WARE

The standard red-washed ware is essentially the same as the straw-tempered smoothed ware except for the application of a red wash on the exterior. The red pigment is usually fugitive and matte in appearance. The fine variety of this ware is rare and the vessels comparatively smaller and thinner. The paste, too, is denser with less straw. As a

---

120. See Dollfus 1975, fig. 53:11–13 (Jafarabad, levels 3m–n); Dollfus 1983, figs. 68:3–4, 79:8, 83:3, 5 (Tappeh Bandebal, levels 16, 14–13); and Weiss 1976, fig. 11 (Qabr-e Sheikheyn). Presumably, a black burnished variety of this ware also occurs in Deh Luran; see Hole, Flannery, and Neely 1969: 168–69 (Tappeh Sabz, Bayat phase).

rule, both surfaces of open vessels are covered with a red wash. The color is deeper than that applied to the standard variety and ranges from red to brown to purple red. Often the red wash is burnished to a high sheen.

## STRAW-TEMPERED RED-BANDED/LINE WARE

A hallmark of the Archaic Susiana 2 phase, the surface treatment of straw-tempered red-banded/line ware vessels distinguishes this group from the standard red-washed ware. In fact, the decorated examples of the straw-tempered smoothed ware fall into this category. The decoration usually, but not always, consists of a single band (but sometimes more complex patterns) applied to the exterior. The bands usually have jagged edges, which can result from smearing the pigment with fingers or a piece of cloth instead of a brush. A few examples of this decorated ware have bands with straight edges, presumably belonging to the end of the phase, and is transitional to the Archaic Susiana 3; we have no stratigraphic evidence to support this assumption.

A variant of this ware has more complex painted patterns. The exclusively geometric designs are drawn using at least two different types of brush. Again, it seems that by the middle of the Archaic Susiana 2 phase, this ware had developed out of the former.

## STRAW-TEMPERED PAINTED-BURNISHED WARE

The appearance of this specific, handsome ware and its variants marks the beginning of the Archaic Susiana 1 phase.[121] The ware is the same as all the Archaic straw-tempered wares; it is the surface treatment and its specific and complex painted patterns that readily distinguish this class of pottery from the rest. The color of the paste varies, as usual, from light buff to yellowish tan, brown, or orange. The core is almost always gray or even black. The straw face of the fabric is carefully covered with a uniform slip, over which geometric designs of varying complexity are painted in dark brown and sometimes jet black, and then burnished, hence the designation.

## STRAW-TEMPERED PAINTED-BURNISHED VARIANT

At Chogha Mish, straw-tempered painted-burnished variant ware occurs with the standard painted-burnished ware. Excavations at Chogha Bonut showed that the painted-burnished variant appeared earlier and the standard painted-burnished ware developed later during the Archaic Susiana 1 phase, when the site of Chogha Mish was first occupied.

The painted-burnished variant employs the same clay as the standard painted-burnished, but it is less burnished and the slip is not as uniform nor as thick. While the examples of the painted-burnished show a limited repertoire of designs that are usually confined to the upper part of the vessel, the painted-burnished variant exhibits a larger and freer repertoire of designs, sometimes covering the entire surface of the vessel. Rows of wavy horizontal and vertical lines are the most common element of design.

## MATTE-PAINTED WARE

Archaic Susiana 3, the final phase of the Archaic Susiana period, was dominated by two distinct wares: (1) close-line ware, and (2) matte-painted ware. Apart from its distinct repertoires of shapes and painted patterns, this class of pottery is distinguished from other straw-tempered wares of the Archaic Susiana period by a comparatively much finer vegetal tempering agent. The ware is predominantly yellowish buff in color on the surface and brownish buff in the core, with occasional gray cores. The tan or yellowish buff surface is sometimes mottled orange or pinkish buff. The name of the ware is derived from the distinctly dull gray or black paint applied to the surface. A subtype of this ware (not as common) bears a surface decoration that combines a red wash on the lower body (sometimes on the lip) and the painted design above.

## DENSE-SANDY WARE

Occurring first during the Archaic Susiana 2 phase, this distinct ware appears alongside the straw-tempered red-banded ware. The main characteristic of this ware is its fine mineral tempering agent that is almost invisible to

121. For Archaic 0 and Formative Susiana, see Alizadeh 2003a.

the naked eye. Based on the surface treatment, four subtypes of this ware can be distinguished as follows: (1) plain ware, (2) fugitive red-washed ware, (3) fugitive red-lined ware, and (4) dark-painted ware.

Some plain ware sherds have faint traces of a red wash and thus may have originally been red washed. Dark-painted ware is the rarest type and is distinguished by a fast pigment and simple "windowpane" decoration, which closely resembles some decorative designs of the Cheshmeh Ali period in the Central Plateau.[122] This ware also occurs in Deh Luran and is dated to the "Chogha Mami Transitional" phase (Hole 1977, figs. 52:A, 53:A, I). The context of this ware is uncertain at Chogha Mish, but in Deh Luran it is closely associated with the typical close-line ware, suggesting that this particular ware was part of the larger, more dominant repertoire of the close-line ware.

## CLOSE-LINE WARE

Close-line ware is entirely different from all other Archaic wares. It appears suddenly in both Susiana and Deh Luran. If this ware was introduced into southwestern Iran from the Mandali region of Mesopotamia (Hole 1977: 12), then it may have entered Deh Luran and Susiana from the Mehran plain in the province of Ilam, north of Deh Luran. A regional survey in the Mehran plain and my own visits to a number of prehistoric sites in the region, however, failed to reveal any pottery similar to the close-line ware.

The paste ranges from buff to grayish and greenish buff and rarely orange buff. It is tempered with fine grits, sometimes sand. Some of the vessel shapes and decorations are similar to those of the following Early Susiana period and therefore the two wares may sometimes be confused with one another. In such cases, in the absence of stratigraphic information, particularly in surface surveys, one can distinguish the two by the difference in size and color of the tempering agents, as well as the absence of vegetal tempering in the close-line ware paste. The paint is black or dark brown and applied with such skill that even when lines are drawn close to one another (hence the appellation) the edges are crisp and never run or touch one another.

122. See Ghirshman 1938, pl. 54 A:2, B:4.

# CHAPTER FOUR

# DEVELOPMENT OF SHARED ARTISTIC TRADITIONS IN DECORATED POTTERY IN SOUTHWEST ASIA

## PART 1: MESOPOTAMIAN PREHISTORIC ARTISTIC AND TECHNICAL DEVELOPMENT

### INTRODUCTION

From the beginning of village life and the invention of pottery sometime in the late eighth millennium B.C. until the mid-sixth millennium B.C., prehistoric regional cultures in Iran and Mesopotamia shared a number of characteristics and artistic trends in material culture, especially in decorated pottery vessels. This chapter is devoted to an analysis of the technical and artistic development of Susiana prehistoric pottery and its differences and similarities to other pottery assemblages in the neighboring regions. This discussion, however, may be better understood against a general overview of the common trends in the artistic creation of material culture in early Mesopotamia.

The variety of individual cultures in the Near East matches that of its varied geographical areas. Mesopotamia is divided into two major parts, south and north, not because of any sharp natural boundaries, but because of the differences in material cultural assemblages these two regions display, as well as differences in the historical trajectory of both regions.

Early Neolithic farming villages seem to have begun earlier — during the Jarmo period — in the high altitudes of the Zagros Mountains in Iraqi Kurdestan (ca. 1,000 m above sea level) than those in the south. During the following Hassuna period, settlements were established at much lower altitudes (ca. 200–300 m above sea level) on the east and west banks of the Tigris. The sphere of cultural interactions in southwest Asia seems to have begun in the succeeding Samarran period, when the material culture of northeastern Mesopotamia exhibits links with that of early Susiana villages. Samarran culture overlapped with and was finally replaced by the Halaf culture, which was oriented westward with a probable diffusion center in the Habur area of eastern Syria. Halaf culture also diffused northward into eastern Anatolia. Unlike the south, there is not a continuous cultural development in the north. For example, all three cultural phases — Hassuna, Samarra, and Halaf — overlap for a time before they are completely replaced. Only in the south, in the sequence of the five phases of Ubaid (Ubaid 0–4, also known as el-Oueili, Eridu, Haji Mohammed, Middle and Late Ubaid), is there a continuous line of development. The Halaf culture in northern Mesopotamian overlapped with the Ubaid 2/Haji Mohammed culture and was finally replaced by that of Ubaid 3 culture from the south.[123]

### NORTHERN MESOPOTAMIA

#### JARMO PHASE

The archaeological deposits at the highland village of Jarmo, in the foothills of the Zagros Mountains, primarily consist of two phases: aceramic and ceramic. The initial phase of pottery manufacture at Jarmo is considered too advanced and sophisticated to be the beginning.[124] The earliest painted pottery at Jarmo is a soft, straw-tempered buff ware with a limited range of decoration that consists of simple geometric lines, "blobs," and the well-known "tadpoles." This simple decorated ware has parallels in the Iranian Zagros Mountains at Tappeh Sarab near Kerman-

123. The presence at Tepe Gawra of the typical Ubaid 2/Haji Mohammed) tortoise vessels suggests that the southern cultural contact/influence in the north may have started even earlier.

124. See Adams 1983: 213.

shah,[125] but most important, at Chogha Bonut in lowland Susiana. In shape, type of ware, and painted decoration, the smear-painted ware of the Formative Susiana phase is similar to that of Jarmo, though unlike the latter, smear-painted ware was not the first class of pottery that appeared at Bonut.[126] This suggests a common ancestor for these geographically widely separated sites. Furthermore, the well-known T-shaped figurines, as well as the finger-shaped figurines, occur at all these early Neolithic sites.

## Hassuna Phase

The Hassuna cultural phase of the north has pottery with painted and incised geometric decorations. There are also some animal and human figurines, but otherwise no other representations. The Hassuna pottery assemblage does not show any continuity from the preceding Jarmo phase and may have its origins in the central northern plain of Mesopotamia in the cultural phase represented by such early sites as Tell Maghzaliyah, Umm Dabaghiyah, and Tappeh Yarim.[127] Some of the cylindrical pottery vessels with slightly flaring rim from Tell Hassuna have close parallels in the Archaic Susiana 0 phase at Chogha Bonut and the Mohammad Jafar phase of Deh Luran.[128] Surprisingly, the typical late Archaic 3/Early Susiana stone hoes with a narrow tang, splayed blade, and bitumen coating occurred at the earlier level Ia at Tell Hassuna (Lloyd and Safar 1945, fig. 19:5). Otherwise, if there was a closer connection between northern Mesopotamia and southwestern Iran, it is not reflected in the material culture.

## Samarran Phase

The next cultural phase, Samarra, overlapped with the Hassuna phase before replacing it. Nevertheless, Samarran artistic traditions do not seem to have evolved from Hassunan ones, even though the precursors of some of the geometric compositions of the Samarran pottery[129] are found in the Hassuna pottery assemblage. With the Samarran culture, we see a well-developed style of pottery decoration that is for the most part markedly tectonic in arrangement. The simplest composition is the superimposed goats on a sherd from Chogha Mami (Oates 1969, pl. 31:A). Graves at the type-site Samarra have yielded bowls that illustrate the different ways of decorating circular fields on the interiors of bowls (Herzfeld 1930). Frequently, the center of the circle is not emphasized but is framed by the linear bodies of two or four goats, whose long, curved horns emphasize the circumference of the circle and give a torsional feeling to the pattern. In other cases, the center is occupied by a square, to each corner of which is attached a triangle; long necks and horns together with little tails change the geometric triangles into goats. In another case, the center is marked by a swastika, and stylized birds with fish dangling from their beaks provide radial elements, a composition that later develops into complex patterns in Susiana and southern Mesopotamia. The arrangement of the painted, stylized figures of women with long flowing hair is analogous to the circle of goats. The representational motifs are set into a framework of geometric elements such as "pegs" and meanders that are densely arranged in sharply defined borders. Only one bowl, found at Tell es-Sawwan, bears on its interior surface many birds without any marked tectonic arrangement. It is far more "fussy" than the normal Samarran compositions.

Occasionally, a human face was painted on Samarran vessels. A fragmentary Samarran jar from level V at Tell Hassuna (fig. 3a:YY)[130] is the best-known example of the sophistication of Samarran artists. In its original, intact shape the entire vessel could be seen as a hollow statuette in the round representing a human with a bulbous body and thick neck. The hair, parted in the middle, is represented by a series of vertical chevrons. The face is detailed and highly decorated. The "coffee-bean" eyes (so characteristic of the later Ubaid figurines), eyebrows, tattooed cheeks, and hair anticipate the later Chogha Mami (Oates 1969, pl. 25:a–f) and Archaic Susiana 3 clay figurines, culminating in the late Ubaid clay figurines of southern Mesopotamia.

More surprising than the terra-cotta figures are those carved in stone from the contemporary graves at Tell es-Sawwan (el-Wailly and Abu es-Soof 1965). These female figures are rendered in a fashion that is neither markedly abstract nor markedly realistic. Some have their arms at their sides while others hold them crossed at the waist. The most elaborate element of these figurines is the inlaid eyes. The stone figurines have no contemporary parallels

125. See Braidwood and Howe 1960, pl. 15:12–17; Braidwood et al. 1983, fig. 105; and especially Lamberg-Karlovsky and Sabloff 1979, pl. 2.7; Mortensen 1964, fig. 17:a–c.
126. See Alizadeh 2003a.
127. Munchaev, Merpert, and Bader 1984; Kirkbride 1972, 1973a, 1973b, 1975; Bader 1993; Bader, Merpert, and Munchaev 1981.
128. Compare, for example, Lloyd and Safar 1945, fig. 3:5; and Hole, Flannery, and Neely 1969, fig. 44:D.
129. Namely the use of chevrons, zigzags, diagonal lines, pendant triangles, and wide hatched crossing bands on the interior of some bowls (Lloyd and Safar 1945, fig. 2).
130. See also Lloyd and Safar 1945, fig. 1:2.

and their characteristic inlaid eyes recur much later, in Late Uruk and Early Dynastic stone statues in Mesopotamia, with no apparent intermediate links.

### Halaf Phase

The Halaf period brings to northern Mesopotamia a new style of pottery decoration, which Helene Kantor conversationally characterized as "more Rococo and much fussier than Samarra." Nevertheless, there must have been a phase when Halaf potters absorbed some of the Samarran traditions. To be sure, the squaring-of-the-circle scheme, that is, the central square with triangles attached to the corners, known from both Samarran and the contemporary cultures of Eridu in the south and Early Susiana in the southeast, reappears on the famous polychrome Halaf bowls (Mallowan and Rose 1933, pls. 14–15). The central rosette with either a few or many rays, used in the third phase of the Ubaid period (Ubaid 2/Haji Mohammed) and in the early Middle Susiana phase, occurs frequently on the Halaf bowls. These center motifs are accompanied by small motifs, including dotted circles, resulting in a finely subdivided network of patterns. For the most part, the circular designs are radially symmetrical and torsional elements are much rarer than in the earlier Samarran culture.

Naturalistic motifs appear in the Halaf style but are rather limited. The most common animal motif is the bucranium, which was stylized in a variety of ways. Snakes and birds also appear. Many small birds fill a triangular panel on the closely painted sides of jars from Tell Hassan (Fiorina 1984, fig. 31; 1987, fig. 5). However, none of these examples prepares us for a unique straight-sided bowl found at Arpachiya (Hijjara 1997, pl. 48A). A number of panels on the exterior of this vessel are filled with geometric elements or bucrania, but one has what may be called an episodic representation in which, presumably, the "highlights" of a narrative are depicted; the missing parts of the narrative would have to be supplied by the prehistoric viewer. The scene is found on a large jar; the upper part depicts two men who seem to clamber in order to dip into the contents of a gigantic high-neck jar. Another representational scene consists of a striding hunter shooting at a feline, flanked by a bovine and two women standing on either side of an upright loom. The flat bottom of the painted jar has an enigmatic design that seems to be a structure with steps leading up to an altar or emblem. We cannot identify this last motif, but the sudden appearance of representations painted individually without any regard to formal considerations shows us how little we know of the range of the arts of the Halaf period.

The Halaf culture is thus distinguished by a sophisticated tradition of pottery painting characterized by a strongly abstract orientation in which the limited number of representational motifs are geometricized. However, as mentioned before, the unique bowl from Hijjara's excavations at Arpachiya proves the unexpected existence of a primarily representational aspect with quite complex groups of motifs. We must assume that comparably painted vessels existed. The analogies between the Hijjara bowl and the flask in the form of a woman from Tappeh Yarim indicate a consistency of style. The influence of the Halaf style spread far, even to the northern coast of Syria, at Ras Shamra and in the Amuq. It remains doubtful that Halaf tradition "crossed" the Tigris, much less appeared in the Zagros as what is known locally as "J" ware (Levine and Young 1987). However, it does not seem to have bequeathed any lasting legacy to the decorative art of the later periods. Instead, it is replaced in northern Mesopotamia by a developed stage of the Ubaid material culture — particularly the pottery and architectural styles — from the south, and in the west by later stages of the local sequence.

## SOUTHERN MESOPOTAMIA

### Ubaid 0 (el-Oueili) Phase

The art historian will have to look at the northern Mesopotamian prehistoric cultures to find antecedents to the explosive representational art of the Uruk period in the south, for to date, none of the prehistoric cultures of lower Mesopotamia offer any clues to the Uruk representational art.

In southern Mesopotamia, recent excavations at the site of Tell el-Oueili have brought to light a cultural stage antedating the earliest known Ubaid phase at Eridu (i.e., Ubaid 1). Finally, the long-hypothesized early phase of the southern sequence is taking substance. The pottery decoration, so far as we know it, is purely geometric and reminiscent of the geometric motifs of the close-line ware of the Archaic Susiana 3 phase in Khuzestan, but in a simplified and degenerated state. A comparative analysis of the Samarran-related close-line ware in Susiana and Deh Luran, the Chogha Mami Transitional ware from the Mandali region of central Mesopotamia, and the pottery of Ubaid 0 at el-Oueili reveal the limited nature of the repertoire of designs in southern Mesopotamia. This, however, may be considered as regional variations of a single tradition, for the great Samarran architectural tradition of Tell es-Sawwan with large, multi-room structures and corner buttresses continued later at Chogha Mami (Oates 1969, pl. 24) and Tell el-Oueili (Vallet 1996).

## UBAID 1 (ERIDU) PHASE

The Ubaid culture provides an outstanding line of continuity in the development of pottery and, especially, architecture. At Eridu the superimposed shrines begin with a very modest room that gradually was enlarged until the typical Uruk monumental shrine was reached. Furthermore, the large tripartite structures found at Tell el-Oueili (Vallat 1996, fig. 7), far more monumental in their layout than one would expect to see in a residential unit, are striking precursors of the tripartite plan typical of Late Uruk temples and possibly administrative buildings of the Eanna complex at Warka.

The next stage of cultural development in southern Mesopotamia (Ubaid 1/Eridu phase) exhibits strong ties with the previous phases. The deeper levels at Eridu represent the second phase of the Ubaid culture, where the pottery decoration is purely geometric. An important family of bowls that is known also in the Early Susiana period at Chogha Mish establishes a contemporaneity and a strong artistic link.

## UBAID 2 (HAJI MOHAMMED) PHASE

The Ubaid 2 phase, best known at the sites of Eridu, Ras el-ʾAmiya, and Haji Mohammed, has — like its predecessor — a geometric system of pottery painting and is strongly tectonic. Circular fields are squared by using central rectangles, from the corners of which triangles emerge — the same scheme that was already prominent in the Eridu phase and much earlier, in the Samarran phase in the north. In the contemporary early Middle Susiana phase in neighboring Khuzestan, there was much greater variety of squaring-of-the-circle patterns. Another frequent scheme in the Ubaid 2/Haji Mohammed phase is the radial composition on the interior of wide open bowls. In still other cases, the central circle of the interior of large bowls is occupied by a diaper pattern of windmills. Although the Haji Mohammed phase of the Ubaid culture has close links with the early Middle Susiana phase in Khuzestan, the two traditions already show separate lines of development. In the Susiana area, the decorative tradition was to become more complicated, while in Mesopotamia it was simplified.

## UBAID 3–4 PHASES

In the third, standard phase of Ubaid (Ubaid 3) and later (Ubaid 4), painted motifs are greatly simplified. Wide horizontal and wavy bands encircle vessels. Broad washes of paint were used, occasionally with a reserve circle in which a rosette was placed. In contrast, in both the Susiana and Deh Luran areas, contemporary phases have a highly developed decorative style with a number of representational motifs, namely, fish, tortoises, birds, goats, bulls, bucrania, panthers, human beings holding hands (dancing?),[131] and later, in the Late Susiana 1 phase, highly stylized goats and birds set into a closely knit frame of registers and panels. There is hardly a trace of this decorative wealth in the Ubaid phase of Mesopotamia.

The Late Ubaid phase has yielded distinctive terra-cotta figurines, the famous lizard-headed women and men. Female figures are much more common; the arms are crossed, either under the breasts or to hold a nursing child. The heads are greatly elongated, the faces are lengthened into snouts, and the eyes are represented by coffee bean-shaped pellets. Similar pellets also adorn the shoulders. The assumption that the heads are those of lizards has prompted speculation as to the superhuman character of the figures. The possibility exists that these are not really lizard heads but strongly simplified human heads. The deformed skulls that have been found in Deh Luran, and another from Chogha Mish that belongs to the contemporary late Middle Susiana phase, suggest the possibility that these Ubaid figurines may represent actual physical characteristics of some special members of the society (possibly the elite).

131. See Garfinkel 2003.

### TERMINAL UBAID PHASE

The Ubaid period merges into a little-known transitional phase with gray- and red-burnished wares, which in turn merges into the Uruk period. If we are to find some continuity from the prehistoric periods to the Uruk period, it is much more likely to trace it in the south where the Ubaid culture developed. In the north the sequence is not that of consecutive stages in a single material cultural tradition, but rather different traditions with different geographical centers. It is clear that we could hardly expect any continuous development. In southwest Asia, Susiana is another region where a long sequence of stages of a single tradition can be followed, namely, the Susiana tradition of Khuzestan adjacent to southern Iraq.

When we turn from architecture to representational art, which flourished in such an unbelievably rich fashion in the Uruk period, prototypes hardly seem to be present. As mentioned above, the painted patterns on the standard Ubaid pottery are of simple schemes. There is only one source where we could look for antecedents for the glyptic art of the Uruk period, namely, the stamp seals typical of both the Late Ubaid and Late Susiana 2 phase. In Iraq they are best known from northern sites where the Ubaid culture had been acclimatized at the expense of the western-oriented Halaf tradition. They bear a wide variety of motifs, including humans and animals that are often scattered on the field without any organized pattern. In the final phase of the Susiana prehistoric sequence, Late Susiana 2, stamp seals were also sometimes elaborately carved.

## PART 2: STYLISTIC ANALYSIS OF SUSIANA PREHISTORIC POTTERY

### INTRODUCTION

Prehistoric Susiana painted pottery provides one of the most delightful mediums and a powerful tool to study and trace millennia-old decorative traditions and their evolution in southwestern Iran. The large and varied corpus of Susiana prehistoric painted pottery also allows the archaeologist to study stylistic changes and to link them to stratigraphic observations, particularly the elusive transitional phases from one period to the next. Although the discovery of transitional phases is not crucial in the interpretation of the internal history of a given site, it is of utmost importance to establish a refined comparative chronology that can be used in dating surface collections in the interpretation of regional and interregional development and contact.

The Chogha Mish pottery corpus is extensively analyzed and presented in *Chogha Mish* I. Here, we limit our discussion to some general aspects of the various painted styles, decorative schemes, and techniques, as well as to the analysis of what we believe can be considered transitional style from one phase to the next. In addition, we also address the circumstances that resulted in the abandonment of Chogha Mish as Susiana's regional center and the establishment of Susa on the opposite side of the plain.

The early ceramic assemblages as reported from Chogha Bonut, Chogha Mish, and Tappeh Tuleii (KS-372), a small, low mound some 50 km northwest of Chogha Mish (fig. 2), consist of classes of pottery vessels with a number of distinct shapes and painted designs that seem to represent an unbroken and evolutionary sequence from the Formative to the Archaic Susiana 3 phase when the close-line ware (or Chogha Mami Transitional ware, as it is known in Deh Luran) was introduced into the sequence. Specific classes in the early Susiana pottery assemblage include: (1) the formative maroon-on-cream painted ware, (2) the Archaic Susiana 0 painted-burnished variant ware, and (3) the Archaic Susiana 1 painted-burnished ware (Alizadeh 2003a). These wares are well attested at Chogha Bonut, Tuleii, and Chogha Mish, but are poorly represented in Deh Luran.

### FORMATIVE SUSIANA PHASE

The Formative Susiana phase corresponds to the appearance of pottery in lowland Susiana and so far has been documented only at Chogha Bonut. A general explanation of this and the following Archaic Susiana 0 phase is necessary for an understanding of the re-evaluation of the periodization suggested by Kantor. The term "Formative Susiana" was coined by Kantor prior to the excavations at Chogha Bonut and was applied to the basal levels at Chogha Mish, which were characterized by a mixture of the painted-burnished variant ware and the standard painted-burnished ware. The stratified evidence from Chogha Bonut indicates that the painted-burnished variant was preceded by at least two distinct ceramic phases and therefore the term "Formative" cannot apply to the cultural stage characterized by the painted-burnished variant ware, clearly a latecomer. Based on our understanding of the pottery sequence at Chogha Bonut and Chogha Mish, we suggest the term "Formative Susiana" for the phase characterized by the coarse straw-tempered, straw-tempered red-burnished, and smear-painted wares. The latter seems to have been an experimental stage in decorating pottery vessels, as it appears to have been short-lived and so far is found only at Chogha Bonut. The discovery, existence, and stratigraphic position of this and the following Archaic Susiana 0 phase and their characteristic cultural assemblages are extensively discussed and analyzed in the final publication of Chogha Bonut and need no reiteration (Alizadeh 2003a).

When Chogha Mish was occupied in the early seventh millennium B.C., lowland Susiana had already been colonized by two small communities of farmers at Chogha Bonut and possibly at Tappeh Tuleii, a small settlement west of the provincial town of Dezful, northwest of Chogha Mish.[132] So far, the earliest evidence of human activity in the plain of Susiana comes from only one site, Chogha Bonut. The initial phase seems to have been aceramic with hearths, flint blades, and stone vessels (Kantor 1976/77: 23; Alizadeh 1996/97, 1997, 2003a). The following period, the Formative Susiana, is characterized by a simple decorated pottery, known as film-painted ware (Kantor 1976; 1976/77: 23; Alizadeh 2003a). Although very little is known about this early phase of settlement in Susiana, its existence is important in the study of the origins of agriculture and village life in Susiana and its relation to similar developments in the Zagros Mountains.

The earliest ceramic evidence from Chogha Bonut is classified on the basis of stratigraphy and stylistic variations. A plain, friable pottery constitutes the earliest stage of pottery manufacture in lowland Susiana. Some pieces of this class of pottery bear traces of red ochre, but with no discernible pattern. Another class of pottery, straw-tempered red-burnished ware, soon appears and overlaps with this coarse ware. The appearance at Chogha Bonut of solid architecture coincides with the appearance of another distinct pottery type, smear-painted ware.[133] Examples of this class of pottery are decorated using a finger as brush, hence the appellation, a technique that may have been employed on some of the famous Jarmo "tadpole" decorated vessels. Overlapping with and finally succeeding the smear-painted ware is the maroon-on-cream painted ware, known also from Deh Luran, and the painted-burnished variant ware, marking the beginning of shared artistic tradition with the early Deh Luran sites.

## ARCHAIC SUSIANA PERIOD

The entire Archaic Susiana period is characterized by the presence of a plain, vegetal-tempered ware, already present in the Formative Susiana phase. The occurrence of this ware throughout the sequence without any major changes in fabric or in shape suggests that Archaic Susiana represents a developing cultural phase with no break. The stratified succession of a series of decorated wares, however, has been used to distinguish four major phases. Based on stratigraphic position and stylistic analysis of the archaeological materials, the Archaic Susiana period is divided into four phases, the Archaic Susiana 0 (Alizadeh 2003a) and Archaic Susiana 1–3 (Kantor 1972/73). The earliest, Archaic Susiana 0, was found at Chogha Bonut, Tappeh Tuleii, and possibly Boneh Fazl Ali. Evidence of the Archaic Susiana 1–3 was found at Chogha Mish.

### ARCHAIC SUSIANA 0 PHASE

The Archaic Susiana 0 phase[134] is characterized primarily by the painted-burnished variant ware found at Chogha Bonut, Tappeh Tuleii, and Chogha Mish. The development of this comparatively sophisticated ware out of the preceding simpler wares is analogous to the appearance of the sophisticated Samarran pottery at Tell Hassuna in northern Mesopotamia and the appearance of the Archaic Susiana 3 close-line ware in southwestern Iran. While the painted-burnished variant ware appears with the maroon-on-red ware at Chogha Bonut, at the basal levels of Chogha Mish it is mixed with the standard painted-burnished ware, which is absent from Chogha Bonut and Tappeh Tuleii.

132. Tappeh Tuleii has been identified by its excavator as a "herders' camp" (Hole 1974, 1975). But this identification is not certain and the possibility remains that the site may be a permanent farming village (Wheeler Pires-Ferreira 1976/77) occupied somewhat later than Chogha Bonut (see Alizadeh 2003a).

133. Kantor termed this characteristic ware "film-painted ware" to underline the fact that on some of the examples the paint is so thin that the underlying surface can be seen. But the term seems to be misleading and, in any case, most of the sherds of this type have thick paint, hence the descriptive term "smear-painted." We chose the term "smear" to describe its highly characteristic technique of painting.

134. To avoid confusion in terminology and to underline the continuity of the cultural phase characterized by the painted-burnished variant with the following Archaic Susiana 1, characterized by the standard painted-burnished ware, we suggest "Archaic Susiana 0," following the example of the French for the el-Oueili phase (i.e., Ubaid 0).

Exact parallels for the painted-burnished variant ware and the maroon-on-cream painted ware have been found at Tappeh Tuleii (Hole 1974, figs. 11–14). In the nearby Deh Luran plain, the painted-burnished variant ware is scarce, but the maroon-on-cream ware is well represented. Thus, the evidence from these sites can now be fitted into the early cultural sequence of Khuzestan as established by the combined finds from Chogha Mish and Chogha Bonut.

The majority of the examples of the painted-burnished variant vessels are decorated with a series of closely spaced horizontal wavy lines, usually limited to the upper body of the vessel (fig. 3b:OO, BBBB–CCCC, III, PPPP). The wavy lines may either be continuous or divided into metopes with a series of vertical bands (fig. 3b:CCCC, PPPP). Both matte and shiny paint occur. Related to this decoration is a subfamily that can be divided into at least four groups based on the primary decorative scheme. These include (1) vessels decorated with a solid band of paint below the lip; (2) a negative chevron band or multiple bands reserved in a solid panel of paint (fig. 3b:OO); (3) those with overall decoration consisting of horizontal registers and pendant triangles; and, much less frequent, (4) vessels decorated with meanders whose interstices are filled with horizontal bands.[135] The edges of the border lines are often scalloped and the space between them reserved, anticipating not only some features of the standard painted-burnished ware, but also the tradition of fine reserved lines seen in the designs of the Archaic 3 close-line ware and the Early Susiana pottery. Of all the decorative schemes observed in this early stage of decorative art, the chevron — negative and positive, also known from the later Samarran pottery and sometimes consisting of several parallel lines — was perhaps the most enduring composition in prehistoric Susiana.

No sherds of standard painted-burnished ware were found at Chogha Bonut. At Chogha Mish, the painted-burnished variant co-existed with the standard painted-burnished ware, but it is not known for how long, or whether the standard painted-burnished ware existed from the beginning of the occupation. In any case, by the time the standard painted-burnished variant appeared in Susiana, Chogha Bonut and Tappeh Tuleii had been deserted.

## Archaic Susiana 1 Phase

The Archaic Susiana 1 phase is marked by the standard painted-burnished ware, a decorated, straw-tempered ware that is usually slipped and highly burnished (figs. 3b:OOOO; 73). The primary decorative composition on the examples of this ware consists of widely spaced fringed panels, rickrack zigzags, and zigzag registers superimposed by bands filled with various elements such as florets and what appear to be horizontally placed birds in flight.[136] This general composition continued in various combinations until the end of the prehistoric sequence, around 4000 B.C. The interior lips of most examples are decorated with either a solid band or a combination of solid band and two or three pendant semicircles (fig. 73:C), another Archaic Susiana motif that continued well into the Middle Susiana period.[137]

A series of closely placed stepped designs, each separated from the next by thin reserved lines, combines the much later Middle and Late Susiana stepped motifs with the Archaic and Early Susiana technique of meticulously rendered reserved borders.[138] Such taxing effort was replaced in the Middle Susiana period by incision, using a sharp stylus to scratch the intended reserved lines, a major distinction between some of the similar compositions of the Early and Middle Susiana periods.

Another enduring and recurring feature of the painted-burnished decorative repertoire is the group of pendant solid scallops or triangles (sometimes with a hook) on the interior lip or the exterior lower painted panel (fig. 73:B–C).[139] This simple decorative motif was used in a number of compositions throughout the prehistoric sequence. With the sole exception of possible stylized birds, no animal or human forms are depicted on the examples of the painted-burnished ware.

135. For an analysis of the meander and scalloped wavy lines, see *Chogha Mish* I: 243–44, fig. 36.
136. See *Chogha Mish* I, pl. 224:G–I.
137. See *Chogha Mish* I, pl. 224:C.
138. See *Chogha Mish* I, pls. 223:K; 224:C–F.
139. See *Chogha Mish* I, pls. 223:B–C; 224:D–E; 226:E–G.

## ARCHAIC SUSIANA 2 PHASE

The primary decorated vessels of the Archaic Susiana 2 phase belong to the red-line/band ware (figs. 3b:NN: 72:E–I, K). These vessels have a dense sandy fabric and are decorated primarily with a red paint. The most frequent motif is bands of chevrons bordered by solid triangles (fig. 72:D–E). The reserved zigzags and multiple zigzags in a broad panel of the Archaic Susiana 1 phase developed further in this phase into chevron friezes and became firmly established throughout the entire prehistoric sequence. During the following Archaic Susiana 3 phase, chevron friezes were bordered on top and bottom by rows of solid or hatched triangles (fig. 71:B), a composition that continues in various forms into the Middle and Late Susiana periods (cf. fig. 3b:NN with T, SSS–TTT, and 3a:HHHH). The evolved composition of chevron friezes is also prominent in the Samarran pottery.

The multiple stepped patterns of the previous phase, the Archaic Susiana 1, are now simplified and rendered as simple stepped lines.[140] A new motif of diagonal bands with basketry-like hatching is introduced (fig. 72:K)[141] and continues in use until the end of the Archaic period; it is seen on some of the examples of the matte-painted ware (fig. 71:E) and close-line ware in both Susiana and Deh Luran,[142] as well as on some Samarran vessels. The typical meander motif of the Archaic Susiana 1 also continues into this and later phases.[143] On the basis of its context, Kantor dated to this phase the base of a plate that was decorated with four human figures.[144] If this sherd did belong to this phase, then it represents the earliest unequivocal human representation on pottery in southwestern Iran.

## ARCHAIC SUSIANA 3 PHASE

The matte-painted and the close-line wares, two wares entirely different in fabric and to a lesser extent in decoration, represent the final phase of the Archaic Susiana period. The former ware has vegetal inclusions and the latter has fine mineral tempering. The matte-painted ware is the direct descendant of the earlier painted-burnished and red-line wares, while the close-line ware has features new to the repertoire of painted designs and shapes. Nevertheless, examples (e.g., fig. 72:a) of the close-line ware exhibit similarities in decorative motifs, composition, and technique to the earlier wares, as well as to those of its contemporary, the matte-painted ware.

### Matte-painted Ware

As in the earlier red-line ware, variously decorated chevron friezes bordered by solid, hatched, or negative triangles are the most common decoration (fig. 3b:HHH). The earlier fringed crosshatched panels of the painted-burnished ware (*Chogha Mish* I, pl. 223:B–C) evolved into a motif of solid "footed rectangles" (figs. 3b:YYY, 71:A)[145] bordered by broad bands. This motif continues and recurs in the Middle Susiana period in a variety of complex shapes and fringes.[146] The use of pendant scallops on the interior lip of open vessels, too, continues from the Archaic Susiana 2 phase and survives until the late Middle Susiana phase. The composition of triangles bordering single, double, or clusters of chevrons, so basic in the earlier Archaic phase and the Samarran phase, continues in this phase. In such compositions, the triangles might be reserved, solid, or occupied by filling motifs, a practice that continues well into the Late Susiana period (fig. 3a:TT).

Another prominent design of matte-painted ware consists of a bold checkerboard of crosshatched and reserved rectangles, usually with a single filling geometric motif (fig. 3b:ZZZ), a variation of the earlier "footed rectangles" (fig. 3b:YYY). This specific motif develops further in the Early Susiana period, when the geometric filling elements were replaced by a single or a column of flying birds (fig. 3b:AAAA). Human forms, perhaps already known from the Archaic Susiana 2 phase, are depicted with the same style of mannerism on some of the examples of this ware (fig. 3b:HHH).[147] Similar human forms also occur at the contemporary Chogha Mami (see Oates 1969, pl. 31:B).[148]

140. See *Chogha Mish* I, pl. 218:C.
141. See *Chogha Mish* I, pl. 217:E–F.
142. See *Chogha Mish* I, pl. 212:J; Hole 1977, figs. 52:a; 53:a; pl. 37:a, c, i.
143. Compare *Chogha Mish* I, pl. 218:A with 226 and 176:X.
144. See *Chogha Mish* I, pl. 217:I.
145. For a variant of this motif, see *Chogha Mish* I, pl. 213:D.
146. See *Chogha Mish* I, pl. 173:K–L.
147. The fragment published in the first volume (*Chogha Mish* I, pl. 217:I) with similar human figures painted on the interior base of an open form was misassigned. It is indeed part of the close-line ware assemblage.
148. A base plate dated by Kantor to the Archaic Susiana 2 phase (*Chogha Mish* I, pl. 217:I) is decorated on the interior base with four humans. The left and right arms of the individuals to the right and left are raised. Judging by the reserved triangles indicating the genitals, they seem to be female. This is almost exactly the way a group of two females flanking a male on contemporary potsherds from Chogha Mami is depicted (Oates 1969, pl. 31:B). What sets the Chogha Mish example apart is the curious mirror image of the four figures.

## Close-line Ware

The matte-painted ware is a direct descendant of the earlier Archaic Susiana tradition, but the close-line ware has no clear direct antecedent in the earlier phases. Apart from the fact that the constituent lines of the various compositions on close-line vessels are much more carefully drawn than those of the Samarran ware, the only major difference between the two ceramic styles is the almost total absence of animal and human figures from the close-line ware repertoire.[149] In addition, the typical Samarran central designs on the base of open forms are also extremely rare in close-line ware. What connects the Samarran pottery to the close-line ware is therefore not the similarities of certain individual motifs, but rather the shared grammar of designs that dictates certain combinations of motifs in the two styles of decoration.

The close-line ware also appears in southern Mesopotamia (Tell el-Oueili), central Mesopotamia (Chogha Mami), and Deh Luran (Chogha Sefid), where it is known as "Chogha Mami Transitional" ware. Although in general, close-line ware shows affinities with the ceramics of the Samarran period in upper Mesopotamia, recent excavations at Tell el-Oueili, near Larsa, have revealed stratified layers that predate the Ubaid 1/Eridu period and contain pottery similar to the close-line ware of Chogha Mish (Calvet 1983, 1985/86, 1986). It must be noted, however, that the complexity and variety of the close-line ware decorative schemes, as well as its high quality, are unmatched by what is known at Tell el-Oueili, but much closer to those from Chogha Sefid, in Deh Luran.

The close-line ware exhibits a tremendous burst of new decorative motifs and compositions, as well as new shapes. A close look reveals some underlying similarities in structure and grammar of design to the matte-painted and the earlier wares as well. Carinated bowls were usually adorned on the interior with the distinct decoration that consists of pendant hatched triangles, groups of three or four straight vertical lines, usually linked by cross strokes, and horizontal wavy lines (fig. 3b:II–MM, GGG). While these interior decorative elements are new, the typical earlier combination of a solid band, scallops, or semicircles on the interior lips of some close-line examples are not (fig. 3b:MM, OOOO).[150]

On the exterior of some specimens, single, double, or even triple groups of diagonal lines separated by blank panels are prominent (figs. 3b:MM; 66:A, C, H). This motif continues into the following Early Susiana period (figs. 3a:R; 56:D). A variant of this motif combines decorated pendant triangles (on the interior) with a row of single, double, or clusters of Xs on the exterior (fig. 3b:II, KK). The combination of the Xs and pendant triangles continues into the Early Susiana, but now the triangles are simplified and usually have a dripping appendage or are linked to a rectangular pattern painted on the interior base of open forms (fig. 3a:HH). Such triangles are rare at Jafarabad levels 6–4, but the X motif occurs there in various combinations, albeit in a degenerated fashion. The composition of Xs combined with pendant triangles does not occur in either southern Mesopotamia or Deh Luran in the following Early Susiana period.

Another prominent Archaic Susiana 3 decorative composition at Chogha Mish, which occurs only on carinated bowls with their upper walls slightly turned inward, is the alternating panels of crosshatching and linked vertical lines (fig. 3b:DDD, abstract humans?). A modified version of this motif continues into the Early Susiana period at both Chogha Mish and Jafarabad (see Dollfus 1975, fig. 25:1, 4). Again, this particular composition is absent in southern Mesopotamia.

Typical decoration for closed forms consists of a solid band, a double register with alternating groups of paired and multiple lines ("pegs"), and a zone in which a wide reserved zigzag is filled with chevrons. This decorative scheme also occurs on some carinated bowls (fig. 3b:LL); it is not only related to the simple scheme found on many Samarran bowls, but also to the earlier, simple patterns seen on some Archaic Susiana 0 and Archaic Susiana 2 phase vessels (cf. fig. 3b:NN–OO, III with T, LL). Another specific Archaic Susiana scheme that occurs at Chogha Mish on cylindrical and hemispherical vessels is the frieze of opposing single or clusters of chevrons, separated by "hourglasses" and lozenges (fig. 3b:EEE–FFF). Such compositions continue into the Early Susiana period, as seen at both Chogha Mish and Jafarabad (see Dollfus 1975, figs. 21:6, 22:6, 23:8, 25:8, 28:3). They also occur in southern Mesopotamia but are absent from the published corpus from Deh Luran. The clusters of opposed diagonal lines separated by crosshatched triangles (fig. 3b:WWW), and its variants (fig. 3b:W–X, RRR–TTT, VVV), occur mostly on jars with flaring necks. When broad crosshatched bands (fig. 3b:TTT, VVV) replace the cluster of diagonal lines,

149. A glaring exception is a "scorpion" painted on a shoulder fragment found at Chogha Mish. See *Chogha Mish* I, pl. 211:S. Contemporary levels at Chogha Sefid in the Deh Luran plain also yielded a base plate decorated with long-legged birds and what appears to be a stylized human figure (Hole 1977, pl. 36:L–O).

150. For much more similar examples, see *Chogha Mish* I, pls. 210:C, E; 211:H, M–N.

they exhibit affinities in both structure and composition to the basic pattern of chevrons bordering reserved triangles of the Archaic Susiana 2 phase.[151]

The obvious affinities of the grammar of designs among the Samarran, Chogha Mami Transitional, close-line, and Tell el-Oueili wares cannot be considered as either incidental or simple imitation, though imitation, emulation, and movement of artisans (through interregional marriage, for example) may have contributed to the similarities we observe. Nevertheless, a common heritage for these early cultures cannot be ruled out. While the close-line ware and the Chogha Mami Transitional ware from the Mandali region in central Mesopotamia share many characteristics with the Samarran pottery, the painted ware of the Ubaid 0 at el-Oueili is only broadly similar to these. Whether the simple and limited repertoire of painted motifs and compositions of the el-Oueili ware is a reflection of geography or chronology is still an open question. However, given the fact that the levels with this pottery at el-Oueili were stratigraphically immediately below the levels with the Eridu pottery, we may consider geography as a contributing factor for the differences. What is more, based on the existing repertoire of painted motifs of the el-Oueili ware, it is difficult to imagine it as the direct ancestor of the complex and sophisticated Eridu ware.

## EARLY SUSIANA PERIOD

The Early Susiana pottery tradition is directly related to that of the Archaic period. A hybrid of the Archaic Susiana ceramic traditions developed in this period. Early Susiana pottery is clearly a direct descendant of the Archaic Susiana 3 ceramics, with the close-line ware as the main source of inspiration. Although the Early Susiana ceramic has many similarities with that of Ubaid 1/Eridu phase in southern Mesopotamia, many Early Susiana painted decorative motifs and compositions,[152] as well as the dominant plain, flanged vessels (figs. 3b:LLLL; 64:A-K) have no parallels there.[153] Such specific plain vessels are direct descendants of the Archaic deep carinated vessels and are limited in distribution to the Susiana region (fig. 3b:MMMM–NNNN). Despite a great number of similarities in this period among the potteries of Susiana, Deh Luran, and southern Mesopotamia, regional development along separate lines existed. It was not until the following late Middle Susiana phase, when the highlands became integrated into the sphere of interaction in southwestern Iran, that the Susiana pottery became distinct from that of contemporary Mesopotamia and developed along different lines, resulting in the mature pottery tradition of the Late Susiana 2 phase, best exemplified at Susa.

Direct descendants from the Archaic Susiana 3 phase are the Early Susiana bell-shaped bowls that are completely covered with decoration on both surfaces (fig. 3a:R). The interior decoration consists of tightly spaced horizontal brush strokes to form a solid mass of paint with narrow "slots" left unpainted. The outside decoration consists of multiple coalescing diagonal strokes separated by reserved diagonal bands filled with what appears to be schematic flying birds or other filling elements.

Prominent among the artistic developments of Early Susiana potters was the technique of transforming the interior circular base of open vessels into a square (figs. 3a:D; 59:A–D). This effect was achieved by drawing two pairs of widely spaced parallel lines that cross at right angles to produce four equilateral pendant triangles whose apices touch the four corners of the square. This decorative scheme, which may have been inspired by the earlier Samarran tradition (fig. 3b:H–J), became the basis for the complex circular patterns that are very prominent in the Middle Susiana period.

The technique of meticulously rendering reserved lines that border various elements of design retained its importance and continued, but the finely drawn parallel lines, typical of the Archaic Susiana 3 close-line ware, had become sloppy and almost coalesce (fig. 3b:T–U). Other designs, such as the alternating triangles bordered with solid bands, continued even into the Middle and Late Susiana period (cf. figs. 3b:W with 3a:P, TT, and 3b:T). In the Middle Susiana example, the crosshatched triangles are sometimes replaced by reserved ones (fig. 3a:N–P).

Bold contrasts between negative and positive elements of design that begin in the Archaic 3 matte-painted ware develop and become typical of the Early Susiana decorative tradition (figs. 55–56). The interior design of pendant triangles, the hallmark of the Archaic 3 close-line ware, and the exterior design of continuous Xs persist in the Early Susiana period, but were never combined on a single vessel at Chogha Mish (figs. 58:C; 59).[154] One sherd decorated

151. See *Chogha Mish* I, pl. 217:G–H.
152. For examples, see figures 3a:U; 3b:FF, AAA; 65:A–E; and 58:C.
153. The same is probably true about Deh Luran, but the limited number of published examples preclude a definitive conclusion.
154. At Jafarabad, the two patterns do occur on a single vessel (Dollfus 1975, fig. 29:3). It comes from Level 6, the basal level, and as such may be a surviving fragment of the earlier phase. All other examples with the X motif have plain interior; see Dollfus 1975, fig. 27:1–9.

with Xs presumably comes from an early Middle Susiana context at Jawi (Dollfus 1983, fig. 15:7), indicating that vessels decorated with Xs may have persisted even into the beginning of the Middle Susiana period. Another prominent Early Susiana type lip sherd from Jawi (Dollfus 1983, fig. 15:7) corroborates this suggestion.

Other surviving decorative elements and schemes from Archaic Susiana (and possibly Samarra) include single, double, or even triple groups of diagonal lines separated by blank panels (fig. 3a:Q–R); a frieze of opposing chevrons separated by "hourglasses" and lozenges; and continuous clusters of zigzags and chevrons bordered by cross-hatched triangles (fig. 3b:T).

Vertical tab handles appear in this phase (figs. 3a:EE; 63:D, H) and continue into the Middle Susiana period (figs. 3a:DD; 50:D). Decorated rectangular and, more commonly, circular pottery lids also appear in this phase (figs. 3a:FF; 62). They are curiously absent from Deh Luran and only one fragment of the rectangular type is reported from Jafarabad level 4 (Dollfus 1975, fig. 30:3), but they do occur at the nearby site of Jawi (Dollfus 1983, fig. 16:5). These lids are also completely absent from Mesopotamia and thus appear to be a Susian invention.

Elaborate decorations that completely cover the interior of some open forms developed in the Early Susiana period out of the more restrained Archaic Susiana tradition (figs. 3a:D; 58:H; 59:D; 60:F–G). The exterior of such vessels is usually decorated with a horizontal register filled with a zigzag band, normally thicker than the bordering bands (fig. 58:D–F, I). Again, such bowls do not occur at Jafarabad and only one example is reported from Jawi (Dollfus 1983, fig. 15:2).

## MIDDLE SUSIANA PERIOD

Based on stylistic changes in pottery and stratigraphic observations, the Middle Susiana period is divided into early and late phases — Kantor's Middle Susiana 2 is incorporated into the early phase. In terms of pottery, the early Middle Susiana phase is a direct continuation of the preceding Early Susiana period and shares many features with the contemporary southern Mesopotamian pottery, that is, the Ubaid 2/Haji Mohammed phase. The second phase, late Middle Susiana, was a time of both substantial change and continuity in the pottery and in the regional status of Chogha Mish.

Various types of shallow and deep bowls with flaring walls bear the hallmark of Middle Susiana decorative designs that cover most of the interior and the exterior above the carination (fig. 3a:A–C, K–P). The interiors of these vessels are densely painted with a tripartite scheme corresponding to the base, the curvature below the carination, and the main walls of the vessels. Two concentric bands enclose the interior central field. The inner band is joined by cusps that radiate from the central design and the outer band is either free floating or joined to other elements. Among the various types of ceramic vessels in the entire Susiana sequence, such bowls exhibit the most varied and complex decorative schemes. The same can be claimed for the similar Ubaid 2/Haji Mohammed open bowls in southern Mesopotamia.

Specific to the early Middle Susiana decorative repertoire are the lip frieze of reserved crescents (fig. 3:O), occasionally grading to pendant triangles, and the oval fields in the central quadrants filled with fish, birds, and other subsidiary motifs on the interior of open bowls (fig. 3a:A–D). While the reserved crescents are common in both Susiana and southern Mesopotamia, filled ovals are found only at Chogha Mish. This specific decorative feature disappeared in the following late Middle Susiana phase.

Another specific feature of the early Middle Susiana bowls is the technique of covering the exterior of some open forms with large panels of paint with small reserved triangles between them (fig. 3a:C, O). Bowls decorated with such panels usually have a dense lattice grid of crossing diagonal lines on the interior walls. In the following late Middle Susiana phase, these grids become much more open and by the end of the phase the crossing diagonal lines are replaced by clusters of crossing diagonal lines separated by empty space (fig. 3a:M–N). Toward the end of the phase, the cusps are substantially attenuated.

Tab handles continue from the Early Susiana period with more elaborate decorations than before (figs. 3a:DD; 50:D). They disappear by the end of the Middle Susiana period. The common, intricately decorated lids of the Early Susiana period are replaced by much simpler but deeper lids (fig. 3a:XX). Early Middle Susiana lids have parallels in both Susiana[155] and southern Mesopotamia.[156] More sophisticated lids in the manner of the typical Middle Susiana radiating design also occur (fig. 3a:WW) but are extremely rare.

---

155. Dollfus 1978, fig. 17:7, Tappeh Bandebal levels 16–11.

156. Stronach 1961, pl. 57:7–9; Ziegler 1953, pl. 25:C.

Tortoise jars appear in the early Middle Susiana phase and continue until the end of the period (figs. 3a:BB–CC; 52). Their defining features include a lentoid body, hole mouth, and large flaring spout. They are well known in both southern (at Eridu and Ras al-ʾAmiya)[157] and northern Mesopotamia (at Gawra).[158] In Susiana the only site other than Chogha Mish that has these vessels is Jawi, north of Susa.[159] In the first part of the Middle Susiana period, the decoration of these vessels consists of a broad wash of paint that covers both the spout and the entire body above the carination (figs. 3a:CC; 52:A, D). Reserved narrow vertical bands or horizontal wavy lines provide the decorative patterns. Later in the sequence, the meticulously reserved lines seen on the Archaic and Early Susiana vessels are replaced by incised lines (fig. 3a:CC), though a few vessels still bear the reserved lines. The few tortoise vessels dated to the late Middle Susiana phase (figs. 3a:BB; 52:H, I) are invariably decorated with motifs typical of the phase.

Another Middle Susiana innovation is a peculiar class of pottery objects that, for lack of a better term, we call "stands." Their highly specialized form has a concave top with a circular hole in the middle and an open base (figs. 3a:AA; 51). The top is always highly decorated and the cylindrical walls of the base are almost always decorated with a row of zigzags bordered by two wide bands, a pattern already known from the Archaic period. If they served as stands for porous pottery vessels (not common in the period) and the hole is designed to drain the moisture, the need to decorate a covered space becomes superfluous. Such vessels seem to be limited to Chogha Mish; they are not reported from Mesopotamia.

A certain class of ring-based bowls appears by the end of the early Middle Susiana phase and as such may be considered transitional to the following late Middle Susiana phase (fig. 3a:NNN). This specific form, with its specific decorative design, is at home in Fars during the Tall-e Bakun B2 and Tall-e Gap phases. The walls of these bowls are unusually straight. The exterior walls are left plain save for two bands covering the lip and the ring base; the interior decoration consists of comparatively large motifs organized with reference to the lip, a scheme that contrasts sharply with the standard Susiana practice where the focal pattern is usually the center of the bowl. In this new group, the center of the vessel is left unpainted. In several examples, the areas of the three pendant triangles are subdivided into four smaller triangles; the middle one is left blank, but the three surrounding triangles are filled with crosshatching. Later in the phase, and particularly in the Late Susiana 1 phase, these divided crosshatched triangles are applied to a number of shapes and with more complex combinations of motifs (fig. 3a:OOO–PPP). Such triangles appear in Fars at the beginning of the Bakun B2 phase, perhaps slightly earlier than late Middle Susiana, but the earliest exact parallels are found on the famous Samarran high-neck jar from Tell Hassuna.[160] At least one millennium separates the Samarran and Middle Susiana periods, but it must be noted that the Samarran style of pottery decoration did not evolve from the preceding Hassuna phase and may have an Iranian origin, though no intervening culture has been found in Iran to fill the gap.

## POST-MIDDLE SUSIANA DEVELOPMENT

An understanding of the burst of innovative motifs and compositions of the post-Middle Susiana period rests on the overall cultural development in this phase. During the early Middle Susiana phase, the interregional pottery tradition of the earlier phases continued. Close parallels still existed between the ceramics of Susiana, Deh Luran ("Khazineh Phase"), and southern Mesopotamia (Ubaid 2/Haji Mohammed and Eridu levels XII–IX). The change in the Susiana ceramic tradition was part of larger regional developments. A number of surveys indicate that this phase was a time of population increase in southwestern Iran.[161] It was also a period of expansion and possibly migration from Mesopotamia to more marginal regions, such as those along the Persian Gulf coast (Burkholder 1972; Burkholder and Golding 1971; Oates et al. 1977). By the middle of the period, the number of sites in Susiana reached a maximum. Chogha Mish grew to be the largest settlement, a development paralleled in Deh Luran where at least two sites grew to more than 3 ha (Hole 1987: 37, 40). The sheer size of Chogha Mish, about 15 ha in this period, makes it the largest population center in southwestern Iran. Though the architecture is mostly residential, the evidence of a 10 × 15 m monumental structure (the Burnt Building) with thick plastered walls (1.50 m thick) suggests the existence of non-domestic architecture as well. The stacks of jars found in a back room of the Burnt Building imply storage facilities and perhaps distribution of goods, but the presence of many complete flint blades, flint chips, and nodules gives an indication of a workshop as well (Kantor 1989/90: 33–34).

---

157. Safar, Mustafa, and Lloyd 1981, figs. 72–73; Stronach 1961, pl. 56:3–5.
158. Tobler 1950, pl. 69:24.
159. Dollfus 1983, fig. 18:6–8; 23:7, 10.
160. Figure 3a:YY; see also Lloyd and Safar 1945, fig. 1:2.
161. Adams 1962; Hole 1987; Dittmann 1984; Alizadeh 1992. See also Kouchoukos 1998 for a comprehensive review of the survey results.

As described in *Chapter 1*, violence may have ended the Middle Susiana period at Chogha Mish, as suggested by the evidence of fire in the Burnt Building. This large Middle Susiana center, along with some contemporary sites, was abandoned, not to be re-occupied for perhaps several centuries. A similar development occurred in Deh Luran. These events culminated in major changes in the Susiana society by the fifth millennium B.C.

By the end of the early Middle Susiana phase, the interregional artistic tradition that was shared for at least a millennium between southwestern Iran and Mesopotamia seems to have ceased. There appears to have been a reorientation in the interregional contact. This development may have been the result, among other things, of the rising regional elite who sought resources that could be found only in the highlands. The following Late Susiana period was a time of increasing contact with the highlands, as suggested by the general similarities among the regional ceramics of southwestern Iran. A general westward shift of the settlements in Susiana also occurred. The large cemeteries of Hakalān and Parchineh in the Zagros Mountains appeared in the first half of the fifth millennium B.C.[162] As we discuss in *Chapter 1*, these cemeteries were not associated with any settlement and are located in an area unsuitable for grain agriculture, suggesting their use by mobile pastoralists. Similar cemeteries of later historical periods in this region reinforce this attribution.

## LATE SUSIANA PERIOD

Any interpretation of post-Middle Susiana archaeological data, from the lowlands in general and from Chogha Mish in particular, must in part depend on an understanding of the break in the sequence at Chogha Mish between the Middle and Late Susiana periods, on the one hand, and on the westward movement of settlements during that hiatus on the other. Thus, the following observations are offered in an effort to account for these events.

The painted ceramics of the Late Susiana period can be divided into two related but separate groups with known stratigraphic niches. One group is characteristic of the earlier part of the period, that is, the Late Susiana 1 phase, which begins more or less with the abandonment of Chogha Mish after the Burnt Building was destroyed by fire and sealed. The second group represents the entire prehistoric sequence at Susa and its contemporary sites, just prior to the Terminal Susa phase (ca. 4000–3900 B.C.).

Excavations at Chogha Mish and other sites in Khuzestan, as well as the ceramics collected from numerous surveys, demonstrate that the vessel types and painted designs that Le Breton attributed to his Susiana sequence "d" can be divided into two distinct classes of pottery representing two chronologically sequential phases. The characteristic shapes and decorative motifs that comprise Le Breton's earlier phase d can now be attributed to the late Middle Susiana phase. In Susiana this class of pottery is known from Chogha Mish, Jafarabad (levels 3m–n), Jawi (period II), Tappeh Bandebal (period II, levels 27–16), Farrukhabad (Farukh phase), and Tappeh Sabz (Bayat phase) in Deh Luran.

Numerous surveys have discovered examples of Le Breton's later phase d ceramics, but only three sites provide stratigraphically controlled evidence of this pottery class. In Khuzestan, comparative material comes from Tappeh Bandebal and Qabr-e Sheikheyn. In Deh Luran, Farrukhabad is the only site that has produced stratified materials for this phase.

The stylistic distinction between the pottery assemblages of the two phases is made based on both vessel shapes and painted designs. Some typical examples of the Late Susiana 1 phase ceramics that come from the Gremliza collection (Alizadeh 1992) are illustrated here (figs. 4–5).[163] The repertoire of the painted motifs of the Late Susiana 1 phase is large and varied. Naturalistic, stylized, and geometric motifs occur. The most characteristic examples of this class are bowls with a sharp carination near the base and numerous dots as a subsidiary design element.

Assigning surface collections to various chronological phases and periods in the absence of comparative stratified materials is, of course, filled with pitfalls. To avoid a stylistic selection in order to isolate a chronological phase, we rely mostly on the excavated materials from Tappeh Bandebal, Farrukhabad, and occasionally Qabr-e Sheikheyn. However, searching for parallels and diagnostics only among stratified materials is serviceable up to the point of establishing a chronological niche for the survey materials. The numbers of published examples from Bandebal and, particularly, Farrukhabad are limited. Even with a greater number of examples, the strong possibility remains that not all characteristics are represented at any given site. Therefore, pieces not represented in the excavated materials

162. Haerinck and Overlaet 1996; Vanden Berghe 1970, 1973a, 1973b, 1975.

163. Examples illustrated in figures 4–5 are *not* from Chogha Mish. The figures include pottery vessels discovered by Dr. Gremliza (Alizadeh 1992) in his survey of Susiana and are illustrated here for comparative purposes.

are included in the pottery repertoire of this later phase based on stylistic similarities and their absence from sites with a known stratigraphic hiatus between the late Middle Susiana and Late Susiana 2/Susa 1 phase (e.g., Chogha Mish and Jafarabad). Admittedly, relying on negative evidence is not an ideal way to date unrepresented pieces. It is, nevertheless, warranted and practical because of the well-known pottery sequence of Susiana and our knowledge of its relative chronology.

The change in the ceramic tradition seems to coincide with, or was the result of, changes in settlement pattern and some regional developments. Chogha Mish was abandoned after the conflagration of its Burnt Building, marking the end of the Middle Susiana period.[164] The site was re-occupied sometime during the Late Susiana 2 phase, probably when Susa was already a full-fledged town. Evidence from archaeological surface surveys indicates that during the period between the desertion of Chogha Mish and the founding of Susa no one site attained — as far as size is concerned — a central position as did Chogha Mish before and Susa later, with the possible exception of Chogha Do Sar (see *Chapter 1*). Moreover, there seems to have been a drop in the regional population as well as a general tendency for the settlements to move to the west of the plain (Hole 1987: 85–86).

The distinguishing marks of the Late Susiana period in the Susiana sequence not only include a characteristic change in the spatial distribution of settlements, but also a new class of pottery with stylistic links to the earlier local traditions and to those in the highlands. Nevertheless, there is substantial continuity from the preceding phase in the style and mannerism of decorative motifs. Thus, one might choose to treat this class of pottery as the final manifestation of the Middle Susiana period.

For several reasons, however, we consider the term "Late Susiana 1" more appropriate for this phase and its pottery repertoire, taking into account the following observations: (1) there seems to be more continuity from this phase to the Late Susiana 2 (Susa 1) than there is between this and the preceding late Middle Susiana; (2) a number of important constituents of late Middle Susiana pottery disappear in this phase, while a number of new shapes and painted motifs appear (e.g., fig. 4:A–F, H); and (3) the change in the pottery repertoire coincided with or was the result of some regional and interregional developments such as: (a) the abandonment of Chogha Mish as the largest site in Susiana; (b) the shift of the Susiana settled community from the east to the west; (c) the appearance of isolated cemeteries in highland Iran, suggesting the existence of developed and organized mobile pastoralist groups; (d) the perceived increasing contact with the highlands; (e) the development and specialization of other crafts such as architecture and administrative technology; and (f) the appearance of Late Susiana 1 pottery in the Central Plateau (see *Chapter 1*).

These observations suggest that the end of the Middle Susiana period cannot be considered as one of stylistic change in the ceramic tradition. Rather, the new forms and painted motifs seem to be a reflection of far greater socioeconomic and political changes that were paving the way to urbanization and formation of state organizations that appear one thousand years later. These transformations occurred at a historical juncture when there were signs in southwestern Iran and southern Mesopotamia of increasing socioeconomic complexity.

## Characteristics of Late Susiana 1 Pottery

The most prominent and readily recognizable element among the painted designs of Late Susiana 1 pottery is the dot motif,[165] a decorative scheme consisting of series of small dots usually arranged in horizontal rows accompanying solid elements, or scattered randomly on the surface of the vessel. These dots appear with simple geometric designs and stylized animal motifs. Various combinations of these elements usually appear on bowls with a sharp carination above the base and with cylindrical or slightly incurved walls (fig. 4:A, C–D). They also appear on cylindrical vessels with flat bases. Bowls decorated with multiple painted bands without the dots also occur (fig. 4:E–F). Another typical and new form is a deep, conical goblet with a shaved, pointed base and simple painted geometric decoration.

Bowls decorated with a series of concentric circles inscribing an "hourglass" or a "sun disc" also appear in this phase (fig. 5:A). These bowls seem to be absent from Farrukhabad and Tappeh Bandebal but are common

164. There is probably a Late Susiana 1 phase occupation on the High Mound at Chogha Mish, of which very little material (mostly sherds) was recovered (H. Kantor, pers. comm.). Moreover, recently I found a few sherds decorated with the dot motif in the Chogha Mish collection at the Oriental Institute. Even so, if Chogha Mish continued to be occupied during the Late Susiana 1 phase, it must have been an insignificant settlement. in addition, these few sherds can be attributed to a nomadic camp at the site, as it was an ideal location for camping as it is today.

165. Although in the majority of cases dots are used as filling or subsidiary motifs, following Henry Wright (1981a) we use the term "dot motif" because it is simple and graphic.

at Qabr-e Sheikheyn (Weiss 1976, fig. 20:110–11). Another prominent type, apparently absent in the Deh Luran plain but present in Susiana and in the Zagros Mountains,[166] consists of bowls with either concave or flaring walls (Weiss 1976, fig. 18; Dollfus 1983, figs. 71:8, 81:15). The latter usually have a sharp carination close to the base. Two narrow bands in reserve separate the central motif from the lip and base bands (fig. 4:G–H). The area between these bands is covered with paint, leaving opposed diagonal bands and equilateral triangles in reserve (fig. 4:H). In a variant of this type, the middle frieze is executed in the positive (fig. 5:C). This type is also absent from Chogha Mish and Jafarabad; since it appears in Bandebal levels 17 and 16, it may have started in the Late Middle Susiana phase and subsequently became popular during the Late Susiana 1 phase. Exact parallels and many other variants of this type of shape and decoration occur at Tall-e Bakun B (Egami and Masuda 1962, figs. 15:13, 17:8), Tall-e Gap (Egami and Sono 1962, figs. 14:7, 17:10, pl. 21:1), Tappeh Sialk (Ghirshman 1938, pl. 81:14), and Tappeh Giyan (Contenau and Ghirshman 1935, pl. 48).

Naturally, there is also evidence of continuity from the earlier Middle Susiana pottery tradition. Prominent among the carryovers are: large open bowls with a simple band on the exterior lip and a series of triple or quadruple diagonal lines or festoons hanging from the interior lip (fig. 37:C–D, G); the geometric design consisting of one or two rows of solid lozenges, bordered with multiple horizontal bands (fig. 46:B); small hemispherical jars (fig. 44:N); bowls decorated with a frieze of crosshatched triangles and a sigma motif (Wright 1981a, fig. 18:a–c); and jars with completely painted necks (figs. 46:A, E–F, I; 47; Wright 1981a, fig. 24:A, table 8).

Other prominent late Middle Susiana ceramic types that continue into the Late Susiana 1 include bowls and hemispherical jars with a decorative design that evolve throughout the Susiana sequence. The decoration usually consists of a frieze of large, bold zigzags; large triangles fill the interstices of the zigzags. These triangles are broken up into three smaller crosshatched triangles (figs. 5:D) and its variant (figs. 4:G; 44:R). A simpler version of this design appears first in the Archaic Susiana 3 phase (fig. 67:B) and continues into the Early (fig. 58:I), Middle (fig. 44:R), and Late Susiana periods.[167]

## Stratified Evidence for the Late Susiana 1 Phase

In an earlier study (Alizadeh 1992) we discussed in detail the evidence pertinent to the establishment of a phase between the destruction and subsequent abandonment of Chogha Mish and the establishment of Susa as a new regional center. This new phase not only represents the major spatial rearrangement of population centers and some sociopolitical upheaval in Susiana during the first half of the fifth millennium B.C., but it also represents a class of pottery that is akin to the millennia-old tradition of the lowlands. More importantly it has affinities with the highland ceramic tradition, primarily with that of prehistoric Fars.

The following discussion of the stylistic and stratigraphic position of the new class of pottery was published in Alizadeh 1992. Since then, only one study (Kouchoukos 1998) has addressed these issues. Moreover, no new body of related material has been published from Susiana. Thus we present our argument here in its entirety with some modification based on the analysis of Kouchoukos. The Late Susiana 1 pottery assemblage, as defined and described here, is found stratigraphically above that of the late Middle Susiana. This Late Susiana 1 phase pottery assemblage is extremely rare at Chogha Mish and seems to be absent from Jafarabad, indicating a gap at Jafarabad between levels 3m–n and 3d–l, and between the late Middle Susiana Burnt Building and the Late Susiana 2 occupation of the High Mound at Chogha Mish.

Potteries from Farrukhabad and Tappeh Bandebal help establish a stratigraphic niche for this phase. Bandebal's levels 28–10 have been divided into three periods, Bandebal I–III. Level 28 is assigned to Bandebal I, levels 27–11 to Bandebal II, and level 10 to Bandebal III. Period II is divided into three phases. The earliest, levels 27–19, correspond to the late Middle Susiana phase, levels 18–13 to "transitional" late Middle Susiana, and levels 12–11 to the period between the late Middle Susiana and Late Susiana 2 phase/Susa 1.[168]

Tappeh Bandebal level 16 seems to be basically late Middle Susiana, but with some carryovers into the following phase. Among them, large bowls decorated with sets of concentric parallelograms separated by solid bands

166. For example, see Contenau and Ghirshman 1935, Tappeh Giyan level Vc, pl. 48:22; Vanden Berghe 1975, fig. p. 56.

167. For various later examples of this prominent design, see de Mecquenem et al. 1943, fig. 112:24–25 (Buhalan); Vanden Berghe 1975: 56 (Parchineh, tomb A 30); Dollfus 1975, fig. 22:2 (Jafarabad); Dollfus 1978, fig. 14: (Jowi); Pottier 1923, no. 15 (Susa).

168. In her chronological chart, Dollfus (1983: 166–67, table 41) separates levels 12–11 from level 13 by a broken line. In the text, however, level 13 is added to levels 12–11 to represent her "période 12."

are noteworthy (fig. 4:B; Dollfus 1983, fig. 74:5). Another characteristic motif is found on some decorated bowls whose exterior is covered with paint with opposed hatched diagonal bands in reserve (figs. 4:H; 5:C; Dollfus 1983, fig. 71:8). These bowls do not occur at Farrukhabad but are found at Qabr-e Sheikheyn (Weiss 1976, fig. 18:92). Simple bowls decorated with multiple broad horizontal bands first appear in levels 17 and 16 and continue into level 11; this motif was later accompanied by dots (fig. 4:C–D; Dollfus 1983, figs. 65:1, 74:1–2, 83:9). At Farrukhabad this type is found in layers B 44–37 and A 30–24, indicating that the multiple bands motif appeared a little later than some other characteristic motifs (Wright 1981a, table 8). These bowls are absent from Tappeh Sabz, "Bayat phase," Chogha Mish, and Jawi, but common at Bandebal and Qabr-e Sheikheyn (Weiss 1976, fig. 29:3–4).

The pottery from level 15 at Tappeh Bandebal is not illustrated. Level 14 still has some late Middle Susiana pottery, but the prominent Late Susiana 1 bowls with sharp carination near the base appear in this level (Dollfus 1983, fig. 85:15, 17). It is interesting to note that these bowls, along with other Late Susiana 1 characteristics, appear first in level 19 and become frequent in levels 17–11 (Dollfus 1983, fig. 65:8–9, table 27).

Bold motifs combined with the dot motif, which constitutes an important constituent of the Late Susiana 1 painted designs repertoire, appear for the first time in level 14 at Tappeh Bandebal (fig. 4:A, C; Dollfus 1983, fig. 82:2). Another characteristic of Late Susiana 1 ceramic motifs in level 14 is the combination of opposed hatched bars linked by chevrons whose apices touch the upper and lower framing bands (fig. 5:C; Dollfus 1983, fig. 82:8). This motif and its variants occur at Qabr-e Sheikheyn (Weiss 1976, fig. 18:92–94) but are absent from Farrukhabad. In addition, some painted designs more common in eastern Iran also appeared in level 14. One example, found on a bulbous jar, consists of a row of crosshatched lozenges, probably an abstraction of a "lizard," linked by chevrons (Dollfus 1983, fig. 81:14). This design is absent from Chogha Mish, Jafarabad, and Qabr-e Sheikheyn but common in Kerman and especially in Fars.[169] The decoration consists of one file of crosshatched rectangles that are attached to one another and to the framing elements with small solid squares at their corners (Dollfus 1983, fig. 82:1). One example of this type was found at Chogha Mish (fig. 3a:BBB) and therefore may be a carryover from the late Middle Susiana phase. Late Susiana 1 motifs and shapes become dominant in Bandebal levels 13, 12, and especially 11. They include bowls with sharp carination near the base (Dollfus 1983, fig. 81:15,17), opposed crosshatched bars (Dollfus 1983, figs. 81:15, 82:8), and bowls decorated with dot motifs (Dollfus 1983, fig. 82:2). None of these shapes and motifs occur at either Chogha Mish or Jafarabad.

At Farrukhabad the Late Susiana 1 pottery was found in two excavation areas, A and B. Levels 31–23 in area A and levels 47–37 in area B are dated to the "Farukh phase" (Wright 1981a: 8, 57–60). Whereas Late Susiana 1 was the earliest phase reached in area B, in area A Farukh phase layers were found above the deposits of the late Middle Susiana phase ("Bayat phase" in Deh Luran) with no apparent gap. The site seems to have been abandoned sometime during the Late Susiana 1 phase and was re-occupied during the Protoliterate phase.

At Farrukhabad Late Susiana 1 ceramics were also found mixed with some late Middle Susiana carryovers, but the few published examples do not show the variety in shape and decoration found at Tappeh Bandebal and Qabr-e Sheikheyn. Tall beakers with narrow and pointed bases occur. In many cases, the base is scraped and rounded, but examples with shaved bases also occur (Wright 1981a, figs. 13–14, 24–26). The two examples that are reported from Bandebal (Dollfus 1983, fig. 83:2) and Qabr-e Sheikheyn (Weiss 1976, fig. 29:11) are plain. At Farrukhabad both plain and painted types occur; the latter has a simple design consisting of lip and base bands that border a wavy line framed by four vertical lines (Wright 1981a, fig. 14:a–b). These beakers are reported to be restricted to the Farukh phase (Wright 1981a: 26). Again, they are absent from Chogha Mish and Jafarabad.

The characteristic simple bowls with multiple band motifs and dot motifs also occur (Wright 1981a, fig. 15:H). Dot motifs typically occur on bowls with concave or flaring walls (Wright 1981a, fig. 17:a–g). Wright attributes a specific bold decorative element termed the "step motif" to this phase as well (Wright 1981a, fig. 19:a–f). This motif is not reported from Tappeh Bandebal or Qabr-e Sheikheyn, which may be an accident of discovery.

Certain shapes and decorative motifs of Late Susiana 1 pottery are absent from Farrukhabad as well. If not accidental, the absence of these shapes and motifs suggests regional variation rather than chronological difference. This suggestion is supported by the fact that several typical late Middle Susiana pottery types continue into the Farukh phase with no stratigraphic gap between layers A 33 (late Middle Susiana) and A 31 (Farukh phase).[170] The missing shapes and motifs from Farrukhabad include flat-base cylindrical jars, bowls with a sharp carination near the base

169. For examples, see Caldwell 1967, figs. 4–5; Lamberg-Karlovsky 1970, fig. 37:M; Beale 1986, fig. 4.21:C; Langsdorff and McCown 1942, pl. 61:2; Stein 1936, pls. 21:41, 28:27; Egami and Sono 1962, fig. 20:12.

170. It must be noted that most types missing from Farrukhabad were present in the Louvre pottery collection from Tappeh Khazineh (in the Deh Luran plain).

that is decorated with simple bands (fig. 4:C–F), open bowls ornamented with a series of concentric circles inscribing an "hourglass" or a "sun disc" (fig. 5:A), the combination of various stylized animals and dots, and bowls decorated with opposed hatched diagonal bands. Most of these shapes and motifs occur at Tappeh Bandebal and Qabr-e Sheikheyn (Weiss 1976, figs. 18, 20, 22).

## Evidence of Late Susiana 1 Occupation at Susa

The abandonment of Chogha Mish by the end of the Middle Susiana period cannot, of course, be equated with the disappearance of its large population and its resident ruling elite. If, as we propose, interregional conflict and security were the contributing factors for the Chogha Mish elite to relocate, we may be able to demonstrate this archaeologically, admittedly with the help of circumstantial evidence. It seems that Susa was founded as a large urban center. If the late Middle Susiana inhabitants of Chogha Mish indeed chose to relocate to the site of Susa, it is impossible to determine at what point during the Late Susiana 1 phase this happened. The purpose of this section, then, is to demonstrate that Susa was founded much earlier than is traditionally thought and as such is an excellent candidate as the locus to study the continuity of social complexity that started at Chogha Mish two thousand years earlier.

Susa 1 (Acropole levels 27–25) is known to be chronologically later than Tappeh Bandebal levels 12–11, Qabr-e Sheikheyn levels 5–2, and Farrukhabad levels B 37–47/A 23–31. It is also considered contemporary with Jafarabad levels 3–1, Chogha Mish Late Susiana 2 High Mound, Tappeh Bandebal III level 10, and Qabr-e Sheikheyn level 1. However, the following observations indicate that Susa must have been occupied at the least in the Late Susiana 1 phase when Chogha Mish laid abandoned.

As mentioned, the dot motif is a distinctive decorative element and an unmistakeable hallmark of the Late Susiana 1 pottery repertoire, providing a reliable, stratified diagnostic for this phase. This decorative element is absent from Late Susiana Chogha Mish, Jafarabad levels 3–1, and Tappeh Bandebal III level 10, all contemporary with Susa 1 levels 27–25. On the other hand, it occurs at Bandebal II levels 14–11, Qabr-e Sheikheyn levels 4–2, and Farrukhabad levels B 37–47/A 23–31, all earlier than Susa 1 levels 27–25. The presence of this and other Late Susiana 1 motifs at Susa argues for an earlier date for Susa 1 basal levels than traditionally thought, making Susa 1 partly contemporaneous with the Late Susiana 1 sites just mentioned and therefore much closer in time to the fall of Chogha Mish at the end of the Middle Susiana period.

The presence of the dot motif at Susa is indicated by various examples published from the site.[171] Other early motifs at Susa include bowls decorated with pendant scallops on the interior lip (fig. 3a:Z; Le Breton 1947, fig. 47:8), concentric bold circles framing a central element (fig. 5:A; Le Breton 1947, fig. 48:12–15; Stève and Gasche 1971, pl. 39:17), and bowls decorated with a multiple-band motif (fig. 4:E–F; Stève and Gasche 1971, pl. 34:23).

It can be argued that, as with the late Middle Susiana carryovers, the typical Late Susiana 1 motifs found at Susa are also survivors of the preceding phase and, as such, do not necessarily indicate a chronological presence of the Late Susiana 1 phase. This argument would be strong and convincing if other contemporary sites, such as Chogha Mish, Jafarabad levels 3–1, and Tappeh Bandebal III level 10, had similar assemblages, which they do not. The presence at Susa of the above motifs and shapes, characteristic of the Late Susiana 1 phase, and their absence from Chogha Mish, Jafarabad levels 3–1, and Bandebal III indicate that Susa 1 partly overlaps with the Late Susiana 1 phase and must have been founded sometime during the Late Susiana 1 phase. If further investigation and detailed analysis of the unpublished materials from Susa, or future investigation at the site, provide solid stratigraphic evidence for the above observations, then that evidence will be theoretically significant in the study of socioeconomic and political development in Susiana.

If we are justified in stretching the initial settlement at Susa to an earlier phase, then it is reasonable to suggest that Chogha Mish inhabitants sought to resettle in a less volatile region, away from the troubled area, and so founded Susa on the western part of the plain, if not immediately, then soon after they left Chogha Mish. This suggestion also helps explain the large initial size of Susa and its associated socioeconomic eminence from the onset, a development that must have started prior to the founding of Susa, whether at Chogha Mish or at some as-yet undiscovered site. Admittedly, this hypothesis can only be tested by precise radiocarbon dating from both Chogha Mish and from the deepest level at Susa, which are to date unavailable.

---

171. For examples, see Le Breton 1947, figs. 47:26–30, 32–33; and Stève and Gasche 1971, pls. 40:17–18, 41:35.

Following Veenenbos (1958), Kouchoukos (1998) discusses a geomorphological factor that might have played a role in the changing of settlement patterns in lowland Susiana in the fifth millennium B.C. Veenenbos argues that for much of the earlier Holocene the Susiana plain was rapidly aggrading. Based on an analysis comparing the dated basal levels at excavated sites in Deh Luran and Susiana with the elevations of the surrounding floodplain, Michael Kirkby (1977) concludes that aggradation was already in progress as early as 8000 B.C. and continued at a rate of about 0.6 mm per year until roughly 2000 B.C., when aggradation slowed and the major rivers began to incise the plain.

Kouchoukos (1998: 95–105) argues that while this holds possible for the Dez and Karun rivers, remnant levees show that the Karkheh River was a meandering system. Braided channels form when streams are charged with a high sediment load too coarse to be carried in suspension. In such cases, the load is deposited along the course of the river, forming elongated sediment bars around which the river diverges and recombines. In regions such as Susiana where the river channel gradient is steep and the bank material readily erodable, braided rivers form wide, shallow, and relatively straight valleys. Such river systems are inherently unstable, leading, in times of flood, to extensive deposition of fine sediments and also making them susceptible to abrupt diversions of flow.

According to Veenenbos (1958), the Dez and Karkheh rivers were migrating gradually westward for much of the Holocene period, perhaps due to the tectonic uplift of the eastern region of the plain. This uplifting may have generated a gentle northeast–southwest slope, dictating the direction of any artificial irrigation canals and the frequency of flooded areas to the west of these rivers. Veenenbos also observes that in antiquity the Dez followed the modern course of the Sia Mansur and Shur rivers, situated on either side of Chogha Mish. As for the Karkheh River, Veenenbos reconstructs three successive courses across the plain from the study of its relict levee system. The oldest followed the modern course of the Dez River; the middle course followed the modern Atig and Shaur streams, and the last one is the present course of the river. This suggests that Chogha Mish had been established next to the Dez River before it changed it course; it also suggests that Susa was founded on the east bank of the Karkheh River before that river changed its course to its present position.

Whether the events by the end of the Middle Susiana period were spurred by economic, sociopolitical, or purely geomorphological factors — but most probably the combination of all — the conclusion that Susa was a new home for the inhabitants of Chogha Mish, or at least its elite, seems to be warranted, but calls for further evidence and more specific data.

## Late Susiana 1 and the Highland Connection

As we mentioned before, during the late Middle Susiana phase, lowland Susiana turned its attention from Mesopotamia to highland Iran. Thus we consider the increasing interregional contact between the lowlands and highlands as a contributing factor in the changes that occurred in Susiana between 5000 and 3000 B.C. The perceived increasing interregional contact could have been the result of a myriad of factors, including the rise of the local population and regional elite, their desire for interregional alliances through treaty and/or marriages, and the desire to obtain highland natural resources, including mobile pastoral productions such as meat, wool, and dairy products. Consequently, a network of exchange could have developed in which material goods, ideas, political alliances (or "symbolic understandings" as Wright [1981a: 262] put it), spouses, and craftsmen would be exchanged. Pertinent archaeological evidence for such a network of exchange has eluded archaeologists. Nevertheless, the similarity between the ceramic assemblages of the lowlands and highlands may be attributed to a shared tradition among craftsmen and interregional marriages rather than to mere imitation.

In this presumed network of exchange, the artistic and stylistic influence seems to have been mutual. Evidence, though weak, suggests that some of the new types and decorative motifs and elements in the Late Susiana 1 phase were introduced from the highland, especially from Fars. The use of dots in specific motifs and arrangements, prominent in the Late Susiana 1 assemblage, has a long history in Fars, beginning at Jari B.[172] In Fars the dot motif continued into the Tall-e Bakun B2 and Tall-e Gap phases, contemporary with the Late Susiana 1 phase, and into the following Tall-e Bakun A phase, contemporary with the Susa 1 or Late Susiana 2 phase.[173] At Bakun A, more than one hundred fragments of painted pottery bearing this motif were found in all four architectural levels. Since Bakun

172. See Egami and Masuda 1962, figs. 14:3–4; 15:9.

173. For examples, see Egami and Sono 1962, fig. 17:6–11; and Langsdorff and McCown 1942, pls. 54:15; 62:6–7; 64:5; 65:5; 70:3, 5–6, 15; and 71:3, 10.

A and Susa 1 are more or less contemporaneous, it seems that this motif had a much longer life-span in its presumed homeland than it did in Susiana. Late Susiana 1 motifs also occur in Behbahan, Ram Hormuz (Tall-e Geser, also incorrectly known as Ghazir), Luristan (Tappeh Giyan), and in the Central Plateau (in the Qum area south of Tehran, Kaboli 2000, fig. 29), indicating their wide geographic distribution.[174]

One of the most interesting painted motifs, most probably of highland Fars origin, consists of an earlier version of the well-known Tall-e Bakun A motif of a canine (dog?) chasing or guarding a goat. So far, the only Susiana example was found by Dr. Gremliza (Alizadeh 1992, fig. 59:F) on Chogha Cheshmeh II in central Susiana. On this specimen, in the manner of highland tradition, the goat is rendered as a negative image. Good parallels are found in highland Fars.[175]

Rows of standing and wading birds bordered with solid bands appear first in the late Middle Susiana phase and develop into the long-necked cranes typical of the Late Susiana 2 phase at Susa. Exact parallels for the early version of this motif abound at Tall-e Gap in Fars.[176] Similarly, plain bowls with interior design of a series of clusters of pendant diagonal or vertical lines appear first in late Middle Susiana (fig. 37:C) and continue into the Late Susiana 1 phase. Again, close parallels are found at Tall-e Gap and Tall-e Bakun A.[177]

Other common lowland/highland motifs include a slash motif that decorated the reserved areas between solid rectangles, multiple-band motif, and rows of solid lozenges with elongated horizontal ovals in reserve.[178] This last motif, usually used to decorate bowls, first appeared in the early Middle Susiana phase in Susiana (Jawi I, L 16), Dollfus 1983, fig. 15:9–10) and became popular during the Late Susiana 1 phase in both the highland and lowland.

In conclusion, the later development of the highland states that successfully integrated the lowlands and highlands seems to have its origins in late prehistoric times. The shared artistic and technical tradition of the highlands and lowlands in the fifth millennium B.C. may be taken as a prelude to the rise of the proto-Elamite civilization and the subsequent rise of the various Elamite and Anshanite polities.

174. See Dittmann 1984, figs. 24:8–21; 25:1, 6, 9 (Behbahan); Caldwell 1968, fig. 1 (Tall-e Geser); Contenau and Ghirshman 1935, pls. 49–51 (Tappeh Giyan level Vc).

175. Egami and Sono 1962, fig. 21:5, p. 36:9 (Tall-e Gap); Sumner unpublished survey, site 5K2; Stein 1936, pl. 24:14 (Tall-e Saku), and several others in the British Museum's Stein collection.

176. See Egami and Sono 1962, pl. 36:3–5, 7–8.

177. Egami and Sono 1962, pls. 26:1–4, 27:1–2; Egami and Masuda 1962, fig. 10:1, 11:12; Langsdorff and McCown 1942, pl. 29:1–7.

178. At Farrukhabad (Wright 1981a, fig. 20:D), Tall-e Bakun A (Langsdorff and McCown 1942, pl. 48:12–13), and Tappeh Giyan level Vc (Contenau and Ghirshman 1935, pl. 46).

# CHAPTER FIVE

# ADMINISTRATIVE TECHNOLOGY: SEALS, SEALINGS, AND TOKENS

## INTRODUCTION

The crystallization of village life in the Near East coincided with the appearance of a class of clay objects known as tokens. The new economic and social environment of early Neolithic farming villages seems to have presented a strong incentive for a personal, if not interpersonal, mnemonic notation system, an exigency of life that does not seem to have been necessary in the earlier fluid hunting-gathering Upper Paleolithic communities. Nevertheless, Marshack (1972a–b) has demonstrated that abstract notation systems existed even in the Aurignacian and Magdalenian periods in Europe about 20,000 years ago. As Marshack noted, such a system need not be formal, representing actual numbers, rather it can be "an informal tradition whose basic system is the accumulation of sets and subsets, but the precise form or style of the accumulation was not culturally determined except in general terms" (Marshack 1972a: 825). Only relatively recently were such clay objects systematically analyzed and interpreted as tokens for numerical notation.[179]

Clay tokens of the early Neolithic period are simple in shape and have a wide geographic distribution in the Near East, occurring in the Levant (e.g., Beisamoun, Jericho), Jordan (e.g., Beidha, Ain Ghazal), Syria (e.g., Mureybet, Tappeh Aswad), Anatolia (e.g., Çan Hassan, Demircihöyük),[180] Iraq (e.g., Jarmo, Tell Maghzaliyah, M'lefaat), Iran (e.g., Tappeh Ganj Dareh, Tappeh Asiab, Tappeh Ali Kosh, Chogha Mish, Tappeh Zagheh), and Turkmenistan (e.g., Anau, Jeitun).[181] It is not known whether clay tokens developed in one particular region and then spread throughout the Near East. By the middle of the Neolithic period, around 5500–5000 B.C., clay tokens occur in association with monumental buildings, but the early stages of their development and utilization need not have been encouraged by regional economic impetus. Such simple systems of notation may have developed independently more than once and in more than one particular region. The human brain is hard-wired to seek patterns and to organize them into some sort of manageable form. This fact, coupled with the shared exigencies of daily life, would lead to parallel developments of simple mnemonic methods of recording numerical data with, for example, notches on a stick, a collection of pebbles (Schmandt-Besserat 1974; Lieberman 1980; Oppenheim 1959), or with a collection of variously shaped clay objects that were easy to make, store, carry, and count.

## PREHISTORIC EVIDENCE

The evidence of prehistoric administrative technology at Chogha Mish consists primarily of clay and stone tokens, as well as a few stamp seals and seal impressions. Small baked and unbaked clay tokens occur in all prehistoric Susiana levels (fig. 77:A–F, H–K, O, S). The similarity in shape and size of some of the prehistoric tokens to the ubiquitous Protoliterate tokens is taken by Denise Schmandt-Besserat as evidence of the evolution of these tokens into later abstract signs (see n. 179 for criticisms of her thesis). The most common shapes among the prehistoric tokens found at Chogha Mish are cones (fig. 77:A–F), discs (fig. 77:J–K, S), and spheres (see *Chogha Mish* I, pl. 231). Such tokens have a wide geographic distribution and are reported from many prehistoric sites in the Near East.[182]

Conical and disc-shaped tokens are the most common types in the Archaic period levels. They continue into the Protoliterate phase with only slight changes in size and in general shape. Among the conical tokens, three (fig. 77:C, F, I) are similar to the T-shaped, finger-shaped stalk, and chessman figurines of the Archaic period. While one of

179. For a full treatment of these objects, see Schmandt-Besserat 1977a, 1977b, and 1992; see Friberg 1994 for a critical review of Schmandt-Besserat 1992. See also Englund 1993, 1998: 46–51; Friberg 1984; Michalowski 1993; and Zimansky 1993.

180. Baykal-Seeher and Obladen-Kauder 1996.

181. For comprehensive bibliographic references, see Schmandt-Besserat 1992.

182. See Schmandt-Besserat 1977a: 4ff.; 1992.

these (fig. 77:I; pl. 25:C, lower right) may indeed be an example of the chessman figurines typical of the Archaic Susiana 2 phase, we consider the other two specimens to be tokens because simple conical tokens with a simple or flaring base continue to occur even after the Archaic period when T-shaped and stalk figurines disappear.[183]

No seals or sealings were found at Chogha Mish in the levels earlier than the late Middle Susiana phase. A fragment of what appears to be a round clay tablet (fig. 76:EE; pl. 25:A) is a unique, enigmatic object and may be dated by context to the late Middle Susiana phase since it was found under the floor of a Protoliterate room (see fig. 17:S18:902). Two parallel impressed lines divide the surface into halves, each bearing impressions of a triangular object (stamp seal?). This singular clay object has general parallels in the contemporary Deh Luran. From Tappeh Ali Kosh and Tappeh Sabz a number of flat oval-shaped pebbles were discovered. These objects bear on one side a simple geometric (in one example, floral) incised pattern (Hole, Flannery, and Neely 1969: 200–01, fig. 86). Whether the Chogha Mish "tablet" is related in function to these Deh Luran pebbles is impossible to tell.

Various types of Early Susiana tokens were also found at Chogha Mish (fig. 77:C–E, H, K, S). One example (fig. 77:J) is remarkably similar to Schmandt-Besserat's type III. Tokens of this type bear an incised or impressed cross that Schmandt-Besserat interprets as the Sumerian pictograph for sheep (Schmandt-Besserat 1978: 56, table; 1992: 22, fig. 18.3). One elaborate object (fig. 77:K, pl. 25:G) may have been some type of tool (i.e., spool, sinker, etc.), but clay utilitarian objects are not as a rule painted and usually bear signs of wear. Moreover, both sides of the disc bear a central cross much the same as the one depicted in figure 77:J and as Schmandt-Besserat types III and 3:7 with concave sides (Schmandt-Besserat 1992: 208). The continuation of this type of token from the Early Susiana into the Protoliterate phase can be bridged by similar tokens that occur at Susa; these have a central cross but are less elaborately painted (Schmandt-Besserat 1992: 25, fig. 19). A remarkably close parallel to the token depicted on plate 25:G is reported from a Late Susiana 2 context at both Susa (de Mecquenem 1934, fig. 16:2) and Jafarabad (Dollfus 1971, fig. 21:18), indicating the long evolution of this particular shape and painted pattern from the Early Susiana to the Protoliterate phase.

A truly unique object is a perforated disc-shaped plano-convex token (fig. 77:S). The closest parallel for this token comes from Susa.[184] Dollfus (1971, fig. 21:18) reports an almost identical object from Jafarabad. The difference between the Jafarabad and Chogha Mish objects are the two small depressions the former bears at its center. Another object (fig. 77:O) is tentatively considered to be a token because it is unbaked and thus useless as a sinker; it is also too light to have served as loom weight.

The majority of clay tokens datable to the Middle Susiana period are spherical and disc-shaped.[185] The few Middle and Late Susiana sealings and stamp seals found in the first five seasons of excavations are fully discussed in *Chogha Mish* I.[186] Surprisingly, no sealings or seals datable to the Middle Susiana period were found in the subsequent seasons. The four stamp seals illustrated in figure 76 (A–C, E; pl. 22:C), as well as the stamp seal on plate 22:A, date to the Late Susiana 2 phase. While some of these objects (fig. 76:A, C–D; pl. 22:A) are typical of the late prehistoric period both in the shape and geometric design, one (fig. 76:B; pl. 22:C) is different. The main motif on this seal is a single quadruped. In Iran, stamp seals with animal or human designs apparently first appeared in the final phases of the prehistoric period and continued into the Protoliterate phase.[187] Further, this object does not have a provenance and could well belong to a phase later than the Late Susiana 2 phase.

Only two clay sealings (fig. 76:U, Y) can be assigned to the Late Susiana 2 phase. These sealing fragments unquestionably belong to door sealings with multiple seal impressions, much the same as the late prehistoric door sealings found at Susa and Tall-e Bakun A.[188]

## PROTOLITERATE PHASE

The largest corpus of clay tokens from Chogha Mish belongs to the Protoliterate phase. Protoliterate tokens from Chogha Mish are fully discussed and illustrated in *Chogha Mish* I,[189] where Kantor discusses the Protoliterate seals and sealings not only from the first five seasons, but also those discovered during the later seasons.[190] In the

183. A number of conical tokens with fingernail impressions, discussed by Schmandt-Besserat (1992: 204, types 1:30–32), bear general similarities to figure 74:I.
184. Schmandt-Besserat 1992, fig. 36.3, bottom row, second from right.
185. See also *Chogha Mish* I: 253–54, table 27.
186. *Chogha Mish* I: 256–57, pls. 67, 234.
187. Stamp seals with animal and/or human design occurred much earlier in upper Mesopotamia during the Halaf period; for examples, see Amiet 1961, pl. 1.
188. See Alizadeh 1988a, 1988b, and 2005.
189. *Chogha Mish* I: 120–25, tables 11–12, pls. 40, 134.
190. *Chogha Mish* I: 115–48.

present volume we expand the published corpus of seals and sealings by adding the remaining recognizable pieces in figures 76 and 77. Here, examples found in the sixth and later seasons are illustrated (fig. 77:G, L–R). Two new types are depicted in figure 77 (N–O). They are classified by Schmandt-Besserat[191] as paraboloid tokens; their earliest type is represented by figure 77:I.

The only intact cylinder seal (fig. 76:D) bears superimposed rows of fish, a typical Mesopotamian Late Uruk/Terminal Uruk design.[192] The seal was found in the debris capping the monumental Protoliterate building in the East Area, suggesting the possibility of a later Protoliterate architectural phase there; similar seals were found in level 17 of the Susa Acropolis.[193] Two additional stamp seals (pl. 22:B, D) were also found in a Protoliterate context. The first example (pl. 22:B) is a stamp seal with a geometric design. The back of the seal is provided with a loop handle. The other stamp seal (pl. 22:D) has what seems to be a design composed of two feet depicted pointing in opposite directions. Stamp seals with almost identical designs are also found at Susa and Tappeh Yahya in Kerman.[194]

The various types of sealings found in most of the Protoliterate levels consist of door, bag, bale, and jar sealings, as well as clay balls, bullae (solid egg-shaped tags), and tablets. Six new examples of tablets are discussed here (fig. 76:CC, FF, pl. 22:F-K). One (fig. 76:CC; pl. 22:J) is a flat tablet with four impressions of a seal, the design of which is shown on another (fig. 76:FF; pl. 22:K). The seal impressions on both these objects were not created in the normal manner of rolling the cylinder on the wet clay, but rather in the manner of stamp seals. From the impressions it appears that the entire cylinder was pressed against the clay to make the impression of the whole seal. Similar cylindrical impressions do occur on square and rectangular tablets of the terminal Susa 1 phase, but the impressions on figure 76:CC were made with a plain cylindrical object.[195] The one example that is remarkably similar to these two tablets is reported to have come from Tappeh Sabz in Deh Luran (Porada 1969, plate on p. 57). Whether these tablets are evidence of the initial use of cylinder seals or whether they had special meaning and function is impossible to say with the available data. It must be mentioned that similar seals dated to the Late Susiana 2 phase were found at Susa, Jafarabad,[196] and Tappeh Sabz in Deh Luran (Hole, Flannery, and Neely 1969, fig. 103:N), anticipating the more complex administrative technology of the later Protoliterate phase.

The remaining tablets (pl. 22:E–I) are made of unbaked clay with no seal impression. They only bear numerical notations and as such must belong to the last stages of the Protoliterate period. It is noteworthy that these numerical tablets were found in P17:1102, a rectangular room in the subsidiary building of the monumental Protoliterate building in the East Area (fig. 16). The impressed signs include small circles (pl. 22:E), a combination of small and large circles (pl. 22:F), ovals (pl. 22:G), long strokes (pl. 22:I), and the combination of strokes and circles (pl. 22:H). Similar or identical signs occur on the clay tablets from level IV at Warka,[197] but the Warka tablets bear pictographic signs as well. Some of the clay tablets found in Tappeh Sialk level IV are similar to the Chogha Mish tablets in that they only bear numerical notations.[198] Level IV at Tappeh Sialk is dated to the proto-Elamite period, slightly later than the latest Protoliterate occupation at Chogha Mish. But if numerical tablets preceded those with combined numerals and pictographic signs, then Sialk IV must have started earlier. Susa has also provided similar clay tablets with only numerical signs and no seal impressions from levels 17A–17B.[199]

The representations on Protoliterate cylinder seals provide a vivid picture of the society that created them. It was a society headed by a ruler always represented in the same characteristic manner. He led his community in both religious observances and in battle. The cylinder seal representations also show ordinary individuals engaged in activities of daily life (craftsmen, hunters, and herdsmen). Animals both realistic and fantastic appear in many contexts with natural scenes and abstract compositions. The art bequeathed to us by the Protoliterate phase shows that this was one of the most innovative phases in the ancient Near East.

The bulk of the material illustrating the glyptic art of the Protoliterate phase consists of impressions of cylinder seals on documents (clay balls, bullae, and tablets) and on the sealings of doors, pottery vessels, and bales or packages of various sorts. The largest groups of impressions come from Warka, Susa, and Chogha Mish in the east, and

191. Schmandt-Besserat 1992, fig. 31, 21–22.
192. Similar fish motifs appear at Susa in level 17 of Acropolis (Le Brun 1971, fig. 43:10).
193. See Vallat 1971, fig. 43:10.
194. For Susa, see Amiet 1972, nos. 379, 409–10 (the latter are square in shape). For Tappeh Yahya, see Lamberg-Karlovsky 1971: 91, fig. 2:C.
195. A baked-clay cylinder seal found in a Late Susiana 2 phase level at Jafarabad is the closest to the seal that was used to impress the object in figure 76:CC, FF both in shape, size, and in geometric design (see Dollfus 1971, pl. 9:10, fig. 21:15).
196. See Dollfus 1971, fig. 21:15.
197. Falkenstein 1936, pls. 1–18.
198. See Ghirshman 1938, pl. 92:S.1631, S.1621, S.1619, S.1617; pl. 93:S.1625, S.539, etc.
199. See Vallat 1971, fig. 43:4, 6–7, 9; Scheil 1923, pls. 3:20–21, 23; 4:28–29; 9:70; 25:160; 28:184, and so on. See also Englund (1998) for an extensive treatment of the subject.

the Habuba Kabira sites in the northwest. Despite their small scale and usually fragmentary preservation, impressions document an amazing range of subject matter and style. Actual cylinder seals are rarely found, making their absence a tantalizing problem.

# CHAPTER SIX

# CLAY AND STONE FIGURINES

## OLD ELAMITE PERIOD

From the Old Elamite (Sukkalmah) occupation on the High Mound, a number of fragmentary baked-clay plaques with images of women were recovered. They vary in size and quality of workmanship but are typical for the period. Such figurines and figurine molds have been analyzed in detail (Azarpay 1999; Goodarzi-Tabrizi 1999; *Chogha Mish* I; Spycket 1992, 1995), we need not discuss them here.

The most spectacular object dating to the Old Elamite period is the goat-handled cup made of bituminous stone that was found on the High Mound in the ninth season (pl. 26:B). Though not technically a figurine, it is briefly introduced here; Kantor gives this object full treatment elsewhere.[200] The cup was found near the Protoliterate catch basin in N9:1005 (fig. 8) and, judging by the scattered human bones associated with it, may have been part of the funerary deposit of an Elamite grave. The cup is 14.25 cm high and the goat-shaped handle reaches a height of 16.80 cm; the diameter at the base is 7.30 cm.

Bituminous stone was used as early as the Archaic Susiana 3 phase. Bituminous stone vessels with theriomorphic ornaments and attachments appeared at Chogha Mish during the late fourth millennium B.C. and became widespread in both Iran and Mesopotamia in the second millennium B.C. Though the paucity of evidence does not allow tracing the evolution of such vessels, it seems that Achaemenid ibex-handled vessels were inspired by the Elamite tradition.[201]

## PROTOLITERATE PHASE

From the Protoliterate monumental building (fig. 16) came an outstanding bone figurine of a naked woman, only 3.55 cm high (pl. 26:A). The head is rendered crudely; two shallow depressions represent the eyes; and the eyebrows, lips, and mouth are indicated by deep incisions. The hair on the back is indicated by a gentle, flowing mass; at front, two comparatively narrow locks of hair rest on the breasts. The high-quality, naturalistic modeling of the figurine and its upright stance have close parallels from other sites, namely Uruk and Khafajah. The examples from Khafajah are furnished with a round base and provide the closest parallels for the Chogha Mish figurine.

Another fragmentary figurine of a female (fig. 78:G) found in the same building represents an abstract style much closer to the style of the prehistoric figurines. This baked-clay figurine primarily consists of a cylindrical body the upper sides and top of which are stretched to form the head and arms. Two cone-shaped lumps of clay indicate the breasts.

The Protoliterate animal figurines from Chogha Mish represent either dogs (fig. 80:A) or sheep/cattle (fig. 80:C). Though the animal figurines are well proportioned and naturalistic, no attempt has been made to represent anatomical and facial details. This style is much in accordance with the rendering of animals and humans in the glyptic art of Protoliterate Iran, as opposed to that of Mesopotamia where such features are usually rendered with care.

## MIDDLE AND LATE SUSIANA PERIODS

From the Late Susiana 2 phase deposit on the High Mound, a small but typical range of quadrupeds and occasionally birds or "rod/horn" figurines was discovered (fig. 80:I–J).[202] One figurine (fig. 80:I) looks like a decorated horn. In its broken state it is about 7 cm long, therefore the statuette from which it presumably comes would have been some 20–30 cm long. However, no such statuette, intact or fragmentary, has been found in prehistoric contexts. Furthermore, the thicker end of the object, which would have attached to the head, has a finished surface and there-

200. Kantor 1974/75a, 1974/75b.

201. See Kantor 1977 for a full discussion.

202. See also *Chogha Mish* I: 260.

fore was not broken off from the body. Similar decorated objects with unmistakably finished ends, reported from the Susa Acropolis,[203] make it clear that such "horns" were independent objects; perhaps they are tokens representing horned animals (possibly goats). Several pictographic signs found on proto-Elamite clay tablets from Susa look remarkably like representations of individual notched horns,[204] suggesting that perhaps one of these objects (fig. 80:I) might have been a token.

In the preceding Middle Susiana period the only common figurines represent presumably sheep and cattle; they are either decorated or plain (fig. 80:B, D–E, G–H; pl. 27:B). However, as a representative of Middle Susiana work, there is a less common and more sophisticated terra-cotta pendant in the shape of a bull head (fig. 80:G). It is not an isolated piece since there is one other example.

In contrast to animal figurines, human figurines are extremely rare in the Middle Susiana context at Chogha Mish. The two examples found can both be assigned to the initial phase of the period, early Middle Susiana. The more complete piece is a "violin" figurine with painted dots at the edge (*Chogha Mish* I, pl. 235:G). The head is broken but was presumably a round disc like the fragmentary head found in the ninth season (*Chogha Mish* I, registration number 9087).

It was during the Archaic and Early Susiana periods when figurines in human form seem to have been quite common, so much so that we can trace their gradual evolution over hundreds of years. Alongside the human figurines, both simple and occasionally more elaborate renderings of animals also occur. Outstanding among them is the stone figurine of a boar (fig. 80:F; pl. 27:B). In its overall simplicity, the piece is well proportioned and naturalistically rendered. With the help of a few simple lines, the major characteristics of a wild boar, such as snout, eyes, tail, and underbelly wrinkles, are indicated.[205] The figurine of a boar (fig. 80:F) has a perforation on the rump, suggesting that it may have been used as a pendant.

## EARLY SUSIANA PERIOD

Figurines of the Archaic and Early Susiana periods were found for the most part in the area of the Gully Cut near an underlying structure with a buttressed wall and massive pottery deposits. This may have been an area of special character, but the present data preclude us from any spatial-functional analysis of the context.

Evidence is steadily accumulating to indicate the gradual transition from Archaic to Early Susiana. This can be demonstrated in great detail not only from the pottery, but also from the figurines. For example, the Archaic painted torso (fig. 78:D; pl. 28:K) is very similar to a fragmentary mid-section (fig. 78:A; pl. 28:D), as well as a torso (fig. 78:E; pl. 28:A) of the Early Susiana period; all show the same rendering of the waist with horizontal painted bands and a lower body with vertical stripes.

Two examples of the lower body of a human figurine, complete at the base, have been recovered at Chogha Mish. It is noteworthy that in each case the fragment consists of one-half of the body in lateral section (fig. 78:G–H; pl. 28:C–D). This is no accident; the figures are made from two lateral halves that were pressed together to make the cylindrical figurine. A relatively deep cleft remained where the two sections were not bonded together. This is clearly visible in the fragment of a female statuette; between the bulging breasts one can see the deep cleft where the two parts of the object come together (fig. 78:E; pl. 28:A). This fragment supports the assumption that these figurines may represent women. All have painted details and can be considered lineal descendants of such types as the Archaic 3 examples (fig. 78:D; pl. 28:K).

Excellent parallels for these Early Susiana painted figurines occur at Jafarabad, where torsos with painted costumes show how typical such figures were for the period.[206] Unfortunately, no complete painted figures were found at Jafarabad. However, two figurine heads from Chogha Mish provide more evidence for what a complete figure might have looked like. One head (fig. 78:C; pl. 27:A) is 5 cm high and thus would have belonged to a figure of larger dimensions than the examples discussed above.[207] The neck, painted with a horizontal black band, supports the vertical stance of the head. The head itself is roughly circular with an attenuated crest that is not fully preserved. The facial details consist of eyebrows, "coffee-bean" eyes, and small pellets representing or decorating the ears, as

203. Stève and Gasche 1971, pls. 37:5–9; 93:7–11.

204. For examples, see Scheil 1923: 59, first column and tablet numbers 16, 32, 64, 83, 174, and 188.

205. The striking similarity between the Chogha Mish boar and that found by Robert Braidwood at Tappeh Sarab (near Kermanshah, western Iran), indicates a shared representation style and keen observation among the prehistoric artisans in western Iran (Broman Morales 1990, pl. 2:A).

206. Dollfus 1975, figs. 32, 33:11, pl. 18:1.

207. A composite reconstruction of this head and the mid-section of the body (fig. 78:A, pl. 28:D) is illustrated on the *Frontispiece*.

well as the now-broken nose that projected from the smooth surface of the face. Black paint is used to emphasize these details, as well as the edge of the face. Two broad bands of paint run diagonally from the middle of the forehead toward the ears; two others run vertically from the eyes to the chin. We have no way of telling for certain what these painted bands represent. Possibly they are tattoos or paint actually applied to the face; they could, of course, be merely adornment of the figurine without reflecting any real feature.[208] The broken upper part of the head could have been either a headdress or perhaps a rendering of an artificially elongated skull. Such intentionally deformed skulls have been found at Susiana sites. At Chogha Mish itself a very well-preserved elongated skull was found at the bottom of Trench XXII in Early Susiana context (*Chogha Mish* I, pl. 69).

The second figurine head is smaller and, in contrast to the first, is supported by a diagonally projecting neck. The head itself is disc shaped, slightly concave in the back, and without any real modeling in front. A large nose projects from the middle of the "disc"; the two nostrils are indicated by slight indentations and are emphasized by neat dabs of brown paint. The mouth is indicated in the same way, but less neatly. Round or ovoid pellets form the eyes and the eyebrows. Bold lines running diagonally down from the bridge of the nose cannot be indisputably equated with any natural feature. The periphery of the entire front of the face is painted; the paint runs onto the back of the head where it renders the hair. A cleft running from the top of the nose over the head and down to the nape of the neck is a noteworthy feature reminiscent of the cleft on the otherwise very differently shaped head of the Archaic 3 phase (fig. 79:A). Three diagonal painted lines on the back of the neck probably indicate dress.

The best parallels for the two Early Susiana painted heads from Chogha Mish are the Samarran period heads found at Chogha Mami, though none are identical. The closest in style are four somewhat disc-shaped heads, none of which is as geometric as our examples (Oates 1968, pls. 2–3:a; 1969, pl. 26:a–f). The general similarity is obvious and includes such details as pellets at the ears, the use of paint to represent the hair and to emphasize important parts of the face, and, in some cases, the diagonal stance of the neck. Dissimilarities include the more detailed rendering of the hair with curving locks painted on the forehead and even an indication of a plait of hair fastened on the back of one of the Chogha Mami heads. Perhaps an even more noteworthy difference is the more organic structure of the eyebrows, which connect to the nose, whereas in the Chogha Mish heads what we interpret as eyebrows float as discrete elements well away from the nose.

A fifth head from Chogha Mami, though in its flattened stance is quite unlike the one from Chogha Mish, has a projection issuing from the forehead that may be similar to that which once existed in the larger example (Oates 1969, pl. 25:a–c). Two more heads found at Chogha Mish are covered all over with a red wash rather than with painted patterns. The smaller head (pl. 27:D) is also posed on a diagonally jutting neck and consists of a simple rounded face with the forehead rising up, reminiscent of the Chogha Mami head just mentioned. The sweeping nose with its carefully indicated nostrils is perfectly preserved. The "coffee-bean" eyes are huge in proportion to the rest of the head. There is no indication of a mouth or any other facial feature.

The second and larger red-washed head (fig. 78:B) is more complex and even shows a slight amount of modeling in the chin and on the side of the face. This head is much less geometric than the other, although its eyes are very unrealistic, consisting of great modeled hemispheres crossed diagonally by a narrow, deep incision. The nostrils are indicated by a slight incision; no mouth is indicated, but on the chin a large plug is plastically rendered. Comparable plugs also appear on Chogha Mami heads (Oates 1969, pl. 26:c–d). The larger red-washed head exhibits a feature that so far is unique, namely the use of perforations. Two small holes appear at the ears and five on the top of the forehead. We may speculate that originally additional elements were attached by means of these holes to represent, for example, a headdress or hair. It is tantalizing that we do not know to what kind of figure these two red-washed heads were attached. They are, however, a good indication of the variety of figurines that existed in the Early Susiana period.

Another distinct class of small, seated figurines is represented by two examples. This type probably began in the final phase of the Archaic period but was certainly rare. From the Early Susiana deposit in the Gully Cut comes a tiny figurine, only 2 cm in length, which for its size exhibits very well-modeled buttocks and back (fig. 79:B; pl. 27:F). Large pellets form the feet, the huge breasts, and the three beads of a necklace. Alternatively, these latter can be taken as representing the nose and cheeks of the figurine. This possibility is much stronger because the characteristic head cleft is well preserved just above the three clay "beads." Another, fragmentary, figure in the same seated

208. Facial tattoos are still common among both the Arabic-speaking and Bakhtiyari women in Khuzestan, and it is not farfetched to consider the painted lines on these figurines as the same.

pose was also recovered (fig. 79:C). Excavations at Chogha Mami have revealed an elaborate figure painted all over and with the feet and arms indicated (Oates 1969, pl. 28:a–b, torsos). Several of the Chogha Mami torsos have necklaces represented by pellets more realistic in their proportions than on the Chogha Mish miniature figure (Oates 1969, pls. 28:c–d; 29:a–e).

No indisputable male figurines have been found at Chogha Mish. However, the general shape of one figurine (fig. 79:L; *Chogha Mish* I, pl. 236:C) is similar to that of the simple standing female figurines, but without the usual triangular region representing female genitalia. These figurines are usually unpainted, bend slightly forward, and have an incision at the back to indicate buttocks. They may date to Early Susiana, although they come from a mixed context. The buttocks are clearly modeled, but a raised button in front is either furnished with a shallow hole or with an incised cross. It is perhaps more logical to consider this feature as a navel rendered out of proportion.

Already in the Archaic Susiana period, relatively simple unbaked-clay renderings of animals occur and some are also known from the Early Susiana period. Fortunately some specimens were found that indicate the complexity of rendering animals in Archaic Susiana 3 and Early Susiana phases. A fragment of close-line ware painted with bands and dashes could not have been part of a vessel but can be reconstructed as the hindquarters or the horn of an animal figurine (fig. 80:J). If this specimen indeed represents the horn of an animal, the proportions of the original must have reached those of a statuette. In the seventh season of excavations, another mysterious fragment of close-line ware, which could not possibly be part of a vessel, was recovered (fig. 80:K). It is elaborately painted and possibly represents the hindquarters of an animal. This reconstruction is based on another painted piece of a horn found in the tenth season of excavations. The ware and the painted patterns on these three pieces are strikingly similar. A fragment of this size would have belonged to a figurine about 10 cm in length, therefore we can guess that the larger horn fragment might have belonged to a figurine some 18 cm in length. Such a figure would indeed have been an imposing work.

## ARCHAIC SUSIANA PERIOD

The Archaic Susiana period at Chogha Mish can be divided into three phases on the basis of the stratified finds of pottery and architectural remains.[209] The figurines from the Archaic Susiana 2 phase have a quite abstract and characteristic chessman shape (fig. 79:J–K, M–N). This class of Archaic figurines consists of a simple cylinder with a slightly concave top and base; in some pieces deep punctuations seem to represent the eyes, the nose, or the mouth. The vertical incised lines at the base of one figurine (fig. 79:M) might represent dress. Already in the Archaic 2 phase there seems to have been a tendency for slightly more naturalistic versions of the chessman type. This is indicated by fragmentary figurines in which the lower parts are modeled so as to suggest a narrow waist (fig. 79:J; pl. 8:I; *Chogha Mish* I, pl. 237:H).

In the final phase of the Archaic period there is a considerable evolution of the figurines and several different types can be distinguished. The chessman type has now developed into figures with a distinct head, upper torso, and skirted lower body. Based on the available evidence, the Archaic Susiana 3 human figurines can be divided into the three main categories of unpainted incised, painted, and painted-incised.

Much interest is devoted to suggesting details of the textile covering the lower part of the figure. One complete figure of this type has a triangular head with a pinched out flange in front to represent the nose (fig. 79:A). No other facial features are shown. In addition to the unpainted figures of the Archaic Susiana 3 phase we also see the introduction of painting, as on a relatively large head of the same triangular shape (fig. 78:D). Here, too, only the nose is pinched out from the head; all other details are indicated by paint except for the slight cleft marking the top of the head. Unfortunately, the lower body is missing, thus we can only guess that it might have been similar to the fragmentary figurine with a tapered waist (fig. 79:A). The lower body is slightly triangular in section. The hips swell out and the sides undulate down, presumably to a broad base, as seen in a similar figurine (fig. 78:F). A triangular area covered with paint and delineated with incised lines represents the pubic area. An incised vertical line below the pubic area separates the legs. The vertical and horizontal painted stripes can be taken as corresponding to the textile details of the dress.

209. An additional, earlier phase of the Archaic Susiana period was discovered at Chogha Bonut during the 1995 Oriental Institute-ICHTO joint project. This phase, termed the Archaic 0 phase, and represented by distinct, but related pottery, does not occur at Chogha Mish. See *Chapters 1* and *4*.

Two examples (fig. 79:F, H) are somewhat incongruous with the rest of the Archaic figurines. The latter (fig. 79:H) is stylistically much closer to the conical-skirted and chessman figurines. It consists of a conical lump of clay with a rough base. The breasts are molded out of the cone and the usual mid-section incision is applied between the breasts. The neck is indicated by a very shallow depression just above the chest. The lower body (or possibly skirt) is decorated with a few fingernail impressions. The other figurine (fig. 79:F), if indeed it is a figurine, is quite abstract. It is a solid clay cylinder, the top of which — presumably the head — is missing. The top of the preserved portion bulges slightly, suggesting a pelvic area. The cylinder is decorated with a ladder-like incised pattern on three sides. The fourth side, presumably the front, is decorated with a double ladder-like pattern. If this specimen is a figurine, then the incised decoration should be interpreted as patterns or fringes of the garment, similar to the Early Susiana figurine (fig. 79:D).

T-shaped or thorn-shaped clay and stone figurines are the most prominent type of all Archaic Susiana figurines (pl. 27:C). Whether such objects were meant to represent female humans is not clear. There are a few characteristics shared by other, less ambiguous female figurines of the same period that lend support to this interpretation. They occur in all phases of the Archaic Susiana period at Chogha Mish but began earlier, for they also occur in the preceding, Formative Susiana phase at the neighboring site of Chogha Bonut (Alizadeh 2003a, fig. 30:A–C).

As the name implies, these figurines have an elongated base from which a tapering projection rises perpendicular to the base. The apex of this projection is usually plain, as is the base. In some specimens, the base is decorated with fingernail impressions with or without a discernible pattern. In such cases, almost invariably the apex of the projection is also decorated.

The decoration of the apex is usually done by fingernail impressions, but sometimes with a combination of nail impressions and clay appliqué, suggesting facial features. The association of decorated base and the decorated apex seems to be consistent throughout the Archaic period. Stylistic analysis of another type of figurine from Chogha Mish, described above, can shed light on the iconography of the T-shaped figurines. The strong similarity between the lower part of chessman and conical-skirted figurines with the base of the T-shaped figurines strongly suggests that the latter represent seated women with splayed skirts.

# CHAPTER SEVEN

# SMALL OBJECTS, STONE TOOLS, AND STONE VESSELS

## PERSONAL ORNAMENTS

Prehistoric ornamental beads are rare at Chogha Mish, even though a large number of undisturbed graves were found in the course of eleven seasons of excavation. The available data do not allow a reasonable speculation as to whether this paucity of personal objects of semi-precious stones in prehistoric Chogha Mish is indicative of a certain type of socioeconomic underpinning at the site. Flannery (1999) argues that the rarity of exotic materials in Near Eastern chiefly societies may have been due to certain cultural behaviors that do not involve material objects, namely piety, skills in negotiation, and great religious knowledge.[210]

A few well-preserved beads from the Archaic and Middle Susiana phases are published in *Chogha Mish* I.[211] The few beads that were discovered in the ninth season belong to the Protoliterate phase (fig. 81:L–O). One example (fig. 81:P) is a painted cylindrical object that may have been either a pendant or a token. Pendants made of mother-of-pearl (fig. 81:Q–S) are more numerous in the prehistoric sequence. Two of these pendants (fig. 81:Q–R) are broken and have rough edges, thus the preserved objects may not represent their original shape.

Several types of studs and labrets of both clay and stone were used as facial decoration during the Archaic through the early Middle Susiana phases.[212] The double-headed (fig. 81:A–B) and T-shaped variants of the stud type (fig. 81:F–H) started in the Archaic period and continued into the Middle Susiana period. One typical stud of the Middle Susiana period (fig. 81:F; pl. 25:C) is representative of a large group of studs. This group is cut from white-veined black stone or dark-veined white stone in such a way as to produce a black or white stalk and a white "eye" with black "iris" or vice versa.

Various types of bracelets made of stone, bituminous stone, and terra-cotta were common throughout the entire Susiana sequence at Chogha Mish.[213] Two illustrated specimens (fig. 81:J–K; pl. 25:D–E) are triangular in section and at Chogha Mish were specific to the Early Susiana period, though other types also occurred in this period and continued into the succeeding Middle Susiana period.[214]

One pendant (fig. 81:I) represents a Protoliterate ornament in the shape of an abbreviated bird. Such pendants are made of both stone and shell.[215]

## CLAY AND TERRA-COTTA OBJECTS

Baked-clay sickles were common items in the Protoliterate tool kit (fig. 82:M–N). They are usually made of the same ware as the Protoliterate standard buff ware but were baked at such high temperatures that the color is usually greenish yellow or greenish buff. Such sickles appeared during the Ubaid 4 phase in Mesopotamia and were also common during the Uruk period. In Susiana, terra-cotta sickles appeared during the Protoliterate phase. The Late Susiana example reported from Jafarabad (Dollfus 1971, fig. 20:22), though generally similar in shape, is different in many details, particularly the bitumen-smeared groove intended to hold the flint blades.

Spools may have been used in textile and possibly kilim manufacture. Two types of "spools" occur at Chogha Mish, solid and perforated. A number of examples of the former type are published in *Chogha Mish* I;[216] one speci-

210. See also Stein 1994 and D'Altroy and Earle 1985.
211. *Chogha Mish* I: 224, pl. 234:W–BB.
212. That these objects were most certainly used for decoration is best illustrated by an Early Susiana terra-cotta example (fig. 81:B; see *Chogha Mish* I, pl. 234:A). Excavations at Chogha Mami also produced a number of clay figurines decorated with such studs (Oates 1969). In addition, one such stud was found against the mandible of a male skeleton at Tappeh Ali Kosh in the Deh Luran plain (Hole, Flannery, and Neely 1969: 235–36, fig. 109).
213. See *Chogha Mish* I: 256–57, table 28, for details.
214. See *Chogha Mish* I, table 28, for the temporal distribution of bracelets in various phases of the Susiana sequence.
215. For similar objects at Susa, see de Mecquenem 1934: 192, fig. 27:24; for Mesopotamia, see Mackay 1931, pl. 74:6 (Jemdet Nasr).
216. *Chogha Mish* I, pl. 126:Y–CC.

men (fig. 82:C) is perforated. Terra-cotta spools at Chogha Mish range in height from 4.7 to 6.2 cm and are usually found in groups of two or more. In Mesopotamia, similar spools, like sickles, occurred in the Late Ubaid phase and became common during the Uruk period; such spools do not seem to have become common in Anatolia until much later.[217]

Terra-cotta discs with a single perforation on the edge (fig. 82:G) is another type of clay object that appears to be related to the manufacture of textiles, perhaps kilims. That they were in fact used in such industry was documented by Marta Hoffman in 1964.[218] Again, this type of loom weight occurred earlier in both Mesopotamia[219] and Susiana;[220] they appeared much later in Minoan Crete.[221] Disc-shaped loom weights and their spherical versions (fig. 82:E) may also have been used as sinkers. The spherical type occurs in earlier contexts and if the disc-shaped type was introduced from Mesopotamia, they did not replace the earlier, round ones.[222]

Numerous painted mosaic cones were discovered at Chogha Mish (fig. 82:I–K). These decorative architectural elements were first discovered at Warka (Loftus 1857: 187; Heinrich 1932, pl. 7), decorating walls, niches, and engaged columns of the Eanna temenos. The abundance of these cones, both on the surface and in all Protoliterate deposits at Chogha Mish, suggests that numerous Protoliterate buildings there were decorated with these cones. Although no complete Protoliterate building was discovered on the High Mound, the dense concentration of baked-clay cones there indicates that they must have come from a monumental building that once stood at the highest point of the site.

Three examples of terra-cotta "pegs" (fig. 82:B, D, H) were found. These well-baked pegs have either a hollow or a solid shaft with a slight depression. Such objects are characteristic of the Protoliterate phase.[223] At Susa one was found in situ inserted into the central hole of a baked-clay square plaque (Stève and Gasche 1971: 150–51, pls. 33:1–16, 38). These objects were presumably set into walls to serve either as fasteners or as decorative architectural elements. At Warka similar but larger pegs (*Flaschenwand*) were placed in rows at the top edges of the high platforms belonging to the successive phases of the White Temple complex (Jordan 1932: 22–23, pls. 9, 17; Heinrich 1937, pl. 44:B).

Three other objects (fig. 82:A, F, L) are singletons. One (fig. 82:A) is reconstructed as a solid disc. It was found in an early Middle Susiana context but may well be intrusive. The absence of wear marks and the fact that it is painted on only one side suggests that the object may have been used as a lid for a small jar. The second enigmatic object (fig. 82:F) is a small baked-clay cone, perhaps a variant of the mosaic wall cone. The third object (fig. 82:L), a strainer, came from a Protoliterate pit that was dug into the prehistoric levels and, as such, may or may not date to the Protoliterate phase.

The pottery vessel in the shape of a hedgehog (fig. 34; pl. 29:A) is of special interest. Although it served to hold and dispense liquid and thus may be considered a ritual vessel,[224] its rarity, its special form, accessories, and meticulous incised decoration set it apart as a special and pleasing object, hence its inclusion in this section. The vessel is made of Protoliterate standard ware. A round hole is provided on top of the vessel (on the back of the animal) and a typical Protoliterate tapering spout is provided in such an ingenious way to represent the snout of the animal. Four tapering stumps and a narrow strip of clay represent the stubby legs and the tail. The projecting appliqués in front are provided with slightly crescent recesses indicating the eyes. This vessel and another vase, published in the first volume,[225] are among the most elaborately incised decorated Protoliterate vessels.

---

217. Lloyd and Safar 1943, pl. 16:B (Tell Uqair); Lenzen 1974, pl. 21:K (Warka); de Genouillac et al. 1934, pl. 44:1 (Tello); Mackay 1931, pl. 70:28–30 (Jemdet Nasr); Woolley 1955: 66, U.14466; 67, U.14941 (Ur, Pit F, Stratum H, late Uruk); Speiser 1935 (Gawra VIII); Schmidt 1932: 122, fig. 150:B 2686–87 (Alishar, Assyrian Colony period).

218. See Hoffmann 1964: 17–22; 33–36, figs. 4–6:42–43, 9–10:46–50, 13–14:18; see also Sheffer 1981.

219. See Boehmer 1972, pl. 45:38, 38w (Warka, Square K XVII, Anu Ziggurat area); Lloyd and Safar 1943, pl. 16b; Lloyd 1978: 46, fig. 14 (Tell Uqair, House A); Huot et al. 1980: 123, fig. 30:G, I (Tell el-Oueili). A variant of this type of tool with two perforations may also have been a loom weight. See Jordan 1932, pl. 20d (Warka, Eanna XVII); Boehmer 1972, pl. 50:140 (Warka, Steingebaude sounding, Layer 5); Woolley 1955: 9, fig. 14 (al-Ubaid).

220. A single disc of this type was found in a late Middle Susiana context in the seventh season of excavations at Chogha Mish.

221. See Warren 1972: 212, 243, fig. 96:7, 75, 77–79; pl. 73:77 (Early Minoan IIa and b). For an Early Minoan II example from Palaikastro and Late Minoan examples from Tylissos, see ibid., p. 212.

222. For a discussion of the various types of looms and their chronological and geographical distribution, see Forbes 1964: 198–206; Hoffman 1964: 5–16, 297–336.

223. Stève and Gasche (1971: 51) argue that at Susa such pegs apparently occur earlier during the Late Susiana 2 phase and continue into the Protoliterate phase.

224. On some Protoliterate cylinder seals and on the Warka stone vase, theriomorphic vessels appear as temple objects.

225. *Chogha Mish* I, pls. 116–19.

## SPINDLE WHORLS

A large corpus of clay and stone spindle whorls is presented and discussed in *Chogha Mish* I.[226] Here, we have chosen a few outstanding examples from the last six seasons of excavations at Chogha Mish, as well as one from a Middle Susiana deposit found at Chogha Bonut.[227] Surprisingly, no spindle whorl dated with any certainty to the Archaic Susiana phases has been recovered from Chogha Mish or Chogha Bonut. At the contemporary levels at Tappeh Ali Kosh in Deh Luran, few perforated discs made of plain potsherds are attributed to this period (Hole, Flannery, and Neely 1969: 205, fig. 88:a–c). Whether this is an accident of discovery or whether during the Archaic period a perishable material was used to manufacture spindle whorls is by no means clear.

The earliest recognizable spindle whorls come from Early Susiana contexts and are too sophisticated to represent early forms of this tool. The Early Susiana whorls come in three major types, each with slight variations: (1) painted plano-convex (fig. 83:F), (2) painted shallow conical (fig. 83:E), and (3) plain star shaped (fig. 83:G; pl. 25:H). Types 1 and 2 almost always have a denticulated circumference, often large enough to resemble cogs. The Early Susiana tradition continued into the Middle Susiana period when there was a considerable increase in the number of shapes and painted designs (fig. 83:A–D, H–I). Many Middle Susiana spindle whorl types became extinct in the following Late Susiana period, when the majority of spindle whorls discovered at Chogha Mish and elsewhere were plain.[228]

## METAL OBJECTS

The only prehistoric metal object found at Chogha Mish is a copper pin dated to the late Middle Susiana phase (*Chogha Mish* I: 250, pl. 65:P). As with the first five seasons, almost all the metal objects came from Protoliterate and later deposits.

A large number of metal objects were discovered from the East Area, but only those that are recognizable are illustrated here (fig. 84:A–D, F–H).[229] The only new type is a copper nail or stud (fig. 84:C) found in a Protoliterate context, although it must be dated to the Old or Middle Elamite period since it resembles copper/bronze nails used at the Inshushinak temple at Susa.[230] Another example (fig. 84:E) is a bronze arrowhead of the Achaemenid period.

## BONE OBJECTS

During the first five seasons of excavations at Chogha Mish, only a few well-preserved and recognizable bone tools were discovered.[231] The same is true of the last six seasons. The high concentration of salt and other minerals at Chogha Mish (and at the nearby Chogha Bonut) may be responsible for the paucity of bone tools. But, with the exception of the Late Susiana 2 phase and the Protoliterate phase,[232] all other phases are represented.[233]

A long, handsomely carved and highly polished double-eyed needle/awl (fig. 85:L), an awl with a shaft (fig. 85:J), and a ladle or spatula (fig. 85:C) belong to the Archaic period. Bone tools from the Early Susiana period are relatively more numerous. Pins or awls (fig. 85:B, D, H, K, M, O–P) are most common. Some (fig. 85:B, D; pl. 25: B) are so thoroughly carved that the original shape of the bone is no longer evident, while others (fig. 85:O–P) still retain the shape of the bone. The most exquisite example of Early Susiana bone-cutting technique is represented by an almost intact needle (fig. 85:I) with the eye still perfectly preserved. The illustrated examples of Middle Susiana bone tools represent all the types discovered during the last six seasons of excavations (fig. 85:E–G, N). Except for the difference in the type of needles of the Early and Middle Susiana periods (cf. fig. 85:F with 85:I), Middle Susiana bone tools are generally similar to those of the Early Susiana.

---

226. *Chogha Mish* I: 106–09; 251–53.
227. For a complete presentation of Chogha Bonut spindle whorls, see Alizadeh 2003a.
228. For a detail discussion and temporal distribution of various types of whorls, see *Chogha Mish* I: 252–53, table 26.
229. For other metal tool types, see *Chogha Mish* I: 105, pls. 29:A–H, 128:A–S.
230. See Jéquier 1900: 119, fig. 220; 134, figs. 333–34; de Morgan 1905: 79, pl. 47:4–7.
231. *Chogha Mish* I: 253–54.
232. A few bone tools dating to the Protoliterate phase were reported in the field books, but no illustrations are available.
233. For a more detailed description and discussion, see *Chogha Mish* I: 110.

# STONE TOOLS

The prehistoric and Protoliterate stone implements from Chogha Mish were analyzed by Daniel Shimabuku and are presented in detail in *Chogha Mish* I.[234] Figure 87 and plate 30 illustrate both the known and published types of stone implements, as well as a few types not presented previously.

Shown in figure 87:A–B are two bitumen-hafted flint blades from a late Middle Susiana context. This type of hafted blade must have at least started in the Early Susiana period because a number of such bitumen-smeared flint blades have been found in deposits dated to that period.

Figure 87:C shows an example of the well-known stone hoes of the Early Susiana period (see also pl. 30:A–B, F–H). The fossilized rope and the bitumen coating the shaft are exquisitely preserved as illustrated, but most of the stone hoes from this period bear only bitumen stains and sometimes only the impression of the rope. An exact parallel for such hoes is reported from a Late Susiana 2 context from Susa (de Mecquenem 1934, fig. 2:1). It is not certain whether hoes with roped handles continued to be manufactured for this long period, or whether this single example from Susa was found in antiquity and was used as a tool. In Susiana such hoes appeared in the late Archaic/Early Susiana period and continued into the Protoliterate phase; they appeared much earlier in northern Mesopotamia (Lloyd and Safar 1945, fig. 19, Hassuna phase).

Whether the example in figure 87:G is some type of a tool or simply a miniature tumbler is not certain. But since it is made of alabaster, it is not likely that it was used as a tool. A fragmentary stone pestle (fig. 87:K) comes from an Early Susiana context, but the type has a long history and appears in the sequence from the Archaic Susiana 1 phase (see also pl. 30:I–M). That the three ceremonial "mace-heads" (fig. 87:D–F) could not have been used as weapons is indicated by the narrow perforation with flaring ends that could hardly accommodate a strong, solid handle for practical use.

The example in figure 87:H, plate 30:D–E, is a variant of the common Archaic/Early Susiana saddle-shaped stone mill. Such objects are common in prehistoric contexts and are found at many sites in western Iran. Another example (pl. 30:N) is a phallus-shaped stone object of uncertain use. The shape may be accidental and the object may well have been used as a hammer or pounder, though admittedly no sign of use is evident on its surface. It is unknown whether the ball-shaped bituminous stone object (fig. 87:I) was used as tool or was shaped into a ball as a convenient way to store bitumen. Similar objects reported from Farrukhabad, in the nearby Deh Luran plain, from the much later "Farrukh phase" (Late Susiana 1 phase), suggest the latter possibility (Wright 1981a: 53, pl. 17b).

Balls made of sandstone (pl. 25:F) were commonly used in prehistory as pounders, but our example has a simple geometric motif incised on the surface in the shape of two triangles joined at their apices. So far, this is the only example of its kind found at Chogha Mish. In the Deh Luran area a number of incised pebbles are reported from Tappeh Ali Kosh and Tappeh Sabz dating to the Bus Mordeh through the Mehmeh phases (i.e., Archaic to Middle Susiana periods).[235] It is unlikely that this object was used as a tool, for its incised sign is exactly like that found on some Early Susiana flanged vessels, where it is called a "potter's mark."[236]

# STONE VESSELS

## PROTOLITERATE PHASE

Several types of stone were used to manufacture stone vessels in the Protoliterate phase, namely sandstone, alabaster, and a type of yellowish translucent stone. The bulk of the Protoliterate stone vessels found at Chogha Mish consist of fragmentary pieces. Few whole vessels survived (fig. 86:G, J, N, P–Q, S–T), showing the range of stone vessel types as well as the skill of craftsmen.

234. *Chogha Mish* I: 261–78.
235. Hole, Flannery, and Neely 1969: 200–02, fig. 86.
236. See *Chogha Mish* I, pl. 203, no. 104. During the first five seasons at Chogha Mish (and much more in the later seasons), about 104 different marks were found on the flanged vessels of the Early Susiana period. If these individual signs represented individual potters, then it is difficult to envision why so many potters were needed in a 5 ha population center. An alternative view would be that these signs represent individual families who shared the same collective pottery kilns and that the marks helped them to identify their own vessels. Kouchoukos (1998: 140) argues that such signs belonged to potters who shared huge bonfires to bake their vessels. But the sheer number of such signs argues against this hypothesis as well.

As with the examples published in *Chogha Mish* I,[237] the majority of whole vessels and vessel fragments consist of open forms, simple flat-base bowls being the most common (fig. 86:J, Q, T). Rounded-base hemispherical bowls, with or without a pouring lip, also occur (fig. 86:N, S). There is one example of a closed form, an exquisite four-lugged miniature jar (fig. 86:G). A vessel with a raised base is represented by a single fragment (fig. 86:P). The interior surface of this fragment is highly polished and thus the base may belong to an open form.

Simple open bowls with a rim band appear in the late Middle Susiana phase (fig. 86:O) and continue into the Protoliterate phase (fig. 86:Q), becoming somewhat taller and deeper. Based on the frequency of occurrence, the band rim seems to be a feature typical for stone bowls; the few pottery vessels with this feature may have been imitations of the stone type.[238] On the other hand, stone vessels with open pouring lips (fig. 86:S; pl. 29:B) may be an imitation of the common pottery type (fig. 26:E).

## PREHISTORIC PERIODS

The small corpus of fragmentary prehistoric stone vessels found at Chogha Mish, particularly those from the Archaic Susiana period, must be an accident of discovery. Excavations at Chogha Bonut (Alizadeh 2003a) and at Tappeh Ali Kosh in Deh Luran (Hole, Flannery, and Neely 1969: 107–08, fig. 42) have shown the skill and craftsmanship of Archaic stone cutters. Here, the only two complete pieces recovered from Archaic Susiana contexts are a shallow miniature bowl (fig. 86:A) and a miniature pot with a sharp carination (fig. 86:I). The most spectacular achievement of the Archaic stone cutter is represented by a fragmentary obsidian open bowl (fig. 86:F). The majority of stone vessels from the last six seasons of excavations at Chogha Mish, including those made of a bituminous stone, date to the Early Susiana period (fig. 86:C–D, K–L). Typical of the Early Susiana period are cylindrical vessels with beaded rims (fig. 86:C–D, K–L).

A limited number of deep and shallow bowls (fig. 86:M, O, R, U) and footed rectangular containers are made of bituminous stone (fig. 86:V) and represent the Middle Susiana assemblage. As with the stone vessels of the Protoliterate phase, all Middle Susiana stone vessels have parallel shapes in the pottery corpus of the period. No whole stone vessels or vessel fragments were found in Late Susiana 2 deposits at Chogha Mish in the course of the last six seasons.

# BASKETRY

Numerous fragments of bitumen bearing impressions of reed matting were found during the sixth season of excavations. The majority of the fragments are flat and thus part of the floor covers (pls. 29:D–E; 30:C) and are all that remain from actual baskets that were covered with bitumen.[239] All the illustrated samples (pls. 29:D–E; 30:C) are dated by context to the Early Susiana period. Smaller, less well-preserved Archaic samples have also been found in Archaic Susiana context in the East Area. Most of the Early Susiana samples are preserved well enough to allow the identification of the weave patterns. As in Deh Luran,[240] the majority of patterns are over-two, under-two twilled reed mat. The earliest exact parallel comes from the Hassuna phase in northern Mesopotamia (Lloyd and Safar 1945: 271, fig. 38).

237. *Chogha Mish* I, pls. 29:O, AA–CC; 124:A–FF; 125:A–E.

238. *Chogha Mish* I: 103, pls. 17:L; 84:O–P.

239. Similar rectangular and round baskets are still used in Khuzestan to carry and store dates.

240. For similar impressions, see Hole, Flannery, and Neely 1969: 220–23, fig. 95:A, pl. 37:D.

# APPENDIX ONE

# PRODUCTION ZONE SOURCING AND INTRAREGIONAL EXCHANGE OF CERAMICS IN THE FOURTH-MILLENNIUM B.C. SUSIANA PLAIN: A CASE STUDY

Royal Omar Ghazal,* Nicholas Kouchoukos,*
Robert J. Speakman,** Michael D. Glascock,** and Christophe Descantes**[241]

## SUMMARY

Instrumental Neutron Activation Analysis (INAA) was conducted at the University of Missouri Research Reactor (MURR) on 200 pottery sherds from the Susiana plain in southwestern Iran, dating to the Late Susiana 2 (Susa 1) and mid-fourth millennium B.C. Previous INAA research by Judith Berman sought to evaluate the organization of ceramic production and distribution on the plain. Berman's analyses indicated that the clay sources in the region were too homogenous to be analytically useful in reconstructing specific compositional ceramic groups. However, subsequent statistical reanalysis of Berman's data by Nicholas Kouchoukos has suggested that there is more compositional diversity and structure than Berman's analyses indicated. This present case study was able to suggest a number of improvements to the sampling design that allowed us to evaluate the efficacy of using INAA in this region. Our analysis of three principal sites in the Susiana plain has allowed us to determine that, despite the underlying homogeneity of the plain's clay sources, sufficient compositional diversity does exist and can contribute significantly to the evaluation of the hypotheses formulated to explain Susiana's fourth-millennium B.C. organization of ceramic production, namely, the "centralization hypothesis" advanced by Gregory Johnson and Henry T. Wright.

## INTRODUCTION

Archaeologists have proposed that specialized modes of craft production and centralized exchange are characteristic features and perhaps motivators of political and social complexity (e.g., Childe 1936, 1951; for overview, see Brumfiel and Earle 1987; Costin and Hagstrum 1995; Earle 1997; Sinopoli 1991). Considerable research has focused upon the institutional or elite management of the economy and how state apparatuses strategically control economic activities and build political power. Studies of craft production in complex societies have generally been geared toward determining the degree to which production was centralized or was subject to administrative control. Luxury items or socially valuable goods have enjoyed the lion's share of this research focus, given that these objects are seen to be instrumental in creating, maintaining, and legitimizing political power. Utilitarian goods, such as pottery vessels, are believed to have a lower exchange value and therefore have not been given the same scrutiny. However, in cultural periods where raw materials for preciosity exchange are lacking or underdeveloped, these more mundane domains of production may prove critical to the development of early states.

Johnson and Wright (Johnson 1973, 1987; Wright and Johnson 1975) have suggested that state development in the Susiana plain was not an event, but rather a protracted process that arose from increased intraregional exchange of mundane goods and commodities, such as pottery. Lacking clear indicators for preciosity exchange, Johnson and

241. * Department of Anthropology, University of Chicago; ** The University of Missouri Research Reactor.

Wright focused their attention on what they believe to be the administrated centralization of ceramic production and attachment of craft specialists to regional centers. In what has come to be known as the "centralization hypothesis," Wright and Johnson (1975; Johnson 1973, 1987) argued that regional centers were the primary locations of ceramic production on the plain. As evidence, they cite the conspicuous lack of cultural materials related to production at rural sites. Indicators of pottery production, such as kilns and pottery wasters, were only discovered at the three largest settlements on the plain, namely Susa (KS-00), Chogha Mish (KS-01), and Tappeh Abu Fanduweh (KS-59). This evidence led Johnson (1973, 1987) to propose that "microstylistic" description of the pottery from fourth-millennium B.C. Susiana could be used to attribute the distribution of certain pottery types to subregional workshops.

Encouraged by Wright and Johnson's novel insight, Judith Berman (1986, 1987) attempted to identify spatial distribution of the pottery manufactured at these workshops through bulk compositional analysis. She conducted INAA on 1,021 sherds and clay samples taken from fifth- and fourth-millennium B.C. contexts in the Susiana plain. Her results proved to be considerably uniform. However, reanalysis of a subset of Berman's data (Kouchoukos 1998) suggests that the sampling strategy and statistics employed in Berman's analysis may have hampered her results; considerable temporal and spatial variability was in fact evident across the plain.

Although Berman's data set was rather large, her sampling strategy had a number of inherent problems. For example, the number of vessel types (approximately seventy) may have introduced too much potential variation into the data set. Moreover, techniques of manufacture, including clay processing, firing procedures, and temper use can contribute significantly to the geochemical signature of a ceramic (Senior 1998; Blackman 1992; Theusen and Heydorn 1991). In addition, the number of sampled sites may have significantly hampered her ability to construct compositional groups. More than a hundred sites were sampled in her analysis, yielding an average ratio of ten sherds per site. Small group sizes make it impossible to analyze the data using the full range of multivariate statistics available.

Encouraged by these observations, we were able to suggest a number of pertinent changes to the sampling design for the present case study, which seeks to evaluate the utility of using INAA to study intraregional production and distribution in the Susiana plain. Our results indicate that INAA can yield meaningful compositional information. Based on our preliminary and tentative results, it appears that pottery in fourth-millennium B.C. Susiana was produced not only at regional centers, but in the rural countryside as well.

## METHODOLOGY

### SAMPLING DESIGN

In the summer of 2004, we conducted an INAA pilot study of 200 sherds dating to the fourth and fifth millennia B.C. Samples were selected for analysis on the basis of the location, relevance to prior research, chronological appropriateness, and availability. Minimum group sizes were chosen to meet or exceed the number of elements analyzed (here, thirty-three). Tables 3–4 provide a site-by-site breakdown of the sampled ware types.

Although the primary concern of this study was the mid-fourth-millennium ceramic assemblage, we felt it necessary to include a small subset of Late Susiana 2 pottery in order to evaluate both temporal and technical variability of Susiana ceramics. The Late Susiana 2 V-geometric beakers have been reported from many sites in Susiana. All V-geometric beaker samples were derived from the Oriental Institute's F. G. L. Gremliza survey collection (see Alizadeh 1992). In order to make the case study more manageable and to restrict the range of technical variability that might contribute to compositional differences, we limited our analysis of mid-fourth-millennium pottery vessels to three types: (1) crosshatch band jars (see fig. 29:B for type), (2) beveled-rim bowls (see fig. 26:D for type), and (3) the aforementioned V-geometric beakers (see *Chogha Mish* I, pl. 162:A for type).[242]

There are several good reasons to select crosshatch band jars and beveled-rim bowls. First, crosshatch band jars are one of the ceramic types that can be confidently attributed to the mid-fourth millennium B.C. and were probably mass produced. The beveled-rim bowl group is more problematic from a chronological standpoint, but they are generally attributed to mid- to late phases of the period. Second, all the samples used in our analysis come from stratified contexts at the regional center of Chogha Mish and the rural site of Tappeh Sharafabad (KS-36). A group of ten beveled-rim bowl sherds from problematic "kiln" contexts taken in the surface survey of Tappeh Abu Fanduweh

242. All material used in this study from the site of Chogha Mish was contributed by the University of Chicago's Oriental Institute. In addition, all Sharafabad and Tappeh Abu Fanduweh material was contributed by the University of Michigan's Museum of Anthropology.

have also been included (Johnson 1973). Finally, both these types have been studied extensively in the past. The Sharafabad crosshatch band jar samples analyzed in this study were also included in Johnson's (1987) microstylistic analysis, Cheryl Coursey's (1997) petrographic analysis, and Berman's (1986) INAA study. We can therefore be confident that our conclusions regarding these ceramics bear directly upon prior observations. In addition, retesting these types was necessary because we eventually intend to calibrate our data set with that of Berman.[243]

### SAMPLE PREPARATION

Our Susiana samples were prepared for INAA according to standard MURR procedures (Glascock 1992; Neff 2000). The analyses conducted at MURR produced elemental concentration values for thirty-three elements. For the purposes of data manipulation, all elemental data were transformed to base-10 logarithm values in order to compensate for differences in magnitude between major elements, such as calcium and iron, and rare elements, such as those in the lanthanide series.[244] In tables 5–13 each sample is identified by a unique identification number that consists of the initials of the principal investigator followed by a sequential three-digit sample number (e.g., ROG158).[245]

## PRELIMINARY RESULTS

Initial groups in the present analysis were determined through the visual selection of groups identified in cluster analysis (CA). Tantalum and rubidium concentrations have proved to be particularly effective in determining initial groups that could be tested using more robust multivariate statistics, such as principle components analysis (PCA). In addition to bivariate plots of elemental concentrations, robust multivariate statistics were employed in this research. Although cluster plots can yield useful information about the structure of a data set, the overall variance-covariance cannot be ascertained in a single bivariate projection (Pollard 1986; cf. Baxter 1992: 144). Principle components analysis provides a multivariate approach for graphing the data by calculating and ranking the orientation and length of axes of greatest variance-covariance in the data (for review, see Baxter 1993; Neff 1994).

The following section describes the basic compositional group structure identified for our Susiana ceramic data (figs. 89–99). Table 4 provides provenance information and elemental concentrations for all the samples in this analysis.

### DATA SET

Figure 89 shows a bivariate plot of tantalum and thorium of the entire data set. The structure of the projected data set reveals two to three possible groupings, and therefore served as the initial reference for the construction of groups. Subsequent permutations of the data revealed that these "groups" were highly correlated with archaeological contexts. Subsequent sections detail the graphic presentation of our results.

### BEVELED-RIM BOWLS

In our analysis, bivariate plots illustrate clear compositional groupings of beveled-rim bowls, which are highly correlated with their site contexts (figs. 90–92). Our projections show that beveled-rim bowls are compositionally distinct for Chogha Mish, Sharafabad, and Tappeh Abu Fanduweh. Although Berman's data proved to be largely

243. INAA research can be conducted at a number of places around the world, but results rarely prove comparable. In addition, detection limits (i.e., the number of elements analyzed) can vary from one institution to the next. Berman's analyses were conducted at the Brookhaven National Laboratory.

244. There has been some debate among specialists regarding the necessity of log transformation of data sets. Pollard (1986; cf. Baxter 1993: 3–4) provides a useful summary of these debates. Baxter (1993: 4) suggests that "a substantive reason for such a transformation is the assumption that naturally occurring trace elements, in the clays that go into making a pot, for example, have a log-normal distribution; if data are highly skew[ed] the transformation will often improve the performance of the method [i.e., PCA]." Notably, Berman's (1986) data were not log transformed.

245. All quantitative analyses for this research were performed in GAUSS, a program designed at MURR to facilitate the identification of compositional groups. In addition to bivariate projections, the GAUSS program provides four different methods for computing principle components analyses: (1) principal components analysis using variance-covariance matrix; (2) principal components analysis using correlation matrix; (3) simultaneous RQ factor analysis with variance-covariance matrix; and (4) simultaneous RQ factor analysis with correlation matrix. Each method contributed results that would appear to confirm the general conclusions gained herein, but markedly different graphic results. The first option (i.e., variance-covariance matrix) was employed in the calculation of all PCA values in this report.

homogenous across the plain, Berman (1986: 243) was also able to suggest that beveled-rim bowls were compositionally homogenous within individual sites, suggesting local production of these wares. Our results concur strongly with her conclusions, indicating clear compositional groupings with a strong correlation between site and type. Berman (1986: 240) suggests that local sources of tempering agents may be the contributing factor in the site-to-site variability in the composition of beveled-rim bowls.

## CROSSHATCH BAND JARS

In Berman's (1986: 249–51)[246] analysis of the crosshatch band jars, two parallel groups appeared in the bivariate scatter-plot of scandium (Sc) versus iron (Fe) — elements that are determined to be highly correlated in the overall data set (fig. 91). As in most of her projections, crosshatch band jar samples can be seen clustering in a linear pattern, but differ from other plots in that two parallel trends can be distinguished (note the lower "group" in the dashed ellipsis at bottom of fig. 93). The original researchers noted that two facts about this group were immediately apparent: (1) many of the samples in this small group came from Sharafabad, and (2) these aberrant projections were all irradiated in the same batch, leading some to speculate that some form of sampling error had taken place. After reanalysis, many of these specimens were omitted from the final analysis (Berman 1986: 251).

One possible reason for the separation of the crosshatch band jars in Berman's data set may have been that the Sharafabad samples (twenty in number) were one of the larger groups of specimens to come from a single location (eighty-seven samples from a total of eleven sites). This in part has influenced our decision to increase the number of samples per site group, rather than including a large number of specimens from several different sites from across the Susiana plain. In our projections (figs. 94–95), crosshatch band jars exhibit a distinctly different clustering pattern when compared to the beveled-rim bowls. We might attribute this variability to differences in resource procurement, workshop organization, paste composition formulas (used by potters), or some other cultural variable (e.g., trade, exchange, etc.).

Much of the projected and statistical overlapping exhibited by the data set can be attributed to the higher degree of compositional variability in the crosshatch band jar samples. In contrast, beveled-rim bowl specimens tend to cluster together much more tightly, suggesting that they may more accurately reflect the compositional structure of their clay sources. Despite their compositional diversity, however, crosshatch band jars from Sharafabad and Chogha Mish demonstrate compositional groupings in both elemental and component projections. Therefore, we can reasonably surmise that, as with the beveled-rim bowls, crosshatch band jars are produced locally and at sites of different size and apparent complexity.

## MID-FOURTH MILLENNIUM B.C. AND LATE SUSIANA 2 AGGREGATE GROUPS

As noted above, the cluster analysis of both beveled-rim bowls and crosshatch band jars shows a high degree of correlation between the archaeological provenance of the sherd and the compositional groups. Beveled-rim bowls and crosshatch band jars have demonstrated strikingly different degrees of variability. Yet, while they can be discriminated visually, beveled-rim bowl and crosshatch band jar compositional groups also have a high degree of association particularly in elemental plots that exhibit linear trends due to the positive correlation. In these linear trends, beveled-rim bowl samples tend to associate at the lower end of the graph, while crosshatch band jars plot higher on the graph. Given their comparative compositional similarities, crosshatch band jar and beveled-rim bowl groups were combined to form aggregate groups.

As aggregate groups, the beveled-rim bowls and crosshatch band jars display a remarkable degree of covariation at the site level (see fig. 96). Indeed, the aggregate groups composed of mid-fourth-millennium B.C. wares can be shown to remain compositionally distinct between sites. Furthermore, they appear to be temporally distinct from the Late Susiana 2 V-geometric beakers in both elemental and principal component projections (see figs. 97–98).

---

246. Note that the elements are not log transformed, as in the original publication.

## UNCLASSIFIED SAMPLES AND GROUPS

Mahalanobis distance statistic samples possessing a probability of one percent or above are considered good candidates for group membership. In addition, specimens whose Mahalanobis distance lay below the one percent probability cutoff *for all groups* were unclassified. Nevertheless, specimens occasionally indicate possible membership in one or more groups. Final group membership then must be determined by the investigators based on the relative magnitude of the probability and the visual projections of the data. Specimens whose group membership cannot be determined, or extreme outliers, are often omitted from the final projection of the data set. For reasons that are often unclear, some specimens may have very good statistics but exhibit very poor projections or cause principal component groupings to vary more significantly than others. In some cases, these unusual specimens can dominate an analysis and make detection of reference groups difficult, if not impossible (Baxter 1993: 7).

In the present study, Mahalanobis distance probabilities confirm that the group structure proposed herein is statistically viable. However, several of the unassigned samples exceed the one percent probability of membership in one or more of the identified groups. Membership probabilities fluctuate dramatically when these samples are assigned to one of the identified groups. Unclassified samples in the present analysis were often shown to have a very strong visual association in selected principal component and bivariate projections to the groups thus far described but could vary widely in graphs of alternate components or elements. One of the difficulties in constructing elemental or component projections is that unclassified samples may appear to be closely related to a particular group statistically but become quite skewed when they are plotted (often in the best projections!). Probability statistics and bivariate/multivariate projections often proved to be inclusive in assigning group membership to these samples. Therefore, these samples were removed from the final analysis of the data set. As too many omissions can give the impression that the data are being unduly manipulated, Baxter (1993: 7) suggests that a compromise approach (employed here; see fig. 99) is to project the outliers and other omitted samples from an analysis in relation to the other data points. The principal component plots of the aggregated site-type groups make for the clearest projection of the data. Therefore, in figure 98, the unclassified data (fifty-two in number) are projected against the three aggregated groups described above. We remain optimistic that with additional analyses of pottery from this region we will be able to classify some of the problematic pottery.

# DISCUSSION

It has been suggested that pottery was not being produced at Sharafabad or other rural sites on the Susiana plain in the fourth millennium B.C. (Johnson 1973; Wright and Johnson 1975), and that the pottery found at these sites was imported from the regional centers of Susa, Chogha Mish, and/or Tappeh Abu Fanduweh. Our results in this sense are provocative because they would clearly suggest that pottery vessels, particularly beveled-rim bowls, were manufactured locally despite the lack of evidence for production, such as kilns and wasters. In our analysis, virtually no migration of samples could be noted between compositional site groups based on beveled-rim bowl specimens alone. Although our data are in contrast with past theories of ceramic production in Susiana (Johnson 1973; Wright and Johnson 1975), the results are in keeping with other arguments for localized beveled-rim bowls production, distribution, and consumption (Beale 1978; Le Brun 1980; Berman 1986).

Crosshatch band jar compositions on the other hand, while also distinctly correlated with sites, show a higher degree of variability relative to the beveled-rim bowl specimens. These compositional differences may reflect migration of samples due to trade, or they may reflect underlying differences in the tempering formulas used to make non-beveled-rim bowl wares. A small portion of samples that relate archaeologically to Chogha Mish and Sharafabad show compositional affinities with the opposing group. While the underlying homogeneity of the plain could explain these "migrating" samples, the possibility of exchange between the two sites could be reasonably entertained. However, a number of alternative interpretations can be formulated on social grounds.

First, it may be possible that the ceramics were all produced at Chogha Mish, but that two different workshops, relying upon different clay sources, produced wares for specific rural markets. Nevertheless, this scenario does not seem likely given the overall homogeneity of clays on the plain. To date, there does not seem to be an appreciable degree of intra-site variability to qualify such a position.

Second, we might suggest that ceramics found at Sharafabad were being acquired from another regional center, such as Susa or Tappeh Abu Fanduweh. Regrettably, samples from Susa could not be acquired in time for this study but will be analyzed in the final publication of the data. A small group of ten beveled-rim bowls from Tappeh Abu

Fanduweh, however, were tested and appeared to be compositionally distinct from the other groups (figs. 90–91). This leaves the hypothesis that Sharafabad ceramics were predominantly of local origin provisionally intact.

Finally, the high degree of variability in the crosshatch band jar group may reflect local organizational differences in manufacturing processes. The absence of kilns and wasters from Sharafabad might indicate that production took place off-site on the surrounding plain, perhaps reflecting decreased labor capacity of these smaller rural sites relative to large urban centers such as Chogha Mish. It should also be noted that excavations at Sharafabad were limited to a few test trenches. Therefore, materials or locations related to ceramic production may remain masked by the overburden of later occupations.

The apparent homogeneity of source clays in the Susiana plain is surely a salient factor masking material exchanges. However, it should be remarked that the underlying homogeneity could in fact be exacerbated by the overall magnitude of intraregional trade, which is no doubt occurring. Increased sampling of beveled-rim bowls would seem to be warranted, as these wares seem to provide the most useful proxy measure for local source clays. We have already noted that beveled-rim bowls act as effective anchor points for establishing compositional groups. Other ware types like the crosshatch band jar have been shown to closely adhere to these "anchors," despite a larger degree of variability. No doubt this is partly due to the vagaries of their chemical composition but may also reflect exchange, trade, or use of alternate clay sources. A better understanding of tempering formulas used in the production of beveled-rim bowls and other wares is necessary for sorting out these issues and will figure prominently in subsequent permutations of this ongoing research.

We should also note that compositional groups do not necessarily imply individual workshops. In fact, we would likely anticipate several workshops operating within a site, some specialized and others non-specialized. The social organization of production at a particular site can profoundly affect a potter's access to clay. Ethnographically, we know that craft specialists often assiduously guard their clay resources (Dietler and Herbich 1998; Miller 1985; Nicklin 1981). In some instances, potters may rely upon several clay sources to produce desired attributes in the ceramic paste (Rice 1987: 115–24). Indeed, we might venture to suggest that the compositional diversity of specialized wares, like crosshatch band jars, could derive from the use of multiple clay resources by potters at different workshops within a site.

A subset of Late Susiana 2 V-geometric beaker data was included in this study in order to lend much-needed diachronic perspective to the analysis. Large samples of Late Susiana 2 pottery could not be gained from individual sites in time for this study, so we sampled collections from sites located along the Dez River south of Sharafabad. The results demonstrate that Late Susiana 2 ceramics were compositionally distinct from the mid-fourth-millennium wares described above, perhaps due to technical differences such as painting, slipping, and firing (Theusen and Heydorn 1991). Compositional differences might also result from changing patterns of clay deposition and exploitation.

## CONCLUSION

Previous INAA studies have concluded that source clays in the Susiana plain were too homogenous to identify the location of production or track the trajectory of material exchanges. One of the primary goals of this case study was to reevaluate the utility of INAA in this region. To that end, we focused our attention on three primary ware types, beveled-rim bowls, crosshatch band jars, and V-geometric beakers. Both beveled-rim bowls and crosshatch band jars exist in relatively high concentrations in survey collections and bear the weight of considerable prior analysis (Beale 1978; Berman 1986, 1987; Coursey 1997; Johnson 1973, 1987; Wright and Johnson 1975). The present research project asks: (1) Can we determine whether Susiana clays are in fact too homogenous to see groups which we can relate to sites on the plain? (2) Are particular wares compositionally dissimilar from other vessels sharing the same archaeological provenance? (3) Do we see samples associated with particular archaeological deposits migrating to other groups, reflecting exchange of ceramics? Provisional results affirm all three of these questions.

We cannot yet claim that the observed pattern of local production prevailed across the entire Susiana plain. Instead, we point out that at least three compositional groups can be seen in elemental and principal component projections of mid-fourth-millennium samples. These compositional groups are closely correlated with the site-groups of Chogha Mish, Sharafabad, and Tappeh Abu Fanduweh. The variability evident in the crosshatch band jars appears consistent with the proposition that intraregional exchange took place but requires further clarification.

Our research has demonstrated the effectiveness of INAA on the Susiana plain at least within the narrow geographic parameters of this investigation. With continued analysis, compositional differences in ceramic materials promise insight into crucial questions concerning the intensity, source, and duration of intraregional and interregional trade and the role that commodities played in the development of regionally expansive states.

## ACKNOWLEDGMENTS

Archaeological samples for this research were provided by the Oriental Institute at the University of Chicago and the Museum of Anthropology at the University of Michigan. This research could not have been undertaken without the generous assistance of Raymond Tindel, Henry T. Wright, Geoff Emberling, Eric Rupley, Abbas Alizadeh, and Toby Hartnell. We acknowledge gratefully the assistance of Rebecca Schmidt, Tessa Schut, Mark Hammond, Jonathan Dake, and the rest of the staff at MURR. Partial funding for this research was provided by a MURR Archeometry Fellowship (NSF grant # B.C.S-0102325), a Leiffer Fellowship from the University of Chicago, and the Lichtstern Fund of the University of Chicago Department of Anthropology.

Table 3. Number of INAA Specimens by Site and Type

| *SITE* | *TYPE* | | | | |
|---|---|---|---|---|---|
| | *Crosshatch Band Jar* | *Beveled-rim Bowl* | *Clay* | *Late Susiana 2 V-Geometric Beaker* | *Subtotal* |
| Chogha Mish (KS-01) | 41 | 25 | — | — | 66 |
| Sharafabad (KS-36) | 39 | 30 | 10 | 9 | 88 |
| Tappeh Abu Fanduweh (KS-59) | — | 10 | — | — | 10 |
| Abul Bashir (KS-562) | — | — | — | 3 | 3 |
| Tappeh Seyfabad (KS-458) | — | — | — | 4 | 4 |
| Gremliza Survey G-III (KS-162) | — | — | — | 1 | 1 |
| Gremliza Survey G-IX (KS-168) | — | — | — | 1 | 1 |
| Tappeh Deylameh Sofla (KS-49) | — | — | — | 1 | 1 |
| Khalte (KS-1450) | — | — | — | 7 | 7 |
| Ishan al-ʿAin (KS-05) | — | — | — | 2 | 2 |
| Chogha Cheshmeh (KS-494) | — | — | — | 7 | 7 |
| Badili (KS-709) | — | — | — | 3 | 3 |
| Beladieh (KS-409) | — | — | — | 3 | 3 |
| Shangar-e Sofla (KS-113) | — | — | — | 1 | 1 |
| Shamʿun (KS-1322) | — | — | — | 1 | 1 |
| Gremliza Survey G1-III (KS-161) | — | — | — | 2 | 2 |
| **Total** | **80** | **65** | **10** | **45** | **200** |

Table 4. Site and Type Information for INAA Samples

| *Sample Identification* | *Site Identification* | *Site Name** | *Northing (meters)* | *Easting (meters)* | *Type* |
|---|---|---|---|---|---|
| ROG001–027 | KS-36 | Tappeh Sharafabad | 3575096 E | 251937 E | CHBJ |
| ROG028–057 | KS-36 | Tappeh Sharafabad | 3575096 N | 251937 E | BRB |
| ROG058–067 | KS-36 | Tappeh Sharafabad | 3575096 N | 251937 E | Clay |
| ROG068–109 | KS-01 | Chogha Mish | 3567891 N | 269610 E | BRB |
| ROG110–133 | KS-01 | Chogha Mish | 3567891 N | 269610 E | CHBJ |
| ROG134–136 | KS-562 | Abul Bashir G97 | 3553866 N | 264382 E | V-GB |
| ROG137 | KS-05 | Ishan al-ʿAin G86-I | 3560284 N | 263390 E | V-GB |
| ROG138 | KS-458 | Tappeh Seyfabad G64-I | 3565285 N | 262792 E | V-GB |
| ROG139 | KS-162 | G-III | 3563399 N | 279982 E | V-GB |
| ROG140 | KS-168 | G-IX | 3560946 N | 258548 E | V-GB |
| ROG141 | KS-49 | Tappeh Deylameh Sofla G26-II | 3557748 N | 258548 E | V-GB |
| ROG142–148 | KS-1450 | Khalte G131 | 3575301 N | 257382 E | V-GB |
| ROG149–155 | KS-494 | Chogha Cheshmeh G86-II | 3559944 N | 263402 E | V-GB |
| ROG156 | KS-05 | Ishan al-ʿAin G86-I | 3560284 N | 263390 E | V-GB |
| ROG157–159 | KS-709 | Badili G79 | 3560555 N | 269737 E | V-GB |
| ROG160–162 | KS-458 | Tappeh Seyfabad G64-I | 3565285 N | 262792 E | V-GB |
| ROG163–165 | KS-409 | Beladieh G62-I | 3563580 N | 265994 E | V-GB |
| ROG166 | KS-113 | Shangar-e Sofla G60 | 3559012 N | 266463 E | V-GB |
| ROG167–175 | KS-36 | Tappeh Sharafabad | 3575096 N | 251937 E | V-GB |
| ROG176 | KS-1322 | Shamʾun G25-II | 3560759 N | 258837 E | V-GB |
| ROG177 | KS-161 & KS-162 | GI-III | 3566016 N | 279469 E | V-GB |
| ROG178 | KS-161 & KS-162 | GI-II | 3566016 N | 279469 E | V-GB |
| ROG179–180 | KS-59 | Tappeh Abu Fanduweh | 3553987 N | 246909 E | BRB |
| ROG181–192 | KS-36 | Tappeh Sharafabad | 3575096 N | 251937 E | CHBJ |
| ROG193–200 | KS-59 | Tappeh Abu Fanduweh | 3553987 N | 246909 E | BRB |

* In the third column, "G" followed by numbers represents sites surveyed by Dr. Gremliza.

Table 5. Elemental Concentration (ppm) Data for Susiana Ceramics

| *Sample Identification* | *Arsenic (As)* | *Lanthanum (La)* | *Lutetium (Lu)* | *Neodymium (Nd)* |
|---|---|---|---|---|
| ROG001 | 4.5299 | 19.8607 | 0.2357 | 17.2148 |
| ROG002 | 4.2102 | 18.5205 | 0.2291 | 16.1184 |
| ROG003 | 6.0339 | 19.4993 | 0.2398 | 16.1589 |
| ROG004 | 5.1929 | 17.6084 | 0.2034 | 15.6621 |
| ROG005 | 7.1128 | 18.7509 | 0.2447 | 16.9654 |
| ROG006 | 6.1243 | 17.3862 | 0.2568 | 17.4510 |
| ROG007 | 5.5243 | 19.6841 | 0.2576 | 17.4017 |
| ROG008 | 5.8582 | 22.0875 | 0.3055 | 20.0616 |
| ROG009 | 5.7197 | 21.1801 | 0.2324 | 18.1206 |
| ROG010 | 5.5801 | 20.4377 | 0.2571 | 17.9633 |
| ROG011 | 6.1719 | 19.2967 | 0.2796 | 19.4060 |
| ROG012 | 6.1261 | 20.5595 | 0.2584 | 17.1143 |
| ROG013 | 5.1786 | 18.6111 | 0.2454 | 16.9066 |
| ROG014 | 5.5095 | 18.6205 | 0.2124 | 17.0103 |
| ROG015 | 5.5553 | 21.5832 | 0.2596 | 19.9743 |
| ROG016 | 6.4589 | 17.4697 | 0.3226 | 17.7943 |
| ROG017 | 4.5879 | 18.1697 | 0.2179 | 17.7392 |
| ROG018 | 7.0431 | 17.7728 | 0.2424 | 16.2229 |
| ROG019 | 6.2401 | 17.8542 | 0.2471 | 17.5632 |
| ROG020 | 5.7792 | 17.8158 | 0.2391 | 16.2970 |
| ROG021 | 5.3545 | 22.8692 | 0.2628 | 21.7049 |
| ROG022 | 8.3307 | 23.0404 | 0.3638 | 21.1895 |
| ROG023 | 4.9080 | 18.8395 | 0.2954 | 17.1303 |
| ROG024 | 5.7585 | 17.1787 | 0.2194 | 14.2600 |
| ROG025 | 5.2246 | 17.5211 | 0.2159 | 15.6882 |
| ROG026 | 5.5040 | 18.6867 | 0.2291 | 17.9001 |
| ROG027 | 4.3468 | 17.0374 | 0.2170 | 15.1487 |
| ROG028 | 12.4919 | 15.6544 | 0.2019 | 15.4860 |
| ROG029 | 3.5439 | 21.0974 | 0.2435 | 19.3697 |
| ROG030 | 23.5206 | 16.7722 | 0.1996 | 16.6797 |
| ROG031 | 9.6875 | 16.8651 | 0.2147 | 15.3269 |
| ROG032 | 12.6999 | 16.0428 | 0.2281 | 14.2718 |
| ROG033 | 6.0598 | 17.3535 | 0.2075 | 17.3729 |
| ROG034 | 25.3231 | 15.6590 | 0.1898 | 15.4687 |
| ROG035 | 16.7857 | 15.7884 | 0.2069 | 14.6872 |
| ROG036 | 6.8348 | 15.9352 | 0.2088 | 14.7764 |
| ROG037 | 22.6414 | 16.5697 | 0.2177 | 15.6396 |

Table 5. Elemental Concentration (ppm) Data for Susiana Ceramics (*cont.*)

| *Sample Identification* | *Arsenic (As)* | *Lanthanum (La)* | *Lutetium (Lu)* | *Neodymium (Nd)* |
|---|---|---|---|---|
| ROG038 | 4.6418 | 19.3208 | 0.2384 | 17.6456 |
| ROG039 | 4.9397 | 18.6191 | 0.2276 | 16.7415 |
| ROG040 | 5.4863 | 15.6806 | 0.2129 | 13.2467 |
| ROG041 | 3.1220 | 21.5835 | 0.2540 | 20.0477 |
| ROG042 | 4.2330 | 20.0939 | 0.2698 | 17.9706 |
| ROG043 | 4.2748 | 16.2940 | 0.2137 | 15.3940 |
| ROG044 | 3.6608 | 16.5298 | 0.2133 | 15.9116 |
| ROG045 | 5.4110 | 15.9624 | 0.2260 | 15.1887 |
| ROG046 | 5.7469 | 18.5362 | 0.2382 | 16.7711 |
| ROG047 | 4.9764 | 16.4146 | 0.2172 | 14.7685 |
| ROG048 | 3.8900 | 18.3850 | 0.2295 | 16.4691 |
| ROG049 | 4.7884 | 15.7218 | 0.1972 | 14.5871 |
| ROG050 | 5.6206 | 17.9454 | 0.2247 | 16.1197 |
| ROG051 | 4.0499 | 16.1791 | 0.1821 | 14.3139 |
| ROG052 | 3.9510 | 16.5152 | 0.2064 | 13.5547 |
| ROG053 | 4.7366 | 20.5615 | 0.2466 | 17.6379 |
| ROG054 | 4.5406 | 18.5006 | 0.2033 | 14.8847 |
| ROG055 | 3.5558 | 21.2581 | 0.2580 | 15.2358 |
| ROG056 | 4.7898 | 16.9830 | 0.1960 | 16.8158 |
| ROG057 | 3.9647 | 16.3999 | 0.2151 | 14.8254 |
| ROG058 | 6.1567 | 17.7586 | 0.2550 | 17.1263 |
| ROG059 | 5.7590 | 18.4366 | 0.2339 | 13.4256 |
| ROG060 | 4.3351 | 18.2151 | 0.2313 | 16.9720 |
| ROG061 | 7.5410 | 18.7842 | 0.2281 | 15.0762 |
| ROG062 | 5.1819 | 20.1979 | 0.2673 | 19.7724 |
| ROG063 | 5.4034 | 19.0096 | 0.2380 | 17.2599 |
| ROG064 | 3.1717 | 16.4237 | 0.2100 | 12.8845 |
| ROG065 | 5.5314 | 15.4883 | 0.2079 | 12.2828 |
| ROG066 | 4.4191 | 18.6736 | 0.2015 | 14.9203 |
| ROG067 | 5.4742 | 17.3479 | 0.2237 | 16.2931 |
| ROG068 | 5.7241 | 21.1409 | 0.2598 | 14.9078 |
| ROG069 | 6.3705 | 20.5892 | 0.2493 | 17.5461 |
| ROG070 | 5.1295 | 20.2706 | 0.2683 | 20.0303 |
| ROG071 | 7.9007 | 18.7999 | 0.2554 | 13.7090 |
| ROG072 | 7.1684 | 18.9287 | 0.2674 | 13.4042 |
| ROG073 | 8.2732 | 25.2651 | 0.3159 | 20.7811 |
| ROG074 | 5.6392 | 22.0270 | 0.2857 | 19.0900 |

Table 5. Elemental Concentration (ppm) Data for Susiana Ceramics (*cont.*)

| *Sample Identification* | *Arsenic (As)* | *Lanthanum (La)* | *Lutetium (Lu)* | *Neodymium (Nd)* |
|---|---|---|---|---|
| ROG075 | 7.1012 | 18.4374 | 0.2501 | 13.2708 |
| ROG076 | 6.8076 | 17.9591 | 0.2309 | 13.7952 |
| ROG077 | 6.6211 | 23.1537 | 0.3232 | 18.8339 |
| ROG078 | 4.2091 | 20.4540 | 0.2658 | 14.2433 |
| ROG079 | 6.2886 | 20.9051 | 0.2876 | 19.5582 |
| ROG080 | 9.4542 | 16.7383 | 0.2390 | 12.6376 |
| ROG081 | 5.4636 | 20.2726 | 0.2402 | 18.8739 |
| ROG082 | 4.1962 | 20.7175 | 0.2634 | 18.2433 |
| ROG083 | 4.3889 | 20.2649 | 0.2425 | 18.7057 |
| ROG084 | 5.2115 | 22.0839 | 0.2854 | 21.8949 |
| ROG085 | 5.3286 | 20.7376 | 0.2498 | 19.5379 |
| ROG086 | 6.8249 | 18.9943 | 0.2418 | 14.7335 |
| ROG087 | 4.4181 | 17.9728 | 0.2274 | 16.7554 |
| ROG088 | 5.3621 | 21.6891 | 0.2747 | 17.5374 |
| ROG089 | 3.2956 | 19.2820 | 0.2576 | 13.5889 |
| ROG090 | 7.6500 | 21.9675 | 0.3028 | 18.3166 |
| ROG091 | 7.1316 | 18.8210 | 0.2444 | 17.6459 |
| ROG092 | 6.4474 | 18.1874 | 0.2316 | 14.9477 |
| ROG093 | 6.0731 | 21.1587 | 0.2546 | 18.7138 |
| ROG094 | 16.6838 | 20.9905 | 0.2548 | 19.7382 |
| ROG095 | 4.4659 | 20.4575 | 0.2518 | 15.9385 |
| ROG096 | 5.6564 | 19.0812 | 0.2238 | 16.2922 |
| ROG097 | 6.8873 | 16.3710 | 0.2032 | 12.5828 |
| ROG098 | 4.7594 | 19.3447 | 0.2759 | 17.7948 |
| ROG099 | 4.5175 | 19.0437 | 0.2290 | 12.9324 |
| ROG100 | 5.9193 | 19.9275 | 0.2402 | 17.4806 |
| ROG101 | 5.1933 | 17.8969 | 0.2357 | 14.6660 |
| ROG102 | 8.7896 | 17.8653 | 0.2900 | 13.7003 |
| ROG103 | 7.8333 | 21.1414 | 0.2812 | 20.3310 |
| ROG104 | 6.7812 | 20.9969 | 0.2812 | 20.2362 |
| ROG105 | 8.1255 | 20.6445 | 0.2664 | 16.6277 |
| ROG106 | 5.2453 | 19.4620 | 0.2661 | 16.6790 |
| ROG107 | 10.0573 | 20.8651 | 0.2979 | 18.7668 |
| ROG108 | 5.0717 | 19.7826 | 0.2810 | 17.3304 |
| ROG109 | 8.3548 | 17.8710 | 0.2737 | 15.9647 |
| ROG110 | 2.4139 | 16.6315 | 0.2361 | 14.7388 |
| ROG111 | 3.4320 | 16.5529 | 0.2231 | 15.5993 |

Table 5. Elemental Concentration (ppm) Data for Susiana Ceramics (*cont.*)

| *Sample Identification* | *Arsenic (As)* | *Lanthanum (La)* | *Lutetium (Lu)* | *Neodymium (Nd)* |
|---|---|---|---|---|
| ROG112 | 9.8178 | 18.0903 | 0.2877 | 15.0448 |
| ROG113 | 5.7781 | 17.3036 | 0.2342 | 16.3733 |
| ROG114 | 7.9638 | 18.1613 | 0.2547 | 15.1774 |
| ROG115 | 5.4500 | 16.2633 | 0.1873 | 12.5909 |
| ROG116 | 15.3812 | 20.9832 | 0.2817 | 17.9850 |
| ROG117 | 6.7842 | 15.9335 | 0.2220 | 14.9633 |
| ROG118 | 11.5656 | 16.7228 | 0.2135 | 15.1407 |
| ROG119 | 6.5257 | 20.4661 | 0.2605 | 18.1346 |
| ROG120 | 3.8930 | 17.0673 | 0.2250 | 16.4503 |
| ROG121 | 6.2519 | 16.3830 | 0.2278 | 14.0393 |
| ROG122 | 4.5575 | 17.1106 | 0.2495 | 14.5553 |
| ROG123 | 4.8350 | 16.7161 | 0.2356 | 15.4670 |
| ROG124 | 5.1517 | 16.4965 | 0.2467 | 14.4430 |
| ROG125 | 7.1831 | 16.2047 | 0.2327 | 15.7188 |
| ROG126 | 6.4219 | 20.9884 | 0.2904 | 18.4015 |
| ROG127 | 8.9797 | 17.0766 | 0.2300 | 17.1585 |
| ROG128 | 4.8983 | 19.5518 | 0.2718 | 16.5974 |
| ROG129 | 6.6310 | 14.2360 | 0.1781 | 12.0784 |
| ROG130 | 4.5529 | 18.3924 | 0.2843 | 16.3642 |
| ROG131 | 7.9399 | 15.6814 | 0.2255 | 13.2786 |
| ROG132 | 5.2005 | 18.7321 | 0.2666 | 17.0379 |
| ROG133 | 4.7140 | 15.9008 | 0.2146 | 13.8531 |
| ROG134 | 7.1214 | 22.9079 | 0.3291 | 21.0212 |
| ROG135 | 0.0000 | 22.3644 | 0.3009 | 20.0695 |
| ROG136 | 6.8389 | 20.9856 | 0.2757 | 18.8033 |
| ROG137 | 8.5038 | 22.9681 | 0.3030 | 20.1231 |
| ROG138 | 0.0000 | 24.4581 | 0.3318 | 23.1318 |
| ROG139 | 1.5724 | 23.2850 | 0.3168 | 20.7768 |
| ROG140 | 26.6859 | 23.4387 | 0.3020 | 20.8761 |
| ROG141 | 8.7624 | 24.5022 | 0.3431 | 21.8624 |
| ROG142 | 16.7480 | 21.9383 | 0.2748 | 20.0748 |
| ROG143 | 4.4962 | 22.9171 | 0.3588 | 20.1401 |
| ROG144 | 7.9489 | 22.7263 | 0.2776 | 20.7657 |
| ROG145 | 8.1783 | 22.1513 | 0.2717 | 21.0169 |
| ROG146 | 3.3799 | 25.3723 | 0.3488 | 24.0882 |
| ROG147 | 0.0000 | 26.4232 | 0.3473 | 24.3677 |
| ROG148 | 4.9327 | 23.5269 | 0.3109 | 18.8486 |

Table 5. Elemental Concentration (ppm) Data for Susiana Ceramics (*cont.*)

| *Sample Identification* | *Arsenic (As)* | *Lanthanum (La)* | *Lutetium (Lu)* | *Neodymium (Nd)* |
|---|---|---|---|---|
| ROG149 | 3.4067 | 22.4351 | 0.2815 | 20.0595 |
| ROG150 | 3.9318 | 23.5122 | 0.3251 | 21.4386 |
| ROG151 | 6.0378 | 25.0744 | 0.2868 | 19.0755 |
| ROG152 | 4.0905 | 24.4007 | 0.3069 | 23.1830 |
| ROG153 | 1.4071 | 22.6099 | 0.2974 | 21.1460 |
| ROG154 | 17.4942 | 19.0757 | 0.2838 | 16.3196 |
| ROG155 | 6.7658 | 23.4197 | 0.2795 | 17.1445 |
| ROG156 | 9.5144 | 22.2505 | 0.2537 | 19.1491 |
| ROG157 | 6.4788 | 24.6245 | 0.2847 | 19.5731 |
| ROG158 | 9.8066 | 24.5063 | 0.3022 | 23.4577 |
| ROG159 | 13.0054 | 22.7322 | 0.3103 | 19.1797 |
| ROG160 | 2.5227 | 24.5972 | 0.2915 | 20.4256 |
| ROG161 | 3.9648 | 24.7255 | 0.3071 | 18.0736 |
| ROG162 | 4.7399 | 23.5420 | 0.3144 | 18.7101 |
| ROG163 | 12.6697 | 22.0043 | 0.2939 | 20.2176 |
| ROG164 | 10.8939 | 22.6779 | 0.3056 | 17.6877 |
| ROG165 | 8.0028 | 19.3736 | 0.2643 | 18.3343 |
| ROG166 | 3.9991 | 25.2890 | 0.3470 | 19.9757 |
| ROG167 | 6.8753 | 23.2805 | 0.3180 | 15.8049 |
| ROG168 | 8.1631 | 22.8804 | 0.2963 | 19.5118 |
| ROG169 | 7.2451 | 22.6747 | 0.2835 | 19.8892 |
| ROG170 | 1.2195 | 25.6817 | 0.3222 | 21.3607 |
| ROG171 | 6.7963 | 24.2910 | 0.3256 | 17.5385 |
| ROG172 | 18.0886 | 25.4088 | 0.3069 | 20.9912 |
| ROG173 | 12.8172 | 23.5170 | 0.2604 | 22.1434 |
| ROG174 | 2.6351 | 23.5081 | 0.3102 | 17.1113 |
| ROG175 | 1.4621 | 26.2684 | 0.3397 | 21.9888 |
| ROG176 | 5.2520 | 25.2673 | 0.2788 | 18.3338 |
| ROG177 | 5.9819 | 26.1244 | 0.3042 | 18.2335 |
| ROG178 | 4.7949 | 24.2100 | 0.2719 | 21.4447 |
| ROG179 | 10.4025 | 19.5776 | 0.2402 | 15.9240 |
| ROG180 | 4.3165 | 18.8377 | 0.2128 | 12.4110 |
| ROG181 | 4.4624 | 19.2623 | 0.2219 | 18.8826 |
| ROG182 | 5.8186 | 23.4254 | 0.3214 | 20.1288 |
| ROG183 | 3.9157 | 21.9863 | 0.2469 | 17.6916 |
| ROG184 | 3.4626 | 21.8314 | 0.2698 | 15.9850 |
| ROG185 | 2.7471 | 21.2749 | 0.2133 | 14.4478 |

Table 5. Elemental Concentration (ppm) Data for Susiana Ceramics (*cont.*)

| *Sample Identification* | *Arsenic (As)* | *Lanthanum (La)* | *Lutetium (Lu)* | *Neodymium (Nd)* |
|---|---|---|---|---|
| ROG186 | 5.0950 | 21.4775 | 0.2832 | 15.4175 |
| ROG187 | 4.5242 | 20.5211 | 0.2034 | 19.7305 |
| ROG188 | 4.1651 | 24.6095 | 0.3049 | 23.6718 |
| ROG189 | 3.8239 | 21.6023 | 0.2486 | 15.3350 |
| ROG190 | 6.4900 | 21.6582 | 0.2796 | 16.2095 |
| ROG191 | 6.0642 | 21.2991 | 0.2418 | 16.5253 |
| ROG192 | 7.5803 | 20.5725 | 0.2232 | 17.1143 |
| ROG193 | 3.2944 | 19.0126 | 0.2381 | 14.4921 |
| ROG194 | 5.4097 | 18.2080 | 0.2222 | 14.0950 |
| ROG195 | 8.7713 | 18.6514 | 0.2220 | 14.6381 |
| ROG196 | 8.0369 | 17.4206 | 0.2187 | 13.4855 |
| ROG197 | 13.1486 | 20.6215 | 0.2646 | 18.9178 |
| ROG198 | 7.2987 | 16.8976 | 0.2122 | 16.7371 |
| ROG199 | 9.5739 | 20.6610 | 0.2640 | 17.4952 |
| ROG200 | 7.1818 | 18.2140 | 0.2349 | 14.5185 |

Table 6. Elemental Concentration (ppm) Data for Susiana Ceramics

| *Sample Identification* | *Samarium (Sm)* | *Uranium (U)* | *Ytterbium (Yb)* | *Cerium (Ce)* |
|---|---|---|---|---|
| ROG001 | 3.6859 | 2.3436 | 1.4225 | 40.5149 |
| ROG002 | 3.5115 | 2.4030 | 1.3653 | 37.3352 |
| ROG003 | 3.6304 | 2.5081 | 1.4344 | 39.8895 |
| ROG004 | 3.2478 | 1.7574 | 1.3033 | 35.5892 |
| ROG005 | 3.6221 | 1.9691 | 1.4821 | 38.4097 |
| ROG006 | 3.3547 | 1.5622 | 1.4535 | 35.1653 |
| ROG007 | 3.7543 | 2.2258 | 1.4745 | 40.7009 |
| ROG008 | 4.1723 | 1.8847 | 1.7320 | 45.1268 |
| ROG009 | 3.9727 | 2.5585 | 1.4913 | 43.4579 |
| ROG010 | 3.8727 | 2.5251 | 1.6075 | 41.5005 |
| ROG011 | 3.6425 | 1.6873 | 1.5969 | 38.6854 |
| ROG012 | 3.8245 | 2.1415 | 1.4858 | 42.1370 |
| ROG013 | 3.5034 | 2.1282 | 1.3840 | 38.3568 |
| ROG014 | 3.4558 | 1.9788 | 1.3937 | 37.4536 |
| ROG015 | 3.8551 | 2.8528 | 1.5896 | 43.7423 |
| ROG016 | 3.3374 | 1.6905 | 1.5107 | 35.3094 |
| ROG017 | 3.4253 | 2.4312 | 1.3608 | 36.9170 |
| ROG018 | 3.4005 | 1.8731 | 1.5100 | 35.7847 |
| ROG019 | 3.4138 | 1.9844 | 1.5446 | 35.6344 |
| ROG020 | 3.3105 | 2.1494 | 1.3821 | 35.8860 |
| ROG021 | 4.2680 | 2.7062 | 1.6720 | 46.8578 |
| ROG022 | 4.4886 | 2.1756 | 2.0374 | 47.3807 |
| ROG023 | 3.5168 | 2.3131 | 1.3795 | 38.0950 |
| ROG024 | 3.2031 | 1.7467 | 1.3077 | 34.8776 |
| ROG025 | 3.3100 | 2.4987 | 1.3754 | 35.7604 |
| ROG026 | 3.5606 | 2.5443 | 1.5423 | 38.3682 |
| ROG027 | 3.2464 | 2.5293 | 1.2969 | 34.5117 |
| ROG028 | 3.0609 | 2.5807 | 1.1646 | 31.6821 |
| ROG029 | 4.0226 | 2.8751 | 1.5680 | 42.6126 |
| ROG030 | 3.2463 | 2.9440 | 1.2311 | 33.5151 |
| ROG031 | 3.2389 | 2.4806 | 1.3363 | 34.2844 |
| ROG032 | 3.1425 | 1.8959 | 1.2318 | 32.5610 |
| ROG033 | 3.2897 | 2.0249 | 1.3803 | 34.9895 |
| ROG034 | 3.1838 | 4.0390 | 1.1794 | 32.5659 |
| ROG035 | 3.1009 | 3.0056 | 1.3126 | 32.1935 |
| ROG036 | 3.1119 | 2.2907 | 1.3228 | 32.4846 |
| ROG037 | 3.2180 | 2.6104 | 1.2542 | 33.4845 |

Table 6. Elemental Concentration (ppm) Data for Susiana Ceramics (*cont.*)

| *Sample Identification* | *Samarium (Sm)* | *Uranium (U)* | *Ytterbium (Yb)* | *Cerium (Ce)* |
|---|---|---|---|---|
| ROG038 | 3.7630 | 2.2636 | 1.4551 | 39.9518 |
| ROG039 | 3.5665 | 2.2853 | 1.4578 | 37.7004 |
| ROG040 | 2.9974 | 1.9155 | 1.2032 | 31.3986 |
| ROG041 | 4.0957 | 3.0153 | 1.5280 | 44.0482 |
| ROG042 | 3.9112 | 3.0241 | 1.5252 | 40.8120 |
| ROG043 | 3.1635 | 2.3589 | 1.2653 | 33.4960 |
| ROG044 | 3.1408 | 2.0278 | 1.2405 | 33.2607 |
| ROG045 | 3.0760 | 1.8617 | 1.2394 | 32.3985 |
| ROG046 | 3.5944 | 3.2429 | 1.3650 | 37.6453 |
| ROG047 | 3.1751 | 1.6994 | 1.2992 | 32.9911 |
| ROG048 | 3.4189 | 2.2026 | 1.4041 | 37.4696 |
| ROG049 | 3.0561 | 2.0030 | 1.2056 | 32.2057 |
| ROG050 | 3.4747 | 2.1350 | 1.3057 | 36.4489 |
| ROG051 | 3.0810 | 1.6983 | 1.1847 | 34.1913 |
| ROG052 | 3.2308 | 2.0431 | 1.3402 | 34.9184 |
| ROG053 | 3.9122 | 2.4360 | 1.6255 | 42.7339 |
| ROG054 | 3.5194 | 2.0031 | 1.4445 | 38.7532 |
| ROG055 | 4.0178 | 2.5056 | 1.6520 | 44.6164 |
| ROG056 | 3.2540 | 2.2062 | 1.3410 | 34.9804 |
| ROG057 | 3.1968 | 2.2594 | 1.3090 | 34.7140 |
| ROG058 | 3.4191 | 2.2713 | 1.3534 | 37.3750 |
| ROG059 | 3.5020 | 2.6245 | 1.4697 | 38.0967 |
| ROG060 | 3.5909 | 2.3643 | 1.4369 | 38.6977 |
| ROG061 | 3.6041 | 2.6706 | 1.2997 | 39.4217 |
| ROG062 | 3.8329 | 2.5135 | 1.5786 | 41.7282 |
| ROG063 | 3.6091 | 2.3594 | 1.4302 | 39.4283 |
| ROG064 | 3.2277 | 2.4625 | 1.3499 | 35.2486 |
| ROG065 | 3.0199 | 2.1923 | 1.2229 | 31.9874 |
| ROG066 | 3.5412 | 2.1828 | 1.4551 | 39.0915 |
| ROG067 | 3.3384 | 2.1572 | 1.3692 | 36.6723 |
| ROG068 | 4.0712 | 1.8354 | 1.7787 | 43.8805 |
| ROG069 | 3.9919 | 2.0512 | 1.7854 | 42.9232 |
| ROG070 | 3.9936 | 2.2621 | 1.8136 | 42.2012 |
| ROG071 | 3.6641 | 2.0552 | 1.5754 | 38.8279 |
| ROG072 | 3.7249 | 2.0199 | 1.6336 | 40.2865 |
| ROG073 | 4.9322 | 2.6371 | 2.0413 | 55.1740 |
| ROG074 | 4.2383 | 2.2180 | 1.9852 | 46.1116 |

Table 6. Elemental Concentration (ppm) Data for Susiana Ceramics (*cont.*)

| *Sample Identification* | *Samarium (Sm)* | *Uranium (U)* | *Ytterbium (Yb)* | *Cerium (Ce)* |
|---|---|---|---|---|
| ROG075 | 3.5496 | 1.8324 | 1.4820 | 37.6826 |
| ROG076 | 3.6359 | 2.0638 | 1.5291 | 38.0739 |
| ROG077 | 4.7283 | 4.1869 | 1.9206 | 47.5714 |
| ROG078 | 3.9039 | 2.0547 | 1.7144 | 42.1761 |
| ROG079 | 4.0446 | 2.2512 | 1.8945 | 43.2176 |
| ROG080 | 3.3975 | 3.3435 | 1.5172 | 34.5226 |
| ROG081 | 3.8347 | 2.4341 | 1.5652 | 41.5992 |
| ROG082 | 3.9162 | 2.2626 | 1.7358 | 44.1341 |
| ROG083 | 3.8279 | 2.4427 | 1.6329 | 40.8480 |
| ROG084 | 4.3094 | 1.9358 | 1.8402 | 45.7757 |
| ROG085 | 3.9438 | 1.6953 | 1.5605 | 43.2334 |
| ROG086 | 3.6188 | 1.8201 | 1.7823 | 39.2446 |
| ROG087 | 3.4307 | 2.4667 | 1.5284 | 37.0586 |
| ROG088 | 4.1796 | 2.3111 | 1.7960 | 44.6738 |
| ROG089 | 3.7619 | 1.9287 | 1.6268 | 40.2894 |
| ROG090 | 4.3266 | 1.7441 | 1.9489 | 45.8291 |
| ROG091 | 3.6335 | 1.8594 | 1.5278 | 38.4995 |
| ROG092 | 3.3703 | 2.3197 | 1.4930 | 37.2442 |
| ROG093 | 4.0916 | 1.8262 | 1.7083 | 43.4346 |
| ROG094 | 4.0865 | 2.3201 | 1.8042 | 44.1399 |
| ROG095 | 3.8996 | 1.9092 | 1.7207 | 42.2503 |
| ROG096 | 3.6560 | 2.2253 | 1.5302 | 39.1964 |
| ROG097 | 3.1458 | 1.7433 | 1.4163 | 33.3473 |
| ROG098 | 3.7887 | 2.5063 | 1.5954 | 40.7932 |
| ROG099 | 3.6472 | 2.2830 | 1.6458 | 39.2983 |
| ROG100 | 3.7822 | 1.9500 | 1.5956 | 41.6906 |
| ROG101 | 3.2627 | 1.8822 | 1.3293 | 36.0990 |
| ROG102 | 3.3506 | 1.8339 | 1.4268 | 36.3604 |
| ROG103 | 4.0431 | 2.3529 | 1.7598 | 43.1593 |
| ROG104 | 3.9990 | 2.1029 | 1.6851 | 43.6822 |
| ROG105 | 3.8664 | 2.2627 | 1.6471 | 41.5141 |
| ROG106 | 3.8331 | 2.3397 | 1.6126 | 40.4077 |
| ROG107 | 4.0524 | 2.4490 | 1.7017 | 43.7475 |
| ROG108 | 3.7010 | 2.2361 | 1.5744 | 39.6915 |
| ROG109 | 3.4951 | 1.9831 | 1.3943 | 36.7899 |
| ROG110 | 3.1617 | 1.8370 | 1.3427 | 33.9559 |
| ROG111 | 3.1972 | 1.8593 | 1.7052 | 33.5761 |

Table 6. Elemental Concentration (ppm) Data for Susiana Ceramics (*cont.*)

| *Sample Identification* | *Samarium (Sm)* | *Uranium (U)* | *Ytterbium (Yb)* | *Cerium (Ce)* |
|---|---|---|---|---|
| ROG112 | 3.5203 | 2.5636 | 1.5218 | 37.1452 |
| ROG113 | 3.3856 | 1.9654 | 1.3547 | 35.9728 |
| ROG114 | 3.5416 | 2.2483 | 1.6932 | 37.9004 |
| ROG115 | 2.9864 | 2.1048 | 1.2089 | 33.5216 |
| ROG116 | 4.1190 | 2.0420 | 1.7383 | 44.3528 |
| ROG117 | 3.0916 | 2.1068 | 1.2706 | 32.7730 |
| ROG118 | 3.2227 | 2.1062 | 1.3565 | 34.4271 |
| ROG119 | 3.9880 | 2.4115 | 1.5780 | 42.5622 |
| ROG120 | 3.3172 | 2.1584 | 1.4729 | 35.3326 |
| ROG121 | 3.1738 | 1.7541 | 1.3586 | 33.5864 |
| ROG122 | 3.3539 | 1.9538 | 1.4676 | 35.4354 |
| ROG123 | 3.2647 | 1.7414 | 1.4567 | 34.9404 |
| ROG124 | 3.2767 | 2.0166 | 1.2798 | 34.2150 |
| ROG125 | 3.2082 | 2.1471 | 1.3625 | 34.0637 |
| ROG126 | 4.0655 | 2.3559 | 1.6924 | 43.9573 |
| ROG127 | 3.3267 | 1.9826 | 1.3698 | 34.8124 |
| ROG128 | 3.7825 | 2.1530 | 1.6894 | 40.4861 |
| ROG129 | 2.7457 | 1.6033 | 1.2529 | 29.0055 |
| ROG130 | 3.5450 | 1.8101 | 1.6204 | 37.4704 |
| ROG131 | 3.0605 | 1.8470 | 1.3339 | 32.0531 |
| ROG132 | 3.6066 | 1.6335 | 1.7025 | 38.7167 |
| ROG133 | 3.0482 | 2.2276 | 1.2365 | 32.8137 |
| ROG134 | 4.4719 | 2.8491 | 1.9409 | 47.5313 |
| ROG135 | 4.2804 | 2.6811 | 1.8316 | 45.7243 |
| ROG136 | 4.0558 | 2.8888 | 1.6140 | 43.9721 |
| ROG137 | 4.2771 | 2.5427 | 1.7831 | 46.5278 |
| ROG138 | 4.7745 | 3.4464 | 2.0164 | 50.3911 |
| ROG139 | 4.5803 | 2.6631 | 1.8398 | 50.6177 |
| ROG140 | 4.4711 | 3.1043 | 1.7759 | 48.9151 |
| ROG141 | 4.6851 | 3.0531 | 2.1808 | 51.3896 |
| ROG142 | 4.1949 | 2.8055 | 1.6791 | 45.6079 |
| ROG143 | 4.6500 | 3.0241 | 2.0441 | 49.7945 |
| ROG144 | 4.2859 | 2.6678 | 1.6605 | 46.4864 |
| ROG145 | 4.3132 | 2.8866 | 1.6241 | 47.0736 |
| ROG146 | 4.9094 | 4.2101 | 2.0619 | 51.5955 |
| ROG147 | 5.0334 | 2.7083 | 2.0217 | 55.1847 |
| ROG148 | 4.4948 | 2.2220 | 1.8490 | 48.6675 |

Table 6. Elemental Concentration (ppm) Data for Susiana Ceramics (*cont.*)

| *Sample Identification* | *Samarium (Sm)* | *Uranium (U)* | *Ytterbium (Yb)* | *Cerium (Ce)* |
|---|---|---|---|---|
| ROG149 | 4.2085 | 2.8252 | 1.7235 | 46.3452 |
| ROG150 | 4.5371 | 2.8037 | 1.8011 | 49.6004 |
| ROG151 | 4.8983 | 2.4292 | 2.0966 | 53.1784 |
| ROG152 | 4.6218 | 2.5600 | 1.8795 | 52.4981 |
| ROG153 | 4.3499 | 2.8947 | 2.0438 | 49.0931 |
| ROG154 | 3.7623 | 2.9088 | 2.0065 | 41.4467 |
| ROG155 | 4.5688 | 2.5198 | 1.9754 | 50.5929 |
| ROG156 | 4.3477 | 3.2551 | 1.8295 | 47.2359 |
| ROG157 | 4.7547 | 3.2669 | 2.1175 | 52.1656 |
| ROG158 | 4.7547 | 3.6816 | 2.1219 | 50.9004 |
| ROG159 | 4.2945 | 2.0747 | 1.9016 | 48.7279 |
| ROG160 | 4.7001 | 2.4916 | 2.1203 | 53.5615 |
| ROG161 | 4.7562 | 2.3996 | 2.1158 | 50.7003 |
| ROG162 | 4.5924 | 2.8003 | 2.0237 | 51.5111 |
| ROG163 | 4.2008 | 3.3020 | 1.7846 | 45.9808 |
| ROG164 | 4.2747 | 2.4829 | 1.6899 | 47.3195 |
| ROG165 | 3.8833 | 2.3073 | 1.7033 | 41.8156 |
| ROG166 | 4.9114 | 2.4840 | 2.2839 | 56.1129 |
| ROG167 | 4.6056 | 2.4287 | 1.9863 | 50.2007 |
| ROG168 | 4.3435 | 2.5362 | 2.1312 | 50.9284 |
| ROG169 | 4.3532 | 2.1966 | 1.8985 | 48.7368 |
| ROG170 | 4.8836 | 2.6485 | 2.0852 | 48.3556 |
| ROG171 | 4.6694 | 2.3213 | 2.0166 | 56.2028 |
| ROG172 | 4.9250 | 1.9746 | 2.1385 | 55.7108 |
| ROG173 | 4.4807 | 2.2054 | 1.8267 | 58.3462 |
| ROG174 | 4.5403 | 2.8219 | 2.1389 | 48.5325 |
| ROG175 | 5.1199 | 2.8098 | 2.2699 | 50.8798 |
| ROG176 | 4.8061 | 3.3375 | 1.9819 | 54.7261 |
| ROG177 | 5.0827 | 2.3583 | 2.3232 | 53.9599 |
| ROG178 | 4.7458 | 3.0180 | 1.7227 | 52.5457 |
| ROG179 | 3.8266 | 2.3210 | 1.7383 | 40.9668 |
| ROG180 | 3.6031 | 2.3127 | 1.6187 | 40.2211 |
| ROG181 | 3.5991 | 2.3091 | 1.3406 | 40.0801 |
| ROG182 | 4.5857 | 2.6756 | 2.1559 | 48.5585 |
| ROG183 | 4.0228 | 2.0842 | 1.6391 | 45.5296 |
| ROG184 | 4.1227 | 2.2984 | 1.6243 | 45.9808 |
| ROG185 | 4.0094 | 2.2194 | 1.6526 | 44.8055 |

Table 6. Elemental Concentration (ppm) Data for Susiana Ceramics (*cont.*)

| *Sample Identification* | *Samarium (Sm)* | *Uranium (U)* | *Ytterbium (Yb)* | *Cerium (Ce)* |
|---|---|---|---|---|
| ROG186 | 4.0142 | 2.9245 | 1.5802 | 45.4221 |
| ROG187 | 3.8322 | 2.1650 | 1.5801 | 42.9468 |
| ROG188 | 4.7401 | 2.4198 | 2.0653 | 51.0233 |
| ROG189 | 4.0367 | 3.5283 | 1.5712 | 45.5750 |
| ROG190 | 4.1325 | 2.6117 | 1.6673 | 46.2083 |
| ROG191 | 3.9115 | 2.1757 | 1.5139 | 44.3637 |
| ROG192 | 4.0406 | 1.9832 | 1.7358 | 44.2554 |
| ROG193 | 3.7528 | 1.5775 | 1.6128 | 41.0409 |
| ROG194 | 3.4857 | 1.8497 | 1.6890 | 37.0884 |
| ROG195 | 3.6939 | 1.9261 | 1.6645 | 40.2622 |
| ROG196 | 3.3979 | 1.7430 | 1.4724 | 36.6369 |
| ROG197 | 4.2725 | 1.9043 | 1.7938 | 46.2369 |
| ROG198 | 3.3078 | 2.0119 | 1.4556 | 35.3465 |
| ROG199 | 4.0928 | 1.6114 | 1.8659 | 44.2843 |
| ROG200 | 3.5609 | 1.2784 | 1.6364 | 38.7035 |

Table 7. Elemental Concentration (ppm) Data for Susiana Ceramics

| *Sample Identification* | *Cobalt (Co)* | *Chromium (Cr)* | *Caesium (Cs)* | *Europium (Eu)* |
|---|---|---|---|---|
| ROG001 | 15.5004 | 138.8081 | 2.5622 | 0.8653 |
| ROG002 | 14.9803 | 141.5449 | 2.0402 | 0.8438 |
| ROG003 | 16.8835 | 156.6406 | 2.7007 | 0.8391 |
| ROG004 | 14.3319 | 130.1825 | 2.1065 | 0.7556 |
| ROG005 | 16.6957 | 193.4029 | 3.1394 | 0.8394 |
| ROG006 | 16.5050 | 201.4255 | 2.5502 | 0.7516 |
| ROG007 | 19.0475 | 140.9895 | 2.7466 | 0.8663 |
| ROG008 | 22.0998 | 217.3806 | 3.4017 | 0.9786 |
| ROG009 | 16.5246 | 141.0731 | 2.9259 | 0.9312 |
| ROG010 | 13.4108 | 201.6492 | 2.0899 | 0.8321 |
| ROG011 | 17.2279 | 208.3401 | 2.9715 | 0.8619 |
| ROG012 | 16.6688 | 143.2565 | 2.8030 | 0.9046 |
| ROG013 | 18.1292 | 149.8398 | 2.6077 | 0.8201 |
| ROG014 | 15.4732 | 128.0338 | 2.7089 | 0.8287 |
| ROG015 | 15.6259 | 142.8032 | 3.8119 | 0.8543 |
| ROG016 | 16.2809 | 209.3920 | 2.6521 | 0.7738 |
| ROG017 | 15.2613 | 122.5138 | 1.9902 | 0.7959 |
| ROG018 | 16.1297 | 212.2199 | 2.5739 | 0.7663 |
| ROG019 | 16.4161 | 216.6579 | 2.8964 | 0.8041 |
| ROG020 | 15.3590 | 155.0233 | 2.5581 | 0.7688 |
| ROG021 | 19.8164 | 172.8772 | 2.8437 | 1.0174 |
| ROG022 | 26.6206 | 271.5164 | 3.4895 | 1.0215 |
| ROG023 | 16.2626 | 136.9561 | 1.7478 | 0.8373 |
| ROG024 | 15.1994 | 141.5224 | 2.3561 | 0.7448 |
| ROG025 | 15.6770 | 151.6525 | 1.9659 | 0.7403 |
| ROG026 | 16.3846 | 164.1922 | 2.5036 | 0.8081 |
| ROG027 | 14.5822 | 145.7366 | 2.1316 | 0.7541 |
| ROG028 | 11.7003 | 137.1456 | 1.6411 | 0.7088 |
| ROG029 | 18.4848 | 181.3820 | 2.3716 | 0.9593 |
| ROG030 | 11.7357 | 154.9066 | 1.6687 | 0.7411 |
| ROG031 | 14.1840 | 149.0807 | 1.5621 | 0.7843 |
| ROG032 | 10.6413 | 142.4041 | 1.6614 | 0.7470 |
| ROG033 | 13.5626 | 131.3617 | 1.8173 | 0.7556 |
| ROG034 | 11.0369 | 131.2863 | 1.7367 | 0.7003 |
| ROG035 | 10.5595 | 143.2831 | 1.6602 | 0.7049 |
| ROG036 | 13.1869 | 142.3740 | 2.1117 | 0.7299 |
| ROG037 | 12.4586 | 147.2613 | 1.8086 | 0.7414 |

Table 7. Elemental Concentration (ppm) Data for Susiana Ceramics (*cont.*)

| *Sample Identification* | *Cobalt (Co)* | *Chromium (Cr)* | *Caesium (Cs)* | *Europium (Eu)* |
|---|---|---|---|---|
| ROG038 | 15.7650 | 164.5423 | 2.1902 | 0.8923 |
| ROG039 | 15.1588 | 118.6640 | 2.1300 | 0.8267 |
| ROG040 | 12.9997 | 113.5442 | 1.7463 | 0.7210 |
| ROG041 | 16.7296 | 166.5632 | 2.6297 | 0.9379 |
| ROG042 | 15.8098 | 159.0262 | 2.2887 | 0.8870 |
| ROG043 | 14.6152 | 133.0696 | 2.2128 | 0.7283 |
| ROG044 | 13.9862 | 148.5668 | 1.9580 | 0.7453 |
| ROG045 | 12.9198 | 134.9215 | 1.9532 | 0.7299 |
| ROG046 | 13.6978 | 127.7426 | 1.5600 | 0.8340 |
| ROG047 | 13.1683 | 130.7933 | 1.9361 | 0.7655 |
| ROG048 | 15.5715 | 136.2340 | 3.1990 | 0.8036 |
| ROG049 | 13.7228 | 133.3620 | 1.7252 | 0.7332 |
| ROG050 | 14.5585 | 140.5333 | 2.1704 | 0.8013 |
| ROG051 | 14.5096 | 121.4904 | 2.1623 | 0.7245 |
| ROG052 | 13.6480 | 123.8721 | 2.0377 | 0.7446 |
| ROG053 | 16.8020 | 163.2346 | 2.3457 | 0.9344 |
| ROG054 | 15.7451 | 148.3048 | 2.0427 | 0.8424 |
| ROG055 | 14.7525 | 164.5158 | 2.8324 | 0.9689 |
| ROG056 | 15.4360 | 142.5216 | 1.7914 | 0.7907 |
| ROG057 | 14.5971 | 140.5027 | 2.0805 | 0.7624 |
| ROG058 | 14.0264 | 147.4347 | 2.6043 | 0.8276 |
| ROG059 | 15.9199 | 141.1044 | 3.3379 | 0.8207 |
| ROG060 | 16.4336 | 159.0451 | 2.6571 | 0.8645 |
| ROG061 | 12.9379 | 127.1241 | 3.5473 | 0.8088 |
| ROG062 | 18.3319 | 144.7485 | 3.7467 | 0.8927 |
| ROG063 | 16.0114 | 157.4272 | 3.2838 | 0.8724 |
| ROG064 | 14.2803 | 143.3046 | 2.6790 | 0.7626 |
| ROG065 | 11.9833 | 149.4096 | 2.2063 | 0.7255 |
| ROG066 | 16.7561 | 140.4850 | 3.0497 | 0.8427 |
| ROG067 | 13.3890 | 138.3940 | 2.9221 | 0.7895 |
| ROG068 | 18.1494 | 196.6110 | 3.8695 | 0.8988 |
| ROG069 | 18.5169 | 203.6189 | 2.7920 | 0.9068 |
| ROG070 | 14.5047 | 294.9379 | 2.5539 | 0.9246 |
| ROG071 | 15.2981 | 175.2909 | 2.5927 | 0.8290 |
| ROG072 | 15.4937 | 193.5357 | 2.7674 | 0.8239 |
| ROG073 | 24.8558 | 225.7107 | 4.2238 | 1.1424 |
| ROG074 | 21.1838 | 182.5949 | 3.9341 | 0.9536 |

Table 7. Elemental Concentration (ppm) Data for Susiana Ceramics (*cont.*)

| *Sample Identification* | *Cobalt (Co)* | *Chromium (Cr)* | *Caesium (Cs)* | *Europium (Eu)* |
|---|---|---|---|---|
| ROG075 | 17.5373 | 176.6899 | 2.5646 | 0.8068 |
| ROG076 | 15.3191 | 176.4243 | 2.9974 | 0.8164 |
| ROG077 | 18.9329 | 206.9436 | 3.2416 | 0.9744 |
| ROG078 | 17.0683 | 192.1239 | 3.7014 | 0.8585 |
| ROG079 | 18.4012 | 181.3731 | 3.4144 | 0.8951 |
| ROG080 | 14.4159 | 138.2848 | 1.8074 | 0.7304 |
| ROG081 | 17.3695 | 194.5173 | 2.9963 | 0.8540 |
| ROG082 | 21.1641 | 169.9186 | 3.2953 | 0.9277 |
| ROG083 | 17.7844 | 189.6910 | 3.4673 | 0.8636 |
| ROG084 | 19.7211 | 198.7360 | 3.8191 | 0.9601 |
| ROG085 | 21.7133 | 240.7629 | 3.5221 | 0.9446 |
| ROG086 | 15.7865 | 157.8230 | 2.6457 | 0.8013 |
| ROG087 | 15.3946 | 184.3171 | 2.2383 | 0.7892 |
| ROG088 | 18.9631 | 185.1865 | 3.7914 | 0.9375 |
| ROG089 | 16.6175 | 174.5499 | 3.0547 | 0.8598 |
| ROG090 | 20.0623 | 258.8474 | 3.0457 | 0.9694 |
| ROG091 | 16.6332 | 164.6816 | 2.4300 | 0.8344 |
| ROG092 | 16.8400 | 132.9855 | 2.7168 | 0.8018 |
| ROG093 | 16.8775 | 195.7594 | 2.1996 | 0.9241 |
| ROG094 | 19.2595 | 180.2110 | 3.7479 | 0.9089 |
| ROG095 | 18.5916 | 194.1872 | 3.7391 | 0.8752 |
| ROG096 | 15.8996 | 168.7277 | 2.7006 | 0.8308 |
| ROG097 | 13.3806 | 152.8755 | 2.3182 | 0.7194 |
| ROG098 | 17.5759 | 193.4494 | 3.2765 | 0.8471 |
| ROG099 | 14.7355 | 153.0792 | 3.8155 | 0.8093 |
| ROG100 | 18.7523 | 171.3837 | 3.8566 | 0.8587 |
| ROG101 | 15.7966 | 162.4270 | 2.9291 | 0.7462 |
| ROG102 | 16.0965 | 161.2065 | 3.1303 | 0.7729 |
| ROG103 | 19.2545 | 194.0255 | 3.5331 | 0.9080 |
| ROG104 | 17.9736 | 191.0259 | 3.7527 | 0.9055 |
| ROG105 | 17.4161 | 179.9186 | 3.1160 | 0.8537 |
| ROG106 | 16.7649 | 186.7007 | 2.7180 | 0.8843 |
| ROG107 | 19.6384 | 199.1727 | 3.9004 | 0.9177 |
| ROG108 | 17.8332 | 179.7243 | 3.6239 | 0.8206 |
| ROG109 | 16.8815 | 130.9189 | 2.5410 | 0.7765 |
| ROG110 | 13.5986 | 159.4787 | 2.7285 | 0.7246 |
| ROG111 | 13.8087 | 157.2913 | 2.0674 | 0.7254 |

Table 7. Elemental Concentration (ppm) Data for Susiana Ceramics (*cont.*)

| *Sample Identification* | *Cobalt (Co)* | *Chromium (Cr)* | *Caesium (Cs)* | *Europium (Eu)* |
|---|---|---|---|---|
| ROG112 | 15.8967 | 241.6074 | 2.6238 | 0.7957 |
| ROG113 | 14.1720 | 142.7581 | 2.4870 | 0.7796 |
| ROG114 | 17.9009 | 152.4784 | 3.3429 | 0.8134 |
| ROG115 | 11.9365 | 127.0451 | 1.9968 | 0.6635 |
| ROG116 | 17.4506 | 174.7826 | 2.5271 | 0.9395 |
| ROG117 | 14.6507 | 143.7367 | 2.0644 | 0.7130 |
| ROG118 | 15.2937 | 141.3258 | 2.4874 | 0.7151 |
| ROG119 | 19.5123 | 170.6369 | 3.2148 | 0.8968 |
| ROG120 | 14.2739 | 175.5372 | 2.2035 | 0.7896 |
| ROG121 | 11.5704 | 154.5943 | 2.2428 | 0.7341 |
| ROG122 | 11.1194 | 158.2926 | 1.9116 | 0.7486 |
| ROG123 | 14.0696 | 150.0575 | 2.7681 | 0.7453 |
| ROG124 | 15.5656 | 136.5320 | 2.7482 | 0.7353 |
| ROG125 | 15.4466 | 135.5916 | 2.5823 | 0.7372 |
| ROG126 | 20.3089 | 179.7289 | 2.5813 | 0.9247 |
| ROG127 | 14.8010 | 204.8866 | 2.3068 | 0.7664 |
| ROG128 | 15.7324 | 173.8047 | 2.6051 | 0.8656 |
| ROG129 | 11.6488 | 134.4205 | 2.0962 | 0.6212 |
| ROG130 | 16.5551 | 212.7159 | 2.4130 | 0.7984 |
| ROG131 | 14.6164 | 131.0338 | 2.3748 | 0.6912 |
| ROG132 | 16.4194 | 161.1602 | 1.8192 | 0.8291 |
| ROG133 | 12.0455 | 173.9357 | 1.8810 | 0.6999 |
| ROG134 | 17.7842 | 285.5405 | 4.2159 | 1.0110 |
| ROG135 | 20.5590 | 176.0008 | 4.4471 | 0.9432 |
| ROG136 | 16.1230 | 217.7533 | 2.8603 | 0.8546 |
| ROG137 | 20.6508 | 217.0267 | 4.6411 | 0.9808 |
| ROG138 | 18.6654 | 195.7686 | 3.8025 | 1.0333 |
| ROG139 | 18.6887 | 187.2038 | 3.9524 | 1.0000 |
| ROG140 | 18.9243 | 214.2910 | 4.0204 | 0.9588 |
| ROG141 | 25.4232 | 224.0777 | 5.5471 | 1.0956 |
| ROG142 | 20.5961 | 207.6954 | 4.3913 | 0.9155 |
| ROG143 | 19.1963 | 231.3815 | 5.0844 | 1.0140 |
| ROG144 | 18.0421 | 218.9436 | 4.7389 | 0.9872 |
| ROG145 | 20.9626 | 200.9581 | 4.7247 | 0.9504 |
| ROG146 | 20.9020 | 287.4565 | 4.3877 | 1.1082 |
| ROG147 | 23.9579 | 214.0290 | 5.0882 | 1.0966 |
| ROG148 | 20.3314 | 228.6479 | 5.0281 | 0.9838 |

Table 7. Elemental Concentration (ppm) Data for Susiana Ceramics (*cont.*)

| *Sample Identification* | *Cobalt (Co)* | *Chromium (Cr)* | *Caesium (Cs)* | *Europium (Eu)* |
|---|---|---|---|---|
| ROG149 | 20.5221 | 206.5753 | 4.5442 | 0.9523 |
| ROG150 | 20.6301 | 193.1092 | 1.7410 | 0.9789 |
| ROG151 | 27.1361 | 262.5999 | 3.3666 | 1.1410 |
| ROG152 | 21.8482 | 235.1117 | 5.0821 | 1.0644 |
| ROG153 | 14.1346 | 212.9194 | 1.7498 | 1.0035 |
| ROG154 | 15.3038 | 176.2746 | 2.3476 | 0.8604 |
| ROG155 | 21.7699 | 256.9426 | 3.8737 | 1.0521 |
| ROG156 | 16.2654 | 185.7875 | 4.4184 | 0.9765 |
| ROG157 | 18.2426 | 212.0995 | 4.6407 | 1.1036 |
| ROG158 | 19.1979 | 209.1768 | 4.4205 | 1.0799 |
| ROG159 | 19.8997 | 175.9654 | 4.9297 | 0.9977 |
| ROG160 | 20.1898 | 194.3937 | 5.0957 | 1.0234 |
| ROG161 | 19.5688 | 288.2147 | 3.7644 | 1.1029 |
| ROG162 | 21.7690 | 226.6096 | 4.6154 | 0.9835 |
| ROG163 | 18.6137 | 176.7227 | 3.4692 | 0.9313 |
| ROG164 | 15.3376 | 196.5437 | 4.1249 | 0.9574 |
| ROG165 | 14.6633 | 190.1596 | 4.4842 | 0.8588 |
| ROG166 | 22.0392 | 208.3317 | 4.1924 | 1.1731 |
| ROG167 | 19.6507 | 251.3361 | 4.4424 | 1.0790 |
| ROG168 | 22.4222 | 210.4433 | 5.3106 | 0.9762 |
| ROG169 | 23.7592 | 218.7852 | 4.9673 | 1.0007 |
| ROG170 | 20.6402 | 210.1738 | 3.3240 | 0.9840 |
| ROG171 | 22.6632 | 206.2639 | 5.6349 | 1.1011 |
| ROG172 | 24.1621 | 204.5014 | 5.4905 | 1.0962 |
| ROG173 | 22.8031 | 182.9324 | 5.3011 | 1.1341 |
| ROG174 | 17.9673 | 155.8676 | 5.5708 | 1.0068 |
| ROG175 | 21.0552 | 207.6516 | 4.7874 | 1.0635 |
| ROG176 | 18.8367 | 211.5260 | 4.9397 | 1.0668 |
| ROG177 | 20.8058 | 283.0499 | 3.9996 | 1.1612 |
| ROG178 | 19.8375 | 228.3201 | 3.6987 | 1.0995 |
| ROG179 | 22.6044 | 221.2434 | 0.6475 | 0.9083 |
| ROG180 | 19.3318 | 219.3890 | 3.7477 | 0.8352 |
| ROG181 | 16.9586 | 141.2582 | 2.8492 | 0.8506 |
| ROG182 | 19.1414 | 366.0635 | 3.9992 | 1.0206 |
| ROG183 | 18.2051 | 151.7435 | 3.0799 | 0.9374 |
| ROG184 | 19.8357 | 172.2331 | 3.3324 | 0.9635 |
| ROG185 | 18.6956 | 168.8977 | 3.2613 | 0.9184 |

Table 7. Elemental Concentration (ppm) Data for Susiana Ceramics (*cont.*)

| *Sample Identification* | *Cobalt (Co)* | *Chromium (Cr)* | *Caesium (Cs)* | *Europium (Eu)* |
|---|---|---|---|---|
| ROG186 | 17.0127 | 159.9698 | 2.8185 | 0.9300 |
| ROG187 | 18.2825 | 173.6349 | 2.7780 | 0.9053 |
| ROG188 | 19.1286 | 311.0328 | 3.9033 | 1.0764 |
| ROG189 | 20.1961 | 165.7458 | 3.3038 | 0.9512 |
| ROG190 | 19.0695 | 178.5772 | 2.9348 | 0.9683 |
| ROG191 | 16.8988 | 151.4529 | 2.9416 | 0.9101 |
| ROG192 | 20.3905 | 246.5988 | 3.0968 | 0.9592 |
| ROG193 | 16.3368 | 304.1426 | 2.0030 | 0.8556 |
| ROG194 | 15.0753 | 250.6235 | 1.1282 | 0.8089 |
| ROG195 | 18.2555 | 263.4122 | 0.4682 | 0.8528 |
| ROG196 | 16.8078 | 207.6945 | 0.5931 | 0.8032 |
| ROG197 | 20.6728 | 240.2098 | 2.1543 | 1.0189 |
| ROG198 | 18.6854 | 200.5004 | 1.9910 | 0.7830 |
| ROG199 | 19.5937 | 340.8228 | 2.8462 | 0.9576 |
| ROG200 | 17.0924 | 302.2438 | 1.4676 | 0.8344 |

Table 8. Elemental Concentration (ppm) Data for Susiana Ceramics

| *Sample Identification* | *Iron (Fe)* | *Hafnium (Hf)* | *Nickel (Ni)* | *Rubidium (Rb)* |
|---|---|---|---|---|
| ROG001 | 35225.0 | 2.6316 | 103.73 | 19.68 |
| ROG002 | 32568.6 | 2.5086 | 80.01 | 29.15 |
| ROG003 | 33328.4 | 2.8425 | 76.73 | 48.43 |
| ROG004 | 31434.5 | 2.2931 | 89.36 | 36.97 |
| ROG005 | 36623.6 | 2.9260 | 124.67 | 54.84 |
| ROG006 | 31498.1 | 2.9896 | 130.50 | 47.33 |
| ROG007 | 35988.0 | 2.6336 | 95.06 | 51.59 |
| ROG008 | 43880.9 | 3.1182 | 163.65 | 41.13 |
| ROG009 | 37491.3 | 2.8413 | 89.08 | 55.31 |
| ROG010 | 34575.9 | 3.1218 | 116.84 | 42.24 |
| ROG011 | 36082.9 | 2.8387 | 112.47 | 53.36 |
| ROG012 | 35740.7 | 2.8042 | 82.26 | 52.11 |
| ROG013 | 35239.3 | 2.6218 | 79.10 | 42.99 |
| ROG014 | 32673.5 | 2.4584 | 103.07 | 27.76 |
| ROG015 | 35373.3 | 2.7418 | 92.24 | 33.24 |
| ROG016 | 32423.5 | 2.8161 | 138.48 | 48.18 |
| ROG017 | 31338.9 | 2.5351 | 89.95 | 27.22 |
| ROG018 | 31809.1 | 2.8520 | 141.47 | 47.27 |
| ROG019 | 32821.4 | 2.8942 | 108.75 | 47.76 |
| ROG020 | 30353.4 | 2.6358 | 81.49 | 46.00 |
| ROG021 | 42271.7 | 3.1160 | 87.69 | 51.99 |
| ROG022 | 49246.1 | 3.4247 | 210.82 | 61.29 |
| ROG023 | 32206.8 | 2.5781 | 91.24 | 34.21 |
| ROG024 | 29366.1 | 2.5147 | 79.82 | 40.35 |
| ROG025 | 30344.9 | 2.6857 | 75.02 | 38.33 |
| ROG026 | 32041.0 | 2.7190 | 77.35 | 44.43 |
| ROG027 | 29508.7 | 2.4971 | 92.45 | 41.23 |
| ROG028 | 25365.3 | 2.3132 | 71.77 | 32.61 |
| ROG029 | 35276.4 | 3.2310 | 81.20 | 18.94 |
| ROG030 | 26116.3 | 2.4263 | 42.25 | 34.22 |
| ROG031 | 27836.3 | 2.6226 | 64.19 | 32.33 |
| ROG032 | 26614.0 | 2.4800 | 43.95 | 35.76 |
| ROG033 | 28883.6 | 2.5280 | 87.60 | 38.13 |
| ROG034 | 24993.8 | 2.2505 | 59.57 | 32.98 |
| ROG035 | 24268.4 | 2.2838 | 71.52 | 33.01 |
| ROG036 | 26267.5 | 2.3166 | 79.11 | 34.16 |
| ROG037 | 27124.2 | 2.4366 | 45.54 | 38.29 |

Table 8. Elemental Concentration (ppm) Data for Susiana Ceramics (*cont.*)

| *Sample Identification* | *Iron (Fe)* | *Hafnium (Hf)* | *Nickel (Ni)* | *Rubidium (Rb)* |
|---|---|---|---|---|
| ROG038 | 32572.5 | 2.8773 | 104.52 | 44.27 |
| ROG039 | 31853.4 | 2.5826 | 87.38 | 44.13 |
| ROG040 | 26443.1 | 2.0762 | 64.91 | 37.81 |
| ROG041 | 36875.6 | 2.9053 | 104.60 | 23.17 |
| ROG042 | 34679.8 | 2.7815 | 78.26 | 33.71 |
| ROG043 | 29172.2 | 2.3242 | 91.18 | 41.50 |
| ROG044 | 27681.6 | 2.4071 | 69.90 | 38.76 |
| ROG045 | 26940.6 | 2.3409 | 71.38 | 36.15 |
| ROG046 | 31704.2 | 2.4333 | 73.41 | 31.78 |
| ROG047 | 27631.3 | 2.3083 | 71.10 | 37.65 |
| ROG048 | 32444.4 | 2.4758 | 90.56 | 47.56 |
| ROG049 | 27358.6 | 2.3592 | 84.84 | 33.03 |
| ROG050 | 30100.5 | 2.6499 | 99.30 | 43.66 |
| ROG051 | 29763.2 | 2.2752 | 64.28 | 39.49 |
| ROG052 | 29641.7 | 2.3248 | 66.24 | 36.24 |
| ROG053 | 35142.9 | 3.0119 | 93.00 | 48.01 |
| ROG054 | 32073.8 | 2.5949 | 54.19 | 40.09 |
| ROG055 | 38086.7 | 2.9312 | 83.85 | 21.69 |
| ROG056 | 29245.1 | 2.4176 | 59.74 | 38.34 |
| ROG057 | 28280.9 | 2.4262 | 72.80 | 33.26 |
| ROG058 | 29623.8 | 2.6873 | 73.14 | 44.41 |
| ROG059 | 32828.5 | 2.5169 | 94.10 | 51.82 |
| ROG060 | 32328.2 | 2.6334 | 105.72 | 42.52 |
| ROG061 | 31094.6 | 2.5107 | 60.24 | 56.68 |
| ROG062 | 35347.2 | 2.8361 | 91.79 | 54.71 |
| ROG063 | 34617.8 | 2.6592 | 65.88 | 55.16 |
| ROG064 | 28320.7 | 2.4638 | 74.36 | 45.44 |
| ROG065 | 25605.9 | 2.3376 | 51.19 | 37.88 |
| ROG066 | 33464.9 | 2.4921 | 77.27 | 47.55 |
| ROG067 | 29850.7 | 2.4240 | 78.19 | 47.95 |
| ROG068 | 38105.1 | 3.1588 | 106.60 | 29.28 |
| ROG069 | 35304.1 | 3.2926 | 88.95 | 44.46 |
| ROG070 | 30538.5 | 3.9622 | 72.29 | 28.43 |
| ROG071 | 34373.7 | 3.0871 | 92.83 | 49.37 |
| ROG072 | 32316.8 | 3.2006 | 90.20 | 32.24 |
| ROG073 | 50393.0 | 4.2480 | 114.47 | 25.29 |
| ROG074 | 40981.3 | 3.2717 | 114.61 | 67.85 |

Table 8. Elemental Concentration (ppm) Data for Susiana Ceramics (*cont.*)

| *Sample Identification* | *Iron (Fe)* | *Hafnium (Hf)* | *Nickel (Ni)* | *Rubidium (Rb)* |
|---|---|---|---|---|
| ROG075 | 33228.2 | 2.7961 | 98.01 | 48.04 |
| ROG076 | 31468.8 | 3.0680 | 89.42 | 51.75 |
| ROG077 | 39286.1 | 3.7224 | 101.06 | 59.90 |
| ROG078 | 35788.0 | 3.1135 | 108.45 | 31.58 |
| ROG079 | 36328.5 | 3.3460 | 89.02 | 59.51 |
| ROG080 | 27494.6 | 2.7745 | 75.93 | 37.44 |
| ROG081 | 33813.2 | 3.3235 | 80.12 | 24.42 |
| ROG082 | 41484.5 | 3.0727 | 104.28 | 57.98 |
| ROG083 | 35134.6 | 3.1190 | 62.46 | 33.37 |
| ROG084 | 39398.2 | 3.4999 | 108.31 | 62.55 |
| ROG085 | 38625.0 | 3.1684 | 130.25 | 40.16 |
| ROG086 | 32406.4 | 2.8438 | 89.83 | 49.08 |
| ROG087 | 32591.6 | 2.8669 | 85.14 | 46.46 |
| ROG088 | 39801.7 | 3.2962 | 102.83 | 66.31 |
| ROG089 | 34330.1 | 2.9927 | 77.17 | 54.59 |
| ROG090 | 36037.3 | 4.1269 | 116.37 | 55.63 |
| ROG091 | 32199.5 | 2.7796 | 95.28 | 44.93 |
| ROG092 | 32916.7 | 2.5579 | 68.72 | 48.80 |
| ROG093 | 34083.6 | 3.4177 | 84.83 | 38.10 |
| ROG094 | 37696.2 | 3.0622 | 76.59 | 62.32 |
| ROG095 | 36079.9 | 3.2591 | 87.62 | 34.11 |
| ROG096 | 32526.8 | 2.7326 | 87.82 | 39.71 |
| ROG097 | 26471.3 | 2.5441 | 70.74 | 42.34 |
| ROG098 | 34002.7 | 3.2525 | 86.70 | 58.43 |
| ROG099 | 32560.1 | 2.9255 | 71.80 | 36.12 |
| ROG100 | 37595.7 | 2.8409 | 103.56 | 18.66 |
| ROG101 | 32258.0 | 2.5196 | 92.27 | 50.65 |
| ROG102 | 31664.8 | 2.7554 | 128.55 | 53.03 |
| ROG103 | 37304.2 | 3.3280 | 82.01 | 55.06 |
| ROG104 | 36990.2 | 3.3684 | 87.79 | 62.16 |
| ROG105 | 35266.9 | 2.9907 | 103.03 | 55.04 |
| ROG106 | 32623.3 | 3.3381 | 78.34 | 39.10 |
| ROG107 | 40039.4 | 3.2914 | 120.10 | 65.85 |
| ROG108 | 34755.5 | 3.1402 | 87.68 | 30.99 |
| ROG109 | 33301.8 | 2.6721 | 95.33 | 48.21 |
| ROG110 | 26720.0 | 2.7308 | 67.48 | 43.51 |
| ROG111 | 27699.1 | 2.7434 | 87.69 | 43.20 |

Table 8. Elemental Concentration (ppm) Data for Susiana Ceramics (*cont.*)

| *Sample Identification* | *Iron (Fe)* | *Hafnium (Hf)* | *Nickel (Ni)* | *Rubidium (Rb)* |
|---|---|---|---|---|
| ROG112 | 32270.6 | 3.1990 | 146.58 | 47.85 |
| ROG113 | 28604.4 | 2.6828 | 61.74 | 46.06 |
| ROG114 | 35584.0 | 2.7514 | 114.71 | 60.16 |
| ROG115 | 24463.8 | 2.2864 | 238.20 | 38.66 |
| ROG116 | 40067.4 | 3.2902 | 110.66 | 63.42 |
| ROG117 | 27718.4 | 2.5652 | 80.95 | 43.18 |
| ROG118 | 30243.3 | 2.5409 | 104.79 | 48.97 |
| ROG119 | 37334.9 | 3.0990 | 88.60 | 32.98 |
| ROG120 | 29283.9 | 3.1105 | 63.60 | 44.89 |
| ROG121 | 26323.0 | 2.7317 | 68.05 | 44.53 |
| ROG122 | 25696.5 | 3.1626 | 79.47 | 30.93 |
| ROG123 | 28591.9 | 2.7236 | 82.56 | 47.35 |
| ROG124 | 29736.7 | 2.6145 | 93.68 | 47.27 |
| ROG125 | 30566.9 | 2.5911 | 76.72 | 46.43 |
| ROG126 | 41977.2 | 3.2457 | 103.56 | 56.55 |
| ROG127 | 28090.2 | 3.3219 | 89.42 | 43.84 |
| ROG128 | 33931.7 | 3.3463 | 56.60 | 51.00 |
| ROG129 | 23950.9 | 2.3752 | 77.59 | 40.79 |
| ROG130 | 31020.1 | 3.4316 | 87.13 | 46.46 |
| ROG131 | 28300.1 | 2.4163 | 66.52 | 40.67 |
| ROG132 | 32995.4 | 2.9598 | 72.59 | 45.81 |
| ROG133 | 25302.5 | 2.7453 | 62.88 | 42.36 |
| ROG134 | 41082.3 | 4.1318 | 122.42 | 22.54 |
| ROG135 | 43191.9 | 3.3815 | 154.12 | 10.85 |
| ROG136 | 39544.5 | 3.5352 | 150.13 | 15.25 |
| ROG137 | 41735.0 | 3.4541 | 153.34 | 19.61 |
| ROG138 | 47227.8 | 3.6152 | 139.44 | 21.01 |
| ROG139 | 47117.5 | 3.4899 | 111.02 | 11.24 |
| ROG140 | 45215.7 | 3.6567 | 134.67 | 18.29 |
| ROG141 | 48853.9 | 3.7726 | 158.51 | 73.47 |
| ROG142 | 43148.0 | 3.4319 | 149.76 | 29.61 |
| ROG143 | 46877.2 | 3.9180 | 162.93 | 22.09 |
| ROG144 | 43051.9 | 3.6177 | 106.22 | 35.97 |
| ROG145 | 45815.6 | 3.5783 | 147.42 | 18.53 |
| ROG146 | 42844.0 | 4.3388 | 120.57 | 27.96 |
| ROG147 | 50017.0 | 4.0986 | 122.86 | 47.02 |
| ROG148 | 46002.9 | 3.6652 | 156.93 | 41.05 |

Table 8. Elemental Concentration (ppm) Data for Susiana Ceramics (*cont.*)

| *Sample Identification* | *Iron (Fe)* | *Hafnium (Hf)* | *Nickel (Ni)* | *Rubidium (Rb)* |
|---|---|---|---|---|
| ROG149 | 45584.1 | 3.4170 | 143.40 | 32.28 |
| ROG150 | 44404.8 | 3.6549 | 103.75 | 31.66 |
| ROG151 | 51764.5 | 3.8080 | 173.23 | 28.31 |
| ROG152 | 48069.6 | 3.8351 | 140.13 | 29.09 |
| ROG153 | 39027.3 | 4.0279 | 105.17 | 20.41 |
| ROG154 | 37038.6 | 3.1044 | 82.50 | 56.56 |
| ROG155 | 42858.1 | 4.2362 | 116.79 | 24.59 |
| ROG156 | 42702.3 | 3.2098 | 89.62 | 23.71 |
| ROG157 | 48786.6 | 3.7514 | 98.87 | 19.91 |
| ROG158 | 47746.9 | 3.7293 | 119.89 | 24.31 |
| ROG159 | 48359.7 | 3.4044 | 110.96 | 21.48 |
| ROG160 | 49589.7 | 3.7340 | 143.89 | 21.66 |
| ROG161 | 40813.3 | 4.1857 | 109.17 | 57.16 |
| ROG162 | 48563.7 | 4.0340 | 112.72 | 18.77 |
| ROG163 | 44846.9 | 3.3172 | 119.09 | 69.26 |
| ROG164 | 46560.0 | 3.5479 | 107.38 | 33.60 |
| ROG165 | 42393.7 | 3.4283 | 112.40 | 27.60 |
| ROG166 | 49335.9 | 4.0826 | 110.14 | 38.72 |
| ROG167 | 42901.6 | 3.9387 | 124.72 | 22.62 |
| ROG168 | 49429.1 | 3.7772 | 100.10 | 28.85 |
| ROG169 | 47139.1 | 3.6000 | 122.17 | 16.05 |
| ROG170 | 45098.7 | 3.6628 | 116.79 | 18.36 |
| ROG171 | 50207.0 | 3.9678 | 91.38 | 31.81 |
| ROG172 | 51035.9 | 3.8721 | 104.35 | 23.96 |
| ROG173 | 47774.0 | 4.1516 | 97.90 | 17.30 |
| ROG174 | 40709.3 | 3.8069 | 75.17 | 12.10 |
| ROG175 | 46054.2 | 3.4986 | 120.36 | 33.63 |
| ROG176 | 49253.8 | 3.7726 | 102.89 | 38.31 |
| ROG177 | 45145.3 | 4.4096 | 114.46 | 32.33 |
| ROG178 | 45558.7 | 3.8843 | 115.00 | 35.47 |
| ROG179 | 37333.0 | 2.9960 | 154.29 | 19.97 |
| ROG180 | 36025.5 | 3.1937 | 120.93 | 16.89 |
| ROG181 | 35128.4 | 2.6614 | 88.02 | 50.39 |
| ROG182 | 39735.8 | 4.4212 | 111.07 | 64.01 |
| ROG183 | 36943.6 | 2.9112 | 85.34 | 58.45 |
| ROG184 | 39165.4 | 2.9323 | 88.11 | 58.83 |
| ROG185 | 38648.3 | 3.1015 | 92.56 | 23.11 |

Table 8. Elemental Concentration (ppm) Data for Susiana Ceramics (*cont.*)

| *Sample Identification* | *Iron (Fe)* | *Hafnium (Hf)* | *Nickel (Ni)* | *Rubidium (Rb)* |
|---|---|---|---|---|
| ROG186 | 37223.5 | 2.8904 | 73.50 | 54.16 |
| ROG187 | 36544.8 | 2.9041 | 73.15 | 50.60 |
| ROG188 | 38228.9 | 4.3116 | 85.67 | 68.14 |
| ROG189 | 39799.1 | 3.2350 | 81.69 | 55.87 |
| ROG190 | 40025.9 | 3.2988 | 95.48 | 53.44 |
| ROG191 | 36251.6 | 2.8774 | 80.24 | 55.36 |
| ROG192 | 38971.7 | 3.2831 | 121.47 | 57.47 |
| ROG193 | 30773.6 | 3.8860 | 98.23 | 18.54 |
| ROG194 | 28395.2 | 3.6095 | 88.34 | 17.45 |
| ROG195 | 32361.8 | 3.6951 | 125.27 | 16.60 |
| ROG196 | 31182.3 | 3.3539 | 87.68 | 19.95 |
| ROG197 | 40948.8 | 3.4062 | 165.79 | 18.23 |
| ROG198 | 32869.8 | 2.7705 | 138.28 | 25.14 |
| ROG199 | 35933.5 | 4.3321 | 134.98 | 7.53 |
| ROG200 | 31504.6 | 3.6951 | 118.17 | 13.90 |

Table 9. Elemental Concentration (ppm) Data for Susiana Ceramics

| *Sample Identification* | *Antimony (Sb)* | *Scandium (Sc)* | *Strontium (Sr)* | *Tantalum (Ta)* |
|---|---|---|---|---|
| ROG001 | 0.4988 | 12.8299 | 736.74 | 0.8741 |
| ROG002 | 0.4275 | 11.8242 | 832.00 | 0.7645 |
| ROG003 | 0.5099 | 12.1031 | 869.84 | 0.8276 |
| ROG004 | 0.5181 | 11.4977 | 695.92 | 0.7580 |
| ROG005 | 0.5803 | 12.6437 | 1078.82 | 0.7381 |
| ROG006 | 0.5181 | 11.4032 | 606.22 | 0.6875 |
| ROG007 | 0.5199 | 12.8891 | 674.66 | 0.8794 |
| ROG008 | 0.6495 | 15.9268 | 539.91 | 0.9229 |
| ROG009 | 0.5957 | 13.5368 | 579.60 | 0.8985 |
| ROG010 | 0.6903 | 11.8687 | 666.01 | 0.6978 |
| ROG011 | 0.5255 | 13.0116 | 709.05 | 0.7979 |
| ROG012 | 0.5072 | 13.0605 | 694.01 | 0.8903 |
| ROG013 | 0.4897 | 12.8096 | 734.36 | 0.8348 |
| ROG014 | 0.5060 | 11.9814 | 660.16 | 0.8126 |
| ROG015 | 0.6135 | 13.1032 | 613.22 | 0.8772 |
| ROG016 | 0.5408 | 11.7344 | 638.76 | 0.7184 |
| ROG017 | 0.4495 | 11.3829 | 790.77 | 0.7684 |
| ROG018 | 0.5149 | 11.4880 | 679.33 | 0.6935 |
| ROG019 | 0.5207 | 11.8741 | 621.80 | 0.6950 |
| ROG020 | 0.5120 | 11.0919 | 653.38 | 0.7471 |
| ROG021 | 0.5726 | 15.3137 | 667.65 | 0.9849 |
| ROG022 | 0.8701 | 18.2219 | 592.86 | 0.7653 |
| ROG023 | 0.5537 | 11.8323 | 724.71 | 0.8111 |
| ROG024 | 0.5052 | 10.7152 | 702.45 | 0.7057 |
| ROG025 | 0.5030 | 11.1416 | 764.16 | 0.7210 |
| ROG026 | 0.5273 | 11.6152 | 916.89 | 0.7618 |
| ROG027 | 0.4408 | 10.7712 | 1034.12 | 0.7191 |
| ROG028 | 0.4483 | 9.2713 | 712.79 | 0.6492 |
| ROG029 | 0.6171 | 12.5280 | 791.99 | 0.8756 |
| ROG030 | 0.4652 | 9.5957 | 920.92 | 0.6666 |
| ROG031 | 0.4677 | 10.1985 | 818.60 | 0.6805 |
| ROG032 | 0.4603 | 9.6632 | 848.48 | 0.6645 |
| ROG033 | 0.4747 | 10.3428 | 835.73 | 0.7352 |
| ROG034 | 0.3887 | 9.3391 | 766.76 | 0.6370 |
| ROG035 | 0.3565 | 9.3175 | 884.12 | 0.6617 |
| ROG036 | 0.3599 | 9.6342 | 550.19 | 0.6551 |
| ROG037 | 0.4655 | 9.8877 | 677.62 | 0.6820 |

Table 9. Elemental Concentration (ppm) Data for Susiana Ceramics (*cont.*)

| *Sample Identification* | *Antimony (Sb)* | *Scandium (Sc)* | *Strontium (Sr)* | *Tantalum (Ta)* |
|---|---|---|---|---|
| ROG038 | 0.5175 | 11.8293 | 708.84 | 0.8382 |
| ROG039 | 0.4949 | 11.5285 | 1174.84 | 0.7804 |
| ROG040 | 0.4008 | 9.7101 | 712.96 | 0.6543 |
| ROG041 | 0.5251 | 13.4505 | 726.14 | 0.8899 |
| ROG042 | 0.4795 | 12.4482 | 733.60 | 0.8443 |
| ROG043 | 0.3555 | 10.5669 | 656.15 | 0.7054 |
| ROG044 | 0.3491 | 10.1331 | 949.06 | 0.6895 |
| ROG045 | 0.3695 | 9.6598 | 628.30 | 0.6736 |
| ROG046 | 0.5418 | 11.3162 | 852.81 | 0.7863 |
| ROG047 | 0.4063 | 10.0453 | 704.20 | 0.6805 |
| ROG048 | 0.3895 | 11.9735 | 554.06 | 0.7924 |
| ROG049 | 0.4312 | 9.8994 | 591.24 | 0.6935 |
| ROG050 | 0.4945 | 10.7661 | 836.18 | 0.7636 |
| ROG051 | 0.4311 | 10.6452 | 639.20 | 0.6795 |
| ROG052 | 0.4059 | 10.6250 | 542.72 | 0.7108 |
| ROG053 | 0.5273 | 12.4122 | 536.21 | 0.8779 |
| ROG054 | 0.5426 | 11.3367 | 724.42 | 0.8124 |
| ROG055 | 0.5904 | 13.6131 | 474.09 | 0.8963 |
| ROG056 | 0.4337 | 10.5553 | 475.52 | 0.7451 |
| ROG057 | 0.4123 | 10.0082 | 500.09 | 0.7290 |
| ROG058 | 0.4171 | 10.5904 | 463.19 | 0.7467 |
| ROG059 | 0.4409 | 11.8926 | 587.20 | 0.8099 |
| ROG060 | 0.4745 | 11.5201 | 510.75 | 0.8371 |
| ROG061 | 0.4859 | 11.3852 | 522.55 | 0.8042 |
| ROG062 | 0.5406 | 12.7369 | 477.13 | 0.8527 |
| ROG063 | 0.4709 | 12.5322 | 482.69 | 0.8572 |
| ROG064 | 0.3720 | 10.1998 | 567.15 | 0.7132 |
| ROG065 | 0.4209 | 9.1222 | 515.64 | 0.6556 |
| ROG066 | 0.4506 | 12.0891 | 551.18 | 0.7973 |
| ROG067 | 0.4207 | 10.7724 | 536.78 | 0.7391 |
| ROG068 | 0.6233 | 13.1960 | 527.72 | 0.7558 |
| ROG069 | 0.6344 | 12.5881 | 662.18 | 0.7431 |
| ROG070 | 0.6367 | 11.0708 | 1010.20 | 0.7421 |
| ROG071 | 0.5735 | 11.9243 | 527.61 | 0.7081 |
| ROG072 | 0.5852 | 11.6499 | 639.63 | 0.6785 |
| ROG073 | 0.9197 | 17.7901 | 424.06 | 1.1811 |
| ROG074 | 0.6639 | 14.3367 | 635.57 | 0.7886 |

Table 9. Elemental Concentration (ppm) Data for Susiana Ceramics (*cont.*)

| *Sample Identification* | *Antimony (Sb)* | *Scandium (Sc)* | *Strontium (Sr)* | *Tantalum (Ta)* |
|---|---|---|---|---|
| ROG075 | 0.5786 | 11.7212 | 520.91 | 0.7138 |
| ROG076 | 0.4640 | 10.8845 | 606.47 | 0.6466 |
| ROG077 | 0.7451 | 13.8094 | 663.86 | 0.7747 |
| ROG078 | 0.6157 | 12.5036 | 496.85 | 0.7171 |
| ROG079 | 0.5911 | 12.6893 | 764.09 | 0.7150 |
| ROG080 | 0.5596 | 9.6369 | 662.49 | 0.5638 |
| ROG081 | 0.6603 | 11.8625 | 719.54 | 0.6794 |
| ROG082 | 0.5355 | 14.6946 | 550.94 | 1.0082 |
| ROG083 | 0.5730 | 12.2300 | 580.16 | 0.7173 |
| ROG084 | 0.7235 | 13.7731 | 581.94 | 0.7756 |
| ROG085 | 0.6129 | 13.5889 | 528.49 | 0.8524 |
| ROG086 | 0.5065 | 11.3505 | 604.20 | 0.6430 |
| ROG087 | 0.4318 | 11.3529 | 743.70 | 0.6672 |
| ROG088 | 0.6356 | 13.8631 | 617.79 | 0.7840 |
| ROG089 | 0.5522 | 11.9797 | 565.57 | 0.7054 |
| ROG090 | 0.5000 | 12.8300 | 453.52 | 0.8157 |
| ROG091 | 0.5516 | 11.3498 | 494.88 | 0.6742 |
| ROG092 | 0.5222 | 12.0195 | 624.55 | 0.8018 |
| ROG093 | 0.6267 | 11.9469 | 776.87 | 0.7446 |
| ROG094 | 0.4932 | 13.3062 | 540.23 | 0.7366 |
| ROG095 | 0.5941 | 12.5557 | 551.86 | 0.7259 |
| ROG096 | 0.5511 | 11.4402 | 603.84 | 0.6953 |
| ROG097 | 0.5078 | 9.4466 | 562.58 | 0.5879 |
| ROG098 | 0.5279 | 12.0886 | 582.85 | 0.7124 |
| ROG099 | 0.6749 | 11.4871 | 589.02 | 0.6280 |
| ROG100 | 0.6085 | 12.6689 | 486.38 | 0.6952 |
| ROG101 | 0.4912 | 11.0086 | 558.02 | 0.6221 |
| ROG102 | 0.4444 | 11.0163 | 565.55 | 0.5957 |
| ROG103 | 0.6216 | 12.9220 | 635.06 | 0.7561 |
| ROG104 | 0.6717 | 12.8496 | 835.46 | 0.7432 |
| ROG105 | 0.5859 | 12.1483 | 645.77 | 0.7131 |
| ROG106 | 0.6054 | 11.5582 | 827.13 | 0.7140 |
| ROG107 | 0.6005 | 14.1952 | 445.39 | 0.7804 |
| ROG108 | 0.6151 | 12.0362 | 682.34 | 0.6602 |
| ROG109 | 0.6492 | 11.6121 | 854.86 | 0.6875 |
| ROG110 | 0.3524 | 9.5702 | 434.06 | 0.6085 |
| ROG111 | 0.4592 | 9.8873 | 776.35 | 0.6066 |

Table 9. Elemental Concentration (ppm) Data for Susiana Ceramics (*cont.*)

| *Sample Identification* | *Antimony (Sb)* | *Scandium (Sc)* | *Strontium (Sr)* | *Tantalum (Ta)* |
|---|---|---|---|---|
| ROG112 | 0.5709 | 11.5822 | 826.68 | 0.6797 |
| ROG113 | 0.5136 | 10.1719 | 783.52 | 0.6077 |
| ROG114 | 0.5851 | 12.4258 | 847.38 | 0.6928 |
| ROG115 | 0.4212 | 8.7813 | 951.06 | 0.5257 |
| ROG116 | 0.8593 | 14.1528 | 1425.13 | 0.8356 |
| ROG117 | 0.5412 | 9.8089 | 789.50 | 0.5807 |
| ROG118 | 0.5764 | 10.7200 | 903.88 | 0.6379 |
| ROG119 | 0.7142 | 13.1285 | 960.92 | 0.7473 |
| ROG120 | 0.4224 | 10.7589 | 631.04 | 0.7198 |
| ROG121 | 0.4462 | 9.5118 | 755.90 | 0.5913 |
| ROG122 | 0.4574 | 9.3073 | 870.59 | 0.6106 |
| ROG123 | 0.4350 | 10.0949 | 842.31 | 0.6023 |
| ROG124 | 0.4136 | 10.5095 | 670.48 | 0.6153 |
| ROG125 | 0.5246 | 10.7179 | 743.17 | 0.6300 |
| ROG126 | 0.7300 | 14.7281 | 770.37 | 0.8303 |
| ROG127 | 0.4688 | 9.5800 | 598.96 | 0.5843 |
| ROG128 | 0.5277 | 12.1341 | 1021.33 | 0.7435 |
| ROG129 | 0.4589 | 8.6310 | 716.00 | 0.5056 |
| ROG130 | 0.4683 | 10.9425 | 532.99 | 0.6673 |
| ROG131 | 0.4794 | 10.0391 | 933.91 | 0.5679 |
| ROG132 | 0.6053 | 11.6445 | 821.21 | 0.6685 |
| ROG133 | 0.4108 | 9.0524 | 782.82 | 0.5817 |
| ROG134 | 0.7944 | 14.5949 | 695.13 | 0.8466 |
| ROG135 | 0.1900 | 15.7959 | 686.68 | 0.8261 |
| ROG136 | 0.7454 | 14.1203 | 781.74 | 0.7927 |
| ROG137 | 0.6996 | 15.0009 | 641.49 | 0.9691 |
| ROG138 | 0.6792 | 16.9201 | 672.65 | 0.9301 |
| ROG139 | 0.7215 | 16.8324 | 508.64 | 0.8702 |
| ROG140 | 0.5062 | 16.3659 | 782.37 | 0.8961 |
| ROG141 | 0.8409 | 17.7383 | 327.58 | 0.9274 |
| ROG142 | 0.9652 | 15.2646 | 753.39 | 0.8365 |
| ROG143 | 0.4849 | 16.4661 | 525.65 | 1.0025 |
| ROG144 | 0.8647 | 15.5165 | 457.67 | 0.8932 |
| ROG145 | 0.9229 | 16.0116 | 582.54 | 0.8758 |
| ROG146 | 0.5820 | 15.2154 | 559.30 | 0.9465 |
| ROG147 | 0.8048 | 18.0870 | 390.32 | 1.0390 |
| ROG148 | 0.6940 | 16.0714 | 848.36 | 0.9419 |

Table 9. Elemental Concentration (ppm) Data for Susiana Ceramics (*cont.*)

| *Sample Identification* | *Antimony (Sb)* | *Scandium (Sc)* | *Strontium (Sr)* | *Tantalum (Ta)* |
|---|---|---|---|---|
| ROG149 | 0.6456 | 16.3432 | 786.36 | 0.9526 |
| ROG150 | 0.5722 | 16.0139 | 999.72 | 0.8658 |
| ROG151 | 0.7866 | 18.5367 | 767.67 | 1.0786 |
| ROG152 | 0.7729 | 17.0211 | 792.76 | 0.9967 |
| ROG153 | 0.4041 | 14.1947 | 1171.22 | 0.8832 |
| ROG154 | 0.7612 | 13.2163 | 1697.20 | 0.7387 |
| ROG155 | 0.8208 | 15.3905 | 928.52 | 0.9137 |
| ROG156 | 0.8341 | 15.0713 | 692.19 | 0.8118 |
| ROG157 | 0.8628 | 17.6022 | 880.80 | 1.0851 |
| ROG158 | 0.7938 | 17.2476 | 1219.94 | 1.0515 |
| ROG159 | 0.9844 | 17.3592 | 770.02 | 0.8644 |
| ROG160 | 0.4002 | 17.6148 | 610.32 | 0.9998 |
| ROG161 | 0.7278 | 14.5516 | 750.11 | 0.9260 |
| ROG162 | 0.7761 | 17.1879 | 541.84 | 0.9103 |
| ROG163 | 0.9154 | 15.7773 | 872.62 | 0.8478 |
| ROG164 | 1.0549 | 16.5183 | 759.69 | 0.8901 |
| ROG165 | 0.8612 | 15.0488 | 859.61 | 0.8319 |
| ROG166 | 0.7377 | 18.1605 | 671.04 | 1.0474 |
| ROG167 | 0.7355 | 15.3406 | 280.52 | 0.9278 |
| ROG168 | 0.9749 | 17.4621 | 371.22 | 0.8962 |
| ROG169 | 0.8734 | 16.7714 | 439.25 | 0.8865 |
| ROG170 | 1.0285 | 15.9813 | 411.60 | 0.9188 |
| ROG171 | 0.8152 | 18.0543 | 421.39 | 0.9852 |
| ROG172 | 1.2806 | 18.4218 | 428.53 | 1.0170 |
| ROG173 | 0.7409 | 17.4067 | 415.62 | 0.9488 |
| ROG174 | 0.6015 | 14.9673 | 604.04 | 0.8309 |
| ROG175 | 0.9181 | 16.6440 | 570.59 | 1.0186 |
| ROG176 | 0.8243 | 17.0283 | 1242.06 | 0.9760 |
| ROG177 | 0.7981 | 15.8570 | 813.16 | 0.9390 |
| ROG178 | 0.7370 | 15.9372 | 943.53 | 0.9632 |
| ROG179 | 0.4253 | 13.3663 | 669.43 | 0.7955 |
| ROG180 | 0.5792 | 12.6991 | 855.87 | 0.7054 |
| ROG181 | 0.4492 | 12.6249 | 555.21 | 0.8841 |
| ROG182 | 0.6544 | 14.2226 | 648.42 | 0.8612 |
| ROG183 | 0.5186 | 13.4405 | 822.96 | 0.8833 |
| ROG184 | 0.5058 | 14.1053 | 626.89 | 0.9435 |
| ROG185 | 0.5380 | 13.8420 | 936.14 | 0.9174 |

Table 9. Elemental Concentration (ppm) Data for Susiana Ceramics (*cont.*)

| *Sample Identification* | *Antimony (Sb)* | *Scandium (Sc)* | *Strontium (Sr)* | *Tantalum (Ta)* |
|---|---|---|---|---|
| ROG186 | 0.4914 | 13.4957 | 770.72 | 0.9253 |
| ROG187 | 0.4991 | 13.3093 | 494.61 | 0.8718 |
| ROG188 | 0.5807 | 14.1893 | 950.66 | 0.8760 |
| ROG189 | 0.4963 | 14.1504 | 580.10 | 0.9741 |
| ROG190 | 0.5423 | 14.2956 | 695.26 | 0.9925 |
| ROG191 | 0.5109 | 13.1936 | 805.99 | 0.8661 |
| ROG192 | 0.5788 | 14.1437 | 545.63 | 0.8212 |
| ROG193 | 0.4891 | 11.0210 | 1093.80 | 0.6924 |
| ROG194 | 0.5126 | 10.2122 | 1604.02 | 0.6297 |
| ROG195 | 0.4652 | 11.4588 | 868.43 | 0.6984 |
| ROG196 | 0.4721 | 11.0817 | 1168.57 | 0.6824 |
| ROG197 | 0.6382 | 14.0842 | 1117.65 | 0.9573 |
| ROG198 | 0.5019 | 11.7131 | 1202.17 | 0.7018 |
| ROG199 | 0.6303 | 12.7594 | 996.36 | 0.7379 |
| ROG200 | 0.5368 | 11.2998 | 861.31 | 0.7151 |

Table 10. Elemental Concentration (ppm) Data for Susiana Ceramics

| *Sample Identification* | *Terbium (Tb)* | *Thorium (Th)* | *Zinc (Zn)* | *Zirconium (Zr)* |
|---|---|---|---|---|
| ROG001 | 0.4742 | 5.0939 | 77.39 | 71.73 |
| ROG002 | 0.4287 | 4.6548 | 99.44 | 79.43 |
| ROG003 | 0.5067 | 5.1973 | 87.16 | 94.04 |
| ROG004 | 0.4326 | 4.5689 | 116.88 | 73.30 |
| ROG005 | 0.4519 | 5.4059 | 97.10 | 80.83 |
| ROG006 | 0.5559 | 4.8235 | 104.92 | 64.56 |
| ROG007 | 0.6033 | 5.2776 | 114.36 | 71.32 |
| ROG008 | 0.5172 | 6.3034 | 102.68 | 73.77 |
| ROG009 | 0.4458 | 5.5649 | 84.76 | 78.19 |
| ROG010 | 0.4796 | 5.9177 | 107.29 | 83.02 |
| ROG011 | 0.4746 | 5.1116 | 106.10 | 79.26 |
| ROG012 | 0.4443 | 5.2081 | 103.48 | 71.98 |
| ROG013 | 0.4605 | 4.7460 | 86.85 | 89.24 |
| ROG014 | 0.5589 | 4.6865 | 87.83 | 64.86 |
| ROG015 | 0.5075 | 5.8739 | 89.10 | 88.18 |
| ROG016 | 0.4063 | 4.9261 | 91.11 | 74.48 |
| ROG017 | 0.3936 | 4.6715 | 112.89 | 92.36 |
| ROG018 | 0.4705 | 5.0331 | 85.45 | 74.11 |
| ROG019 | 0.4258 | 5.0738 | 88.80 | 64.38 |
| ROG020 | 0.4683 | 4.6799 | 95.59 | 68.93 |
| ROG021 | 0.5468 | 5.8798 | 115.17 | 112.28 |
| ROG022 | 0.6165 | 6.9576 | 88.98 | 98.79 |
| ROG023 | 0.5107 | 4.7362 | 96.85 | 75.37 |
| ROG024 | 0.3713 | 4.4260 | 98.26 | 67.07 |
| ROG025 | 0.4086 | 4.7979 | 96.18 | 62.14 |
| ROG026 | 0.5056 | 4.8524 | 81.33 | 98.55 |
| ROG027 | 0.4149 | 4.4793 | 90.90 | 58.04 |
| ROG028 | 0.3873 | 3.8993 | 85.37 | 80.30 |
| ROG029 | 0.5131 | 5.2811 | 97.05 | 79.21 |
| ROG030 | 0.5004 | 4.0102 | 89.62 | 71.07 |
| ROG031 | 0.5295 | 4.2057 | 133.48 | 71.54 |
| ROG032 | 0.4084 | 4.0557 | 85.12 | 57.58 |
| ROG033 | 0.4036 | 4.4128 | 132.03 | 71.54 |
| ROG034 | 0.4180 | 3.9306 | 90.72 | 73.77 |
| ROG035 | 0.4233 | 4.0068 | 91.98 | 67.42 |
| ROG036 | 0.3971 | 3.9754 | 92.31 | 70.33 |
| ROG037 | 0.4252 | 4.0490 | 109.73 | 56.45 |

Table 10. Elemental Concentration (ppm) Data for Susiana Ceramics (*cont.*)

| *Sample Identification* | *Terbium (Tb)* | *Thorium (Th)* | *Zinc (Zn)* | *Zirconium (Zr)* |
|---|---|---|---|---|
| ROG038 | 0.5501 | 5.0305 | 108.90 | 102.84 |
| ROG039 | 0.4803 | 4.7026 | 101.99 | 69.07 |
| ROG040 | 0.3963 | 3.9002 | 125.15 | 65.98 |
| ROG041 | 0.5145 | 5.4876 | 83.18 | 98.25 |
| ROG042 | 0.5081 | 5.3028 | 87.91 | 75.73 |
| ROG043 | 0.4255 | 4.2187 | 107.92 | 77.08 |
| ROG044 | 0.4061 | 4.1189 | 107.64 | 73.15 |
| ROG045 | 0.4497 | 4.1328 | 124.09 | 73.84 |
| ROG046 | 0.4479 | 4.6223 | 71.91 | 62.97 |
| ROG047 | 0.4205 | 4.0679 | 105.25 | 47.33 |
| ROG048 | 0.4230 | 4.8559 | 121.47 | 61.72 |
| ROG049 | 0.4305 | 3.9391 | 98.22 | 62.07 |
| ROG050 | 0.4524 | 4.5193 | 83.65 | 72.05 |
| ROG051 | 0.3937 | 4.2369 | 121.51 | 69.33 |
| ROG052 | 0.4275 | 4.4111 | 131.59 | 83.74 |
| ROG053 | 0.6428 | 5.1743 | 103.47 | 93.77 |
| ROG054 | 0.4958 | 4.5487 | 78.88 | 83.99 |
| ROG055 | 0.6346 | 5.4507 | 102.65 | 124.59 |
| ROG056 | 0.5075 | 4.2100 | 93.38 | 89.80 |
| ROG057 | 0.4558 | 4.5182 | 92.60 | 94.95 |
| ROG058 | 0.4726 | 4.2974 | 91.84 | 94.82 |
| ROG059 | 0.4592 | 4.7943 | 98.89 | 90.15 |
| ROG060 | 0.4887 | 4.5738 | 137.65 | 87.66 |
| ROG061 | 0.4930 | 5.1194 | 98.91 | 86.28 |
| ROG062 | 0.5474 | 5.5594 | 115.18 | 85.00 |
| ROG063 | 0.5455 | 4.8231 | 108.50 | 77.71 |
| ROG064 | 0.4192 | 4.2445 | 109.16 | 97.13 |
| ROG065 | 0.4011 | 3.6707 | 78.43 | 84.92 |
| ROG066 | 0.4632 | 4.8261 | 113.40 | 88.35 |
| ROG067 | 0.4329 | 4.4177 | 90.85 | 77.99 |
| ROG068 | 0.5462 | 6.2468 | 92.10 | 97.74 |
| ROG069 | 0.5152 | 5.9326 | 95.91 | 92.12 |
| ROG070 | 0.5595 | 5.4258 | 86.49 | 119.04 |
| ROG071 | 0.5221 | 5.4944 | 99.57 | 88.06 |
| ROG072 | 0.6176 | 5.3572 | 92.93 | 90.52 |
| ROG073 | 0.6030 | 7.6414 | 77.95 | 126.14 |
| ROG074 | 0.5502 | 6.5605 | 111.14 | 93.74 |

Table 10. Elemental Concentration (ppm) Data for Susiana Ceramics (*cont.*)

| *Sample Identification* | *Terbium (Tb)* | *Thorium (Th)* | *Zinc (Zn)* | *Zirconium (Zr)* |
|---|---|---|---|---|
| ROG075 | 0.5249 | 5.4047 | 94.00 | 96.20 |
| ROG076 | 0.5043 | 5.0810 | 76.45 | 95.53 |
| ROG077 | 0.6548 | 6.4342 | 125.22 | 111.99 |
| ROG078 | 0.6763 | 5.7787 | 79.83 | 87.77 |
| ROG079 | 0.5577 | 6.1215 | 99.88 | 110.93 |
| ROG080 | 0.4555 | 4.5832 | 75.55 | 80.23 |
| ROG081 | 0.6564 | 5.6783 | 92.10 | 98.97 |
| ROG082 | 0.4438 | 5.4256 | 85.76 | 104.76 |
| ROG083 | 0.5051 | 5.6169 | 75.11 | 87.77 |
| ROG084 | 0.6344 | 6.4707 | 87.15 | 97.01 |
| ROG085 | 0.6129 | 5.5026 | 71.11 | 86.60 |
| ROG086 | 0.5064 | 5.3962 | 79.94 | 72.63 |
| ROG087 | 0.4474 | 5.0953 | 97.59 | 92.38 |
| ROG088 | 0.5689 | 6.2941 | 116.72 | 112.55 |
| ROG089 | 0.5104 | 5.4999 | 80.11 | 105.56 |
| ROG090 | 0.5766 | 6.5894 | 86.68 | 108.53 |
| ROG091 | 0.4866 | 5.0030 | 92.85 | 87.16 |
| ROG092 | 0.4575 | 4.7869 | 83.79 | 84.11 |
| ROG093 | 0.6863 | 5.6713 | 69.98 | 98.37 |
| ROG094 | 0.4926 | 6.0296 | 138.90 | 106.56 |
| ROG095 | 0.6704 | 5.8551 | 81.21 | 104.75 |
| ROG096 | 0.5047 | 5.3680 | 83.59 | 90.08 |
| ROG097 | 0.4155 | 4.5305 | 80.35 | 79.49 |
| ROG098 | 0.6348 | 5.5495 | 89.23 | 102.33 |
| ROG099 | 0.4852 | 5.6460 | 65.21 | 86.22 |
| ROG100 | 0.5003 | 5.7168 | 80.38 | 83.68 |
| ROG101 | 0.3902 | 5.0022 | 81.11 | 64.85 |
| ROG102 | 0.4733 | 5.1090 | 91.93 | 76.13 |
| ROG103 | 0.5548 | 6.0764 | 96.08 | 88.02 |
| ROG104 | 0.5508 | 6.0578 | 95.85 | 89.65 |
| ROG105 | 0.5861 | 5.7266 | 91.38 | 68.89 |
| ROG106 | 0.5641 | 5.5200 | 62.99 | 75.26 |
| ROG107 | 0.6285 | 6.4384 | 104.53 | 87.75 |
| ROG108 | 0.5162 | 5.5448 | 79.81 | 87.40 |
| ROG109 | 0.4747 | 5.3262 | 81.41 | 67.46 |
| ROG110 | 0.4344 | 4.4361 | 81.78 | 70.27 |
| ROG111 | 0.5345 | 4.6949 | 78.24 | 85.21 |

Table 10. Elemental Concentration (ppm) Data for Susiana Ceramics (*cont.*)

| *Sample Identification* | *Terbium (Tb)* | *Thorium (Th)* | *Zinc (Zn)* | *Zirconium (Zr)* |
|---|---|---|---|---|
| ROG112 | 0.4762 | 5.1647 | 100.30 | 85.46 |
| ROG113 | 0.4855 | 4.8895 | 97.29 | 70.94 |
| ROG114 | 0.4571 | 5.5262 | 125.78 | 76.97 |
| ROG115 | 0.3624 | 4.1565 | 74.78 | 71.78 |
| ROG116 | 0.6161 | 6.4700 | 81.32 | 92.02 |
| ROG117 | 0.3732 | 4.6587 | 89.24 | 61.01 |
| ROG118 | 0.4468 | 4.8505 | 93.27 | 65.47 |
| ROG119 | 0.5686 | 6.0379 | 79.31 | 79.46 |
| ROG120 | 0.5471 | 4.6640 | 87.89 | 99.73 |
| ROG121 | 0.4141 | 4.6061 | 81.34 | 48.75 |
| ROG122 | 0.5158 | 4.6275 | 79.34 | 76.67 |
| ROG123 | 0.4701 | 4.7911 | 105.25 | 66.21 |
| ROG124 | 0.5151 | 4.8886 | 100.06 | 70.15 |
| ROG125 | 0.4410 | 4.8791 | 101.36 | 53.94 |
| ROG126 | 0.5222 | 6.4025 | 99.19 | 86.25 |
| ROG127 | 0.5006 | 4.9074 | 86.01 | 84.05 |
| ROG128 | 0.5110 | 5.6371 | 108.03 | 96.41 |
| ROG129 | 0.3772 | 3.9837 | 78.48 | 67.32 |
| ROG130 | 0.4649 | 5.3308 | 99.77 | 91.59 |
| ROG131 | 0.3760 | 4.5945 | 95.02 | 76.49 |
| ROG132 | 0.4959 | 5.4087 | 102.87 | 86.95 |
| ROG133 | 0.5222 | 4.3587 | 82.18 | 88.34 |
| ROG134 | 0.6451 | 6.9592 | 57.24 | 151.55 |
| ROG135 | 0.6054 | 7.1436 | 84.62 | 66.55 |
| ROG136 | 0.5908 | 6.7007 | 59.39 | 109.88 |
| ROG137 | 0.6499 | 6.7114 | 81.72 | 108.35 |
| ROG138 | 0.8306 | 7.6594 | 67.82 | 107.41 |
| ROG139 | 0.7302 | 7.8532 | 46.58 | 79.21 |
| ROG140 | 0.6656 | 7.4023 | 55.78 | 97.86 |
| ROG141 | 0.6883 | 7.9274 | 97.92 | 98.01 |
| ROG142 | 0.5129 | 6.9465 | 77.73 | 105.61 |
| ROG143 | 1.0978 | 7.8175 | 54.37 | 124.21 |
| ROG144 | 0.5534 | 7.0337 | 67.95 | 78.99 |
| ROG145 | 0.5065 | 7.2455 | 66.73 | 116.80 |
| ROG146 | 0.6196 | 7.2442 | 80.79 | 124.47 |
| ROG147 | 0.6192 | 8.6627 | 82.17 | 90.88 |
| ROG148 | 0.6307 | 7.6145 | 73.83 | 72.63 |

Table 10. Elemental Concentration (ppm) Data for Susiana Ceramics (*cont.*)

| *Sample Identification* | *Terbium (Tb)* | *Thorium (Th)* | *Zinc (Zn)* | *Zirconium (Zr)* |
|---|---|---|---|---|
| ROG149 | 0.6698 | 6.9642 | 72.64 | 96.17 |
| ROG150 | 0.6753 | 7.5046 | 66.45 | 97.90 |
| ROG151 | 0.6395 | 7.2222 | 76.52 | 104.64 |
| ROG152 | 0.6099 | 7.5082 | 89.02 | 103.03 |
| ROG153 | 0.5783 | 7.0445 | 67.72 | 126.25 |
| ROG154 | 0.4644 | 6.0466 | 80.96 | 73.94 |
| ROG155 | 0.6137 | 7.2191 | 63.90 | 114.84 |
| ROG156 | 0.5500 | 6.7961 | 79.63 | 94.76 |
| ROG157 | 0.6170 | 7.5728 | 61.87 | 106.81 |
| ROG158 | 0.6009 | 7.4244 | 58.88 | 78.62 |
| ROG159 | 0.5849 | 7.5927 | 61.83 | 89.68 |
| ROG160 | 0.5976 | 8.3617 | 82.81 | 125.23 |
| ROG161 | 0.7627 | 6.7976 | 86.36 | 120.37 |
| ROG162 | 0.5855 | 7.7937 | 70.40 | 101.92 |
| ROG163 | 0.5875 | 7.0627 | 59.28 | 92.08 |
| ROG164 | 0.5116 | 7.4252 | 48.58 | 90.96 |
| ROG165 | 0.4946 | 6.9676 | 52.26 | 100.89 |
| ROG166 | 0.6839 | 8.0822 | 75.87 | 118.28 |
| ROG167 | 0.6568 | 7.2546 | 58.98 | 105.91 |
| ROG168 | 0.5594 | 7.8239 | 90.62 | 95.23 |
| ROG169 | 0.5760 | 7.5532 | 103.74 | 104.24 |
| ROG170 | 0.5989 | 7.0237 | 87.39 | 99.85 |
| ROG171 | 0.6240 | 8.8609 | 86.50 | 105.06 |
| ROG172 | 0.7109 | 8.9529 | 100.61 | 106.03 |
| ROG173 | 0.8761 | 8.8500 | 102.20 | 115.41 |
| ROG174 | 0.7954 | 7.5121 | 82.06 | 92.62 |
| ROG175 | 0.5928 | 7.2481 | 78.81 | 116.06 |
| ROG176 | 0.6029 | 8.2847 | 65.65 | 118.51 |
| ROG177 | 0.6875 | 7.5286 | 77.93 | 145.47 |
| ROG178 | 0.6368 | 7.1197 | 70.13 | 105.13 |
| ROG179 | 0.5251 | 5.2978 | 92.28 | 85.43 |
| ROG180 | 0.4710 | 5.5456 | 80.99 | 85.91 |
| ROG181 | 0.4314 | 4.9059 | 84.64 | 75.86 |
| ROG182 | 0.6260 | 6.6808 | 89.37 | 144.19 |
| ROG183 | 0.5437 | 5.6516 | 93.49 | 93.71 |
| ROG184 | 0.7274 | 5.6595 | 92.64 | 107.38 |
| ROG185 | 0.4777 | 5.4920 | 83.89 | 87.32 |

Table 10. Elemental Concentration (ppm) Data for Susiana Ceramics (*cont.*)

| *Sample Identification* | *Terbium (Tb)* | *Thorium (Th)* | *Zinc (Zn)* | *Zirconium (Zr)* |
|---|---|---|---|---|
| ROG186 | 0.5494 | 5.8403 | 88.04 | 97.80 |
| ROG187 | 0.5895 | 5.1789 | 96.13 | 96.25 |
| ROG188 | 0.7088 | 7.0241 | 93.65 | 124.31 |
| ROG189 | 0.5187 | 5.7703 | 91.24 | 87.51 |
| ROG190 | 0.5661 | 5.7736 | 116.17 | 103.53 |
| ROG191 | 0.5091 | 5.6403 | 86.73 | 97.60 |
| ROG192 | 0.7045 | 5.8544 | 131.01 | 84.98 |
| ROG193 | 0.4706 | 5.5130 | 59.64 | 107.52 |
| ROG194 | 0.4671 | 4.8763 | 69.52 | 75.54 |
| ROG195 | 0.5339 | 5.2309 | 81.59 | 107.19 |
| ROG196 | 0.4676 | 5.0562 | 85.72 | 95.75 |
| ROG197 | 0.5740 | 6.1911 | 69.78 | 102.46 |
| ROG198 | 0.4550 | 4.7227 | 76.64 | 85.07 |
| ROG199 | 0.5592 | 5.8740 | 71.17 | 149.03 |
| ROG200 | 0.5805 | 5.2098 | 70.26 | 79.96 |

Table 11. Elemental Concentration (ppm) Data for Susiana Ceramics

| *Sample Identification* | *Aluminum (Al)* | *Barium (Ba)* | *Calcium (Ca)* | *Dysprosium (Dy)* |
|---|---|---|---|---|
| ROG001 | 42053.8 | 182.7 | 137337.3 | 2.4290 |
| ROG002 | 41962.6 | 207.4 | 146481.9 | 2.6534 |
| ROG003 | 45541.5 | 176.0 | 152829.3 | 2.9541 |
| ROG004 | 45213.5 | 200.4 | 159506.5 | 2.7641 |
| ROG005 | 47457.9 | 314.6 | 122009.4 | 2.7132 |
| ROG006 | 41660.5 | 181.8 | 138567.0 | 2.8484 |
| ROG007 | 48285.0 | 105.8 | 130193.1 | 2.6654 |
| ROG008 | 57588.0 | 216.7 | 119133.2 | 3.5432 |
| ROG009 | 52210.2 | 199.9 | 119827.5 | 2.7102 |
| ROG010 | 50008.8 | 156.4 | 138212.7 | 2.8159 |
| ROG011 | 46564.2 | 181.3 | 144188.4 | 3.1630 |
| ROG012 | 49760.5 | 175.7 | 135796.3 | 2.9656 |
| ROG013 | 47733.0 | 139.0 | 152023.8 | 2.5977 |
| ROG014 | 46371.6 | 172.6 | 151034.9 | 2.7521 |
| ROG015 | 50973.0 | 165.1 | 143210.7 | 2.7609 |
| ROG016 | 44944.3 | 167.8 | 134348.3 | 3.1022 |
| ROG017 | 42998.5 | 177.1 | 152158.0 | 2.6459 |
| ROG018 | 45285.7 | 174.5 | 144533.3 | 2.7035 |
| ROG019 | 43904.9 | 188.2 | 144038.7 | 2.7387 |
| ROG020 | 40119.1 | 205.3 | 164978.8 | 2.1672 |
| ROG021 | 52719.5 | 188.1 | 119007.4 | 3.2268 |
| ROG022 | 66803.5 | 178.4 | 117243.0 | 3.2740 |
| ROG023 | 42813.7 | 151.0 | 148087.7 | 2.1491 |
| ROG024 | 39903.9 | 119.9 | 170669.7 | 2.4841 |
| ROG025 | 40688.8 | 112.7 | 154740.1 | 2.4262 |
| ROG026 | 45538.5 | 183.6 | 159147.5 | 2.4863 |
| ROG027 | 39175.3 | 162.1 | 171945.1 | 2.3908 |
| ROG028 | 35853.8 | 62.5 | 170693.6 | 2.0120 |
| ROG029 | 46141.8 | 335.7 | 180661.5 | 3.2474 |
| ROG030 | 34729.2 | 182.3 | 173568.9 | 2.5438 |
| ROG031 | 37094.4 | 126.3 | 148353.1 | 2.1925 |
| ROG032 | 34027.3 | 123.4 | 166870.8 | 2.5073 |
| ROG033 | 39218.8 | 92.4 | 163723.6 | 2.5496 |
| ROG034 | 35066.7 | 209.1 | 167164.2 | 2.2208 |
| ROG035 | 36613.2 | 140.9 | 164182.5 | 2.6508 |
| ROG036 | 36112.0 | 223.1 | 171565.1 | 2.1487 |
| ROG037 | 38815.6 | 159.3 | 155223.4 | 2.2431 |

Table 11. Elemental Concentration (ppm) Data for Susiana Ceramics (*cont.*)

| *Sample Identification* | *Aluminum (Al)* | *Barium (Ba)* | *Calcium (Ca)* | *Dysprosium (Dy)* |
|---|---|---|---|---|
| ROG038 | 44298.3 | 162.7 | 124947.6 | 2.7859 |
| ROG039 | 43908.2 | 161.4 | 162042.9 | 2.6014 |
| ROG040 | 35407.8 | 93.1 | 174226.9 | 2.3036 |
| ROG041 | 51680.7 | 140.0 | 149998.3 | 2.6583 |
| ROG042 | 48009.6 | 144.8 | 144556.0 | 3.2201 |
| ROG043 | 41876.0 | 79.1 | 177665.0 | 2.1888 |
| ROG044 | 35776.8 | 198.8 | 168224.9 | 1.9001 |
| ROG045 | 34909.6 | 143.5 | 167207.5 | 2.4493 |
| ROG046 | 43921.3 | 211.7 | 161883.2 | 2.4751 |
| ROG047 | 36103.5 | 203.5 | 157413.7 | 2.2016 |
| ROG048 | 43607.4 | 137.2 | 150377.3 | 2.2934 |
| ROG049 | 33400.9 | 123.3 | 163940.9 | 2.4950 |
| ROG050 | 42561.2 | 200.2 | 166914.2 | 2.7431 |
| ROG051 | 38924.2 | 105.8 | 169042.1 | 2.5530 |
| ROG052 | 36396.6 | 120.1 | 157114.6 | 2.7102 |
| ROG053 | 45234.6 | 190.0 | 145861.6 | 2.6881 |
| ROG054 | 40785.9 | 204.8 | 173215.8 | 2.6743 |
| ROG055 | 51658.4 | 95.3 | 150680.1 | 2.9300 |
| ROG056 | 34349.0 | 167.9 | 165419.1 | 2.6530 |
| ROG057 | 36782.4 | 86.9 | 168970.7 | 2.4238 |
| ROG058 | 32857.5 | 165.7 | 206635.6 | 2.1335 |
| ROG059 | 39937.3 | 464.2 | 213173.2 | 2.5666 |
| ROG060 | 40261.4 | 181.8 | 196300.4 | 3.5366 |
| ROG061 | 41496.4 | 276.7 | 200650.9 | 2.4576 |
| ROG062 | 49641.0 | 235.2 | 180652.9 | 2.9528 |
| ROG063 | 43152.2 | 100.3 | 175382.7 | 2.7121 |
| ROG064 | 36366.2 | 132.9 | 187159.0 | 2.7073 |
| ROG065 | 31846.1 | 107.9 | 202905.8 | 2.5092 |
| ROG066 | 42434.8 | 170.0 | 195909.3 | 2.4757 |
| ROG067 | 37721.2 | 90.3 | 190595.8 | 2.3885 |
| ROG068 | 52692.0 | 333.3 | 127284.3 | 3.1711 |
| ROG069 | 49393.2 | 533.4 | 148022.2 | 3.2479 |
| ROG070 | 47837.1 | 466.2 | 154794.2 | 3.4597 |
| ROG071 | 48748.1 | 240.7 | 147149.8 | 2.7472 |
| ROG072 | 65588.5 | 177.9 | 101033.5 | 3.6724 |
| ROG073 | 48402.9 | 206.2 | 147591.8 | 2.8486 |
| ROG074 | 57446.7 | 309.7 | 138725.2 | 3.2615 |

Table 11. Elemental Concentration (ppm) Data for Susiana Ceramics (*cont.*)

| *Sample Identification* | *Aluminum (Al)* | *Barium (Ba)* | *Calcium (Ca)* | *Dysprosium (Dy)* |
|---|---|---|---|---|
| ROG075 | 43867.6 | 215.3 | 113471.2 | 2.5513 |
| ROG076 | 45957.5 | 681.5 | 125120.6 | 2.4946 |
| ROG077 | 56076.7 | 851.7 | 91937.6 | 3.2053 |
| ROG078 | 53625.1 | 462.9 | 134788.3 | 3.4453 |
| ROG079 | 55937.0 | 471.7 | 141046.5 | 2.7397 |
| ROG080 | 40713.4 | 483.1 | 168300.1 | 2.2145 |
| ROG081 | 50460.6 | 136.5 | 130243.6 | 3.1473 |
| ROG082 | 50719.6 | 153.1 | 102375.2 | 3.0559 |
| ROG083 | 53348.5 | 343.3 | 146920.2 | 3.5650 |
| ROG084 | 57786.1 | 374.3 | 122986.0 | 3.6673 |
| ROG085 | 53435.9 | 524.5 | 124414.4 | 2.8966 |
| ROG086 | 47593.4 | 743.9 | 149647.0 | 2.7446 |
| ROG087 | 45025.2 | 532.3 | 161939.3 | 2.8044 |
| ROG088 | 55418.2 | 436.9 | 116682.5 | 3.2265 |
| ROG089 | 51332.6 | 617.5 | 142622.0 | 2.7225 |
| ROG090 | 50967.9 | 475.2 | 131668.0 | 3.5874 |
| ROG091 | 43890.5 | 211.0 | 113120.1 | 2.9395 |
| ROG092 | 42664.1 | 228.8 | 189290.3 | 2.6011 |
| ROG093 | 48296.6 | 712.7 | 134329.6 | 3.3973 |
| ROG094 | 54375.7 | 627.5 | 125490.3 | 3.1428 |
| ROG095 | 50695.3 | 526.8 | 143562.4 | 2.8019 |
| ROG096 | 48880.2 | 875.9 | 152596.2 | 2.8770 |
| ROG097 | 37555.0 | 308.5 | 166898.1 | 2.5979 |
| ROG098 | 52324.3 | 497.0 | 145687.7 | 3.3813 |
| ROG099 | 47621.6 | 797.6 | 142965.2 | 2.7877 |
| ROG100 | 52618.5 | 131.2 | 141937.6 | 3.0002 |
| ROG101 | 41743.4 | 306.5 | 143323.8 | 2.5102 |
| ROG102 | 43802.0 | 240.7 | 141676.0 | 2.4301 |
| ROG103 | 56287.9 | 217.4 | 136542.6 | 2.8401 |
| ROG104 | 53263.1 | 618.7 | 135954.0 | 3.1432 |
| ROG105 | 51752.7 | 393.7 | 129671.2 | 3.0647 |
| ROG106 | 45471.6 | 520.6 | 145010.2 | 2.9209 |
| ROG107 | 56200.7 | 276.4 | 122907.2 | 3.4422 |
| ROG108 | 48658.6 | 463.6 | 144158.7 | 3.0188 |
| ROG109 | 50653.8 | 736.8 | 186624.5 | 2.7414 |
| ROG110 | 42350.0 | 206.6 | 160530.5 | 2.4426 |
| ROG111 | 41277.7 | 491.0 | 188038.7 | 2.4553 |

Table 11. Elemental Concentration (ppm) Data for Susiana Ceramics (*cont.*)

| *Sample Identification* | *Aluminum (Al)* | *Barium (Ba)* | *Calcium (Ca)* | *Dysprosium (Dy)* |
|---|---|---|---|---|
| ROG112 | 49754.8 | 333.0 | 148066.7 | 2.8853 |
| ROG113 | 42577.5 | 325.8 | 165864.5 | 2.4572 |
| ROG114 | 51110.9 | 348.3 | 142004.1 | 2.7845 |
| ROG115 | 33996.2 | 446.8 | 198050.5 | 2.2186 |
| ROG116 | 57554.2 | 455.2 | 142347.9 | 3.4317 |
| ROG117 | 38449.8 | 452.4 | 167620.0 | 2.6127 |
| ROG118 | 43449.5 | 286.9 | 152382.4 | 2.6116 |
| ROG119 | 51529.8 | 545.5 | 161473.7 | 2.8929 |
| ROG120 | 42276.8 | 511.0 | 164104.6 | 2.3383 |
| ROG121 | 38914.0 | 340.5 | 169145.5 | 2.8561 |
| ROG122 | 41643.2 | 629.3 | 168837.9 | 3.1124 |
| ROG123 | 39971.3 | 307.5 | 163483.5 | 2.5974 |
| ROG124 | 41707.0 | 229.5 | 164066.8 | 2.2411 |
| ROG125 | 46161.4 | 412.1 | 163919.5 | 2.4458 |
| ROG126 | 57162.1 | 781.2 | 141698.2 | 3.3773 |
| ROG127 | 42809.7 | 474.5 | 158987.2 | 2.5884 |
| ROG128 | 48960.6 | 450.9 | 147221.2 | 2.9390 |
| ROG129 | 38418.7 | 217.0 | 183395.7 | 2.1267 |
| ROG130 | 48602.7 | 438.9 | 130200.5 | 2.7341 |
| ROG131 | 41186.5 | 389.6 | 186435.6 | 2.7222 |
| ROG132 | 49500.0 | 594.1 | 170863.9 | 2.7974 |
| ROG133 | 41407.4 | 478.8 | 174522.1 | 2.6809 |
| ROG134 | 60352.9 | 140.9 | 120656.6 | 3.5804 |
| ROG135 | 64648.9 | 61.7 | 165514.6 | 2.7106 |
| ROG136 | 58938.6 | 99.0 | 154953.0 | 3.1480 |
| ROG137 | 62100.3 | 115.3 | 151886.6 | 3.9142 |
| ROG138 | 66926.2 | 317.8 | 116349.0 | 3.6504 |
| ROG139 | 66099.5 | 0.0 | 121655.6 | 3.0130 |
| ROG140 | 68078.6 | 52.8 | 125437.3 | 3.5825 |
| ROG141 | 75735.8 | 284.1 | 129178.1 | 3.7951 |
| ROG142 | 61098.7 | 1016.9 | 144860.8 | 3.1222 |
| ROG143 | 70205.9 | 95.2 | 116157.0 | 3.6345 |
| ROG144 | 65192.6 | 105.4 | 141867.8 | 4.3208 |
| ROG145 | 66909.0 | 0.0 | 142768.0 | 2.9800 |
| ROG146 | 62716.9 | 393.4 | 131808.6 | 4.1598 |
| ROG147 | 74459.7 | 199.9 | 112518.7 | 3.8473 |
| ROG148 | 68615.1 | 1320.4 | 130139.3 | 3.4406 |

Table 11. Elemental Concentration (ppm) Data for Susiana Ceramics (*cont.*)

| *Sample Identification* | *Aluminum (Al)* | *Barium (Ba)* | *Calcium (Ca)* | *Dysprosium (Dy)* |
|---|---|---|---|---|
| ROG149 | 63747.9 | 533.1 | 142281.6 | 3.1680 |
| ROG150 | 64322.7 | 318.0 | 141915.1 | 3.1133 |
| ROG151 | 69014.4 | 158.7 | 130741.1 | 3.6829 |
| ROG152 | 65192.2 | 222.5 | 125956.3 | 3.3562 |
| ROG153 | 56161.2 | 226.6 | 133402.6 | 3.1876 |
| ROG154 | 49610.7 | 870.4 | 166261.6 | 2.8541 |
| ROG155 | 66843.6 | 661.6 | 125996.8 | 3.2451 |
| ROG156 | 60392.2 | 180.7 | 147913.7 | 3.1478 |
| ROG157 | 67754.7 | 192.7 | 132660.3 | 3.4286 |
| ROG158 | 65963.0 | 220.9 | 132501.0 | 3.7493 |
| ROG159 | 69515.6 | 681.3 | 144601.1 | 3.8570 |
| ROG160 | 76269.2 | 371.1 | 118911.3 | 3.2945 |
| ROG161 | 58633.0 | 213.9 | 122244.1 | 3.7639 |
| ROG162 | 71227.2 | 133.7 | 115106.1 | 3.4762 |
| ROG163 | 62577.2 | 349.7 | 147553.6 | 3.4586 |
| ROG164 | 66646.9 | 260.2 | 129327.3 | 3.0347 |
| ROG165 | 65530.7 | 298.0 | 113938.2 | 3.3706 |
| ROG166 | 70218.4 | 718.2 | 119733.6 | 3.7712 |
| ROG167 | 58880.8 | 154.9 | 109464.4 | 3.6006 |
| ROG168 | 72499.1 | 193.2 | 113786.8 | 3.2324 |
| ROG169 | 68606.4 | 418.9 | 133762.0 | 3.1205 |
| ROG170 | 72260.7 | 207.9 | 114002.4 | 3.8417 |
| ROG171 | 76435.1 | 183.5 | 127016.3 | 3.7309 |
| ROG172 | 77205.2 | 248.0 | 128920.3 | 4.1627 |
| ROG173 | 65445.8 | 79.6 | 133335.8 | 2.9758 |
| ROG174 | 67856.9 | 151.3 | 139231.3 | 3.6717 |
| ROG175 | 64903.4 | 150.5 | 133833.6 | 3.4170 |
| ROG176 | 70358.3 | 1142.7 | 111266.1 | 3.7155 |
| ROG177 | 64252.4 | 233.7 | 109126.2 | 3.7410 |
| ROG178 | 64742.5 | 326.3 | 124775.0 | 3.3430 |
| ROG179 | 50262.0 | 123.5 | 155812.3 | 3.1777 |
| ROG180 | 51997.7 | 226.9 | 170764.3 | 2.8185 |
| ROG181 | 47571.0 | 159.4 | 134758.1 | 2.8201 |
| ROG182 | 57558.3 | 556.3 | 94101.2 | 3.6497 |
| ROG183 | 47338.8 | 219.6 | 142815.9 | 3.3279 |
| ROG184 | 51032.4 | 0.0 | 122624.2 | 3.1532 |
| ROG185 | 50018.4 | 159.8 | 142572.8 | 2.8484 |

Table 11. Elemental Concentration (ppm) Data for Susiana Ceramics (*cont.*)

| *Sample Identification* | *Aluminum (Al)* | *Barium (Ba)* | *Calcium (Ca)* | *Dysprosium (Dy)* |
|---|---|---|---|---|
| ROG186 | 52587.4 | 218.4 | 142637.1 | 3.0203 |
| ROG187 | 42949.5 | 166.4 | 115894.2 | 2.8011 |
| ROG188 | 58836.3 | 2196.8 | 82060.6 | 3.6408 |
| ROG189 | 49563.1 | 174.1 | 123637.0 | 3.2238 |
| ROG190 | 50888.7 | 117.2 | 131008.0 | 3.1958 |
| ROG191 | 47877.8 | 172.9 | 152072.2 | 3.0383 |
| ROG192 | 52017.8 | 432.8 | 99772.3 | 3.6100 |
| ROG193 | 45575.9 | 193.1 | 180093.3 | 2.7343 |
| ROG194 | 43530.1 | 111.9 | 154904.7 | 2.8148 |
| ROG195 | 45517.9 | 129.1 | 141759.1 | 2.5219 |
| ROG196 | 46802.2 | 580.9 | 146883.5 | 2.2540 |
| ROG197 | 49293.1 | 73.6 | 162882.4 | 4.0122 |
| ROG198 | 41026.2 | 784.3 | 175980.3 | 2.5669 |
| ROG199 | 53207.1 | 230.0 | 165421.0 | 3.5497 |
| ROG200 | 46594.6 | 194.8 | 146310.5 | 2.4236 |

Table 12. Elemental Concentration (ppm) Data for Susiana Ceramics

| *Sample Identification* | *Potassium (K)* | *Manganese (Mn)* | *Sodium (Na)* | *Titanium (Ti)* |
|---|---|---|---|---|
| ROG001 | 13474.8 | 642.43 | 8752.6 | 3430.9 |
| ROG002 | 17589.8 | 455.62 | 5404.2 | 3045.9 |
| ROG003 | 18509.3 | 688.97 | 7198.3 | 3246.0 |
| ROG004 | 15889.4 | 652.60 | 7032.5 | 3691.9 |
| ROG005 | 21149.4 | 573.56 | 8840.2 | 3350.1 |
| ROG006 | 18635.1 | 546.87 | 6873.0 | 3117.3 |
| ROG007 | 21173.4 | 688.34 | 8727.5 | 3831.1 |
| ROG008 | 16203.0 | 719.44 | 7580.9 | 4294.4 |
| ROG009 | 20356.2 | 684.50 | 9206.9 | 4111.3 |
| ROG010 | 20936.2 | 551.13 | 9518.3 | 3063.9 |
| ROG011 | 18146.9 | 658.52 | 8014.0 | 3328.8 |
| ROG012 | 21134.6 | 620.30 | 6543.6 | 4034.4 |
| ROG013 | 16587.4 | 710.46 | 7850.8 | 4045.3 |
| ROG014 | 16944.1 | 598.57 | 6649.7 | 3614.2 |
| ROG015 | 12785.2 | 585.37 | 8938.9 | 3688.9 |
| ROG016 | 17875.8 | 545.25 | 7078.1 | 3120.2 |
| ROG017 | 17796.6 | 548.44 | 6074.5 | 3465.9 |
| ROG018 | 20252.5 | 541.70 | 7020.0 | 3266.9 |
| ROG019 | 18310.6 | 537.84 | 6584.5 | 3434.7 |
| ROG020 | 15645.5 | 653.44 | 6250.6 | 3478.9 |
| ROG021 | 21039.3 | 624.89 | 6902.5 | 3969.9 |
| ROG022 | 16726.3 | 1043.17 | 9625.5 | 3290.9 |
| ROG023 | 19529.1 | 700.23 | 7571.4 | 2923.7 |
| ROG024 | 16376.8 | 678.64 | 6099.1 | 3067.0 |
| ROG025 | 20821.3 | 659.79 | 7031.1 | 3516.1 |
| ROG026 | 20132.8 | 660.68 | 6581.9 | 4364.6 |
| ROG027 | 18584.9 | 540.67 | 7236.8 | 3379.6 |
| ROG028 | 16961.8 | 612.39 | 6180.7 | 2611.1 |
| ROG029 | 11238.9 | 757.82 | 8629.4 | 4133.6 |
| ROG030 | 19414.7 | 582.38 | 6131.0 | 3456.4 |
| ROG031 | 23051.7 | 630.38 | 12713.4 | 3099.2 |
| ROG032 | 20766.7 | 588.76 | 8407.6 | 3301.1 |
| ROG033 | 18064.7 | 617.79 | 9603.2 | 2656.7 |
| ROG034 | 18659.7 | 545.91 | 6283.2 | 2800.3 |
| ROG035 | 18990.5 | 535.05 | 6517.3 | 2905.8 |
| ROG036 | 17471.9 | 565.73 | 6071.4 | 3093.5 |
| ROG037 | 22793.4 | 604.27 | 7462.9 | 2727.5 |

Table 12. Elemental Concentration (ppm) Data for Susiana Ceramics (*cont.*)

| *Sample Identification* | *Potassium (K)* | *Manganese (Mn)* | *Sodium (Na)* | *Titanium (Ti)* |
|---|---|---|---|---|
| ROG038 | 19047.3 | 622.82 | 6472.3 | 4180.1 |
| ROG039 | 17843.9 | 657.60 | 7116.3 | 3716.5 |
| ROG040 | 15867.4 | 566.23 | 5343.0 | 2888.1 |
| ROG041 | 14956.8 | 694.92 | 7732.1 | 4183.4 |
| ROG042 | 17425.5 | 741.30 | 6882.5 | 3707.7 |
| ROG043 | 17857.8 | 612.51 | 4868.0 | 3394.0 |
| ROG044 | 16152.9 | 588.28 | 5777.7 | 3367.6 |
| ROG045 | 15361.5 | 595.87 | 4982.3 | 2862.8 |
| ROG046 | 15916.9 | 634.74 | 6959.1 | 3091.8 |
| ROG047 | 16372.7 | 631.92 | 6368.6 | 3328.7 |
| ROG048 | 17030.6 | 581.70 | 5149.7 | 3482.9 |
| ROG049 | 16255.0 | 578.37 | 6997.5 | 2718.2 |
| ROG050 | 15614.6 | 632.68 | 7629.8 | 3031.1 |
| ROG051 | 18964.4 | 659.89 | 8002.3 | 3466.6 |
| ROG052 | 19505.2 | 601.97 | 7397.0 | 2831.6 |
| ROG053 | 20247.7 | 735.54 | 6639.3 | 3620.7 |
| ROG054 | 17953.8 | 645.67 | 6642.5 | 3101.0 |
| ROG055 | 17873.1 | 729.96 | 9397.2 | 3594.2 |
| ROG056 | 17296.7 | 632.35 | 7947.7 | 2636.5 |
| ROG057 | 15694.0 | 572.62 | 6363.3 | 2898.0 |
| ROG058 | 13583.2 | 543.62 | 5074.1 | 2642.3 |
| ROG059 | 15489.4 | 624.75 | 5972.5 | 3679.8 |
| ROG060 | 17624.2 | 710.49 | 7152.5 | 3856.0 |
| ROG061 | 15676.2 | 613.93 | 6775.5 | 3742.4 |
| ROG062 | 18998.7 | 739.68 | 6716.0 | 3720.5 |
| ROG063 | 16007.0 | 780.07 | 4403.5 | 3267.4 |
| ROG064 | 13806.2 | 643.00 | 3799.2 | 3864.4 |
| ROG065 | 10901.7 | 564.00 | 3847.3 | 2206.9 |
| ROG066 | 15424.2 | 723.22 | 3983.0 | 3945.6 |
| ROG067 | 12277.9 | 772.64 | 3497.8 | 3720.2 |
| ROG068 | 14029.6 | 740.32 | 8169.5 | 3014.0 |
| ROG069 | 15213.1 | 779.98 | 4680.4 | 3327.1 |
| ROG070 | 15411.5 | 644.31 | 8612.3 | 3316.6 |
| ROG071 | 20492.0 | 668.86 | 5778.9 | 3348.3 |
| ROG072 | 18215.8 | 884.35 | 12890.1 | 5185.3 |
| ROG073 | 17790.1 | 640.55 | 9996.3 | 2791.3 |
| ROG074 | 22525.8 | 904.49 | 4861.2 | 3890.6 |

Table 12. Elemental Concentration (ppm) Data for Susiana Ceramics (*cont.*)

| *Sample Identification* | *Potassium (K)* | *Manganese (Mn)* | *Sodium (Na)* | *Titanium (Ti)* |
|---|---|---|---|---|
| ROG075 | 17088.9 | 653.26 | 5481.9 | 2880.8 |
| ROG076 | 15574.0 | 656.81 | 5312.7 | 2720.2 |
| ROG077 | 22335.6 | 942.27 | 4726.1 | 3752.1 |
| ROG078 | 14207.9 | 767.80 | 7847.9 | 3139.6 |
| ROG079 | 18603.1 | 924.15 | 5441.9 | 3402.4 |
| ROG080 | 18428.6 | 1008.59 | 5855.0 | 2281.6 |
| ROG081 | 13400.2 | 759.51 | 9041.2 | 2821.8 |
| ROG082 | 16803.4 | 737.22 | 3876.6 | 4149.4 |
| ROG083 | 13242.1 | 759.41 | 7661.7 | 3370.9 |
| ROG084 | 20197.6 | 878.40 | 5902.6 | 4167.3 |
| ROG085 | 10630.0 | 730.52 | 5613.7 | 4010.4 |
| ROG086 | 16677.5 | 709.03 | 4179.2 | 2798.0 |
| ROG087 | 15751.3 | 489.55 | 4240.4 | 3530.3 |
| ROG088 | 22619.9 | 832.22 | 5570.5 | 3312.2 |
| ROG089 | 17111.4 | 704.33 | 4486.5 | 3124.6 |
| ROG090 | 16259.6 | 818.42 | 5190.4 | 3847.8 |
| ROG091 | 17009.1 | 630.60 | 5400.5 | 3307.3 |
| ROG092 | 19211.6 | 628.69 | 3661.7 | 3461.1 |
| ROG093 | 21022.2 | 747.77 | 6773.2 | 3249.0 |
| ROG094 | 20187.5 | 755.36 | 4581.2 | 3463.6 |
| ROG095 | 12907.0 | 802.59 | 8399.5 | 3487.2 |
| ROG096 | 16657.8 | 681.28 | 4765.9 | 3039.4 |
| ROG097 | 14167.1 | 583.23 | 4016.6 | 2736.2 |
| ROG098 | 18658.3 | 855.75 | 5734.1 | 2595.7 |
| ROG099 | 16422.8 | 597.90 | 6026.2 | 3374.4 |
| ROG100 | 7863.8 | 728.17 | 8751.9 | 3271.3 |
| ROG101 | 15933.0 | 546.11 | 4128.3 | 2720.3 |
| ROG102 | 16475.5 | 632.46 | 4771.2 | 2636.7 |
| ROG103 | 18478.9 | 860.58 | 5498.6 | 3617.7 |
| ROG104 | 18805.8 | 914.00 | 5653.8 | 3449.9 |
| ROG105 | 20839.6 | 735.31 | 5059.0 | 3067.8 |
| ROG106 | 15737.4 | 717.85 | 5824.1 | 3666.4 |
| ROG107 | 21264.9 | 730.86 | 5527.3 | 3656.8 |
| ROG108 | 11460.6 | 787.52 | 7869.2 | 2845.8 |
| ROG109 | 18200.8 | 711.88 | 4249.6 | 3076.5 |
| ROG110 | 13081.3 | 495.66 | 4171.2 | 2519.6 |
| ROG111 | 15871.5 | 618.24 | 4057.7 | 3141.1 |

Table 12. Elemental Concentration (ppm) Data for Susiana Ceramics (*cont.*)

| *Sample Identification* | *Potassium (K)* | *Manganese (Mn)* | *Sodium (Na)* | *Titanium (Ti)* |
|---|---|---|---|---|
| ROG112 | 19198.0 | 584.71 | 6175.8 | 3303.2 |
| ROG113 | 18630.1 | 645.46 | 5746.4 | 3060.5 |
| ROG114 | 23090.1 | 751.59 | 4858.0 | 3153.3 |
| ROG115 | 15357.0 | 515.91 | 4609.6 | 2200.8 |
| ROG116 | 27885.9 | 847.56 | 5340.0 | 3376.1 |
| ROG117 | 18378.2 | 640.95 | 5383.4 | 2545.7 |
| ROG118 | 22347.4 | 701.27 | 5555.5 | 2377.0 |
| ROG119 | 13844.1 | 775.18 | 7136.2 | 3097.5 |
| ROG120 | 15889.7 | 561.41 | 4307.7 | 3115.2 |
| ROG121 | 16090.1 | 615.53 | 4569.8 | 2487.9 |
| ROG122 | 15539.3 | 609.19 | 5563.8 | 2660.4 |
| ROG123 | 16965.7 | 645.87 | 5298.8 | 2784.5 |
| ROG124 | 18199.0 | 666.39 | 3792.1 | 3367.3 |
| ROG125 | 20705.3 | 677.73 | 4366.5 | 3047.3 |
| ROG126 | 23106.3 | 763.87 | 3665.7 | 3556.8 |
| ROG127 | 14653.5 | 887.69 | 5341.0 | 2517.0 |
| ROG128 | 24604.5 | 683.69 | 5357.2 | 3467.2 |
| ROG129 | 18151.2 | 529.65 | 4371.0 | 2804.7 |
| ROG130 | 18353.4 | 776.71 | 4799.4 | 3421.0 |
| ROG131 | 17135.0 | 646.84 | 4088.2 | 2783.4 |
| ROG132 | 21791.1 | 745.87 | 4247.8 | 3009.6 |
| ROG133 | 14569.3 | 593.22 | 4792.7 | 2966.0 |
| ROG134 | 19395.9 | 664.54 | 11350.0 | 3986.9 |
| ROG135 | 6126.0 | 787.33 | 14526.7 | 3597.8 |
| ROG136 | 16302.8 | 709.21 | 11713.6 | 3500.5 |
| ROG137 | 11058.6 | 733.58 | 11257.4 | 4410.4 |
| ROG138 | 17171.6 | 701.98 | 12191.7 | 3876.5 |
| ROG139 | 12704.5 | 822.93 | 12186.4 | 4027.7 |
| ROG140 | 11660.7 | 731.62 | 11409.1 | 3850.3 |
| ROG141 | 16340.6 | 904.36 | 3930.2 | 3849.6 |
| ROG142 | 7087.4 | 733.23 | 8328.3 | 3805.2 |
| ROG143 | 15202.5 | 863.16 | 8788.6 | 3951.1 |
| ROG144 | 17472.6 | 727.09 | 9590.8 | 4636.8 |
| ROG145 | 12916.2 | 730.55 | 11334.2 | 4505.5 |
| ROG146 | 9232.6 | 711.43 | 9308.2 | 4855.8 |
| ROG147 | 13656.7 | 873.67 | 9860.4 | 5150.6 |
| ROG148 | 13152.9 | 817.43 | 7362.5 | 4022.3 |

Table 12. Elemental Concentration (ppm) Data for Susiana Ceramics (*cont.*)

| *Sample Identification* | *Potassium (K)* | *Manganese (Mn)* | *Sodium (Na)* | *Titanium (Ti)* |
|---|---|---|---|---|
| ROG149 | 8031.8 | 720.44 | 8910.0 | 4182.4 |
| ROG150 | 15627.5 | 866.74 | 9596.7 | 4122.9 |
| ROG151 | 13128.9 | 788.78 | 9819.1 | 4973.3 |
| ROG152 | 15070.6 | 796.26 | 9097.1 | 4119.5 |
| ROG153 | 20631.0 | 655.04 | 9238.6 | 3941.6 |
| ROG154 | 17647.8 | 679.74 | 3687.4 | 3518.3 |
| ROG155 | 17374.0 | 840.06 | 13500.8 | 3652.2 |
| ROG156 | 13298.6 | 709.80 | 8141.5 | 3774.9 |
| ROG157 | 16570.1 | 676.55 | 9905.5 | 4861.7 |
| ROG158 | 14934.4 | 689.45 | 9550.6 | 4660.2 |
| ROG159 | 8769.2 | 779.44 | 8964.4 | 3785.5 |
| ROG160 | 15215.6 | 790.19 | 10830.2 | 4020.9 |
| ROG161 | 21990.9 | 570.12 | 9958.6 | 4397.4 |
| ROG162 | 18897.4 | 776.40 | 11528.1 | 4816.0 |
| ROG163 | 25132.3 | 802.35 | 4587.3 | 3203.7 |
| ROG164 | 17554.9 | 676.34 | 8670.3 | 3686.1 |
| ROG165 | 16280.5 | 554.21 | 8768.3 | 3974.5 |
| ROG166 | 12869.6 | 792.59 | 10243.8 | 4902.4 |
| ROG167 | 13970.7 | 804.25 | 20678.5 | 4088.2 |
| ROG168 | 13370.6 | 806.94 | 17553.3 | 3167.3 |
| ROG169 | 5578.0 | 669.42 | 11750.1 | 3722.1 |
| ROG170 | 14587.2 | 849.16 | 14220.6 | 4751.5 |
| ROG171 | 7881.8 | 911.79 | 15334.0 | 4213.4 |
| ROG172 | 8494.1 | 876.95 | 11370.3 | 4291.4 |
| ROG173 | 16478.5 | 674.66 | 15303.8 | 4009.1 |
| ROG174 | 8263.7 | 673.37 | 13881.4 | 3978.6 |
| ROG175 | 22585.5 | 773.13 | 11582.1 | 4486.3 |
| ROG176 | 21773.0 | 680.15 | 7812.1 | 4335.3 |
| ROG177 | 17641.4 | 603.74 | 9905.0 | 4331.1 |
| ROG178 | 12758.6 | 739.87 | 6113.9 | 4320.7 |
| ROG179 | 8748.7 | 811.10 | 7922.4 | 3296.9 |
| ROG180 | 7641.3 | 755.39 | 10856.8 | 3751.7 |
| ROG181 | 17441.8 | 588.39 | 9160.7 | 3344.0 |
| ROG182 | 21894.6 | 684.03 | 9550.6 | 4534.0 |
| ROG183 | 19242.5 | 709.80 | 6295.6 | 3829.1 |
| ROG184 | 23069.3 | 757.25 | 9576.9 | 4454.8 |
| ROG185 | 15806.5 | 720.44 | 11794.6 | 3868.5 |

Table 12. Elemental Concentration (ppm) Data for Susiana Ceramics (*cont.*)

| *Sample Identification* | *Potassium (K)* | *Manganese (Mn)* | *Sodium (Na)* | *Titanium (Ti)* |
|---|---|---|---|---|
| ROG186 | 20049.8 | 698.45 | 7436.5 | 4222.4 |
| ROG187 | 18822.0 | 747.55 | 11735.2 | 3877.7 |
| ROG188 | 20297.8 | 504.59 | 11502.5 | 3892.1 |
| ROG189 | 19613.7 | 746.10 | 9396.8 | 4465.0 |
| ROG190 | 21366.1 | 701.81 | 6751.9 | 4463.9 |
| ROG191 | 21733.6 | 727.38 | 5169.9 | 3686.0 |
| ROG192 | 22951.7 | 764.94 | 8255.6 | 4015.0 |
| ROG193 | 8296.9 | 716.19 | 10221.0 | 3611.6 |
| ROG194 | 6062.2 | 650.70 | 8884.7 | 2781.8 |
| ROG195 | 7038.6 | 831.78 | 11492.2 | 3837.9 |
| ROG196 | 7130.1 | 719.08 | 14799.8 | 2475.1 |
| ROG197 | 5259.3 | 852.26 | 9093.3 | 3913.7 |
| ROG198 | 6877.6 | 757.75 | 7054.4 | 3664.6 |
| ROG199 | 1114.9 | 870.27 | 9279.0 | 3564.4 |
| ROG200 | 5032.3 | 754.26 | 13955.5 | 3082.7 |

Table 13. Elemental Concentration (ppm) Data for Susiana Ceramics

| *Sample Identification* | *Vanadium (V)* | *Sample Identification* | *Vanadium (V)* |
|---|---|---|---|
| ROG001 | 94.66 | ROG041 | 105.84 |
| ROG002 | 97.83 | ROG042 | 99.63 |
| ROG003 | 110.26 | ROG043 | 96.27 |
| ROG004 | 99.12 | ROG044 | 83.74 |
| ROG005 | 101.02 | ROG045 | 84.77 |
| ROG006 | 88.24 | ROG046 | 93.66 |
| ROG007 | 105.39 | ROG047 | 100.29 |
| ROG008 | 113.07 | ROG048 | 101.38 |
| ROG009 | 110.08 | ROG049 | 98.42 |
| ROG010 | 80.56 | ROG050 | 74.25 |
| ROG011 | 106.25 | ROG051 | 94.92 |
| ROG012 | 93.99 | ROG052 | 93.10 |
| ROG013 | 117.21 | ROG053 | 79.60 |
| ROG014 | 90.09 | ROG054 | 78.26 |
| ROG015 | 104.61 | ROG055 | 90.77 |
| ROG016 | 95.83 | ROG056 | 92.08 |
| ROG017 | 92.91 | ROG057 | 98.33 |
| ROG018 | 96.75 | ROG058 | 90.32 |
| ROG019 | 91.17 | ROG059 | 115.89 |
| ROG020 | 102.79 | ROG060 | 94.93 |
| ROG021 | 117.97 | ROG061 | 114.51 |
| ROG022 | 146.03 | ROG062 | 123.63 |
| ROG023 | 107.07 | ROG063 | 121.96 |
| ROG024 | 94.62 | ROG064 | 98.73 |
| ROG025 | 105.38 | ROG065 | 91.94 |
| ROG026 | 107.63 | ROG066 | 114.31 |
| ROG027 | 92.41 | ROG067 | 102.05 |
| ROG028 | 91.35 | ROG068 | 117.87 |
| ROG029 | 75.22 | ROG069 | 79.42 |
| ROG030 | 107.94 | ROG070 | 76.73 |
| ROG031 | 83.45 | ROG071 | 88.86 |
| ROG032 | 126.59 | ROG072 | 114.91 |
| ROG033 | 74.58 | ROG073 | 72.60 |
| ROG034 | 117.64 | ROG074 | 109.88 |
| ROG035 | 97.34 | ROG075 | 87.56 |
| ROG036 | 93.60 | ROG076 | 83.82 |
| ROG037 | 122.20 | ROG077 | 86.70 |

Table 13. Elemental Concentration (ppm) Data for Susiana Ceramics (*cont.*)

| *Sample Identification* | *Vanadium (V)* | *Sample Identification* | *Vanadium (V)* |
|---|---|---|---|
| ROG038 | 110.22 | ROG078 | 89.56 |
| ROG039 | 95.99 | ROG079 | 87.05 |
| ROG040 | 93.57 | ROG080 | 71.61 |
| ROG081 | 88.56 | ROG135 | 148.04 |
| ROG082 | 106.32 | ROG136 | 108.86 |
| ROG083 | 96.72 | ROG137 | 106.82 |
| ROG084 | 93.45 | ROG138 | 147.94 |
| ROG085 | 103.44 | ROG139 | 146.52 |
| ROG086 | 84.23 | ROG140 | 146.28 |
| ROG087 | 85.22 | ROG141 | 130.99 |
| ROG088 | 108.32 | ROG142 | 113.32 |
| ROG089 | 98.40 | ROG143 | 134.26 |
| ROG090 | 100.99 | ROG144 | 118.82 |
| ROG091 | 97.31 | ROG145 | 127.21 |
| ROG092 | 101.42 | ROG146 | 143.88 |
| ROG093 | 83.54 | ROG147 | 137.98 |
| ROG094 | 151.67 | ROG148 | 137.11 |
| ROG095 | 99.05 | ROG149 | 133.73 |
| ROG096 | 85.07 | ROG150 | 139.17 |
| ROG097 | 86.63 | ROG151 | 130.52 |
| ROG098 | 85.53 | ROG152 | 136.68 |
| ROG099 | 103.19 | ROG153 | 121.10 |
| ROG100 | 105.30 | ROG154 | 110.37 |
| ROG101 | 84.47 | ROG155 | 124.42 |
| ROG102 | 93.71 | ROG156 | 114.84 |
| ROG103 | 92.91 | ROG157 | 160.83 |
| ROG104 | 106.85 | ROG158 | 136.80 |
| ROG105 | 100.02 | ROG159 | 122.25 |
| ROG106 | 81.88 | ROG160 | 142.43 |
| ROG107 | 117.99 | ROG161 | 132.12 |
| ROG108 | 89.11 | ROG162 | 142.01 |
| ROG109 | 89.07 | ROG163 | 120.49 |
| ROG110 | 73.82 | ROG164 | 123.38 |
| ROG111 | 74.12 | ROG165 | 132.15 |
| ROG112 | 101.36 | ROG166 | 134.76 |
| ROG113 | 83.23 | ROG167 | 110.05 |
| ROG114 | 119.94 | ROG168 | 127.83 |

Table 13. Elemental Concentration (ppm) Data for Susiana Ceramics (*cont.*)

| *Sample Identification* | *Vanadium (V)* | *Sample Identification* | *Vanadium (V)* |
|---|---|---|---|
| ROG115 | 81.00 | ROG169 | 133.12 |
| ROG116 | 115.09 | ROG170 | 133.95 |
| ROG117 | 95.39 | ROG171 | 136.62 |
| ROG118 | 115.59 | ROG172 | 133.40 |
| ROG119 | 102.55 | ROG173 | 105.00 |
| ROG120 | 90.28 | ROG174 | 129.95 |
| ROG121 | 91.51 | ROG175 | 132.68 |
| ROG122 | 62.35 | ROG176 | 132.52 |
| ROG123 | 91.49 | ROG177 | 123.26 |
| ROG124 | 81.05 | ROG178 | 116.18 |
| ROG125 | 89.15 | ROG179 | 76.30 |
| ROG126 | 103.30 | ROG180 | 80.49 |
| ROG127 | 87.99 | ROG181 | 122.34 |
| ROG128 | 91.60 | ROG182 | 124.14 |
| ROG129 | 90.02 | ROG183 | 93.61 |
| ROG130 | 89.72 | ROG184 | 109.08 |
| ROG131 | 92.00 | ROG185 | 98.18 |
| ROG132 | 74.75 | ROG186 | 103.26 |
| ROG133 | 79.82 | ROG187 | 90.71 |
| ROG134 | 106.18 | ROG188 | 106.71 |
| ROG189 | 111.78 | ROG195 | 57.50 |
| ROG190 | 129.32 | ROG196 | 39.32 |
| ROG191 | 95.61 | ROG197 | 67.90 |
| ROG192 | 100.33 | ROG198 | 68.41 |
| ROG193 | 81.99 | ROG199 | 47.89 |
| ROG194 | 48.48 | ROG200 | 74.07 |

# APPENDIX TWO

# MASTER LIST OF LOCI FROM CHOGHA MISH SEASONS 2–11 IN CHRONOLOGICAL ORDER

| *Season* | *Area* | *Provenance* | *Elevation* | *Type of Deposit or Feature* |
|---|---|---|---|---|
| **Probably Archaic Susiana** | | | | |
| Ch.M. V | Trench XXV | R20:515 East | 76.86 | Occupational debris |
| Ch.M. 1996 VII | Gully Cut | S22:701 | 75.46 | Occupational debris |
| **Archaic Susiana 1** | | | | |
| Ch.M. IV | Gully Cut | S22:402+403 | 72.88 | Occupational debris |
| Ch.M. IV | Gully Cut | S22:402+403 | 72.88–72.00 | Occupational debris |
| Ch.M. IV | Gully Cut | S22:402+403 | 72.88 | Occupational debris |
| Ch.M. IV | Gully Cut | S22:403 | 74.13–73.53 | Occupational debris |
| Ch.M. IV | Gully Cut | S22:403 | 73.23 | Occupational debris |
| Ch.M. IV | Gully Cut | S22:403 | 73.13–72.88 | Occupational debris |
| Ch.M. IV | Gully Cut | S22:403 | 72.53 | Occupational debris |
| Ch.M. IV | Gully Cut | S22:404 | 73.43 | Occupational debris |
| Ch.M. IV | Gully Cut | S22:404 | 73.43–73.13 | Occupational debris |
| Ch.M. IV | Gully Cut | S22:404 | 72.83 | Occupational debris |
| Ch.M. IV | Gully Cut | S22:405 East | 73.00–72.80 | Occupational debris |
| Ch.M. IV | Gully Cut | S22:405 Middle | 73.95 | Occupational debris |
| Ch.M. IV | Gully Cut | S22:405 Middle | 73.70 | Occupational debris |
| Ch.M. IV | Gully Cut | S22:405 Middle | 73.70–73.45 | Occupational debris |
| Ch.M. IV | Gully Cut | S22:404 | 73.43 | Occupational debris |
| Ch.M. IV | Gully Cut | S22:405 Middle | 73.30 | Occupational debris |
| Ch.M. V | Gully Cut | S22:502 | 73.30–73.20 | Occupational debris |
| Ch.M. V | Gully Cut | S22:502 | 73.20–72.89 | Occupational debris |
| Ch.M. V | Gully Cut | S22:502 | 72.89 | Occupational debris |
| Ch.M. V | Gully Cut | S22:502 | 72.89–72.47 | Occupational debris |
| Ch.M. V | Gully Cut | S22:502 | 72.47–72.18 | Occupational debris |
| Ch.M. V | Gully Cut | S22:503 | 72.40–72.05 | Occupational debris |
| Ch.M. V | Gully Cut | S22:503 | N/A | Occupational debris |
| Ch.M. V | Gully Cut | S22:503 | 72.99–72.69 | Occupational debris |
| Ch.M. V | Gully Cut | S22:503 | 72.69–72.40 | Occupational debris |
| Ch.M. V | Gully Cut | S22:503 | 72.49 | Occupational debris |
| Ch.M. V | Gully Cut | S22:503 | 72.40–72.05 | Occupational debris |

| *Season* | *Area* | *Provenance* | *Elevation* | *Type of Deposit or Feature* |
|---|---|---|---|---|
| **Archaic Susiana 1** (*cont.*) | | | | |
| Ch.M. V | Gully Cut | S22:506 | 73.30–72.96 | Occupational debris |
| Ch.M. V | Gully Cut | S22:506 | 73.24–72.96 | Occupational debris |
| Ch.M. V | Gully Cut | S22:506 | 72.96–72.72 | Occupational debris |
| Ch.M. V | Gully Cut | S22:507 | 72.96–72.72 | Occupational debris |
| Ch.M. V | Gully Cut | S22:508 | 73.44–73.06 | Occupational debris |
| Ch.M. V | Gully Cut | S22:508 | 73.29–73.24 | Occupational debris |
| Ch.M. V | Gully Cut | S22:508 | 73.06–72.84 | Occupational debris |
| Ch.M. V | Gully Cut | S22:508 | 72.84 | Occupational debris |
| Ch.M. V | Gully Cut | S22:508 | 72.74–72.59 | Occupational debris |
| Ch.M. V | Gully Cut | S22:508 | 72.59–72.40 | Occupational debris |
| Ch.M. V | Gully Cut | S22:511 | 72.49–72.20 | Occupational debris |
| Ch.M. V | Gully Cut | S22:511 | 72.40 | Occupational debris |
| Ch.M. V | Gully Cut | S22:511 | 72.40–72.23 | Occupational debris |
| Ch.M. V | Gully Cut | S22:511 | 72.23 | Occupational debris |
| Ch.M. V | Gully Cut | S22:511 | 71.70 | Occupational debris |
| **Archaic Susiana 1–2** | | | | |
| Ch.M. IV | Gully Cut | S22:401 | 74.88–74.63 | Occupational debris |
| Ch.M. IV | Gully Cut | S22:404 | 74.93–74.38 | Occupational debris |
| Ch.M. IV | Gully Cut | S22:405 Middle | 74.85–74.60 | Occupational debris |
| Ch.M. V | Trench XXXII | R23:503 | 76.93 | Room |
| Ch.M. V | Trench XXXII | R23:504 | 76.85 | Room |
| Ch.M. VI | Gully Cut | S22:601 | 73.12 | Occupational debris |
| Ch.M. VI | Gully Cut | S22:601 | 73.00 | Occupational debris |
| Ch.M. VII | Trench XXXII | R23:708 | 76.09 | Occupational debris |
| **Archaic 2** | | | | |
| Ch.M. IV | Sounding G | S-T21 | 72.60–72.50 | Occupational debris |
| Ch.M. IV | Sounding G | S-T21 | 72.50 | Occupational debris |
| Ch.M. IV | Gully Cut | S22:404 | 75.13 | Occupational debris |
| Ch.M. V | Trench XXXII | R23:501 | N/A | Settlement area |
| Ch.M. V | Trench XXXII | R23:504 | N/A | Room |
| Ch.M. V | Trench XXXII | Q23:504 | N/A | Room |
| Ch.M. V | Trench XXXII | R23:504 East | 75.92 | Room |
| Ch.M. V | Trench XXXII | R23:504 East | 75.90 | Room |
| Ch.M. V | Gully Cut | S22:502 | 74.43 | Occupational debris |
| Ch.M. V | Gully Cut | S22:502 | 74.43 | Occupational debris |
| Ch.M. V | Gully Cut | S22:502 | 74.41 | Hard surface (floor?) |

| *Season* | *Area* | *Provenance* | *Elevation* | *Type of Deposit or Feature* |
|---|---|---|---|---|
| **Archaic 2** (*cont.*) | | | | |
| Ch.M. V | Gully Cut | S22:502 | 74.40–74.26 | Occupational debris |
| Ch.M. V | Gully Cut | S22:502 | 74.26–74.01 | Occupational debris |
| Ch.M. V | Gully Cut | S22:502 | 74.20–74.11 | Occupational debris |
| Ch.M. V | Gully Cut | S22:502 | 74.11–73.68 | Occupational debris |
| Ch.M. V | Gully Cut | S22:502 | 74.11–73.60 | Occupational debris |
| Ch.M. V | Gully Cut | S22:502 | 73.96–73.83 | Occupational debris |
| Ch.M. V | Gully Cut | S22:502 | 73.83–73.60 | Occupational debris |
| Ch.M. V | Gully Cut | S22:502 | 73.83–73.36 | Occupational debris |
| Ch.M. V | Gully Cut | S22:502 | 73.60–73.50 | Occupational debris |
| Ch.M. V | Gully Cut | S22:502 | 73.50–73.30 | Occupational debris |
| Ch.M. V | Gully Cut | S22:506 | 74.12 | Ash deposit |
| Ch.M. V | Gully Cut | S22:506 | 74.06 | Ash deposit |
| Ch.M. V | Gully Cut | S22:506 | 73.79–73.30 | Occupational debris |
| Ch.M. V | Gully Cut | S22:508 | 74.22–73.96 | Occupational debris |
| Ch.M. V | Gully Cut | S22:508 | 73.96–73.73 | Occupational debris |
| Ch.M. V | Gully Cut | S22:508 | 73.73–73.29 | Occupational debris |
| Ch.M. V | Gully Cut | S23:505 | 74.50–73.83 | Occupational debris |
| Ch.M. V | Gully Cut | S23:505 | 74.31 | Occupational debris |
| Ch.M. VI | Gully Cut | S22:601 | 73.67 | Occupational debris |
| Ch.M. VI | Gully Cut | S22:601 | 74.38 | Occupational debris |
| Ch.M. VI | Gully Cut | S22:601 | 74.07–73.77 | Occupational debris |
| Ch.M. VI | Gully Cut | S22:601 | 73.80–73.55 | Occupational debris |
| Ch.M. VI | Gully Cut | S22:601 | 73.67 | Occupational debris |
| Ch.M. VI | Gully Cut | S22:601 | 73.46 | Occupational debris |
| Ch.M. VI | Gully Cut | S22:602 | 74.12 | Occupational debris |
| Ch.M. VI | Gully Cut | S22:602 | 73.95 | Occupational debris |
| Ch.M. VI | Gully Cut | S22:602 | 73.63 | Occupational debris |
| Ch.M. VII | Trench XXI | Q22:708 | N/A | Occupational debris |
| Ch.M. VII | Trench XXXII | Q22:708 | N/A | Occupational debris |
| Ch.M. VII | Trench XXXII | Q23:713 | N/A | Occupational debris |
| **Archaic Susiana 2–3** | | | | |
| Ch.M. IV | Sounding H | T21–22 North | 71.95–71.65 | Occupational debris |
| Ch.M. V | Gully Cut | S22:502 South | 74.78 | Occupational debris |
| Ch.M. V | Gully Cut | S22:505 | 74.60 | Hard surface (floor?) |
| Ch.M. V | Gully Cut | S22:505 | N/A | Indeterminate |
| Ch.M. V | Gully Cut | S22:508 | 74.84–74.61 | Occupational debris |

| *Season* | *Area* | *Provenance* | *Elevation* | *Type of Deposit or Feature* |
|---|---|---|---|---|
| **Archaic Susiana 2–3** (*cont.*) | | | | |
| Ch.M. V | Gully Cut | S22:508 | 74.61–74.42 | Occupational debris |
| Ch.M. V | Gully Cut | S22:508 | 74.43–74.22 | Occupational debris |
| Ch.M. VI | Trench XXI | P22:614 | 79.80 | Occupational debris |
| Ch.M. VI | Trench XXI | P22:614 | 79.80 | Occupational debris |
| Ch.M. VI | Trench XXI | P22:614 | 79.70 | Occupational debris |
| Ch.M. VI | Trench XXI | P22:614 | 79.50 | Room |
| Ch.M. VI | Trench XXV | R20:608 | 77.60 | Living surface |
| Ch.M. VI | Trench XXV | R20:608 | 77.03 | Living surface |
| Ch.M. VI | Trench XXV | R20:608 | 76.62 | Living surface |
| **Archaic Susiana** | | | | |
| Ch.M. IV | Sounding G | S-T21 | 74.20–73.95 | Occupational debris |
| Ch.M. IV | Sounding G | S-T21 | 73.95–73.70 | Occupational debris |
| Ch.M. IV | Sounding G | S-T21 | 73.70–73.45 | Occupational debris |
| Ch.M. IV | Sounding G | S-T21 | 73.45–73.35 | Occupational debris |
| Ch.M. IV | Sounding G | S-T21 | 73.35–73.15 | Occupational debris |
| Ch.M. IV | Sounding G | S-T21 | 73.15–72.90 | Occupational debris |
| Ch.M. IV | Sounding G | S-T21 | 72.90 | Occupational debris |
| Ch.M. IV | Sounding G | S-T21 | 72.90–72.60 | Occupational debris |
| Ch.M. V | Trench XXXII | R23:501 | 77.52 | Pebble surface |
| Ch.M. V | Trench XXXII | R23:501 | 77.20 | Occupational debris |
| Ch.M. V | Gully Cut | S22:501 | 75.81–75.41 | Occupational debris |
| Ch.M. V | Gully Cut | S22:501 | 75.42–75.14 | Occupational debris |
| Ch.M. V | Gully Cut | S22:501 | 75.14–74 .71 | Occupational debris |
| Ch.M. V | Gully Cut | S22:501 | 74.81 | Occupational debris |
| Ch. M, V | Gully Cut | S22:501 | 74.78–74.43 | Occupational debris |
| Ch.M. V | Gully Cut | S22:501 | 74.71 | Occupational debris |
| Ch.M. V | Gully Cut | S22:504 | 75.84 | Occupational debris |
| Ch.M. V | Gully Cut | S22:505 | 74.72–74.60 | Occupational debris |
| Ch.M. V | Gully Cut | S22:507 | 75.64 | Occupational debris |
| Ch.M. V | Gully Cut | S22:507 | 75.43 | Burial |
| Ch.M. V | Gully Cut | S22:507 | 75.43 | Occupational debris |
| Ch.M. V | Gully Cut | S22:507 | 75.23–75.14 | Occupational debris |
| Ch.M. V | Gully Cut | S22:507 | 75.14–74.79 | Occupational debris |
| Ch.M. V | Gully Cut | S22:508 | 75.14–74.79 | Occupational debris |
| Ch.M. V | Gully Cut | S22:508 | 75.14–74.79 | Occupational debris |
| Ch.M. V | Gully Cut | S22:508 | 74.89–74.61 | Occupational debris |

| *Season* | *Area* | *Provenance* | *Elevation* | *Type of Deposit or Feature* |
|---|---|---|---|---|
| **Archaic Susiana** (*cont.*) | | | | |
| Ch.M. V | Gully Cut | S22:508 | 74.70 | Occupational debris |
| Ch.M. V | Gully Cut | S22:508 North | 75.01 | Occupational debris |
| Ch.M. V | Gully Cut | S22:508 South | 75.14–74.79 | Occupational debris |
| Ch.M. V | Gully Cut | S22:512 | 75.88–75.36 | Occupational debris |
| Ch.M. V | Gully Cut | S22:512 | 75.68–75.46 | Occupational debris |
| Ch.M. V | Gully Cut | S22:512 | 75.46–75.39 | Occupational debris |
| Ch. M, V | Gully Cut | S22:512 | 75.46–75.06 | Occupational debris |
| Ch.M. V | Gully Cut | S22:512 | 75.39–75.24 | Occupational debris |
| Ch.M. V | Gully Cut | S22:512 | 75.24–74.59 | Occupational debris |
| Ch.M. V | Gully Cut | S22:512 | 75.16 | Occupational debris |
| Ch.M. V | Gully Cut | S22:512 | 75.09 | Occupational debris |
| Ch.M. V | Gully Cut | S22:512 | 74.91–74.71 | Occupational debris |
| Ch.M. V | Gully Cut | S22:512 | 74.59 | Occupational debris |
| Ch.M. V | Gully Cut | S22:512 | N/A | Occupational debris |
| Ch.M. V | Gully Cut | S22:512 North | 75.36–74.91 | Occupational debris |
| Ch.M. VI | Gully Cut | S22:601 | 75.32 | Occupational debris |
| Ch.M. VI | Gully Cut | S22:601 | 74.96–74.67 | Occupational debris |
| Ch.M. VI | Gully Cut | S22:601 | 74.87 | Occupational debris |
| Ch.M. VI | Gully Cut | S22:601 | 74.72 | Occupational debris |
| Ch.M. VI | Gully Cut | S22:602 | 75.32 | Occupational debris |
| Ch.M. VI | Gully Cut | S22:602 | 74.71 | Occupational debris |
| Ch.M. VI | Gully Cut | S22:602 | 74.67–74.18 | Occupational debris |
| Ch.M. VI | Gully Cut | S22:602 | 74.45 | Occupational debris |
| Ch.M. VI | Trench XXI | P22:612 | 79.45 | Room |
| Ch.M. VI | Trench XXI | P22:617 | 79.36 | Room |
| Ch.M. VI | Trench XXI | P22:620 | 81.00 | Room |
| Ch. M, VI | Trench XXI | P22:620 | 80.95 | Room |
| Ch.M. VI | Trench XXI | P22:620 | 80.83 | Room |
| Ch.M. VI | Trench XXI | P22:620 | 80.80 | Room |
| Ch.M. VI | Trench XXI | P22:628 | 79.91 | Room |
| Ch.M. VI | Trench XXI | P22:628 | 79.58 | Occupational debris |
| Ch.M. VI | Trench XXI | Q22:602 | 79.90 | Occupational debris |
| Ch.M. VI | Trench XXV | S20:619 | 75.20 | Occupational debris |
| Ch.M. VI | Trench XXXII | R23:601 | 76.20 | Occupational debris |
| Ch.M. VI | Trench XXXII | R23:601 | 76.11 | Occupational debris |
| Ch.M. VII | Gully Cut | S22:703 | 75.25 | Occupational debris |

| *Season* | *Area* | *Provenance* | *Elevation* | *Type of Deposit or Feature* |
|---|---|---|---|---|
| **Archaic Susiana** (*cont.*) | | | | |
| Ch.M. VII | Gully Cut | S22:703 | 75.23 | Occupational debris |
| Ch.M. VII | Gully Cut | S22:703 | 74.86 | Occupational debris |
| Ch.M. VII | Trench XXI | Q23:713 | 77.66 | Occupational debris |
| Ch.M. VII | Trench XXI | Q23:713 | 77.59 | Occupational debris |
| Ch.M. VII | Trench XXI | Q23:713 South | 77.79 | Occupational debris |
| Ch.M. VIII | Gully Cut | S22:824 | 75.19 | Occupational debris |
| Ch.M. VIII | Gully Cut | S22:824 | 75.08 | Occupational debris |
| Ch.M. VIII | Gully Cut | S22:824 | 74.98 | Occupational debris |
| Ch.M. VIII | Gully Cut | S22:824 | 74.83 | Occupational debris |
| Ch.M. VIII | Gully Cut | S22:824 West | 75.11 | Occupational debris |
| Ch.M. VIII | Gully Cut | S22:826 | 73.62 | Occupational debris |
| Ch.M. VIII | Trench XXI | Q22:802 | 76.87 | Occupational debris |
| Ch.M. VIII | Trench XXI | Q22:802 | 76.32 | Occupational debris |
| Ch.M. VIII | Trench XXI | Q22:803 | 77.48 | Occupational debris |
| Ch.M. VIII | Trench XXI | Q23:808 East | 77.11 | Occupational debris |
| Ch.M. VIII | Trench XXI | Q23:810 | 77.80 | Occupational debris |
| Ch.M. VIII | Trench XXI | Q23:810 | 77.68 | Occupational debris |
| Ch.M. VIII | Trench XXI | Q23:810 East | 77.60 | Occupational debris |
| Ch.M. VIII | Trench XXI | Q23:814 | 77.59 | Room |
| Ch.M. VIII | Trench XXI | Q23:814 | 77.32 | Room |
| Ch.M. VIII | Trench XXXVII | Q24:801 West | 79.19 | Occupational debris |
| Ch.M. VIII | Trench XXXVII | Q24:801 West | 78.98 | Occupational debris |
| Ch.M. VIII | Trench XXXVII | Q24:801 West | 77.63 | Occupational debris |
| Ch.M. VIII | Trench XXXVII | Q24:801 West | 77.45 | Occupational debris |
| Ch.M. VIII | Trench XXXVII | Q24:801 West | 77.22 | Occupational debris |
| Ch.M. VIII | Trench XXXVII | Q24:801 West | 77.00 | Occupational debris |
| Ch.M. VIII | Trench XXXVII | Q24:801 West | 76.68 | Occupational debris |
| Ch.M. VIII | Trench XXXVII | Q24:801 West | 76.53 | Occupational debris |
| Ch.M. VIII | Trench XXXVII | Q24:801 West | 76.19 | Occupational debris |
| Ch.M. VIII | Trench XXXVII | Q24:801 West | 75.99 | Occupational debris |
| Ch.M. VIII | Trench XXXVII | Q24:801 West | 75.79 | Occupational debris |
| Ch.M. VIII | Trench XXXVII | Q24:802 East | 77.18 | Occupational debris |
| Ch.M. VIII | Trench XXXVII | Q24:802 East | 76.75 | Occupational debris |
| **Archaic 3 + Miscellaneous** | | | | |
| Ch.M. VII | TrenchXXXII | R23:710 | 77.82 | Occupational debris |
| Ch.M. VII | TrenchXXXII | R23:710 | 77.46 | Occupational debris |

| *Season* | *Area* | *Provenance* | *Elevation* | *Type of Deposit or Feature* |
|---|---|---|---|---|
| **Archaic Susiana 3 – Early Susiana Transition** | | | | |
| Ch.M. IV | Sounding G | S-T21 | 74.30–74.20 | Occupational debris |
| Ch.M. VIII | Trench XXI | Q22:80 | 78.44 | Occupational debris |
| Ch.M. VIII | Trench XXI | Q22:803 | 78.76 | Occupational debris |
| Ch.M. VIII | Trench XXI | Q22:806 | 79.11 | Room |
| Ch.M. VIII | Trench XXI | Q22:806 | 79.07 | Room |
| Ch.M. VIII | Trench XXI | Q23:801 | 78.78 | Wall |
| Ch.M. VIII | Trench XXI | Q23:80 South | 78.69 | Surface wash |
| Ch.M. VIII | Trench XXI | Q23:802 | 78.82 | Surface wash |
| Ch.M. VIII | Trench XXI | Q23:802 | 78.70 | Occupational debris |
| Ch.M. VIII | Trench XXI | Q23:802 | 78.33 | Occupational debris |
| Ch.M. VIII | Trench XXI | Q23:802 | 78.30 | Occupational debris |
| Ch.M. VIII | Trench XXI | Q23:803 North | 78.80 | Occupational debris |
| Ch.M. VIII | Trench XXI | Q23:806 | 79.22 | Occupational debris |
| Ch.M. VIII | Trench XXI | Q23:806 | 78.92 | Occupational debris |
| Ch.M. VIII | Trench XXI | Q23:808 | 78.24 | Occupational debris |
| Ch.M. VIII | Trench XXI | Q23:808 East | 78.01 | Occupational debris |
| Ch.M. VIII | Trench XXI | Q23:809 | 78.16 | Room |
| Ch.M. VIII | Trench XXI | Q23:810 | 78.27 | Occupational debris |
| Ch.M. VIII | Trench XXI | Q23:810 | 78.18 | Occupational debris |
| Ch.M. VIII | Trench XXI | Q23:810 | 77.90 | Occupational debris |
| Ch.M. VIII | Trench XXI | Q23:810 | 77.47 | Occupational debris |
| Ch.M. VIII | Trench XXI | Q23:810 | 77.43 | Occupational debris |
| Ch.M. VIII | Trench XXI | Q23:810 East | 78.07 | Occupational debris |
| Ch.M. VIII | Trench XXI | Q23:810 West | 78.03 | Occupational debris |
| Ch.M. VIII | Trench XXI | Q23:810 West | 77.71 | Occupational debris |
| Ch.M. VIII | Trench XXI | Q23:821 | 78.59 | Room |
| Ch.M. VIII | Trench XXI | Q23:821 | 78.43 | Room |
| Ch.M. VIII | Gully Cut | S22:801 South | 76.65 | Room |
| Ch.M. VIII | Gully Cut | S22:802 | 76.85 | Protoliterate pit(?) |
| Ch.M. VIII | Gully Cut | S22:803 | 76.61 | Protoliterate pit(?) |
| Ch.M. VIII | Gully Cut | S22:806 | 76.90–65.00 | Open court |
| Ch.M. VIII | Gully Cut | S22:806 East | 76.64 | Room? |
| Ch.M. VIII | Gully Cut | S22:807 | 76.68 | Cubical |
| Ch.M. VIII | Gully Cut | S22:808 | 75.91 | Protoliterate pit |
| Ch.M. VIII | Gully Cut | S22:808 | 75.46 | Occupational debris |
| Ch.M. VIII | Gully Cut | S22:808 | 75.28 | Occupational debris |

| *Season* | *Area* | *Provenance* | *Elevation* | *Type of Deposit or Feature* |
|---|---|---|---|---|
| **Archaic Susiana 3 – Early Susiana Transition** (*cont.*) | | | | |
| Ch.M. VIII | Gully Cut | S22:808 | 75.15 | Occupational debris |
| Ch.M. VIII | Gully Cut | S22:808 | 75.06 | Occupational debris |
| Ch.M. VIII | Gully Cut | S22:808 North | 75.47 | Occupational debris |
| Ch.M. VIII | Gully Cut | S22:808 North | 75.28 | Occupational debris |
| Ch.M. VIII | Gully Cut | S22:808 North | 75.13 | Occupational debris |
| Ch.M. VIII | Gully Cut | S22:808 | 75.51 | Occupational debris |
| Ch.M. VIII | Gully Cut | S22:810 | 76.55 | Yard and kiln(?) area |
| Ch.M. VIII | Gully Cut | S22:811 | 76.96 | Room |
| Ch.M. VIII | Gully Cut | S22:812 | 76.90 | Open court |
| Ch.M. VIII | Gully Cut | S22:813 | 76.90 | Open court/room |
| Ch.M. VIII | Gully Cut | S22:814 | 76.60 | Room |
| Ch.M. VIII | Gully Cut | S22:815 | 76.62 | Room |
| Ch.M. VIII | Gully Cut | S23:815 South | 76.58 | Occupational debris |
| Ch.M. VIII | Gully Cut | S22:816 | 76.55 | Room |
| Ch.M. VIII | Gully Cut | S22:818 | 76.65 | Room |
| Ch.M. VIII | Gully Cut | S22:819 | 76.85 | Activity area/room |
| Ch.M. VIII | Gully Cut | S22:821 | 76.00 | Area between walls |
| Ch.M. VIII | Gully Cut | S22:822 | 76.45 | Room |
| Ch.M. VIII | Gully Cut | S22:823 | 75.30 | Occupational debris |
| Ch.M. VIII | Gully Cut | S22:823 | 76.10 | Hearth/kiln(?) |
| Ch.M. VIII | Gully Cut | S22:823 | 75.08 | Occupational debris |
| Ch.M. VIII | Gully Cut | S22:823 | 74.98 | Occupational debris |
| Ch.M. VIII | Gully Cut | S22:823 | 74.84 | Occupational debris |
| Ch.M. VIII | Gully Cut | S22:823 North | 75.03 | Kiln(?) area |
| Ch.M. VIII | Gully Cut | S22:823 North | 74.51 | Occupational debris |
| Ch.M. VIII | Gully Cut | S22:823 South | 75.37 | Occupational debris |
| Ch.M. VIII | Gully Cut | S22:823 South | 75.24 | Occupational debris |
| Ch.M. VIII | Gully Cut | S22:823 South | 74.92 | Occupational debris |
| Ch.M. VIII | Gully Cut | S22:823 South | 74.79 | Occupational debris |
| Ch.M. VIII | Gully Cut | S22:823 South | 74.63 | Occupational debris |
| Ch.M. VIII | Gully Cut | S22:823 West | 74.89 | Occupational debris |
| Ch.M. VIII | Gully Cut | S22:825 | 76.30 | Room |
| Ch.M. VIII | Gully Cut | S22:826 | 75.90 | Alley |
| Ch.M. VIII | Gully Cut | S22:826 | 74.12 | Occupational debris |
| Ch.M. VIII | Gully Cut | S22:826 | 74.08 | Occupational debris |
| Ch.M. VIII | Gully Cut | S22:827 | 74.85 | Room |

| *Season* | *Area* | *Provenance* | *Elevation* | *Type of Deposit or Feature* |
|---|---|---|---|---|
| **Archaic Susiana 3 – Early Susiana Transition** (*cont.*) | | | | |
| Ch.M. VIII | Gully Cut | S22:827 | 74.85 | Room |
| Ch.M. VIII | Gully Cut | S22:828 | 75.30 | Long Hall |
| Ch.M. VIII | Gully Cut | S22:830 | 74.92 | Occupational debris |
| Ch.M. VIII | Gully Cut | S22:830 South | 74.99 | Occupational debris |
| Ch.M. VIII | Gully Cut | S22:830 South | 74.81 | Occupational debris |
| Ch.M. VIII | Gully Cut | S22:830 Middle | 74.99 | Occupational debris |
| Ch.M. VIII | Gully Cut | S22:831 North | 75.02 | Occupational debris |
| Ch.M. VIII | Gully Cut | S22:831 South | 75.70 | Burnt area |
| Ch.M. VIII | Gully Cut | S23:824 | 775.00 | Open area next to burial |
| Ch.M. IX | Gully Cut | S22:901 | 75.60 | Kiln(?) area |
| Ch.M. IX | Gully Cut | S22:902 Northeast | 75.00 | Open area |
| Ch.M. IX | Gully Cut | S22:902 Southwest | 75.00 | Open area |
| Ch.M. IX | Gully Cut | S22:903 | 75.82 | Open area |
| Ch.M. IX | Gully Cut | S22:904 | 74.50 | Protoliterate pit |
| Ch.M. IX | Gully Cut | S22:905 | 75.85 | Open area |
| Ch.M. IX | Gully Cut | S22:907 | 75.35 | Open area |
| Ch.M. IX | Gully Cut | S22:908 | 75.40 | Long bricks |
| Ch.M. IX | Gully Cut | S22:912 | 75.30 | Open court |
| Ch.M. IX | Gully Cut | S22:914 | 75.45 | Open area |
| Ch.M. IX | Gully Cut | S22:916 | 74.90 | Entrance to room |
| Ch.M. IX | Gully Cut | S22:918 | 77.22 | Room |
| Ch.M. IX | Gully Cut | S22:923 | 75.35 | Long Hall |
| Ch.M. IX | Gully Cut | S22:929 | 75.40 | Entrance to Long Hall |
| **Early Susiana** | | | | |
| Ch.M. V | Trench XXI | Q23:504 | 79.92–79.55 | Supra floor fill |
| Ch.M. V | Trench XXXI | P27:505 | 78.35–78.30 | Settlement area |
| Ch.M. V | Trench XXXI | P27:505 | 78.30–77.90 | Surface near wall |
| Ch.M. VI | Trench XXI | P22:602 | 81.95 | Room |
| Ch.M. VI | Trench XXI | P22:602 | 81.25 | Room |
| Ch.M. VI | Trench XXI | P22:602 West | 82.18 | Surface wash |
| Ch.M. VI | Trench XXI | P22:604 | 81.58 | Room |
| Ch.M. VI | Trench XXI | P22:605 | 81.15 | Room |
| Ch.M. VI | Trench XXI | P22:606 | 80.42 | Occupational debris |
| Ch.M. VI | Trench XXI | P22:606 | 81.77 | Occupational debris |
| Ch.M. VI | Trench XXI | P22:606 | 80.86 | Pottery deposit |
| Ch.M. VI | Trench XXI | P22:606 | 80.54 | Occupational debris |

| *Season* | *Area* | *Provenance* | *Elevation* | *Type of Deposit or Feature* |
|---|---|---|---|---|
| **Early Susiana** (*cont.*) | | | | |
| Ch.M. VI | Trench XXI | P22:606 | 80.51 | Pottery deposit |
| Ch.M. VI | Trench XXI | P22:606 | 80.50 | Occupational debris |
| Ch.M. VI | Trench XXI | P22:606 | 80.38 | Floor |
| Ch.M. VI | Trench XXI | P22:606 | 80.34 | Occupational debris |
| Ch.M. VI | Trench XXI | P22:606 North | 81.06 | Occupational debris |
| Ch.M. VI | Trench XXI | P22:606 South | 81.24 | Occupational debris |
| Ch.M. VI | Trench XXI | P22:606 South | 81.06 | Occupational debris |
| Ch.M. VI | Trench XXI | P22:606 Middle | 80.46 | Occupational debris |
| Ch.M. VI | Trench XXI | Northwest of P22:606 | 81.42 | Occupational debris |
| Ch.M. VI | Trench XXI | North of P22:606 | 81.33 | Occupational debris |
| Ch.M. VI | Trench XXI | P22:607 | 81.43 | Room |
| Ch.M. VI | Trench XXI | P22:607 | 80.81 | Room |
| Ch.M. VI | Trench XXI | P22:607 North | 81.54–81.29 | Room |
| Ch.M. VI | Trench XXI | P22:608 | 81.11 | Room |
| Ch.M. VI | Trench XXI | P22:608 North | 81.16 | Room |
| Ch.M. VI | Trench XXI | P22:608 North | 81.13 | Room |
| Ch.M. VI | Trench XXI | P22:608 North | 81.08 | Room |
| Ch.M. VI | Trench XXI | P22:608 North | 80.78 | Room |
| Ch.M. VI | Trench XXI | P22:608 North | 80.62 | Room |
| Ch.M. VI | Trench XXI | P22:608 North | 80.50 | Room |
| Ch.M. VI | Trench XXI | P22:609 | 81.16 | Occupational debris |
| Ch.M. VI | Trench XXI | P22:609 | 80.34 | Room |
| Ch.M. VI | Trench XXI | P22:611 | 81.10 | Occupational debris |
| Ch.M. VI | Trench XXI | P22:611 | 80.81 | Occupational debris |
| Ch.M. VI | Trench XXI | P22:611 | 80.66 | Occupational debris |
| Ch.M. VI | Trench XXI | P22:611 | 80.58 | Occupational debris |
| Ch.M. VI | Trench XXI | P22:611 | 80.50 | Occupational debris |
| Ch.M. VI | Trench XXI | P22:611 | 80.38 | Occupational debris |
| Ch.M. VI | Trench XXI | P22:611 | 80.37 | Occupational debris |
| Ch.M. VI | Trench XXI | P22:611 South | 80.15 | Occupational debris |
| Ch.M. VI | Trench XXI | P22:612 | 80.18 | Occupational debris |
| Ch.M. VI | Trench XXI | P22:615 | 81.43 | Surface wash |
| Ch.M. VI | Trench XXI | P22:620 | 82.14 | Room |
| Ch.M. VI | Trench XXI | P22:620 Northwest | 82.02–81.42 | Room |
| Ch.M. VI | Trench XXI | P22:621 West | 82.19 | Surface wash |
| Ch.M. VI | Trench XXI | P22:622 | 80.79 | Room |

| *Season* | *Area* | *Provenance* | *Elevation* | *Type of Deposit or Feature* |
|---|---|---|---|---|
| **Early Susiana** (*cont.*) | | | | |
| Ch.M. VI | Trench XXI | P22:622 | 80.74 | Room |
| Ch.M. VI | Trench XXI | P22:623 | 82.02 | Room |
| Ch.M. VI | Trench XXI | P22:623 | 81.72 | Room |
| Ch.M. VI | Trench XXI | P22:624 | 82.00 | Room |
| Ch.M. VI | Trench XXI | P22:625 | 81.88 | Room |
| Ch.M. VI | Trench XXI | P22:625 | 81.75 | Room |
| Ch.M. VI | Trench XXI | P22:625 | 81.23 | Room |
| Ch.M. VI | Trench XXI | P22:626 | 81.69–81.35 | Room |
| Ch.M. VI | Trench XXI | P22:626 | 80.87 | Room |
| Ch.M. VI | Trench XXI | P22:628 | 80.67 | Room |
| Ch.M. VI | Trench XXI | P22:629 | 81.68 | Occupational debris |
| Ch.M. VI | Trench XXI | P22:629 | 81.37 | Occupational debris |
| Ch.M. VI | Trench XXI | P22:629 South | 80.89 | Occupational debris |
| Ch.M. VI | Trench XXI | P22:629 Southwest | 80.84 | Occupational debris |
| Ch.M. VI | Trench XXI | Q22:601 | 80.89 | Occupational debris |
| Ch.M. VI | Trench XXI | Q22:601 | 80.69 | Occupational debris |
| Ch.M. VI | Trench XXI | Q22:602 | 81.02 | Occupational debris |
| Ch.M. VI | Trench XXI | Q22:602 | 80.29 | Occupational debris |
| Ch.M. VI | Trench XXI | Q22:603 | 80.33 | Surface wash |
| Ch.M. VI | Trench XXI | Q22:603 | 80.06 | Occupational debris |
| Ch.M. VI | Trench XXI | Q22:603 | 79.70 | Room |
| Ch.M. VI | Trench XXI | Q23:604 | 80.81 | Surface wash |
| Ch.M. VI | Trench XXV | S20:607 | 78.74 | Pebble surface |
| Ch.M. VI | Trench XXV | S20:617 | 78.40 | Occupational debris |
| Ch.M. VII | Trench XXI | P23:702 | 80.58 | Occupational debris |
| Ch.M. VII | Trench XXI | Q22:706 | 79.36 | Surface wash |
| Ch.M. VII | Trench XXI | Q22:707 | 79.71 | Surface wash |
| Ch.M. VII | Trench XXI | Q22:707 | 79.47 | Occupational debris |
| Ch.M. VII | Trench XXI | Q23:702 | 79.84 | Surface wash |
| Ch.M. VII | Trench XXI | Q23:702 | 79.51 | Surface wash |
| Ch.M. VII | Trench XXI | Q23:703 | 79.40 | Room floor |
| Ch.M. VII | Trench XXI | Q23:703 | 79.32 | Occupational debris |
| Ch.M. VII | Trench XXI | Q23:703 | 78.92 | Occupational debris |
| Ch.M. VII | Trench XXI | Q23:703 | 78.84 | Occupational debris |
| Ch.M. VII | Trench XXI | Q23:704 | 79.33 | Room |
| Ch.M. VII | Trench XXI | Q23:707 | 79.62 | Room |

| *Season* | *Area* | *Provenance* | *Elevation* | *Type of Deposit or Feature* |
|---|---|---|---|---|
| **Early Susiana** (*cont.*) | | | | |
| Ch.M. VII | Trench XXI | Q23:707 | 79.30 | Room |
| Ch.M. VII | Trench XXI | Q23:709 | 79.99 | Occupational debris |
| Ch.M. VII | Trench XXI | Q23:710 | 79.78 | Room |
| Ch.M. VII | Trench XXI | Q23:710 | 79.49 | Room |
| Ch.M. VII | Trench XXI | Q23:711 | 78.00 | Occupational debris |
| Ch.M. VII | Trench XXXVI | G29:702 | 77.07 | Occupational debris |
| Ch.M. VII | Trench XXXVI | G29:702 | 76.84 | Occupational debris |
| Ch.M. VII | Trench XXXVI | G29:703 North | 76.86 | Occupational debris |
| Ch.M. VII | Trench XXXVI | G29:703 North | 76.82 | Occupational debris |
| Ch.M. VIII | Trench XXI | Q22:805 | 79.35 | Room |
| Ch.M. VIII | Trench XXI | Q22:805 | 79.29 | Room |
| Ch.M. VIII | Trench XXI | Q22:805 | 78.74 | Room |
| Ch.M. VIII | Trench XXI | Q23:803 Southwest | 80.14 | Surface wash |
| Ch.M. VIII | Trench XXI | Q23:804 | 79.10 | Surface wash |
| Ch.M. VIII | Trench XXI | Q23:805 | 78.80 | Room |
| Ch.M. VIII | Trench XXI | Q23:805 | 78.68 | Room |
| Ch.M. VIII | Trench XXI | Q23:809 | 78.24 | Room |
| Ch.M. VIII | Trench XXI | Q23:812 | 79.49 | Lane/alley |
| Ch.M. VIII | Trench XXI | Q23:813 | 79.89 | Brick platform |
| Ch.M. VIII | Trench XXI | Q23:813 | 79.80 | Brick platform |
| Ch.M. VIII | Trench XXI | Q23:813 | 79.38 | Brick platform |
| Ch.M. VIII | Trench XXI | Q23:817 | 79.00 | Surface wash |
| Ch.M. VIII | Trench XXI | Q23:818 | 79.17 | Room |
| Ch.M. VIII | Trench XXI | Q23:818 South | 78.60 | Occupational debris |
| Ch.M. VIII | Trench XXI | Q23:819 | 79.27 | Supra floor fill |
| Ch.M. VIII | Trench XXI | Q23:819 | 79.26 | Supra floor fill |
| Ch.M. VIII | Trench XXI | Q23:820 | 79.28 | Occupational debris |
| Ch.M. VIII | Trench XXI | Q23:820 | 79.05 | Room |
| Ch.M. VIII | Trench XXI | Q23:820 | 78.80 | Room |
| Ch.M. VIII | Trench XXI | Q23:820 | 78.63 | Room |
| Ch.M. VIII | Trench XXI | Q23:821 | 79.17 | Room |
| Ch.M. VIII | Trench XXI | Q23:821 | 78.78 | Room |
| Ch.M. VIII | Trench XXI | Q23:823 | 78.58 | Room |
| Ch.M. VIII | Trench XXI | Q23:823 | 78.15 | Room |
| Ch.M. VIII | Trench XXI | Q23:824 | 78.10 | Room |
| Ch.M. VIII | Trench XXI | Q23:827 | 78.75 | Room |

| *Season* | *Area* | *Provenance* | *Elevation* | *Type of Deposit or Feature* |
|---|---|---|---|---|
| **Early Susiana** (*cont.*) | | | | |
| Ch.M. VIII | Trench XXI | Q23:827 | 78.45 | Room |
| Ch.M. VIII | Trench XXI | Q23:829 | 77.91 | Room |
| Ch.M. VIII | Trench XXI | Q23:831 | 80.70 | Occupational debris |
| Ch.M. VIII | Trench XXXVII | Q24:802 East | 77.82 | Occupational debris |
| Ch.M. VIII | Trench XXXVII | Q24:802 East | 77.77 | Occupational debris |
| Ch.M. VIII | Trench XXXVII | Q24:802 East | 77.75 | Occupational debris |
| Ch.M. VIII | Trench XXXVII | Q24:802 East | 77.49 | Occupational debris |
| Ch.M. VIII | Trench XXXVII | Q24:802 East | 77.40 | Occupational debris |
| Ch.M. VIII | Trench XXXVII | Q25:801 | 77.39 | Occupational debris |
| Ch.M. VIII | Trench XXXVII | Q25:801 | 77.12 | Occupational debris |
| Ch.M. VIII | Gully Cut | S22:802 | 75.98 | Occupational debris |
| Ch.M. VIII | Gully Cut | S22:802 | 75.86 | Occupational debris |
| Ch.M. VIII | Gully Cut | S22:802 | 75.85 | Occupational debris |
| Ch.M. VIII | Gully Cut | S22:806 North | 76.60 | Occupational debris |
| Ch.M. VIII | Gully Cut | S22:808 | 76.70 | Occupational debris |
| Ch.M. VIII | Gully Cut | S22:808 | 75.91 | Occupational debris |
| Ch.M. VIII | Gully Cut | S22:808 | 75.67 | Occupational debris |
| Ch.M. VIII | Gully Cut | S22:808 | 75.60 | Occupational debris |
| Ch.M. VIII | Gully Cut | S22:808 South | 75.68 | Occupational debris |
| Ch.M. VIII | Gully Cut | S22:810 | 76.51 | Supra floor fill |
| Ch.M. VIII | Gully Cut | S22:810 | 76.47 | Room floor |
| Ch.M. VIII | Gully Cut | S22:810 | 76.30 | Occupational debris |
| Ch.M. VIII | Gully Cut | S22:813 | 75.86 | Occupational debris |
| Ch.M. VIII | Gully Cut | S22:813 | 75.66 | Occupational debris |
| Ch.M. VIII | Gully Cut | S22:814 | 76.85 | Room |
| Ch.M. VIII | Gully Cut | S22:814 | 76.75 | Room |
| Ch.M. VIII | Gully Cut | S22:814 | 76.42 | Room |
| Ch.M. VIII | Gully Cut | S22:815 | 76.65 | Room floor |
| Ch.M. VIII | Gully Cut | S22:815 North | 76.59 | Supra floor fill |
| Ch.M. VIII | Gully Cut | S22:815 South | 76.44 | Occupational debris |
| Ch.M. VIII | Gully Cut | S22:816 | 76.59 | Room floor |
| Ch.M. VIII | Gully Cut | S22:818 | 76.30 | Occupational debris |
| Ch.M. VIII | Gully Cut | S22:818 | 76.11 | Occupational debris |
| Ch.M. VIII | Gully Cut | S22:818 | 75.59 | Occupational debris |
| Ch.M. VIII | Gully Cut | S22:819 | 75.78 | Occupational debris |
| Ch.M. VIII | Gully Cut | S22:819 North | 76.08 | Occupational debris |

| *Season* | *Area* | *Provenance* | *Elevation* | *Type of Deposit or Feature* |
|---|---|---|---|---|
| **Early Susiana** (*cont.*) | | | | |
| Ch.M. VIII | Gully Cut | S22:819 East | 75.65 | Occupational debris |
| Ch.M. VIII | Gully Cut | S22:819 Middle | 75.78 | Occupational debris |
| Ch.M. VIII | Gully Cut | S22:821 | 76.35 | Occupational debris |
| Ch.M. VIII | Gully Cut | S22:821 | 76.41 | Room |
| Ch.M. VIII | Gully Cut | S22:821 | 76.32 | Room |
| Ch.M. VIII | Gully Cut | S22:821 North | 76.22 | Room |
| Ch.M. VIII | Gully Cut | S22:822 North | 76.18 | Room |
| Ch.M. VIII | Gully Cut | S22:822 East | 76.16 | Wall |
| Ch.M. VIII | Gully Cut | S22:822 South | 76.22 | Hearth area |
| Ch.M. VIII | Gully Cut | S22:822 South | 76.02 | Occupational debris |
| Ch.M. VIII | Gully Cut | S22:822 South | 75.95 | Occupational debris |
| Ch.M. VIII | Gully Cut | S22:822 West | 76.10 | Wall |
| Ch.M. VIII | Gully Cut | S22:822 Middle | 76.22 | Room |
| Ch.M. VIII | Gully Cut | S22:822 | 75.98 | Occupational debris |
| Ch.M. VIII | Gully Cut | S22:822 | 75.84 | Occupational debris |
| Ch.M. VIII | Gully Cut | S22:822 | 75.77 | Occupational debris |
| Ch.M. VIII | Gully Cut | S22:823 | 75.74 | Occupational debris |
| Ch.M. VIII | Gully Cut | S22:823 | 75.62 | Occupational debris |
| Ch.M. VIII | Gully Cut | S22:823 | 75.60 | Occupational debris |
| Ch.M. VIII | Gully Cut | S22:823 North | 76.06 | Occupational debris |
| Ch.M. VIII | Gully Cut | S22:823 | 75.62 | Occupational debris |
| Ch.M. VIII | Gully Cut | S22:823 | 75.60 | Occupational debris |
| Ch.M. VIII | Gully Cut | S22:823 North | 75.06 | Occupational debris |
| Ch.M. VIII | Gully Cut | S22:823 North | 75.81 | Occupational debris |
| Ch.M. VIII | Gully Cut | S22:823 North | 75.47 | Occupational debris |
| Ch.M. VIII | Gully Cut | S22:823 West | 75.94 | Occupational debris |
| Ch.M. VIII | Gully Cut | S22:823 West | 75.90 | Occupational debris |
| Ch.M. VIII | Gully Cut | S22:823 Middle | 75.44 | Occupational debris |
| Ch.M. VIII | Gully Cut | S22:823 Middle | 75.43 | Occupational debris |
| Ch.M. VIII | Gully Cut | S22:825 | 75.95 | Occupational debris |
| Ch.M. VIII | Gully Cut | S22:826 | 75.14 | Occupational debris |
| Ch.M. VIII | Gully Cut | S22:826 | 75.02 | Occupational debris |
| Ch.M. VIII | Gully Cut | S22:826 | 74.66 | Occupational debris |
| Ch.M. VIII | Gully Cut | S22:826 East | 75.14 | Occupational debris |
| Ch.M. VIII | Gully Cut | S22:826 West | 75.49 | Occupational debris |
| Ch.M. VIII | Gully Cut | S22:826 West | 75.09 | Occupational debris |

| *Season* | *Area* | *Provenance* | *Elevation* | *Type of Deposit or Feature* |
|---|---|---|---|---|
| **Early Susiana** (*cont.*) | | | | |
| Ch.M. VIII | Gully Cut | S22:827 | 75.75 | Room |
| Ch.M. VIII | Gully Cut | S22:827 | 75.51 | Room |
| Ch.M. VIII | Gully Cut | S22:827 | 75.49 | Room |
| Ch.M. VIII | Gully Cut | S22:827 | 75.13 | Room |
| Ch.M. VIII | Gully Cut | S22:827 | 75.10 | Room |
| Ch.M. VIII | Gully Cut | S22:827 | 74.93 | Room |
| Ch.M. VIII | Gully Cut | S22:827 | 74.78 | Occupational debris |
| Ch.M. VIII | Gully Cut | S22:827 | 74.76 | Occupational debris |
| Ch.M. VIII | Gully Cut | S22:827 West | 75.98 | Room |
| Ch.M. VIII | Gully Cut | S22:827 West | 75.75 | Room |
| Ch.M. VIII | Gully Cut | S22:828 | 75.30 | Brick platform |
| Ch.M. VIII | Gully Cut | S22:829 | 76.35 | Occupational debris |
| Ch.M. VIII | Gully Cut | S22:830 North | 75.38 | Occupational debris |
| Ch.M. VIII | Gully Cut | S22:830 Middle | 75.55 | Occupational debris |
| Ch.M. VIII | Gully Cut | S22:830 Middle | 75.28 | Occupational debris |
| **Early Susiana + Miscellaneous** | | | | |
| Ch.M. VII | Trench XXI | Q22:707 | 79.56 | Surface wash |
| Ch.M. VII | Trench XXI | Q23:804 | 79.39 | Surface wash |
| Ch.M. VII | Trench XXI | Q23:804 | 79.00 | Surface wash |
| Ch.M. VII | Trench XXI | Q23:820 | 79.48 | Surface wash |
| Ch.M. VII | Trench XXI | Q23:827 | 78.91 | Surface wash |
| **Early Susiana – Early Middle Susiana Transition** | | | | |
| Ch.M. IV | Trench XIII | K22:409 | 79.59 | Settlement area |
| Ch.M. V | Trench XIII | K23:509 | 80.15 | Room |
| Ch.M. V | Trench XIII | K23:509 | 79.90 | Room |
| Ch.M. V | Trench XIII | K23:509 | 79.87 | Room |
| Ch.M. V | Trench XIII | L22:506 | 80.00 | Room |
| Ch.M. VII | Trench XXXVI | G29:701 | 74.93 | Occupational debris |
| Ch.M. VII | Trench XXXII | R23:701 | 76.77 | Occupational debris |
| Ch.M. VII | Trench XXXII | R23:701 | 76.66 | Occupational debris |
| **Early Middle Susiana** | | | | |
| Ch.M. IV | Sounding G | S-T21 | 75.95–75.65 | Settlement area |
| Ch.M. IV | Trench XIII | K22:403 | 81.19–80.99 | Room |
| Ch.M. IV | Trench XIII | West of K22:403 | 81.30 | Near wall |
| Ch.M. IV | Trench XIII | K22:405 | 81.35–80.50 | Inside kiln(?) |
| Ch.M. V | Trench XIII | K22:501 | 81.10 | Occupational debris |

| *Season* | *Area* | *Provenance* | *Elevation* | *Type of Deposit or Feature* |
|---|---|---|---|---|
| **Early Middle Susiana** (*cont.*) | | | | |
| Ch.M. V | Trench XIII | K22:502 | 81.27 | Near wall |
| Ch.M. V | Trench XIII | K22:502 | 81.00 | Near wall |
| Ch.M. V | Trench XIII | K23:506 | 81.60–80.80 | Near wall |
| Ch.M. V | Trench XIII | K23:506 | 81.36 | Room |
| Ch.M. V | Trench XIII | K23:506 | 81.20–80.40 | Room |
| Ch.M. V | Trench XIII | K23:506 | 80.75 | Room |
| Ch.M. V | Trench XIII | K23:506 | 80.43–80.05 | Room |
| Ch.M. V | Trench XIII | K23:506 | 80.30 | Room |
| Ch.M. V | Trench XIII | K23:507 | 80.98 | Room |
| Ch.M. V | Trench XIII | K23:510 | 80.46 | Settlement area |
| Ch.M. V | Trench XIII | L22:504 | 81.12 | Room |
| Ch.M. V | Trench XIII | L22:504 | 80.05 | Room |
| Ch.M. V | Trench XIII | L22:506 | 81.90 | Room |
| Ch.M. V | Trench XIII | L22:506 | 80.54 | Room |
| Ch.M. V | Trench XXI | P23:501 | 82.49 | Settlement area |
| Ch.M. V | Trench XXI | P23:501 | 82.39 | Settlement area |
| Ch.M. V | Trench XXI | P23:501 | 82.04 | Settlement area |
| Ch.M. V | Trench XXI | P23:502 | 82.24 | Hearth area |
| Ch.M. V | Trench XXI | P23:502 | 81.75 | Hearth area |
| Ch.M. V | Trench XXI | P23:502 | 81.75 | Hearth area |
| Ch.M. V | Trench XXI | P23:503 | 82.25 | Settlement area |
| Ch.M. V | Trench XXI | P23:504 | 82.24 | Room |
| Ch.M. V | Trench XXI | P23:504 | 82.20 | Room |
| Ch.M. V | Trench XXI | P23:505 | 82.15 | Room |
| Ch.M. V | Trench XXXI | P27:501 | 78.34 | Settlement area |
| Ch.M. V | Trench XXXI | P27:501 North | 78.57–78.27 | Settlement area |
| Ch.M. V | Trench XXXI | P27:501 North | 78.53–78.10 | Near wall |
| Ch.M. V | Trench XXXI | P27:503 | 78.34 | Floor |
| Ch.M. VI | Trench XXI | P22:601 | 81.69–81.21 | Occupational debris |
| Ch.M. VI | Trench XXI | P22:602 | 81.44 | Room |
| Ch.M. VI | Trench XXI | P22:605 | 81. 93 | Surface wash |
| Ch.M. VI | Trench XXI | P22:606 | 82.42–81.92 | Surface wash |
| Ch.M. VI | Trench XXI | P22:606 | 82.42 | Surface wash |
| Ch.M. VI | Trench XXI | P22:606 | 81.92 | Occupational debris |
| Ch.M. VI | Trench XXI | P22:606 Northwest | 82.08–81.42 | Occupational debris |
| Ch.M. VI | Trench XXI | P22:606 West | 82.18 | Surface wash |

| Season | Area | Provenance | Elevation | Type of Deposit or Feature |
|---|---|---|---|---|
| **Early Middle Susiana** (*cont.*) | | | | |
| Ch.M. VI | Trench XXI | P22:606 Middle | 82.42 | Surface wash |
| Ch.M. VI | Trench XXI | P22:611 | 82.19 | Surface wash |
| Ch.M. VI | Trench XXI | P22:611 | 81.51 | Occupational debris |
| Ch.M. VI | Trench XXI | P23:601 | 83.04 | Surface wash |
| Ch.M. VI | Trench XXI | P23:601 | 82.92 | Surface wash |
| Ch.M. VI | Trench XXI | P23:601 | 82.84 | Occupational debris |
| Ch.M. VI | Trench XXI | P23:601 | 82.31 | Occupational debris |
| Ch.M. VI | Trench XXI | P23:601 | 82.19 | Occupational debris |
| Ch.M. VI | Trench XXI | P23:601 | 82.16 | Occupational debris |
| Ch.M. VI | Trench XXI | P23:601 | 81.89 | Occupational debris |
| Ch.M. VI | Trench XXI | P23:601 | 81.22–81.70 | Occupational debris |
| Ch.M. VI | Trench XXI | P23:602 | 82.02 | Occupational debris |
| Ch.M. VI | Trench XXI | P23:602 | 82.02 | Occupational debris |
| Ch.M. VI | Trench XXI | P23:602 | 81.70 | Occupational debris |
| Ch.M. VI | Trench XXI | P23:602 | 81.63 | Occupational debris |
| Ch.M. VI | Trench XXI | P23:602 | 81.50 | Occupational debris |
| Ch.M. VI | Trench XXI | P23:602 | 81.31 | Occupational debris |
| Ch.M. VI | Trench XXI | P23:602 | 80.55 | Occupational debris |
| Ch.M. VI | Trench XXI | P23:602 South | 81.52 | Occupational debris |
| Ch.M. VI | Trench XXI | P23:603 | 82.22 | Occupational debris |
| Ch.M. VI | Trench XXI | P23:603 | 82.19 | Occupational debris |
| Ch.M. VI | Trench XXI | P23:604 | 81.89 | Occupational debris |
| Ch.M. VI | Trench XXI | P23:604 | 81.74 | Occupational debris |
| Ch.M. VI | Trench XXI | P23:604 | 81.69 | Occupational debris |
| Ch.M. VI | Trench XXI | P23:604 | 81.31 | Occupational debris |
| Ch.M. VI | Trench XXI | P23:604 North | 82.84 | Surface wash |
| Ch.M. VI | Trench XXI | P23:604 South | 82.84 | Surface wash |
| Ch.M. VI | Trench XXI | P23:604 South | 82.18–81.83 | Occupational debris |
| Ch.M. VI | Trench XXI | P23:604 South | 82.12 | Occupational debris |
| Ch.M. VI | Trench XXI | P23:604 South | 81.69–81.23 | Occupational debris |
| Ch.M. VI | Trench XXI | P23:604 South | 81.58 | Occupational debris |
| Ch.M. VI | Trench XXI | P23:604 Middle | 82.84 | Surface wash |
| Ch.M. VI | Trench XXI | P23:604 | 82.44 | Surface wash |
| Ch.M. VI | Trench XXI | P23:606 | 82.05 | Occupational debris |
| Ch.M. VI | Trench XXI | P23:606 | 81.50 | Occupational debris |
| Ch.M. VI | Trench XXI | P23:606 | 81.32 | Occupational debris |

| *Season* | *Area* | *Provenance* | *Elevation* | *Type of Deposit or Feature* |
|---|---|---|---|---|
| **Early Middle Susiana** (*cont.*) | | | | |
| Ch.M. VI | Trench XXI | P23:606 | 81.26 | Occupational debris |
| Ch.M. VI | Trench XXI | P23:607 | 83.05–82.75 | Surface wash |
| Ch.M. VI | Trench XXI | P23:607 | 82.16 | Occupational debris |
| Ch.M. VI | Trench XXI | P23:607 | 82.04 | Occupational debris |
| Ch.M. VI | Trench XXI | P23:607 | 81.64 | Occupational debris |
| Ch.M. VI | Trench XXI | P23:607 | 81.82 | Room |
| Ch.M. VI | Trench XXI | Q22:602 South | 81.82 | Occupational debris |
| Ch.M. VI | Trench XXI | Q23:602 | 80.25 | Occupational debris |
| Ch.M. VI | Trench XXI | Q23:602 | 79.53 | Occupational debris |
| Ch.M. VII | Trench XXI | P23:702 | 81.13 | Occupational debris |
| Ch.M. VII | Trench XXXVI | G29:703 South | 76.23 | Occupational debris |
| **Early Middle Susiana Mixed** | | | | |
| Ch.M. V | Trench XIII | K23:502 | 81.70 | Settlement area |
| Ch.M. VI | Trench XXXII | R23:601 | 77.17–76.94 | Occupation debris |
| Ch.M. VI | Trench XXI | P23:607 | 82.75 | Surface wash |
| **Late Middle Susiana** | | | | |
| Ch.M. II | Trench II | R10–11 Plot 2E | 79.10 | Occupational debris |
| Ch.M. II | Trench XVI | O27 South | 78.60 | Settlement area |
| Ch.M. III | Trench XXI | P-Q23:301 | 81.50 | Settlement area |
| Ch.M. IV | Trench XIII | K22:400 | 82.54–82.44 | Settlement area |
| Ch.M. IV | Trench XIII | K22:400 | 82.29–82.09 | Settlement area |
| Ch.M. IV | Sounding G | S-T21 | 77.50–76.70 | Settlement area |
| Ch.M. IV | Sounding G | S-T21 | 76.25–76.10 | Settlement area |
| Ch.M. IV | Sounding G | S-T21 | 76.10 | Settlement area |
| Ch.M. IV | Sounding G | S-T21 | 76.00 | Settlement area |
| Ch.M. IV | Sounding G | S-T21 | 76.00–75.95 | Settlement area |
| Ch.M. V | Trench XIII | K22:501 | 82.00 | Occupational debris |
| Ch.M. V | Trench XIII | K22:501 | 81.59 | Occupational debris |
| Ch.M. V | Trench XIII | K22:501 | 81.52 | Occupational debris |
| Ch.M. V | Trench XIII | K22:501 | 81.40 | Occupational debris |
| Ch.M. V | Trench XIII | L22:501 | 82.50 | Settlement area |
| Ch.M. V | Trench XIII | L22:501 | 82.46–82.16 | Settlement area |
| Ch.M. V | Trench XIII | L22:502 | 82.00 | Settlement area |
| Ch.M. V | Trench XIII | L22:505 | 82.17 | Room |
| Ch.M. V | Trench XIII | L23:502 | 81.30 | Settlement area |
| Ch.M. V | Trench XIII | L23:504 | 82.34 | Settlement area |

| *Season* | *Area* | *Provenance* | *Elevation* | *Type of Deposit or Feature* |
|---|---|---|---|---|
| **Late Middle Susiana** (*cont.*) | | | | |
| Ch.M. V | Trench XXV | R20:515 | 79.69 | Settlement area |
| Ch.M. V | Trench XXV | R20:515 | 79.40 | Settlement area |
| Ch.M. V | Trench XXV | R20:515 North | 79.60 | Settlement area |
| Ch.M. V | Trench XXV | R20:515 East | 78.75 | Pit |
| Ch.M. V | Trench XXXI | P27:507 | 79.60–79.44 | Settlement area |
| Ch.M. V | Trench XXXI | P27:507 | 79.34–79.13 | Settlement area |
| Ch.M. VI | Trench XXV | R20:603 | 79.08 | Occupational debris |
| Ch.M. VI | Trench XXV | R20:604 | 78.48 | Occupational debris |
| Ch.M. VI | Trench XXV | S20:601 | 79.20–78.66 | Surface wash |
| Ch.M. VI | Trench XXV | S20:601 | 79.11–78.89 | Occupational debris |
| Ch.M. VI | Trench XXV | S20:601 | 79.10 | Surface wash |
| Ch.M. VI | Trench XXV | S20:601 | 79.04 | Surface wash |
| Ch.M. VI | Trench XXV | S20:601 | 78.99–78.60 | Occupational debris |
| Ch.M. VI | Trench XXV | S20:601 | 78.92–78.72 | Occupational debris |
| Ch.M. VI | Trench XXV | S20:601 | 78.90 | Occupational debris |
| Ch.M. VI | Trench XXV | S20:601 | 78.78 | Occupational debris |
| Ch.M. VI | Trench XXV | S20:601 | 78.74–78.35 | Occupational debris |
| Ch.M. VI | Trench XXV | S20:601 | 78.67 | Occupational debris |
| Ch.M. VI | Trench XXV | S20:601 | 78.60 | Occupational debris |
| Ch.M. VI | Trench XXV | S20:601 | 78.56–78.42 | Occupational debris |
| Ch.M. VI | Trench XXV | S20:601 | 78.56 | Occupational debris |
| Ch.M. VI | Trench XXV | S20:601 | 78.47 | Occupational debris |
| Ch.M. VI | Trench XXV | S20:601 | 78.33 | Occupational debris |
| Ch.M. VI | Trench XXV | S20:601 | 78.30 | Occupational debris |
| Ch.M. VI | Trench XXV | S20:601 | 78.2 | Occupational debris |
| Ch.M. VI | Trench XXV | S20:601 | 78.12 | Occupational debris |
| Ch.M. VI | Trench XXV | S20:601 | 78.06 | Occupational debris |
| Ch.M. VI | Trench XXV | S20:601 | 77.89 | Occupational debris |
| Ch.M. VI | Trench XXV | S20:601 | 77.81 | Occupational debris |
| Ch.M. VI | Trench XXV | S20:601 South | 79.13–78.61 | Occupational debris |
| Ch.M. VI | Trench XXV | S20:602 | 79.12 | Room |
| Ch.M. VI | Trench XXV | S20:602 | 78.60 | Room |
| Ch.M. VI | Trench XXV | S20:603 | 79.20 | Pit |
| Ch.M. VI | Trench XXV | S20:603 | 78.91 | Pit |
| Ch.M. VI | Trench XXV | Southwest of S20:603 | 79.06 | Hard surface (floor?) |
| Ch.M. VI | Trench XXV | S20:605 | 79.20 | Occupational debris |

| *Season* | *Area* | *Provenance* | *Elevation* | *Type of Deposit or Feature* |
|---|---|---|---|---|
| **Late Middle Susiana** (*cont.*) | | | | |
| Ch.M. VI | Trench XXV | S20:605 | 79.05 | Occupational debris |
| Ch.M. VI | Trench XXV | S20:605 | 79.05 | Occupational debris |
| Ch.M. VI | Trench XXV | S20:606 | 78.88 | Ash deposit |
| Ch.M. VI | Trench XXV | S20:608 | 79.60 | Mudbrick pavement |
| Ch.M. VI | Trench XXV | S20:608 | 79.20 | Mudbrick pavement |
| Ch.M. VI | Trench XXV | S20:608 | 79.12 | Mudbrick pavement |
| Ch.M. VI | Trench XXV | S20:608 | 79.07 | Mudbrick pavement |
| Ch.M. VI | Trench XXV | S20:608 | 79.97 | Mudbrick pavement |
| Ch.M. VI | Trench XXV | S20:608 Southwest | 79.17 | Mudbrick pavement |
| Ch.M. VI | Trench XXV | S20:608 West | 79.27–78.88 | Mudbrick pavement |
| Ch.M. VI | Trench XXV | S20:608 Middle | 79.04 | Mudbrick pavement |
| Ch.M. VI | Trench XXV | S20:608 | 78.36 | Occupational debris |
| Ch.M. VI | Trench XXV | S20:609 | 78.11 | Occupational debris |
| Ch.M. VI | Trench XXV | S20:609 | 78.07 | Occupational debris |
| Ch.M. VI | Trench XXV | S20:609 | 77.89 | Occupational debris |
| Ch.M. VI | Trench XXV | S20:609 | 77.60 | Occupational debris |
| Ch.M. VI | Trench XXV | S20:609 | 77.48 | Occupational debris |
| Ch.M. VI | Trench XXV | S20:609 | 77.23 | Occupational debris |
| Ch.M. VI | Trench XXV | S20:609 | 77.05 | Occupational debris |
| Ch.M. VI | Trench XXV | S20:609 West | 78.07 | Occupational debris |
| Ch.M. VI | Trench XXV | S20:609 | 79.73 | Occupational debris |
| Ch.M. VI | Trench XXV | S20:610 | 78.73 | Occupational debris |
| Ch.M. VI | Trench XXV | S20:610 | 78.44 | Room |
| Ch.M. VI | Trench XXV | S20:610 | 77.81 | Occupational debris |
| Ch.M. VI | Trench XXV | S20:612 | 77.60 | Occupational debris |
| Ch.M. VI | Trench XXV | S20:612 | 77.52 | Occupational debris |
| Ch.M. VI | Trench XXV | S20:612 | 77.40 | Occupational debris |
| Ch.M. VI | Trench XXV | S20:612 | 77.26 | Pebble surface |
| Ch.M. VI | Trench XXV | S20:612 | 77.25 | Occupational debris |
| Ch.M. VI | Trench XXV | S20:612 | 77.05 | Occupational debris |
| Ch.M. VI | Trench XXV | S20:612 | 76.87 | Occupational debris |
| Ch.M. VI | Trench XXV | S20:612 | 76.82 | Occupational debris |
| Ch.M. VI | Trench XXV | S20:613 | 78.17 | Granary(?) |
| Ch.M. VI | Trench XXV | S20:614 | 78.03 | Occupational debris |
| Ch.M. VI | Trench XXV | S20:615 | 78.13 | Occupational debris |
| Ch.M. VI | Trench XXV | S20:615 | 78.13 | Occupational debris |

| *Season* | *Area* | *Provenance* | *Elevation* | *Type of Deposit or Feature* |
|---|---|---|---|---|
| **Late Middle Susiana** (*cont.*) | | | | |
| Ch.M. VI | Trench XXV | S20:615 | 78.00 | Occupational debris |
| Ch.M. VI | Trench XXV | S20:615 | 77.83 | Occupational debris |
| Ch.M. VI | Trench XXV | S20:615 | 77.68 | Occupational debris |
| Ch.M. VI | Trench XXV | S20:615 | 77.53 | Occupational debris |
| Ch.M. VI | Trench XXV | S20:615 | 77.28 | Occupational debris |
| Ch.M. VI | Trench XXV | S20:618 | 76.90 | Occupational debris |
| Ch.M. VI | Trench XXV | S20:618 | 76.50 | Occupational debris |
| Ch.M. VI | Trench XXV | S20:618 | 76.30 | Occupational debris |
| Ch.M. VI | Trench XXV | S20:619 | 76.70 | Occupational debris |
| Ch.M. VI | Trench XXV | S20:620 | 77.92 | Occupational debris |
| Ch.M. VI | Trench XXV | S20:620 | 77.86 | Occupational debris |
| Ch.M. VI | Trench XXV | S20:621 | 79.16 | Occupational debris |
| Ch.M. VI | Trench XXV | S20:621 | 79.04 | Occupational debris |
| Ch.M. VI | Trench XXV | S20:621 | 78.85 | Occupational debris |
| Ch.M. VI | Trench XXV | S20:621 | 78.75 | Occupational debris |
| Ch.M. VI | Trench XXV | S20:621 | 78.70 | Occupational debris |
| Ch.M. VI | Trench XXV | S20:621 | 78.64 | Occupational debris |
| Ch.M. VI | Trench XXV | S20:621 | 78.60 | Occupational debris |
| Ch.M. VI | Trench XXV | S20:621 | 78.60 | Occupational debris |
| Ch.M. VI | Trench XXV | S20:621 | 78.42 | Occupational debris |
| Ch.M. VI | Trench XXV | S20:621 | 78.40 | Occupational debris |
| Ch.M. VI | Trench XXV | S20:621 | 78.32 | Occupational debris |
| Ch.M. VI | Trench XXV | S20:621 | 78.25 | Occupational debris |
| Ch.M. VI | Trench XXV | S20:621 | 78.20 | Occupational debris |
| Ch.M. VI | Trench XXV | S20:621 | 78.09 | Occupational debris |
| Ch.M. VI | Trench XXV | S20:621 | 78.04 | Occupational debris |
| Ch.M. VI | Trench XXV | S20:621 | 78.04 | Occupational debris |
| Ch.M. VI | Trench XXV | S20:621 | 77.90 | Occupational debris |
| Ch.M. VI | Trench XXV | S20:621 | 77.85 | Occupational debris |
| Ch.M. VI | Trench XXV | S20:621 | 77.76 | Occupational debris |
| Ch.M. VI | Trench XXV | S20:621 West | 78.42 | Occupational debris |
| Ch.M. VI | Trench XXV | S20:622 | 78.84 | Occupational debris |
| Ch.M. VI | Trench XXV | S20:622 | 78.43 | Room |
| Ch.M. VI | Trench XXV | S20:622 | 78.34 | Room |
| Ch.M. VI | Trench XXV | S20:622 | 78.10 | Room |
| Ch.M. VI | Trench XXV | S20:622 | 77.90–77.70 | Room |

| *Season* | *Area* | *Provenance* | *Elevation* | *Type of Deposit or Feature* |
|---|---|---|---|---|
| **Late Middle Susiana** (*cont.*) | | | | |
| Ch.M. VI | Trench XXV | S20:622 | 77.70 | Room |
| Ch.M. VI | Trench XXV | S20:622 | N/A | Room |
| Ch.M. VI | Trench XXXIII | S19:601 North | 76.55 | Occupational debris |
| Ch.M. VI | Trench XXXIII | S19:601 North | 76.10 | Occupational debris |
| Ch.M. VI | Trench XXXIII | S19:601 North | 76.08 | Occupational debris |
| Ch.M. VI | Trench XXXIII | S19:601 North | 75.59 | Occupational debris |
| Ch.M. VI | Trench XXXIII | S19:601 South | 75.82 | Occupational debris |
| Ch.M. VI | Trench XXXIII | South of S19:603 | 77.25 | Occupational debris |
| Ch.M. VI | Trench XXXIII | South of S19:603 | 76.91 | Occupational debris |
| Ch.M. VI | Trench XXXIII | South of S19:603 | 76.88 | Occupational debris |
| Ch.M. VI | Trench XXXIII | South of S19:603 | 76.84 | Occupational debris |
| Ch.M. VI | Trench XXXIII | South of S19:603 | 76.74 | Occupational debris |
| Ch.M. VI | Trench XXXIII | South of S19:603 | 76.29 | Occupational debris |
| Ch.M. VI | Trench XXXIII | South of S19:603 | 75.79 | Occupational debris |
| Ch.M. VI | Trench XXXIII | South of S19:603 | 74.48 | Occupational debris |
| Ch.M. VI | Trench XXXIII | South of S19:603 | 73.82 | Occupational debris |
| Ch.M. VI | Trench XXXIII | South of S19:603 | 73.30 | Occupational debris |
| Ch.M. VI | Trench XXXIII | S19:604 | 77.30 | Occupational debris |
| Ch.M. VI | Trench XXXIII | S19:604 | 76.14 | Occupational debris |
| Ch.M. VI | Trench XXXIII | S19:604 | 75.36 | Occupational debris |
| Ch.M. VI | Trench XXXIII | S19:604 | 73.02 | Occupational debris |
| Ch.M. VI | Trench XXXIII | S18:602 | 77.39 | Occupational debris |
| Ch.M. VI | Trench XXXIII | S18:602 South | 76.32 | Occupational debris |
| Ch.M. VI | Trench XXXIII | S18:603 | 77.06 | Occupational debris |
| Ch.M. VI | Trench XXXIII | S18:603 | 76.93 | Occupational debris |
| Ch.M. VI | Trench XXXIII | S18:603 | 76.75 | Occupational debris |
| Ch.M. VI | Trench XXXIII | S19:601 | 76.93 | Occupational debris |
| Ch.M. VI | Trench XXXIII | S19:601 North | 76.60 | Occupational debris |
| Ch.M. VI | Trench XXXIII | S19:601 North | 76.50 | Occupational debris |
| Ch.M. VI | Trench XXXIII | S19:601 South | 76.79 | Occupational debris |
| Ch.M. VI | Trench XXXIII | S19:601 South | 76.69 | Occupational debris |
| Ch.M. VI | Trench XXXIII | S19:601 South | 76.54 | Occupational debris |
| Ch.M. VI | Trench XXXIII | S19:601 South | 76.30 | Occupational debris |
| Ch.M. VI | Trench XXXIII | S19:601 South | 76.22 | Occupational debris |
| Ch.M. VI | Trench XXXIII | S19:602 | 75.74 | Occupational debris |
| Ch.M. VI | Trench XXXIII | S19:602 North | 76.65 | Occupational debris |

| *Season* | *Area* | *Provenance* | *Elevation* | *Type of Deposit or Feature* |
|---|---|---|---|---|
| **Late Middle Susiana** (*cont.*) | | | | |
| Ch.M. VI | Trench XXXIII | S19:602 North | 75.74 | Occupational debris |
| Ch.M. VI | Trench XXXIII | S19:602 South | 76.95 | Occupational debris |
| Ch.M. VI | Trench XXXIII | R19:601 East | 76.32 | Occupational debris |
| Ch.M. VI | Trench XXXIII | S18:602 | 75.70 | Occupational debris |
| Ch.M. VI | Trench XXXIII | S18:602 North | 75.91 | Occupational debris |
| Ch.M. VI | Trench XXXIII | S18:602 North | 75.85 | Occupational debris |
| Ch.M. VI | Trench XXXIII | S18:602 North | 75.58 | Occupational debris |
| Ch.M. VI | Trench XXXIII | S18:602 North | 75.35 | Occupational debris |
| Ch.M. VI | Trench XXXIII | S18:602 South | 75.91 | Occupational debris |
| Ch.M. VI | Trench XXXIV | S18:604 | 77.45 | Surface wash |
| Ch.M. VI | Trench XXXIV | S18:604 | 76.49 | Occupational debris |
| Ch.M. VI | Trench XXXIV | T19:602 | 76.55 | Wall |
| Ch.M. VI | Trench XXXIV | T19:602 | 76.20 | Occupational debris |
| Ch.M. VI | Trench XXXIV | T19:602 | 75.45 | Occupational debris |
| Ch.M. VI | Trench XXXIV | T19:602 | 75.07 | Occupational debris |
| Ch.M. VI | Trench XXXIV | T19:602 | 74.42 | Occupational debris |
| Ch.M. VI | Trench XXXIV | T19:602 | 73.58 | Occupational debris |
| Ch.M. VI | Trench XXXIV | T19:652 | 77.45 | Surface wash |
| Ch.M. VI | Trench XXXV | R19:601 | 77.55 | Surface wash |
| Ch.M. VI | Trench XXXV | R19:601 | 76.81 | Occupational debris |
| Ch.M. VI | Trench XXXV | R19:601 | 76.13 | Occupational debris |
| Ch.M. VI | Trench XXXV | R19:601 | 74.85 | Occupational debris |
| Ch.M. VI | Trench XXXV | R19:601 | 74.35 | Occupational debris |
| Ch.M. VI | Trench XXXV | R19:601 East | 75.47 | Occupational debris |
| Ch.M. VI | Trench XXXV | R19:601 East | 74.35 | Occupational debris |
| Ch.M. VI | Trench XXXV | R19:601 West | 77.55 | Surface wash |
| Ch.M. VI | Trench XXXV | R19:601 West | 76.47 | Occupational debris |
| Ch.M. VI | Trench XXXV | R20:600 | 77.55 | Surface wash |
| Ch.M. VI | Trench XXXV | R20:610 | 77.55 | Surface wash |
| Ch.M. VI | Trench XXXV | R20:610 | 77.50 | Occupational debris |
| Ch.M. VI | Trench XXXV | R20:610 | 77.55 | Surface wash |
| Ch.M. VI | Trench XXXV | R20:610 | 76.13 | Occupational debris |
| Ch.M. VI | Trench XXXV | R20:610 | 75.88 | Occupational debris |
| Ch.M. VI | Trench XXXV | R20:610 | 75.67 | Occupational debris |
| Ch.M. VI | Trench XXXV | R20:610 East | 75.25 | Occupational debris |
| Ch.M. VI | Trench XXXV | Northeast of R20:610 | 77.08 | Occupational debris |

| *Season* | *Area* | *Provenance* | *Elevation* | *Type of Deposit or Feature* |
|---|---|---|---|---|
| **Late Middle Susiana** (*cont.*) | | | | |
| Ch.M. VII | Trench XXI | P23:701 | 82.85 | Surface wash |
| Ch.M. VII | Trench XXI | P23:701 | 82.54 | Occupational debris |
| Ch.M. VII | Trench XXXVI | G27:701 | 81.62 | Inside kiln area |
| Ch.M. VII | Trench XXXVI | G27:701 East | 81.71 | Occupational debris |
| Ch.M. VII | Trench XXXVI | G27:701 East | 81.26 | Inside kiln area |
| Ch.M. VII | Trench XXXVI | G27:702 | 81.65 | Supra floor fill |
| Ch.M. VII | Trench XXXVI | G27:702 | 81.18 | Supra floor fill |
| Ch.M. VII | Trench XXXVI | G27:702 | 80.96 | Floor |
| Ch.M. VII | Trench XXXVI | G27:703 | 81.47 | Supra floor fill |
| Ch.M. VII | Trench XXXVI | G27:703 | 81.17 | Supra floor fill |
| Ch.M. VII | Trench XXXVI | G28:702 | 80.49 | Occupational debris |
| Ch.M. VII | Trench XXXVI | G28:702 | 80.41 | Occupational debris |
| Ch.M. VII | Trench XXXVI | G28:702 | 79.65 | Occupational debris |
| Ch.M. VII | Trench XXXVI | G28:703 | 79.02 | Occupational debris |
| Ch.M. VII | Trench XXXVI | G28:705 | 79.87 | Pit |
| Ch.M. VII | Trench XXXVI | G28:705 | 79.60 | Pit |
| Ch.M. VII | Trench XXXVI | G28:705 | 79.42–78.30 | Pit |
| Ch.M. VII | Trench XXXVI | G28:705 | 79.42 | Pit |
| Ch.M. VII | Trench XXXVI | G28:705 | 77.75 | Pit |
| Ch.M. VII | Trench XXXVI | G28:705 | 77.73 | Pit |
| Ch.M. VII | Trench XXXVI | G28:705 | 77.70 | Pit |
| Ch.M. VII | Trench XXXVI | G28:705 | 76.08 | Pit |
| Ch.M. VII | Trench XXXVI | G28:705 | 75.74 | Pit |
| Ch.M. VII | Trench XXXVI | G28:705 | 75.50 | Pit |
| Ch.M. VII | Trench XXXVI | G28:705 | 74.39 | Pit |
| Ch.M. VII | Trench XXXVI | G27:702 | 82.27 | Surface wash |
| Ch.M. VII | Trench XXXVI | G27:703 | 80.68 | Hard surface |
| Ch.M. VII | Trench XXXVI | G28:703 | 80.68 | Hard surface |
| Ch.M. VII | Trench XXXVI | G28:703 North | 77.42 | Occupational debris |
| Ch.M. VII | Trench XXXVI | G28:703 North | 76.94 | Occupational debris |
| Ch.M. VII | Trench XXXVI | G28:704 South | 76.83 | Occupational debris |
| Ch.M. VII | Trench XXXVI | G28:704 | 77.54 | Occupational debris |
| Ch.M. VII | Trench XXXVI | G28:704 | 77.19 | Occupational debris |
| Ch.M. VII | Trench XXXVI | G28:704 | 76.57 | Occupational debris |
| Ch.M. VII | Trench XXXVI | G28:704 | 76.26 | Occupational debris |
| Ch.M. VII | Trench XXXVI | G28:704 | 76.25 | Occupational debris |

| *Season* | *Area* | *Provenance* | *Elevation* | *Type of Deposit or Feature* |
|---|---|---|---|---|
| **Late Middle Susiana** (*cont.*) | | | | |
| Ch.M. VII | Trench XXXVI | G28:704 | 75.61 | Occupational debris |
| Ch.M. VII | Trench XXXVI | G28:704 | 75.55 | Occupational debris |
| Ch.M. VII | Trench XXXVI | G28:704 | 75.27 | Occupational debris |
| Ch.M. VII | Trench XXXVI | G28:706 South | 77.17 | Occupational debris |
| Ch.M. VII | Trench XXXVI | G28:707 | 79.54 | Occupational debris |
| Ch.M. VII | Trench XXXVI | G28:707 | 76.40 | Pit |
| Ch.M. VII | Trench XXXVI | G28:707 | 75.90 | Pit |
| Ch.M. VII | Trench XXXVI | G29:701 | 75.07 | Pit |
| Ch.M. VII | Trench XXXVI | G29:701 | 76.98 | Occupational debris |
| Ch.M. VII | Trench XXXVI | G29:701 | 76.88 | Occupational debris |
| Ch.M. VII | Trench XXXVI | G29:701 | 76.25 | Occupational debris |
| Ch.M. VII | Trench XXXVI | G29:701 | 75.88 | Occupational debris |
| Ch.M. VII | Trench XXXVI | G29:701 | 75.37 | Occupational debris |
| Ch.M. VII | Trench XXXVI | G29:701 North | 77.97 | Occupational debris |
| Ch.M. VII | Trench XXXVI | G29:701 South | 78.66 | Occupational debris |
| Ch.M. VII | Trench XXXVI | G29:701 South | 78.03 | Occupational debris |
| Ch.M. VII | Trench XXXVI | G29:701 South | 77.63 | Occupational debris |
| Ch.M. VII | Trench XXXVI | G29:703 | 77.47 | Occupational debris |
| Ch.M. VIII | Trench XXXVII | Q24:802 Northwest | 76.40 | Pit |
| Ch.M. VIII | Trench XXXVII | Q24:802 East | 78.32 | Indeterminable |
| Ch.M. VIII | Trench XXXVII | Q24:802 East | 78.07 | Hearth |
| Ch.M. VIII | Trench XXXVII | Q25:801 | 77.47 | Supra floor fill |
| Ch.M. VIII | Trench XXXVII | Q25:801 East | 77.64 | Occupational debris |
| Ch.M. VIII | Trench XXXVII | Q25:801 East | 76.27 | Pit |
| Ch.M. VIII | Trench XXXVII | Q25:802 | 81.84 | Pit |
| Ch.M. VIII | Trench XXXVII | Q25:802 | 81.80 | Pit |
| Ch.M. VIII | Trench XXXVII | Q25:802 | 79.99 | Pit |
| Ch.M. VIII | Trench XXXVII | Q25:802 | 77.84 | Pit |
| Ch.M. VIII | Trench XXXVII | Q25:802 | 77.57 | Occupational debris |
| Ch.M. VIII | Trench XXXVII | Q25:802 | 77.40 | Pit |
| Ch.M. VIII | Trench XXXVII | Q25:802 | 77.35 | Occupational debris |
| Ch.M. VIII | Trench XXXVII | Q25:802 | 77.02 | Pit |
| Ch.M. VIII | Trench XXXVII | Q25:802 | 76.10 | Pit |
| Ch.M. VIII | Trench XXXVII | Q25:802 East | 77.04 | Pit |
| Ch.M. VIII | Trench XXXVII | Q25:802 East | 76.94 | Pit |
| Ch.M. VIII | Trench XXXVII | Q25:802 East | 76.59 | Pit |
| Ch.M. VIII | Trench XXXVII | Q25:802 East | 76.32 | Pit |

| Season | Area | Provenance | Elevation | Type of Deposit or Feature |
|---|---|---|---|---|
| **Late Middle Susiana** (*cont.*) | | | | |
| Ch.M. VIII | Trench XXXVII | Q25:802 East | 76.24 | Pit |
| Ch.M. VIII | Trench XXXVII | Q25:802 East | 75.70 | Pit |
| Ch.M. VIII | Trench XXXVII | Q25:802 East | 75.17 | Pit |
| Ch.M. VIII | Trench XXXVII | Q25:802 East | 74.92 | Pit |
| Ch.M. VIII | Trench XXXVII | Q25:802 East | 74.56 | Pit |
| Ch.M. VIII | Trench XXXVII | Q25:802 East | 74.12 | Pit |
| Ch. M. VIII | Trench XXXVII | Q25:802 West | 78.18 | Pit |
| Ch.M. VIII | Trench XXXVII | Q25:802 West | 77.25 | Occupational debris |
| Ch.M. VIII | Trench XXXVII | Q25:802 West | 77.13 | Occupational debris |
| Ch.M. VIII | Trench XXXVII | Q25:802 West | 76.94 | Occupational debris |
| Ch.M. VIII | Trench XXXVII | Q25:802 West | 76.07 | Pit |
| Ch.M. VIII | Trench XXXVII | East of Q25:803 | 79.77 | Pit |
| Ch.M. VIII | Gully Cut | S22:801 | 76.81 | Room |
| Ch.M. VIII | Gully Cut | S22:802 North | 76.95 | Occupational debris |
| Ch.M. VIII | Gully Cut | S22:802 North | 76.93 | Occupational debris |
| Ch.M. VIII | Gully Cut | S22:802 North | 76.82 | Occupational debris |
| Ch.M. VIII | Gully Cut | S22:805 | 77.35 | Inside kiln area |
| Ch.M. VIII | Gully Cut | S22:805 | 77.35 | Inside kiln area |
| Ch.M. VIII | Gully Cut | S22:805 | 76.96 | Ash deposit |
| Ch.M. VIII | Gully Cut | S22:805 North | 77.35 | Inside kiln area |
| Ch.M. VIII | Gully Cut | S22:806 North | 76.89 | Inside kiln area |
| Ch.M. VIII | Gully Cut | S22:806 | 77.24 | Occupational debris |
| Ch.M. VIII | Gully Cut | S22:806 | 76.97 | Occupational debris |
| Ch.M. VIII | Gully Cut | S22:806 | 77.89 | Occupational debris |
| Ch.M. VIII | Gully Cut | S22:806 | 76.63 | Occupational debris |
| Ch.M. VIII | Gully Cut | S22:806 | 76.54 | Occupational debris |
| Ch.M. VIII | Gully Cut | S22:806 East | 76.63 | Hearth area |
| Ch.M. VIII | Gully Cut | S22:807 | 77.18 | Near wall |
| Ch.M. VIII | Gully Cut | S22:807 | 76.98 | Room |
| Ch.M. VIII | Gully Cut | S22:809 | 76.80 | Occupational debris |
| Ch.M. VIII | Gully Cut | S22:809 | 76.70 | Occupational debris |
| Ch.M. VIII | Gully Cut | S22:809 | 76.66 | Room |
| Ch.M. VIII | Gully Cut | S22:809 | 76.41 | Room |
| Ch.M. VIII | Gully Cut | S22:809 | 76.37 | Fill over room floor |
| Ch.M. VIII | Gully Cut | S22:811 | 77.10 | Room |
| Ch.M. VIII | Gully Cut | S22:811 | 76.63 | Room |

| *Season* | *Area* | *Provenance* | *Elevation* | *Type of Deposit or Feature* |
|---|---|---|---|---|
| **Late Middle Susiana** (*cont.*) | | | | |
| Ch.M. VIII | Gully Cut | S22:812 | 77.14 | Wall |
| Ch.M. VIII | Gully Cut | S22:812 | 76.72 | Occupational debris |
| Ch.M. VIII | Gully Cut | S22:812 | 76.71 | Occupational debris |
| Ch.M. VIII | Gully Cut | S22:812 | 76.62 | Occupational debris |
| Ch.M. VIII | Gully Cut | S22:812 | 76.49 | Occupational debris |
| Ch.M. VIII | Gully Cut | S22:812 | 76.34 | Occupational debris |
| Ch.M. VIII | Gully Cut | S22:812 | 76.19 | Occupational debris |
| Ch.M. VIII | Gully Cut | S22:812 West | 76.42 | Occupational debris |
| Ch.M. VIII | Gully Cut | S22:812 West | 76.19 | Occupational debris |
| Ch.M. VIII | Gully Cut | S22:817 | 76.48 | Occupational debris |
| Ch.M. VIII | Gully Cut | S22:819 | 77.61 | Surface wash |
| Ch.M. VIII | Gully Cut | S22:819 | 77.61 | Surface wash |
| Ch.M. VIII | Gully Cut | S22:819 | 76.86 | Occupational debris |
| Ch.M. VIII | Gully Cut | S22:819 | 76.71 | Occupational debris |
| Ch.M. VIII | Gully Cut | S22:819 | 76.63 | Occupational debris |
| Ch.M. VIII | Gully Cut | S22:819 | 76.54 | Occupational debris |
| Ch.M. VIII | Gully Cut | S22:819 | 76.33 | Occupational debris |
| Ch.M. VIII | Gully Cut | S22:819 | 76.06 | Occupational debris |
| Ch.M. VIII | Gully Cut | S22:820 West | 75.97 | Occupational debris |
| Ch.M. VIII | Gully Cut | S22:821 | 77.48 | Surface wash |
| **Middle Susiana + Mixed** | | | | |
| Ch.M. V | Trench XXV | R20:515 | 80.04 | Surface wash |
| Ch.M. V | Trench XXV | R20:515 | 79.15 | Settlement area |
| Ch.M. V | Trench XXV | R20:515 | 78.97 | Settlement area |
| Ch.M. V | Trench XXXI | P27:501 | 78.87 | Settlement area |
| Ch.M. V | Trench XXXI | P27:501 | 78.65 | Settlement area |
| Ch.M. V | Trench XXXI | P27:501 Southwest | 79.04 | Settlement area |
| Ch.M. VI | Trench XXV | R20:602 | 80.08 | Surface wash |
| Ch.M. VI | Trench XXV | R20:602 | 79.64 | Occupational debris |
| Ch.M. VI | Trench XXV | R20:602 | 78.89 | Occupational debris |
| Ch.M. VI | Trench XXV | R20:606 | 78.93 | Inside kiln area |
| **Late Susiana 2** | | | | |
| Ch.M. II | Trench I | R10–11 Plot 4 | 82.85 | Occupational debris |
| Ch.M. II | Trench II | R10–11 Plot 4 | 84.70 | Occupational debris |
| Ch.M. II | Trench II | R10–11 Plots 5–6 | 83.40 | Occupational debris |
| Ch.M. III | Trench XXIII | N10 East | 81.37 | Occupational debris |

| *Season* | *Area* | *Provenance* | *Elevation* | *Type of Deposit or Feature* |
|---|---|---|---|---|
| **Late Susiana 2** (*cont.*) | | | | |
| Ch.M. IV | Trench XXIII | N10 West extension | 85.40 | Burial |
| Ch.M. X | Trench XXIII | N10:1001 South | 81.25 | Parthian pit |
| Ch.M. X | Trench XXIII | N10:1001 | 83.09 | Surface |
| Ch.M. X | Trench XXIII | N10:1002 | 84.50 | Pit |
| Ch.M. X | Trench XXIII | N10:1003 | 84.02 | Floor in room |
| Ch.M. X | Trench XXIII | N10:1004 | 83.74 | Floor in room |
| Ch.M. X | Trench XXIII | N10:1004 East | 83.80 | Mudbrick detritus |
| Ch.M. X | Trench XXIII | N10:1005 | 84.10 | Floor in room |
| Ch.M. X | Trench XXIII | N10:1007–08 | 84.30 | Ash |
| Ch.M. X | Trench XXIII | N10:1008–9 | 82.28 | Floor in room |
| Ch.M. X | Trench XXIII | N10:1010 | 83.10 | Floor in room |
| Ch.M. X | Trench XXIII | N10:1011 | 83.10 | Floor in room |
| Ch.M. X | Trench XXIII | N10:1012 | 82.28 | Floor in room |
| Ch.M. X | Trench XXIII | N10:1014 | 82.28 | Floor in room |
| **Probably Protoliterate** | | | | |
| Ch.M. III | Trench V | 0.30 B.S. | N/A | Near PL pits and wall stumps |
| Ch.M. V | Trench XIII | K23:502 | 82.53 | Settlement area |
| Ch.M. VIII | Gully Cut | S22:802 North | 76.73 | Occupational debris |
| **Protoliterate** | | | | |
| Ch.M. II | Trench X | G26–27 Middle | 80.25 | Vicinity of BRBs deposit |
| Ch.M. II | East Area | R17:203 | 83.40 | BRBs |
| Ch.M. II | East Area | R17:203+204 | 83.40–82.50 | Vicinity of pit and wall stumps |
| Ch.M. II | East Area | R17:204+205 | 83.90 | Vicinity of pit and wall stumps |
| Ch.M. II | East Area | R17:208 | 84.21 | Pit (with BRBs, etc.) |
| Ch.M. II | East Area | R17:208 | 84.21–82.71 | Pit (with BRBs, etc.) |
| Ch.M. II | East Area | R17:208 | 83.71–83.61 | Pit (with BRBs, etc.) |
| Ch.M. II | East Area | R17:208 | 83.61 | Pit (with BRBs, etc.) |
| Ch.M. III | East Area | P18:301 | 82.00–80.00 | Pottery |
| Ch.M. III | East Area | P18:301 | 81.90–81.50 | Pottery |
| Ch.M. III | East Area | P18:301 | 81.20 | Pottery deposit |
| Ch.M. III | East Area | R18:305 | 83.40–82.30 | Area near wall |
| Ch.M. III | East Area | R18:305 | 82.75 | Area of pit and wall stumps |
| Ch.M. III | East Area | West of R18:305 | 83.40–82.20 | Area of pit and wall stumps |

| Season | Area | Provenance | Elevation | Type of Deposit or Feature |
|---|---|---|---|---|
| **Protoliterate** (*cont.*) | | | | |
| Ch.M. III | East Area | R19–Q18:301–307 | 81.50 | Area of pit and wall stumps |
| Ch.M. III | Trench VI | K14 West | 81.00–79.50 | Settlement area |
| Ch.M. III | Trench IX | H14:302 | 80.80 | Settlement area |
| Ch.M. III | Trench IX | H14:305 South | 81.40 | Occupational debris |
| Ch.M. III | Trench XIX | Q18 | 0.50 B.S. | Area of pit and wall stumps |
| Ch.M. III | Trench XIX | Q18 | 1.30 B.S. | Area of pit and wall stumps |
| Ch.M. IV | West Area | H15:401 | 80.21–79.17 | Pit |
| Ch.M. IV | West Area | H15:401 | 81.41–80.50 | Pit (with BRBs, etc.) |
| Ch.M. IV | West Area | H15:402 | 80.56–80.16 | Baked-brick drain |
| Ch.M. IV | West Area | East of J14:404 | 80.31 | Vicinity of PL drain |
| Ch.M. IV | East Area | Q18:401 | 80.37 | Surface wash |
| Ch.M. IV | East Area | Q18:402 | 81.23 | Vicinity of PL pit and wall stumps |
| Ch.M. IV | East Area | R17:405 | 83.36–82.64 | Baked-brick installation |
| Ch.M. IV | East Area | R17:408 | 83.40–80.90 | Pit |
| Ch.M. IV | East Area | R18:401 | 80.25–80.00 | Near wall |
| Ch.M. IV | East Area | R18:406 | 82.07–81.67 | Settlement area |
| Ch.M. IV | East Area | R18:413 | 82.85–82.75 | Near room |
| Ch.M. IV | East Area | R18:415 | 82.35–81.40 | PL pit (BRBs, etc.) |
| Ch.M. IV | East Area | R19:401 | 81.75 | Settlement area |
| Ch.M. IV | East Area | S17:401 South | 82.50 | Room |
| Ch.M. IV | East Area | S17:402 | 83.10 | Settlement area |
| Ch.M. IV | East Area | S17:401 | 82.60–82.32 | Room |
| Ch.M. IV | East Area | S18:402 | 82.70 | Room |
| Ch.M. IV | East Area | S18:404 | 82.80–82.00 | Well |
| Ch.M. IV | Trench IX | J15:401 | 81.50–81.15 | Settlement area |
| Ch.M. IV | Trench IX | J15:401 | 81.30–80.65 | Lane |
| Ch.M. IV | Trench IX | East of J15:401 | 80.90–80.80 | Vicinity of PL pits and wall stumps |
| Ch.M. IV | Trench IX | J15:402 | 80.78–80.22 | Rectangular bin-like structure |
| Ch.M. IV | Trench IX | H14:401 | 80.71–80.61 | Vicinity of PL drain |
| Ch.M. IV | Trench IX | H14:406 | 81.27–80.52 | Room |
| Ch.M. IV | Trench XIII | K23:400 | 83.10–82.90 | Settlement area |
| Ch.M. IV | Trench XIII | K23:400 | 82.90–82.80 | Settlement area |

| *Season* | *Area* | *Provenance* | *Elevation* | *Type of Deposit or Feature* |
|---|---|---|---|---|
| **Protoliterate** (*cont.*) | | | | |
| Ch.M. IV | Trench XX | R18 | B.S. | Vicinity of PL pit and wall stumps |
| Ch.M. IV | Trench XXV | R20:401 | 79.08–78.95 | Backed-brick drain |
| Ch.M. IV | Trench XXV | R20:401 | 78.24 | Near wall |
| Ch.M. IV | Trench XXV | R20:402 | 79.23–79.03 | Settlement area |
| Ch.M. IV | Trench XXV | R20:402 South | 78.03–75.69 | PL pit (BRBs, etc.) |
| Ch.M. IV | Trench XXV | R20:403 | 78.67–78.33 | Near wall |
| Ch.M. IV | Trench XXV | R21:401 South | 79.13–78.33 | Settlement area |
| Ch.M. IV | Trench XXV | R21:401 South | 78.00 | Settlement area |
| Ch.M. IV | Trench XXV | R21:402 | 79.23 | Vicinity of PL pit and wall stumps |
| Ch.M. IV | Trench XXV | R21:402 | 78.93 | Vicinity of PL pit and wall stumps |
| Ch.M. IV | Trench XXV | R21:402 North | 78.03–77.78 | Vicinity of PL pit and wall stumps |
| Ch.M. IV | Trench XXV | R21:402 North | 77.23 | Vicinity of PL pit and wall stumps |
| Ch.M. IV | Trench XXV | R21:402 South | 77.78 | Vicinity of PL pit and wall stumps |
| Ch.M. IV | Trench XXV | R21:404 | 78.23 | Inside kiln area |
| Ch.M. IV | Trench XXV | South of R21:404 | 77.73 | Kiln area |
| Ch.M. IV | Trench XXV | R21:405 | 77.43 | Pit |
| Ch.M. IV | Trench XXV | R21:408 | 75.23–74.78 | Pit |
| Ch.M. IV | Trench XXV | R21:401 | 78.03 | Settlement area |
| Ch.M. V | Gully Cut | S22:501 | 6.77–75.81 | Vicinity of PL baked bricks |
| Ch.M. V | Gully Cut | S22:501 | 77.11–76.77 | Surface or slope wash |
| Ch.M. V | Gully Cut | S22:501 | 76.76–76.71 | Vicinity of PL baked bricks |
| Ch.M. V | Gully Cut | S22:501 | 76.71–76.66 | Surface- or slope wash |
| Ch.M. V | Gully Cut | S22:501 | 76.66–76.51 | Vicinity of PL baked bricks |
| Ch.M. V | Gully Cut | S22:501 | 76.51–76.26 | Vicinity of PL baked bricks |
| Ch.M. V | Gully Cut | S22:501 | 76.26–76.01 | Vicinity of PL baked bricks |
| Ch.M. V | Gully Cut | S22:504 | 77.25–76.82 | Surface or slope wash |
| Ch.M. V | Gully Cut | S22:504 | 76.82–76.42 | Vicinity of PL baked bricks |
| Ch.M. V | Gully Cut | S22:504 | 76.42–75.84 | Vicinity of PL baked bricks |
| Ch.M. V | Gully Cut | S22:507 | 76.50–76.43 | Occupational debris |

| *Season* | *Area* | *Provenance* | *Elevation* | *Type of Deposit or Feature* |
|---|---|---|---|---|
| **Protoliterate** (*cont.*) | | | | |
| Ch.M. V | Gully Cut | S22:509 | 76.54–76.14 | Vicinity of PL baked bricks |
| Ch.M. V | Gully Cut | S22:509 | 76.21–75.71 | Vicinity of PL baked bricks |
| Ch.M. V | Gully Cut | S22:512 | 76.51 | Occupational debris |
| Ch.M. V | Sounding I | S-T26 | 75.50 | Slop wash |
| Ch.M. V | Sounding I | S-T26 | 74.40 | Slope wash |
| Ch.M. V | Sounding I | S-T26 | 73.40 | Slope wash |
| Ch.M. V | Sounding I | S-T26 | 73.10 | Slope wash |
| Ch.M. V | Sounding I | S-T26 | 71.40 | Slope wash |
| Ch.M. V | Sounding I | S-T26 | 70.50 | Slope wash |
| Ch.M. V | Sounding I | S-T26 | 70.30 | Slope wash |
| Ch.M. V | Trench V | R20:506 | 78.46 | Settlement area |
| Ch.M. V | Trench V | R20:506 | 78.46 | Settlement area |
| Ch.M. V | Trench V | R20:506 | 78.40 | Settlement area |
| Ch.M. V | Trench V | R20:509 | 79.28 | Surface wash |
| Ch.M. V | Trench V | R20:509 | 78.59 | Pit |
| Ch.M. V | Trench V | R20:510 | 79.37 | PL pit (BRBs, etc.) |
| Ch.M. V | Trench V | R20:510 | 78.75 | PL pit (BRBs, etc.) |
| Ch.M. V | Trench V | R20:510 | 78.71 | PL pit (BRBs, etc.) |
| Ch.M. V | Trench V | R20:510 | 78.17 | PL pit (BRBs, etc.) |
| Ch.M. V | Trench V | R20:510 | 78.05 | PL pit (BRBs, etc.) |
| Ch.M. V | Trench V | R20:510 | 77.64 | PL pit (BRBs, etc.) |
| Ch.M. V | Trench V | R20:510 | 77.64 | PL pit (BRBs, etc.) |
| Ch.M. V | Trench V | West of R20:510 | 79.48 | PL pit (BRBs, etc.) |
| Ch.M. V | Trench V | R20:513 | 79.70 | Settlement area |
| Ch.M. V | Trench V | R20:513 | 79.04 | Settlement area |
| Ch.M. V | Trench V | R20:513 | 78.84 | Settlement area |
| Ch.M. V | Trench V | R20:513 | 78.46 | PL pit (BRBs, etc.) |
| Ch.M. V | Trench V | North of R20:513 | 79.68 | Settlement area |
| Ch.M. V | Trench V | South of R20:513 | 79.36 | Settlement area |
| Ch.M. V | Trench V | South of R20:513 | 78.66 | Settlement area |
| Ch.M. V | Trench V | South of R20:513 | 78.66 | Settlement area |
| Ch.M. V | Trench V | West of R20:513 | 78.81 | Settlement area |
| Ch.M. V | Trench XIII | K23:501 | 82.99–82.83 | Settlement area |
| Ch.M. V | Trench XIII | K23:501 | 82.98–82.83 | Settlement area |
| Ch.M. V | Trench XIII | K23:501 | 82.83 | Settlement area |
| Ch.M. V | Trench XIII | K23:501 | 82.83–82.73 | Settlement area |
| Ch.M. V | Trench XIII | K23:501 | 82.73 | Settlement area |

| *Season* | *Area* | *Provenance* | *Elevation* | *Type of Deposit or Feature* |
|---|---|---|---|---|
| **Protoliterate** (*cont.*) | | | | |
| Ch.M. V | Trench XIII | K23:501 | 82.73–82.63 | Settlement area |
| Ch.M. V | Trench XIII | K23:501 | 82.63 | Settlement area |
| Ch.M. V | Trench XIII | K23:502 | 82.58–82.33 | Settlement area |
| Ch.M. V | Trench XIII | K23:503 | 82.38 | Settlement area |
| Ch.M. V | Trench XIII | K23:503 | 82.23–82.03 | Settlement area |
| Ch.M. V | Trench XIII | K23:503 | 82.03–81.83 | Settlement area |
| Ch.M. V | Trench XIII | K23:505 | 83.02 | Settlement area |
| Ch.M. V | Trench XIII | K23:506 | 80.40–80.36 | Pit |
| Ch.M. V | Trench XIII | L23:501 | 82.98–82.63 | Settlement area |
| Ch.M. V | Trench XXV | R21:503 | 77.81–75.25 | Pit |
| Ch.M. V | Trench XXV | R21:503 | 77.41 | Pit |
| Ch.M. V | Trench XXV | R21:503 | 76.01 | Pit |
| Ch.M. V | Trench XXV | R21:503 | 75.41 | Pit |
| Ch.M. V | Trench XXV | R21:505 | 77.00–76.07 | PL pit (BRBs, etc) |
| Ch.M. V | Trench XXV | R21:505 | 76.70 | PL pit (BRBs, etc) |
| Ch.M. V | Trench XXV | R21:505 | 76.28 | PL pit (BRBs, etc) |
| Ch.M. V | Trench XXV | R21:509 | 76.97–75.40 | PL pit (BRBs, etc.) |
| Ch.M. V | Trench XXV | R21:509 | 76.86–76.03 | PL pit (BRBs, etc.) |
| Ch.M. V | Trench XXV | R21:509 | 76.86–74.74 | PL pit (BRBs, etc.) |
| Ch.M. V | Trench XXV | R21:509 | 76.86–75.75 | PL pit (BRBs, etc.) |
| Ch.M. V | Trench XXV | R21:509 | 76.03–75.75 | PL pit (BRBs, etc.) |
| Ch.M. V | Trench XXV | R21:509 | 75.75 | PL pit (BRBs, etc.) |
| Ch.M. V | Trench XXV | R21:509 | 75.75–75.67 | PL pit (BRBs, etc.) |
| Ch.M. V | Trench XXV | R21:509 | 75.67 | PL pit (BRBs, etc.) |
| Ch.M. V | Trench XXV | R21:509 | 75.40 | PL pit (BRBs, etc.) |
| Ch.M. V | Trench XXV | R21:509 | 75.17 | PL pit (BRBs, etc.) |
| Ch.M. V | Trench XXV | R21:509 | 75.17–74.74 | PL pit (BRBs, etc.) |
| Ch.M. V | Trench XXV | R20:506 | 79.21 | Settlement area |
| Ch.M. V | Trench XXV | West of R20:513 | 78.60 | Settlement area |
| Ch.M. V | Trench XXXI | P27:502 | 79.14 | Ash deposit |
| Ch.M. V | Trench XXXI | P27:502 | 80.14 | Ash deposit |
| Ch.M. V | Trench XXXI | P27:502 | 79.31 | Ash deposit |
| Ch.M. V | Trench XXXI | P27:502 | 79.31 | Ash deposit |
| Ch.M. V | Trench XXXI | P27:502 | 79.24–79.14 | Ash deposit |
| Ch.M. V | Trench XXXI | P27:502 | 79.19 | Ash deposit |
| Ch.M. V | Trench XXXI | P27:502 South | 79.51–79.24 | Ash deposit |
| Ch.M. V | Trench XXXI | P27:503 South | 78.85 | Near wall |

| *Season* | *Area* | *Provenance* | *Elevation* | *Type of Deposit or Feature* |
|---|---|---|---|---|
| **Protoliterate** (*cont.*) | | | | |
| Ch.M. V | Trench XXXI | P27:504 | 79.14–78.10 | Pit |
| Ch.M. V | Trench XXXI | P27:504 | 79.04 | Occupational debris |
| Ch.M. V | Trench XXXI | P27:504 East | 78.80 | Pit |
| Ch.M. V | Trench XXXI | P27:506 | 79.21–79.00 | Surface or slope wash |
| Ch.M. VI | Trench XXXI | P27:601 | 80.19 | Surface wash |
| Ch.M. VI | Trench XXXI | P27:601 | 79.70 | Occupational debris |
| Ch.M. VI | Trench XXXIII | S18:603 North | 77.70 | Occupational debris |
| Ch.M. VII | Trench XXXVI | G27:701 | 82.62 | Surface wash |
| Ch.M. VII | Trench XXXVI | G27:704 | 82.62–81.33 | Pit |
| Ch.M. VII | Trench XXXVI | G27:704 | 81.98 | Pit |
| Ch.M. VII | Trench XXXVI | G27:704 | 81.65 | Pit |
| Ch.M. VII | Trench XXXVI | G27:704 | 81.33 | Pit |
| Ch.M. VII | Trench XXXVI | G27:704 | 80.75 | Pit |
| Ch.M. VII | Trench XXXVI | G27:704 | 80.62 | Pit |
| Ch.M. VII | Gully Cut | S22:701 | 77.13 | Surface wash |
| Ch.M. VII | Gully Cut | S22:701 | 76.53–75.95 | Occupational debris |
| Ch.M. VII | East Area | Q17:701 | 83.92 | Surface wash |
| Ch.M. VII | East Area | Q17:701 | 83.78 | Surface wash |
| Ch.M. VII | East Area | Q17:701 | 83.75 | Surface wash |
| Ch.M. VII | East Area | Q17:701 | 83.57 | Occupational debris |
| Ch.M. VII | East Area | Q17:701 | 83.18 | Occupational debris |
| Ch.M. VII | East Area | Q17:701 | 82.91 | Occupational debris |
| Ch.M. VII | East Area | R17:701 | 83.28 | Occupational debris |
| Ch.M. VII | East Area | R17:701 East | 84.45 | Surface wash |
| Ch.M. VII | East Area | R17:701 East | 83.80 | Room floor |
| Ch.M. VII | East Area | R17:701 East | 83.60 | Hard surface (floor?) |
| Ch.M. VII | East Area | R17:701 East | 83.56 | Occupational debris |
| Ch.M. VII | East Area | R17:701 West | 84.04 | Surface wash |
| Ch.M. VII | East Area | R17:701 West | 83.23 | Room |
| Ch.M. VII | East Area | R17:702 | 84.02 | Inside kiln area |
| Ch.M. VII | East Area | R17:702 | 83.74 | Inside kiln area |
| Ch.M. VII | East Area | R17:703 | 83.91 | Room |
| Ch.M. VII | East Area | R17:704 | 84.30 | Surface wash |
| Ch.M. VII | East Area | R17:704 | 82.35 | Occupational debris |
| Ch.M. VII | East Area | R17:704 East | 84.30 | Surface wash |
| Ch.M. VII | East Area | R17:704 East | 83.64 | Occupational debris |
| Ch.M. VII | East Area | R17:704 East | 83.34 | Occupational debris |

| *Season* | *Area* | *Provenance* | *Elevation* | *Type of Deposit or Feature* |
|---|---|---|---|---|
| **Protoliterate** (*cont.*) | | | | |
| Ch.M. VII | East Area | R17:704 East | 82.85 | Occupational debris |
| Ch M. VII | East Area | R17:704 West | 83.97 | Room |
| Ch.M. VII | East Area | R17:704 West | 83.85 | Room |
| Ch.M. VII | East Area | R17:704 West | 83.84 | Room |
| Ch.M. VII | East Area | R17:704 West | 83.54 | Room |
| Ch.M. VII | East Area | R17:704 West | 83.49 | Room |
| Ch.M. VII | East Area | R17:704 West | 83.43 | Room |
| Ch.M. VII | East Area | R17:704 West | 83.25 | Room |
| Ch.M. VII | East Area | R17:704 West | 82.90 | Room |
| Ch.M. VII | East Area | R17:705 | 83.77 | Occupational debris |
| Ch.M. VII | East Area | R17:705 | 83.65 | Occupational debris |
| Ch.M. VII | East Area | R17:705 | 83.10 | Occupational debris |
| Ch.M. VII | East Area | R17:705 | 82.71 | Occupational debris |
| Ch.M. VII | East Area | R17:706 | 83.78 | Room |
| Ch.M. VII | East Area | R17:707 | 82.84 | Room floor |
| Ch.M. VII | East Area | R17:709 | 83.43 | Occupational debris |
| Ch.M. VII | East Area | R17:710 | 83.14 | Occupational debris |
| Ch.M. VII | East Area | R17:710 | 83.04 | Occupational debris |
| Ch.M. VII | East Area | R17:710 | 82.96 | Occupational debris |
| Ch.M. VII | East Area | R17:710 | 82.89 | Occupational debris |
| Ch.M. VII | East Area | R17:711 | 83.52 | Occupational debris |
| Ch.M. VII | East Area | R17:711 | 83.49 | Occupational debris |
| Ch.M. VII | East Area | R17:711 | 83.17 | Occupational debris |
| Ch.M. VII | East Area | R17:712 | 82.82 | Room |
| Ch.M. VII | East Area | R17:713 | 82.64–82.15 | Pit |
| Ch.M. VII | East Area | R17:714 | 83.74 | Occupational debris |
| Ch.M. VII | East Area | R17:714 | 83.50 | Room |
| Ch.M. VII | East Area | R17:714 | 83.39 | Room |
| Ch.M. VII | East Area | R17:714 | 82.66 | Room |
| Ch.M. VII | East Area | R17:714 | 82.64 | Room floor |
| Ch.M. VII | East Area | R17:714 | 0.00 | Room |
| Ch.M. VII | East Area | R17:715 | 82.58 | Room |
| Ch.M. VII | East Area | R17:716 | 84.30 | Surface wash |
| Ch.M. VII | East Area | R17:716 | 83.97 | Occupational debris |
| Ch.M. VII | East Area | R17:716 | 83.91 | Occupational debris |
| Ch.M. VII | East Area | R17:717 | 83.50 | Room |
| Ch.M. VII | East Area | R17:717 | 83.18 | Room |

| *Season* | *Area* | *Provenance* | *Elevation* | *Type of Deposit or Feature* |
|---|---|---|---|---|
| **Protoliterate** (*cont.*) | | | | |
| Ch.M. VII | East Area | R17:717 | 82.81 | Room |
| Ch.M. VII | East Area | R17:718 | 83.76 | Occupational debris |
| Ch.M. VII | East Area | R17:720 | 82.40 | Pit |
| Ch.M. VII | East Area | R17:721 | 83.68 | Occupational debris |
| Ch.M. VII | East Area | S17:702 | 82.77 | Room |
| Ch.M. VII | Trench XXXII | R23:703 | 77.00 | Pit |
| Ch.M. VII | Trench XXXII | R23:711 | 77.95 | Surface wash |
| Ch.M. VII | Trench XXXII | R23:703 South | 75.80–75.67 | PL pit (BRBs, etc.) |
| Ch.M. VIII | East Area | P17:805 | 82.66 | Surface wash |
| Ch.M. VIII | East Area | P17:805 | 82.36 | Pit |
| Ch.M. VIII | East Area | Q17:801 Plot 1 | 84.11 | Surface wash |
| Ch.M. VIII | East Area | Q17:801 Plot 1 | 83.88 | Occupational debris |
| Ch.M. VIII | East Area | Q17:801 Plot 5 | 83.75 | Surface wash |
| Ch.M. VIII | East Area | Q17:801 Plot 5 | 83.57 | Surface wash |
| Ch.M. VIII | East Area | Q17:802 | 83.36 | Pit |
| Ch.M. VIII | East Area | Q17:802 | 83.19 | Pit |
| Ch.M. VIII | East Area | Q17:802 | 83.09 | Pit |
| Ch.M. VIII | East Area | Q17:803 | 83.41 | Pit |
| Ch.M. VIII | East Area | Q17:803 | 83.37 | Pit |
| Ch.M. VIII | East Area | Q17:803 | 83.08 | Pit |
| Ch.M. VIII | East Area | Q17:803 | 83.01 | Pit |
| Ch.M. VIII | East Area | Q17:803 | 82.91 | Pit |
| Ch.M. VIII | East Area | Q17:803 | 82.75 | Pit |
| Ch.M. VIII | East Area | Q17:803 | 82.70 | Pit |
| Ch.M. VIII | East Area | Q17:803 | 82.58 | Pit |
| Ch.M. VIII | East Area | Q17:803 | 82.56 | Pit |
| Ch.M. VIII | East Area | Q17:803 | 82.54 | Pit |
| Ch.M. VIII | East Area | Q17:803 | 82.42 | Pit |
| Ch.M. VIII | East Area | Q17:804 | 83.11 | Inside kiln |
| Ch.M. VIII | East Area | Q17:804 | 83.00 | Vicinity of PL drain |
| Ch.M. VIII | East Area | Q17:804 South | 82.98 | Inside kiln |
| Ch.M. VIII | East Area | Q17:804 South | 82.85 | Inside kiln |
| Ch.M. VIII | East Area | Q17:805 | 83.03 | Room floor |
| Ch.M. VIII | East Area | Q17:805 | 82.87 | Room floor |
| Ch.M. VIII | East Area | Q17:805 | 82.84 | Room floor |
| Ch.M. VIII | East Area | Q17:805 | 82.64 | Room floor |
| Ch.M. VIII | East Area | Q17:806 | 83.00 | Room floor |

| *Season* | *Area* | *Provenance* | *Elevation* | *Type of Deposit or Feature* |
|---|---|---|---|---|
| **Protoliterate** (*cont.*) | | | | |
| Ch.M. VIII | East Area | Q17:806 | 82 .84 | Room floor |
| Ch.M. VIII | East Area | Q17:807 | 83.04 | Occupational debris |
| Ch.M. VIII | East Area | Q17:810 | 82.88 | Inside kiln |
| Ch.M. VIII | East Area | Q17:811 | 82.69 | Supra floor fill |
| Ch.M. VIII | East Area | Q17:811 | 82.32 | Supra floor fill |
| Ch.M. VIII | East Area | Q17:813 | 82.90 | Surface wash |
| Ch.M. VIII | East Area | Q17:813 | 82.51 | Supra floor fill |
| Ch.M. VIII | East Area | Q17:814 | 83.46 | Surface wash |
| Ch.M. VIII | East Area | Q17:814 | 83.30 | Pit |
| Ch.M. VIII | East Area | Q17:814 | 83.27 | Surface wash |
| Ch.M. VIII | East Area | Q17:814 | 83.03 | Pit |
| Ch.M. VIII | East Area | Q17:816 | 83.23 | Occupational debris |
| Ch.M. VIII | East Area | Q17:816 | 82.67 | Room floor |
| Ch.M. VIII | East Area | Q17:816 | 82.59 | Room floor |
| Ch.M. VIII | East Area | Q17:817 | 83.06 | Room |
| Ch.M. VIII | East Area | Q17:817 | 83.00 | Room |
| Ch.M. VIII | East Area | Q17:817 | 82.49 | Room |
| Ch.M. VIII | East Area | Q17:819 | 82.79 | Surface wash |
| Ch.M. VIII | East Area | Q17:821 | 82.37–81.78 | Pit |
| Ch.M. VIII | East Area | Q17:822 | 82.34 | Kiln area |
| Ch.M. VIII | East Area | Q17:824 | 83.07 | Occupational debris |
| Ch.M. VIII | East Area | Q17:826 | 82.20 | Room |
| Ch.M. VIII | East Area | R16:801 | 84.18 | Surface wash |
| Ch.M. VIII | East Area | R16:801 | 83.91 | Surface wash |
| Ch.M. VIII | East Area | R16:801 | 83.79 | Occupational debris |
| Ch.M. VIII | East Area | R16:801 | 83.76 | Room |
| Ch.M. VIII | East Area | R16:802 | 83.73 | Pit |
| Ch.M. VIII | East Area | R16:802 | 83.51 | Pit |
| Ch.M. VIII | East Area | R16:804 | 83.53 | Room |
| Ch.M. VIII | East Area | R16:804 | 83.09 | Room |
| Ch.M. VIII | East Area | R16:805 | 83.80 | Room |
| Ch.M. VIII | East Area | R16:805 | 83.15 | Room |
| Ch.M. VIII | East Area | R16:806 | 83.54 | Room |
| Ch.M. VIII | East Area | R16:806 | 83.49 | Room |
| Ch.M. VIII | East Area | R16:807 | 82.69 | Pit |
| Ch.M. VIII | East Area | R17:801 Plot 1 | 84.02 | Surface wash |

| *Season* | *Area* | *Provenance* | *Elevation* | *Type of Deposit or Feature* |
|---|---|---|---|---|
| **Protoliterate** (*cont.*) | | | | |
| Ch.M. VIII | East Area | R17:801 Plot 1 South | 83.68 | Room |
| Ch.M. VIII | East Area | R17:801 Plot 3 | 84.08 | Surface wash |
| Ch.M. VIII | East Area | R17:801 | N/A | Ashy pit lined with bricks (kiln?) |
| Ch.M. VIII | East Area | R17:803 | 83.49 | Ashy pit lined with bricks (kiln?) |
| Ch.M. VIII | East Area | R17:803 | 83.28 | Ashy pit lined with bricks (kiln?) |
| Ch.M. VIII | East Area | R17:803 | 82.99 | Ashy pit lined with bricks (kiln) |
| Ch.M. VIII | East Area | R17:804 | 83.68 | Room |
| Ch.M. VIII | East Area | R17:805 | 83.68 | Room |
| Ch.M. VIII | East Area | R17:806 | 83.61 | Room |
| Ch.M. VIII | East Area | R17:808 | 84.00 | Room |
| Ch.M. VIII | East Area | R17:808 | 83.15 | Room |
| Ch.M. VIII | East Area | R17:808 | 83.01 | Room |
| Ch.M. VIII | East Area | R17:810 | 83.02 | Room |
| Ch.M. VIII | East Area | R17:812 | 83.47 | Occupational deposit |
| Ch.M. VIII | East Area | R17:813 | 82.56 | Room floor |
| Ch.M. VIII | East Area | R17:814 | 83.91 | Room |
| Ch.M. VIII | Gully Cut | S22:801 | 77.22 | Surface wash |
| Ch.M. VIII | Gully Cut | S22:801 North | 77.22 | Surface wash |
| Ch.M. VIII | Gully Cut | S22:802 | 77.20 | Occupational debris |
| Ch.M. VIII | Gully Cut | S22:802 South | 76.78 | Occupational debris |
| Ch.M. VIII | Gully Cut | S22:803 | 77.01 | Pit |
| Ch.M. VIII | Gully Cut | S22:803 | 76.41 | Pit |
| Ch.M. VIII | Gully Cut | S22:804 | 76.49 | Pit |
| Ch.M. IX | High Mound | N9:901 | 90.20 | Mudbrick detritus |
| Ch.M. IX | High Mound | N9:903 | 90.15 | Mudbrick detritus |
| Ch.M. IX | High Mound | N9:904 | 90.15 | Mudbrick detritus |
| Ch.M. IX | High Mound | N9:905 | 90.38 | Baked-brick pavement |
| Ch.M. IX | High Mound | N9:907 | 89.80 | Occupational debris |
| Ch.M. IX | High Mound | N9:908 | 89.80 | Occupational debris |
| Ch.M. XI | East Area | P17:1101 | 81.74 | Pottery deposit in long room |
| Ch.M. XI | East Area | P17:1102 | 81.65 | Mudbrick detritus |
| Ch.M. XI | East Area | P17:1103 | 81.56 | Beaten earth floor |

| Season | Area | Provenance | Elevation | Type of Deposit or Feature |
|---|---|---|---|---|
| **Protoliterate** (*cont.*) | | | | |
| Ch.M. XI | East Area | P17:1103 North | 81.70 | Mudbrick detritus |
| Ch.M. XI | East Area | P17:1104 | 81.54 | Beaten earth floor |
| Ch.M. XI | East Area | P17:1106 | 81.60 | Occupational debris |
| **Protoliterate and Miscellaneous** | | | | |
| Ch.M. V | Gully Cut | S22:507 | 75.97 | Occupational debris |
| Ch.M. VII | Gully Cut | S22:701 | 76.43 | Occupational debris |
| **Mixed Protoliterate and Iron III / Achaemenid** | | | | |
| Ch.M. III | East Area | P18:203 | 81.00 | Settlement area |
| Ch.M. IV | Trench XIII | K23:400 | 82.80–82.55 | Settlement area |
| Ch.M. IV | Trench XIII | L23:400 | 83.59–83.44 | Settlement area |
| Ch.M. IV | Trench V:A | P17:401 | 82.20–81.80 | Occupational debris |
| Ch.M. IV | Trench V:A | P17:401 | 82.17 | Packed earth platform |
| Ch.M. V | Trench XIII | L22:501 | 83.21–83.06 | Settlement area |
| Ch.M. V | Trench XIII | L22:501 | 83.06–82.96 | Settlement area |
| Ch.M. V | Trench XIII | L22:501 | 82.96–82.76 | Settlement area |
| Ch.M. VIII | East Area | Q17:801 Plot 2 | 83.87 | Occupational debris |
| Ch.M. VIII | East Area | Q17:801 Plot 2 | 83.44 | Occupational debris |
| Ch.M. VIII | East Area | Q17:801 Plot 3 | 83.99 | Surface wash |
| Ch.M. VIII | East Area | Q17:801 Plot 3 | 83.69 | Occupational debris |
| Ch.M. VIII | East Area | Q17:801 Plot 4 | 83.69 | Surface wash |
| Ch.M. VIII | East Area | Q17:801 Plot 5 | 83.50 | Surface wash |
| Ch.M. VIII | East Area | Q17:801 Plot 6 | 83.58 | Surface wash |
| Ch.M. VIII | East Area | Q17:801 Plot 6 | 83.28 | Occupational debris |
| Ch.M. VIII | East Area | Q17:801 Plot 6 | 83.17 | Occupational debris |
| Ch.M. VIII | East Area | Q17:801 Plot 7 | 83.58 | Occupational debris |
| Ch.M. VIII | East Area | Q17:801 Plot 7 | 83.57 | Surface wash |
| Ch.M. VIII | East Area | Q17:801 Plot 7 | 83.31 | Occupational debris |
| Ch.M. VIII | East Area | R17:801 Plot 3 | 83.82 | Room |
| **Iron III / Achaemenid** | | | | |
| Ch.M. III | East Area | Q18:305 | 82.00–80.00 | Room |
| Ch.M. III | East Area | Q18:305 | 81.15–81.00 | Room |
| Ch.M. VIII | East Area | P17:802 | 83.27 | Occupational debris |
| Ch.M. VIII | East Area | P17:802 | 82.82 | Occupational debris |
| Ch.M. VIII | East Area | P17:802 | 82.45 | Occupational debris |
| Ch.M. VIII | East Area | Q17:807 | 83.50 | Room floor |
| Ch.M. VIII | East Area | Q17:807 | 83.13 | Hearth |

| *Season* | *Area* | *Provenance* | *Elevation* | *Type of Deposit or Feature* |
|---|---|---|---|---|
| **Iron III / Achaemenid** (*cont.*) | | | | |
| Ch.M. VIII | East Area | Q17:812 | 82.69 | Pit |
| Ch.M. VIII | East Area | Q17:825 | 83.27 | Surface wash |
| Ch.M. VIII | East Area | Q17:825 | 82.68 | Occupational debris |
| Ch.M. VIII | East Area | Q17:825 North | 82.72 | Pit |
| Ch.M. VIII | Trench XXXVII | Q24:801 East | N/A | Pit |
| Ch.M. VIII | Trench XXXVII | Q24:802 West | 78.21 | Pit |
| Ch.M. VIII | Trench XXXVII | Q24:802 West | 77.98 | Pit |
| Ch.M. VIII | Trench XXXVII | Q24:802 West | 77.59 | Pit |
| Ch.M. VIII | Trench XXXVII | Q24:802 West | 76.89 | Pit |
| Ch.M. VIII | Trench XXXVII | Q24:802 West | 76.64 | Pit |
| Ch.M. VIII | Trench XXXVII | Q24:803 | 78.61 | Pit |
| Ch.M. VIII | Trench XXXVII | Q24:803 | 77.82 | Pit |
| **Old Elamite (Sukkalmah)** | | | | |
| Ch.M. III | High Mound | O7:301 | 91.30 | Fallen bricks |
| Ch.M. III | High Mound | O7:302 | 91.20 | Mudbrick detritus |
| Ch.M. IV | High Mound Southeast P10:402 | 87.60 | Fallen bricks | |
| Ch.M. IV | High Mound Southeast | P10:402 | 87.23 | Burial no. 432 |
| Ch.M. X | High Mound | O8:1002 | 91.45 | Hard surface |
| Ch.M. X | High Mound | O8:1003 | 91.50 | Mudbrick detritus |
| Ch.M. X | High Mound | O8:1004 North | 91.10 | Mudbrick detritus |
| Ch.M. X | High Mound | O8:1007 | 91.28 | Brick pavement |
| Ch.M. X | High Mound | O9:1007 North | 90.80 | Mudbrick detritus |
| Ch.M. X | High Mound | O9:1010 | 90.80 | Mudbrick detritus |
| **Indeterminate** | | | | |
| Ch.M. V | Sounding I | S-T26 | N/A | Slope wash |
| Ch.M. V | Trench XXV | R20:805 | 77.97 | Surface wash |
| Ch.M. V | Trench XXV | R20:514 | 76.27 | Settlement area |
| Ch.M. VI | Trench XXI | Q23:606 | 81.33 | Occupational debris |
| Ch.M. VI | Trench XXI | P22:608 | 79.98 | Occupational debris |
| Ch.M. VI | Trench XXV | R20:603 | 75.70 | Settlement area |
| Ch.M. VI | Trench XXV | R20:601 | 80.14 | Surface wash |
| Ch.M. VI | Trench XXV | R20:601 | 79.26 | Occupational debris |
| Ch.M. VI | Trench XXV | R20:601 | 78.80 | Occupational debris |
| Ch.M. VI | Trench XXV | R20:601 West | 78.48 | Occupational debris |
| Ch.M. VI | Trench XXV | S20:603 | 79.95 | Occupational debris |
| Ch.M. VI | Trench XXV | South of S20:603 | 78.74–78.31 | Occupational debris |

| *Season* | *Area* | *Provenance* | *Elevation* | *Type of Deposit or Feature* |
|---|---|---|---|---|
| **Indeterminate** (*cont.*) | | | | |
| Ch.M. VI | Trench XXV | S20:611 | 78.74–78.31 | Occupational debris |
| Ch.M. VI | Trench XXV | S20:612 | 78.98 | Near wall |
| Ch.M. VI | Trench XXV | S20:612 | 76.60 | Occupational debris |
| Ch.M. VI | Trench XXV | S20:618 | 75.60 | Occupational debris |
| Ch.M. VI | Trench XXV | S20:618 | 76.63 | Occupational debris |
| Ch.M. VI | Trench XXV | S20:618 | 75.60 | Occupational debris |
| Ch.M. VI | Trench XXV | S20:618 | 75.56 | Occupational debris |
| Ch.M. VI | Trench XXV | S20:619 | 75.46 | Occupational debris |
| Ch.M. VI | Trench XXV | S20:619 | 76.10 | Occupational debris |
| Ch.M. VI | Trench XXV | S20:619 | 75.85 | Occupational debris |
| Ch.M. VI | Trench XXV | S20:619 | 75.59 | Occupational debris |
| Ch.M. VI | Trench XXXIII | S19:601 West | 78.48 | Occupational debris |
| Ch.M. VI | Trench XXXIII | S19:601 North | 75.07 | Occupational debris |
| Ch.M. VI | Trench XXXIII | S19:601 North | 74.47 | Occupational debris |
| Ch.M. VI | Trench XXXIII | S19:601 North | 73.95 | Occupational debris |
| Ch.M. VI | Trench XXXIII | S19:602 North | 77.21 | Occupational debris |
| Ch.M. VI | Trench XXXIII | S19:602 North | 77.03 | Occupational debris |
| Ch.M. VII | Trench XXXVI | G27:701 | 82.19 | Occupational debris |
| Ch.M. VII | Trench XXXVI | G28:704 | 79.81 | Surface wash |
| Ch.M. VII | Trench XXXVI | G28:704 | 79.69 | Surface wash |
| Ch.M. VII | Trench XXXVI | G28:704 | 76.96 | Surface wash |
| Ch.M. VIII | Trench XXI | P22:801 | 80.26 | Occupational debris |
| Ch.M. VIII | Trench XXI | Q22:804 North | 78.83 | Occupational debris |
| Ch.M. VIII | Trench XXI | Q22:804 South | 78.47 | Occupational debris |
| Ch.M. VIII | Trench XXI | Q23:802 North | 78.49 | Occupational debris |
| Ch.M. VIII | Trench XXI | Q23:803 Southwest | 79.53 | Surface wash |
| Ch.M. VIII | Trench XXXVII | Q24:801 | 78.67 | Occupational debris |
| Ch.M. VIII | Trench XXXVII | Q24:801 | 78.67 | Occupational debris |
| Ch.M. VIII | Trench XXXVII | Q24:802 | 78.89 | Surface wash |
| Ch.M. VIII | Trench XXXVII | Q25:803 | 79.34 | Surface wash |
| Ch.M. VIII | Trench XXXVII | Q25:801 | 78.30 | Surface wash |
| Ch.M. VIII | Gully Cut | S22:619 | 76.36 | Occupational debris |
| **Mixed** | | | | |
| Ch.M. VI | Trench XXI | P22:623 | 82.82 | Surface wash |
| Ch.M. VI | Trench XXI | Q22:605 North | 79.39 | Room |
| Ch.M. VI | Trench XXI | Q22:605 North | 79.06 | Room |

| Season | Area | Provenance | Elevation | Type of Deposit or Feature |
|---|---|---|---|---|
| **Mixed** (*cont.*) | | | | |
| Ch.M. VI | Trench XXI | Q22:605 South | 80.11 | Surface wash |
| Ch.M. VI | Trench XXI | Q22:608 | 80.11 | Surface wash |
| Ch.M. VI | Trench XXI | Q22:608 | 79.95–79.57 | Occupational debris |
| Ch.M. VI | Trench XXV | R20:603 | 78.56 | Occupational debris |
| Ch.M. VII | Trench XXXII | R23:710 | 76.10 | Occupational debris |
| Ch.M. VII | Trench XXXII | R23:711 | 77.59 | Occupational debris |
| Ch.M. VII | Trench XXXII | R23:711 | 77.53 | Occupational debris |
| Ch.M. VII | Trench XXXII | R23:711 | 77.02 | Occupational debris |
| Ch.M. VII | Trench XXXII | R23:711 | 76.20 | Occupational debris |
| Ch.M. VII | Trench XXXII | R23:711 West | 78.00 | Occupational debris |
| Ch.M. VII | Trench XXXII | R23:712 | 78.29 | Occupational debris |
| Ch.M. VII | Trench XXXII | R23:712 | 77.86 | Occupational debris |
| Ch.M. VII | Trench XXXII | R23:712 | 76.27 | Occupational debris |
| Ch.M. VII | Trench XXXII | R23:712 North | 75.77 | Occupational debris |
| Ch.M. VIII | Trench XXI | Q22:801 | 78.84 | Surface wash |
| Ch.M. VIII | Trench XXI | Q22:802 | 78.99 | Surface wash |
| Ch.M. VIII | Trench XXI | Q22:802 | 78.83 | Surface wash |
| Ch.M. VIII | Trench XXI | Q22:802 | 78.39 | Occupational debris |
| Ch.M. VIII | Trench XXI | Q22:802 South | 78.16–78.06 | Occupational debris |
| Ch.M. VIII | Trench XXI | Q22:803 North | 79.09 | Settlement area |
| Ch.M. VIII | Trench XXI | Q22:803 North | 78.72 | Occupational debris |
| Ch.M. VIII | Trench XXI | Q22:804 South | 78.56 | Occupational debris |
| Ch.M. VIII | Trench XXI | Q23:804 | 79.69 | Surface wash |
| Ch.M. VIII | Trench XXI | Q23:816 | 77.28 | Occupational debris |
| Ch.M. VIII | Trench XXI | Q23:816 | 76.86 | Occupational debris |
| Ch.M. VIII | Trench XXI | Q23:820 | 79.81 | Surface wash |
| Ch.M. VIII | Trench XXI | Q23:823 | 78.72 | Surface wash |
| Ch.M. VIII | Trench XXI | Q23:825 | 78.43 | Occupational debris |
| Ch.M. VIII | Trench XXI | Q23:825 | 78.36 | Occupational debris |
| Ch.M. VIII | Trench XXI | Q23:825 | 77.97 | Occupational debris |
| Ch.M. VIII | Gully Cut | S22:823 West | 76.35 | Occupational debris |
| **Mixed Susiana** | | | | |
| Ch.M. V | Trench XXV | R20:512 | 78.41 | Settlement area |
| Ch.M. VI | Trench XXXII | R23:601 South | 76.52 | Pit |
| **Archaic Susiana** | | | | |
| Ch.M. V | Gully Cut | S22:502 | N/A | Occupational debris |

| *Season* | *Area* | *Provenance* | *Elevation* | *Type of Deposit or Feature* |
|---|---|---|---|---|
| **Archaic Susiana** (*cont.*) | | | | |
| Ch.M. V | Gully Cut | S22:507 | N/A | Occupational debris |
| Ch.M. V | Trench XXXII | R23:504 | 77.25 | Room |
| Ch.M. VI | Trench XXV | S20:617 | 77.04 | Occupational debris |
| Ch.M. VI | Trench XXXII | R23:601 | 77.66 | Surface wash |
| Ch.M. VII | Trench XXI | Q22:702 | N/A | Occupational debris |
| Ch.M. VII | Trench XXI | Q22:702 | N/A | Occupational debris |
| Ch.M. VII | Trench XXI | Q22:705 | N/A | Occupational debris |
| Ch.M. VII | Trench XXXII | R23:710 | 77.95 | Occupational debris |
| Ch.M. VIII | Trench XXI | Q22:807 | N/A | Occupational debris |
| Ch.M. VIII | Trench XXI | Q22:808 | N/A | Room |
| Ch.M. VIII | Trench XXI | Q22:810 | N/A | Room |
| Ch.M. VIII | Trench XXI | Q22:811 | N/A | Occupational debris |
| Ch.M. VIII | Trench XXI | Q23:822 | N/A | Occupational debris |
| Ch.M. VIII | Trench XXI | Q23:822 | N/A | Occupational debris |
| **Mixed Archaic Susiana / Early Susiana** | | | | |
| Ch.M. V | Gully Cut | S22:502 | 74.78 | Fallen brickwork |
| Ch.M. V | Gully Cut | S22:502 | 74.76 | Fallen brickwork |
| Ch.M. VI | Trench XXI | P22:613 | 80.22 | Room |
| Ch.M. VI | Trench XXI | P22:614 | 80.92 | Occupational debris |
| Ch.M. VI | Trench XXI | P22:618 | 80.19 | Occupational debris |
| Ch.M. VI | Trench XXI | P22:618 | 80.18 | Occupational debris |
| Ch.M. VI | Trench XXI | P22:618 | 79.63 | Occupational debris |
| Ch.M. VI | Trench XXI | P22:620 | 80.18 | Room |
| Ch.M. VI | Trench XXI | P22:620 | 81.01 | Room |
| Ch.M. VI | Trench XXI | P22:628 | 80.89 | Occupational debris |
| Ch.M. VI | Trench XXI | P22:628 | 80.17 | Room |
| Ch.M. VI | Trench XXI | P22:629 | 80.20 | Occupational debris |
| Ch.M. VI | Trench XXI | P22:629 | 80.16 | Occupational debris |
| Ch.M. VI | Trench XXI | P22:630 | 80.38 | Occupational debris |
| Ch.M. VI | Trench XXI | Q22:606 | 80.35 | Occupational debris |
| Ch.M. VI | Trench XXI | Q22:606 | 80.20 | Room |
| Ch.M. VI | Trench XXV | S20:617 | 78.08 | Occupational debris |
| Ch.M. VI | Trench XXV | S20:617 | 77.90 | Occupational debris |
| Ch.M. VII | Trench XXI | Q22:704 | 79.95 | Surface wash |
| Ch.M. VII | Trench XXI | Q22:704 | 79.49 | Occupational debris |
| Ch.M. VII | Trench XXI | Q22:707 | 79.30 | Occupational debris |

| *Season* | *Area* | *Provenance* | *Elevation* | *Type of Deposit or Feature* |
|---|---|---|---|---|
| **Mixed Archaic Susiana / Early Susiana** (*cont.*) | | | | |
| Ch.M. VII | Trench XXI | Q22:707 | 79.07 | Occupational debris |
| Ch.M. VII | Trench XXI | Q22:707 South | 79.40 | Occupational debris |
| Ch.M. VII | Trench XXXII | R23:702 | 76.78 | Occupational debris |
| Ch.M. VIII | Trench XXI | Q22:801 | 78.73 | Occupational debris |
| Ch.M. VIII | Trench XXI | Q22:801 | 78.60 | Occupational debris |
| Ch.M. VIII | Trench XXI | Q22:801 | 78.38 | Occupational debris |
| Ch.M. VIII | Trench XXI | Q22:803 | 78.16–78.06 | Occupational debris |
| Ch.M. VIII | Trench XXI | Q22:803 | 78.16 | Occupational debris |
| Ch.M. VIII | Trench XXI | Q22:803 North | 78.38 | Occupational debris |
| Ch.M. VIII | Trench XXI | Q22:803 South | 78.96 | Occupational debris |
| Ch.M. VIII | Trench XXI | Q22:803 South | 78.61 | Occupational debris |
| Ch.M. VIII | Trench XXI | Q22:803 South | 78.52 | Occupational debris |
| Ch.M. VIII | Trench XXI | Q22:803 South | 78.16–78.06 | Occupational debris |
| Ch.M. VIII | Trench XXI | Q22:803 South | 78.16 | Occupational debris |
| Ch.M. VIII | Trench XXI | Q22:803 South | 78.06 | Occupational debris |
| Ch.M. VIII | Trench XXI | Q22:803 South | 77.91 | Occupational debris |
| Ch.M. VIII | Trench XXI | Q22:804 North | 79.04 | Occupational debris |
| Ch.M. VIII | Trench XXI | Q22:804 North | 78.24 | Occupational debris |
| Ch.M. VIII | Trench XXI | Q22:804 South | 79.33 | Occupational debris |
| Ch.M. VIII | Trench XXI | Q22:804 | 79.01 | Occupational debris |
| Ch.M. VIII | Trench XXI | Q23:801 | 79.15 | Surface wash |
| Ch.M. VIII | Trench XXI | Q23:803 | 78.95 | Occupational debris |
| Ch.M. VIII | Trench XXI | Q23:808 | 78.31 | Occupational debris |
| Ch.M. VIII | Trench XXI | Q23:809 West | 78.56 | Occupational debris |
| Ch.M. VIII | Trench XXI | Q23:814 | 78.83 | Room |
| Ch.M. VIII | Trench XXI | Q23:820 | 77.83 | Occupational debris |
| Ch.M. VIII | Trench XXI | Q23:821 | 79.13 | Room |
| Ch.M. VIII | Trench XXI | Q23:822 | 78.26 | Occupational debris |
| Ch.M. VIII | Trench XXXVII | Q24:802 East | 77.33 | Occupational debris |
| Ch.M. VIII | Gully Cut | S22:824 | 75.53 | Occupational debris |
| **Mixed Archaic / Early / Middle Susiana** | | | | |
| Ch.M. VI | Trench XXV | R20:605 | 77.80 | Occupational debris |
| Ch.M. VI | Trench XXXII | R23:601 | 76.95 | Occupational debris |
| Ch.M. VI | Trench XXXII | R23:601 | 76.94 | Occupational debris |
| Ch.M. VI | Trench XXXII | R23:601 | 76.55 | Occupational debris |
| Ch.M. VI | Trench XXXII | R23:601 Northeast | 76.42 | Occupational debris |

| *Season* | *Area* | *Provenance* | *Elevation* | *Type of Deposit or Feature* |
|---|---|---|---|---|
| **Mixed Archaic / Early / Middle Susiana** (*cont.*) | | | | |
| Ch.M. VII | Trench XXXII | R23:701 | 76.49 | Occupational debris |
| Ch.M. VII | Trench XXXII | R23:701 | 76.16 | Occupational debris |
| Ch.M. VII | Trench XXXII | R23:702 | 77.12 | Occupational debris |
| Ch.M. VII | Trench XXXII | R23:702 | 76.37 | Occupational debris |
| Ch.M. VII | Trench XXXII | R23:702 | 76.19 | Occupational debris |
| Ch.M. VII | Trench XXXII | R23:702 | 76.13 | Occupational debris |
| Ch.M. VII | Trench XXXII | R23:704 | 75.97 | Occupational debris |
| Ch.M. VII | Trench XXXII | R23:704 | 75.47 | Occupational debris |
| Ch.M. VII | Trench XXXII | R23:704 | 75.44 | Occupational debris |
| Ch.M. VII | Trench XXXII | R23:704 | 75.44 | Occupational debris |
| Ch.M. VII | Trench XXXII | R23:704 | 75.19 | Occupational debris |
| Ch.M. VII | Trench XXXII | R23:704 | 75.03 | Occupational debris |
| Ch.M. VII | Trench XXXII | R23:704 | 74.90 | Occupational debris |
| Ch.M. VII | Trench XXXII | R23:705 | 76.00 | Occupational debris |
| Ch.M. VII | Trench XXXII | R23:705 | 75.63 | Occupational debris |
| Ch.M. VII | Trench XXXII | R23:705 | 75.32 | Occupational debris |
| Ch.M. VII | Trench XXXII | R23:706 | 76.72 | Occupational debris |
| Ch.M. VII | Trench XXXII | R23:706 | 76.64 | Occupational debris |
| Ch.M. VII | Trench XXXII | R23:706 | 76.19 | Occupational debris |
| Ch.M. VII | Trench XXXII | R23:706 | 75.89 | Occupational debris |
| Ch.M. VII | Trench XXXII | R23:706 | 75.31 | Occupational debris |
| Ch.M. VIII | Gully Cut | S22:823 West | 76.35 | Occupational debris |
| Ch.M. VIII | Gully Cut | S22:832 | 77.58 | Surface wash |
| Ch.M. VIII | Trench XXI | Q22:803 | 79.48 | Surface wash |
| Ch.M. VIII | Trench XXI | Q22:803 South | 78.31 | Occupational debris |
| Ch.M. VIII | Trench XXI | Q23:829 | 78.37 | Occupational debris |
| **Mixed Early / Middle Susiana** | | | | |
| Ch.M. V | Trench XXXI | P27:501 | N/A | Settlement area |
| Ch.M. V | Trench XXXI | P27:505 | 79.10 | Settlement area |
| Ch.M. VI | Trench XXI | P22:601 | 82.55 | Surface wash |
| Ch.M. VI | Trench XXI | P22:601 | 82.25 | Surface wash |
| Ch.M. VI | Trench XXI | P22:601 | 82.23 | Surface wash |
| Ch.M. VI | Trench XXI | P22:602 | 81.77 | Room |
| Ch.M. VI | Trench XXI | P22:603 | 81.77–81.40 | Occupational debris |
| Ch.M. VI | Trench XXI | P22:604 | 82.15 | Surface wash |
| Ch.M. VI | Trench XXI | P22:606 North | 81.77 | Occupational debris |

| *Season* | *Area* | *Provenance* | *Elevation* | *Type of Deposit or Feature* |
|---|---|---|---|---|
| **Mixed Early / Middle Susiana** (*cont.*) | | | | |
| Ch.M. VI | Trench XXI | P22:606 North | 81.73 | Occupational debris |
| Ch.M. VI | Trench XXI | P22:606 Northeast | 81.52 | Occupational debris |
| Ch.M. VI | Trench XXI | P22:606 South | 81.69 | Occupational debris |
| Ch.M. VI | Trench XXI | P22:609 | 81.67 | Room |
| Ch.M. VI | Trench XXI | P22:611 | 81.14 | Occupational debris |
| Ch.M. VI | Trench XXI | P22:611 | 80.94 | Occupational debris |
| Ch.M. VI | Trench XXI | P22:621 West | 82.19 | Surface wash |
| Ch.M. VI | Trench XXI | P22:623 East | 82.46 | Surface wash |
| Ch.M. VI | Trench XXI | P22:623 West | 82.73 | Surface wash |
| Ch.M. VI | Trench XXI | P22:625 | 81.91 | Room |
| Ch.M. VI | Trench XXI | P23:601 | 81.77 | Occupational debris |
| Ch.M. VI | Trench XXI | P23:602 | 81.07 | Occupational debris |
| Ch.M. VI | Trench XXI | P23:602 | 81.00 | Occupational debris |
| Ch.M. VI | Trench XXI | P23:606 | 81.22 | Occupational debris |
| Ch.M. VI | Trench XXI | P23:606 | 80.69 | Occupational debris |
| Ch.M. VI | Trench XXI | P23:609 | 81.24 | Occupational debris |
| Ch.M. VI | Trench XXI | P23:609 | 80.93 | Occupational debris |
| Ch.M. VI | Trench XXI | P23:611 | 80.54 | Occupational debris |
| Ch.M. VI | Trench XXI | Q22:601 | 81.24 | Occupational debris |
| Ch.M. VI | Trench XXI | Q22:602 North | 80.80 | Surface wash |
| Ch.M. VI | Trench XXI | Q22:603 | 81.42 | Surface wash |
| Ch.M. VI | Trench XXI | Q23:601 | 81.40–80.63 | Surface wash |
| Ch.M. VII | Trench XXXII | R23:701 | 77.20 | Occupational debris |
| Ch.M. VII | Trench XXXII | R23:701 | 76.88 | Occupational debris |
| Ch.M. VII | Trench XXXII | R23:702 | 76.63 | Occupational debris |
| Ch.M. VII | Trench XXXVI | G29:702 | 77.42 | Occupational debris |
| Ch.M. VII | Trench XXXVI | G29:703 North | 76.66 | Occupational debris |
| Ch.M. VIII | Trench XXI | Q22:802 | 77.63 | Occupational debris |
| Ch.M. VIII | Trench XXI | Q23:804 | 78.75 | Occupational debris |
| Ch.M. VIII | Trench XXI | Q23:820 | 79.65 | Surface wash |
| Ch.M. VIII | Trench XXI | Q23:821 | 79.36 | Surface wash |
| Ch.M. VIII | Trench XXI | Q23:821 | 79.31 | Surface wash |
| Ch.M. VIII | Trench XXI | Q24:802 | 78.30 | Occupational debris |
| Ch.M. VIII | Trench XXI | Q25:801 | 77.78 | Occupational debris |
| Ch.M. VIII | Gully Cut | S22:801 North | 76.83 | Occupational debris |
| Ch.M. VIII | Gully Cut | S22:801 East | 76.88 | Occupational debris |

| *Season* | *Area* | *Provenance* | *Elevation* | *Type of Deposit or Feature* |
|---|---|---|---|---|
| **Mixed Early / Middle Susiana** (*cont.*) | | | | |
| Ch.M. VIII | Gully Cut | S22:806 West | 76.95 | Occupational debris |
| Ch.M. VIII | Gully Cut | S22:806 West | 76.73 | Floor |
| Ch.M. VIII | Gully Cut | S22:813 | 76.33 | Room |
| Ch.M. VIII | Gully Cut | S22:813 | 76.29 | Room |
| Ch.M. VIII | Gully Cut | S22:813 | 76.05 | Supra floor fill |
| Ch.M. VIII | Gully Cut | S22:813 East | 76.31 | Occupational debris |
| Ch.M. VIII | Gully Cut | S22:819 West | 75.79 | Occupational debris |
| **Early Susiana + Protoliterate** | | | | |
| Ch.M. V | Trench XXV | R20:511 | 77.96 | Occupational debris |
| Ch.M. V | Trench XXV | R20:511 | 77.84 | Occupational debris |
| Ch.M. V | Trench XXXI | P27:504 | 78.00 | Settlement area |
| Ch.M. VI | Trench XXI | P22:623 North | 82.82 | Surface wash |
| Ch.M. VII | Trench XXXII | R23:711 | 76.58 | Occupational debris |
| Ch.M. VIII | Trench XXI | Q23:803 North | 79.00 | Surface wash |
| **Mixed Archaic / Middle Susiana** | | | | |
| Ch.M. V | Trench XXXII | R23:502 | 77.20 | Settlement area |
| Ch.M. V | Trench XXXII | R23:502 | 76.91 | Settlement area |
| **Mixed Archaic Susiana / Protoliterate** | | | | |
| Ch.M. IV | Trench XXV | R21:411 | 77.53 | Fallen brickwork |
| Ch.M. IV | Gully Cut | S22:401 East | 75.40 | Occupational debris |
| Ch.M. V | Trench XXV | R20:504 | 77.80 | Room |
| Ch.M. V | Trench XXV | R20:510 | 76.10 | Pit |
| Ch.M. VII | Trench XXXII | R23:711 | 77.40 | Occupational debris |
| Ch.M. VII | Trench XXXII | R23:711 | 77.05 | Occupational debris |
| Ch.M. VII | Gully Cut | S22:701 | 75.71 | Occupational debris |
| **Mixed Archaic Susiana 3 / Protoliterate** | | | | |
| Ch.M. V | Gully Cut | S22:507 | 75.89–75.79 | Occupational debris |
| Ch.M. V | Gully Cut | S22:507 | 75.79 | Occupational debris |
| **Middle Susiana / Protoliterate** | | | | |
| Ch.M. VI | Trench XXXIII | S18:603 North | 76.55 | Occupational debris |
| Ch.M. VI | Trench XXXIII | S18:603 North | 76.36 | Occupational debris |
| Ch.M. VI | Trench XXXIII | S18:603 North | 76.08 | Occupational debris |
| Ch.M. VI | Trench XXXIII | S18:603 South | 76.53 | Occupational debris |
| Ch.M. VI | Trench XXXIII | S18:603 South | 76.48 | Occupational debris |
| Ch.M. VI | Trench XXXIII | S19:601 | 77.40 | Occupational debris |
| Ch.M. VI | Trench XXXIII | S19:601 | 77.35 | Occupational debris |

| *Season* | *Area* | *Provenance* | *Elevation* | *Type of Deposit or Feature* |
|---|---|---|---|---|
| **Middle Susiana / Protoliterate** (*cont.*) | | | | |
| Ch.M. VI | Trench XXXV | R20:610 | 76.20 | Occupational debris |
| Ch.M. VI | Trench XXXV | R20:610 | 75.16 | Occupational debris |
| Ch.M. IV | Trench XIII | L23:400 | 83.24–83.90 | Settlement area |
| Ch.M. V | Trench XIII | K23:502 | 82.42–81.48 | Settlement area |
| Ch.M. V | Trench XIII | K23:503 | 82.33–82.23 | Settlement area |
| Ch.M. V | Trench XIII | K23:506 | 81.46 | Room |
| Ch.M. V | Trench XIII | L23:502 | 82.23 | Settlement area |
| Ch.M. V | Trench XXV | R20:501 | 79.23 | Settlement area |
| Ch.M. V | Trench XXV | R20:505 | 78.48 | Settlement area |
| Ch.M. V | Trench XXV | R20:505 | 78.10 | Settlement area |
| Ch.M. V | Trench XXXII | R23:502 | 77.55 | Settlement area |
| Ch.M. V | Sounding I | S-T26 | 72.70 | Slope wash |
| Ch.M. V | Sounding I | S-T26 | 72.10 | Slope wash |
| Ch.M. V | Sounding I | S-T26 | 69.95 | Slope wash |
| Ch.M. V | Sounding I | S-T26 | 69.50 | Slope wash |
| Ch.M. V | Sounding I | S-T26 | 69.10 | Slope wash |
| Ch.M. VI | Trench XXV | R20:602 | 80.12 | Surface wash |
| Ch.M. VI | Trench XXXIII | S19:601 South | 77.55 | Occupational debris |
| Ch.M. VI | Trench XXXIV | T19:601 | 77.45 | Surface wash |
| Ch.M. VI | Trench XXXIV | T19:601 | 75.97 | Occupational debris |
| Ch.M. VI | Trench XXXIV | T19:601 | 74.90 | Occupational debris |
| Ch.M. VII | Trench XXXII | R23:701 | 77.59 | Occupational debris |
| Ch.M. VII | Trench XXXII | R23:702 | 77.38 | Occupational debris |
| Ch.M. VII | Trench XXXII | R23:710 | 78.40 | Surface wash |
| Ch.M. VII | Gully Cut | S22:701 | 75.91 | Occupational debris |
| Ch.M. VIII | Trench XXXVII | Q24:801 | 79.66 | Surface wash |
| Ch.M. VIII | Trench XXXVII | Q24:801 | 79.57 | Surface wash |
| Ch.M. VIII | Trench XXXVII | Q24:801 | 79.00 | Surface wash |
| Ch.M. VIII | Trench XXXVII | Q25:804 | 77.97 | Surface wash |
| Ch.M. VIII | Gully Cut | S22:802 | 77.08 | Occupational debris |
| Ch.M. VIII | Gully Cut | S22:802 | 77.03 | Occupational debris |
| Ch.M. VIII | Gully Cut | S22:802 | 76.99 | Occupational debris |
| Ch.M. VIII | Gully Cut | S22:802 | 76.91 | Occupational debris |
| Ch.M. VIII | Gully Cut | S22:802 | 76.75 | Occupational debris |
| Ch.M. VIII | Gully Cut | S22:802 | 76.70 | Occupational debris |
| Ch.M. VIII | Gully Cut | S22:802 | 76.55 | Occupational debris |

| *Season* | *Area* | *Provenance* | *Elevation* | *Type of Deposit or Feature* |
|---|---|---|---|---|
| **Middle Susiana / Protoliterate** (*cont.*) | | | | |
| Ch.M. VIII | Gully Cut | S22:802 | 76.51 | Occupational debris |
| Ch.M. VIII | Gully Cut | S22:802 North | 77.51 | Surface wash |
| Ch.M. VIII | Gully Cut | S22:802 North | 77.30 | Occupational debris |
| Ch.M. VIII | Gully Cut | S22:802 North | 77.01 | Occupational debris |
| Ch.M. VIII | Gully Cut | S22:806 | 77.20 | Surface wash |
| Ch.M. VIII | Gully Cut | S22:806 North | 77.51 | Surface wash |
| Ch.M. VIII | Gully Cut | S22:806 North | 77.26 | Surface wash |
| **Mixed Susiana / Protoliterate** | | | | |
| Ch.M. V | Trench XXV | R20:501 | 77.34 | Room |
| Ch.M. V | Trench XXV | North of R20:501 | 77.50 | Room |
| Ch.M. V | Trench XXV | R20:502 | 76.18 | Circular bitumen floor |
| Ch.M. V | Trench XXV | R20:505 | 79.28 | Settlement area |
| Ch.M. V | Trench XXV | R20:505 | 78.00 | Settlement area |
| Ch.M. V | Trench XXV | Northwest of R20:507 | 78.70 | Settlement area |
| Ch.M. V | Trench XXV | South of R20:507 | 78.70 | Settlement area |
| Ch.M. V | Trench XXV | R20:508 | 79.32 | Settlement area |
| Ch.M. V | Trench XXV | R20:508 | 79.32 | Pit |
| Ch.M. V | Trench XXV | R20:510 | 77.25 | Occupational debris |
| Ch.M. V | Trench XXV | R21:501 | 77.50 | Room |
| Ch.M. V | Trench XXV | R21:506 | 76.41 | Occupational debris |
| Ch.M. V | Trench XXV | R21:506 | 76.30 | Occupational debris |
| Ch.M. V | Trench XXV | R21:506 East | 75.65 | Settlement area |
| Ch.M. V | Trench XXV | R21:508 | 76.41–76.00 | Settlement area |
| Ch.M. V | Trench XXV | R21:508 | 76.41–75.29 | Settlement area |
| Ch.M. V | Trench XXV | R21:508 | 76.12–76.00 | Settlement area |
| Ch.M. V | Trench XXV | R21:508 | 75.29–75.19 | Settlement area |
| Ch.M. V | Trench XXXI | P27:506 | 79.00 | Settlement area |
| Ch.M. V | Trench XXXII | R23:501 | 78.20 | Surface or slope wash |
| Ch.M. V | Trench XXXII | R23:502 | 77.21 | Settlement area |
| Ch.M. V | Gully Cut | S22:501 | 76.01–75.86 | Occupational debris |
| Ch.M. VI | Trench XXI | P22:604 | 81.71 | Surface wash |
| Ch.M. VI | Trench XXV | R20:606 | 78.42 | Occupational debris |
| Ch.M. VIII | Gully Cut | S22:801 | 76.32 | Occupational debris |
| Ch.M. VIII | Gully Cut | S22:801 South | 76.57 | Occupational debris |
| Ch.M. VIII | Gully Cut | S22:802 | 76.31 | Occupational debris |
| Ch.M. VIII | Gully Cut | S22:802 North | 76.00 | Occupational debris |

| *Season* | *Area* | *Provenance* | *Elevation* | *Type of Deposit or Feature* |
|---|---|---|---|---|
| **Early / Middle Susiana + Protoliterate** | | | | |
| Ch.M. V | Trench XIII | K23:502 | 82.37–81.68 | Settlement area |
| Ch.M. V | Trench XIII | K23:502 | 80.70 | Settlement area |
| Ch.M. V | Trench XXXI | P27:501 North | 79.85–79.00 | Settlement area |
| **Mixed Early Middle Susiana / Protoliterate** | | | | |
| Ch.M. V | Trench XIII | K23:502 | 81.53 | Settlement area |
| Ch.M. V | Trench XIII | K23:502 | 81.12 | Settlement area |
| Ch.M. V | Trench XIII | K23:502 | 81.05 | Settlement area |
| Ch.M. V | Trench XIII | L22:502 | 81.66 | Settlement area |
| Ch.M. VI | Trench XXXI | P27:602 | 79.53 | Surface wash |
| **Mixed Late Middle Susiana / Protoliterate** | | | | |
| Ch.M. VI | Trench XXXIII | S18:601 | 77.49–77.35 | Occupational debris |
| Ch.M. VI | Trench XXXIII | S18:601 | 77.39 | Occupational debris |
| Ch.M. VI | Trench XXXIII | S18:601 | 77.15 | Occupational debris |
| Ch.M. VI | Trench XXXIII | S18:601 North | 76.97 | Occupational debris |
| Ch.M. VI | Trench XXXIII | S18:601 North | 76.68 | Occupational debris |
| Ch.M. VI | Trench XXXIII | S18:601 South | 77.19 | Occupational debris |
| Ch.M. VI | Trench XXXIII | S18:601 South | 76.85 | Occupational debris |
| Ch.M. VI | Trench XXXIII | S18:601 South | 76.40 | Occupational debris |
| Ch.M. VI | Trench XXXIII | S18:601 | 76.95 | Occupational debris |
| Ch.M. VI | Trench XXXIII | S18:602 | 76.89 | Occupational debris |
| Ch.M. VI | Trench XXXIII | S18:602 | 76.68 | Occupational debris |
| Ch.M. VI | Trench XXXIII | S18:602 | 76.48 | Occupational debris |
| Ch.M. VI | Trench XXXIII | S18:602 | 76.48 | Occupational debris |
| Ch.M. VI | Trench XXXIII | S18:602 North | 78.00 | Occupational debris |
| Ch.M. VI | Trench XXXIII | S18:602 North | 77.60 | Occupational debris |
| Ch.M. VI | Trench XXXIII | S18:602 North | 76.32 | Occupational debris |
| Ch.M. VI | Trench XXXIII | S18:602 South | 77.70 | Occupational debris |
| Ch.M. VI | Trench XXXIII | S18:602 Middle | 76.32 | Occupational debris |
| Ch.M. VI | Trench XXXIII | S18:602 Middle | 76.20 | Occupational debris |
| Ch.M. VI | Trench XXXIII | S18:603 | 77.35 | Occupational debris |
| Ch.M. VI | Trench XXXIII | S18:603 | 77.34 | Occupational debris |
| **Approaching or In Virgin Soil** | | | | |
| Ch.M. V | Gully Cut | S23:509 | 73.38–72.35 | Hard packed clean clay |
| Ch.M. VI | Gully Cut | S22:701 | 72.40 | Occupational debris |
| Ch.M. VII | Gully Cut | S22:702 | 72.84–72.64 | Occupational debris |
| Ch.M. VII | Gully Cut | S22:702 | 72.61 | Occupational debris |

| *Season* | *Area* | *Provenance* | *Elevation* | *Type of Deposit or Feature* |
|---|---|---|---|---|
| **Middle Susiana + Protoliterate + Late** | | | | |
| Ch.M. II | Trench XIII | K22:201 West | 83.20 | Settlement area |
| Ch.M. IV | Trench XIII | K22:400 | 83.44–83.29 | Settlement area |
| **Mixed Protoliterate / Late** | | | | |
| Ch.M. IV | Sounding A | L15 | 79.15 | Occupation debris |
| **Probably Iron III / Achaemenid** | | | | |
| Ch.M. VIII | East Area | R17:804 South | 83.34 | Inside kiln area |

# APPENDIX THREE

# FAUNAL REMAINS

The several thousand faunal remains from the excavation of Chogha Mish, too numerous to include here, are presented in an electronic file hosted on the Oriental Institute's Web site: http://oi.uchicago.edu/research/pubs/catalog/oip/oip130.html. A summary of the faunal remains is sorted by period in table 14.

Table 14. Summary of Faunal Remains by Period

| Period | Total of Indentification | *Bos* | *Bovid* | *Camelus* sp. | *Canis aureus* | *Canis familiaris* | *Cervus* | *Dama* | *Equus equus* | *Equus hemionus* or *asinus* | *Equus hemionus* | *Equus* sp. | *Gazelle* | *Gerbillus* sp. | *Goat* | *Hemiechinus* sp. | *Hystrix indica* | *Indeterminate* | Large *Canid* | Large *Felid* |
|---|---|---|---|---|---|---|---|---|---|---|---|---|---|---|---|---|---|---|---|---|
| Ach. | 1,121 | 195 | 1 | 3 | — | 3 | — | — | 6 | — | 2 | 65 | 1 | — | 13 | — | — | 15 | 3 | — |
| Approaching or in virgin soil | 74 | — | — | — | — | — | — | — | — | — | — | — | — | — | — | — | — | — | — | — |
| AS | 214 | 4 | — | — | — | — | — | — | — | — | — | 1 | 2 | — | 1 | — | — | 3 | 2 | — |
| AS 1 | 930 | 33 | — | — | 1 | — | — | — | — | — | — | 29 | 19 | — | 34 | — | — | 14 | 1 | — |
| AS 1–2 | 53 | 2 | — | — | — | — | — | — | — | — | — | — | — | — | 1 | — | — | — | — | — |
| AS 2 | 1,448 | 24 | — | — | — | — | — | — | — | — | 9 | 5 | 21 | — | 30 | — | — | — | — | — |
| AS 2–3 | 267 | 2 | — | — | — | — | — | — | — | — | — | 2 | 4 | — | 2 | — | 1 | 50 | — | — |
| AS 3 | 1,836 | 59 | — | — | — | 9 | — | — | — | — | — | 6 | 18 | — | 30 | — | — | 23 | 3 | — |
| AS 3 + Misc. | 36 | 2 | — | — | — | — | — | — | — | — | — | — | 1 | — | 1 | — | — | — | — | — |
| Elamite | 29 | 14 | — | — | — | — | — | — | — | — | — | — | — | — | — | — | — | — | — | — |
| EMS | 1,219 | 69 | — | — | — | — | — | — | — | 5 | — | 10 | 20 | — | 3 | — | — | 44 | — | — |
| EMS + Misc. | 22 | — | — | — | — | — | — | — | — | — | — | — | — | — | — | — | — | — | — | — |
| ES | 3,406 | 270 | — | — | — | 21 | — | 1 | — | 1 | — | 4 | 52 | — | 19 | 1 | — | 28 | 35 | — |
| ES + Misc. | 81 | 7 | — | — | — | — | — | — | — | — | — | 7 | — | — | 1 | — | — | — | 2 | — |
| ES + PL | 127 | 14 | — | — | — | — | — | — | — | — | — | — | 1 | — | — | — | — | — | — | — |
| ES/AS 3 Trans. | 1,923 | 134 | 1 | — | — | 15 | — | — | — | — | — | 4 | 57 | — | 16 | — | — | 8 | 22 | 1 |
| ES/MS Trans. | 126 | 10 | — | — | — | — | — | — | — | — | — | — | 1 | — | 4 | — | — | 2 | — | — |
| Indeterminate | 473 | 26 | — | — | — | — | — | — | — | — | — | 1 | 1 | — | 2 | — | — | 2 | 2 | — |
| LMS | 555 | 29 | — | — | — | — | — | — | 1 | — | — | 1 | 3 | — | 5 | — | — | 1 | — | — |
| LS | 13 | — | — | — | — | — | — | — | — | — | — | — | 1 | — | — | — | — | — | — | — |
| Mixed | 537 | 23 | 1 | — | — | 4 | — | — | — | — | — | 9 | 4 | — | 5 | — | — | 2 | 24 | 1 |
| Mixed Ach./PL | 359 | 15 | — | — | — | — | — | — | — | — | — | 4 | — | — | 1 | — | — | 21 | 1 | — |
| Mixed ES/AS | 986 | 120 | — | 1 | — | 90 | — | — | 1 | — | — | 26 | 17 | — | 2 | — | — | 6 | 50 | 4 |
| Mixed LS/PL | 1 | — | — | — | — | — | — | — | — | — | — | — | — | — | — | — | — | — | — | — |
| Mixed MS | 53 | 1 | — | — | — | — | — | — | — | — | — | 1 | — | — | — | — | — | — | — | — |
| Mixed MS/AS | 90 | 2 | — | — | — | — | — | — | — | — | — | — | — | — | — | — | — | 1 | — | — |
| Mixed MS/ES | 737 | 30 | 1 | — | — | — | — | — | — | — | — | 2 | 6 | — | 3 | — | — | 16 | 7 | — |
| Mixed MS/ES/AS | 480 | 21 | — | — | — | 6 | — | — | — | — | — | 4 | 10 | — | 3 | — | — | 1 | 11 | 5 |
| Mixed PL/AS | 99 | 5 | — | — | — | — | — | — | — | — | — | — | 1 | — | | — | — | — | — | — |
| Mixed PL/AS 3 | 34 | — | — | — | — | — | — | — | — | — | — | — | — | — | 1 | — | — | — | — | — |
| Mixed PL/EMS | 53 | 5 | — | — | — | — | — | — | — | — | — | — | — | — | 3 | — | — | 1 | — | — |
| Mixed PL/LMS | 351 | 24 | — | — | — | — | — | — | — | — | — | 14 | 2 | — | — | — | — | — | — | — |
| Mixed PL/MS | 1,001 | 62 | — | — | — | — | — | — | — | — | 1 | 6 | 6 | — | 10 | — | — | 39 | — | — |
| MS | 5,777 | 315 | 11 | — | — | 5 | — | — | — | — | — | 9 | 32 | — | 37 | 11 | — | 36 | 12 | — |
| MS + Misc. | 83 | 8 | — | — | — | — | — | — | — | — | — | 1 | 1 | — | 1 | — | — | 5 | — | — |
| MS + PL | 78 | 4 | — | — | — | — | — | — | — | — | — | — | — | — | 1 | — | — | — | — | — |
| PL | 6,262 | 497 | 1 | — | — | 7 | 1 | 2 | — | 1 | 9 | 46 | 43 | 1 | 62 | — | — | 168 | 7 | — |
| PL + LS + MS | 4 | — | — | — | — | — | — | — | — | — | — | — | — | — | — | — | — | — | — | — |
| PL + Misc. | 32 | — | — | — | — | — | — | — | — | — | — | — | — | — | 1 | — | — | — | — | — |
| PL + MS + ES | 28 | 3 | — | — | — | — | — | — | — | — | — | — | 1 | — | — | — | — | 7 | — | — |
| Prob. Ach. | 37 | 3 | — | — | — | — | — | — | — | — | — | 1 | — | — | — | — | — | — | — | — |
| Prob. AS | 57 | 1 | — | — | — | — | — | — | — | — | — | 1 | — | — | — | — | — | — | — | — |
| Prob. PL | 18 | — | — | — | — | — | — | — | — | — | — | 1 | 1 | 12 | — | — | — | — | — | — |

Table 14. Summary of Faunal Remains by Period (*cont.*)

| Large Mammal | *Lepus* sp. | Medium *Artiodactyl* | Medium *Canid* | Medium Carnivore | Medium Mammal | Missing | *Mus* sp. | *Mustelid* | *Nesokia indica* | Rodent | Sheep | Sheep-Goat | Sheep-Goat-Gazelle | Small *Artiodactyl* | Small *Canid* | Small Carnivore | Small *Felid* | Small Mammal | *Suid* | *Sus scrota* | *Tatera indica* | *Vulpes* sp. | *Vulpes vulpes* |
|---|---|---|---|---|---|---|---|---|---|---|---|---|---|---|---|---|---|---|---|---|---|---|---|
| 81 | — | — | 12 | — | 307 | — | — | — | — | 2 | 7 | 316 | 7 | — | — | — | — | — | — | 82 | — | — | — |
| 17 | — | — | — | — | 40 | — | — | — | — | — | 1 | 14 | 1 | — | — | — | — | — | — | 1 | — | — | — |
| 10 | — | — | 1 | — | 133 | — | — | — | — | — | — | 33 | 19 | — | — | — | — | 3 | — | 2 | — | — | — |
| 43 | — | — | 15 | 2 | 385 | — | — | — | — | 1 | 8 | 320 | 22 | — | — | — | — | 2 | — | 1 | — | — | — |
| 4 | — | — | 2 | — | 19 | — | — | — | — | — | — | 16 | 7 | — | — | — | 1 | 1 | — | — | — | — | — |
| 60 | 1 | 1 | 6 | — | 731 | — | — | — | — | 3 | 2 | 434 | 110 | — | — | — | — | 6 | — | 4 | — | 1 | — |
| 15 | — | — | — | — | 87 | 1 | — | — | 1 | — | — | 93 | 9 | — | — | — | — | — | — | — | — | — | — |
| 114 | — | 1 | 15 | — | 800 | — | — | — | — | 6 | 7 | 531 | 155 | — | 1 | — | — | 17 | — | 41 | — | — | — |
| 1 | — | — | 1 | — | 23 | — | — | — | — | — | — | 5 | 1 | — | — | — | — | — | — | 1 | — | — | — |
| 14 | — | — | — | — | — | — | — | — | — | — | — | 1 | — | — | — | — | — | — | — | — | — | — | — |
| 164 | 1 | 1 | 3 | — | 581 | — | — | — | — | 15 | 2 | 199 | 30 | 1 | — | — | — | 20 | 2 | 49 | — | — | — |
| 1 | — | — | 1 | — | 13 | — | — | — | — | — | — | 7 | — | — | — | — | — | — | — | — | — | — | — |
| 455 | — | 1 | 12 | — | 1,698 | 3 | — | 1 | — | 30 | 4 | 545 | 129 | — | 5 | — | — | 10 | 1 | 80 | — | — | — |
| 10 | — | — | — | — | 40 | — | — | — | — | — | — | 9 | 5 | — | — | — | — | — | — | — | — | — | — |
| 17 | — | — | — | — | 70 | — | — | — | — | — | — | 22 | 3 | — | — | — | — | — | — | — | — | — | — |
| 244 | — | 2 | 6 | — | 843 | — | — | — | — | 2 | 2 | 391 | 115 | — | 2 | — | 1 | 3 | — | 50 | — | 4 | — |
| 11 | — | — | 2 | — | 55 | — | — | — | — | 4 | — | 19 | 17 | — | — | — | — | — | — | 1 | — | — | — |
| 59 | — | — | 4 | — | 227 | — | — | — | — | 5 | — | 100 | 17 | — | — | — | — | — | — | 27 | — | — | — |
| 90 | — | — | — | — | 289 | — | — | — | — | 5 | — | 99 | 20 | — | 1 | — | — | — | — | 11 | — | — | — |
| — | — | — |  | — | 5 | — | — | — | — | — | — | 5 |  | — | — | — | — | — | — | 2 | — | — | — |
| 23 | — | — | 4 | — | 284 | — | — | — | — | 12 | 1 | 115 | 18 | 1 | — | — | — | — | — | 6 | — | — | — |
| 54 | — | — | — | — | 183 | — | — | — | — | — | — | 65 | 3 | — | — | — | — | — | — | 12 | — | — | — |
| 42 | — | — | 4 | 1 | 390 | — | — | — | — | — | 3 | 175 | 25 | — | 2 | — | — | 1 | — | 25 | — | 1 | — |
| — | — | — | — | — | 1 | — | — | — | — | — | — | — | — | — | — | — | — | — | — | — | — | — | — |
| 2 | — | — | — | — | 34 | — | — | — | — | 1 | — | 13 | — | — | — | — | — | 1 | — | — | — | — | — |
| 3 | — | — | — | — | 56 | — | — | — | — | 1 | — | 25 | 2 | — | — | — | — | — | — | — | — | — | — |
| 61 | — | — | 1 | — | 452 | — | 1 | — | — | 1 | 1 | 134 | 10 | — | 1 | — | — | 3 | — | 7 | — | — | — |
| 34 | — | — | 19 | 1 | 238 | — | — | — | — | 3 | 1 | 85 | 19 | — | — | — | — | — | — | 18 | 1 | — | — |
| 7 | — | — | 5 | — | 46 | — | — | — | — | — | — | 31 | 3 | — | — | — | — | — | 1 | — | — | — | — |
| 2 | — | — | — | — | 18 | — | — | — | — | — | — | 12 | — | — | — | — | — | — | — | 1 | — | — | — |
| 2 | — | — | — | — | 27 | — | — | — | — | 2 | — | 11 | — | — | — | — | — | 2 | — | — | — | — | — |
| 90 | — | — | 2 | — | 163 | — | — | — | — | 1 | — | 38 | 6 | — | — | — | — | 2 | — | 9 | — | — | — |
| 129 | — | 1 | 9 | — | 508 | — | — | — | — | 17 | 2 | 186 | 5 | — | 1 | — | 1 | 8 | — | 10 | — | — | — |
| 669 | — | 1 | 34 | — | 2,689 | 11 | — | — | — | 45 | 3 | 1,286 | 235 | — | 1 | — | — | 29 | 3 | 297 | 3 | 3 | — |
| 18 | — | — | 1 | — | 32 | — | — | — | — | — | — | 13 | 2 | — | — | — | — | — | — | 1 | — | — | — |
| 15 | — | — | — | — | 38 | — | — | — | — | 1 | — | 13 | 5 | — | — | — | — | — | — | 1 | — | — | — |
| 824 | — | — | 23 | — | 2,662 | — | — | — | — | 15 | 51 | 1,642 | 102 | — | 2 | 1 | 1 | 14 | 2 | 66 | — | — | 12 |
| 3 | — | — | — | — | 1 | — | — | — | — | — | — | — | — | — | — | — | — | — | — | — | — | — | — |
| 1 | — | — | — | — | 20 | — | — | — | — | — | — | 6 | 2 | — | — | — | — | 2 | — | — | — | — | — |
| 7 | — | — | — | — | 3 | — | — | — | — | — | — | 6 | — | — | — | — | — | 1 | — | — | — | — | — |
| 15 | — | — | — | — | 15 | — | — | — | — | — | — | 3 | — | — | — | — | — | — | — | — | — | — | — |
| 7 | — | — | — | — | 25 | — | — | — | — | — | — | 20 | 3 | — | — | — | — | — | — | — | — | — | — |
| — | — | — | — | — | — | — | — | — | — | — | — | — | — | — | — | — | — | — | — | — | — | 4 | — |

# INDEX OF LOCI AND ILLUSTRATED FINDS

| *Locus* | *Elevation* | *Reg. No.* | *Description* | *Illustration* |
|---|---|---|---|---|
| G29:701 | 78.03 | VII-9 | Baked-clay "plug." Middle Susiana | Fig. 81:H |
| G29:701 South | 77.47 | 7398 | Bone token. Early Susiana(?) | Fig. 77:J |
| G29:703 | B.S. | 7061 | Pottery vessel. Early Middle Susiana | Fig. 50:F, pl. 20:I |
| Gully Cut | Surface | 8023 | Pottery vessel. Late Middle Susiana | Fig. 40:L |
| Gully Cut | Surface | 8427 | Open pottery vessel. Early Susiana | Fig. 55:D |
| Gully Cut | Dump | 9162 | White stone bead. Date(?) | Fig. 81:M |
| Gully Cut | N/A | N/A | Unbaked clay chessman figurine. Archaic Susiana/Early Susiana | Fig. 79:L |
| Gully Cut | Surface | VI-91 | Stone pestle. Early Susiana | Pl. 30:L |
| H10:102 | 0.35 B.S. | BF-1001 | Closed pottery vessel. Middle Susiana | Fig. 45:G |
| H10:102 | N/A | BF-1010 | Pottery vessel. Archaic Susiana 3 | Fig. 69:J |
| H15:408 | 1.03 B.S. | VI-52 | Pottery vessel. Protoliterate | Fig. 28:D |
| H16:101 | N/A | BF-1 | Close-line open bowl. Archaic Susiana 3 | Fig. 66:H |
| High Mound | Surface | 1202 | Pottery vessel. Old Elamite (Sukkalmah) | Fig. 25:I |
| High Mound | Surface | 1211 | Pottery vessel. Old Elamite (Sukkalmah) | Fig. 25:H |
| High Mound | B.S. | 3843 | Pottery vessel. Parthian | Fig. 19:K |
| High Mound | B.S. | 3844 | Pottery vessel. Parthian | Fig. 19:N |
| High Mound | N/A | 6751 | Pottery vessel. Late Middle Susiana | Pl. 19:N |
| High Mound | N/A | IX-20 | Pink stone stamp seal. Late Susiana 2 | Pl. 22:A |
| High Mound | Surface | VII-2 | Door sealing fragment with impression of stamp seal. Late Susiana(?) | Fig. 76:U |
| High Mound | Surface | VIII-14 | Stone stamp seal with perforated handle. Late Susiana(?) | Fig. 76:A |
| High Mound | Surface | VIII-41 | Baked-clay stamp seal. Late Susiana(?) | Fig. 76:C |
| J15:301 | Kiln | 3883 | Pottery vessel. Parthian | Fig. 19:M |
| J15:301 | Kiln | 3884 | Pottery vessel. Parthian | Fig. 19:L |
| J15:408 | 1.03 B.S. | 4330 | Pottery vessel. Old Elamite (Sukkalmah) | Fig. 25:C |
| J19:306 | 0.40 B.S. | 3842 | Pottery vessel. Middle Susiana | Fig. 40:F |
| K14:403 | 0.85 B.S. | VI-44 | Pottery vessel. Protoliterate | Fig. 29:I |
| K22:402 | 1.35 B.S. | 4640 | Pottery vessel. Late Middle Susiana | Fig. 37:P |
| K22:402 | N/A | 4658 | Jar sealing fragment. Late Susiana/Protoliterate | Pl. 23:F |
| K23:400 | 1.35 B.S. | 41137 | Open bowl. Late Iron Age/Achaemenid | Fig. 24:A |
| K23:501 | 0.25 B.S. | VI-67 | Pottery vessel. Protoliterate | Fig. 32:J |
| K23:502 | 0.90 B.S. | 5612 | Pottery vessel. Late Iron Age/Achaemenid | Fig. 23:M |
| K23:502 | 0.90 B.S. | VI-59 | Pottery vessel. Protoliterate | Fig. 31:K |
| L22:504 | 81.16 | VI-88 | Sinker/weight stone. Middle Susiana | Pl. 25:I |
| L23:400 | 0.45 B.S. | 41138 | Open bowl. Late Iron Age/Achaemenid | Fig. 20:H |
| M9:901 | 83.68 | 9676 | Pottery vessel. Late Susiana 2 | Fig. 35:E |
| N8:1005 | 90.44 | X-32 | Pottery vessel. Old Elamite (Sukkalmah) | Fig. 25:T |
| N8:903 | 98.80 | 9505 | Pottery vessel. Protoliterate | Fig. 32:A |
| N8:903 | 88.00 | 9691 | Pottery vessel. Protoliterate | Fig. 27:E |
| N8:903 | 88.00 | 9693 | Pottery vessel. Protoliterate | Fig. 32:K |
| N9:? | 90.40 | X-15 | Pottery vessel. Old Elamite (Sukkalmah) | Fig. 25:E |
| N9:1001 | Grave 1001 | 10087 | Pottery vessel. Old Elamite (Sukkalmah) | Fig. 25:U |
| N9:1001 North | 90.83 | X-9 | Pottery vessel. Old Elamite (Sukkalmah) | Fig. 25:S |
| N9:1004 | 90.40 | X-14 | Pottery vessel. Old Elamite (Sukkalmah) | Fig. 25:D |
| N9:1004 | 90.84 | X-16 | Pottery vessel. Old Elamite (Sukkalmah) | Fig. 25:R |
| N9:1006 | 90.30 | X-22 | Pottery vessel. Old Elamite (Sukkalmah) | Fig. 25:G |
| N9:1006 South | 90.88 | 10064 | Pottery vessel. Old Elamite (Sukkalmah) | Fig. 25:F |
| N10:? | High Mound | 6752 | Pottery vessel. Late Susiana 2 | Pl. 19:A |
| N10:1002 North | 85.18 | 10018 | Pottery vessel. Old Elamite (Sukkalmah) | Fig. 25:J |
| N10:1004 | 89.73 | X-15 | Pottery vessel. Protoliterate | Fig. 32:C |
| O18:205 | B.S. | 3927 | Open bowl. Late Iron Age/Achaemenid | Fig. 20:L |
| P9:401 | B.S. | 4693 | Pottery vessel. Old Elamite (Sukkalmah) | Fig. 25:P |
| P10:401 | B.S. | 4690 | Pottery vessel. Old Elamite (Sukkalmah) | Fig. 25:L |
| P17:806 | 83.28 | 11243 | Crescent-shaped clay token. Protoliterate | Pl. 24:A |
| P17:901 | 79.37 | 9177 | Pottery vessel. Middle Susiana | Fig. 36:J |
| P17:901 | 81.85 | 9478 | Pottery vessel. Late Iron Age/Achaemenid | Fig. 23:R |
| P17:901 | 81.83 | 9479 | Pottery vessel. Protoliterate | Fig. 33:I |
| P17:901 | 81.85 | 9481 | Pottery vessel. Protoliterate | Fig. 32:B |

| *Locus* | *Elevation* | *Reg. No.* | *Description* | *Illustration* |
|---|---|---|---|---|
| P17:901 | 81.51 | 9500 | Pottery vessel. Protoliterate | Fig. 26:H |
| P17:901 | N/A | 9908 | Open bowl. Late Iron Age/Achaemenid | Fig. 24:H |
| P17:902 | 82.48 | 9195 | Baked-clay figurine of sheep(?). Protoliterate context | Fig. 80:C |
| P17:902 | 81.61 | 9514 | Plain pottery vessel. Late Middle Susiana | Fig. 53:H |
| P17:902 | 81.15 | 9873 | Bulla with impression of men working. Protoliterate | Fig. 76:N |
| P17:902 | 81.61 | N/A | Pottery vessel. "Pseudo-" beveled-rim bowl. Protoliterate | Fig. 26:B |
| P17:1102 | 81.64 | IX-17 | Slightly baked clay tablet or token. Protoliterate | Pl. 22:F |
| P17:1102 | 81.08 | IX-23 | Gray stone button seal. Protoliterate | Pl. 22:B |
| P17:1102 | 81.90 | IX-24 | Unbaked numerical tablet. Protoliterate | Pl. 22:I |
| P17:1102 | 81.08 | IX-25 | Black stone stamp seal. Protoliterate | Pl. 22:D |
| P17:1102 | 81.90 | IX-26 | Unbaked numerical tablet. Protoliterate | Pl. 22:H |
| P17:1102 | 81.60 | N/A | Unbaked clay "tablet." Protoliterate | Pl. 22:E |
| P17:1102 | 81.60 | N/A | Unbaked clay "tablet." Protoliterate | Pl. 22:G |
| P17:1104 | 81.55 | XI-16 | Pottery vessel. Protoliterate | Fig. 27:J |
| P17:1108 | 81.70 | N/A | Pottery vessel. Protoliterate | Pl. 29:C |
| P17:1112 | 80.72 | XI-19 | Pottery vessel. Late Iron Age/Achaemenid | Fig. 23:L |
| P18:203 | N/A | 2646 | Open bowl. Late Iron Age (Neo-Elamite)/Achaemenid | Fig. 21:E |
| P22:? | Surface | VI-93 | Stone pestle. Middle Susiana | Pl. 30:M |
| P22:601 | 82.55 | VI-8 | Spindle Whorl. Middle Susiana context, but is Early Susiana | Fig. 83:G |
| P22:601 | 82.55 | VI-8 | Baked-clay spindle whorl. Early Susiana | Pl. 25:H |
| P22:602 | 81.44 | 6477 | Pottery vessel. Early Middle Susiana | Fig. 37:L |
| P22:602 | 81.44 | 6480 | Tortoise pottery vessel. Early Middle Susiana | Fig. 52:E |
| P22:602 | 81.44 | 6484 | Pottery vessel. Early Middle Susiana | Fig. 42:E |
| P22:604 | B.S. | 6268 | Pottery vessel. Early Middle Susiana | Fig. 37:I |
| P22:605 | 80.95 | VI-32 | Bitumen bracelet. Early Susiana | Fig. 81:K, pl. 25:D |
| P22:605 | 80.95 | VI-33 | Bitumen bracelet. Early Susiana | Fig. 81:J, pl. 25:E |
| P22:606 | 80.00 | 6872/VI-19 | Pottery vessel. Archaic 3–Early Susiana transitional | Fig. 67:C |
| P22:606 | 82.17 | 6044 | Pottery vessel. Early Middle Susiana | Fig. 38:L |
| P22:606 | 80.86 | 6048 | Open pottery vessel. Early/Middle Susiana transitional | Fig. 58:J |
| P22:606 | 80.42 | 6067 | Pottery vessel. Early/Middle Susiana transitional | Fig. 43:L |
| P22:606 | 80.00 | 6100 | Pottery vessel. Archaic 3–Early Susiana transitional | Fig. 67:B |
| P22:606 | 80.86 | 6123 | Plain pottery vessel. Early Susiana | Fig. 64:J |
| P22:606 | 80.86 | 6132 | Open pottery vessel. Early Susiana | Fig. 57:G |
| P22:606 | 80.65 | 6146 | Plain pottery vessel. Early Susiana | Fig. 65:T |
| P22:606 | 80.85 | 6175 | Decorated pottery lid. Early Susiana | Fig. 62:H |
| P22:606 | N/A | 6178 | Open pottery vessel. Early Susiana | Fig. 59:D |
| P22:606 | 79.50 | 6180 | Plain pottery vessel. Archaic Susiana 3 | Fig. 74:E |
| P22:606 | 80.10 | 6226 | Plain pottery vessel. Early Susiana | Fig. 65:E |
| P22:606 | 81.33 | 6228 | Plain pottery vessel. Early Susiana | Fig. 64:B |
| P22:606 | 80.12 | 6229 | Plain pottery vessel. Early Susiana | Fig. 65:F |
| P22:606 | 80.50 | 6422 | Plain pottery vessel. Early Susiana | Fig. 65:M |
| P22:606 | 80.00 | 6422 | Matte-painted pottery vessel. Archaic Susiana 3 | Fig. 70:B |
| P22:606 | 81.52 | 6533 | Open pottery vessel. Early Susiana | Fig. 59:A |
| P22:606 | N/A | 6845 | Plain pottery vessel. Early Susiana | Fig. 65:A |
| P22:606 | N/A | 6860 | Open pottery vessel. Early Susiana | Fig. 60:D |
| P22:606 | 80.86 | 6862 | Open pottery vessel. Early Susiana | Fig. 58:K |
| P22:606 | 81.14 | 6863 | Open pottery vessel. Early Susiana | Fig. 58:F |
| P22:606 | 81.77 | 6864 | Decorated pottery lid. Early Susiana | Fig. 62:C |
| P22:606 | 80.85 | 6865 | Decorated pottery lid. Early Susiana | Fig. 62:F |
| P22:606 | 80.85 | 6868 | Plain pottery vessel. Early Susiana | Fig. 64:K |
| P22:606 | 80.52 | 6870 | Plain pottery vessel. Early Susiana | Fig. 65:N |
| P22:606 | 80.00 | VI-19/6872 | Pottery vessel. Archaic 3–Early Susiana transitional | Pl. 20:D |
| P22:606 | 80.85 | VI-38 | Decorated pottery lid. Early Susiana | Fig. 62:G, pl. 20:C |
| P22:606 | 80.55 | VI-39 | Plain pottery vessel. Archaic Susiana | Fig. 74:F |
| P22:606 | 81.42 | VI-5 | Pottery vessel. Early Susiana | Pl. 27:D |
| P22:606 | B.S. | VI-74 | Pottery vessel. Early Middle Susiana | Pl. 20:A |
| P22:606 | 81.73 | VIII-39 | Pottery vessel. Early Susiana | Pl. 21:H |

| *Locus* | *Elevation* | *Reg. No.* | *Description* | *Illustration* |
|---|---|---|---|---|
| P22:606 North | 81.73 | 6126 | Plain pottery vessel. Early Susiana | Fig. 64:H |
| P22:606 North | 81.73 | 6183 | Plain pottery vessel. Middle Susiana | Fig. 53:P |
| P22:606 North | 81.75 | VI-34 | Plain pottery vessel. Early Susiana | Fig. 64:D |
| P22:606 South | N/A | 6869 | Plain pottery vessel. Early Susiana | Fig. 64:L |
| P22:606 South | 81.06 | VI-36 | Plain pottery vessel. Early Susiana | Fig. 64:E |
| P22:607 | N/A | 6021 | Pottery vessel. Early Susiana | Fig. 63:D |
| P22:608 | 81.11 | 6098 | Open pottery vessel. Early Susiana | Fig. 58:D |
| P22:608 | 81.11 | 6101 | Pottery vessel. Early Susiana | Fig. 63:I |
| P22:608 | 81.14 | 6184 | Pottery vessel. Early Susiana | Fig. 63:A |
| P22:608 Middle | 80.20 | 6025 | Plain pottery vessel. Archaic Susiana | Fig. 74:C |
| P22:608 North | 81.13 | 6019 | Open pottery vessel. Early Susiana | Fig. 57:J |
| P22:608 North | 81.32 | 6035 | Open pottery vessel. Early Susiana | Fig. 56:J |
| P22:609 | 81.42 | 6022 | Open pottery vessel. Early Susiana | Fig. 56:M |
| P22:609 | 81.83 | 6085 | Open pottery vessel. Early Susiana | Fig. 56:L |
| P22:609 | 81.13 | 6110 | Open pottery vessel. Early Susiana | Fig. 55:J |
| P22:609 | 80.74 | 6111 | Closed pottery vessel. Early Susiana | Fig. 61:H |
| P22:609 | 81.40 | 6462 | Pottery vessel. Early Susiana | Pl. 21:F–G |
| P22:609 | 81.30 | N/A | Open pottery vessel. Early Susiana | Fig. 57:B |
| P22:611 | 80.37 | 6082 | Open pottery vessel. Early Susiana | Fig. 59:B |
| P22:611 | 80.37 | 6167 | Open pottery vessel. Early Susiana | Fig. 58:I |
| P22:611 | 80.66 | 6230 | Plain pottery vessel. Early Susiana | Fig. 64:A |
| P22:611 | 80.38 | 6231 | Plain pottery vessel. Early Susiana | Fig. 65:B |
| P22:611 | 80.50 | 6241 | Plain pottery vessel. Early Susiana | Fig. 64:G |
| P22:611 | 80.50 | 6248 | Open pottery vessel. Early Susiana | Fig. 61:M |
| P22:611 | 80.58 | 6291 | Plain pottery vessel. Early Susiana | Fig. 65:J |
| P22:611 | 82.19 | 6336 | Pottery vessel. Early to Middle Susiana transitional | Fig. 50:B |
| P22:611 | 80.81 | 6861 | Open pottery vessel. Early Susiana | Fig. 61:D |
| P22:611 | 80.57 | VI-102 | Pottery vessel. Early Susiana | Fig. 63:J, pl. 20:B |
| P22:611 West | 81.14 | 6867 | Plain pottery vessel. Early Susiana | Fig. 64:I |
| P22:612 South | 79.25 | N/A | Matte-painted pottery vessel. Archaic Susiana 3 | Fig. 71:B |
| P22:614 | 80.30 | VI-40 | Plain pottery vessel. Early Susiana | Fig. 65:P |
| P22:615 | 81.14 | 6074 | Pottery vessel. Middle Susiana | Fig. 48:C |
| P22:620 | 81.00 | 6139 | Pottery vessel. Archaic Susiana 3 | Fig. 69:G |
| P22:620 | 81.43 | 6765 | Bitumen fragments with basket impression. Early Susiana | Pls. 29:D–E, 30:C |
| P22:622 | 80.94 | VII-51 | Hafted flint hoe with bitumen and rope impressions. Early Susiana | Pl. 30:A |
| P22:623 | 80.50 | VI-16 | Stone hoe. Early Susiana | Fig. 87:C |
| P22:624 | 81.62 | 6141 | Pottery vessel. Early Middle Susiana | Fig. 39:C |
| P22:624 | 80.85 | 6300 | Lid(?) fragment. Early Middle Susiana | Fig. 82:A |
| P22:625 | 81.75 | 6223 | Plain pottery vessel. Early Susiana | Fig. 65:R |
| P22:625 | 82.09 | VI-14 | Bone object. Middle Susiana | Fig. 85:A |
| P22:626 | 81.96 | 6850 | Closed pottery vessel. Late Middle Susiana | Fig. 45:F |
| P22:626 Southwest | 80.85 | VI-79 | Stone hoe. Early Susiana | Fig. 87:L |
| P23:601 | 81.80 | 6018 | Open pottery vessel. Early Susiana | Fig. 56:C |
| P23:601 | B.S. | 6395 | Closed pottery vessel. Late Middle Susiana | Fig. 44:G |
| P23:601 | B.S. | VI-2 | Baked-clay figurine of bull or ram. Middle Susiana | Fig. 80:B, pl. 27:E |
| P23:602 | 81.70 | VI-43 | Closed pottery vessel. Early Middle Susiana | Fig. 44:P, pl. 20:G |
| P23:603 | 82.22 | 6144 | Open pottery vessel. Early Susiana | Fig. 57:H |
| P23:603 | N/A | 6301 | Tortoise pottery vessel. Middle Susiana | Fig. 52:J |
| P23:604 | B.S. | 6009 | Pottery vessel. Archaic Susiana 3 | Fig. 69:I |
| P23:604 | B.S. | 6012 | Pottery vessel. "Sauce boat" vessel fragment. Early Middle Susiana | Fig. 50:E |
| P23:604 | B.S. | 6364 | Pottery vessel. Late Middle Susiana | Fig. 43:I |
| P23:606 | 82.05 | 6046 | Plain pottery vessel. Late Middle Susiana | Fig. 53:J |
| P23:606 | 82.05 | 6197 | Open bowl. Late Iron Age/Achaemenid | Fig. 24:K |
| P23:606 | 81.32 | 6202 | Pottery vessel. Ladle fragment. Early Middle Susiana | Fig. 50:D |
| P23:606 | 81.12 | 6221 | Pottery vessel. Late Middle Susiana | Fig. 42:L |
| P23:606 | 82.05 | 6859 | Plain pottery vessel. Late Middle Susiana | Fig. 53:V |
| P23:607 | 82.65 | 6223 | Pottery vessel. Early/Late Middle Susiana transitional | Fig. 43:D |

| Locus | Elevation | Reg. No. | Description | Illustration |
|---|---|---|---|---|
| P23:607 | 83.05 | 6224 | Closed pottery vessel. Early Middle Susiana | Fig. 44:E |
| P23:704 | 75.44 | 7140 | Pottery vessel. Probably Archaic/Early Susiana transitional | Fig. 63:B |
| P27:501 | 1.27 B.S. | 5525 | Pottery vessel. Late Middle Susiana | Fig. 42:O |
| P27:502 | 79.14 | 5510 | Stone vessel. Middle Susiana | Fig. 86:R |
| Q16:1001 | 83.15 | X-4 | Pottery vessel. Protoliterate | Fig. 31:H |
| Q16:1007 | 83.64 | X-2 | Pottery vessel. Protoliterate | Fig. 32:F |
| Q16:1103 | 83.49 | 11206 | Pottery vessel. Protoliterate | Fig. 26:J |
| Q17:801 | 83.57 | 8160 | Pottery vessel. Late Iron Age/Achaemenid | Fig. 23:F |
| Q17:801 | 83.31 | 8430 | Pottery vessel. Late Iron Age/Achaemenid | Fig. 23:N |
| Q17:801 | 83.57 | 8431 | Open bowl. Late Iron Age/Achaemenid | Fig. 24:C |
| Q17:801 | 83.57 | 8435 | Pottery vessel. Late Iron Age/Achaemenid | Fig. 22:N |
| Q17:801 | 83.57 | 8522 | Pottery vessel. Protoliterate or possibly Achaemenid | Fig. 27:C |
| Q17:801 | 83.31 | 8533 | Open bowl. Late Iron Age/Achaemenid | Fig. 20:I |
| Q17:801 | 83.28 | 8639 | Open bowl. Late Iron Age/Achaemenid | Fig. 24:I |
| Q17:801 | 83.31 | 8642 | Pottery vessel. Late Iron Age/Achaemenid | Fig. 23:G |
| Q17:801 | 83.57 | 8644 | Pottery vessel. Protoliterate | Fig. 27:B |
| Q17:801 | 83.87 | 8665a | Pottery vessel. Protoliterate | Fig. 33:C |
| Q17:801 | 83.30 | 8709 | Open bowl. Late Iron Age/Achaemenid | Fig. 24:G |
| Q17:803 | 83.41 | 8176 | Pottery vessel. Protoliterate | Fig. 29:C |
| Q17:803 | 83.40 | 8396 | Pottery vessel. Protoliterate | Fig. 33:B |
| Q17:803 | 83.37 | 8643 | Pottery vessel. Protoliterate | Fig. 31:A |
| Q17:803 | 83.78 | 8662 | Pottery vessel. Protoliterate | Fig. 26:I |
| Q17:804 | 82.78 | 8395 | Pottery vessel. Protoliterate | Fig. 33:J |
| Q17:804 | 82.73 | 8645 | Pottery vessel. Protoliterate | Fig. 27:A |
| Q17:804 South | 82.85 | VIII-55 | Copper pin/nail. Protoliterate | Fig. 84:G |
| Q17:806 | 82.84 | 8156 | Open bowl. Late Iron Age/Achaemenid | Fig. 24:M |
| Q17:806 | 83.57 | 8610 | Pottery vessel. Protoliterate | Fig. 31:I |
| Q17:806 | 83.57 | 8663 | Pottery vessel. Protoliterate | Fig. 32:H |
| Q17:806 | 81.15 | 9873 | Bulla with cylinder-seal impression of workshop. Protoliterate | Pl. 24:D |
| Q17:806 | 83.30 | 11245 | Jar sealing fragment with cylinder-seal impression of workshop. Protoliterate | Pl. 24:B |
| Q17:806 | 83.28 | 81189 | Conical clay token. Protoliterate | Pl. 24:E |
| Q17:808 | 83.32 | 8390 | Pottery vessel. Late Iron Age/Achaemenid | Fig. 23:S |
| Q17:811 | 82.69 | 8048 | Pottery vessel. Late Iron Age/Achaemenid | Fig. 22:G |
| Q17:811 | 82.69 | 8056 | Pottery vessel. Late Susiana 2 | Fig. 35:C |
| Q17:811 | 82.69 | 8058 | Open bowl. Late Iron Age/Achaemenid | Fig. 20:D |
| Q17:811 | 86.69 | 8337 | Pottery vessel. Late Iron Age/Achaemenid | Fig. 22:F |
| Q17:812 | 82.65 | 8049 | Pottery vessel. Late Iron Age/Achaemenid | Fig. 23:J |
| Q17:813 | 82.51 | 8661 | Pottery vessel. Protoliterate | Fig. 30:G |
| Q17:816 | 82.55 | 8567 | Pottery vessel. Protoliterate | Fig. 28:E |
| Q17:816 | 82.55 | 8611 | Pottery vessel. Protoliterate | Fig. 31:J |
| Q17:816 | 82.59 | VIII-72 | Alabaster miniature jar(?). Protoliterate | Fig. 87:G |
| Q17:903 | 83.75 | 9111 | Open bowl. Late Iron Age/Achaemenid | Fig. 20:B |
| Q17:903 | 83.38 | IX-28 | Pottery vessel. Protoliterate | Fig. 26:D |
| Q17:903 East | 83.63 | IX-9 | Pottery vessel. Protoliterate | Fig. 31:B |
| Q17:903 West | 83.64 | 9021 | Baked-clay spool. Protoliterate | Fig. 82:C |
| Q17:905 West | 82.96 | 9013 | Pottery vessel. Protoliterate | Fig. 26:F |
| Q17:907 | 83.60 | 9031 | Pottery vessel. Late Iron Age/Achaemenid | Fig. 23:K |
| Q17:907 Northeast | 83.60 | 9217 | Baked-clay object. Protoliterate | Fig. 82:F |
| Q17:1001 | 82.65 | X-1 | Libation(?) vessel. Protoliterate | Fig. 34, pl. 29:A |
| Q17:1001 | 82.69 | X-10 | Pottery vessel. Protoliterate | Fig. 27:H |
| Q17:1001 | 82.69 | X-25 | Pottery vessel. Protoliterate | Fig. 27:G |
| Q17:1001 | 82.69 | X-5 | Pottery vessel. Protoliterate | Fig. 27:F |
| Q17:1002 North | 83.58 | X-6 | Baked-clay sinker/loom weight. Protoliterate | Fig. 82:E |
| Q17:1106 | 82.70 | N/A | Pottery vessel. Protoliterate | Fig. 33:F |
| Q18:205 | Surface | 2485 | Pottery vessel. Late Iron Age/Achaemenid | Fig. 23:Q |
| Q18:305 | B.S. | 2587 | Open bowl. Late Iron Age (Neo-Elamite)/Achaemenid | Fig. 21:C |
| Q18:305 | 1.0 B.S. | 2623 | Open bowl. Late Iron Age (Neo-Elamite)/Achaemenid | Fig. 21:I |

| Locus | Elevation | Reg. No. | Description | Illustration |
|---|---|---|---|---|
| Q18:305 | 0.35 B.S. | 3644 | Open bowl. Late Iron Age/Achaemenid | Fig. 24:J |
| Q18:305 | 82.00 | 3885 | Pottery vessel. Late Iron Age/Achaemenid | Fig. 22:O |
| Q18:305 | 1.0 B.S. | 3934 | Pottery vessel. Late Iron Age/Achaemenid | Fig. 23:H |
| Q18:305 | N/A | 3935 | Open bowl. Late Iron Age (Neo-Elamite)/Achaemenid | Fig. 21:F |
| Q18:305 | 1.80 B.S. | 3937 | Open bowl. Late Iron Age (Neo-Elamite)/Achaemenid | Fig. 21:H |
| Q18:314 | Sifting | III-831 | Seal impression on bale (flat) sealing. Protoliterate | Fig. 76:I |
| Q18:1106 | 81.50 | 11198 | Pottery vessel. Protoliterate | Fig. 33:L |
| Q19:301 | 0.20 B.S. | 3822 | Pottery "stand." Late Middle Susiana | Fig. 51:C |
| Q19:901 | N/A | 9009 | Pottery vessel. Late Middle Susiana | Fig. 41:J |
| Q21:101 | Fireplace | 1206 | Pottery vessel. Old Elamite (Sukkalmah) | Fig. 25:A |
| Q21:101 | Fireplace | 1213 | Pottery vessel. Old Elamite (Sukkalmah) | Fig. 25:O |
| Q21:102 | 0.90 B.S. | 1207 | Pottery vessel. Old Elamite (Sukkalmah) | Fig. 25:M |
| Q21:102 | Surface | 1212 | Pottery vessel. Old Elamite (Sukkalmah) | Fig. 25:B |
| Q22:601 | 80.89 | 6026 | Decorated pottery lid. Early Susiana | Fig. 62:E |
| Q22:602 | 79.57 | 6447 | Pottery vessel. Archaic Susiana 2 | Fig. 72:J |
| Q22:602 | 80.47 | N/A | Plain pottery vessel. Early Susiana | Fig. 65:K |
| Q22:602 | 78.80 | N/A | Stone ball with incised mark. Early Susiana | Pl. 25:F |
| Q22:602 | 80.45 | VI-23 | Plain pottery vessel. Early Susiana | Fig. 65:L |
| Q22:602 | 79.50 | VI-25 | Plain pottery vessel. Archaic Susiana 3 | Fig. 75:D |
| Q22:602 | 8047 | VI-26 | Stone pestle. Early Susiana | Pl. 30:I |
| Q22:602 | 80.47 | VI-27 | Stone mill made of medium- to large-grained sandstone. Early Susiana | Pl. 30:D–E |
| Q22:602 | 80.47 | VI-29 | Open pottery vessel. Early Susiana | Fig. 61:A |
| Q22:602 | 80.47 | VI-30 | Open pottery vessel. Early Susiana | Fig. 61:C |
| Q22:602 North | 80.41 | VI-15 | Stone pestle. Early Susiana | Pl. 30:N |
| Q22:603 | 81.42 | 6190 | Decorated pottery lid. Early Susiana | Fig. 62:B |
| Q22:605 | 80.11 | VI-84 | Stone celt. Early Susiana | Fig. 87:M |
| Q22:606 North | 80.35 | VI-83 | Stone celt. Early Susiana | Fig. 87:N |
| Q22:608 | 79.57 | 6164 | Painted-burnished pottery vessel. Archaic Susiana 1 | Fig. 73:A, pl. 20:F |
| Q22:614 | 80.77 | VI-80 | Stone hoe. Early Susiana | Fig. 87:O |
| Q22:701 | N/A | VII-53 | Stone hoe. Early Susiana | Fig. 87:J, pl. 30:F |
| Q22:702 | 79.23 | VII-34 | Mother-of-pearl disc. Early Susiana | Fig. 81:S |
| Q22:702 | 79.11 | VII-50 | Stone hoe with bitumen stain on handle. Early Susiana | Pl. 30:H |
| Q22:702 | 79.11 | VII-52 | Hafted flint hoe with bitumen and rope impressions. Early Susiana | Pl. 30:B |
| Q22:703 | 79.28 | VII-37 | Clay token. Early Susiana(?) | Fig. 77:S |
| Q22:704 | 79.34 | VII-11 | Stone token. Early Susiana | Fig. 77:E |
| Q22:708 | 79.40 | VII-25 | Plain pottery vessel. Archaic Susiana 3 | Fig. 75:G |
| Q22:804 North | 77.48 | 8667 | Pottery vessel. Archaic Susiana 3 | Fig. 72:A |
| Q22:804 South | 78.56 | VIII-16 | Stone vessel. Early Susiana | Fig. 86:E |
| Q23:504 | 79.27 | V-100 | Baked-clay figurine. Early Susiana | Fig. 78:B |
| Q23:601 | 81.40 | 6187 | Tortoise pottery vessel. Early Middle Susiana | Fig. 52:G |
| Q23:702 | 79.08 | 7261 | Open pottery vessel. Early Susiana | Fig. 56:B |
| Q23:703 | 79.40 | 7075 | Open pottery vessel. Early Susiana | Fig. 60:C |
| Q23:709 | 79.99 | VII-35 | Bone object. Early Susiana | Fig. 85:D |
| Q23:712 | 78.29 | 7253 | Pottery vessel. Archaic Susiana 3 | Fig. 68:A |
| Q23:713 | 77.59 | 7216 | Open pottery vessel. Probably transitional Archaic/Early Susiana | Fig. 60:F |
| Q23:713 | 76.98 | VII-90 | Baked-clay token(?). Early Susiana | Fig. 77:K, pl. 25:G |
| Q23:801 | 78.47 | VIII-6 | Whitish stone. Early Susiana | Fig. 87:F |
| Q23:802 | 78.30 | 8155 | Plain pottery vessel. Archaic Susiana 3 | Fig. 74:D |
| Q23:802 | 78.30 | 8660 | Plain pottery vessel. Archaic Susiana 3 | Fig. 75:P |
| Q23:802 | 78.30 | VIII-18 | Stone vessel. Early Susiana | Fig. 86:K |
| Q23:802 | 78.30 | VIII-19 | Stone vessel. Early Susiana | Fig. 86:L |
| Q23:802 | 78.29 | VIII-5 | Dark gray stone. Early Susiana | Fig. 87:E |
| Q23:803 | 78.72 | VIII-39 | Spindle whorl. Early Susiana | Fig. 83:F |
| Q23:804 | 78.60 | 8070 | Matte-painted pottery vessel. Archaic Susiana 3 | Fig. 70:G |
| Q23:804 | 78.50 | N/A | Matte-painted pottery vessel. Archaic Susiana 3 | Fig. 71:C |
| Q23:805 | 78.80 | 8265 | Plain pottery vessel. Early Susiana | Fig. 65:Q |
| Q23:810 | 77.90 | 8092 | Close-line open bowl. Archaic Susiana 3 | Fig. 66:C |

| Locus | Elevation | Reg. No. | Description | Illustration |
|---|---|---|---|---|
| Q23:810 | 77.69 | 81013 | Close-line open bowl. Archaic Susiana 3 | Fig. 66:J |
| Q23:810 | 78.25 | VI-28/A34802 | Matte-painted pottery vessel. Archaic Susiana 3 | Fig. 70:F, pl. 20:E |
| Q23:815 | 77.31 | 8110 | Close-line open bowl. Archaic Susiana 3 | Fig. 66:D |
| Q23:820 | 79.31 | 8665 | Ball of bitumen stone. Early Susiana | Fig. 87:I |
| Q23:820 | 79.28 | VIII-68 | T-shaped figurine. Archaic Susiana 1–2 | Pl. 27:C |
| Q23:821 | 78.42 | VIII-42 | White stone "plug" with two heads. Early Susiana | Fig. 81:A |
| Q23:821 | 78.59 | VIII-61 | Stone token. Early Susiana | Fig. 77:H |
| Q23:821 | 79.19 | VIII-67 | Black-and-white stone "plug." Early Susiana | Fig. 81:D |
| Q23:827 East | 78.82 | 8399 | Plain pottery vessel. Early Susiana | Fig. 64:C |
| Q24:801 | 79.00 | 8116 | Pottery "stand." Late Middle Susiana | Fig. 51:D |
| Q24:801 | 76.26 | 8259 | Pottery vessel. Late Iron Age/Achaemenid | Fig. 22:K |
| Q24:801 | 79.00 | 8651 | Pottery vessel. Early/Middle Susiana transitional | Fig. 43:G |
| Q24:801 East | 77.30 | 8873 | Plain pottery vessel. Early Susiana | Fig. 65:O |
| Q24:801 West | 77.22 | 8248 | Open pottery vessel. Probably intermediate between Archaic/Early Susiana | Fig. 56:H |
| Q24:801 West | 77.22 | 8289 | Pottery vessel. Archaic Susiana 3 | Fig. 69:F |
| Q24:802 | 77.40 | 8249 | Plain pottery vessel. Archaic Susiana 3 | Fig. 75:K |
| Q24:802 East | 78.07 | 8027 | Open pottery vessel. Early Susiana | Fig. 57:F |
| Q24:803 | 78.61 | 8170 | Open bowl. Late Iron Age/Achaemenid | Fig. 20:C |
| Q24:803 | 78.61 | 8170 | Open bowl. Late Iron Age/Achaemenid | Fig. 24:F |
| Q25:801 | 76.62 | 8775 | Close-line open bowl. Archaic Susiana 3 | Fig. 66:E |
| Q25:802 | 75.70 | 8833 | Plain pottery vessel. Early Middle Susiana | Fig. 53:L |
| Q25:802 | 77.00 | 8956 | Closed pottery vessel. Middle Susiana | Fig. 44:N |
| Q25:802 | 77.00 | 8957 | Plain pottery vessel. Late Middle Susiana | Fig. 54:D |
| Q25:802 West | 77.10 | 8251 | Tortoise pottery vessel. Middle Susiana | Fig. 52:F |
| Q9:1010 | B.S. | X-11 | Pottery vessel. Old Elamite (Sukkalmah) | Fig. 25:Q |
| R16:1105 | 83.50 | XI-10 | Pottery vessel. Protoliterate | Fig. 29:B |
| R16:801 | 82.80 | 10092 | Jar sealing fragment. Protoliterate | Pl. 23:A |
| R16:801 | 82.75 | 81185 | Jar sealing fragment. Protoliterate | Pl. 23:D |
| R16:801 | 82.80 | 81186 | Jar sealing fragment. Protoliterate | Pl. 23:C |
| R16:801 | 82.75 | N/A | Jar sealing fragment. Protoliterate | Pl. 23:E |
| R16:803 | 82.45 | 10093 | Door sealing fragment with rope and peg impressions. Protoliterate | Pl. 23:G |
| R16:803 | 82.45 | 10916 | Door sealing fragment. Protoliterate | Pl. 23:H |
| R16:807 | 82.69 | VIII-83 | Baked clay. Protoliterate | Fig. 80:A |
| R16:901 | 84.21 | 9898 | Clay ball fragment with impression of birds (chicken?). Protoliterate | Fig. 76:M |
| R16:902 | 83.87 | 9193 | Pottery vessel. Protoliterate | Fig. 32:I |
| R16:903 | 83.16 | 9203 | Pottery vessel. Protoliterate | Fig. 26:G |
| R16:903 | 83.26 | 9495 | Stone token or pendant. Protoliterate | Fig. 77:G |
| R16:905 | 83.13 | 9215 | Pottery vessel. Protoliterate | Fig. 82:H |
| R16:906 | 83.87 | 9192 | Pottery vessel. Protoliterate | Fig. 33:E |
| R16:907 | 83.13 | 9215 | Pottery vessel. Protoliterate | Fig. 82:D |
| R16:909 | 84.21 | 9901 | Jar sealing fragment with impression of procession. Protoliterate | Fig. 76:T |
| R16:910 | 83.59 | 9899 | Flat sealing with impression of building facade(?). Protoliterate | Fig. 76:Q |
| R16:910 | 83.59 | 9900 | Clay ball fragment with impression of superimposed animals. Protoliterate | Fig. 76:R |
| R16:910 | 83.46 | 9903 | Clay ball fragment with impression of two rows of sacks of grain(?). Protoliterate | Fig. 76:K |
| R16:912 | 82.85 | 9015 | Pottery vessel. Protoliterate | Fig. 26:E |
| R16:912 | 84.03 | 9024 | Pottery vessel. Protoliterate | Fig. 28:A |
| R17:215 | 83.80 | 2579 | Pottery vessel. Parthian | Fig. 19:F |
| R17:407 | 1.20 B.S. | VI-89 | Discoidal socket/weight. Protoliterate | Pl. 25:K |
| R17:408 | 82.90 | VI-47 | Pottery vessel. Protoliterate | Fig. 26:A |
| R17:701 | 84.12 | 7211 | Pottery vessel. Protoliterate | Fig. 82:J |
| R17:701 | 84.12 | 7212 | Pottery vessel. Protoliterate | Fig. 82:I |
| R17:701 | 83.85 | 7390b | Fragment of bale sealing with much eroded impression. Protoliterate | Fig. 76:L |
| R17:704 | 83.25 | VII-60 | Baked-clay figurine. Protoliterate | Fig. 79:G |
| R17:704 | 82.90 | VII-84 | Stone vessel. Protoliterate | Fig. 86:G |
| R17:704 | 82.50 | VIII-92 | Left-handed sickle. Protoliterate | Fig. 82:M |
| R17:704 West | 83.49 | 7389 | Fragment of bale sealing with stamp seal impression. Protoliterate | Fig. 76:BB, pl. 23:B |

| *Locus* | *Elevation* | *Reg. No.* | *Description* | *Illustration* |
|---|---|---|---|---|
| R17:705 | 82.92 | VII-66 | Copper pin. Protoliterate | Fig. 84:F |
| R17:705 | 83.77 | VII-67 | White stone cylinder seal. Protoliterate | Fig. 76:D |
| R17:705 | 83.77 | VII-69 | Stone token or pendant. Protoliterate | Fig. 77:N |
| R17:710 | 82.96 | 7331 | Pottery vessel. Late Iron Age/Achaemenid | Fig. 22:C |
| R17:710 | 82.89 | VII-77 | Clay token. Protoliterate | Fig. 77:M |
| R17:711 | 83.49 | VII-68 | Gray black stone pendant in shape of bird. Protoliterate | Fig. 81:I |
| R17:713 | 82.64 | 7390a | Jar sealing with much eroded impression. Protoliterate | Fig. 76:P |
| R17:714 | 82.65 | 7387 | Clay ball with two different seal impressions of procession and herding. Protoliterate | Fig. 76:AA, pl. 24:F |
| R17:714 | 82.65 | 7388 | Clay ball with impression of battle scene. Protoliterate | Fig. 76:DD |
| R17:714 | 82.64 | VII-94 | Left-handed sickle. Protoliterate | Fig. 82:N |
| R17:716 | 84.30 | VII-75 | Clay token. Protoliterate | Fig. 77:L |
| R17:719 | 83.76 | 7394 | Pottery vessel. Protoliterate | Fig. 33:G |
| R17:803 | 83.28 | 8664 | Bottle stopper/sealing with impression of cloth. Protoliterate | Fig. 76:X |
| R17:803 | 82.99 | 8881 | Open bowl. Late Iron Age/Achaemenid | Fig. 20:O |
| R17:805 | 83.68 | 8432 | Open bowl. Late Iron Age/Achaemenid | Fig. 20:N |
| R17:807 | 83.80 | VIII-17 | Stone vessel. Protoliterate | Fig. 86:S, pl. 29:B |
| R17:808 | 83.15 | VIII-20 | Stone vessel. Protoliterate | Fig. 86:Q |
| R17:808 | 83.68 | VIII-82 | Pottery vessel. Protoliterate | Fig. 82:K |
| R17:914 | 83.39 | VII-88 | Copper/bronze pin. Protoliterate | Fig. 84:H |
| R17:1101 | 83.44 | XI-9 | Pottery vessel. Protoliterate | Fig. 33:K |
| R17:1110 | 82.10 | XI-13 | Pottery vessel. Protoliterate | Fig. 29:A |
| R17:1115 | 83.00 | N/A | Stone vessel. Protoliterate | Fig. 86:N |
| R18:304 | 0.50 B.S. | 3913 | Pottery vessel. Late Iron Age/Achaemenid | Fig. 23:T |
| R18:305 | 1.60 B.S. | 3661 | Open bowl. Late Iron Age (Neo-Elamite)/Achaemenid | Fig. 21:A |
| R18:305 | 0.75 B.S. | 3901 | Pottery vessel. Late Iron Age/Achaemenid | Fig. 23:C |
| R18:305 | 1.75 B.S. | III-804 | Jar sealing with much eroded impression probably of animals. Protoliterate | Fig. 76:O |
| R18:307 | B.S. | 3974 | Open bowl. Late Iron Age/Achaemenid | Fig. 24:L |
| R18:307 | 0.55 B.S. | 4299 | Pottery vessel. Protoliterate | Fig. 29:G |
| R18:414 | N/A | VI-62 | Pottery vessel. Protoliterate | Fig. 29:F |
| R18:901 | 81.33 | 9123 | Plain pottery vessel. Late Middle Susiana | Fig. 53:O |
| R18:901 | 80.52 | 9176 | Plain pottery vessel. Late Middle Susiana | Fig. 54:E |
| R18:901 | 81.10 | 9185a | Pottery vessel. Late Middle Susiana | Fig. 37:O |
| R18:901 | 80.52 | IX | Pottery vessel. Late Middle Susiana | Fig. 38:H |
| R18:901 | 81.51 | IX-115 | Plain pottery vessel. Late Middle Susiana | Fig. 53:F |
| R18:901 | 81.51 | IX-118 | Plain pottery vessel. Late Middle Susiana | Fig. 54:G |
| R18:901 | 81.52 | IX-32 | Plain pottery vessel. Late Middle Susiana | Fig. 53:G |
| R18:901 | 80.52 | IX-34 | Plain pottery vessel. Early Middle Susiana | Fig. 53:M |
| R18:901 | 81.10 | IX-41 | Pottery vessel. Late Middle Susiana | Fig. 37:K |
| R18:901 | 80.46 | IX-48 | Plain pottery vessel. Early Middle Susiana | Fig. 53:K |
| R18:901 | 80.52 | IX-52 | Pottery vessel. Late Middle Susiana | Fig. 40:M |
| R18:902 | 81.22 | 9032 | Pottery vessel. Protoliterate | Fig. 31:E |
| R18:902 | 81.22 | 9185b | Pottery vessel. Late Middle Susiana | Fig. 37:Q |
| R18:902 | 81.22 | 9205 | Plain pottery vessel. Late Middle Susiana | Fig. 53:I |
| R18:902 | 81.22 | 9675 | Pottery vessel. Late Middle Susiana | Fig. 37:M |
| R18:903 | 81.05 | 9090 | Black stone stamp seal. Late Susiana(?) | Fig. 76:E |
| R18:903 | 81.38 | 9561 | Baked-clay horn. Protoliterate context, but probably Middle or Late Susiana | Fig. 80:I |
| R18:904 | 81.78 | 9093 | Baked clay. Middle Susiana | Fig. 80:E |
| R18:904 | 82.05 | 9902 | Jar sealing fragment with impression of human, much eroded. Protoliterate | Fig. 76:Z |
| R18:905 | 81.55 | 9513 | Plain pottery vessel. Late Middle Susiana | Fig. 54:J |
| R18:906 | 80.02 | 9146 | Pottery vessel. Protoliterate | Fig. 32:E |
| R18:906 | 80.02 | 9501 | Pottery vessel. Protoliterate | Fig. 32:L |
| R18:906 | 81.66 | 9502 | Stone vessel. Protoliterate | Fig. 86:J |
| R18:906 | 81.46 | IX-133 | Pottery vessel. Protoliterate | Fig. 31:L |
| R18:906 | 81.22 | IX-40 | Pottery vessel. Late Middle Susiana | Fig. 40:B |
| R18:906 | 79.46 | IX-75 | Pottery vessel. Protoliterate | Fig. 31:D |

| Locus | Elevation | Reg. No. | Description | Illustration |
|---|---|---|---|---|
| R18:908 | 81.13 | IX-105 | Closed pottery vessel. Late Middle Susiana | Fig. 44:T |
| R18:908 | 81.13 | 9045 | Bitumen hafted flint tool. Late Middle Susiana | Fig. 87:B |
| R18:908 | 81.13 | 9046 | Bitumen hafted flint tool. Late Middle Susiana | Fig. 87:A |
| R18:908 | 80.34 | 9172 | Closed pottery vessel. Late Middle Susiana | Fig. 46:A |
| R18:908 | 80.91 | 9187 | Pottery vessel. Middle Susiana | Fig. 49:D |
| R18:908 | 80.88 | 9208 | Pottery vessel. Middle Susiana | Fig. 36:L |
| R18:908 | 81.13 | 9295 | Closed pottery vessel. Late Middle Susiana and Late Susiana 1 | Fig. 44:R |
| R18:908 | 81.13 | 9297 | Closed pottery vessel. Late Middle Susiana | Fig. 44:D |
| R18:908 | 80.91 | 9874 | Door sealing fragment with much eroded seal impression. Protoliterate | Fig. 76:V |
| R18:908 South | 81.13 | 9044 | Spindle whorl. Late Middle Susiana | Fig. 83:C |
| R18:908 South | 81.76 | 9150 | Plain pottery vessel. Late Middle Susiana | Fig. 53:N |
| R18:909 | 80:07 | 9189 | Pottery vessel. Protoliterate | Fig. 29:D |
| R18:909 | 80.98 | IX-58 | Pottery vessel. Protoliterate | Fig. 33:A |
| R18:910 | 80.34 | 9677 | Closed pottery vessel. Early Middle Susiana | Fig. 46:C |
| R18:912 | 81.22 | 9036 | Spindle whorl. Late Middle Susiana | Fig. 83:H |
| R18:913 | 80.23 | 9064 | Clay token. Protoliterate | Fig. 77:P |
| R18:913 | 81.10 | 9173 | Pottery vessel. Late Middle Susiana | Fig. 48:E |
| R18:914 | 81.88 | 9509 | Closed pottery vessel. Late Middle Susiana | Fig. 46:I |
| R18:916 | 80.24 | 9098 | Pottery vessel. Late Iron Age/Achaemenid | Fig. 22:D |
| R18:916 | 80.24 | 9133 | Pottery vessel. Protoliterate | Fig. 30:D |
| R18:916 | 81.71 | IX-103 | Pottery vessel. Late Middle Susiana | Fig. 37:D |
| R18:919 | 82.76 | 9114 | Bone object. Middle Susiana | Fig. 85:N |
| R18:920 | 81.97 | 9137 | Copper pin. Protoliterate | Fig. 84:B |
| R18:921 | 81.13 | 9135 | Spindle whorl. Late Middle Susiana | Fig. 83:A |
| R18:921 | 80.27 | 9166 | Plain pottery vessel. Late Middle Susiana | Fig. 54:M |
| R18:921 | 81.13 | 9467 | Turquoise bead. Protoliterate | Fig. 81:O |
| R18:921 | 81.13 | 9468 | Yellowish white stone bead. Protoliterate | Fig. 81:L |
| R18:921 | 80.35 | N/A | Pottery vessel. Late Middle Susiana | Pl. 19:G |
| R18:921 | 80.40 | N/A | Pottery vessel. Late Middle Susiana | Pl. 19:L |
| R19:? | N/A | 3801 | Pottery vessel. Late Iron Age/Achaemenid | Fig. 22:Q |
| R19:301 | N/A | N/A | Pottery vessel. Old Elamite (Sukkalmah) | Fig. 25:K |
| R19:401 | 1.0 B.S. | 6130 | Pottery vessel. Protoliterate | Fig. 26:C |
| R19:601 | 1.0 B.S. | 6847 | Pottery vessel. Protoliterate | Fig. 28:F |
| R19:903 | 79.52 | 9480 | Stone vessel. Protoliterate | Fig. 86:T |
| R19:903 | 79.89 | IX-132 | Pottery vessel. Protoliterate | Fig. 30:B |
| R19:905 | 79.44 | 9151 | Pottery vessel. Protoliterate | Fig. 31:C |
| R19:905 | 80.15 | 9154 | Pottery vessel. Protoliterate | Fig. 26:K |
| R19:905 | 79.44 | 9543 | Plain pottery vessel. Late Middle Susiana | Fig. 53:C |
| R19:905 | 80.19 | IX-104 | Pottery vessel. Protoliterate | Fig. 28:C |
| R19:905 | 80.15 | IX-89 | Pottery vessel. Protoliterate | Fig. 32:D |
| R19:910 | 80.34 | 9677 | Pottery vessel. Early Middle Susiana | Pl. 21:D |
| R20:401 | B.S. | 4654 | Open bowl. Late Iron Age/Achaemenid | Fig. 24:B |
| R20:510 | 77.64 | 5359 | Pottery vessel. Late Iron Age/Achaemenid | Fig. 22:I |
| R20:510 | 78.68 | 5694 | Pottery vessel. Protoliterate | Fig. 33:D |
| R20:515 | 79.15 | 6177 | Pottery vessel. Lid fragment. Early Middle Susiana | Fig. 50:G |
| R20:601 | 78.48 | 6525 | Pottery vessel. Late Middle Susiana | Fig. 43:K |
| R20:602 | B.S. | 6050 | Pottery vessel. Late Middle Susiana | Fig. 42:A, pl. 19:F |
| R20:602 | B.S. | 6051 | Pottery vessel. Late Middle Susiana | Fig. 42:Q, pl. 19:J |
| R21:301 South | B.S. | 3083 | Close-line open bowl. Archaic Susiana 3 | Fig. 66:B |
| R22:401 | 74.15 | 4520 | Painted-burnished pottery vessel. Archaic Susiana 1 | Fig. 73:C |
| R22:401 | 74.13 | 41050 | Painted-burnished pottery vessel. Archaic Susiana 1 | Fig. 73:B |
| R22:401 | 2.2 B.S. | VI-92 | Stone pestle. Early Susiana | Pl. 30:J |
| R23:502 | 0.65 B.S. | N/A | Stone vessel. Early Susiana | Fig. 86:B |
| R23:601 | 77.39 | 6298 | Pottery vessel. Early/Late Middle Susiana transitional | Fig. 43:E |
| R23:602 | 76.92 | VII-8 | Black stone "plug." Middle Susiana | Fig. 81:G, pl. 25:C |
| R23:701 | 76.77 | 7065 | Pottery vessel. Early Middle Susiana | Fig. 38:K |
| R23:701 | 76.77 | 7066 | Pottery vessel. Early Middle Susiana | Fig. 39:A |

| Locus | Elevation | Reg. No. | Description | Illustration |
|---|---|---|---|---|
| R23:701 | 77.66 | 7119 | Pottery vessel. Early/Late Middle Susiana | Fig. 37:J |
| R23:701 | 77.59 | 7133 | Pottery vessel. Early Middle Susiana | Fig. 42:I |
| R23:701 | 77.59 | 7152 | Plain pottery vessel. Early Susiana | Fig. 65:C |
| R23:702 | 77.63 | 7067 | Pottery vessel. Early to Middle Susiana transitional | Fig. 38:E |
| R23:702 | 77.63 | 7074 | Pottery vessel. Middle Susiana | Fig. 36:H |
| R23:702 | 77.63 | 7084 | Tortoise pottery vessel. Middle Susiana | Fig. 52:C |
| R23:702 | 77.78 | 7128 | Closed pottery vessel. Early Middle Susiana | Fig. 44:H |
| R23:702 | 77.78 | 7130 | Tortoise pottery vessel. Middle Susiana | Fig. 52:H |
| R23:702 | 77.82 | VII-7 | Baked-clay token or "thorn"-shaped figurine. Early Susiana(?) | Fig. 77:F, pl. 25:C |
| R23:703 | 77.36 | 7403 | Closed pottery vessel. Late Middle Susiana | Fig. 44:M |
| R23:704 | 75.47 | 7004 | Pottery vessel. Early Middle Susiana | Fig. 36:K |
| R23:705 | 76.00 | 7069 | Open pottery vessel. Early Susiana | Fig. 60:E |
| R23:706 | 76.64 | VII-59 | Unbaked clay chessman figurine. Archaic Susiana 2 | Fig. 79:M |
| R23:710 | 77.95 | 7105 | Close-line open bowl. Archaic Susiana 3 | Fig. 66:I |
| R23:710 | 77.82 | 7251 | Close-line open bowl. Archaic Susiana 3 | Fig. 66:A |
| R23:710 West | 78.18 | 7068 | Stone vessel. Early Susiana | Fig. 86:D |
| R23:710 West | 78.18 | 7185 | Baked clay animal figurine. Early Susiana | Fig. 80:K |
| R23:710 West | 78.18 | N/A | Stone vessel. Early Susiana | Fig. 86:C |
| R27:702 | 77.63 | 7070 | Tortoise pottery vessel. Early Middle Susiana | Fig. 52:A |
| R27:704 | 74.90 | 7161 | Plain pottery vessel. Early Susiana | Fig. 65:U |
| Round Building | N/A | 2676 | Pottery vessel. Late Iron Age/Achaemenid | Fig. 22:L |
| Round Building | N/A | 5501 | Pottery vessel. Late Iron Age/Achaemenid | Fig. 22:M |
| S17:404 | 82.28 | 41030 | Horned conical clay token. Protoliterate | Pl. 24:C |
| S17:405 | N/A | VI-51 | Pottery vessel. Protoliterate | Fig. 28:B |
| S17:901 | 81.20 | 9629 | Pottery vessel. Late Susiana 2 | Fig. 35:B |
| S17:901 | 81.20 | 9630 | Pottery vessel. Late Susiana 2 | Fig. 35:D |
| S17:901 | 81.20 | 9631 | Pottery vessel. Late Susiana 2 | Fig. 35:A, pl. 19:B |
| S18:403 | B.S. | 9001 | Pottery vessel. Late Iron Age/Achaemenid | Fig. 22:E |
| S18:901 | 83.87 | 9194 | Barrel-shaped baked-clay bead. Protoliterate | Fig. 81:P |
| S18:902 | 81.14 | 9904 | Sealing with four impressions of decorated cylindrical object (cylinder seal?). Protoliterate | Fig. 76:CC, pl. 22:J |
| S18:902 | 81.14 | 9905 | Sealing(?) with four impressions. Protoliterate | Fig. 76:FF, pl. 22:K |
| S18:902 | 80.40 | IX-127 | Plain pottery vessel. Early Middle Susiana | Fig. 54:A |
| S18:902 | 80.97 | IX-31 | Plain pottery vessel. Late Middle Susiana | Fig. 54:K |
| S18:904 | 81.12 | IX-30 | Plain pottery vessel. Late Middle Susiana | Fig. 53:U |
| S18:904 West | 81.12 | IX-131 | Closed pottery vessel. Late Middle Susiana | Fig. 47:D |
| S18:905 West | 81.07 | 9909 | Closed pottery vessel. Late Middle Susiana | Fig. 47:C |
| S18:905 West | 81.07 | IX-113 | Closed pottery vessel. Late Middle Susiana | Fig. 46:E |
| S18:905 West | 81.07 | IX-114 | Closed pottery vessel. Late Middle Susiana | Fig. 47:vB |
| S18:905 West | 81.07 | IX-115 | Closed pottery vessel. Late Middle Susiana | Fig. 46:F |
| S18:905 West | 81.86 | IX-126 | Closed pottery vessel. Late Middle Susiana | Fig. 47:A |
| S18:906 | 81.50 | IX-128 | Plain pottery vessel. Middle Susiana | Fig. 54:I |
| S18:907 | 80.59 | 9420 | Pottery vessel. Late Middle Susiana | Fig. 40:N |
| S18:907 | 81.45 | IX-56 | Plain pottery vessel. Late Middle Susiana | Fig. 53:B |
| S18:915 | 82.00 | 9153 | Pottery vessel. Middle Susiana | Fig. 36:A |
| S18:915 | 81.69 | 9178 | Plain pottery vessel. Late Middle Susiana | Fig. 54:C |
| S18:915 | 82.00 | 9547 | Pottery vessel. Middle Susiana | Fig. 36:I |
| S18:916 | 81.71 | 9026 | Stone vessel. Middle Susiana | Fig. 86:M |
| S18:916 | 81.60 | 9152 | Pottery vessel. Middle Susiana | Fig. 36:E |
| S18:916 | 80.10 | 9171 | Closed pottery vessel. Late Middle Susiana | Fig. 46:B |
| S18:916 | 81.86 | 9464 | Turquoise bead. Protoliterate | Fig. 81:N |
| S18:916 | 81.71 | 9534 | Pottery vessel. Late Middle Susiana | Fig. 40:K |
| S18:916 | 81.71 | 9624 | Pottery vessel. Late Middle Susiana | Fig. 37:G |
| S18:918 | 81.12 | 9051 | Stone vessel. Protoliterate | Fig. 86:P |
| S18:918 | 81.12 | 9110 | Clay token. Protoliterate | Fig. 77:Q |
| S18:918 | 81.12 | 9167 | Pottery vessel. Late Middle Susiana | Fig. 49:F |
| S18:918 | 81.10 | 9206 | Pottery vessel. Late Middle Susiana | Fig. 42:M |

| *Locus* | *Elevation* | *Reg. No.* | *Description* | *Illustration* |
|---|---|---|---|---|
| S18:918 | 80.09 | 9517 | Closed pottery vessel. Middle Susiana | Fig. 44:A |
| S18:918 | 80.09 | 9518 | Closed pottery vessel. Middle Susiana | Fig. 44:B |
| S18:918 | 80.09 | 9520 | Pottery vessel. Middle Susiana | Fig. 36:B |
| S18:918 | 81.65 | 9542 | Pottery vessel. Middle Susiana | Fig. 36:D |
| S18:918 South | 81.58 | 9551 | Closed pottery vessel. Middle Susiana | Fig. 44:I |
| S18:919 | 80.05 | 9580 | Pottery vessel. Lid. Early to Middle Susiana transitional | Fig. 50:A |
| S20:601 | 79.24 | 6002 | Pottery vessel. Late Middle Susiana | Fig. 41:H |
| S20:601 | 0.20 B.S. | 6004 | Closed pottery vessel. Late Middle Susiana | Fig. 44:S |
| S20:601 | 0.20 B.S. | 6005 | Pottery vessel. Late Middle Susiana | Fig. 37:A |
| S20:601 | 78.56 | 6013 | Pottery vessel. Late Middle Susiana | Fig. 37:B |
| S20:601 | 0.40 B.S. | 6036 | Pottery vessel. Late Middle Susiana | Pl. 19:H |
| S20:601 | 78.33 | 6040 | Pottery vessel. Late Middle Susiana | Fig. 42:C, pl. 19:E |
| S20:601 | 76.63 | 6084 | Pottery vessel. Late Middle Susiana | Fig. 38:C |
| S20:601 | 78.47 | 6131 | Pottery vessel. Early Middle Susiana | Fig. 38:D |
| S20:601 | 74.38 | 6370 | Pottery vessel. Archaic Susiana 2 | Fig. 72:C |
| S20:601 | 73.63 | 6372 | Pottery vessel. Archaic Susiana 2 | Fig. 72:G |
| S20:601 | 74.38 | 6432 | Close-line open bowl. Archaic Susiana 3 | Fig. 66:G |
| S20:601 | 78.06 | 6744 | Pottery vessel. Early Middle Susiana(?) | Fig. 49:C |
| S20:601 | 0.40 B.S. | 6836 | Door sealing with stamp seal impressions. Late Susiana(?) | Fig. 76:Y |
| S20:601 | 78.33 | 6848 | Closed pottery vessel. Late Middle Susiana | Fig. 44:Q |
| S20:601 | 0.40 B.S. | 6856 | Pottery vessel. Early Middle Susiana | Fig. 42:K |
| S20:601 | 0.20 B.S. | VI-1 | Baked-clay bull figurine/pendant. Middle Susiana | Fig. 80:G |
| S20:605 | 78.66 | 6003 | Pottery vessel. Late Middle Susiana | Fig. 41:G |
| S20:605 | 79.05 | 6015 | Plain pottery vessel. Late Middle Susiana | Fig. 54:B |
| S20:605 | 79.05 | 6224 | Plain pottery vessel. Late Middle Susiana | Fig. 54:N |
| S20:605 | 79.20 | 6490 | Pottery vessel. Late Middle Susiana | Fig. 43:A |
| S20:605 | 79.05 | 6851 | Closed pottery vessel. Late Middle Susiana | Fig. 45:K |
| S20:606 | N/A | 6498 | Pottery vessel. Late Middle Susiana | Fig. 48:B |
| S20:607 | 78.74 | 6466 | Decorated pottery lid. Early Susiana | Fig. 62:A |
| S20:607 | 78.74 | 6469 | Open pottery vessel. Early Susiana | Fig. 57:E |
| S20:607 | 78.74 | 6866 | Plain pottery vessel. Early Susiana | Fig. 64:F |
| S20:608 East | 78.73 | N/A | Bale sealing fragment with impression of tops of "staff." Protoliterate | Fig. 76:W |
| S20:609 | 78.67 | 6093 | Pottery vessel. Late Middle Susiana | Fig. 42:V |
| S20:609 | 78.90 | 6094 | Pottery vessel. Late Middle Susiana | Fig. 42:U |
| S20:609 | 77.89 | 6451 | Pottery vessel. Late Middle Susiana | Fig. 40:H |
| S20:609 | 77.05 | 6532 | Pottery vessel. Early Middle Susiana | Fig. 38:N |
| S20:609 | 78.07 | 6839 | Closed pottery vessel. Middle Susiana | Fig. 44:L |
| S20:609 | 77.05 | VI-13 | Bone object. Early Susiana | Fig. 85:B, pl. 25:B |
| S20:609 West | 78.07 | 6853 | Pottery vessel. Early to Middle Susiana transitional | Fig. 50:C |
| S20:609 West | 78.07 | 6409a | Tortoise pottery vessel. Middle Susiana | Fig. 52:B |
| S20:609 West | 78.07 | 6409a | Tortoise pottery vessel. Middle Susiana | Fig. 52:I |
| S20:615 | 78.13 | 6441 | Pottery vessel. Early to Middle Susiana transitional | FFig. 38: |
| S20:618 | 75.20 | 6522 | Pottery vessel. Form and decoration Early Susiana/Middle Susiana transitional | Fig. 37:F |
| S20:619 | 75.20 | 6058 | Close-line open bowl. Archaic Susiana 3 | Fig. 66:M |
| S20:620 | 78.20 | 6068 | Pottery vessel. Archaic Susiana 3 | Fig. 69:C |
| S20:620 | 78.20 | 6113 | Pottery vessel. Late Middle Susiana | Fig. 38:M |
| S20:620 | 78.20 | 6114 | Plain pottery vessel. Late Middle Susiana | Fig. 53:S |
| S20:620 | 77.92 | 6116 | Closed pottery vessel. Late Middle Susiana | Fig. 45:H |
| S20:620 | 78.20 | 6858 | Plain pottery vessel. Late Middle Susiana | Fig. 53:A |
| S20:620 | 77.86 | VI-41 | Pottery vessel. Late Middle Susiana | Fig. 41:E, pl. 19:K |
| S20:620 | 77.40 | VI-42 | Pottery vessel. Late Middle Susiana | Fig. 42:T |
| S20:621 | 77.85 | 6147 | Pottery vessel. Late Middle Susiana | Fig. 41:F |
| S20:621 | 77.85 | 6148 | Pottery vessel. Late Middle Susiana | Fig. 40:D |
| S20:621 | 78.40 | 6151 | Pottery vessel. Late Middle Susiana | Fig. 41:K |
| S20:621 | 78.85 | 6857 | Pottery vessel. Late Middle Susiana | Fig. 41:I |
| S20:621 | 78.70 | 6871 | Plain pottery vessel. Early Susiana | Fig. 65:S |
| S22:505 | N/A | N/A | Closed pottery vessel. Late Middle Susiana | Fig. 45:A |

| *Locus* | *Elevation* | *Reg. No.* | *Description* | *Illustration* |
|---|---|---|---|---|
| S22:601 | 73.60 | 6232 | Pottery vessel. Archaic Susiana 2 | Fig. 72:I |
| S22:601 | 73.21 | 6239 | Plain pottery vessel. Archaic Susiana 3 | Fig. 75:Q |
| S22:601 | 73.63 | 6240 | Plain pottery vessel. Archaic Susiana 3 | Fig. 75:V |
| S22:601 | 73.63 | 6426 | Matte-painted pottery vessel. Archaic Susiana 3 | Fig. 70:C |
| S22:601 | 73.63 | 6427 | Pottery vessel. Archaic Susiana 2 | Fig. 72:D |
| S22:601 | 73.46 | 6433 | Pottery vessel. Archaic Susiana 2 | Fig. 72:E |
| S22:601 | 73.63 | 6435 | Pottery vessel. Archaic Susiana 2 | Fig. 72:F |
| S22:601 | 73.46 | 6439 | Plain pottery vessel. Archaic Susiana 3 | Fig. 75:U |
| S22:601 | 73.67 | 6841 | Pottery vessel. Archaic Susiana 2 | Fig. 72:H |
| S22:601 | 73.67 | N/A | Pottery vessel. Archaic Susiana 1 | Fig. 68:C |
| S22:601 | 75.67 | N/A | Pottery vessel. Archaic Susiana 2 | Fig. 72:K |
| S22:601 | 74.38 | VI-100 | Clay tablet with impressed patterns of stippled triangles and bands. Probably Archaic Susiana | Fig. 76:EE, pl. 25:A |
| S22:601 | 74.93 | VI-3 | Baked-clay waist and lower body of female figurine. Early Susiana | Fig. 78:F, pl. 28:J |
| S22:609 | 78.07(?) | 6542 | Plain pottery vessel. Archaic Susiana | Fig. 74:B |
| S22:622 | 78.34 | 6092 | Open pottery vessel. Early/Middle Susiana | Fig. 55:F |
| S22:701 | 76.68 | VII-32 | Mother-of-pearl pendant. Early Susiana | Fig. 81:Q |
| S22:701 | 76.43 | VII-97 | Pottery vessel. Protoliterate | Fig. 30:A |
| S22:701 | 76.43 | VII-97 | Pottery vessel. Protoliterate | Fig. 31:N |
| S22:702 | Surface | 7400 | Pottery vessel. Late Middle Susiana | Fig. 43:B |
| S22:703 | 75.25 | 7079 | Pottery vessel. Archaic Susiana 3 | Fig. 69:E |
| S22:703 | 75.25 | 7091 | Plain pottery vessel. Archaic Susiana 3 | Fig. 75:T |
| S22:703 | 74.86 | 7178 | Plain pottery vessel. Archaic Susiana 3 | Fig. 75:E |
| S22:714 | 75.76 | VII-58 | Baked-clay token or figurine. Archaic Susiana | Fig. 77:I |
| S22:803 | 75.91 | 8001 | Open pottery vessel. Early Susiana | Fig. 60:A |
| S22:803 | 76.15 | 8007 | Open pottery vessel. Early Susiana | Fig. 58:H |
| S22:803 | 76.16 | 8009 | Pottery vessel. Late Middle Susiana | Fig. 40:G |
| S22:803 | 70.41 | 8051 | Pottery vessel. Protoliterate | Fig. 30:C |
| S22:803 | 76.16 | 8568 | Pottery vessel. Protoliterate | Fig. 29:H |
| S22:803 | 77.01 | 8572 | Pottery vessel. Protoliterate | Fig. 31:F |
| S22:805 | 76.88 | 8725 | Pottery vessel. Early Middle Susiana | Fig. 39:D |
| S22:806 | 77.70 | 8086 | Pottery vessel. Late Middle Susiana | Fig. 49:B |
| S22:806 | 76.93 | 8789 | Pottery vessel. Late Middle Susiana | Fig. 41:C |
| S22:806 East | 76.65 | 8181 | Pottery vessel. Late Middle Susiana | Fig. 40:C |
| S22:806 North | 76.93 | 81012 | Plain pottery vessel. Late Middle Susiana | Fig. 53:D |
| S22:808 | 75.91 | 8030 | Open pottery vessel. Early Susiana | Fig. 55:H |
| S22:808 | 75.67 | 8062 | Open pottery vessel. Early Susiana | Fig. 55:A |
| S22:808 | 75.67 | 8063 | Open pottery vessel. Early Susiana | Fig. 56:F |
| S22:808 | 75.67 | 8064 | Open pottery vessel. Early Susiana | Fig. 57:A |
| S22:808 | 75.55 | 8184 | Open pottery vessel. Early Susiana | Fig. 55:E |
| S22:808 | 75.55 | 8227 | Close-line open bowl. Archaic Susiana 3 | Fig. 66:K |
| S22:808 | 75.91 | 8230 | Open pottery vessel. Early Susiana | Fig. 56:D |
| S22:808 | 75.94 | 8239 | Open pottery vessel. Early Susiana | Fig. 57:I |
| S22:808 | 75.46 | 8734 | Pottery vessel. Archaic/Early Susiana transitional | Fig. 63:F |
| S22:808 | 75.46 | 8738 | Open pottery vessel. Early Susiana | Fig. 60:B |
| S22:808 | 75.46 | 8802 | Pottery vessel. Archaic/Early Susiana transitional | Fig. 63:E |
| S22:808 | 75.60 | 8870 | Open pottery vessel. Early Susiana | Fig. 56:G |
| S22:808 | 75.77 | VIII-1 | Baked-clay figurine of seated female. Early Susiana | Fig. 79:B, pl. 27:F |
| S22:808 North | 74.99 | 8695 | Torso of a baked-clay female figurine. Early Susiana | Fig. 78:E, pl. 28:A |
| S22:809 | 77.21 | IX-53 | Stone vessel. Late Middle Susiana | Fig. 86:U |
| S22:809 | 76.77 | VIII-21 | Stone vessel. Middle Susiana | Fig. 86:O |
| S22:812 | 76.65 | 8002 | Closed pottery vessel. Late Middle Susiana | Fig. 44:K |
| S22:813 | 76.30 | IX-26 | Sandstone mill. Early Susiana | Fig. 87:H |
| S22:813 | 76.29 | VIII-49 | Bone object. Middle Susiana | Fig. 85:F |
| S22:816 | 77.19 | 9141 | Stone vessel. Late Middle Susiana | Fig. 86:V |
| S22:819 | 76.71 | 8589 | Spindle whorl. Early Middle Susiana | Fig. 83:D |
| S22:819 | 76.33 | 8677 | Pottery vessel. Early Middle Susiana | Fig. 37:E |

| Locus | Elevation | Reg. No. | Description | Illustration |
|---|---|---|---|---|
| S22:819 | B.S. | 8923 | Spindle whorl. Late Middle Susiana | Fig. 83:B |
| S22:819 | 76.06 | VIII-50 | Bone object. Early Susiana | Fig. 85:I |
| S22:819 North | 76.06 | VIII-56 | Copper pin. Old Elamite(?) | Fig. 84:C |
| S22:821 | 76.35 | 8862 | Open pottery vessel. Early Susiana | Fig. 61:J |
| S22:822 | 76.18 | 8114 | Open pottery vessel. Archaic/Early Susiana transitional | Fig. 58:A |
| S22:822 | 76.18 | VIII-54 | White stone with dark veins. Early Susiana | Fig. 81:C |
| S22:823 | 75.98 | 8104 | Open pottery vessel. Early Susiana | Fig. 58:E |
| S22:823 | 75.84 | 8117 | Open pottery vessel. Archaic/Early Susiana transitional | Fig. 58:C |
| S22:823 | 75.84 | 8183 | Plain pottery vessel. Early Susiana | Fig. 65:I |
| S22:823 | 75.43 | 8252 | Open pottery vessel. Early Susiana | Fig. 61:I |
| S22:823 | 75.94 | 8254 | Open pottery vessel. Early Susiana | Fig. 59:C |
| S22:823 | 75.51 | 8255 | Open pottery vessel. Early Susiana | Fig. 58:G |
| S22:823 | 75.90 | 8260 | Open pottery vessel. Early Susiana | Fig. 56:A |
| S22:823 | 74.84 | 8283 | Open pottery vessel. Early Susiana | Fig. 61:L |
| S22:823 | 74.98 | 8287 | Open pottery vessel. Early Susiana | Fig. 56:I |
| S22:823 | 74.98 | 8308 | Open pottery vessel. Early Susiana | Fig. 61:N |
| S22:823 | 75.08 | 8348 | Matte-painted pottery vessel. Archaic Susiana 3 | Fig. 70:D |
| S22:823 | 74.98 | 8350 | Open pottery vessel. Archaic/Early Susiana transitional | Fig. 58:B |
| S22:823 | 74.98 | 8358 | Plain pottery vessel. Archaic Susiana 2 | Fig. 75:B |
| S22:823 | 75.44 | 8360 | Open pottery vessel. Early Susiana | Fig. 61:O |
| S22:823 | 75.30 | 8440 | Plain pottery vessel. Archaic Susiana 3 | Fig. 75:J |
| S22:823 | 76.35 | 8467 | Bone object. Early Susiana | Fig. 85:P |
| S22:823 | 76.35 | 8468 | Bone object. Early Susiana | Fig. 85:M |
| S22:823 | 75.43 | 8490 | Open pottery vessel. Early Susiana | Fig. 56:K |
| S22:823 | 75.13 | 8497 | Close-line open bowl. Archaic Susiana 3 | Fig. 66:L |
| S22:823 | 75.90 | 8578 | Closed pottery vessel. Early Susiana | Fig. 61:F |
| S22:823 | 74.87 | 8605 | Pottery vessel. Archaic Susiana 3 | Fig. 68:D |
| S22:823 | 76.35 | 8640 | Closed pottery vessel. Early Susiana | Fig. 61:G |
| S22:823 | 74.51 | 8641 | Closed pottery vessel. Early Susiana | Fig. 61:E |
| S22:823 | 75.94 | 8648 | Open pottery vessel. Early Susiana | Fig. 56:E |
| S22:823 | 75.43 | 8758 | Open pottery vessel. Early Susiana | Fig. 61:K |
| S22:823 | 74.92 | 8760 | Pottery vessel. Archaic Susiana 3 | Fig. 69:A |
| S22:823 | 75.84 | 8762 | Plain pottery vessel. Early Susiana | Fig. 65:D |
| S22:823 | 75.03 | 8769 | Open pottery vessel. Early Susiana | Fig. 57:D |
| S22:823 | 75.08 | VIII-4 | Brownish gray sandstone. Archaic Susiana 3 | Fig. 87:D |
| S22:823 | 75.94 | VIII-57 | Bone object. Early Susiana | Fig. 85:H |
| S22:823 | 74.79 | VIII-58 | Copper. Protoliterate | Fig. 84:D |
| S22:823 | 76.35 | VIII-60 | Stone figurine of boar. Archaic/Early Susiana | Fig. 80:F, pl. 27:B |
| S22:823 | 74.79 | VIII-63 | Mother-of-pearl pendant. Archaic Susiana | Fig. 81:R |
| S22:823 North | 75.74 | 8043 | Baked-clay waist and lower body of female figurine. Early Susiana | Fig. 78:G, pl. 28:C |
| S22:823 North | 76.35 | 8465 | Bone object. Early Susiana | Fig. 85:O |
| S22:823 North | 75.03 | 8761 | Open pottery vessel. Early Susiana | Fig. 55:G |
| S22:823 North | 75.81 | VIII-38 | Spindle whorl. Early Susiana | Fig. 83:E |
| S22:823 North | 75.74 | VIII-84 | Mid-section of female figurine. Early Susiana | Fig. 78:A, pl. 28:D |
| S22:823 West | 75.90 | 8298 | Plain pottery vessel. Early Susiana | Fig. 65:H |
| S22:823 West | 74.24 | 8448 | Open pottery vessel. Early Susiana | Fig. 55:C |
| S22:824 | 75.08 | 8238 | Close-line open bowl. Archaic Susiana 3 | Fig. 66:F |
| S22:824 | 74.98 | VIII-62 | Stone token. Archaic Susiana | Fig. 77:B |
| S22:825 | 76.35 | 8099 | Open pottery vessel. Probably transitional Archaic/Early Susiana | Fig. 60:G |
| S22:825 | 76.24 | 8137 | Open pottery vessel. Early Susiana | Fig. 55:I |
| S22:825 | 76.30 | N/A | Pottery vessel. Early Susiana | Pl. 21:C |
| S22:826 | 75.49 | 8128 | Open pottery vessel. Early Susiana | Fig. 55:B |
| S22:826 | 74.68 | 8938 | Open pottery vessel. Early Susiana | Fig. 57:C |
| S22:826 | 74.66 | VIII-85 | Baked-clay head of human figurine. Early Susiana | Fig. 78:C, pl. 27:A |
| S22:827 | 74.30 | 8174 | Baked-clay waist and body of female figurine. Archaic/Early Susiana | Fig. 78:H, pl. 28:B |
| S22:827 | 74.30 | 8856 | Open pottery vessel. Archaic/Early Susiana transitional | Fig. 61:B |
| S22:827 | 74.30 | VIII-52 | White stone "plug." Archaic Susiana 3 | Fig. 81:B |

| *Locus* | *Elevation* | *Reg. No.* | *Description* | *Illustration* |
|---|---|---|---|---|
| S22:831 | 75.41 | 8471 | Unbaked clay chessman figurine. Archaic Susiana 2 | Fig. 79:K |
| S22:831 North | 75.02 | 8292 | Plain pottery vessel. Archaic Susiana 3 | Fig. 75:H |
| S22:831 North | 75.02 | VIII-74 | Baked-clay figurine of female. Early Susiana | Fig. 79:D |
| S22:902 | 77.43 | 9018 | Closed pottery vessel. Middle Susiana | Fig. 44:C |
| S22:902 | 77.51 | 9028 | Baked-clay token. Early Susiana | Fig. 77:C |
| S22:902 | 76.83 | 9080 | Bone object. Middle Susiana | Fig. 85:G |
| S22:902 | 76.83 | 9184 | Pottery vessel. Early Middle Susiana | Fig. 49:A |
| S22:902 | 77.08 | 9333 | Closed pottery vessel. Late Middle Susiana | Fig. 45:I |
| S22:902 Northeast | 77.65 | 9358 | Pottery vessel. Middle Susiana | Fig. 49:E |
| S22:903 | 75.39 | 9134 | Pottery vessel. Early Susiana | Fig. 63:L |
| S22:904 | 76.96 | 9144 | Pottery vessel. Protoliterate | Fig. 30:F |
| S22:904 | 74.72 | 11068 | Plain pottery vessel. Archaic Susiana 3 | Fig. 75:F |
| S22:904 | 76.22 | IX-59 | Strainer. Protoliterate | Fig. 82:L |
| S22:908 | 76.90 | 9033 | Stand/cup(?) fragment. Protoliterate | Fig. 82:B |
| S22:908 | 74.45 | 9282 | Matte-painted pottery vessel. Archaic Susiana 3 | Fig. 71:E |
| S22:909 | 74.57 | 9107 | Plain pottery vessel. Archaic Susiana 2 | Fig. 75:A |
| S22:909 | 73.70 | 9138 | Figurine. Archaic Susiana 2 | Pl. 28:G–H |
| S22:909 | 75.00 | 9312 | Matte-painted pottery vessel. Archaic Susiana 3 | Fig. 70:A, pl. 21:E |
| S22:909 | 74.40 | 9343 | Pottery vessel. Archaic Susiana 3 | Fig. 67:A |
| S22:909 Middle | 74.40 | 9043 | Stone vessel. Archaic Susiana 3 | Fig. 86:I |
| S22:909 Middle | N/A | 9061 | Unbaked clay token. Archaic Susiana | Fig. 77:O |
| S22:909 South | 75.13 | 9008 | Unbaked clay chessman figurine. Archaic Susiana 2 | Fig. 79:J, pl. 28:I |
| S22:909 South | 75.00 | 9277 | Plain pottery vessel. Early Susiana | Fig. 65:G |
| S22:910 South | 74.68 | 9060 | Unbaked clay chessman figurine. Archaic Susiana 3 | Fig. 79:N |
| S22:911 | 74.00 | 9268 | Matte-painted pottery vessel. Archaic Susiana 3 | Fig. 71:A |
| S22:911 | 74.00 | 9269 | Pottery vessel. Archaic Susiana 3 | Fig. 69:B |
| S22:912 | 74.52 | 9047 | Stone vessel. Archaic Susiana 3 | Fig. 86:A |
| S22:912 | 74.57 | 9237 | Pottery vessel. Archaic Susiana 3 | Fig. 69:D |
| S22:912 | 74.74 | 9328 | Pottery vessel. Archaic Susiana 2 | Fig. 72:B |
| S22:912 | 74.52 | 9364 | Pottery vessel. Archaic Susiana 3 | Fig. 69:K |
| S22:912 | 73.72 | 9512 | Pottery vessel. Archaic Susiana 3 | Fig. 68:B, pl. 21:J |
| S22:912 East | 74.46 | 9040 | Baked-clay human figurine. Archaic Susiana 3 | Fig. 79:F, pl. 28:F |
| S22:912 East | 74.46 | 9253 | Baked-clay horn. Archaic Susiana/Early Susiana | Fig. 80:J |
| S22:912 East | 75.55 | N/A | Baked-clay figurine. Early Susiana | Pl. 28:E |
| S22:912, S22:916 | 73.72, 73.70 | 9512/9370 | Pottery vessel. Archaic Susiana 3 | Fig. 68:B |
| S22:913 | 74.54 | 9039 | Head and torso of highly stylized human figurine. Archaic Susiana 3 | Fig. 78:D, pl. 28:K |
| S22:913 | 74.21 | 9063 | Unbaked clay figurine, presumably female. Early Susiana | Fig. 79:C |
| S22:914 | 75.76 | 9101 | Bone object. Early Susiana | Fig. 85:K |
| S22:914 | 73.70 | 9183 | Bone object. Archaic Susiana | Fig. 85:C |
| S22:914 | 73.70 | 9225 | Plain pottery vessel. Archaic Susiana 2 | Fig. 75:C |
| S22:914 | 74.77 | 9267 | Pottery vessel. Archaic/Early Susiana transitional | Fig. 63:C |
| S22:914 | 74.02 | 9511 | Matte-painted pottery vessel. Archaic Susiana 3 | Fig. 71:D |
| S22:916 | 76.19 | 9126 | Unbaked clay chessman figurine. Archaic/Early Susiana | Fig. 79:I |
| S22:916 | 77.19 | 9127 | Baked-clay female figurine. Archaic Susiana 3 | Fig. 79:A |
| S22:916 | 77.19 | 9128 | Baked-clay figurine of dog(?). Middle Susiana | Fig. 80:H |
| S22:916 | 73.70 | 9370 | Pottery vessel. Archaic Susiana 3 | Pl. 21:K |
| S22:916 | 74.94 | 9465 | Bone object. Archaic Susiana | Fig. 85:J |
| S22:918 | 76.53 | 9115 | Stone pestle fragment. Early Susiana | Fig. 87:K |
| S22:919 | 76.61 | 9783 | Pottery vessel. Early Susiana | Pl. 21:B |
| S22:923 | 74.52 | 9494 | Baked-clay token. Archaic Susiana | Fig. 77:A |
| S22:923 | 75.22 | 9739 | Pottery vessel. Early Susiana | Pl. 21:A |
| S22:923 | 74.54 | IX-102 | Plain pottery vessel. Archaic Susiana 3 | Fig. 74:A |
| S22:926 | 77.09 | 9454 | Bone object. Middle Susiana | Fig. 85:E |
| S22:926 | 77.03 | 9806 | Pottery vessel. Late Middle Susiana | Fig. 42:B |
| S22:929 | 74.90 | 11212 | Pottery vessel. Archaic Susiana 1 | Pl. 21:I |
| S22:1101 | 78.95 | N/A | Plain pottery vessel. Archaic Susiana 3 | Fig. 75:I |
| S22:1102 | 73.40 | 11006 | Plain pottery vessel. Archaic Susiana 3 | Fig. 75:O |
| S22:1103 | 73.20 | 11064 | Plain pottery vessel. Archaic Susiana 3 | Fig. 75:L |

| Locus | Elevation | Reg. No. | Description | Illustration |
|---|---|---|---|---|
| S22:1103 | 72.74 | 11180 | Plain pottery vessel. Archaic Susiana 3 | Fig. 75:S |
| S22:1103 | 72.89 | 11186 | Plain pottery vessel. Archaic Susiana 2(?) | Fig. 75:R |
| S22:1103 | 74.20 | N/A | Baked-clay human figurine. Archaic Susiana 3 | Fig. 79:H |
| S22:1107 | 72.20 | 11179 | Plain pottery vessel. Archaic Susiana 3 | Fig. 75:N |
| S22:1108 | 72.68 | 11142 | Plain pottery vessel. Archaic Susiana 3 | Fig. 75:M |
| S22:1108 East | 72.27 | 11158 | Pottery vessel. Archaic Susiana 1 | Fig. 68:E |
| S23:605 | 79.05 | 6128 | Pottery vessel. Early Middle Susiana | Fig. 39:E |
| S23:Steps | 75.46 | 5125 | Matte-painted pottery vessel. Archaic Susiana 3 | Fig. 70:E |
| Sdg. A | B.S. | 2652 | Open bowl. Late Iron Age/Achaemenid | Fig. 24:O |
| Sdg. A | 0.85 B.S. | 41136 | Pottery vessel. Parthian | Fig. 19:D |
| Sdg. E | N/A | II | Pottery vessel. Parthian | Fig. 19:B |
| Sdg. E | B.S. | II | Pottery vessel. Parthian | Fig. 19:H |
| Sdg. E | B.S. | II | Pottery vessel. Parthian | Fig. 19:J |
| Sdg. F | B.S. | 2577 | Pottery vessel. Late Iron Age/Achaemenid | Fig. 22:H |
| Sdg. F | Surface | 2608 | Pottery vessel. Late Iron Age/Achaemenid | Fig. 23:P |
| Sdg. G | 0.55 B.S. | 4115 | Pottery "stand." Late Middle Susiana | Fig. 51:F |
| Sdg. G | 1.40 B.S. | 4264 | Pottery vessel. Middle Susiana | Fig. 36:F |
| Sdg. G | 77.15 | 4462 | Pottery vessel. Late Middle Susiana | Fig. 41:A |
| Sdg. H | 0.90 B.S. | 4116 | Pottery "stand." Late Middle Susiana | Fig. 51:E |
| Sdg. H | B.S. | 4461 | Pottery vessel. Late Middle Susiana | Fig. 42:P |
| Sdg. H | 0.50 B.S. | 41173 | Closed pottery vessel. Early Middle Susiana | Fig. 45:L |
| Surface | N/A | N/A | Closed pottery vessel. Late Middle Susiana | Fig. 45:D |
| Tr. II | 2.50 B.S. | 1219 | Pottery vessel. Old Elamite (Sukkalmah) | Fig. 25:N |
| Tr. V | B.S. | 2484 | Open bowl. Late Iron Age/Achaemenid | Fig. 20:F |
| Tr. V | 0.70 B.S. | 2556 | Open bowl. Late Iron Age/Achaemenid | Fig. 20:M |
| Tr. V | 0.40 B.S. | 2557 | Open bowl. Late Iron Age/Achaemenid | Fig. 20:K |
| Tr. V | 1.40 B.S. | 2593 | Pottery vessel. Late Iron Age/Achaemenid | Fig. 22:J |
| Tr. V | 82.98 | 2619 | Open bowl. Late Iron Age/Achaemenid | Fig. 24:D |
| Tr. V | N/A | 2758 | Open bowl. Late Iron Age/Achaemenid | Fig. 20:J |
| Tr. V | 0.90 B.S. | 2797 | Open bowl. Late Iron Age (Neo-Elamite)/Achaemenid | Fig. 21:K |
| Tr. V | 1.70 B.S. | 3648 | Open bowl. Late Iron Age (Neo-Elamite)/Achaemenid | Fig. 21:G |
| Tr. V | 1.0 B.S. | 3654 | Open bowl. Late Iron Age/Achaemenid | Fig. 24:N |
| Tr. V | 1.20 B.S. | II-213 | Seal impression of female on door sealing. Protoliterate | Fig. 76:J |
| Tr. V | 1.50 B.S. | II-241 | Impression of female with butter-churning vessel on jar sealing. Protoliterate | Fig. 76:G |
| Tr. V, Plot D | 81.40 | 2483 | Open bowl. Late Iron Age/Achaemenid | Fig. 20:A |
| Tr. V, Plot D | 0.50 B.S. | 2589 | Pottery vessel. Late Iron Age/Achaemenid | Fig. 23:D |
| Tr. V, Plot D | 1.0 B.S. | 2618 | Pottery vessel. Late Iron Age/Achaemenid | Fig. 23:E |
| Tr. V, Plot D | 1.0 B.S. | 2638 | Pottery vessel. Late Iron Age/Achaemenid | Fig. 23:O |
| Tr. V, Plot D | N/A | 2669 | Pottery vessel. Late Iron Age/Achaemenid | Fig. 23:B |
| Tr. VI | B.S. | 2625 | Pottery vessel. Late Iron Age/Achaemenid | Fig. 22:P |
| Tr. VI | B.S. | 2631 | Pottery vessel. Parthian | Fig. 19:A |
| Tr. VI | N/A | II-202 | Seal impression of "lamb" on clay ball. Protoliterate | Fig. 76:F |
| Tr. VII | B.S. | 2596 | Open bowl. Late Iron Age/Achaemenid | Fig. 24:E |
| Tr. VII | N/A | 2641 | Open bowl. Late Iron Age (Neo-Elamite)/Achaemenid | Fig. 21:J |
| Tr. VII | 0.90 B.S. | 2657 | Open bowl. Late Iron Age/Achaemenid | Fig. 20:G |
| Tr. VII | N/A | 2667 | Pottery vessel. Late Iron Age/Achaemenid | Fig. 23:A |
| Tr. VIII | 1.0 B.S. | 8237 | Pottery vessel. Parthian | Fig. 19:I |
| Tr. IX | B.S. | 2669 | Pottery vessel. Late Iron Age/Achaemenid | Fig. 22:B |
| Tr. IX | 0.70 B.S. | 3211 | Pottery vessel. Late Middle Susiana | Fig. 38:G |
| Tr. IX | 0.45 B.S. | 4641 | Pottery vessel. Parthian | Fig. 19:E |
| Tr. IX | 0.75 B.S. | IV-24 | Bone object. Archaic Susiana | Fig. 85:L |
| Tr. XI | N/A | 2488 | Open bowl. Late Iron Age/Achaemenid | Fig. 20:E |
| Tr. XIII | N/A | 41043 | Pottery "stand." Late Middle Susiana | Fig. 51:H |
| Tr. XIII | 0.60 B.S. | 2543 | Pottery vessel. Middle Susiana | Fig. 48:A |
| Tr. XIII | 0.85 B.S. | 4232 | Pottery vessel. Early Middle Susiana | Fig. 42:J |
| Tr. XIII | 0.45 B.S. | 4782 | Pottery vessel. Late Iron Age/Achaemenid | Fig. 23:I |
| Tr. XIII | 0.70 B.S. | 6225 | Pottery vessel. Protoliterate | Fig. 32:G |
| Tr. XIII | 82.24 | VI-86 | Stone socket/sinker. Middle Susiana | Pl. 25:J |

| *Locus* | *Elevation* | *Reg. No.* | *Description* | *Illustration* |
|---|---|---|---|---|
| Tr. XIII | 0.95 B.S. | VI-87 | Stone sinker(?). Middle Susiana | Pl. 25:L |
| Tr. XIII | N/A | VI-90 | Stone pestle. Early Middle Susiana | Pl. 30:K |
| Tr. XIII | Surface | VIII-53 | Stone "plug." Date(?) | Fig. 81:E |
| Tr. XIV | B.S. | 2546 | Pottery vessel. Parthian | Fig. 19:C |
| Tr. XVI | Surface | 2523 | Pottery "stand." Late Middle Susiana | Fig. 51:A |
| Tr. XVIII | B.S. | 2621 | Pottery vessel. Late Iron Age/Achaemenid | Fig. 22:A |
| Tr. XVIII | B.S. | N/A | Open bowl. Late Iron Age (Neo-Elamite)/Achaemenid | Fig. 21:D |
| Tr. XXI | Surface | 7155 | Pottery vessel. Early Middle Susiana | Fig. 42:G |
| Tr. XXIV | B.S. | 3836 | Pottery vessel. Parthian | Fig. 19:O |
| Tr. XXIV | B.S. | 31057 | Pottery vessel. Parthian | Fig. 19:G |
| Tr. XXV | 1.00 B.S. | 3360 | Pottery vessel. Archaic Susiana 3 | Fig. 69:H |
| Tr. XXV | 78.56 | 6001 | Pottery vessel. Late Middle Susiana | Fig. 41:B, pl. 19:M |
| Tr. XXV | 76.13 | 6142 | Plain pottery vessel. Late Middle Susiana | Fig. 54:H |
| Tr. XXV | Surface | 8299 | Pottery vessel. Protoliterate | Fig. 33:H |
| Tr. XXV | N/A | N/A | Baked-clay human female figurine. Probably Archaic Susiana 3 | Fig. 79:E |
| Tr. XXVI | N/A | 4117 | Pottery "stand." Late Middle Susiana | Fig. 51:B |
| Tr. XXVI | B.S. | N/A | Open bowl. Late Iron Age (Neo-Elamite)/Achaemenid | Fig. 21:B |
| Tr. XXXIII | 76.40 | 6024 | Pottery vessel. Late Middle Susiana | Fig. 42:R, pl. 19:D |
| Tr. XXXIII | 76.80 | 6027 | Pottery vessel. Late Middle Susiana | Fig. 42:N |
| Tr. XXXIII | 77.68 | 6028 | Pottery vessel. Late Middle Susiana | Fig. 42:S, pl. 19:C |
| Tr. XXXIII | 77.34 | 6029 | Pottery vessel. Early/Late Middle Susiana | Fig. 42:H |
| Tr. XXXIII | 77.40 | 6031 | Pottery vessel. Protoliterate | Fig. 27:I |
| Tr. XXXIII | 77.21 | 6033 | Pottery vessel. Ladle fragment. Early Susiana | Fig. 63:H |
| Tr. XXXIII | 76.32 | 6118 | Pottery vessel. Late Middle Susiana | Pl. 19:I |
| Tr. XXXIII | 77.40 | 6121 | Pottery vessel. Late Middle Susiana | Fig. 37:C |
| Tr. XXXIII | 77.40 | 6121 | Pottery vessel. Late Middle Susiana | Fig. 38:A |
| Tr. XXXIII | 76.83 | 6527 | Pottery vessel. Late Middle Susiana | Fig. 42:D |
| Tr. XXXIII | Surface | 9383 | Pottery vessel. Late Middle Susiana | Fig. 40:E |
| Tr. XXXIII | 77.40 | N/A | Stone vessel. Early Middle Susiana(?) | Fig. 86:H |
| Tr. XXXIII | 77.02 | 6499 | Closed pottery vessel. Late Middle Susiana | Fig. 45:C |
| Tr. XXXIV | Surface | 7100 | Closed pottery vessel. Late Middle Susiana | Fig. 45:E |
| Tr. XXXIV | B.S. | 7266 | Closed pottery vessel. Late Middle Susiana | Fig. 44:J |
| Tr. XXXV | B.S. | 6032 | Pottery vessel. Late Middle Susiana | Fig. 40:A |
| Tr. XXXV | 76.13 | 6133 | Plain pottery vessel. Late Middle Susiana | Fig. 53:T |
| Tr. XXXV | 76.47 | 6134 | Plain pottery vessel. Late Middle Susiana | Fig. 53:R |
| Tr. XXXVI | N/A | VII-1 | White stone "plug" with dark vein used as "eye" of plug. Middle Susiana | Fig. 81:F, pl. 25:C |
| West Area | 1.30 B.S. | 41078 | Pottery "stand." Late Middle Susiana | Fig. 51:G |
| N/A | N/A | 9246 | Pottery vessel. Protoliterate | Fig. 27:D |
| N/A | N/A | IX-111 | Bone female figurine. Protoliterate | Pl. 26:A |
| N/A | N/A | IX-112 | Goat-handled cup. Old Elamite | Pl. 26:B–C |
| N/A | N/A | VII-10 | Token/labret | Pl. 25:C |
| N/A | N/A | VII-11 | Token/labret | Pl. 25:C |
| N/A | N/A | VII-33 | Token/labret | Pl. 25:C |
| N/A | N/A | VII-55 | Token/labret | Pl. 25:C |
| N/A | N/A | VII-57 | Token/labret | Pl. 25:C |
| N/A | N/A | VII-58 | Token/labret | Pl. 25:C |
| N/A | N/A | VII-61 | Token/labret | Pl. 25:C |
| N/A | N/A | VII-65 | Chessman figurine | Pl. 25:C |
| N/A | N/A | VII-9 | Chessman figurine | Pl. 25:C |
| N/A | Surface | 1073 | Pottery vessel. Early Middle Susiana | Fig. 38:J |
| N/A | N/A | 9906 | Baked-clay stamp seal. Late Susiana(?) | Fig. 76:B, pl. 22:C |
| N/A | N/A | BF-2687 | Pottery vessel. Archaic Susiana | Fig. 67:D |
| N/A | Surface | IX-116 | Pottery vessel. Protoliterate | Fig. 31:M |
| N/A | 1.0 B.S. | IX-20 | Plain pottery vessel. Late Middle Susiana | Fig. 54:O |
| N/A | N/A | N/A | Closed pottery vessel. Late Middle Susiana | Fig. 44:F |
| N/A | N/A | N/A | Closed pottery vessel. Late Middle Susiana | Fig. 44:O |

# INDEX OF GEOGRAPHICAL NAMES

# FIGURES

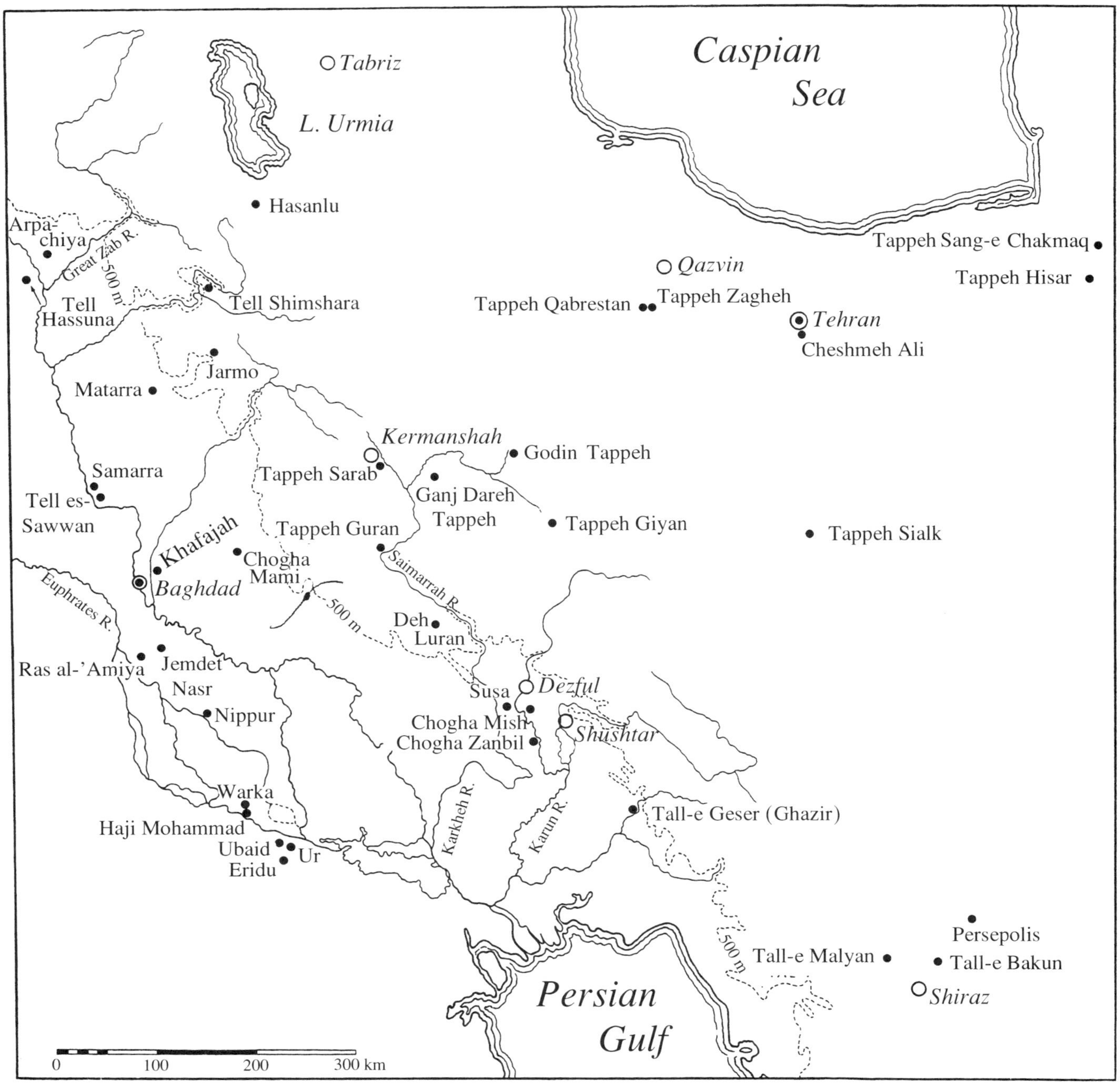


Figure 1. Map Showing the Location of Chogha Mish and Other Major Sites
in Southwestern Iran and Southern Mesopotamia

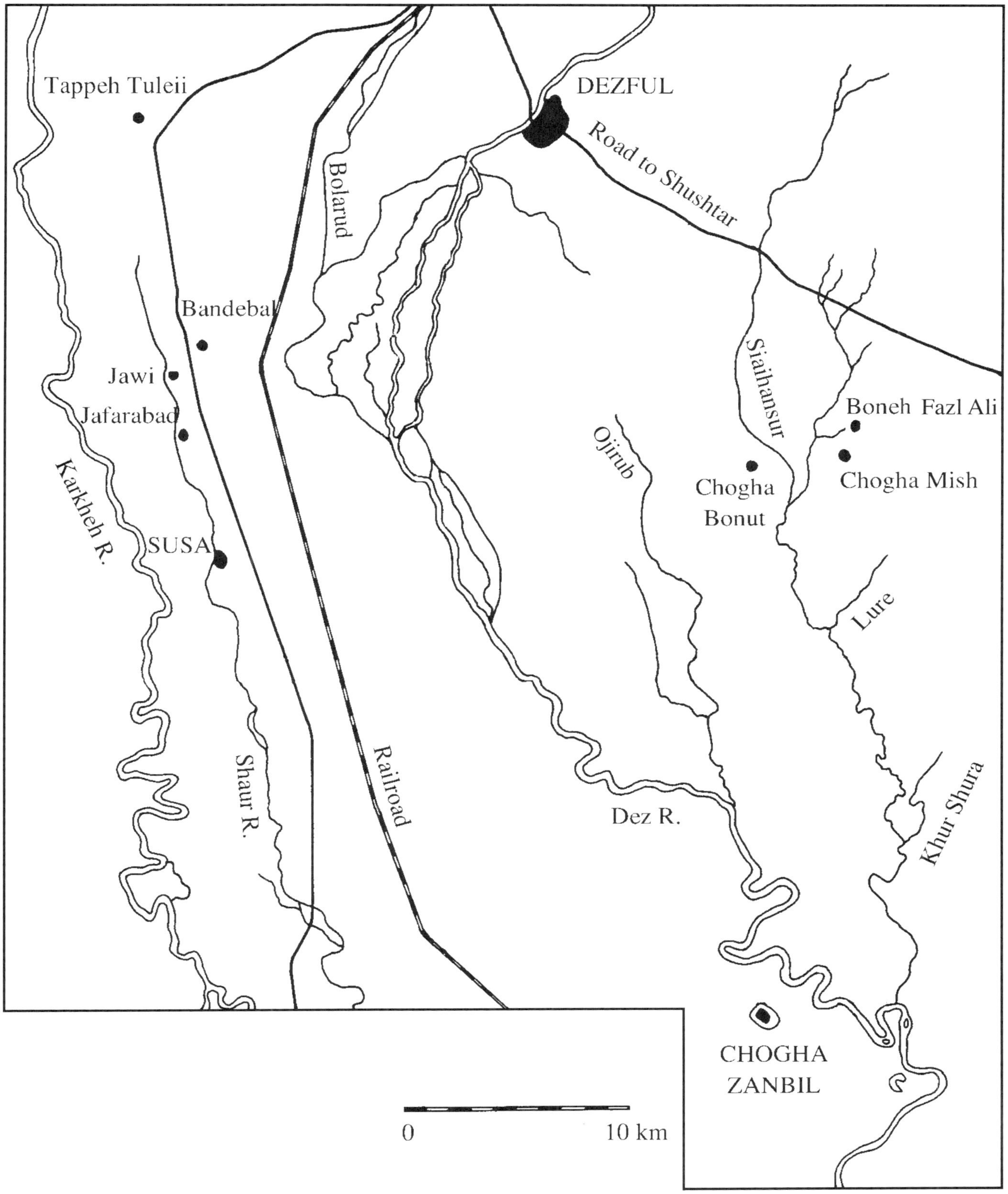


Figure 2. Map of Northern Susiana Plain Showing Locations of Chogha Mish, Chogha Bonut, Boneh Fazl Ali, and Their Environs

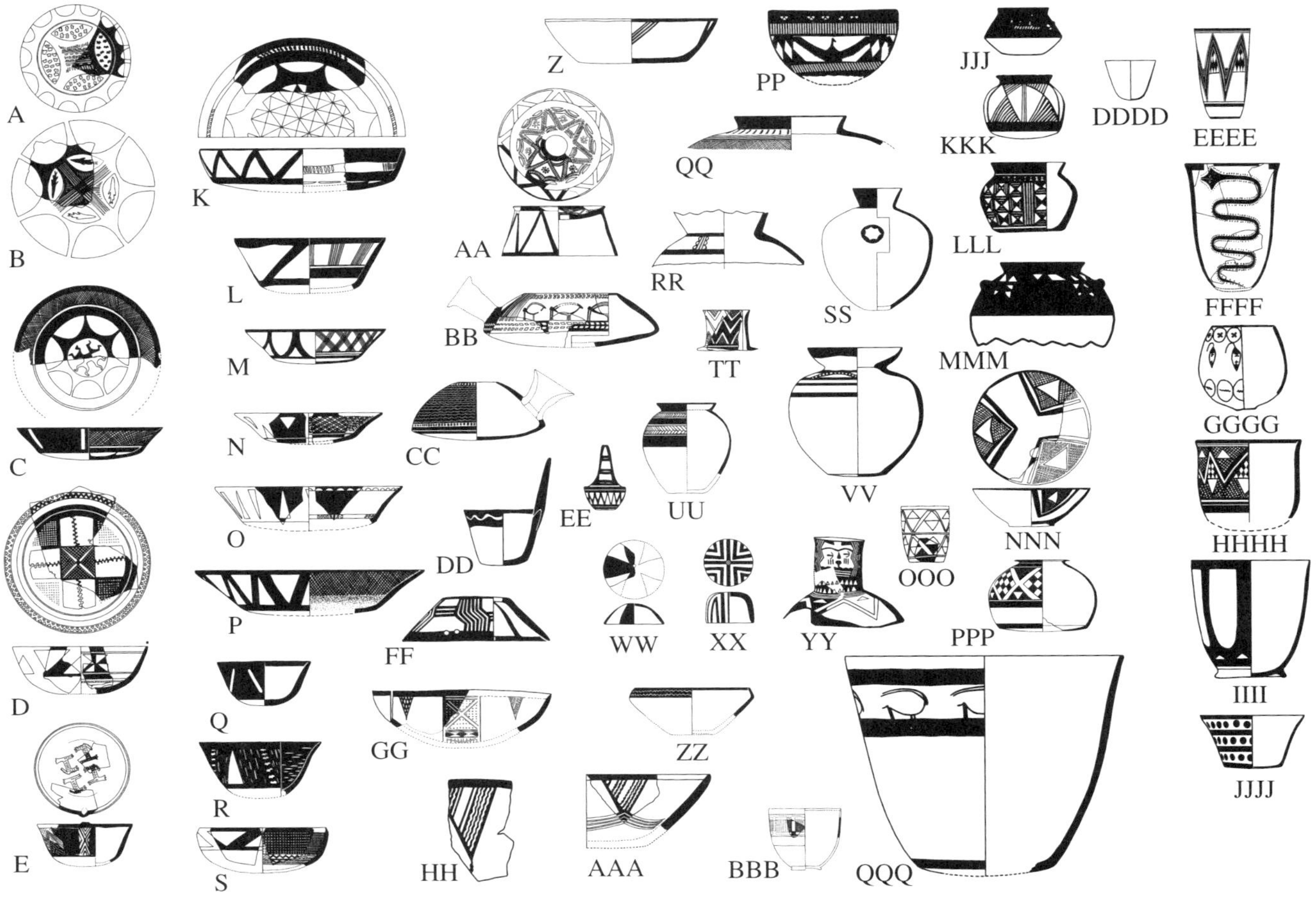


Figure 3a. Synopsis of the Evolution of Pottery Decoration of Prehistoric Susiana. Not to Any Scale

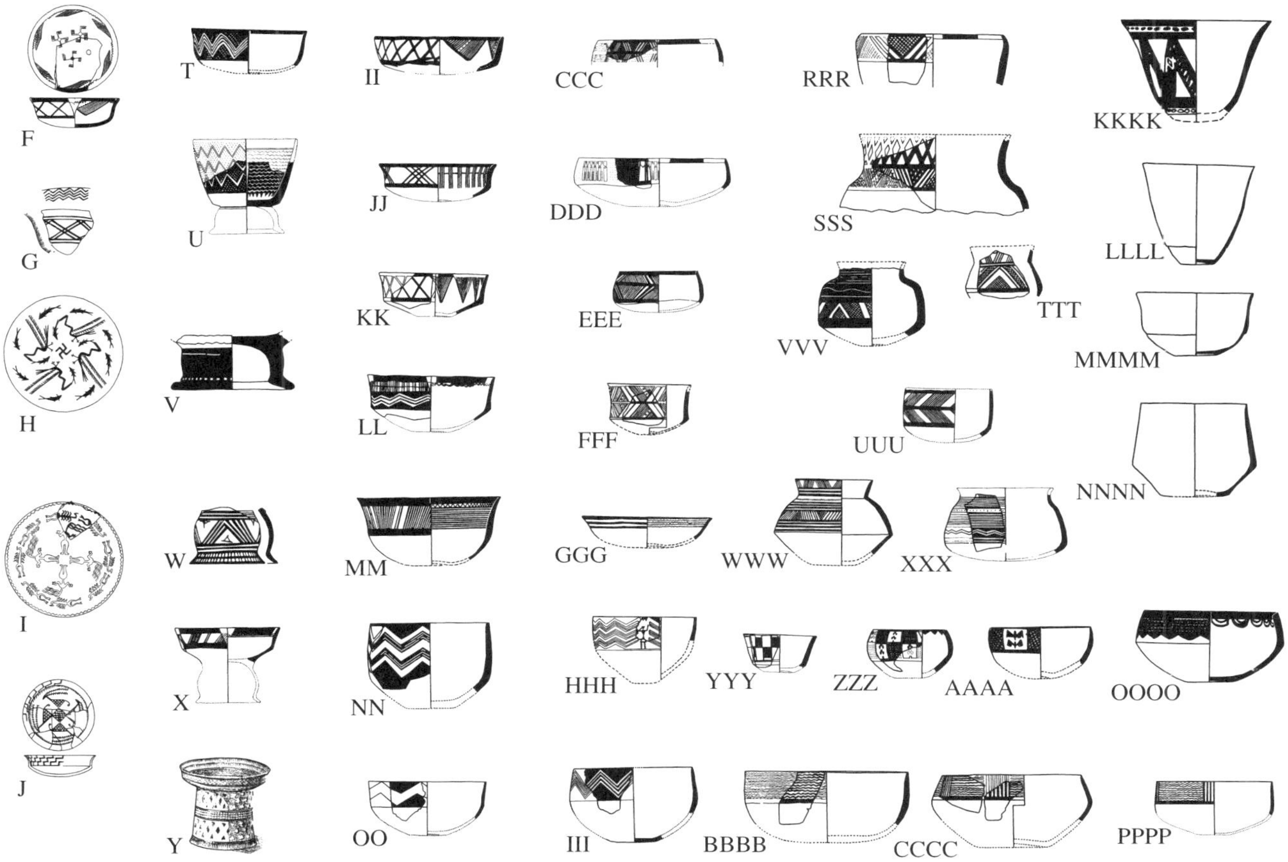


Figure 3b. Synopsis of the Evolution of Pottery Decoration of Prehistoric Susiana. Not to Any Scale (*cont.*)

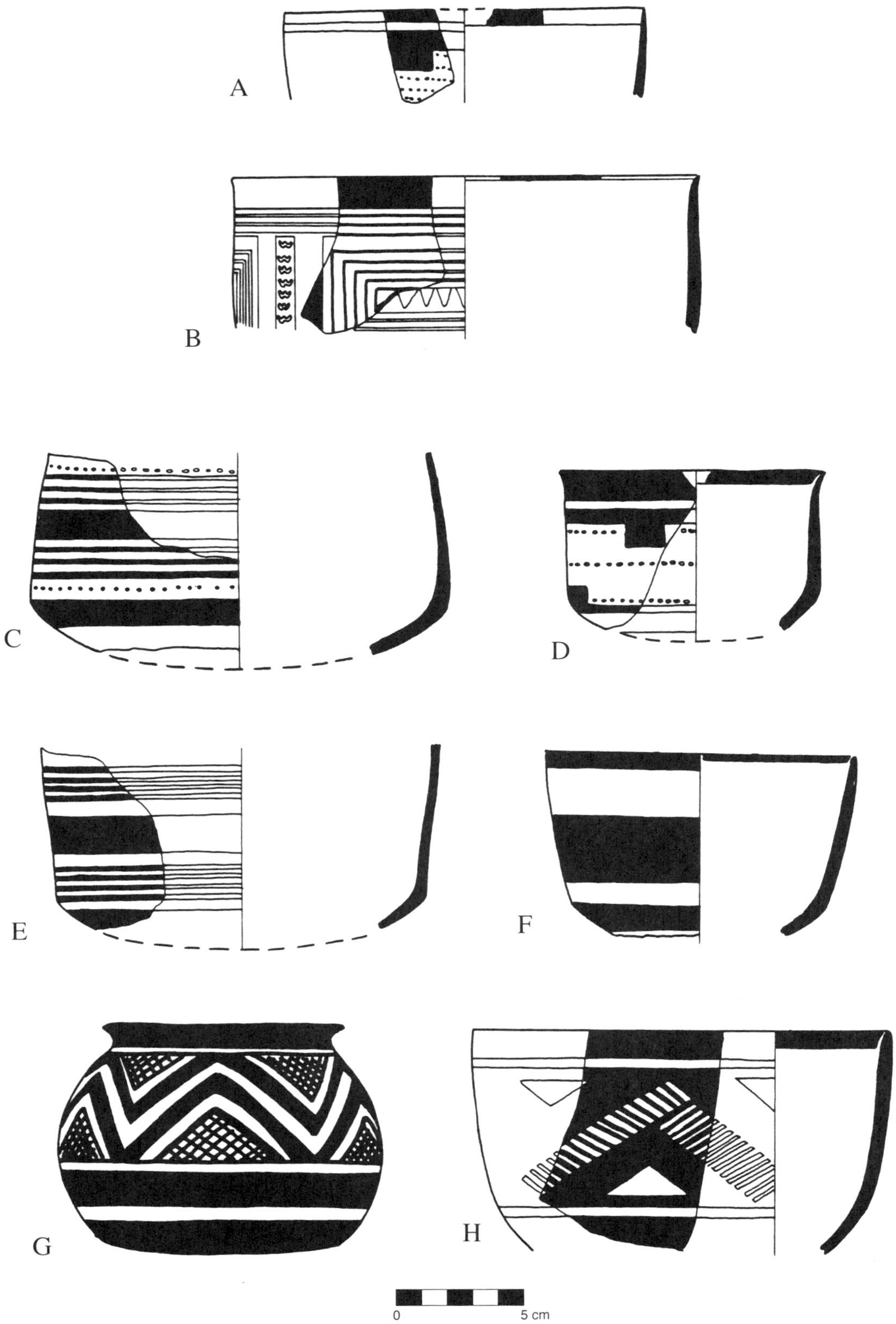


Figure 4. Examples of Late Middle Susiana/Late Susiana 1 Painted Pottery
(from Gremliza's survey of Suziana; see Alizadeh 1992)

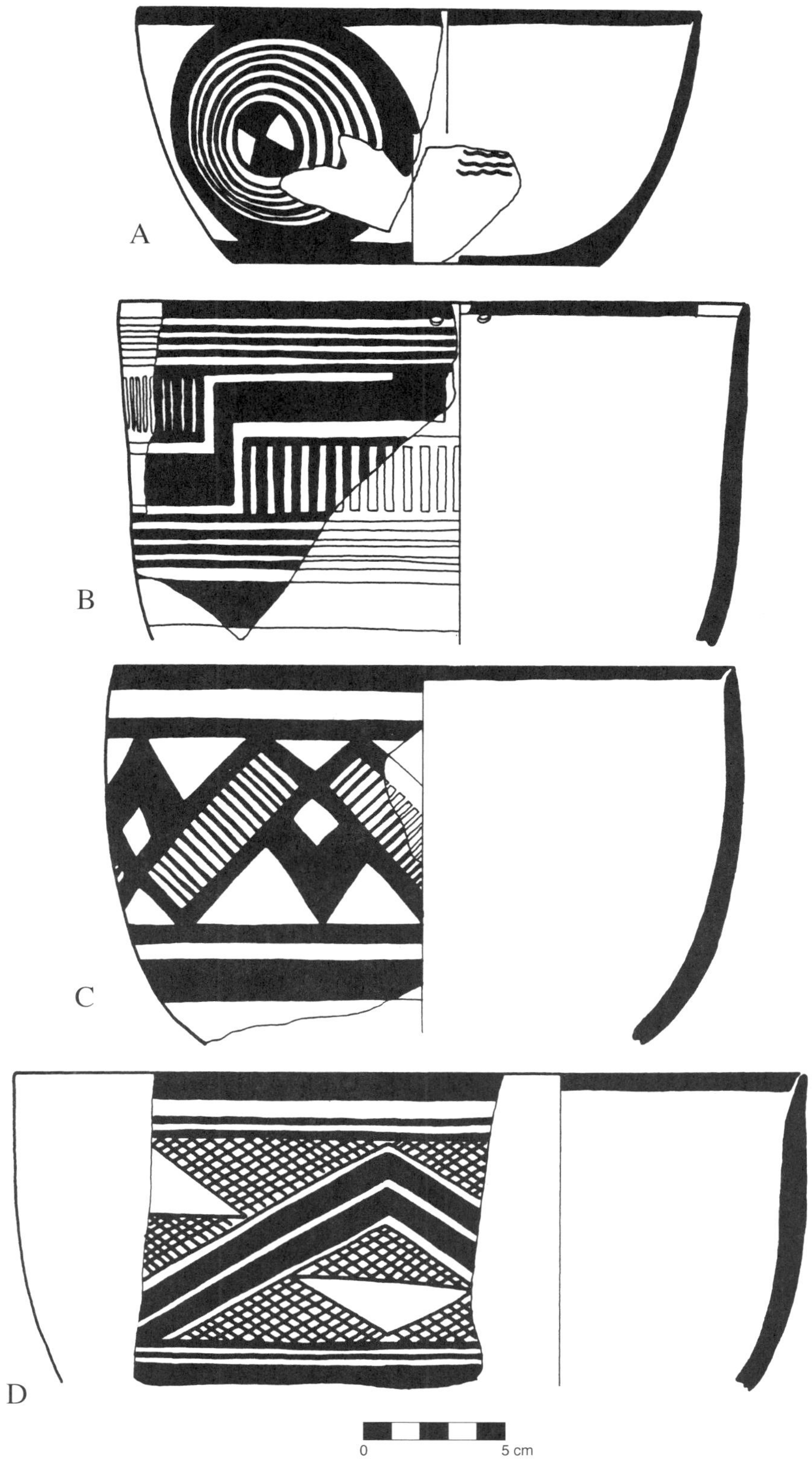


Figure 5. Examples of Late Middle Susiana/Late Susiana 1 Painted Pottery
(from Gremliza's survey of Suziana; see Alizadeh 1992)

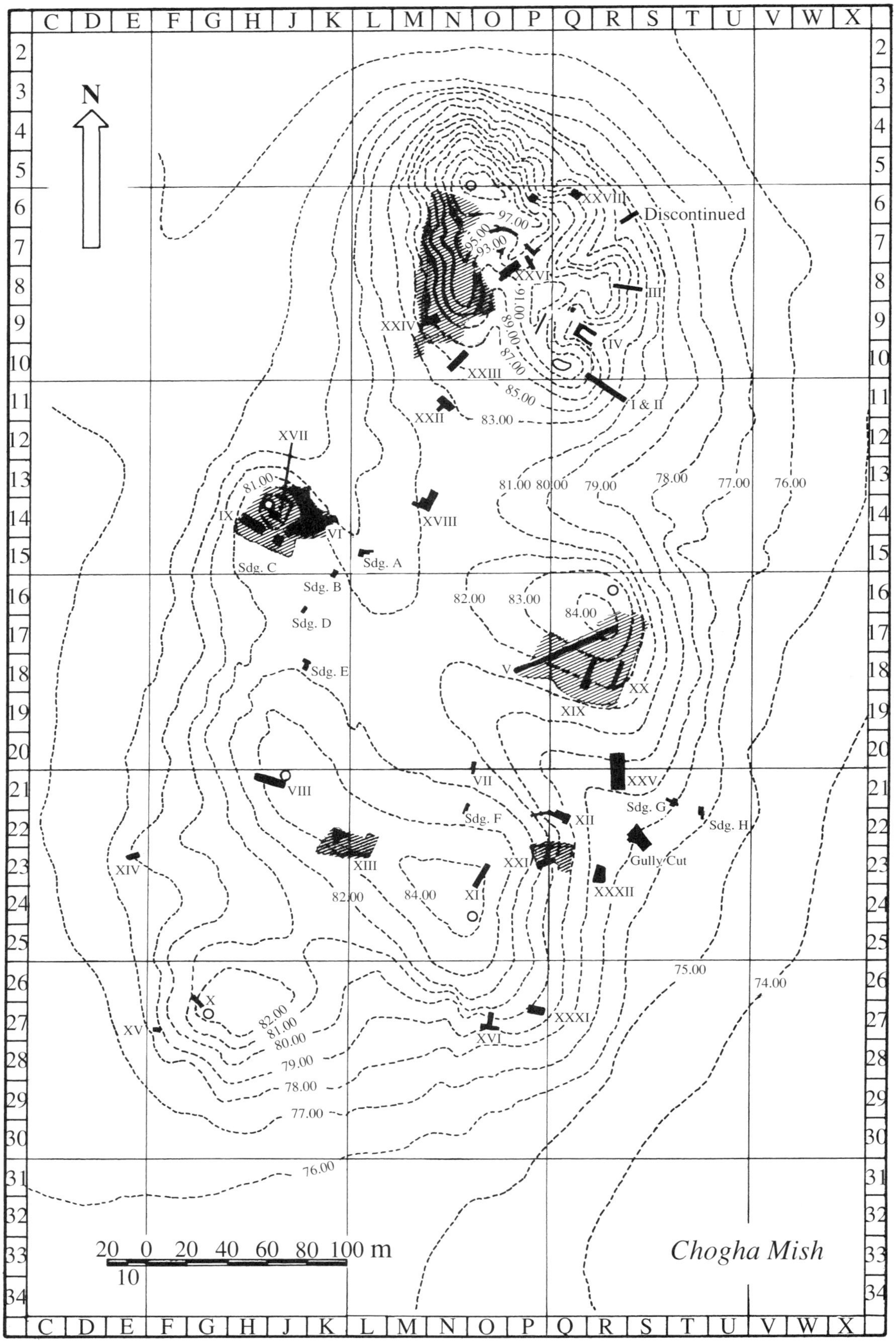


Figure 6. Contour Map of Chogha Mish

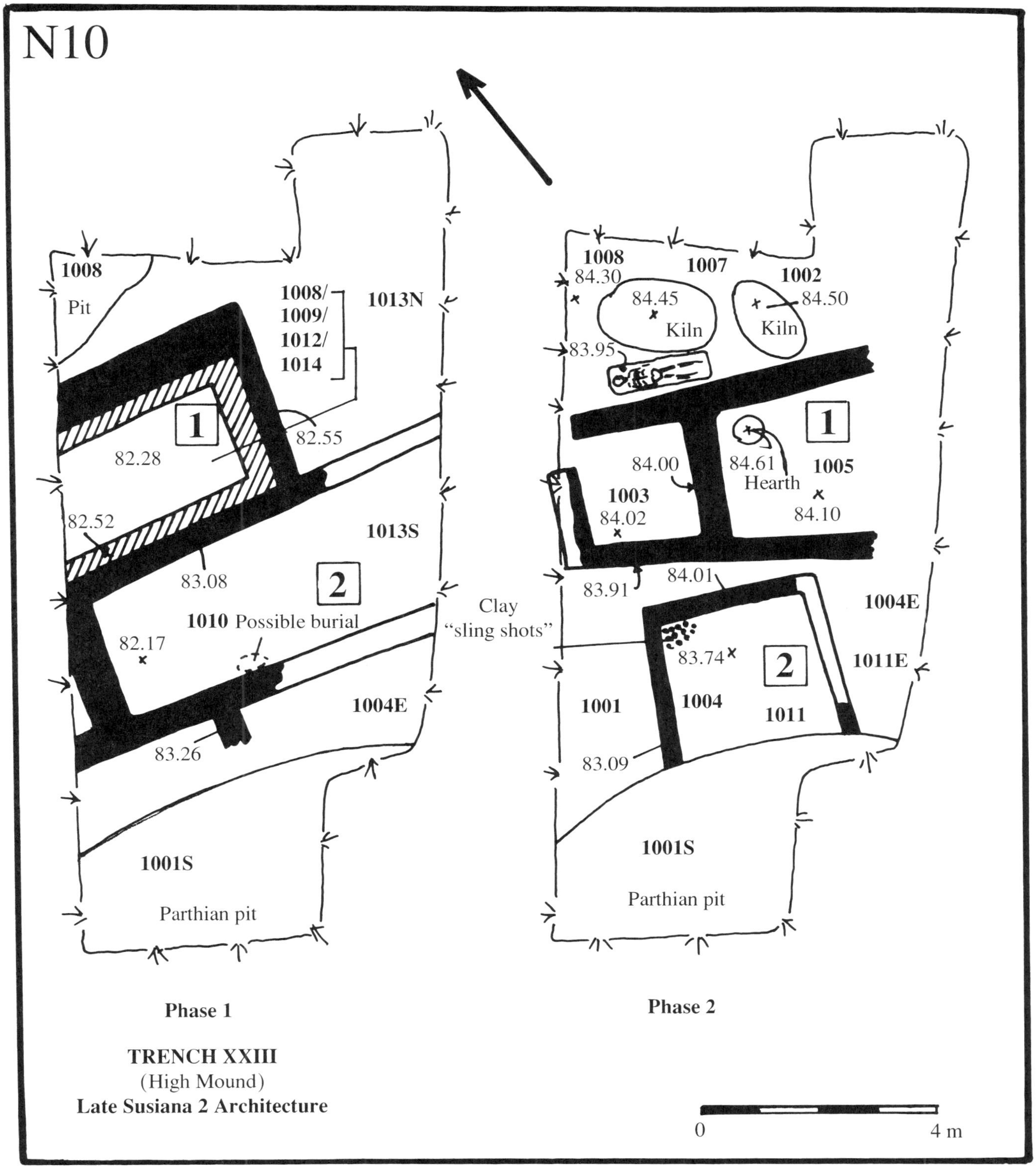


Figure 7. Top Plan of Trench XXIII, High Mound

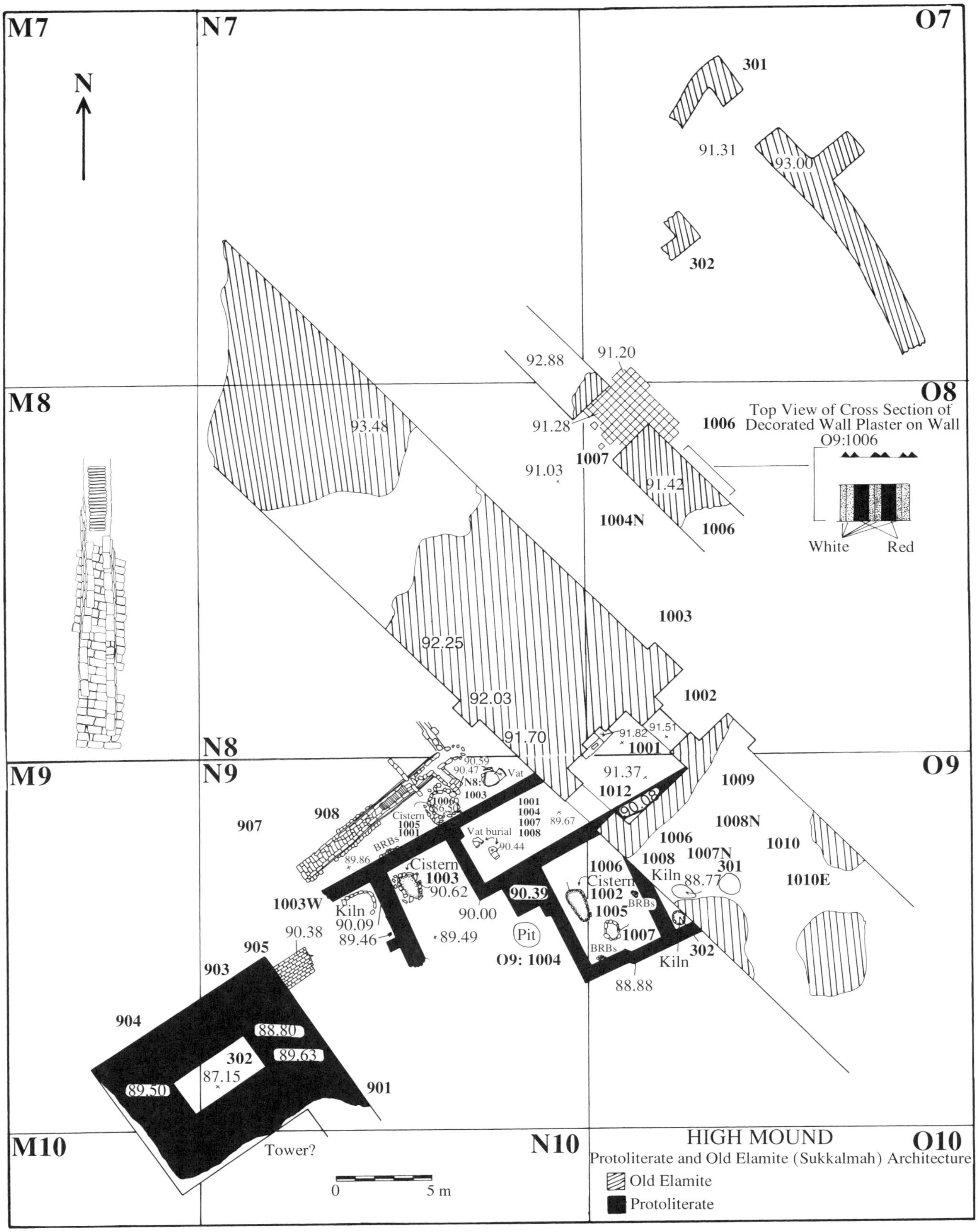


Figure 8. Top Plan of the Old Elamite Fort and Protoliterate Remains, High Mound

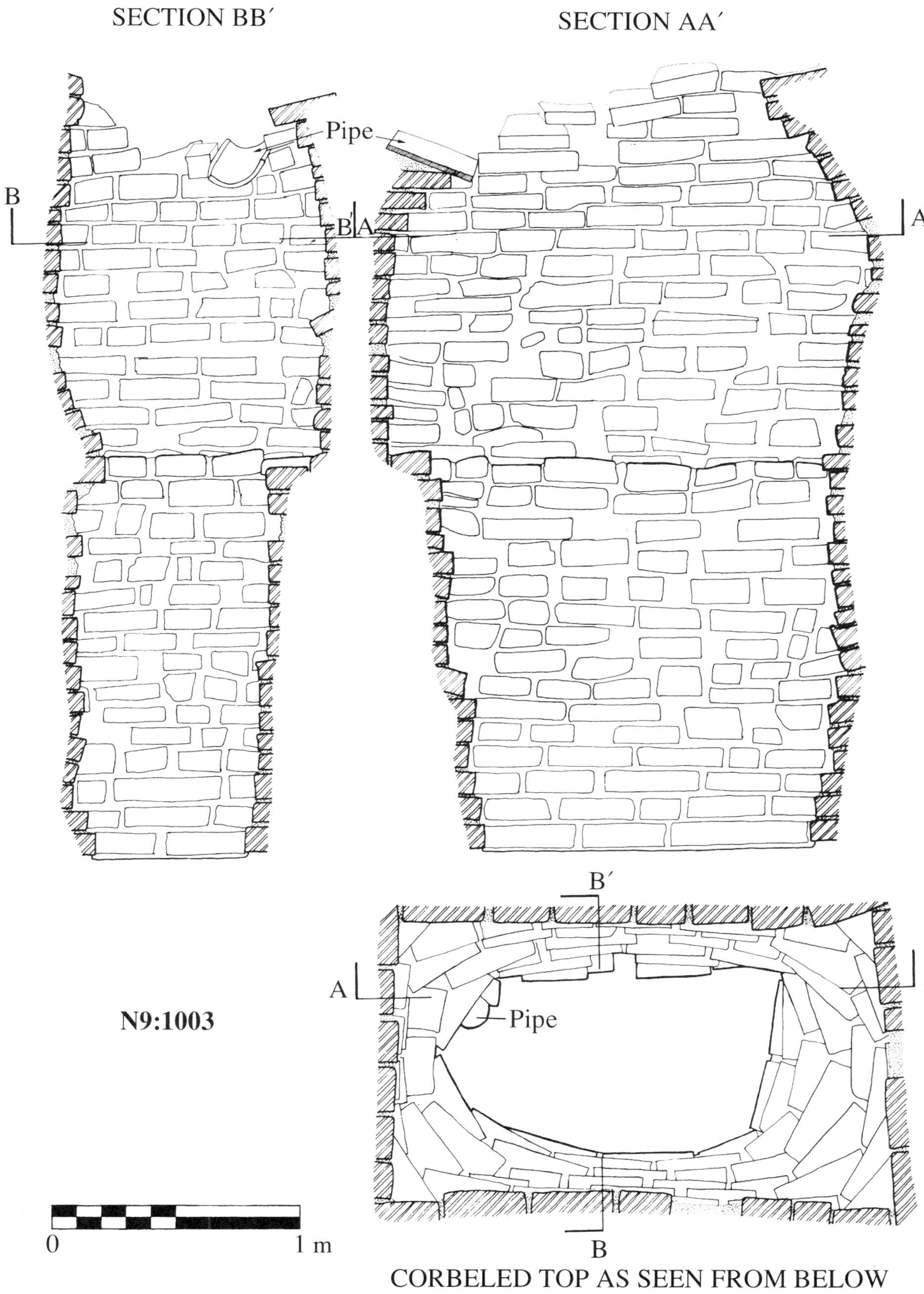


Figure 9. Section Drawings of Elamite Well, N9:1003

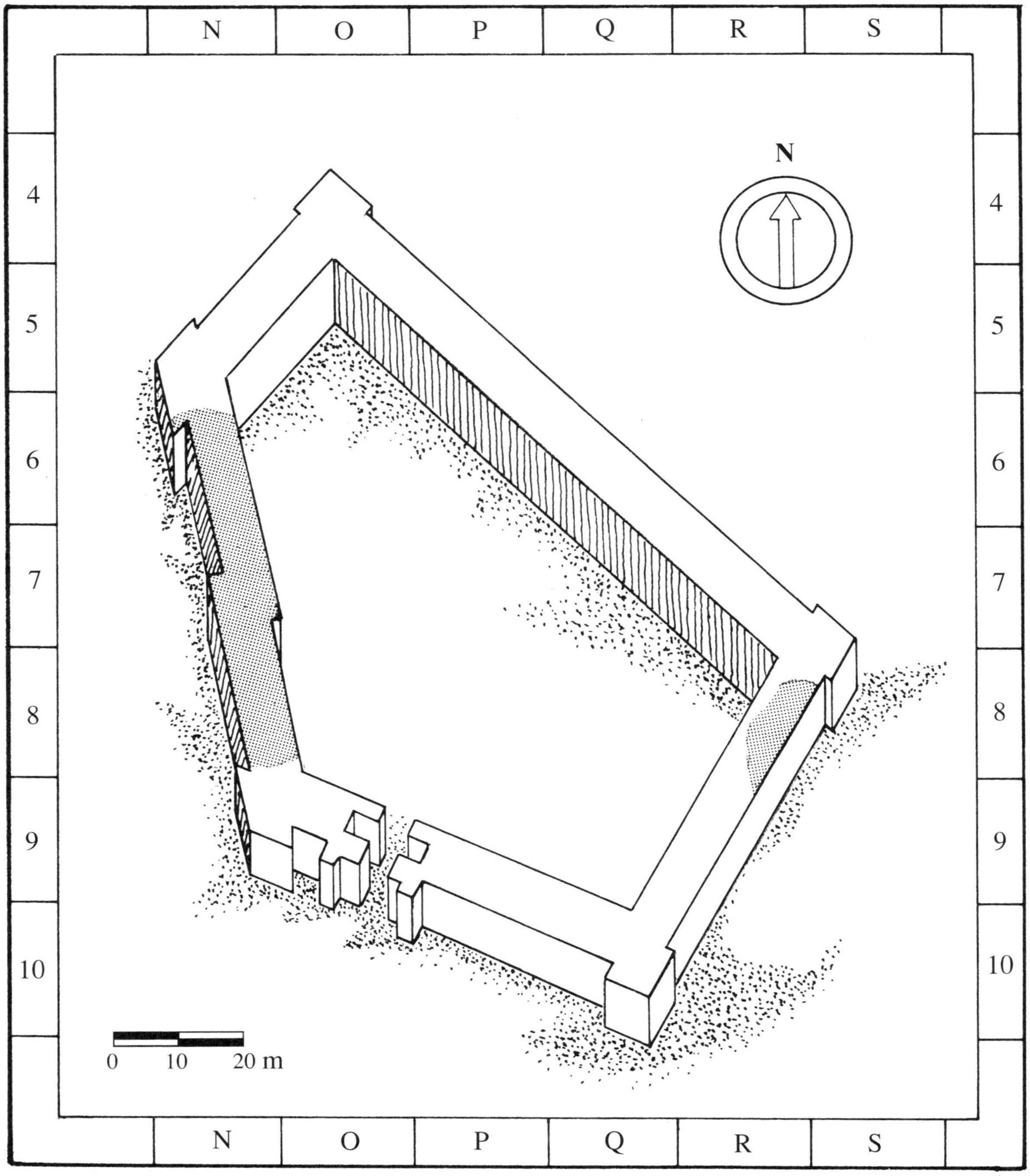


Figure 10. Isometric Plan of the Old Elamite Fort

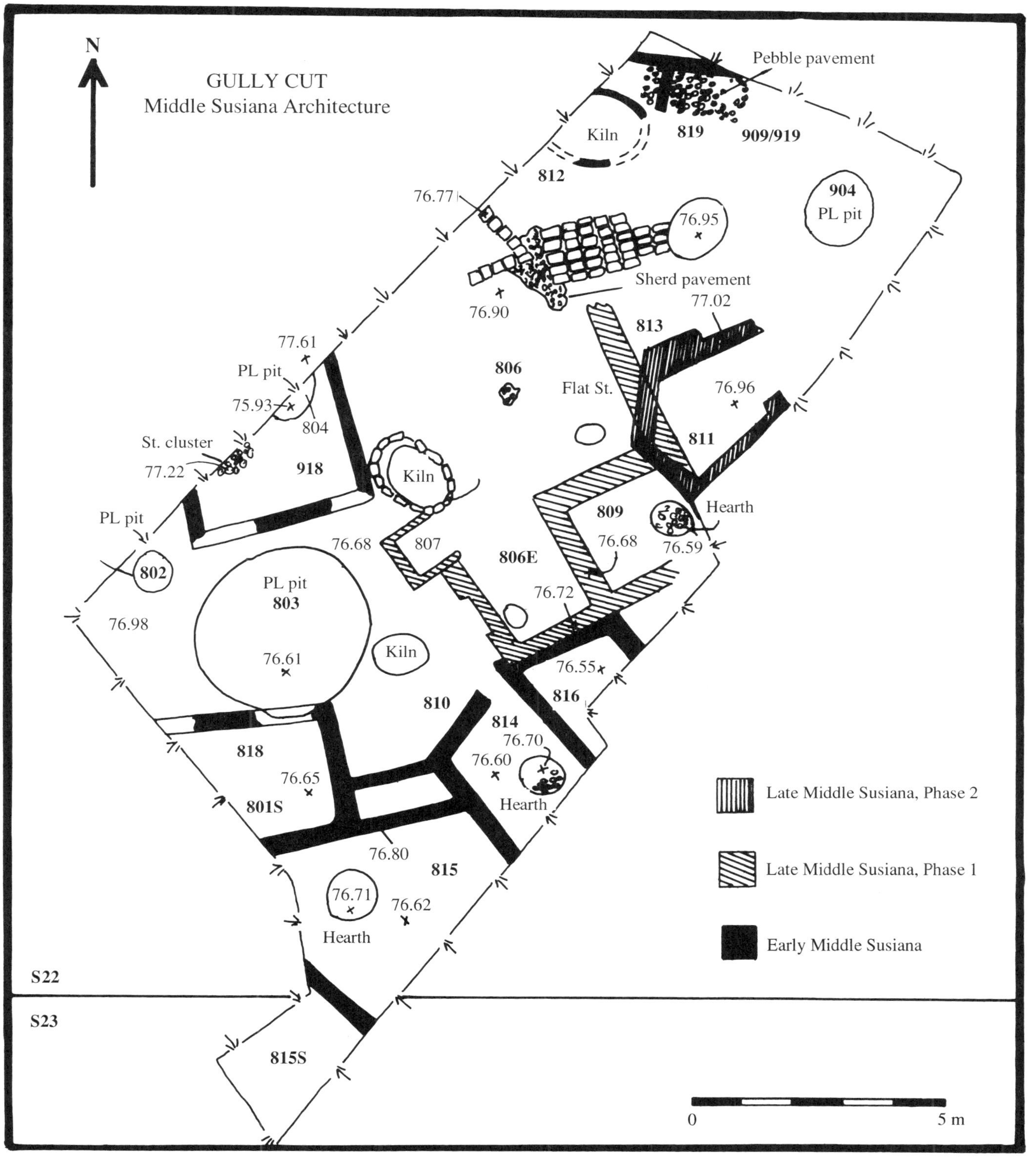


Figure 11. Top Plan of Gully Cut, Middle Susiana

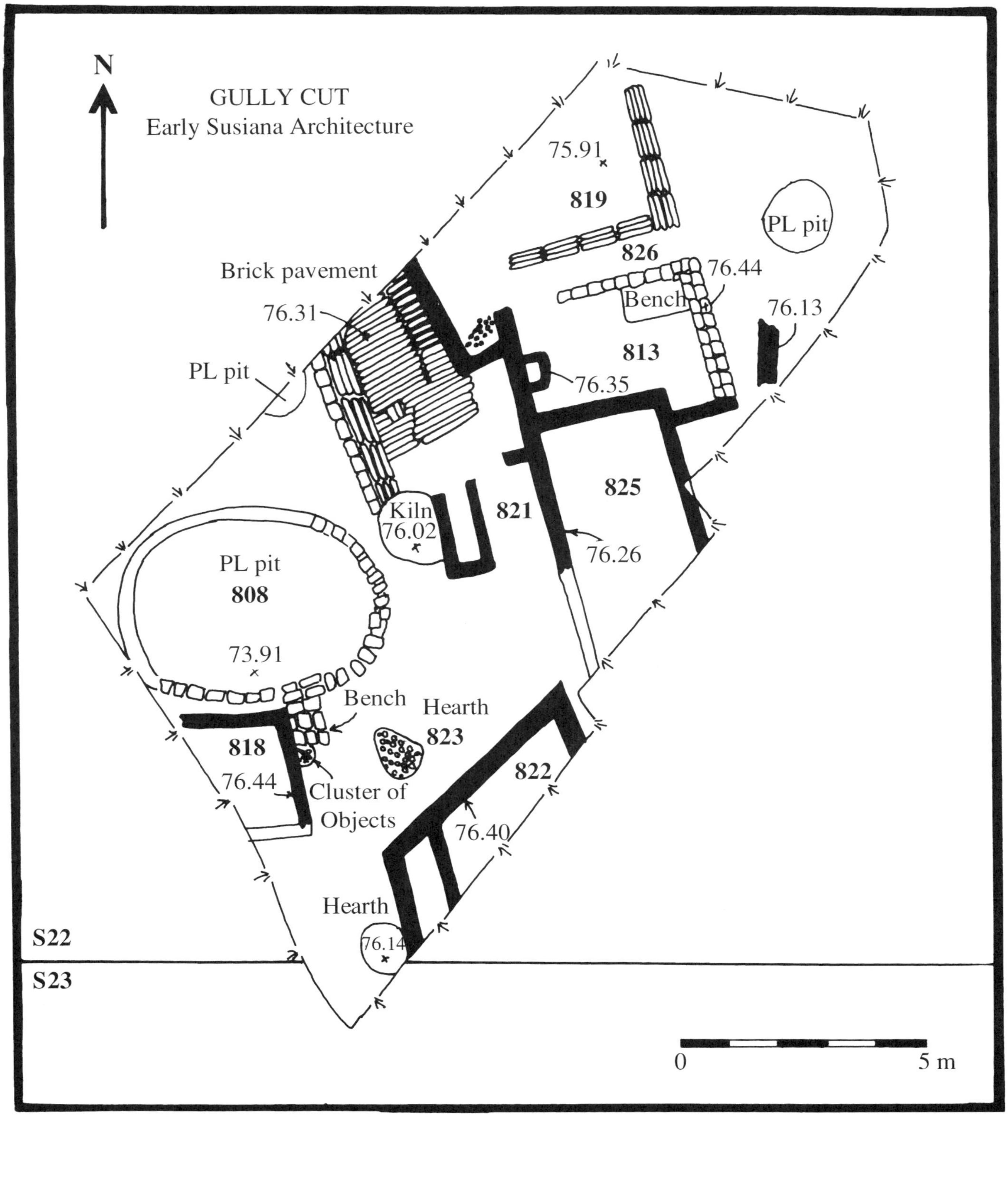


Figure 12. Top Plan of Gully Cut, Early Susiana

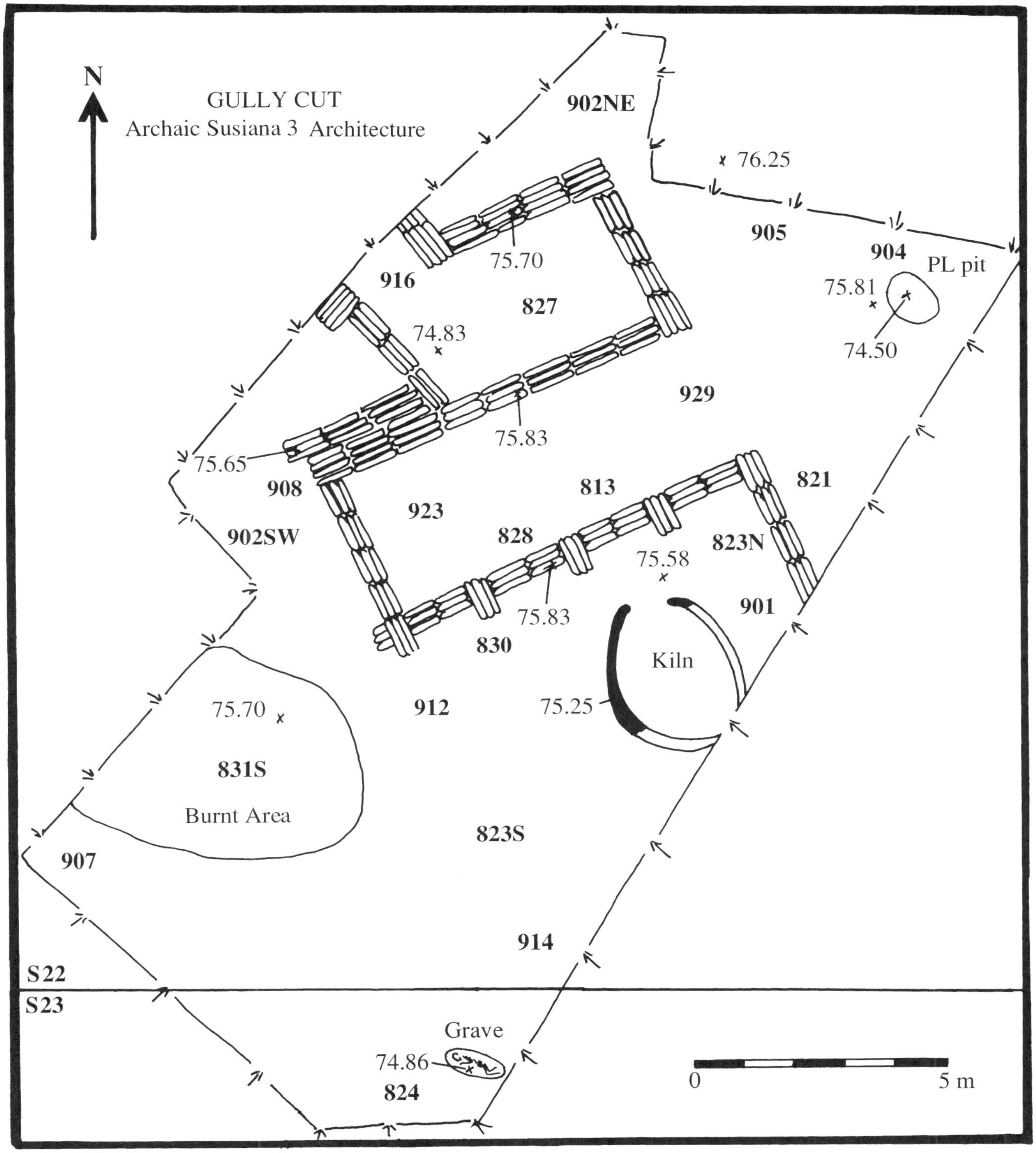


Figure 13. Top Plan of Gully Cut, Archaic Susiana 3

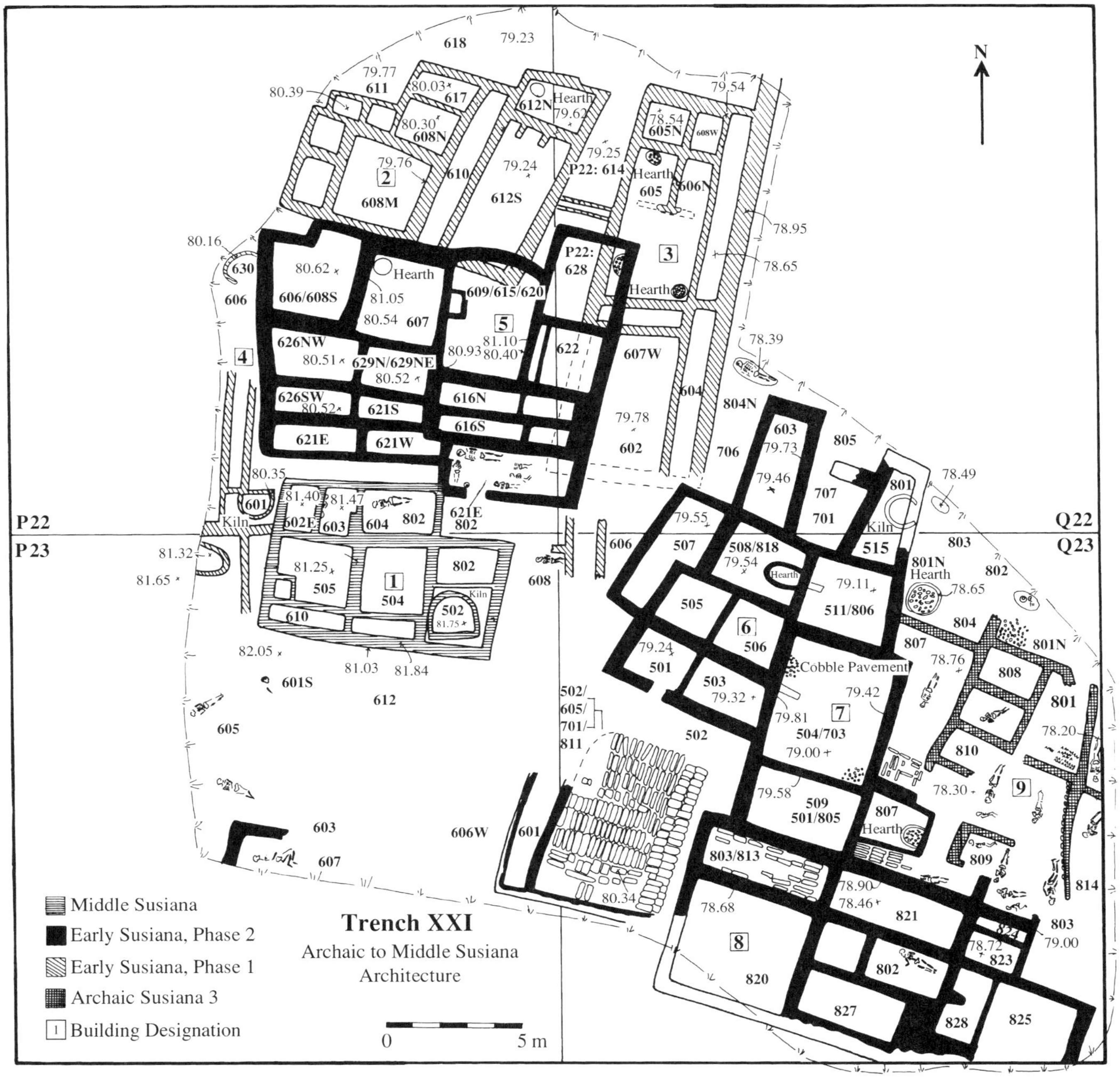


Figure 14. Top Plan of Trench XXI, Archaic to Middle Susiana

Figure 15. Top Plan of Late Middle Susiana Burnt Building

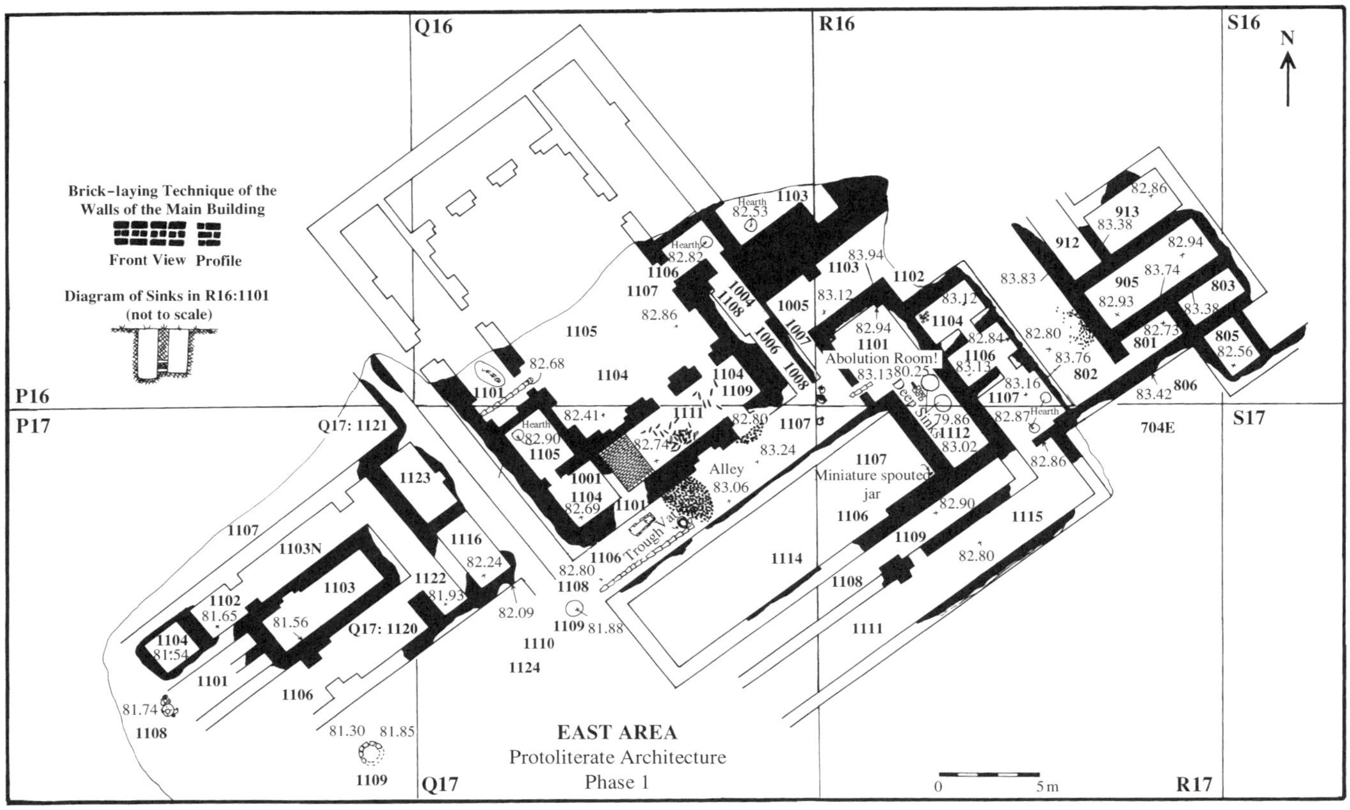


Figure 16. Top Plan of Protoliterate Architectural Complex, Phase 1

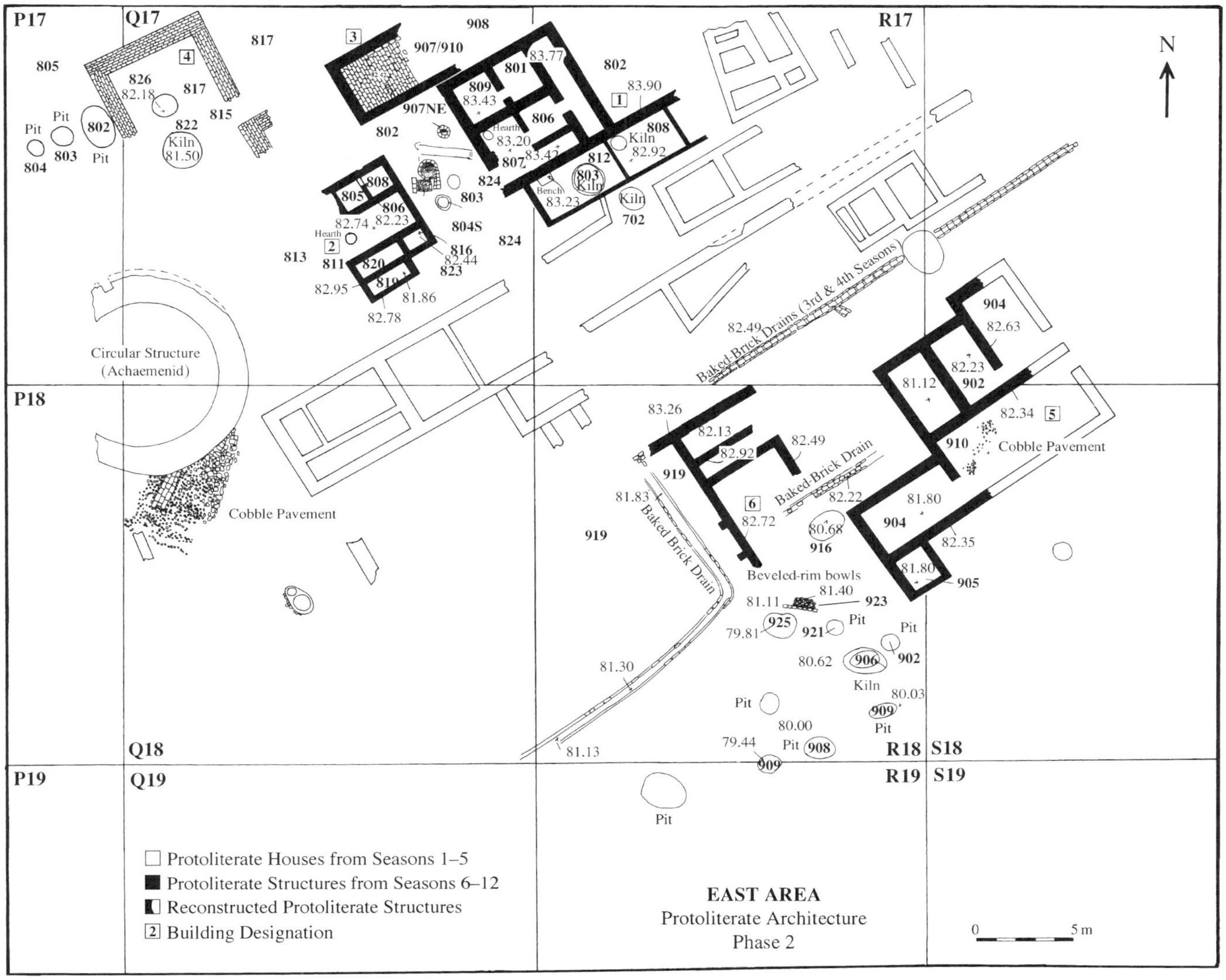


Figure 17. Top Plan of Protoliterate Architectural Complex, Phase 2

Figure 18. Prehistoric Burials

| | *Provenance* | *Elevation* | *Description* |
|---|---|---|---|
| A | Q23:807 | 78.70 | Archaic Susiana 3 |
| B | Q23:801 | 78.40 | Early Susiana |
| C | Q23:809 | 78.75 | Archaic Susiana 3 |
| D | P22:604 | 81.40 | Middle Susiana |
| E | Q22:804 North | 78.59 | Early Susiana |
| F | Q23:803 | 78.25 | Archaic Susiana 3 |
| G | P22:621 | 81.80 | Early Susiana |
| H | P22:621 | 81.78 | Early Susiana |
| I | P23:608 | 79.80 | Early Susiana |
| J | Q23:809 | 78.30 | Archaic Susiana 3 |
| K | P22:621 | 81.75 | Early Susiana |
| L | P22:621 | 81.80 | Early Susiana |
| M | P23:605 | 82.00 | Middle Susiana |
| N | Q23:810 | 78.25 | Archaic Susiana 3 |
| O | Q23:810 | 78.21 | Archaic Susiana 3 |
| P | Q23:810 South | 78.40 | Archaic Susiana 3 |
| Q | Q23:810 South | 78.40 | Archaic Susiana 3; P and Q may be parts of a single burial |
| R | Q23:809 | 78.30 | Archaic Susiana 3 |
| S | P23:607 | 81.00 | Middle Susiana |
| T | S23:824 | 74.86 | Archaic Susiana 3 |

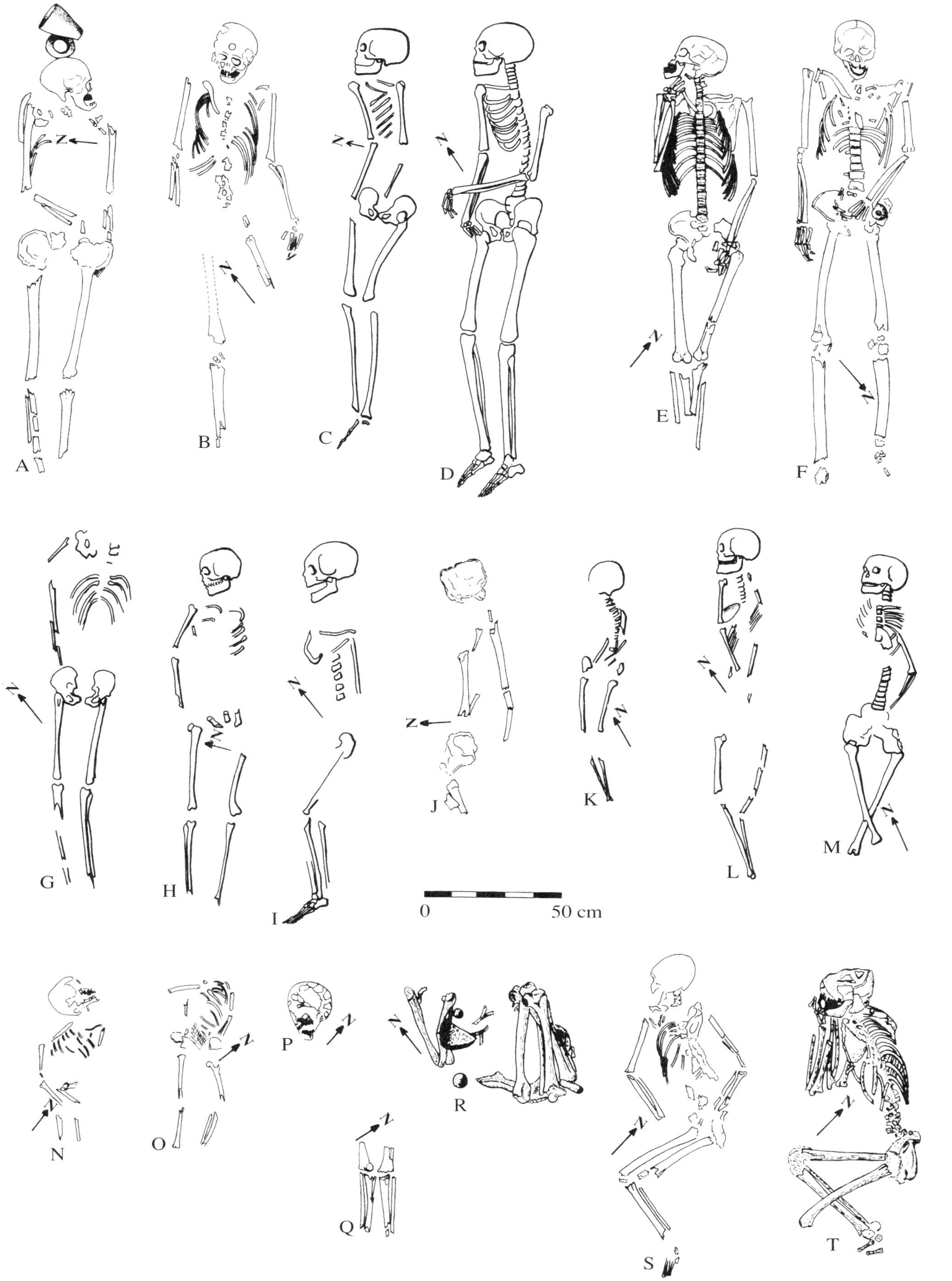


Figure 18. Prehistoric Burials

Figure 19. Parthian Pottery Vessels

| | *Registration Number* | *Provenance* | *Elevation* | *Description* |
|---|---|---|---|---|
| A | 2631 | Tr. VI | B.S. | Buff ware. Buff slip all over. Well baked, gritty with small to medium grits |
| B | II | Sdg. E | N/A | Buff ware. Over-fired greenish buff, gritty, smoothed |
| C | 2546 | Tr. XIV | B.S. | Buff ware. Light gray core, dense. Traces of reddish buff slip on exterior, striations on exterior |
| D | 41136 | Sdg. A | 0.85 B.S. | N/A |
| E | 4641 | Tr. IX | 0.45 B.S. | Buff ware. Sand and grit inclusions. Green glaze on exterior, air bubbles where glaze is thick |
| F | 2579 | R17:215 | 83.80 | Buff ware. Slightly over fired, some scattered medium to large grits. Pale blue glaze on exterior |
| G | 31057 | Tr. XXIV | B.S. | Buff ware. Dark gray core, no visible inclusions, smoothed |
| H | II | Sdg. E | B.S. | Buff ware. Well baked, gritty. Yellowish red wash |
| I | 8237 | Tr. VIII | 1.0 B.S. | Brown buff ware. Grit and sand inclusions, rough surface on exterior |
| J | II | Sdg. E | B.S. | Buff ware. Small to medium grit inclusions, smoothed |
| K | 3843 | High Mound | B.S. | Dark buff ware. Dense, sandy, smoothed |
| L | 3884 | J15:301 | Kiln | Orange buff ware. Dense, small grits and occasional calcite particle inclusions. Slipped all over, striations on exterior and interior. Reconstruction is based on a more complete form. See *Chogha Mish* I, plate 70:O |
| M | 3883 | J15:301 | Kiln | Buff ware. Gritty, smoothed, incised |
| N | 3844 | High Mound | B.S. | Buff ware. Gritty, well baked, smoothed with visible grit drag marks |
| O | 3836 | Tr. XXIV | B.S. | Dark gray ware. Large dark grit with occasional calcite inclusions (crushed shells?), smoothed exterior and interior |

Figure 19. Parthian Pottery Vessels

Figure 20. Late Iron Age/Achaemenid Open Bowls

| | *Registration Number* | *Provenance* | *Elevation* | *Description* |
|---|---|---|---|---|
| A | 2483 | Tr. V, Plot D | 81.40 | Buff ware. Pink buff core. Well baked, no visible inclusions, wheel striations interior and exterior |
| B | 9111 | Q17:903 | 83.75 | Red ware. Grit-tempered, smoothed, slightly burnished |
| C | 8170 | Q24:803 | 78.61 | Buff ware. Buff slipped interior and exterior. Grit and sand inclusions, smoothed with visible wheel striations |
| D | 8058 | Q17:811 | 82.69 | Orange red ware. White slip interior. Dense, grit inclusions |
| E | 2488 | Tr. XI | N/A | Buff ware. Dense. Yellowish buff slip exterior, sand inclusions, smoothed interior and exterior, upper interior burnished |
| F | 2484 | Tr. V | B.S. | Buff ware. Pink buff core. Some grit and sand inclusions, slightly burnished exterior, visible striations |
| G | 2657 | Tr. VII | 0.90 B.S. | Greenish gray ware. Very dense, no visible inclusions, smoothed |
| H | 41138 | L23:400 | 0.45 B.S. | Buff ware. Well baked, some grit inclusions, smoothed |
| I | 8533 | Q17:801 | 83.31 | Standard gray ware. Charcoal gray surface, straw and fine grit temper, smoothed |
| J | 2758 | Tr. V | N/A | Grayish buff ware. Some grit inclusions, smoothed |
| K | 2557 | Tr. V | 0.40 B.S. | Orange buff ware. Coarse. Large grit inclusions, pinkish orange exterior. Interior rough with visible large grits |
| L | 3927 | O18:205 | B.S. | Fine buff ware. No visible inclusions, smoothed exterior, some striations on the upper body |
| M | 2556 | Tr. V | 0.70 B.S. | Buff ware. Dense, sandy with few grits. Scoring and corrugations around rim |
| N | 8432 | R17:805 | 83.68 | Buff ware. Fine grit inclusions, pinkish buff on the surface |
| O | 8881 | R17:803 | 82.99 | Buff ware. Gritty, smoothed. Corrugations below rim |

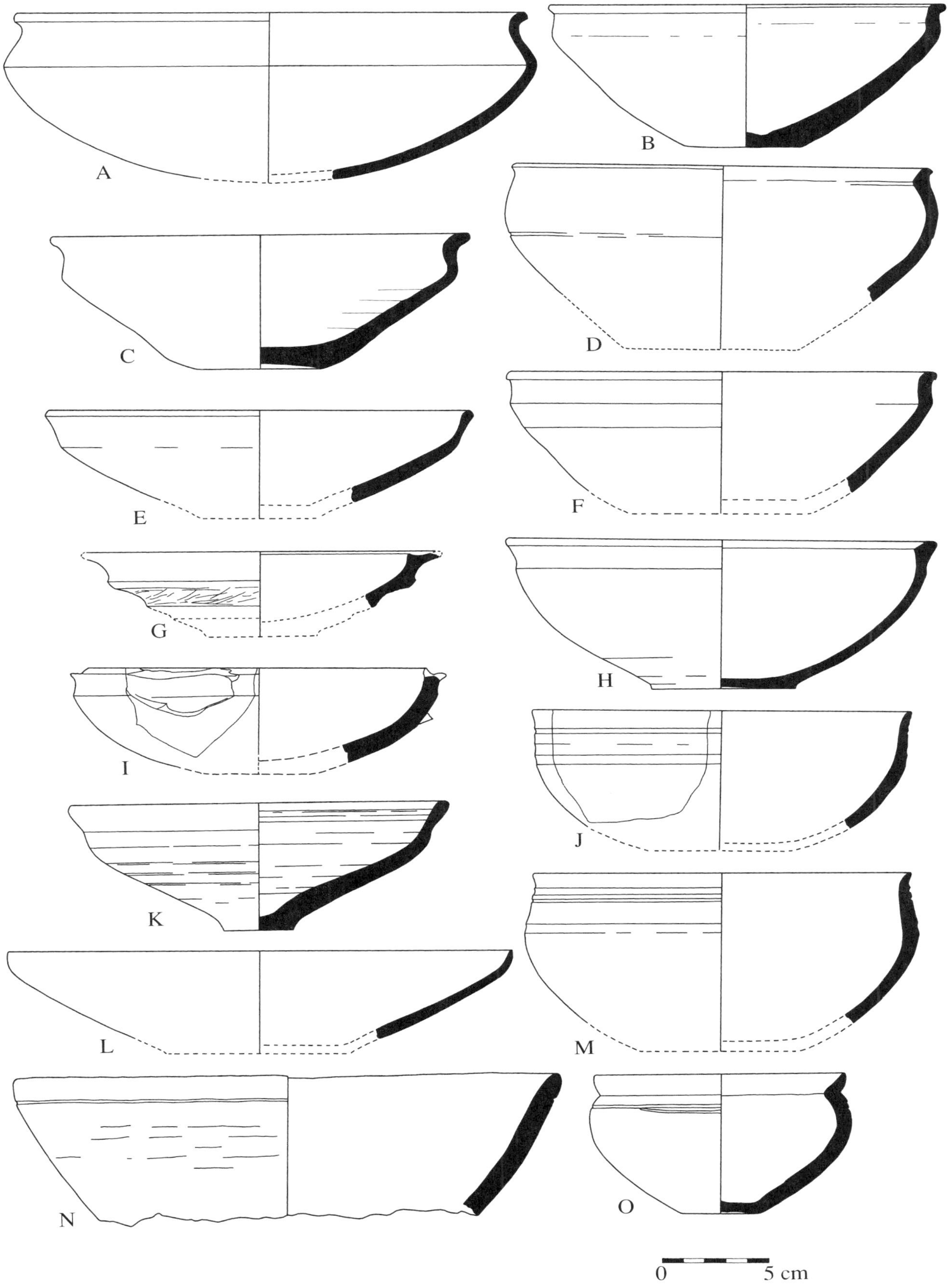


Figure 20. Late Iron Age/Achaemenid Open Bowls

Figure 21. Late Iron Age (Neo-Elamite)/Achaemenid Open Bowls

| | *Registration Number* | *Provenance* | *Elevation* | *Description* |
|---|---|---|---|---|
| A | 3661 | R18:305 | 1.60 B.S. | Buff ware. Well baked, sandy, smoothed |
| B | N/A | Tr. XXVI | B.S. | Greenish buff ware. Well baked, gritty, smoothed. Diameter: 15 cm |
| C | 2587 | Q18:305 | B.S. | Brownish buff ware. Medium and large sized grits included. Slight wheel marks on the exterior |
| D | N/A | Tr. XVIII | B.S. | Brownish buff ware. Cream slip exterior. Well baked, gritty |
| E | 2646 | P18:203 | N/A | Buff ware. Exterior covered with a thin brown slip, interior plain. Small grit inclusions |
| F | 3935 | Q18:305 | N/A | Red ware. Light buff core. Dark, red, and white grit inclusions, sandy face, red slipped on exterior, smoothed, faint traces of burnishing |
| G | 3648 | Tr. V | 1.70 B.S. | Buff ware. Small dark grits as well as some calcite particles included in the paste, smoothed |
| H | 3937 | Q18:305 | 1.80 B.S. | Buff ware. Warm buff core grading to pink toward surface, yellowish buff interior, pinkish buff exterior. Grit inclusions, sandy face, visible striations, lower body scored |
| I | 2623 | Q18:305 | 1.0 B.S. | Buff ware. Over-fired greenish buff, dense, small grit inclusions, surfaces slipped, visible striations |
| J | 2641 | Tr. VII | N/A | Fine red ware. Dense, some sand inclusions, interior, and exterior, buff slipped, striations visible on exterior |
| K | 2797 | Tr. V | 0.90 B.S. | Buff ware. Well baked, grit inclusions, smoothed |

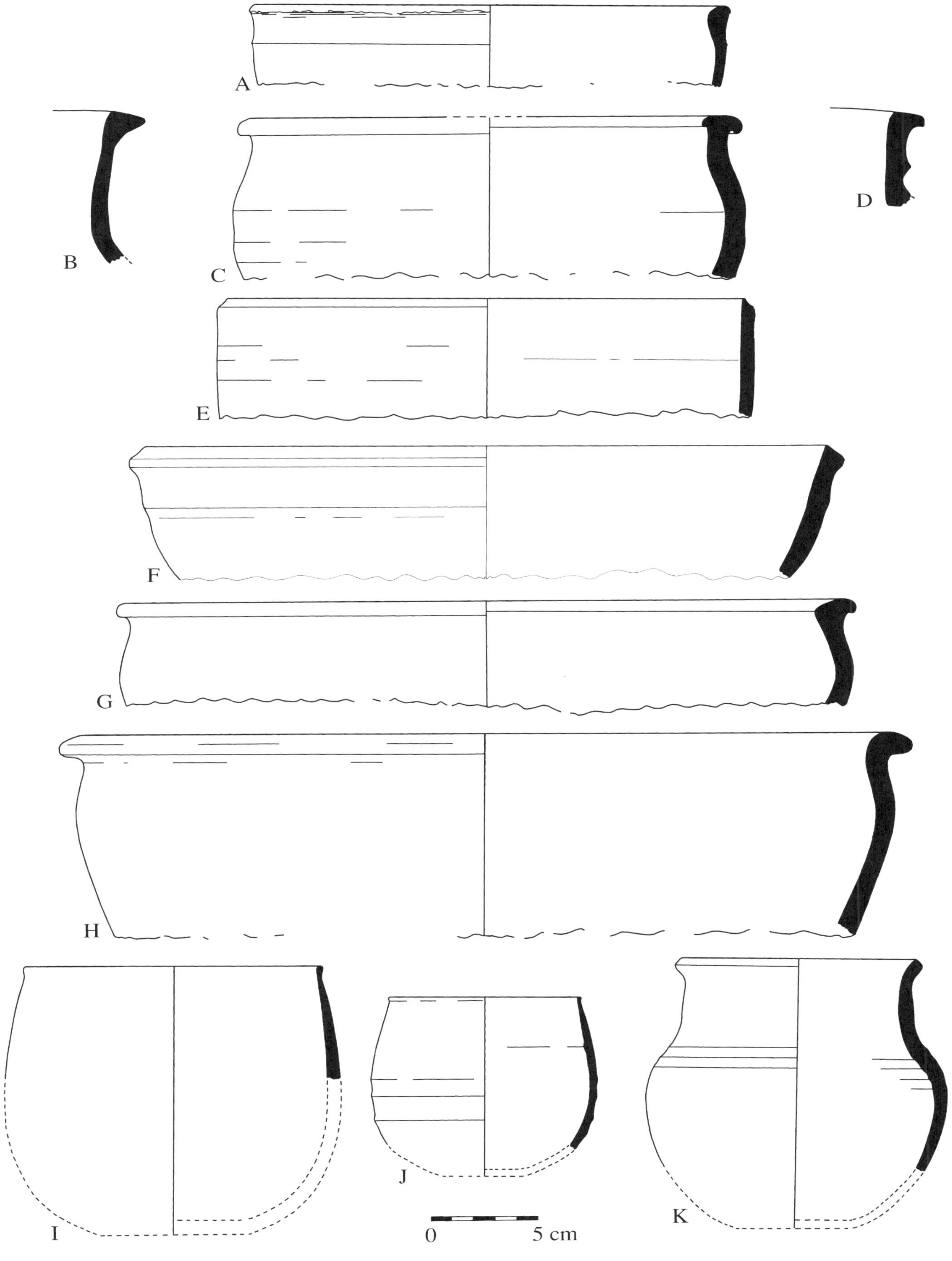


Figure 21. Late Iron Age (Neo-Elamite)/Achaemenid Open Bowls

Figure 22. Late Iron Age/Achaemenid Pottery Vessels

| | *Registration Number* | *Provenance* | *Elevation* | *Description* |
|---|---|---|---|---|
| A | 2621 | Tr. XVIII | B.S. | Buff ware. Buff slip turned greenish buff. Small grit inclusions, wheel corrugations on interior |
| B | 2669 | Tr. IX | B.S. | Buff ware. Slipped all over, mottled surface ranging from orange to greenish buff. Dense, fine grit inclusions |
| C | 7331 | R17:710 | 82.96 | Orange buff ware. Orange slip all over. Dense, small grit and fine chaff inclusions, scraped marks on exterior |
| D | 9098 | R18:916 | 80.24 | Fine red ware. Cream slipped exterior, dark paint. No visible inclusions |
| E | 9001 | S18:403 | B.S. | Fine buff ware. Buff slip on exterior. Sand and occasional grit inclusions, smoothed, wheel marks on interior |
| F | 8337 | Q17:811 | 86.69 | Red ware. Sand and grit inclusions, smoothed |
| G | 8048 | Q17:811 | 82.69 | Buff ware. Red wash on exterior and interior. Grit and sand inclusions |
| H | 2577 | Sdg. F | B.S. | Buff ware. Dark, red, and white grit inclusions, smoothed. Finger prints on handle |
| I | 5359 | R20:510 | 77.64 | Orange red ware. Creamy buff slip on exterior. Grit inclusions |
| J | 2593 | Tr. V | 1.40 B.S. | Buff ware. Probably slipped. Small to medium grit inclusions, smoothed. Slight corrugation marks on exterior |
| K | 8259 | Q24:801 | 76.26 | Red ware. Red slipped. Gray core, sand and grit inclusions, striations on interior |
| L | 2676 | Round Building | N/A | Red ware. Khaki buff core grading to pink toward the surface. Dark grit inclusions, some pinkish white stripes on the bed of spout |
| M | 5501 | Round Building | N/A | Buff ware. Sand inclusions, smoothed. Ville royale II |
| N | 8435 | Q17:801 | 83.57 | Buff ware. Probably slipped. Grit tempered, smoothed |
| O | 3885 | Q18:305 | 82.00 | Buff ware. Buff slipped turned greenish buff. Small grit inclusions, striations on interior |
| P | 2625 | Tr. VI | B.S. | Orange buff ware. Dense, grit tempered, smoothed. Slight traces of burnishing |
| Q | 3801 | R19 | N/A | Buff ware. Coarse, dark coarse grit inclusions, scrape marks on interior |

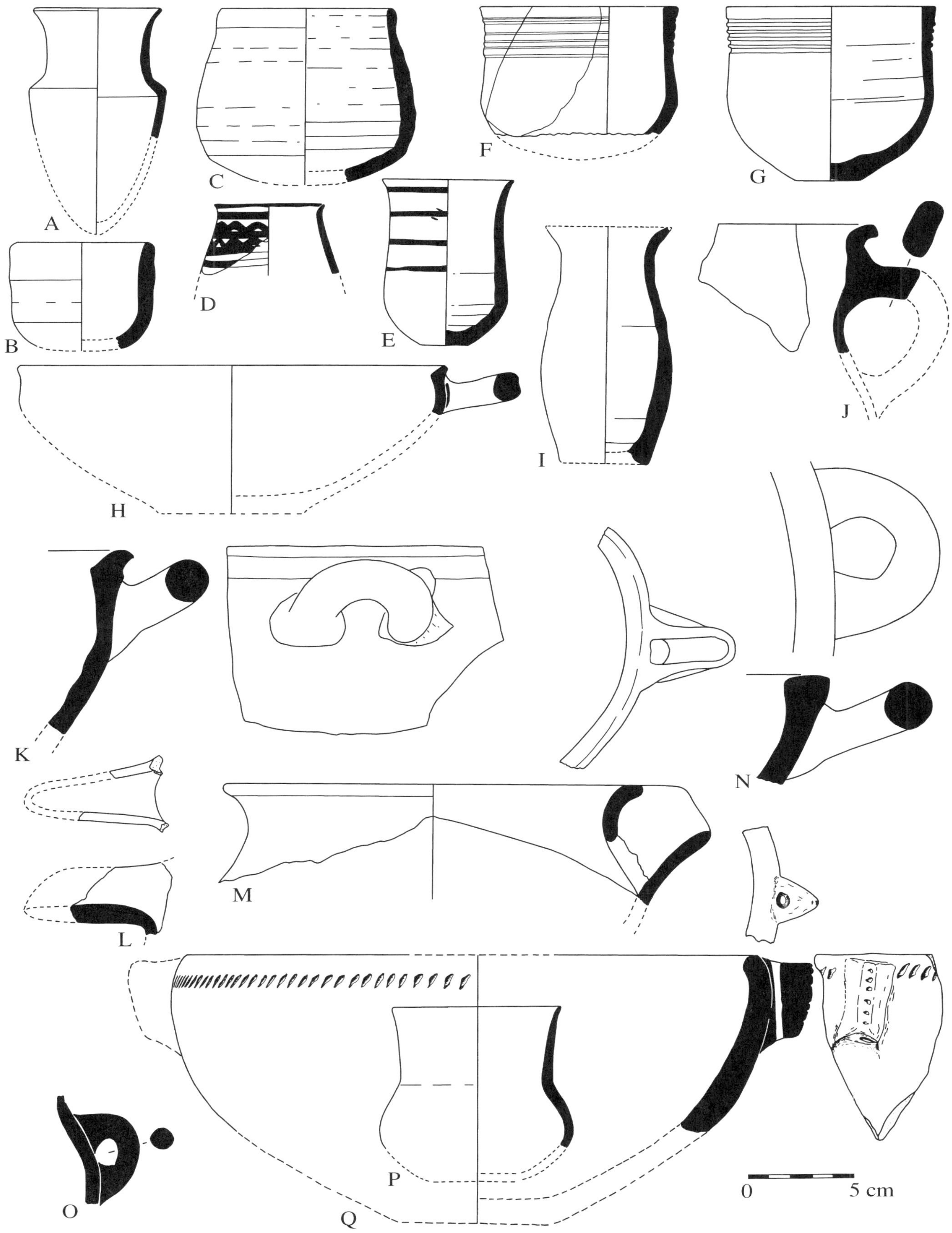


Figure 22. Late Iron Age/Achaemenid Pottery Vessels

Figure 23. Late Iron Age/Achaemenid Pottery Vessels

| | *Registration Number* | *Provenance* | *Elevation* | *Description* |
|---|---|---|---|---|
| A | 2667 | Tr. VII | N/A | Buff ware. Yellowish buff slip exterior. Grit inclusions, sandy face, striation marks on exterior |
| B | 2669 | Tr. V, Plot D | N/A | Red ware. Red core grades to buff toward surface, buff slip on exterior. Grit inclusions, striation marks on exterior |
| C | 3901 | R18:305 | 0.75 B.S. | Buff ware. Uniform core. Small and medium size grit inclusions, smoothed |
| D | 2589 | Tr. V, Plot D | 0.50 B.S. | Buff ware. Buff slip turned over-fired greenish buff. Small to medium size grit inclusions, striation marks on exterior |
| E | 2618 | Tr. V, Plot D | 1.0 B.S. | Buff ware. Buff slip. Small grit inclusions, striation marks on interior and exterior |
| F | 8160 | Q17:801 | 83.57 | Buff ware. Red slip interior and exterior. Sand inclusions, burnished exterior |
| G | 8642 | Q17:801 | 83.31 | Red ware. Sand, grit, and chaff inclusions, gritty face lower body, striation marks upper body |
| H | 3934 | Q18:305 | 1.0 B.S. | Buff ware. Light buff core, multi-color and multi-size grit inclusions, gritty face, striation marks on exterior |
| I | 4782 | Tr. XIII | 0.45 B.S. | Buff ware. Light brown surface. Well baked, dark grit inclusions, gritty face. "Potter's marks"(?) on base |
| J | 8049 | Q17:812 | 82.65 | Buff ware. Buff slip all over. Sand and grit inclusions, striation marks interior and exterior |
| K | 9031 | Q17:907 | 83.60 | Buff ware. Light buff slip with some orange spots. Sand and grit inclusions, smoothed |
| L | XI-19 | P17:1112 | 80.72 | N/A |
| M | 5612 | K23:502 | 0.90 B.S. | Buff ware. Red wash all over. Sand inclusions, smoothed |
| N | 8430 | Q17:801 | 83.31 | Buff ware. Straw-tempered coarse ware with some large grits, striation marks upper body, lower body scraped |
| O | 2638 | Tr. V, Plot D | 1.0 B.S. | Buff ware. Slipped. Light brown surface, grit inclusions, smoothed |
| P | 2608 | Sdg. F | Surface | Red ware. Buff slipped. Small to medium grit inclusions with occasional chaff visible on surface |
| Q | 2485 | Q18:205 | Surface | Buff ware. Probably slipped. Grit tempered, scrape marks on upper body |
| R | 9478 | P17:901 | 81.85 | Buff ware. Buff slip turned greenish due to over firing. Grit tempered |
| S | 8390 | Q17:808 | 83.32 | Buff ware. Buff slip turned greenish due to over firing. Grit tempered, striation marks on interior |
| T | 3913 | R18:304 | 0.50 B.S. | Buff ware. Buff slip turned greenish buff due to over firing. Small to medium size grit tempered; see Stronach and Roaf 1978, fig. 7 |

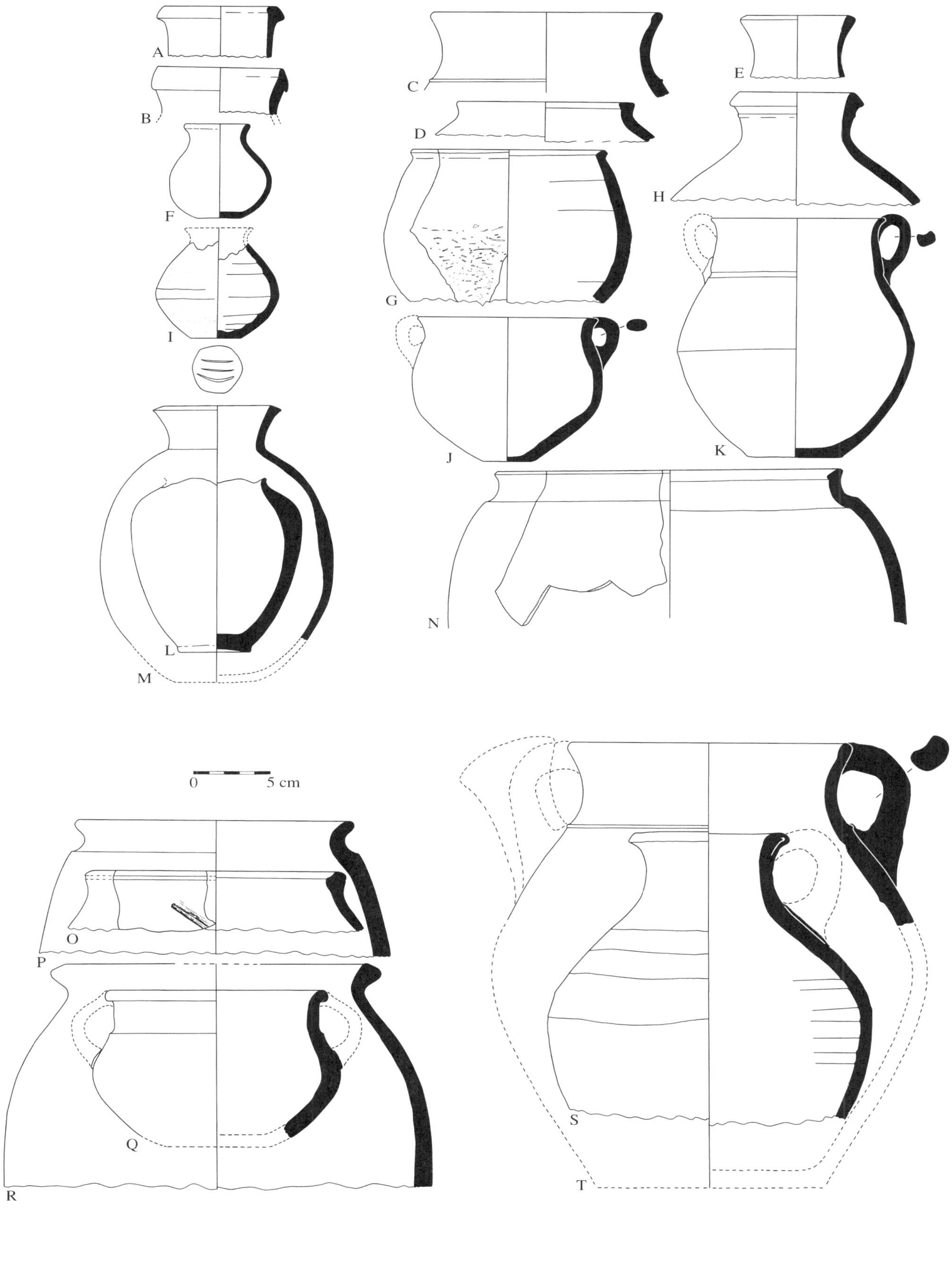


Figure 23. Late Iron Age/Achaemenid Pottery Vessels

Figure 24. Late Iron Age/Achaemenid Open Bowls

| | *Registration Number* | *Provenance* | *Elevation* | *Description* |
|---|---|---|---|---|
| A | 41137 | K23:400 | 1.35 B.S. | Buff ware. Well baked, no visible inclusions, smoothed |
| B | 4654 | R20:401 | B.S. | Buff ware. Creamy slip on exterior and interior. Light buff, sand and grit inclusions, some chaff |
| C | 8431 | Q17:801 | 83.57 | Buff ware. Orange buff surface. Well baked, grit inclusions |
| D | 2619 | Tr. V | 82.98 | Orange buff ware. Well baked, dense, grit inclusions, smoothed |
| E | 2596 | Tr. VII | B.S. | Orange buff ware. Buff slip exterior. Well baked, grit inclusions, visible striations |
| F | 8170 | Q24:803 | 78.61 | Buff ware. Buff slip exterior and interior. Well baked, grit and sand inclusions, smoothed, visible striation marks |
| G | 8709 | Q17:801 | 83.30 | Red ware. Red slip all over. Well baked, no visible inclusions |
| H | 9908 | P17:901 | N/A | N/A |
| I | 8639 | Q17:801 | 83.28 | Red ware. Red slip interior turning to white and flaking. Well baked, grit and sand inclusions |
| J | 3644 | Q18:305 | 0.35 B.S. | Orange buff ware. Dense with metallic ring, well baked, some grit inclusions, scrape marks on lower exterior |
| K | 6197 | P23:606 | 82.05 | Greenish buff ware. Well baked (over fired?), no visible inclusions |
| L | 3974 | R18:307 | B.S. | Buff ware. Well baked, small and large grit inclusions, smoothed |
| M | 8156 | Q17:806 | 82.84 | Buff ware. Buff slip exterior and interior. Well baked, sand inclusions |
| N | 3654 | Tr. V | 1.0 B.S. | Orange ware. Well baked, some sand inclusions, smoothed |
| O | 2652 | Sdg. A | B.S. | Buff ware. Slipped all over. Well baked, light brown buff surface, occasional medium size grit inclusions |

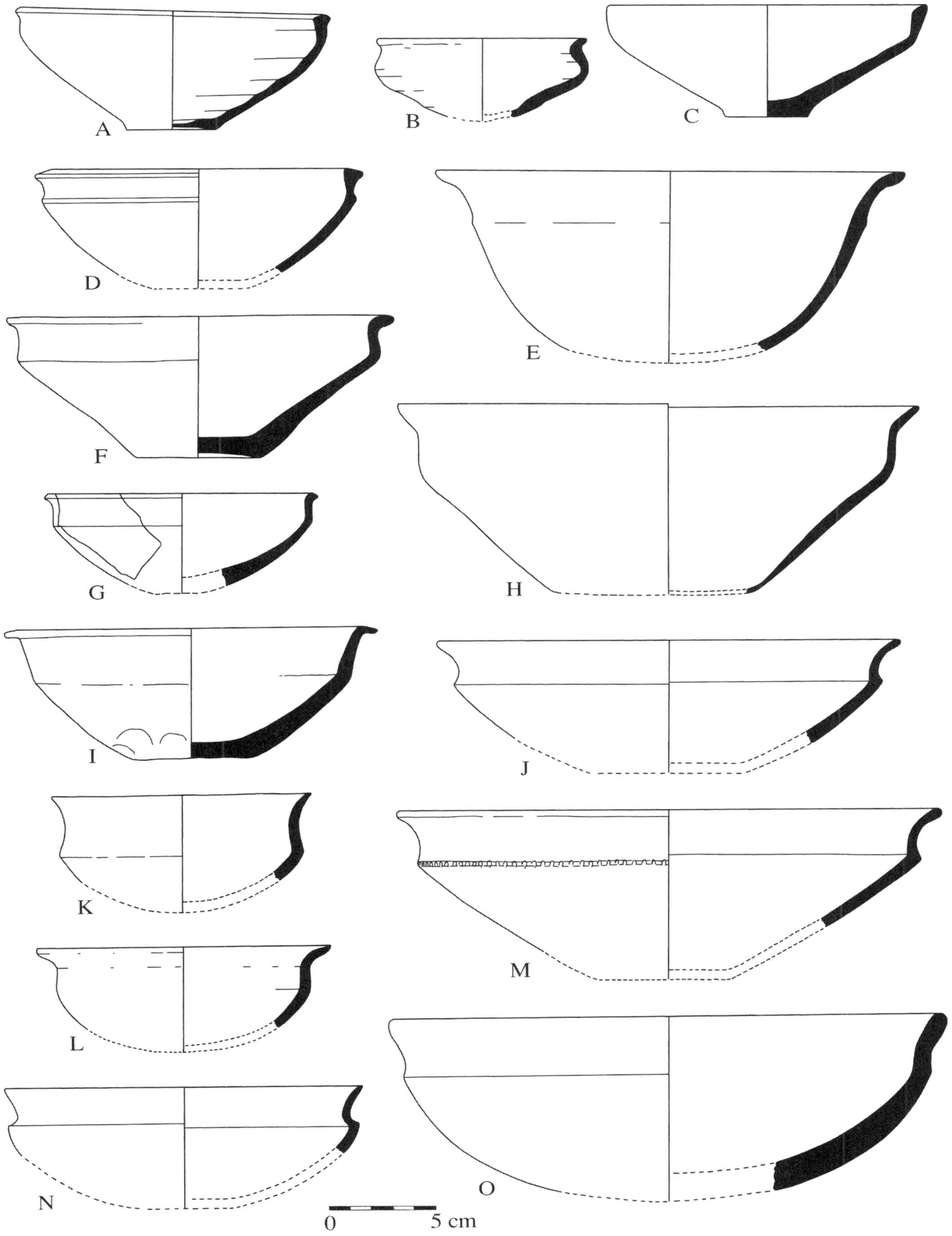


Figure 24. Late Iron Age/Achaemenid Open Bowls

Figure 25. Old Elamite (Sukkalmah) Pottery Vessels

| | *Registration Number* | *Provenance* | *Elevation* | *Description* |
|---|---|---|---|---|
| A | 1206 | Q21:101 | Fireplace | Orange buff ware. Probably slipped. Fine grit tempered |
| B | 1212 | Q21:102 | Surface | Yellowish buff ware. Grit and straw tempered, striation marks below rim |
| C | 4330 | J15:408 | 1.03 B.S. | Buff ware. No slip. Gritty, smoothed |
| D | X-14 | N9:1004 | 90.40 | Buff ware. Tan buff surface, probably slipped. Medium to small grits, scored base |
| E | X-15 | N9 | 90.40 | Buff ware. Buff tan exterior and interior. Grit tempered, smoothed |
| F | 10064 | N9:1006 South | 90.88 | Yellowish buff ware, grading to light orange toward surface. Creamy buff slip exterior. Some fine chaff and grit inclusions |
| G | X-22 | N1006 | 90.30 | Buff ware. Light orange tinge toward exterior. Small to medium grit tempered, striations on interior, scrape marks exterior |
| H | 1211 | High Mound | Surface | Buff ware. Light yellow buff surface. Grit and straw tempered, smoothed |
| I | 1202 | High Mound | Surface | Buff ware. Fine grit tempered, smoothed, wheel corrugations on exterior and interior |
| J | 10018 | N10:1002 North | 85.18 | Buff ware. Traces of cream buff slip exterior. Some grit inclusions, dense, scored base |
| K | N/A | R19:301 | N/A | N/A |
| L | 4690 | P10:401 | B.S. | Creamy buff ware. Straw and grit tempered, dense, striations on both sides, wheel corrugations interior |
| M | 1207 | Q21:102 | 0.90 B.S. | Grayish buff ware. Dense, gritty, fire smudges on exterior |
| N | 1219 | Tr. II | 2.50 B.S. | Buff ware. Slipped. Grit tempered, gritty face, smoothed, grit drag marks on exterior |
| O | 1213 | Q21:101 | Fireplace | Buff ware. Brownish buff surface. Fine straw and grit tempered, interior covered with smudges, striations on interior and exterior |
| P | 4693 | P9:401 | B.S. | Creamy buff ware. Probably slipped. Straw and grit tempered, striations on interior and exterior |
| Q | X-11 | Q9:1010 | B.S. | Buff ware. Probably slipped. Some grit inclusions, striations on interior and exterior |
| R | X-16 | N9:1004 | 90.84 | Buff ware. Creamy buff surface. Some grit inclusions, wheel corrugations interior |
| S | X-9 | N9:1001 North | 90.83 | Buff ware. Straw and grit tempered, striations on exterior and interior |
| T | X-32 | N8:1005 | 90.44 | Buff ware. Creamy buff surface. Straw and grit tempered, smoothed, wheel corrugations on interior |
| U | 10087 | N9:1001 | Grave 1001 | Buff ware. Straw and grit tempered, scored below rim and lower body, wheel corrugations on interior |

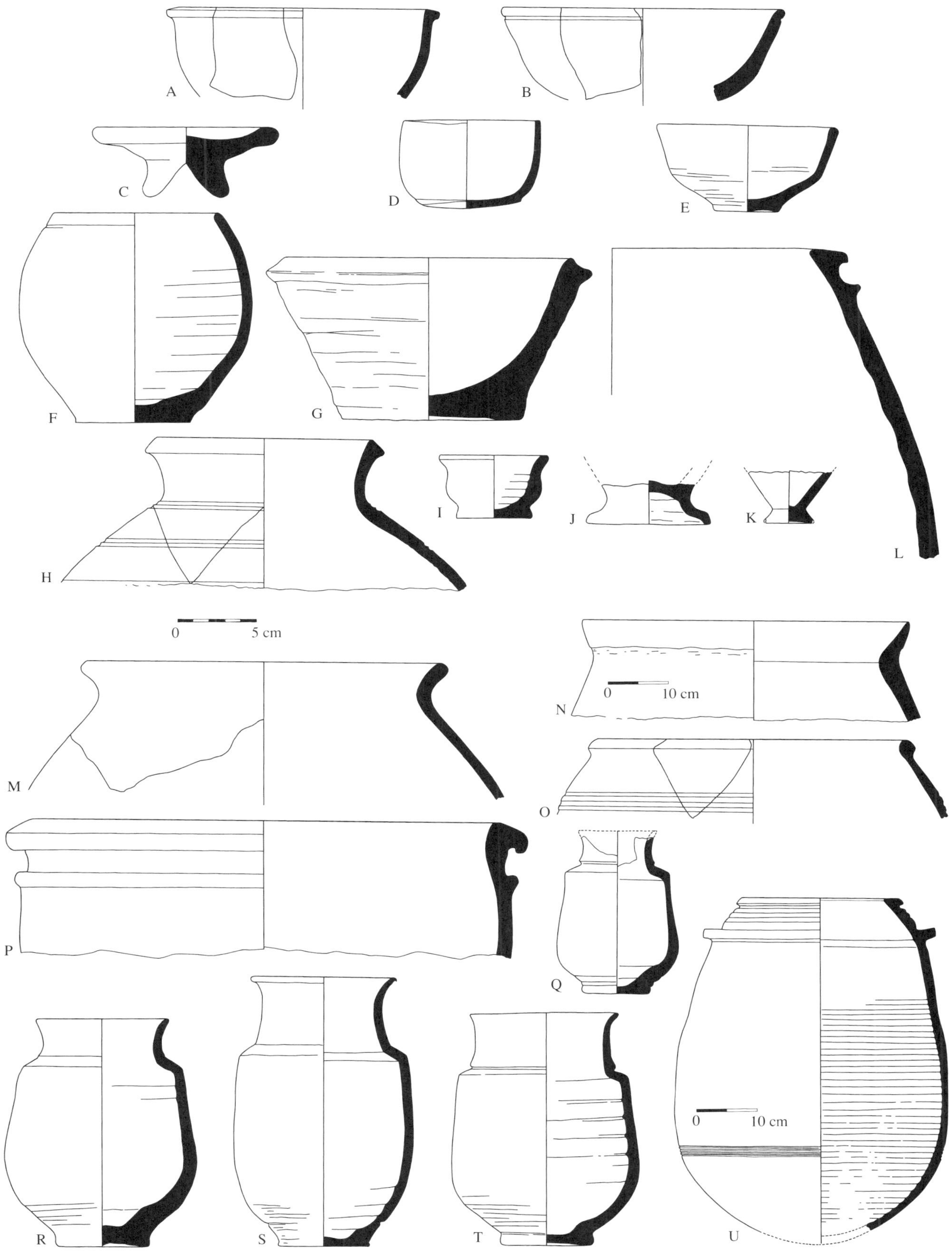


Figure 25. Old Elamite (Sukkalmah) Pottery Vessels

Figure 26. Protoliterate Pottery Vessels

| | *Registration Number* | *Provenance* | *Elevation* | *Description* |
|---|---|---|---|---|
| A | VI-47 | R17:408 | 82.90 | Standard ware. Pinkish buff. Wheel corrugations inside, string-cut base |
| B | N/A | P17:902 | 81.61 | Standard ware. "Pseudo-" beveled-rim bowl |
| C | 6130 | R19:401 | 1.0 B.S. | Standard ware. Buff slip turned greenish buff due to over firing. Fine to medium grits, striations on interior, lower body scraped |
| D | IX-28 | Q17:903 | 83.38 | Coarse ware. Light gray buff, smeared with bitumen on interior and exterior |
| E | 9015 | R16:912 | 82.85 | Standard ware. Buff. Few grits |
| F | 9013 | Q17:905 West | 82.96 | Standard ware. "Pseudo-" beveled-rim bowl |
| G | 9203 | R16:903 | 83.16 | Coarse buff ware. Grit and straw tempered. Rough surface exterior |
| H | 9500 | P17:901 | 81.51 | Standard ware. Buff. Straw tempered |
| I | 8662 | Q17:803 | 83.78 | Buff ware. Pinkish hue on the interior, light pink blotches on the exterior. Striations on the interior |
| J | 11206 | Q16:1103 | 83.49 | Standard ware. Buff. Some grit inclusions. Possibly a lid |
| K | 9154 | R19:905 | 80.15 | Coarse ware. Buff. Chaff tempered, scraped marks on lower body |

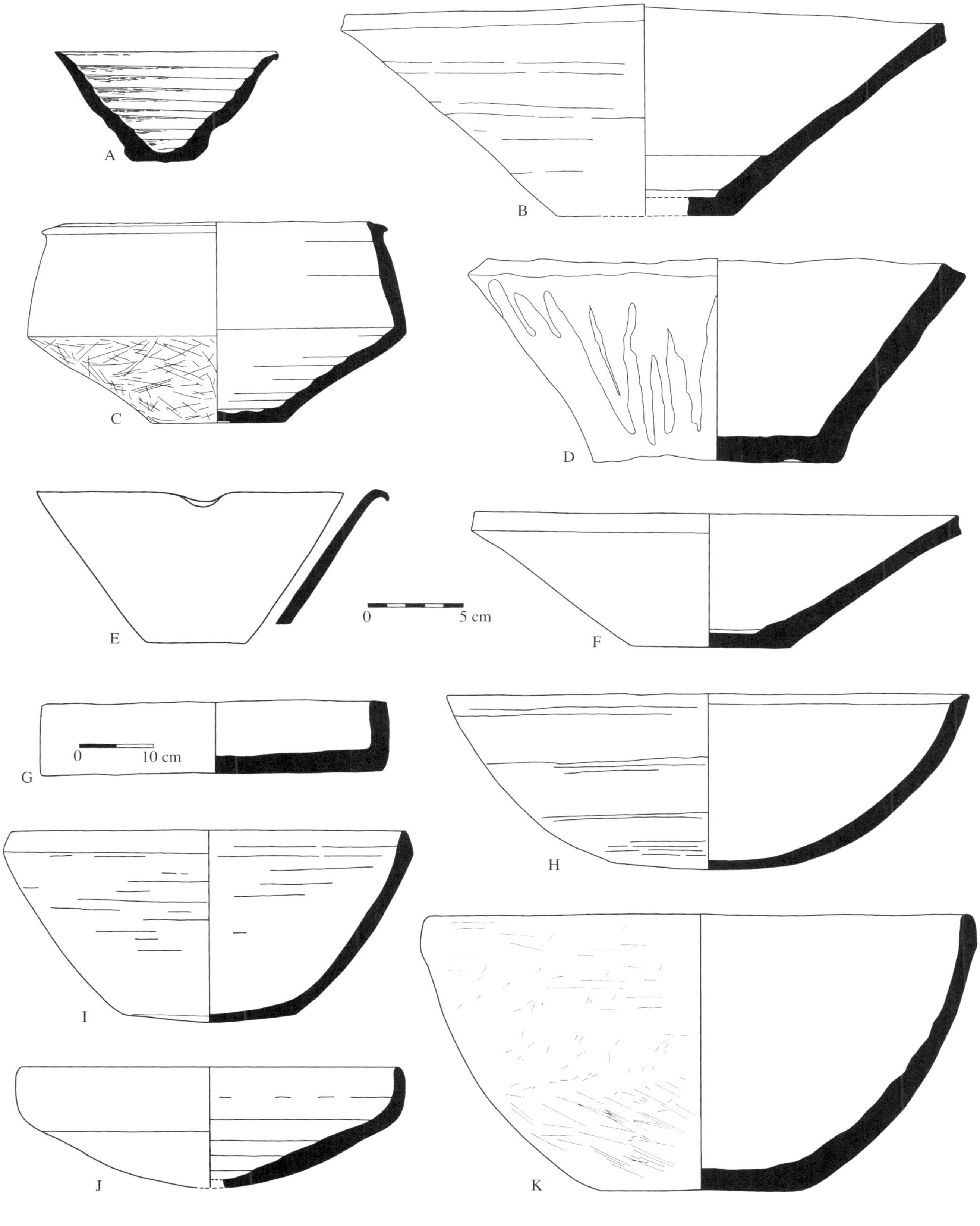


Figure 26. Protoliterate Pottery Vessels

Figure 27. Protoliterate Pottery Vessels

| | *Registration Number* | *Provenance* | *Elevation* | *Description* |
|---|---|---|---|---|
| A | 8645 | Q17:804 | 82.73 | Fine red ware. Red slip. Sand tempered, silky smooth exterior |
| B | 8644 | Q17:801 | 83.57 | Buff ware. Grayish surface, interior slip yellowish buff in color. Sand and grit tempered |
| C | 8522 | Q17:801 | 83.57 | Buff ware. Medium to large grits inclusions, dense, salt encrusted. Possibly Achaemenid |
| D | 9246 | N/A | N/A | N/A |
| E | 9691 | N8:903 | 88.00 | Standard ware. Buff orange. Sand tempered. Smoothed surface, some striations visible on the exterior |
| F | X-5 | Q17:1001 | 82.69 | Standard ware. Buff. Sand and fine grits included. Scraped marks below shoulder, striations on the interior |
| G | X-25 | Q17:1001 | 82.69 | Standard ware. Buff orange. Sand tempered. Smoothed surface, some striations visible on the exterior |
| H | X-10 | Q17:1001 | 82.69 | Standard ware. Pale pink buff. Sand tempered, smoothed |
| I | 6031 | Tr. XXXIII | 77.40 | Standard buff ware. No visible slip, wet smoothed(?) |
| J | XI-16 | P17:1104 | 81.55 | Standard ware. Buff orange. Sand tempered, smoothed |

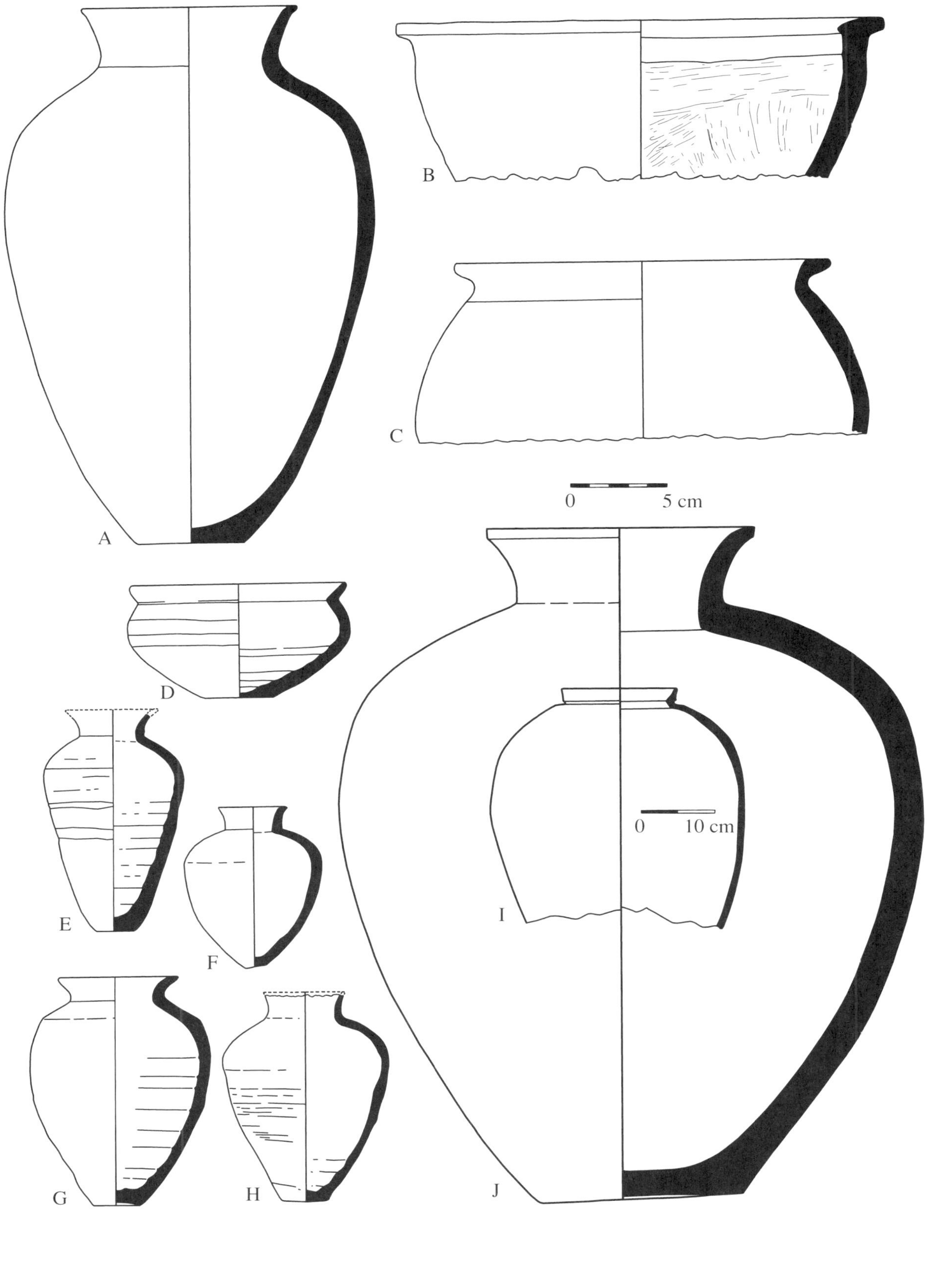


Figure 27. Protoliterate Pottery Vessels

Figure 28. Protoliterate Pottery Vessels

| | *Registration Number* | *Provenance* | *Elevation* | *Description* |
|---|---|---|---|---|
| A | 9024 | R16:912 | 84.03 | Gritty standard ware. Orange buff. Smoothed |
| B | VI-51 | S17:405 | N/A | Gritty standard ware. Reddish brown. Rough body except for the smoothed rim and neck |
| C | IX-104 | R19:905 | 80.19 | Gritty standard ware. Light red. Smoothed |
| D | VI-52 | H15:408 | 1.03 B.S. | Gritty standard ware. Brownish buff. Smoothed |
| E | 8567 | Q17:816 | 82.55 | Coarse ware. Straw-tempered orange brown clay. Scraped marks on body |
| F | 6847 | R19:601 | 1.0 B.S. | Coarse ware. Straw-tempered orange buff ware. Scraped marks on body |

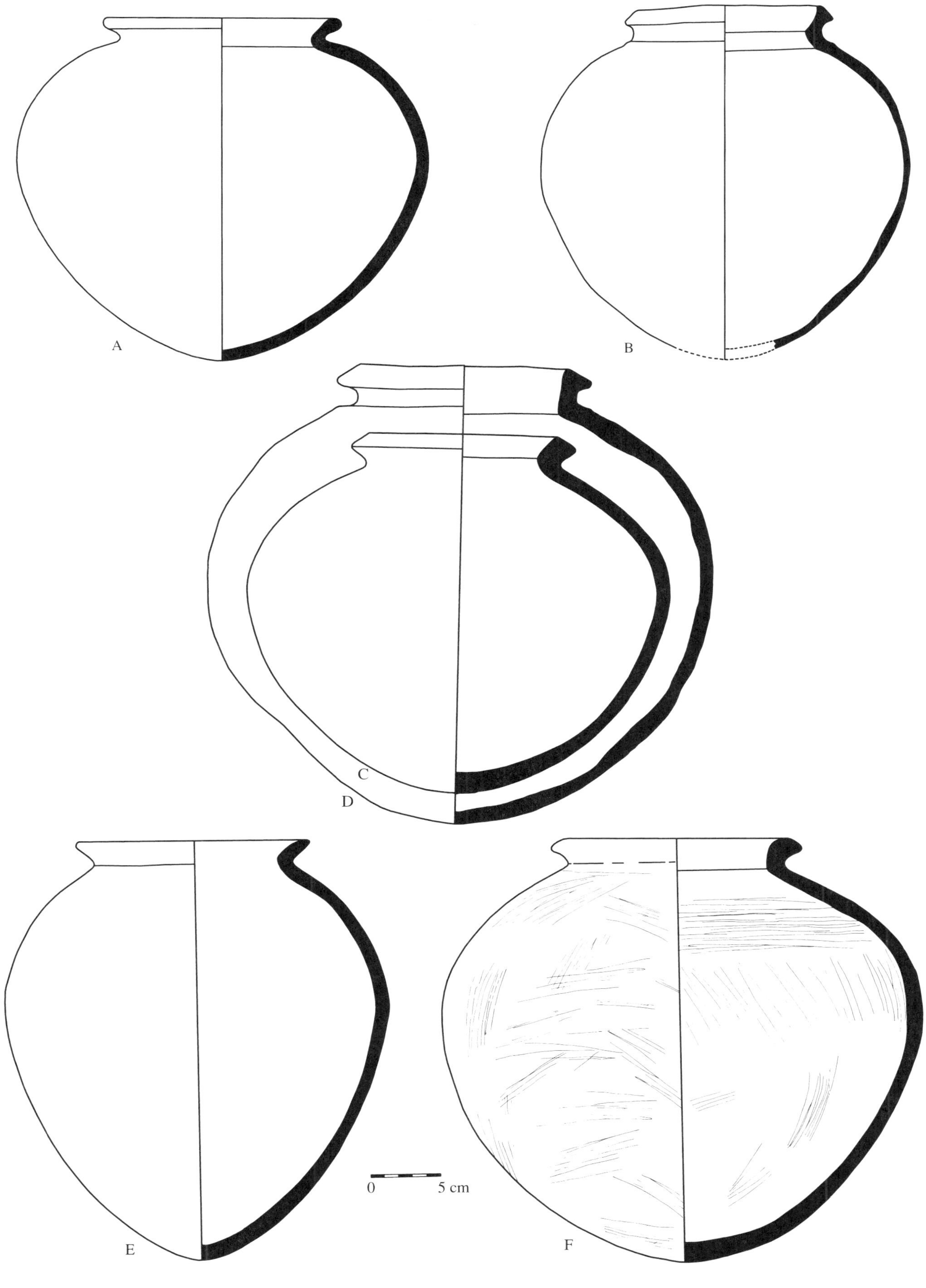


Figure 28. Protoliterate Pottery Vessels

Figure 29. Protoliterate Pottery Vessels

| | *Registration Number* | *Provenance* | *Elevation* | *Description* |
|---|---|---|---|---|
| A | XI-13 | R17:1110 | 82.10 | Standard buff ware. Red wash. Sandy, occasional red grits |
| B | XI-10 | R16:1105 | 83.50 | Standard buff ware. Gritty, dense |
| C | 8176 | Q17:803 | 83.41 | Standard buff ware. Orange buff slip. Grit tempering. Base covered with knobs of various sizes |
| D | 9189 | R18:909 | 80:07 | Standard buff ware. Sandy, smoothed. Shoulder decorated by pinching clay |
| E | X-7 | East Area | N/A | Standard red ware. Sandy, smoothed |
| F | VI-62 | R18:414 | N/A | Standard buff ware. Some grit inclusions, smoothed |
| G | 4299 | R18:307 | 0.55 B.S. | Standard buff ware. Buff slip exterior, buff slip shading into orange. Sand tempered, smoothed. Shoulder decorated with black paint and knobs |
| H | 8568 | S22:803 | 76.16 | Standard buff ware. Surface buff shades to light orange. Sandy, dense |
| I | VI-44 | K14:403 | 0.85 B.S. | Standard buff ware. Surface yellowish buff. Sand tempered |
| J | XI-12 | East Area | N/A | Standard red ware. Sandy, smoothed, wheel striations on the interior |

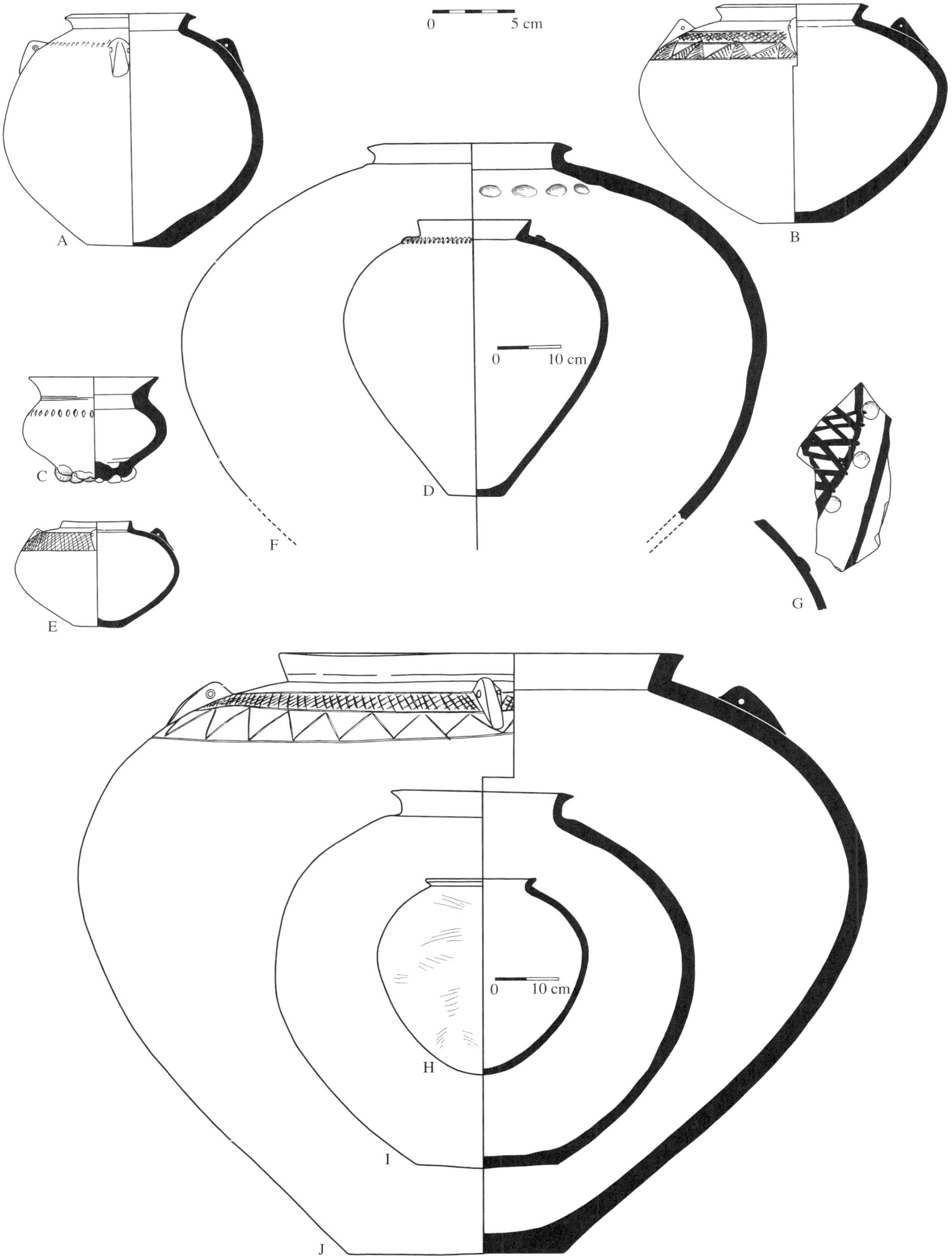


Figure 29. Protoliterate Pottery Vessels

Figure 30. Protoliterate Pottery Vessels

| | *Registration Number* | *Provenance* | *Elevation* | *Description* |
|---|---|---|---|---|
| A | VII-97 | S22:701 | 76.43 | Standard ware. Rather fine, smoothed |
| B | IX-132 | R19:903 | 79.89 | Standard ware. Gritty buff. Incised shoulder |
| C | 8051 | S22:803 | 70.41 | Standard ware. Red slip. Grits and sand inclusions, striations on exterior |
| D | 9133 | R18:916 | 80.24 | Fine buff ware. Sand tempered with occasional grits. Smoothed upper body, scraped lower body |
| E | IX-117 | East Area | N/A | Standard ware. Red slip. Grits and sand inclusions, striations on exterior |
| F | 9144 | S22:904 | 76.96 | Standard buff ware. Sand and grit inclusions, striations on interior and exterior |
| G | 8661 | Q17:813 | 82.51 | Standard red ware. Grit tempered, smoothed, wheel corrugations on interior |
| H | 9030 | R16:914 | 83.50 | Standard red ware. Gritty, heavy corrugations on the interior |

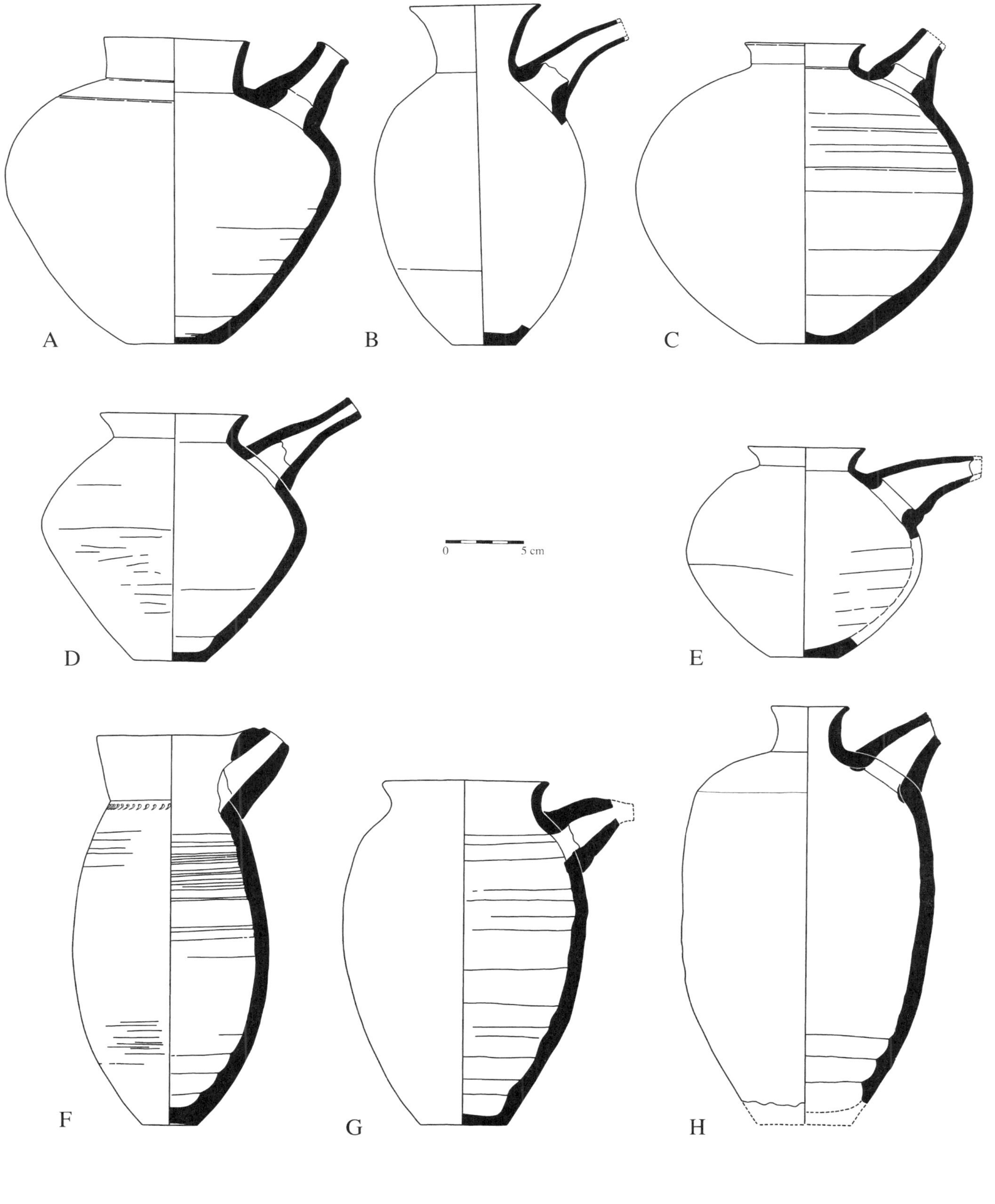


Figure 30. Protoliterate Pottery Vessels

Figure 31. Protoliterate Pottery Vessels

| | *Registration Number* | *Provenance* | *Elevation* | *Description* |
|---|---|---|---|---|
| A | 8643 | Q17:803 | 83.37 | Standard buff ware. Sandy, creamy buff surface, upper body smoothed, lower body scraped |
| B | IX-9 | Q17:903 East | 83.63 | Standard buff ware. Brownish buff core, wet smoothed |
| C | 9151 | R19:905 | 79.44 | Standard buff ware. Sand and grits, very smooth |
| D | IX-75 | R18:906 | 79.46 | Standard buff ware. Yellowish buff surface, sandy |
| E | 9032 | R18:902 | 81.22 | Standard buff ware. Light buff slip shading into light orange on surface. Sand and grit inclusions, smoothed |
| F | 8572 | S22:803 | 77.01 | Fine buff ware. Creamy buff slip. Sand tempered |
| G | VI-56 | East Area | Surface | Standard red ware. Brownish buff core, sandy face |
| H | X-4 | Q16:1001 | 83.15 | Fine buff ware. Buff slipped turned greenish buff on surface. Sand tempered |
| I | 8610 | Q17:806 | 83.57 | Fine buff ware. Creamy buff slip on exterior. Sand tempering with some grits, striations on exterior |
| J | 8611 | Q17:816 | 82.55 | Fine buff ware. Creamy buff slip turned greenish due to over firing. Sandy, smoothed |
| K | VI-59 | K23:502 | 0.90 B.S. | Standard buff ware. Some scattered grits, corrugation marks just below equator |
| L | IX-133 | R18:906 | 81.46 | Standard buff ware. Buff slip turned greenish due to over firing. Sandy, smoothed |
| M | IX-116 | N/A | Surface | Standard buff ware. Sand tempered. Buff slip turned greenish due to over firing |
| N | VII-97 | S22:701 | 76.43 | Standard buff ware. Buff slip. Almost fine, sandy |
| O | 9506 | East Area | N/A | Standard red ware. Sandy, smoothed |

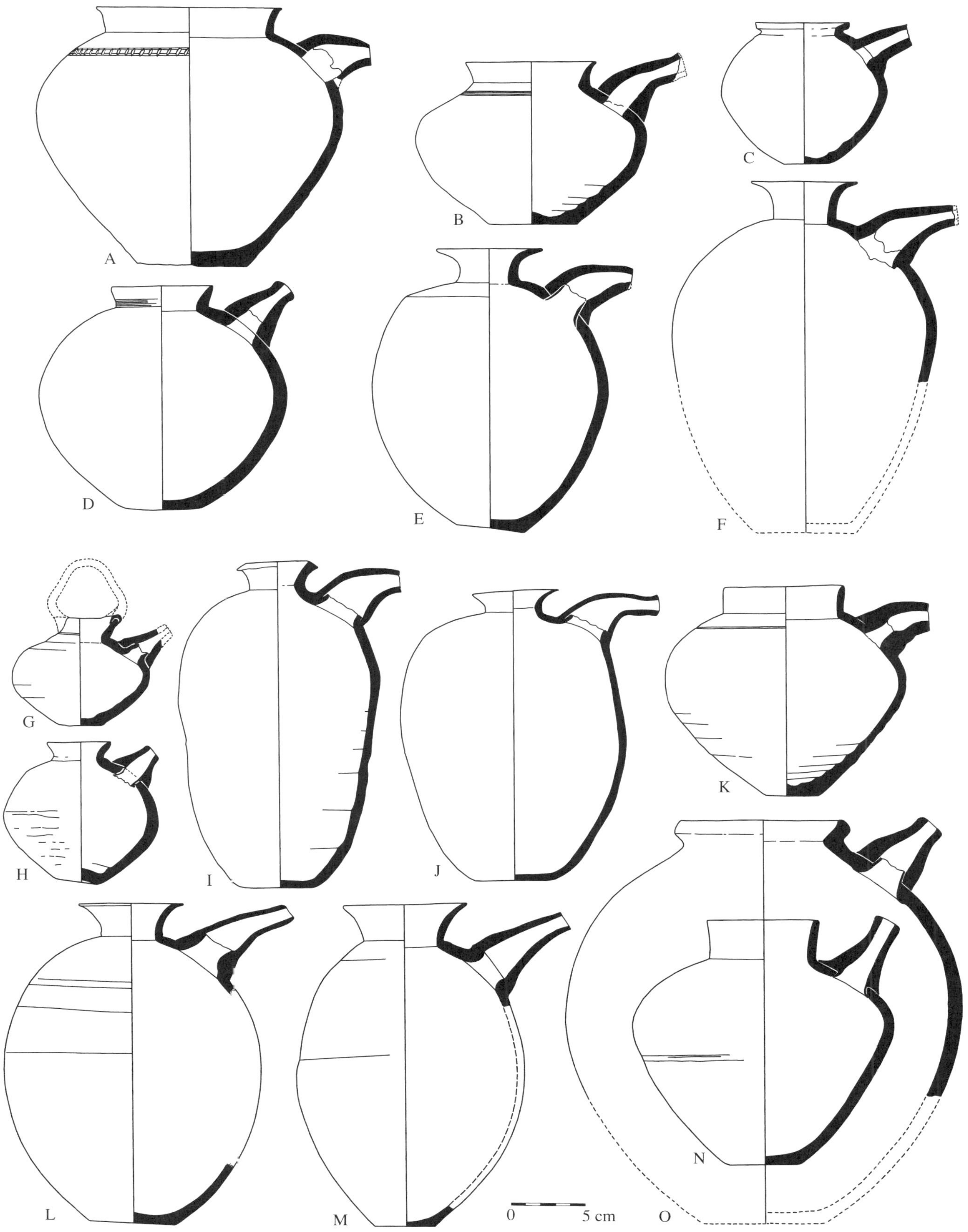


Figure 31. Protoliterate Pottery Vessels

Figure 32. Protoliterate Pottery Vessels

| | *Registration Number* | *Provenance* | *Elevation* | *Description* |
|---|---|---|---|---|
| A | 9505 | N8:903 | 98.80 | Standard buff ware. Gritty, light brownish core grading to buff |
| B | 9481 | P17:901 | 81.85 | Standard ware. Gritty, orange red with buff gray core |
| C | X-15 | N10:1004 | 89.73 | Standard ware. Gritty, brownish buff, wheel corrugations inside |
| D | IX-89 | R19:905 | 80.15 | Standard ware. Gritty, yellowish buff |
| E | 9146 | R18:906 | 80.02 | Standard red ware. Orange buff, incised |
| F | X-2 | Q16:1007 | 83.64 | Standard ware. Gritty, buff |
| G | 6225 | Tr. XIII | 0.70 B.S. | Standard ware. Gritty, some very large. Brownish buff core, orange buff surface, smoothed |
| H | 8663 | Q17:806 | 83.57 | Standard ware. Light buff. Gritty |
| I | 9193 | R16:902 | 83.87 | Fine ware. Light buff, sand and grit tempered. Creamy buff slipped |
| J | VI-67 | K23:501 | 0.25 B.S. | Standard ware. Gritty orange brown, rough surface with fire smudges |
| K | 9693 | N8:903 | 88.00 | Standard ware. Buff orange with light buff brownish core. Grits visible on the surface. No slip |
| L | 9501 | R18:906 | 80.02 | Standard red ware. Gritty, smoothed |

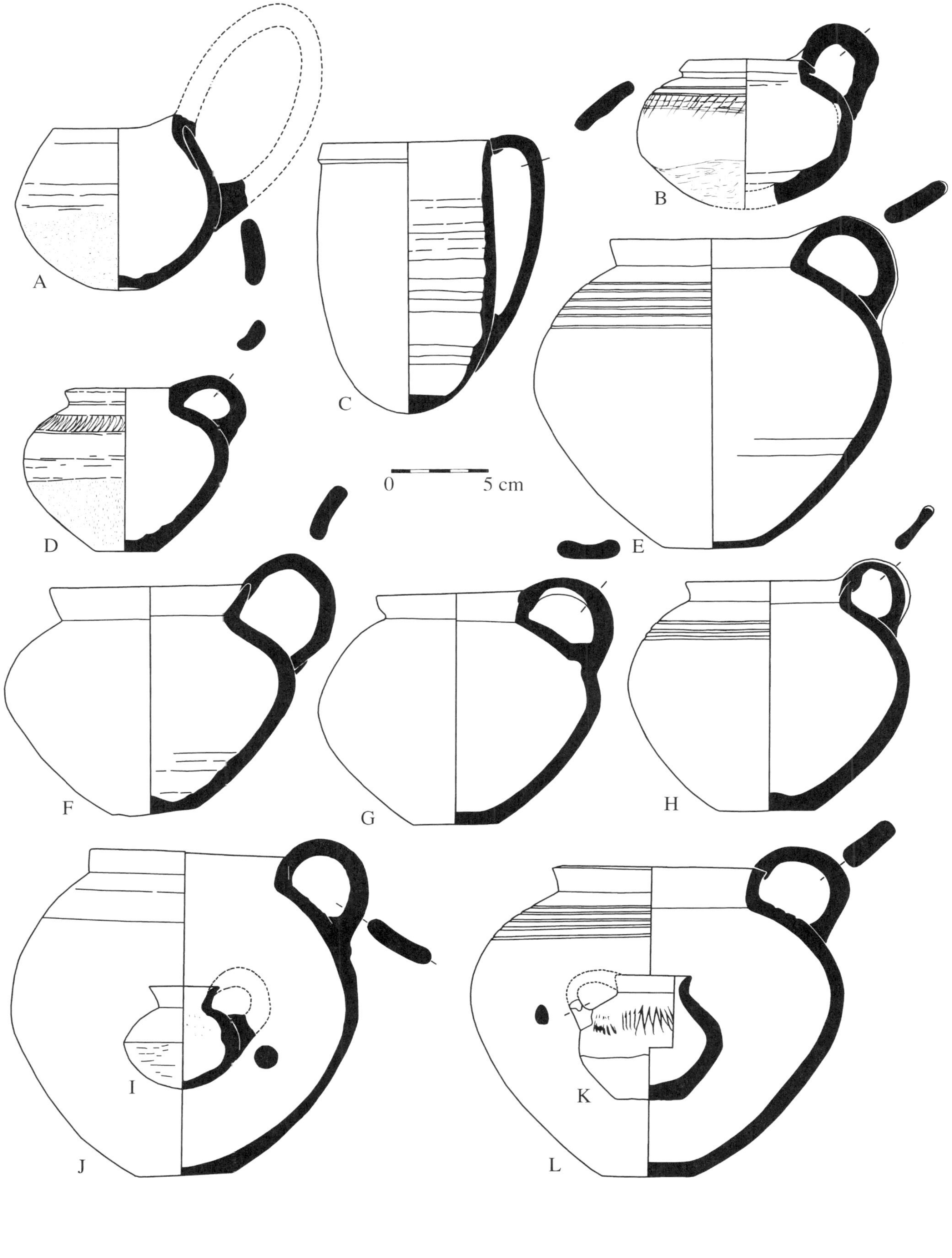


Figure 32. Protoliterate Pottery Vessels

Figure 33. Protoliterate Pottery Vessels

| | *Registration Number* | *Provenance* | *Elevation* | *Description* |
|---|---|---|---|---|
| A | IX-58 | R18:909 | 80.98 | Standard buff ware. Gritty. Smoothed exterior |
| B | 8396 | Q17:803 | 83.40 | Buff ware. Sand and grit inclusions. Prominent wheel marks on interior |
| C | 8665a | Q17:801 | 83.87 | Buff ware. Sand and grits tempering. Wheel marks on the interior. Lower exterior scraped |
| D | 5694 | R20:510 | 78.68 | Light red ware. Dark red wash on exterior with horizontal burnish strokes. Black paint |
| E | 9192 | R16:906 | 83.87 | Red ware. Grit tempered. Flaky surface |
| F | N/A | Q17:1106 | 82.70 | Standard buff ware. Gritty. Water pipe |
| G | 7394 | R17:719 | 83.76 | N/A |
| H | 8299 | Tr. XXV | Surface | N/A |
| I | 9479 | P17:901 | 81.83 | Coarse gray ware. Basin fragment with spout or bellow fragment. Straw tempered. Greenish gray core |
| J | 8395 | Q17:804 | 82.78 | Standard red ware. Red, dark, and white (calcite) grits tempering. Uneven body |
| K | XI-9 | R17:1101 | 83.44 | Coarse ware. Brownish buff. Grits and chaff tempered. Interior "floor" longitudinally stroked |
| L | 11198 | Q18:1106 | 81.50 | Coarse ware. Brownish buff. Grits and chaff tempered. Interior "floor" longitudinally stroked |

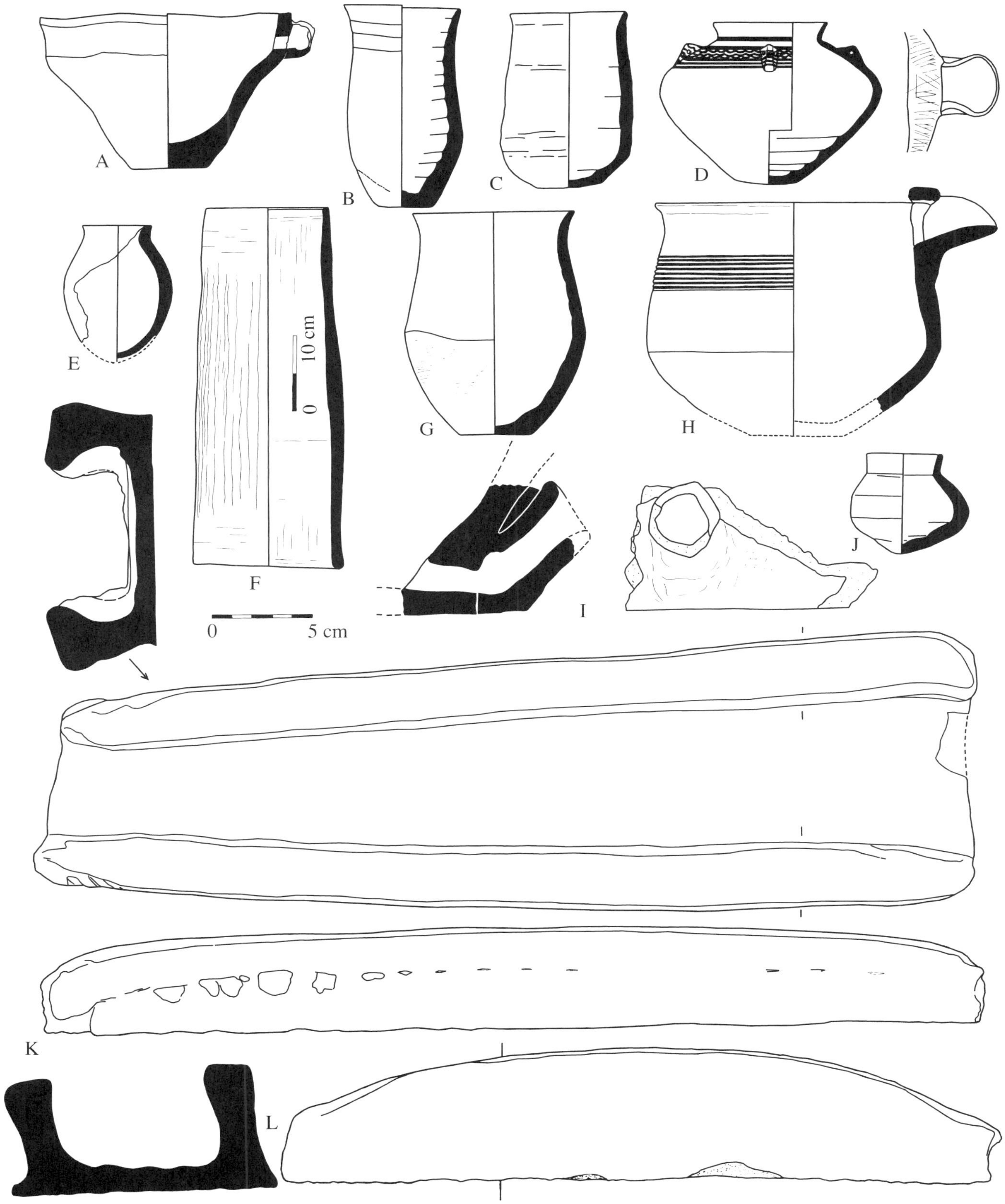


Figure 33. Protoliterate Pottery Vessels

Figure 34. Protoliterate Ritual Vessel

| *Registration Number* | *Provenance* | *Elevation* | *Description* |
|---|---|---|---|
| X-1 | Q17:1001 | 82.65 | Libation(?) vessel. Buff ware. Sand tempered. Creamy buff slipped. Incised. See pl. 29:A for photograph |

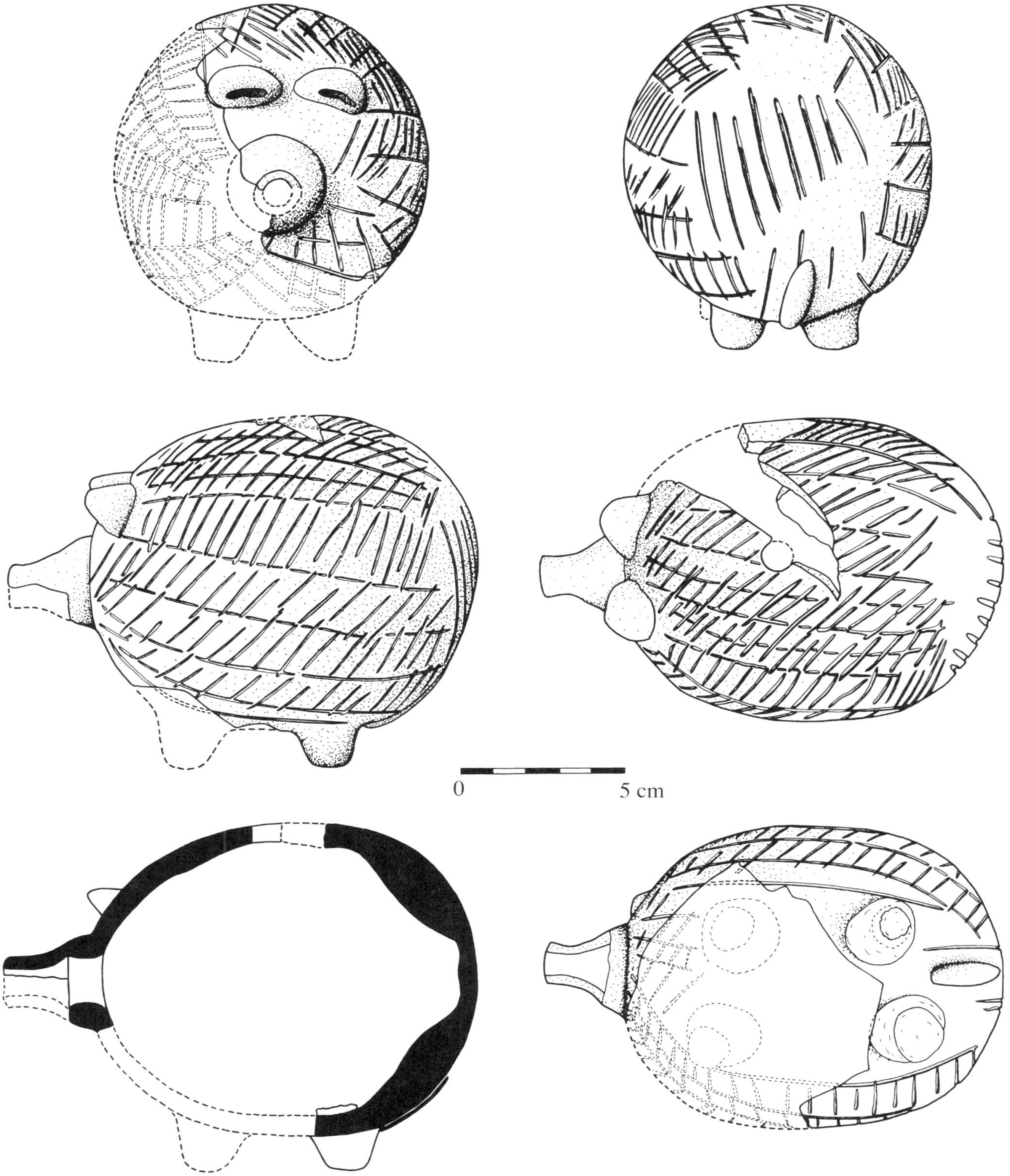


Figure 34. Protoliterate Ritual Vessel

Figure 35. Late Susiana 2 Pottery Vessels

| | *Registration Number* | *Provenance* | *Elevation* | *Description* |
|---|---|---|---|---|
| A | 9631 | S17:901 | 81.20 | Creamy buff fine ware. No visible inclusions, black paint. See plate 19:B for photograph |
| B | 9629 | S17:901 | 81.20 | Creamy buff fine ware. No visible inclusions, black paint |
| C | 8056 | Q17:811 | 82.69 | Fine buff ware. Some sand included. Creamy slip on exterior and interior. Black paint |
| D | 9630 | S17:901 | 81.20 | Light red (2.5 YR 6/6) fine ware. Some sand inclusions, red paint. Susa Acropole II, level VII |
| E | 9676 | M9:901 | 83.68 | Buff ware. Some sand inclusions, smoothed, black paint |

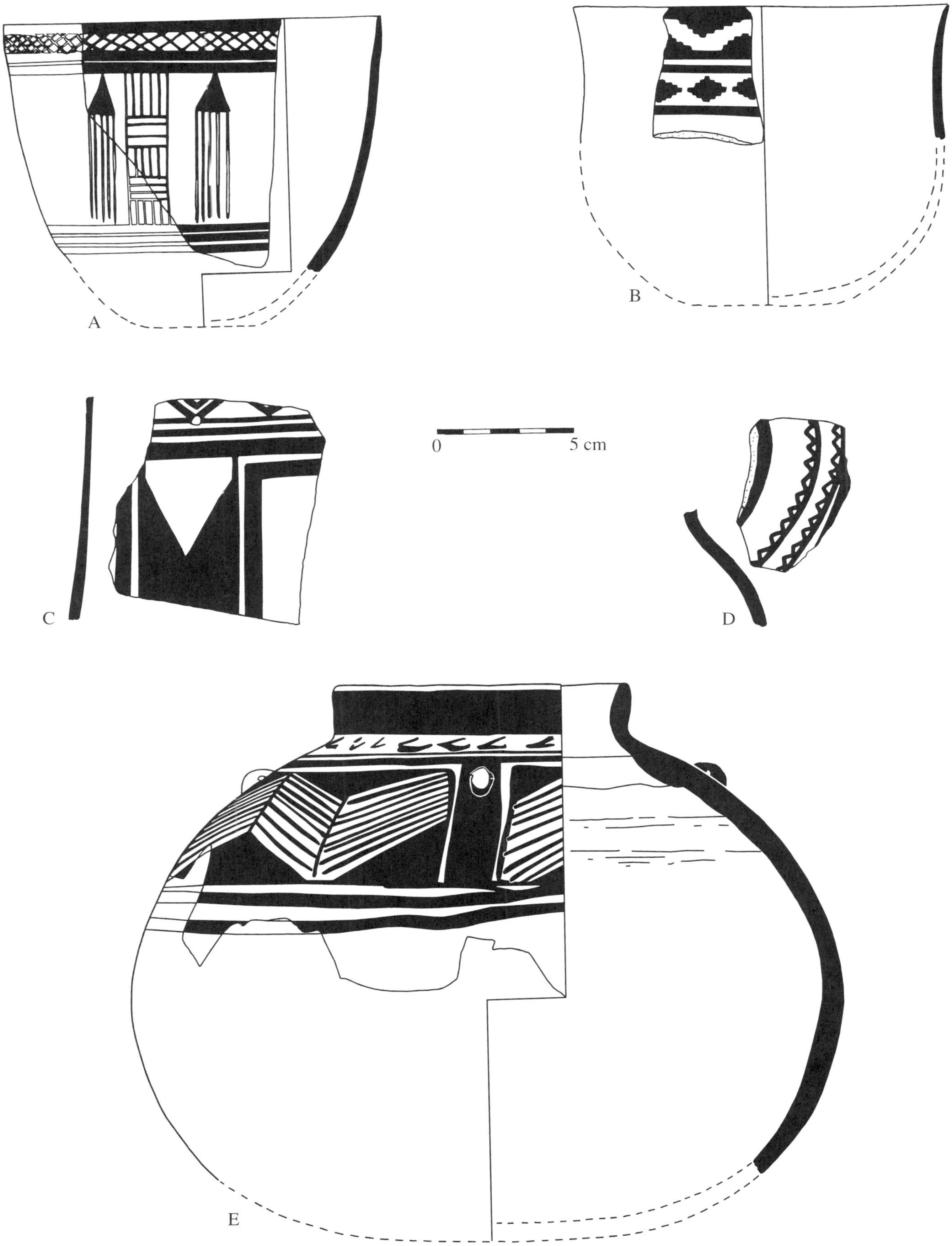


Figure 35. Late Susiana 2 Pottery Vessels

Figure 36. Middle Susiana Pottery Vessels

| | *Registration Number* | *Provenance* | *Elevation* | *Description* |
|---|---|---|---|---|
| A | 9153 | S18:915 | 82.00 | Buff ware. Sand tempered. Creamy buff slip turned greenish buff due to over firing, black paint |
| B | 9520 | S18:918 | 80.09 | Fine buff ware. No visible inclusions. Creamy buff slipped. Black paint |
| C | VII-26 | G28:705 | 79.42 | Buff ware. Dense, no visible inclusions. Yellowish buff slipped. Black paint |
| D | 9542 | S18:918 | 81.65 | Buff ware. Some sand inclusions. Creamy buff slipped. Black paint |
| E | 9152 | S18:916 | 81.60 | Buff ware. Sand tempered with few grits. Buff slipped. Black paint |
| F | 4264 | Sdg. G | 1.40 B.S. | Fine buff ware. Some fine grit inclusions. Creamy buff slipped. Brown matte paint |
| G | 7008 | G27:703 | 81.17 | Fine buff ware. No visible inclusions. Creamy buff slipped. Black broad wash |
| H | 7074 | R23:702 | 77.63 | Buff ware. Small grit tempered. Creamy beige slipped. Brown paint |
| I | 9547 | S18:915 | 82.00 | Buff ware. Some sand inclusions. Creamy buff slip turned slightly green due to over firing. Black paint |
| J | 9177 | P17:901 | 79.37 | Buff ware. Sand tempered. Creamy buff slipped. Black paint |
| K | 7004 | R23:704 | 75.47 | Standard buff ware. Fine grit tempered. Creamy buff slipped. Dark brown paint. Interior decoration achieved by incision through broad wash. Early Middle Susiana |
| L | 9208 | R18:908 | 80.88 | Fine buff ware. No visible inclusions. Creamy buff slip turned slightly green due to over firing. Black paint |

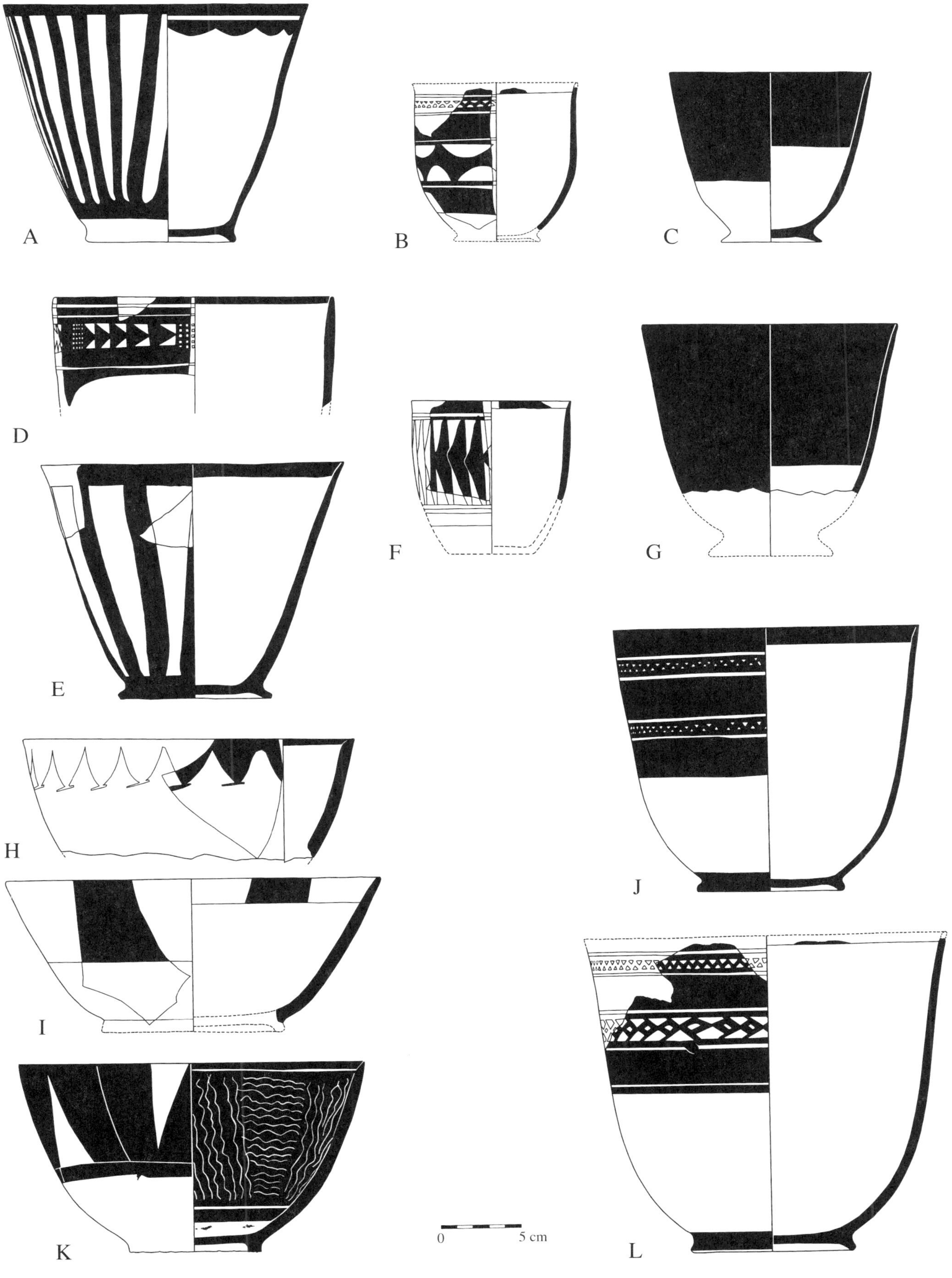


Figure 36. Middle Susiana Pottery Vessels

Figure 37. Middle Susiana Pottery Vessels

| | *Registration Number* | *Provenance* | *Elevation* | *Description* |
|---|---|---|---|---|
| A | 6005 | S20:601 | 0.20 B.S. | Standard buff ware. Sand tempered. Buff slip turned greenish due to over firing. Greenish brown paint. Late Middle Susiana |
| B | 6013 | S20:601 | 78.56 | Standard buff ware. Sand tempered. Creamy buff slip turned greenish due to over firing. Olive black paint. Late Middle Susiana |
| C | 6121 | Tr. XXXIII | 77.40 | Standard buff ware. Sand tempered. Creamy buff slip turned greenish due to over firing. Black paint, somewhat shiny. See also figure 38:A. Late Middle Susiana |
| D | IX-103 | R18:916 | 81.71 | Standard buff ware. Sand tempered. Creamy buff slip turned greenish due to over firing. Black paint. Late Middle Susiana |
| E | 8677 | S22:819 | 76.33 | Standard buff ware. Sand tempered. Creamy buff slipped. Brown paint. Early Middle Susiana |
| F | 6522 | S20:618 | 75.20 | Buff ware. Small grit tempered with occasional traces of chaff. Creamy buff slipped. Black paint. Form and decoration Early Susiana/Middle Susiana Transitional |
| G | 9624 | S18:916 | 81.71 | Standard buff ware. Sand tempered. Buff slipped. Blackpaint. Late Middle Susiana |
| H | 7716 | G28:703 | 77.60 | Standard buff ware. Sand tempered with occasional grits. Buff slipped. Dark paint. Late Middle Susiana |
| I | 6268 | P22:604 | B.S. | Buff ware. Dense. Orange buff surface. Sand tempered with occasional grits. Some air pockets. Dark reddish brown granular paint. Early Middle Susiana |
| J | 7119 | R23:701 | 77.66 | Buff ware. Sand tempered. Buff slipped. Black paint. Early/Late Middle Susiana |
| K | IX-41 | R18:901 | 81.10 | Standard buff ware. Sand tempered with occasional grits. Buff slipped. Dark paint. Late Middle Susiana |
| L | 6477 | P22:602 | 81.44 | Buff ware. Grit tempered with some straw. Buff slipped. Black paint. Early Middle Susiana |
| M | 9675 | R18:902 | 81.22 | Standard buff ware. Sand tempered with occasional grits. Buff slipped. Dark paint. Late Middle Susiana |
| N | 7002 | G28:703 South | 76.98 | Standard buff ware. Sand tempered. Buff slipped. Dark brown paint. For outside decoration, see pl. 20:H. See also figure 39:B. Early/Late Middle Susiana |
| O | 9185a | R18:901 | 81.10 | Standard buff ware. Sand tempered with occasional grits. Buff slipped. Dark paint. Late Middle Susiana |
| P | 4640 | K22:402 | 1.35 B.S. | Standard buff ware. Sand tempered. Buff slipped. Black paint. Late Middle Susiana |
| Q | 9185b | R18:902 | 81.22 | Standard buff ware. Sand tempered with occasional grits. Buff slipped. Dark paint. Late Middle Susiana |
| R | 7051 | G28:705 | 79.42 | Standard buff ware. Sand tempered. Buff slipped. Dark matte paint. Late Middle Susiana |

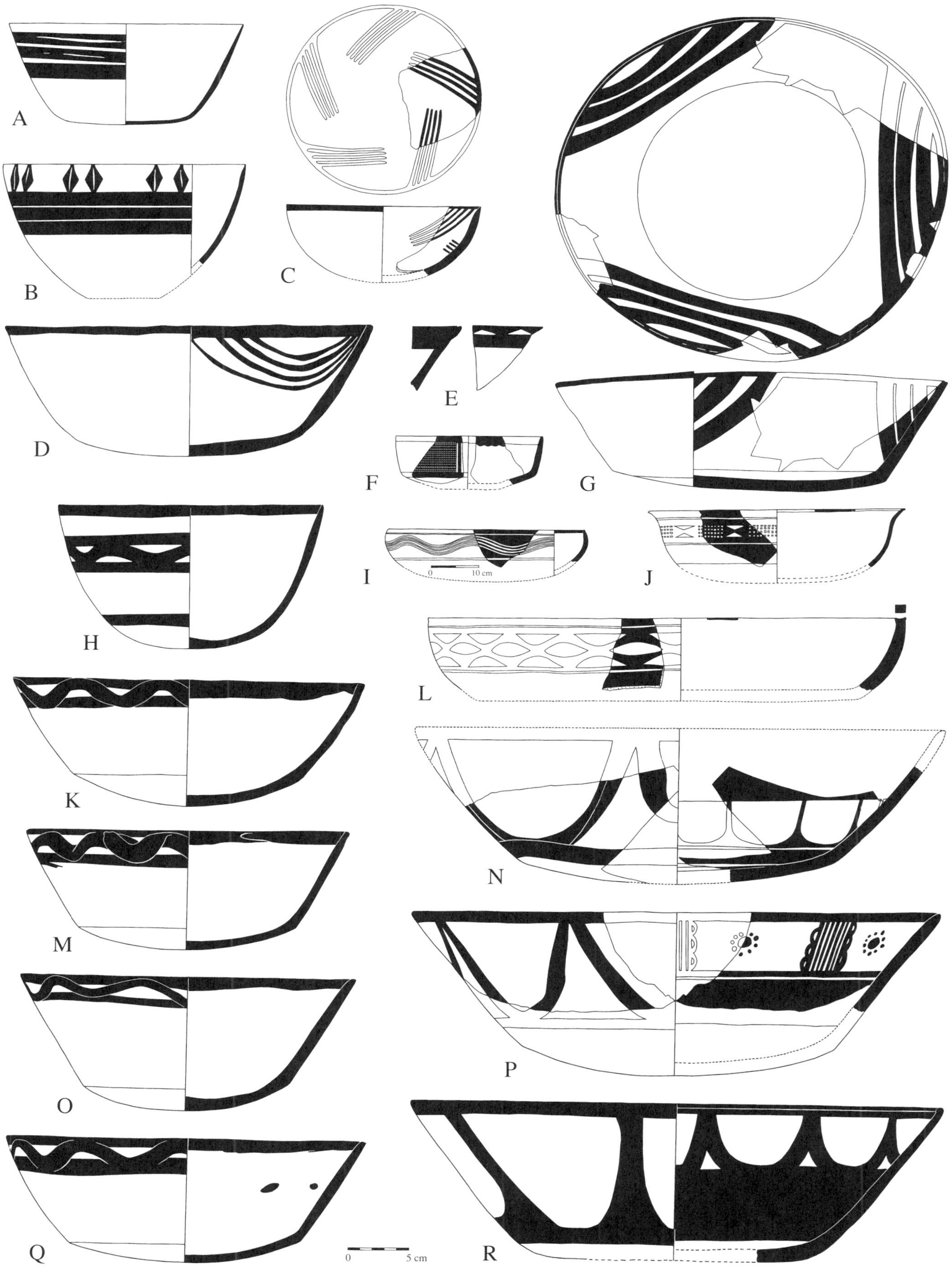


Figure 37. Middle Susiana Pottery Vessels

Figure 38. Middle Susiana Pottery Vessels

| | *Registration Number* | *Provenance* | *Elevation* | *Description* |
|---|---|---|---|---|
| A | 6121 | Tr. XXXIII | 77.40 | Standard buff ware. Sand tempered. Creamy buff slip with a greenish tinge. Black paint. Slightly burnished. See also figure 37:C. Late Middle Susiana |
| B | 7107 | G28:701 | 81.73 | Buff ware. Grit tempered. Probably buff slipped. Black paint |
| C | 6084 | S20:601 | 76.63 | Standard buff ware. Sand tempered. Buff slipped. Black paint. Slightly burnished. Late Middle Susiana |
| D | 6131 | S20:601 | 78.47 | Buff ware. Grit tempered with occasional chaff. Buff slipped, smoothed. Black matte paint. Early Middle Susiana |
| E | 7067 | R23:702 | 77.63 | Standard buff ware. Sand tempered. Buff slipped. Brown paint. Early to Middle Susiana transitional |
| F | 6441 | S20:615 | 78.13 | Standard buff ware. Sand tempered with occasional grits. Cream slipped. Black paint. Early to Middle Susiana transitional |
| G | 3211 | Tr. IX | 0.70 B.S. | Standard buff ware. Sand tempered. Buff slipped with greenish tinge. Brown paint. Late Middle Susiana |
| H | IX | R18:901 | 80.52 | Standard buff ware. Grit tempered. Yellowish buff surface, possibly slipped. Black paint. Late Middle Susiana |
| I | 7003 | G28:701 | 81.27 | Standard buff ware. Some sand. Creamy buff slipped. Brown paint. Scraping marks inside. Late Middle Susiana |
| J | 1073 | N/A | Surface | Standard buff ware. Gritty. Probably slipped light buff. Dark paint. Early Middle Susiana |
| K | 7065 | R23:701 | 76.77 | Buff ware. Grit tempered. Probably slipped. Greenish brown paint. Scraping marks on base. Early Middle Susiana |
| L | 6044 | P22:606 | 82.17 | Fine buff ware. Some sand. Creamy buff slipped. Black paint. Burnished. Early Middle Susiana |
| M | 6113 | S20:620 | 78.20 | Standard buff ware. Sand tempered with some grits. Creamy buff slipped. Smoothed. Black paint. Late Middle Susiana |
| N | 6532 | S20:609 | 77.05 | Standard buff ware. Dense. Small grits tempered. Brown black paint, somewhat shiny. Early Middle Susiana |

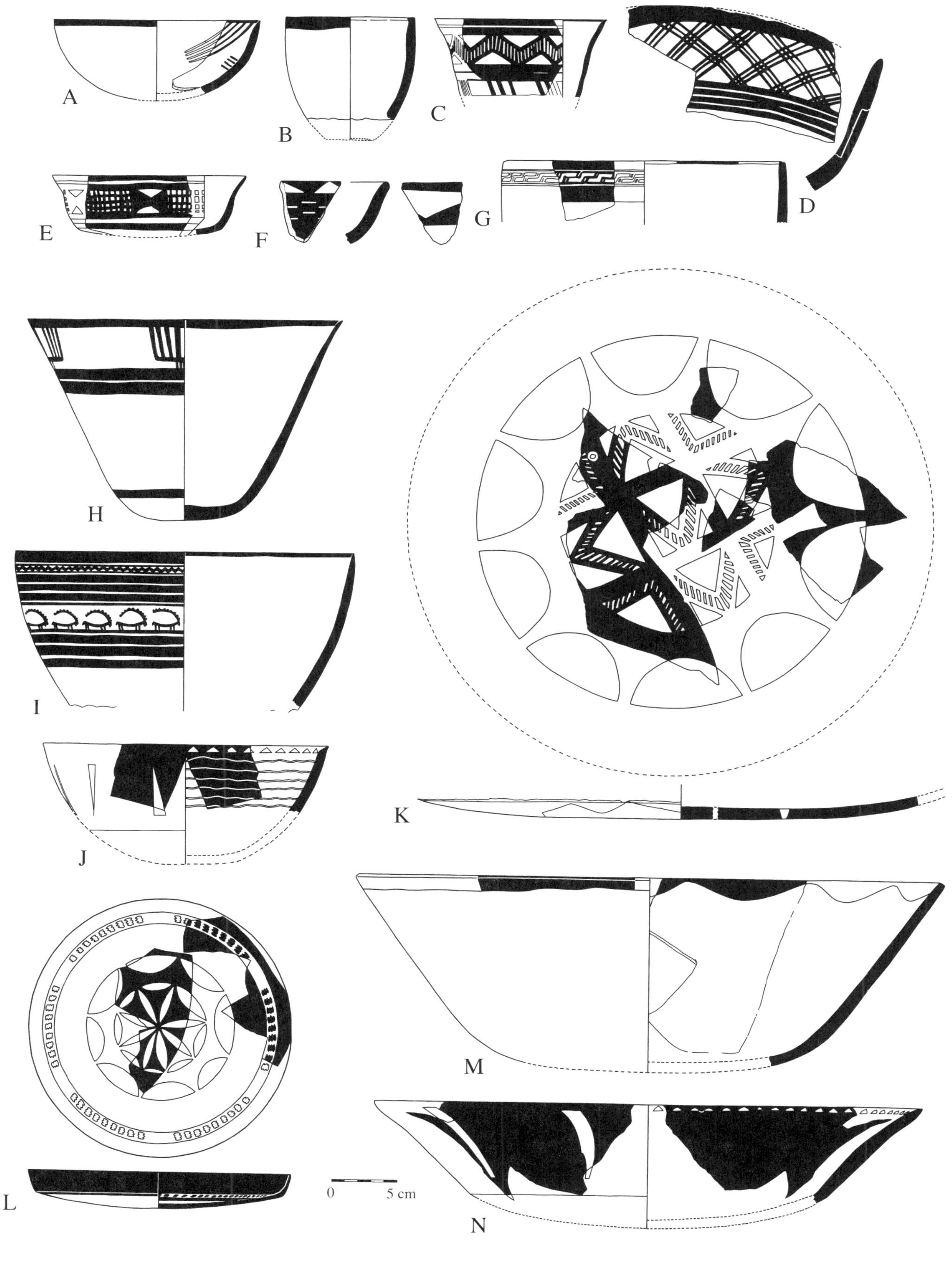


Figure 38. Middle Susiana Pottery Vessels

Figure 39. Middle Susiana Pottery Vessels

| | *Registration Number* | *Provenance* | *Elevation* | *Description* |
|---|---|---|---|---|
| A | 7066 | R23:701 | 76.77 | Standard buff ware. Grit tempered. Scraping marks on base. Olive green paint. Early Middle Susiana |
| B | 7002 | G28:703 South | 76.98 | Standard buff ware. Sand tempered. Creamy buff slipped. Dark brown paint. Early Middle Susiana. For outside decoration, see pl. 20:H. See also figure 37:N |
| C | 6141 | P22:624 | 81.62 | Standard buff ware. Small grit tempered. Creamy buff slipped. Smoothed. Black matte paint. Early Middle Susiana |
| D | 8725 | S22:805 | 76.88 | Standard buff ware. Dense. Sand tempered. Creamy buff slipped. Black paint. Early Middle Susiana |
| E | 6128 | S23:605 | 79.05 | Buff ware. Sand tempered. Smoothed. Brownish black paint. Early Middle Susiana |
| F | 7165 | G27:705 | Surface | Standard buff ware. Sand tempered with some grits. Creamy buff slipped. Black paint. Early Middle Susiana |

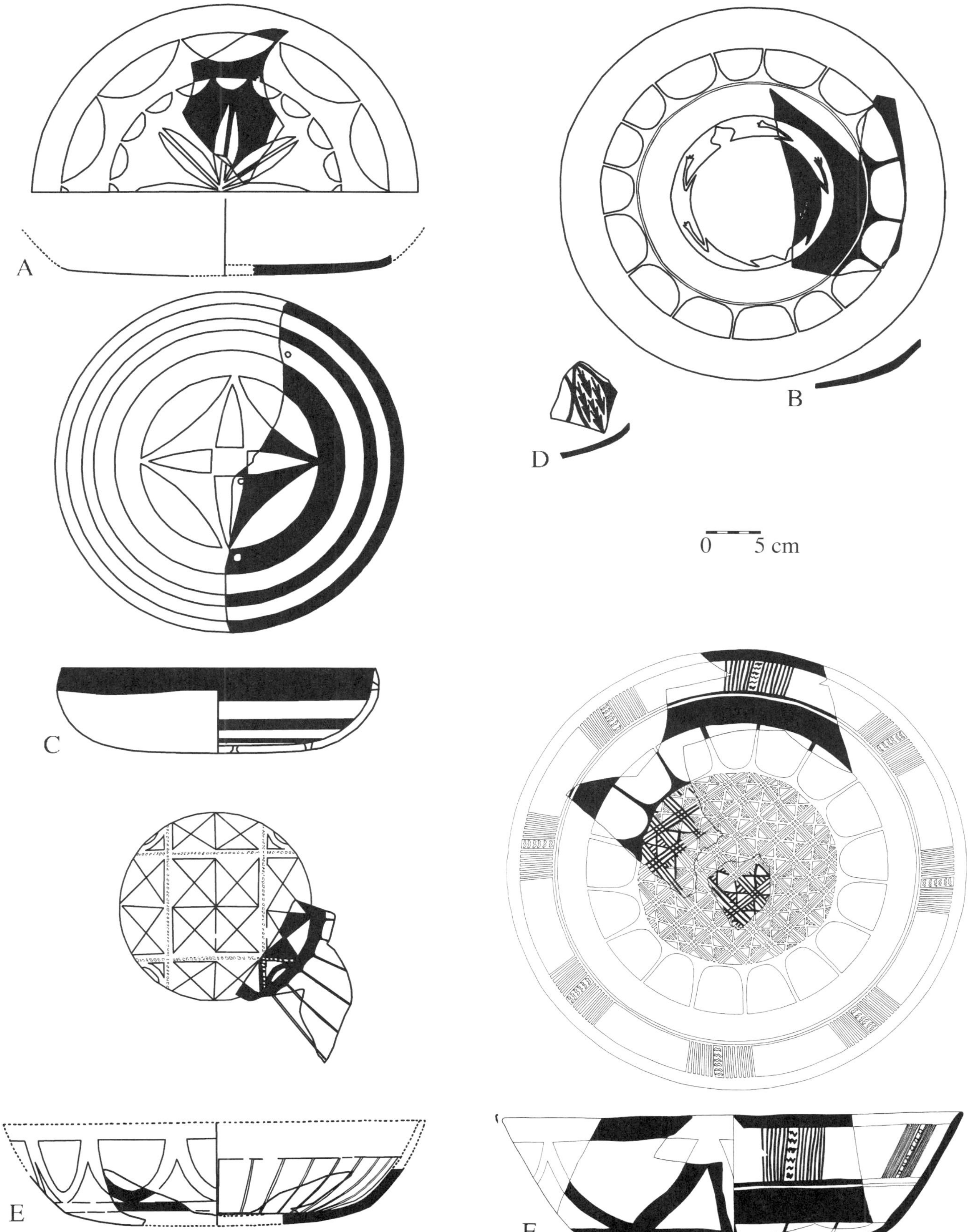


Figure 39. Middle Susiana Pottery Vessels

Figure 40. Middle Susiana Pottery Vessels

| | *Registration Number* | *Provenance* | *Elevation* | *Description* |
|---|---|---|---|---|
| A | 6032 | Tr. XXXV | B.S. | Fine buff ware. No visible inclusions. Creamy buff slipped. Interior greenish tinge. Painted in granulated black matte paint. Late Middle Susiana |
| B | IX-40 | R18:906 | 81.22 | Standard buff ware. Grit tempered. Yellowish buff surface, possibly slipped. Black paint. Late Middle Susiana |
| C | 8181 | S22:806 East | 76.65 | Standard buff ware. Small grit tempered. Greenish buff surface. Olive brown paint. Late Middle Susiana |
| D | 6148 | S20:621 | 77.85 | Fine buff ware. No visible inclusions. Creamy buff slipped. Black paint. Late Middle Susiana |
| E | 9383 | Tr. XXXIII | Surface | Fine buff ware. No visible inclusions. Buff slipped. Black paint. Late Middle Susiana |
| F | 3842 | J19:306 | 0.40 B.S. | Buff ware. Sand and grit tempered. Buff slipped. Black paint. Diameter: 28 cm |
| G | 8009 | S22:803 | 76.16 | Fine buff ware. Sand tempered. Creamy buff slipped. Black paint. Late Middle Susiana |
| H | 6451 | S20:609 | 77.89 | Fine buff ware. Sand tempered. Creamy buff slipped. Black paint. Late Middle Susiana |
| I | 7044 | G27:703 | 82.08 | Standard buff ware. Sand and grit tempered. Buff slipped. Reddish brown paint. Late Middle Susiana |
| J | 7005 | G28:705 | Surface | Standard buff ware. Cream slipped. Dark paint. Scrape marks on lower body. Late Middle Susiana |
| K | 9534 | S18:916 | 81.71 | Standard buff ware. Buff slipped. Black paint. Late Middle Susiana |
| L | 8023 | Gully Cut | Surface | Standard buff ware. Sand tempered with occasional grits. Creamy buff slip with a greenish tinge. Black paint. Late Middle Susiana |
| M | IX-52 | R18:901 | 80.52 | Standard buff ware. Grit tempered. Yellowish buff surface, possibly slipped. Black paint. Late Middle Susiana |
| N | 9420 | S18:907 | 80.59 | Standard buff ware. Sand tempered with some large dark grits. Dark olive brown granular paint. Late Middle Susiana |

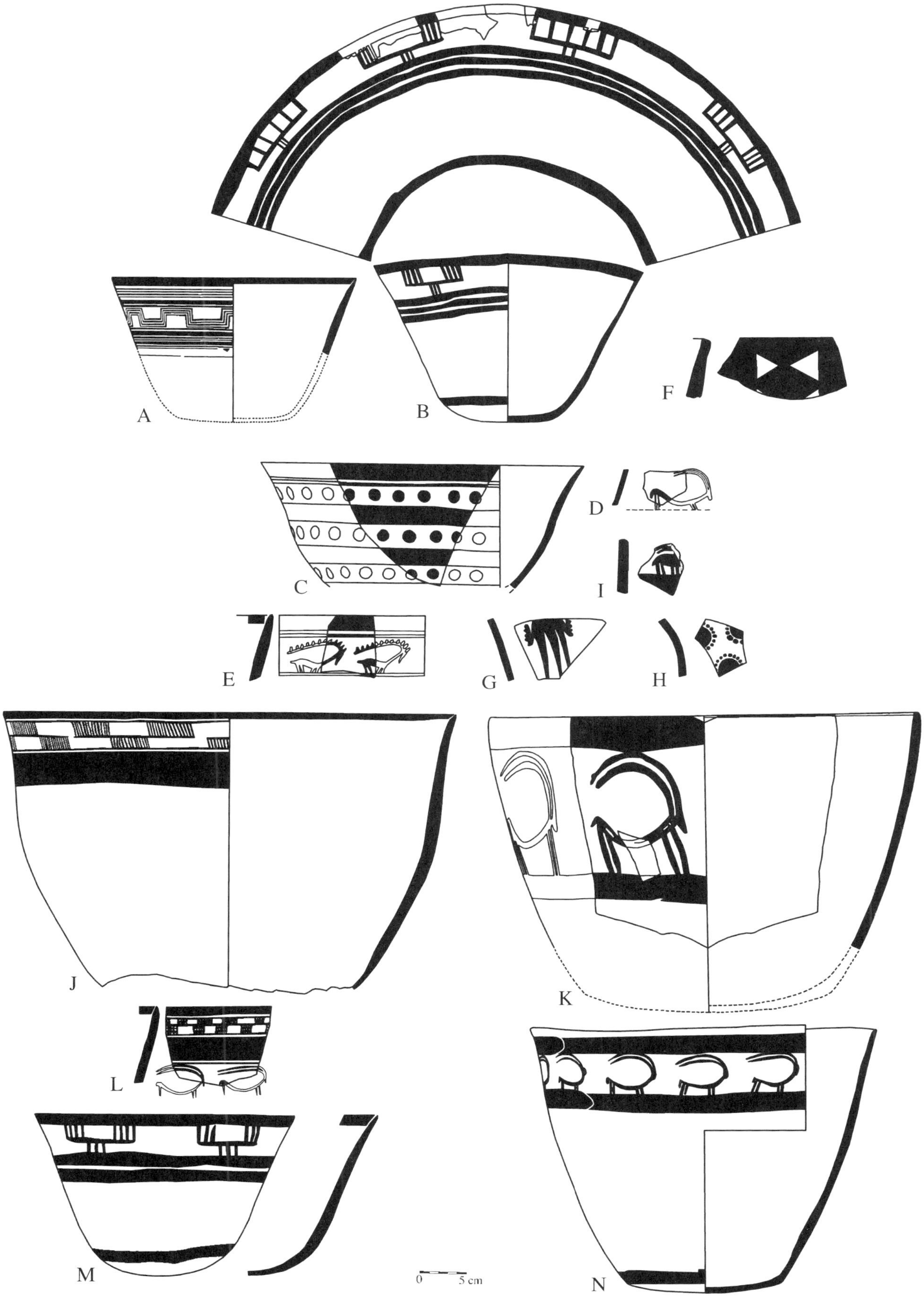


Figure 40. Middle Susiana Pottery Vessels

Figure 41. Middle Susiana Pottery Vessels

| | *Registration Number* | *Provenance* | *Elevation* | *Description* |
|---|---|---|---|---|
| A | 4462 | Sdg. G | 77.15 | Fine buff ware. No visible inclusions. Creamy buff slipped. Black paint. Late Middle Susiana |
| B | 6001 | Tr. XXV | 78.56 | Fine buff ware. No visible inclusions. Creamy buff slipped. Black paint. See plate 19:M for photograph. Late Middle Susiana |
| C | 8789 | S22:806 | 76.93 | Fine buff ware. No visible inclusions. Creamy buff slipped. Black paint. Late Middle Susiana |
| D | 7046 | G28:705 | 79.42 | Fine buff ware. No visible inclusions. Creamy buff slipped. Black paint. Late Middle Susiana |
| E | VI-41 | S20:620 | 77.86 | Fine buff ware. Dense. No visible inclusions. Creamy buff slipped. Somewhat shiny surface. Black granulated paint. See plate 19:K for photograph. Late Middle Susiana |
| F | 6147 | S20:621 | 77.85 | Standard buff ware. Sand tempered. Creamy buff slipped. Smoothed. Dark brown thick matte paint. Late Middle Susiana |
| G | 6003 | S20:605 | 78.66 | Standard buff ware. Sand tempered. Buff slipped. Black paint. Late Middle Susiana |
| H | 6002 | S20:601 | 79.24 | Standard buff ware. Sand tempered. Buff slipped. Black paint. Late Middle Susiana |
| I | 6857 | S20:621 | 78.85 | Standard buff ware. Sand tempered. Buff slipped. Black paint. Late Middle Susiana |
| J | 9009 | Q19:901 | N/A | Fine buff ware. Sand tempered. Creamy buff slipped with a greenish tinge. Black paint. Late Middle Susiana |
| K | 6151 | S20:621 | 78.40 | Fine buff ware. No visible inclusions. Creamy buff slipped. Black paint. Late Middle Susiana |

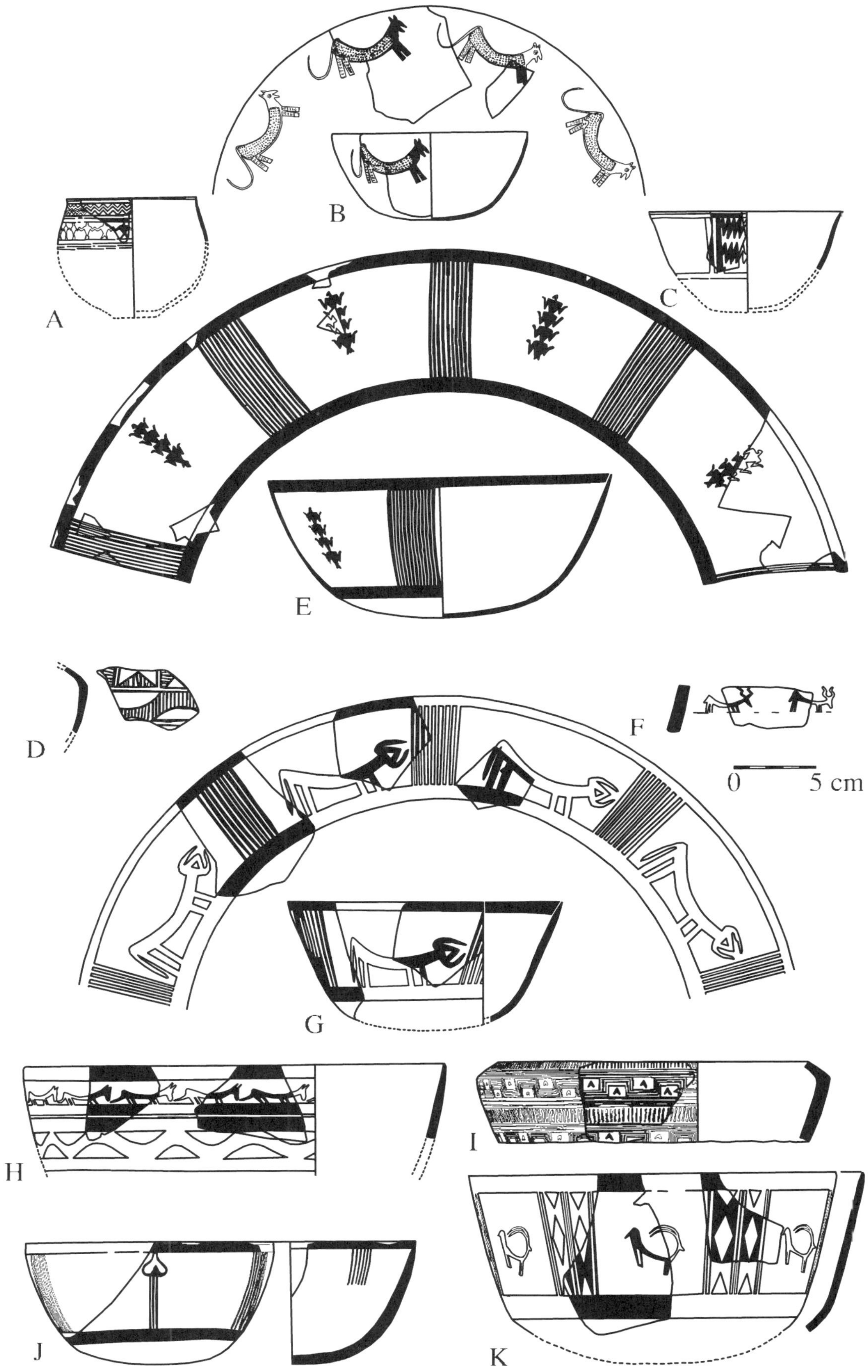


Figure 41. Middle Susiana Pottery Vessels

Figure 42. Middle Susiana Pottery Vessels

| | Registration Number | Provenance | Elevation | Description |
|---|---|---|---|---|
| A | 6050 | R20:602 | B.S. | Fine buff ware. No visible inclusions. Creamy buff slipped. Black matte paint. See plate 19:F for photograph. Late Middle Susiana |
| B | 9806 | S22:926 | 77.03 | Standard buff ware. Sand tempered with few grits. Buff slipped with a greenish tinge. Sunken olive black paint. Late Middle Susiana |
| C | 6040 | S20:601 | 78.33 | Fine buff ware. No visible inclusions. Creamy buff slipped with a greenish tinge. Olive black matte paint. See plate 19:E for photograph. Late Middle Susiana |
| D | 6527 | Tr. XXXIII | 76.83 | Standard buff ware. Sand tempered. Creamy buff slipped. Late Middle Susiana |
| E | 6484 | P22:602 | 81.44 | Standard buff ware. Sand tempered. Creamy buff slipped. Black paint. Early Middle Susiana |
| F | B 1074 | Ch. Bonut/ M10:101 | B.S. | Fine buff ware. No visible inclusions. Creamy buff slipped. |
| G | 7155 | Tr. XXI | Surface | Standard buff ware. Sand tempered. Buff slipped. Black paint. Early Middle Susiana |
| H | 6029 | Tr. XXXIII | 77.34 | Standard buff ware. Sand and grit tempered. Buff slipped. Black granulated paint. Early/Late Middle Susiana |
| I | 7133 | R23:701 | 77.59 | Buff ware. Grit tempered. Buff slipped with a greenish tinge. Early Middle Susiana |
| J | 4232 | Tr. XIII | 0.85 B.S. | Buff ware. Medium grit tempered. Buff slipped. Dark purple brown paint. Early Middle Susiana |
| K | 6856 | S20:601 | 0.40 B.S. | Standard buff ware. Sand tempered. Buff slipped. Dark brown paint. Early Middle Susiana |
| L | 6221 | P23:606 | 81.12 | Fine buff ware. No visible inclusions. Creamy buff slipped. Matte purple paint. Late Middle Susiana |
| M | 9206 | S18:918 | 81.10 | Fine buff ware. No visible inclusions. Creamy buff slipped. Black paint. Late Middle Susiana |
| N | 6027 | Tr. XXXIII | 76.80 | Standard buff ware. Sand tempered. Buff slipped. Black-brown matte paint. Late Middle Susiana |
| O | 5525 | P27:501 | 1.27 B.S. | Standard buff ware. Grit tempered. Buff slipped. Black paint. Late Middle Susiana |
| P | 4461 | Sdg. H | B.S. | Fine buff ware. No visible inclusions. Very light cream buff slipped. Black paint. Late Middle Susiana |
| Q | 6051 | R20:602 | B.S. | Fine buff ware. No visible inclusions. Creamy buff slipped. Black matte paint. See plate 19:J for photograph. Late Middle Susiana |
| R | 6024 | Tr. XXXIII | 76.40 | Fine buff ware. No visible inclusions. Creamy buff slipped. Olive brown granulated paint. See plate 19:D for photograph. Late Middle Susiana |
| S | 6028 | Tr. XXXIII | 77.68 | Fine buff ware. No visible inclusions. Creamy buff slipped. Brown paint. See plate 19:C for photograph. Late Middle Susiana |
| T | VI-42 | S20:620 | 77.40 | Fine buff ware. No visible inclusions. Creamy buff slipped. Black granulated paint, mostly flaked off. Late Middle Susiana |
| U | 6094 | S20:609 | 78.90 | Fine buff ware. No visible inclusions. Creamy buff slipped. Black paint. Late Middle Susiana |
| V | 6093 | S20:609 | 78.67 | Fine buff ware. No visible inclusions. Creamy buff slipped. Black granulated paint, mostly flaked off. Late Middle Susiana |

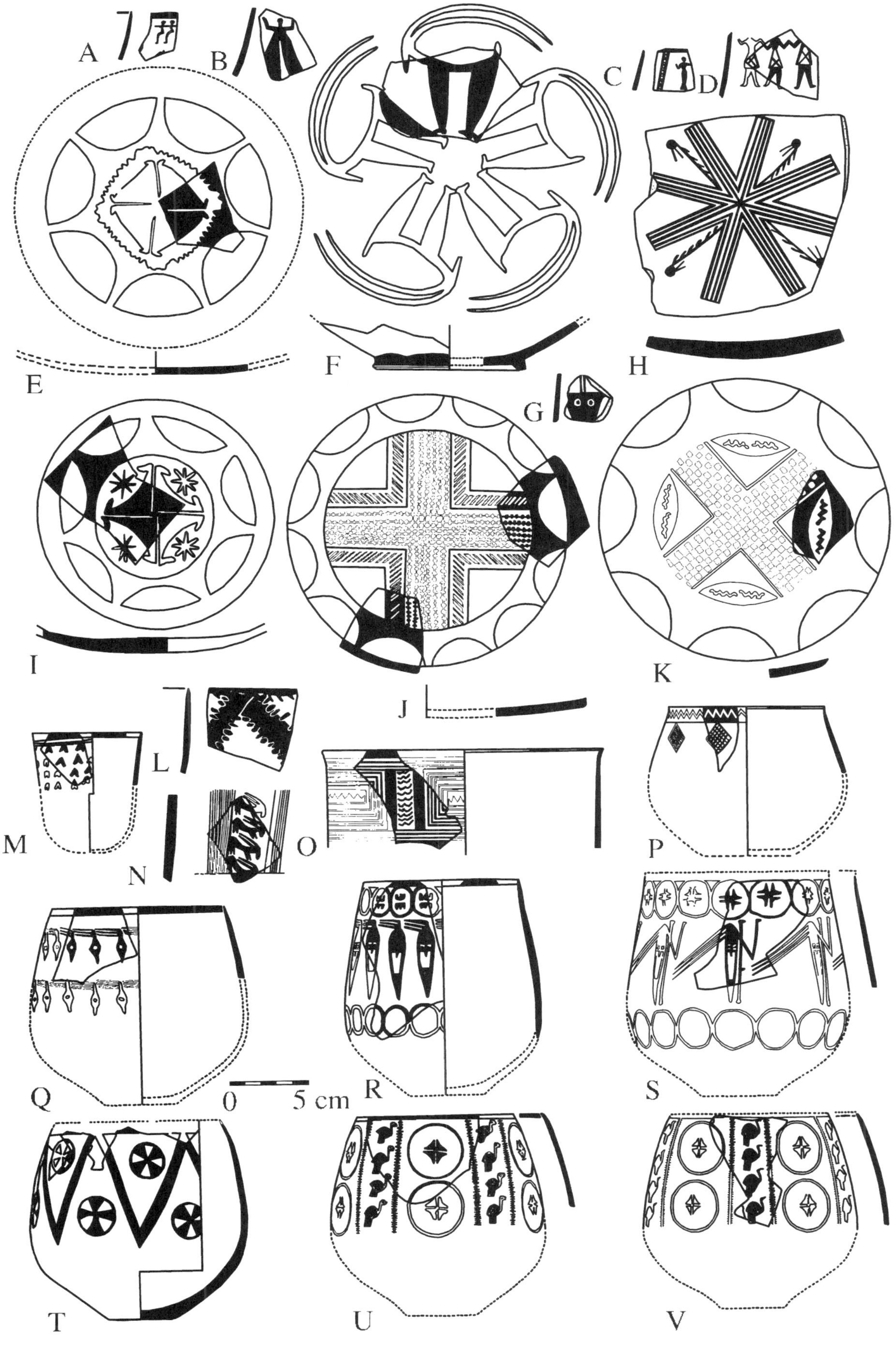


Figure 42. Middle Susiana Pottery Vessels

Figure 43. Middle Susiana Pottery Vessels

| | *Registration Number* | *Provenance* | *Elevation* | *Description* |
|---|---|---|---|---|
| A | 6490 | S20:605 | 79.20 | Standard buff ware. Some sand inclusions. Buff slipped. Black paint. Late Middle Susiana |
| B | 7400 | S22:702 | Surface | Standard buff ware. No visible inclusions. Creamy buff slipped. Late Middle Susiana |
| C | 7104 | G28:704 | 78.19 | Standard buff ware. Sand tempered. Buff slipped. Late Middle Susiana |
| D | 6223 | P23:607 | 82.65 | Standard buff ware. Sand tempered. Buff slipped. Black paint. Early/Late Middle Susiana transitional |
| E | 6298 | R23:601 | 77.39 | Standard buff ware. Creamy buff slipped. Dark brown paint. Early/Late Middle Susiana transitional |
| F | 7104 | G28:704 | 78.19 | Standard buff ware. Creamy buff slipped. Black paint. Late Middle Susiana |
| G | 8651 | Q24:801 | 79.00 | Buff ware. Sand and grit tempered. Creamy buff slip turned greenish buff due to over firing. Black paint. Early/Middle Susiana transitional |
| H | 7206 | G28:702 | 77.73 | Buff ware. Sand and grit tempered. Creamy buff slip turned greenish buff due to over firing. Black paint. Early Middle/Late Middle Susiana |
| I | 6364 | P23:604 | B.S. | Fine buff ware. Scattered small grit inclusions. Buff slipped. Late Middle Susiana |
| J | 7206 a–b | G28:702 | 77.73 | Standard buff ware. Sand tempered with some grits. Buff slipped. Late Middle Susiana |
| K | 6525 | R20:601 | 78.48 | Standard buff ware. Sand tempered with few grits. Buff slipped. Late Middle Susiana |
| L | 6067 | P22:606 | 80.42 | Buff ware. Grit tempered. Buff slipped. Black matte paint. Early/Middle Susiana transitional |

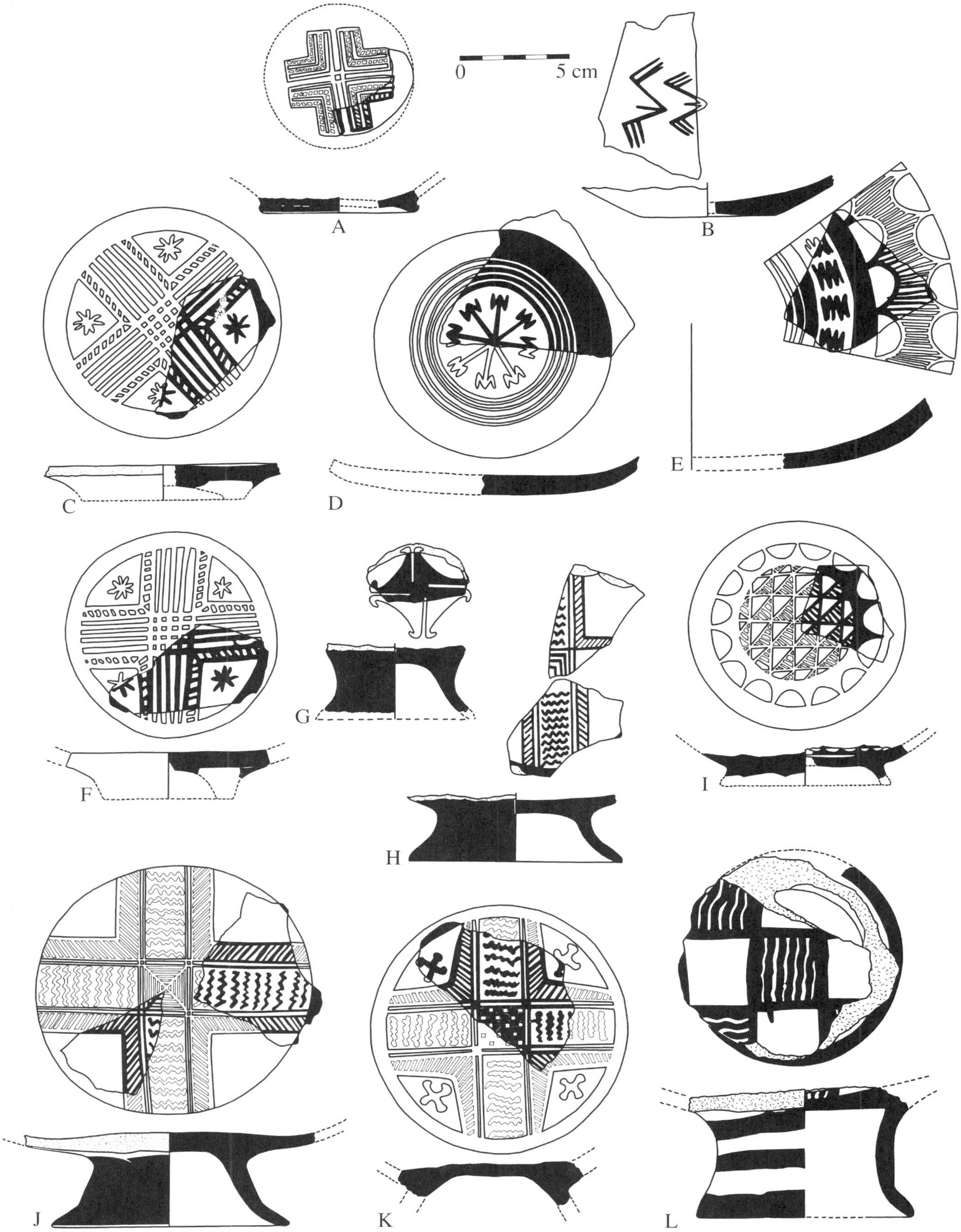


Figure 43. Middle Susiana Pottery Vessels

Figure 44. Middle Susiana Closed Pottery Vessels

| | *Registration Number* | *Provenance* | *Elevation* | *Description* |
|---|---|---|---|---|
| A | 9517 | S18:918 | 80.09 | Standard buff. Sand tempered. Buff slipped. Smoothed. Black paint |
| B | 9518 | S18:918 | 80.09 | Standard buff. Sand tempered. Buff slipped. Smoothed. Black paint |
| C | 9018 | S22:902 | 77.43 | Buff ware. Grit and straw tempered. Handmade |
| D | 9297 | R18:908 | 81.13 | Standard buff ware. Sand tempered. Dense. Creamy buff slipped. Black paint. Late Middle Susiana |
| E | 6224 | P23:607 | 83.05 | Standard buff ware. Sand tempered with scattered grits. Buff slipped. Brown paint. Early Middle Susiana |
| F | N/A | N/A | N/A | Fine buff ware. No visible inclusions. Creamy buff slipped. Dark paint. Late Middle Susiana |
| G | 6395 | P23:601 | B.S. | Standard buff ware. Scattered grits. Creamy buff slipped, with a pinkish hue. Dark paint. Late Middle Susiana |
| H | 7128 | R23:702 | 77.78 | Standard buff ware. Sand tempered with scattered grits. Buff slipped. Black paint. Early Middle Susiana |
| I | 9551 | S18:918 South | 81.58 | Standard buff ware. Sand tempered. Buff slipped. Black paint |
| J | 7266 | Tr. XXXIV | B.S. | Fine buff ware. No visible inclusions. Creamy buff slipped. Black paint. Late Middle Susiana |
| K | 8002 | S22:812 | 76.65 | Standard buff ware. Sand tempered with scattered grits. Buff slipped. Black paint. Late Middle Susiana |
| L | 6839 | S20:609 | 78.07 | Standard buff ware. No visible inclusions. Buff slipped. Dark paint |
| M | 7403 | R23:703 | 77.36 | Fine buff ware. No visible inclusions. Creamy buff slipped. Black paint. Late Middle Susiana |
| N | 8956 | Q25:802 | 77.00 | Fine buff ware. No visible inclusions. Probably slipped |
| O | N/A | N/A | N/A | Standard buff ware. Sand tempered. Buff slipped. Dark paint. Late Middle Susiana |
| P | VI-43 | P23:602 | 81.70 | Standard buff ware. Sand tempered. Buff slipped with a greenish tinge. Black granular paint. See plate 20:G for photograph. Early Middle Susiana |
| Q | 6848 | S20:601 | 78.33 | Standard buff ware. No visible inclusions. Greenish buff paste. Olive green paint. Late Middle Susiana |
| R | 9295 | R18:908 | 81.13 | Fine buff ware. No visible inclusions. Creamy buff slipped. Black paint. Late Middle Susiana and Late Susiana 1 |
| S | 6004 | S20:601 | 0.20 B.S. | Fine buff ware. No visible inclusions. Creamy buff slipped. Black paint. Late Middle Susiana |
| T | IX-105 | R18:908 | 81.13 | Fine buff ware. No visible inclusions. Creamy buff slipped. Dark paint. Late Middle Susiana |

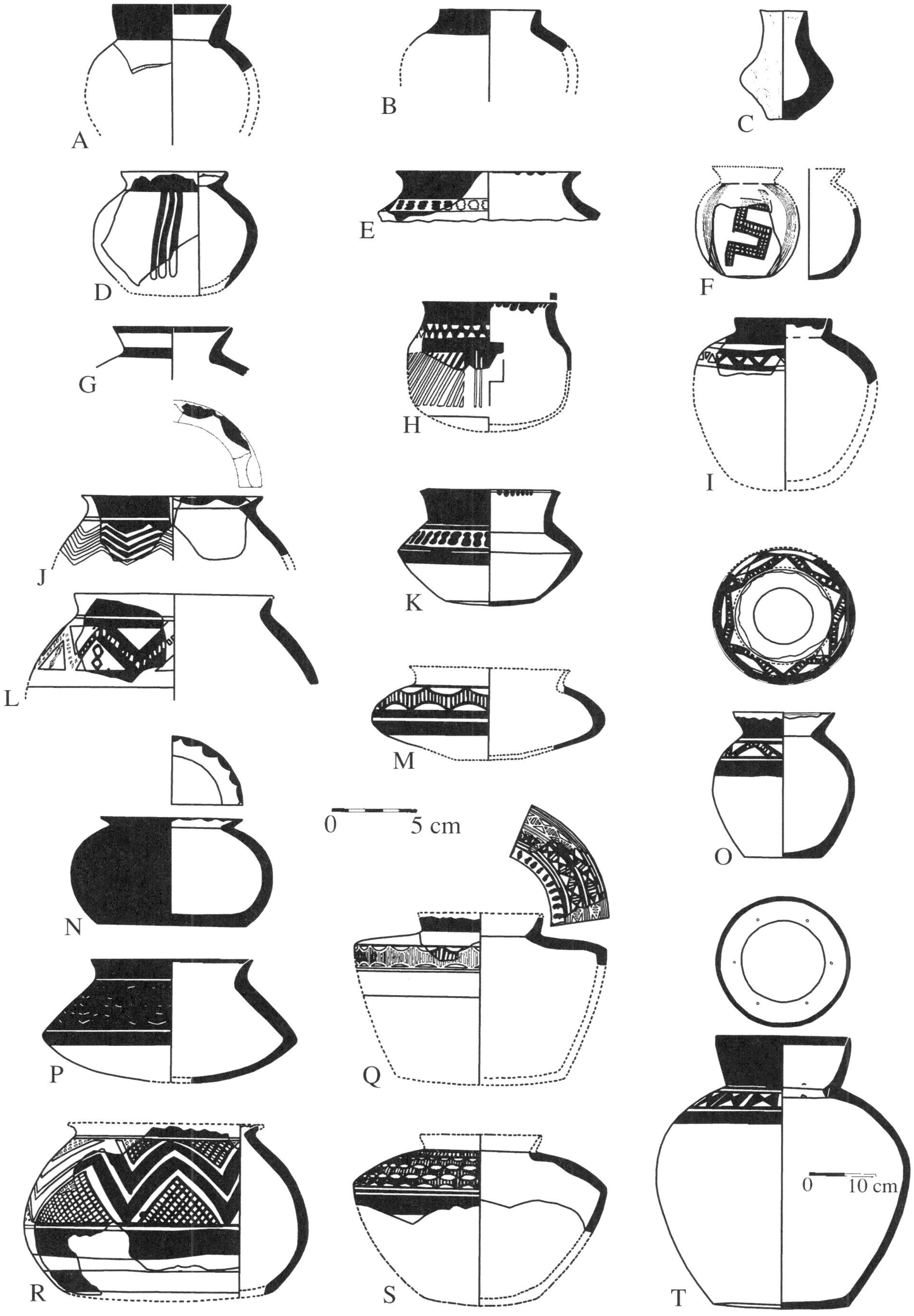


Figure 44. Middle Susiana Closed Pottery Vessels

Figure 45. Middle Susiana Closed Pottery Vessels

| | *Registration Number* | *Provenance* | *Elevation* | *Description* |
|---|---|---|---|---|
| A | N/A | S22:505 | N/A | Standard buff ware. Grit tempered. Gritty face. Buff slipped. Black paint. Late Middle Susiana |
| B | 7015 | G28:702 | 80.41 | Standard buff ware. Sand tempered with few grits. Buff slipped. Brown paint. Late Middle Susiana |
| C | 6499 | Tr. XXXIII | 77.02 | Buff ware. Grit tempered. Buff slipped. Brown paint. Late Middle Susiana |
| D | N/A | Surface | N/A | Fine buff ware. No visible inclusions. Creamy buff slipped. Dark brown paint. Late Middle Susiana |
| E | 7100 | Tr. XXXIV | Surface | Standard buff ware. Sand tempered with few grits. Buff slipped. Black paint. Late Middle Susiana |
| F | 6850 | P22:626 | 81.96 | Buff ware. Sand tempered with a mixture of red, black, and brownish grits, gritty face. Buff slipped. Black paint. Late Middle Susiana |
| G | BF-1001 | H10:102 | 0.35 B.S. | Standard buff ware. Sand tempered, sandy face. Buff slipped. Black paint. Middle Susiana |
| H | 6116 | S20:620 | 77.92 | Buff ware. Grit tempered, gritty face. Buff slipped. Burnished upper body. Late Middle Susiana |
| I | 9333 | S22:902 | 77.08 | Buff ware. Sand tempered. Red wash. Late Middle Susiana |
| J | 7401 | G28:701 | 79.87 | Gray ware. Small grit inclusions. Smoothed. Irregular striations inside. Late Middle Susiana |
| K | 6851 | S20:605 | 79.05 | Standard buff ware. Sand tempered, sandy face. Buff slipped with a greenish tinge. Greenish brown paint. Late Middle Susiana |
| L | 41173 | Sdg. H | 0.50 B.S. | Standard buff ware. Grit tempered. Buff slipped with a greenish tinge. Smoothed. Dark brown paint. Early Middle Susiana |

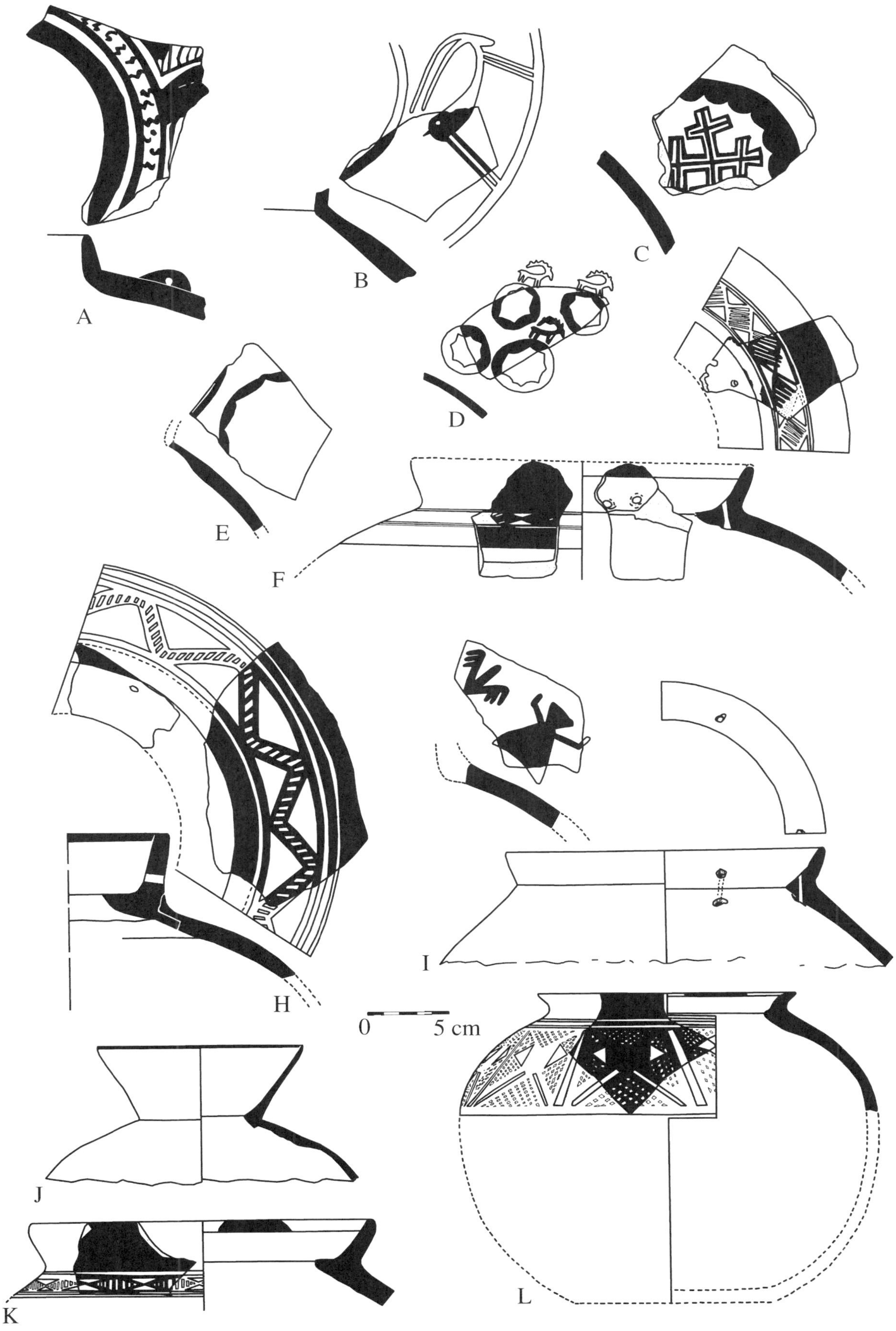


Figure 45. Middle Susiana Closed Pottery Vessels

Figure 46. Middle Susiana Closed Pottery Vessels

| | *Registration Number* | *Provenance* | *Elevation* | *Description* |
|---|---|---|---|---|
| A | 9172 | R18:908 | 80.34 | Standard buff ware. Sand tempered with some grits. Buff slipped. Black paint. Late Middle Susiana |
| B | 9171 | S18:916 | 80.10 | Standard buff ware. Sand tempered with some grits. Creamy buff slipped. Black paint. Late Middle Susiana |
| C | 9677 | R18:910 | 80.34 | Standard buff ware. Sand tempered with some grits. Buff slipped. Dark brown granulated paint. See plate 21:D for photograph. Early Middle Susiana |
| D | 7023 | G28:705 | 77.09 | Standard buff ware. Sand tempered. Orange buff slipped. Brown paint. Late Middle Susiana |
| E | IX-113 | S18:905 West | 81.07 | Standard buff ware. Sand tempered, sandy face lower body. Buff slipped. Brown paint. Late Middle Susiana |
| F | IX-115 | S18:905 West | 81.07 | Standard buff ware. Sand tempered, sandy face lower body. Buff slipped. Brown paint. Late Middle Susiana |
| G | 7402 | G28:701 | 81.27 | Standard buff ware. Sand tempered, sandy face lower body. Buff slipped. Brown paint. Late Middle Susiana |
| H | 7164 | G28:702 | 79.60 | Red ware. Sand tempered with some grits and straw. White slipped or wash all over. Black paint, abraded |
| I | 9509 | R18:914 | 81.88 | Buff ware. Grit tempered. Buff slipped. Black paint. Late Middle Susiana |

Figure 46. Middle Susiana Closed Pottery Vessels

Figure 47. Middle Susiana Closed Pottery Vessels

| | *Registration Number* | *Provenance* | *Elevation* | *Description* |
|---|---|---|---|---|
| A | IX-126 | S18:905 West | 81.86 | Standard buff ware. Sand tempered. Buff slipped. Sandy face lower body. Black paint. Late Middle Susiana |
| B | IX-114 | S18:905 West | 81.07 | Standard buff ware. Sand tempered. Buff slipped. Sandy face lower body. Black paint. Late Middle Susiana |
| C | 9909 | S18:905 West | 81.07 | Standard buff ware. Sand tempered. Buff slipped. Sandy face lower body. Black paint. Late Middle Susiana |
| D | IX-131 | S18:904 West | 81.12 | Standard buff ware. Sand tempered. Buff slipped. Sandy face lower body. Black paint. Late Middle Susiana |

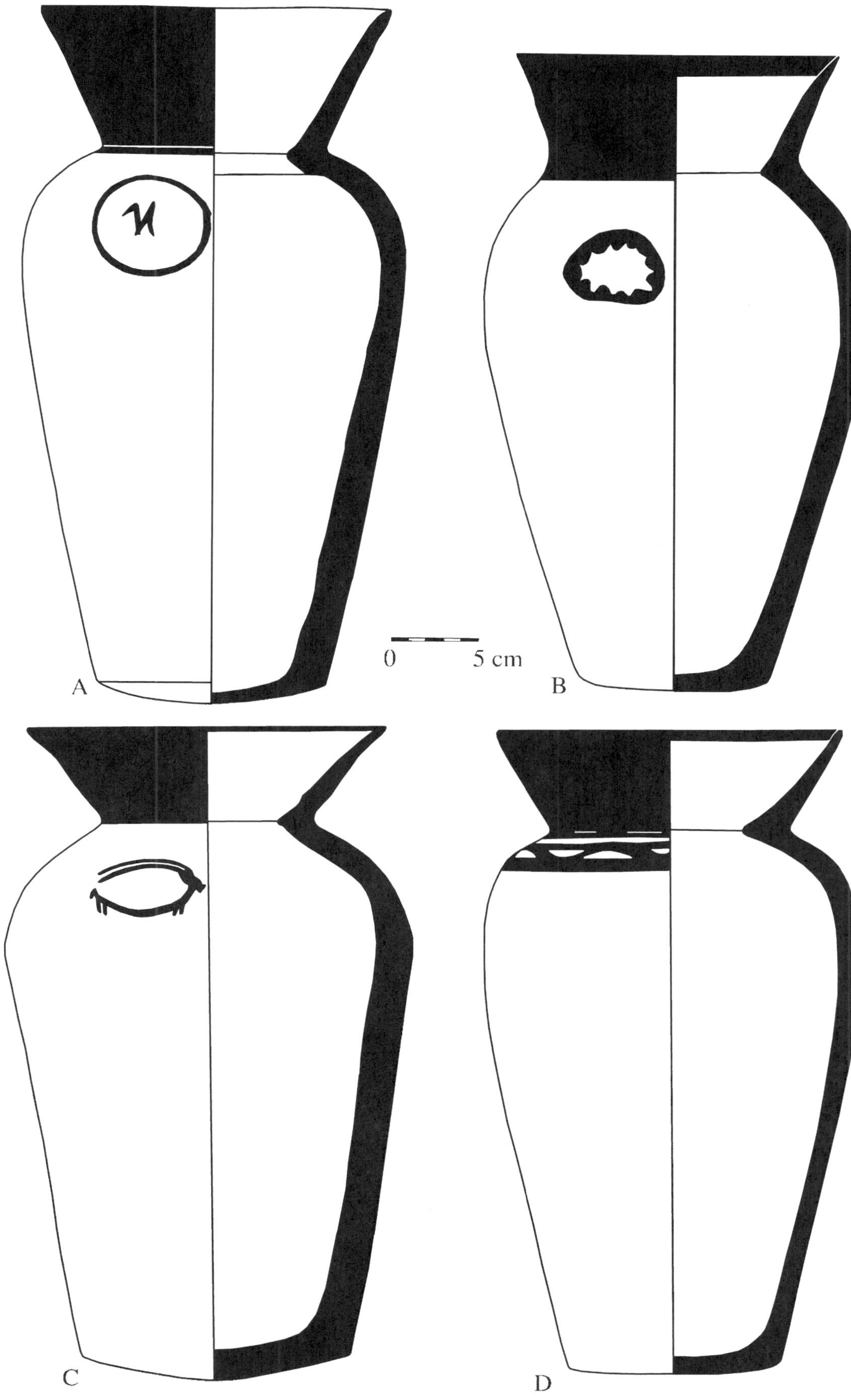


Figure 47. Middle Susiana Closed Pottery Vessels

Figure 48. Middle Susiana Pottery Vessels

| | *Registration Number* | *Provenance* | *Elevation* | *Description* |
|---|---|---|---|---|
| A | 2543 | Tr. XIII | 0.60 B.S. | Standard buff ware. Sand tempered. Dense. Yellowish buff slipped, smoothed. Brown paint |
| B | 6498 | S20:606 | N/A | Standard buff ware. Sand tempered. Buff slipped, smoothed. Scrape marks on both sides. Black paint. Late Middle Susiana |
| C | 6074 | P22:615 | 81.14 | Standard buff ware. Sand and some grits tempered. Red wash on interior. Brownish to plum paint. Early/Middle Susiana transitional |
| D | 7307 | G28:705 | N/A | Standard buff ware. Some grit inclusions. Smoothed. Dark reddish brown paint. Late Middle Susiana |
| E | 9173 | R18:913 | 81.10 | Buff ware. Sand and grit tempered. Buff slipped with a greenish tinge. Black paint. Late Middle Susiana |
| F | VII-16 | G28:705 | 79.42 | Standard buff ware. Sand tempered. Creamy buff slipped. Late Middle Susiana |

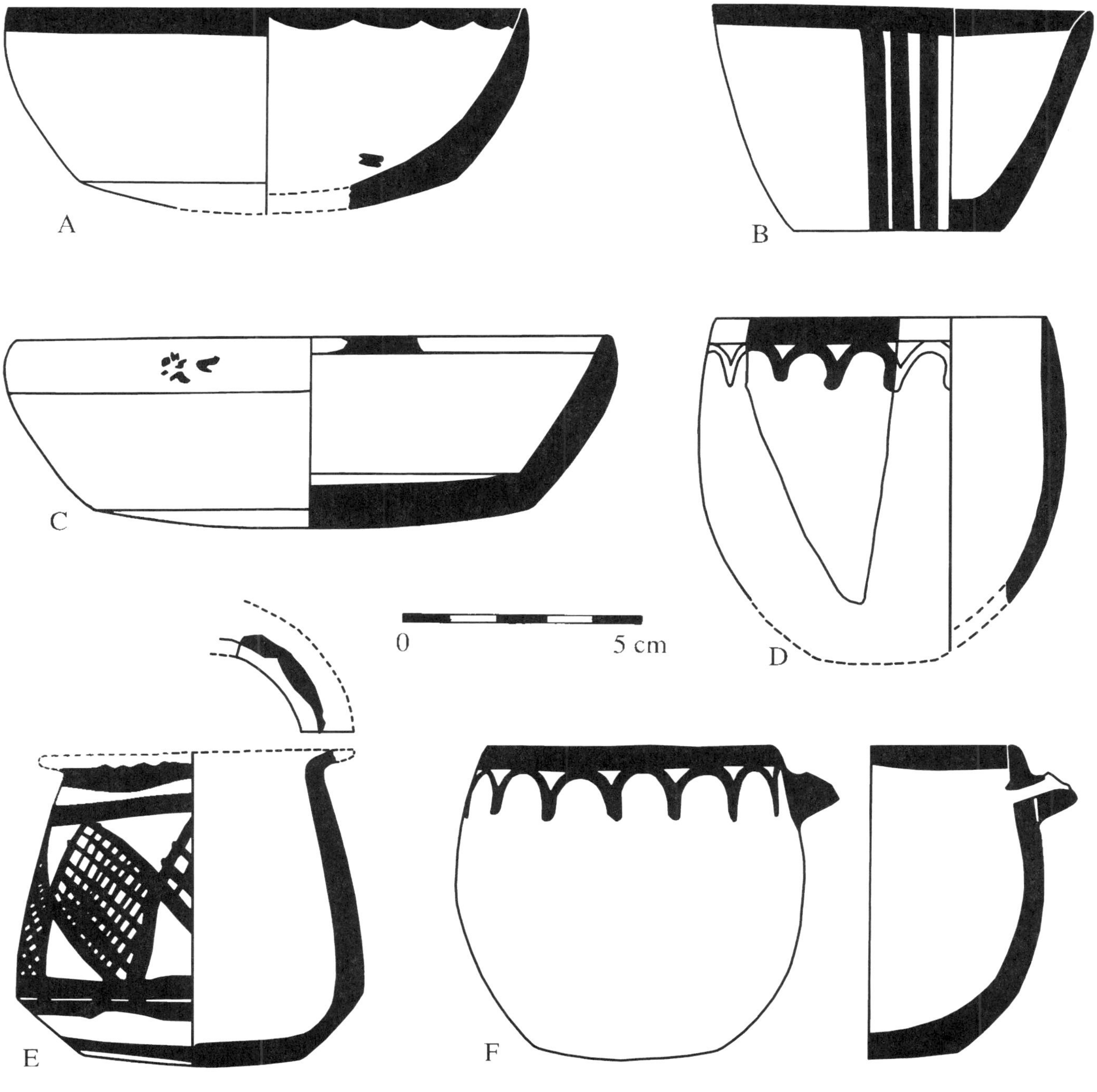


Figure 48. Middle Susiana Pottery Vessels

Figure 49. Middle Susiana Pottery Vessels

| | *Registration Number* | *Provenance* | *Elevation* | *Description* |
|---|---|---|---|---|
| A | 9184 | S22:902 | 76.83 | Standard buff ware. Sand tempered. Buff slipped. Black paint. Early Middle Susiana |
| B | 8086 | S22:806 | 77.70 | Buff ware. Grit tempered. Buff slipped. Black paint. Late Middle Susiana |
| C | 6744 | S20:601 | 78.06 | Standard buff ware. Dense. No visible inclusions. Black paint. Early Middle Susiana(?) |
| D | 9187 | R18:908 | 80.91 | Buff ware. Grit tempered. Black paint. Middle Susiana |
| E | 9358 | S22:902 Northeast | 77.65 | Buff ware. Some chaff and grit inclusions. Buff slipped |
| F | 9167 | S18:918 | 81.12 | Standard buff ware. Sand tempered with occasional grits. Buff slipped. Black paint. Late Middle Susiana |

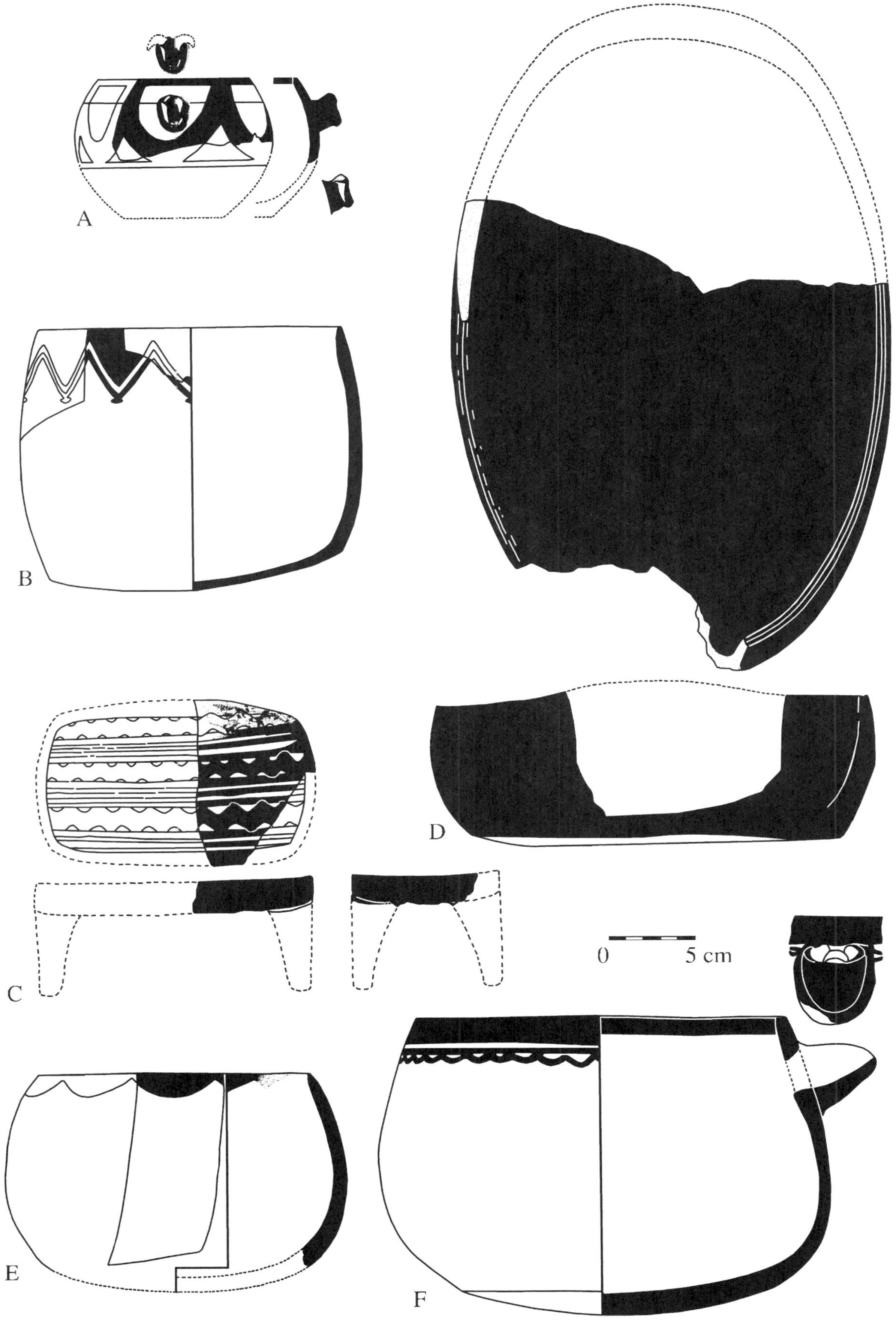


Figure 49. Middle Susiana Pottery Vessels

Figure 50. Middle Susiana Pottery Vessels

| | *Registration Number* | *Provenance* | *Elevation* | *Description* |
|---|---|---|---|---|
| A | 9580 | S18:919 | 80.05 | Lid. Standard buff ware. Sand tempered. Probably buff slipped. Black paint. Early to Middle Susiana transitional |
| B | 6336 | P22:611 | 82.19 | Lid. Standard buff ware. Sand tempered. Probably buff slipped. Slightly pinkish on surface. Black paint. Early to Middle Susiana transitional |
| C | 6853 | S20:609 West | 78.07 | Buff ware. Medium to small dark, brown, and red grits included. Some scattered white particles (calcite) also included. Smoothed. "Comb" scraping marks on neck and lower body. Dark paint. Early to Middle Susiana transitional |
| D | 6202 | P23:606 | 81.32 | Ladle fragment. Buff ware. Some grit inclusions. Red paint. Early Middle Susiana |
| E | 6012 | P23:604 | B.S. | "Sauce boat" vessel fragment. Buff ware. Sand tempered. Buff slipped, smoothed. Gritty black paint. Early Middle Susiana |
| F | 7061 | G29:703 | B.S. | Standard buff ware. Sand tempered. Brown paint. Early Middle Susiana |
| G | 6177 | R20:515 | 79.15 | Lid fragment. Early Middle Susiana |

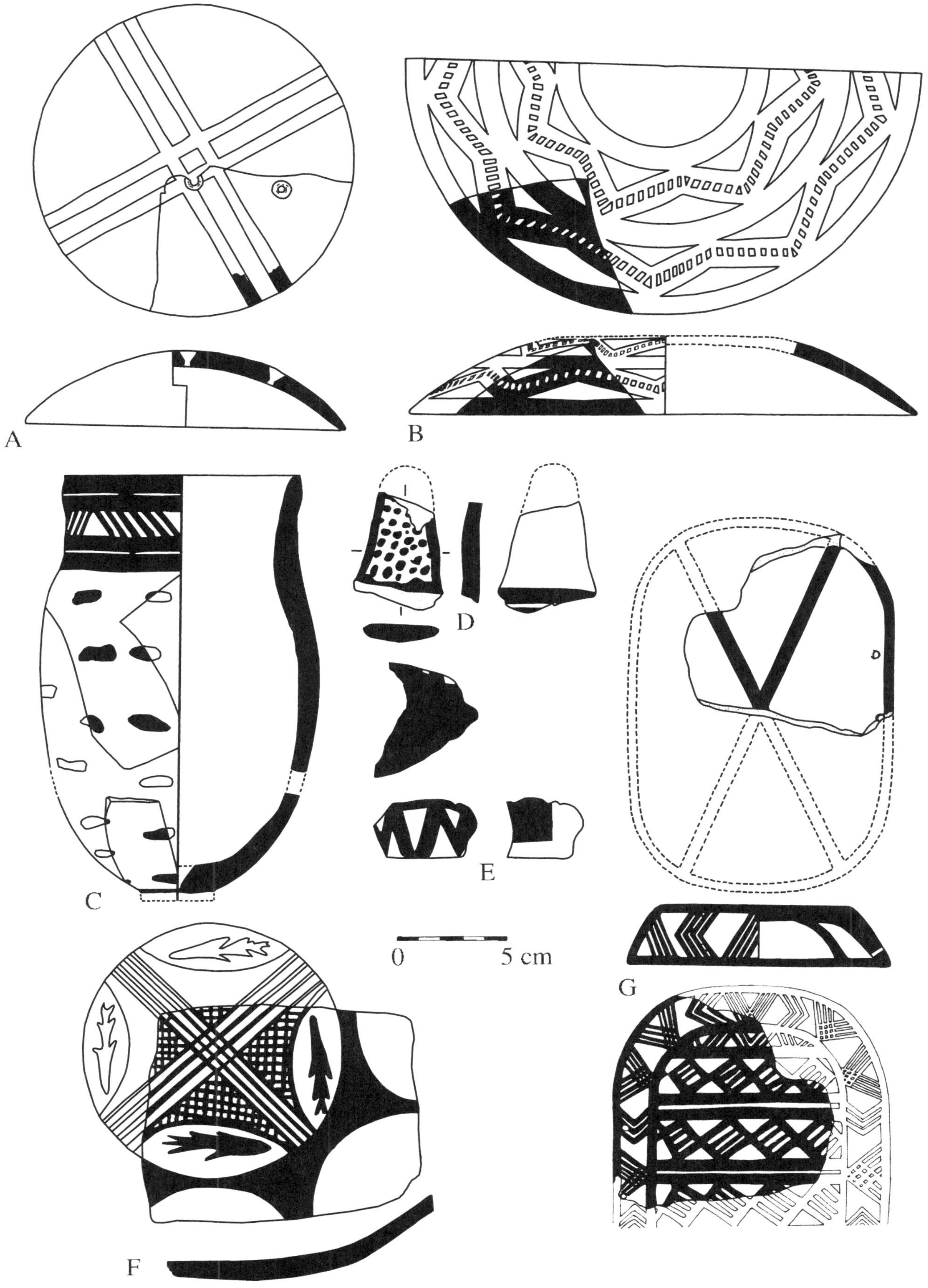


Figure 50. Middle Susiana Pottery Vessels

Figure 51. Middle Susiana Pottery "Stands"

| | *Registration Number* | *Provenance* | *Elevation* | *Description* |
|---|---|---|---|---|
| A | 2523 | Tr. XVI | Surface | Buff ware. Grit tempered. Dense, gritty face. Buff slipped with a greenish tinge. Brown paint. Late Middle Susiana |
| B | 4117 | Tr. XXVI | N/A | Buff ware. Grit tempered. Buff slipped. Black paint. Late Middle Susiana |
| C | 3822 | Q19:301 | 0.20 B.S. | Buff ware. Grit tempered. Dense, gritty face. Buff slipped with a greenish tinge. Brown paint. Late Middle Susiana |
| D | 8116 | Q24:801 | 79.00 | Buff ware. Grit tempered with some chaff. Buff slipped. Black paint. Late Middle Susiana |
| E | 4116 | Sdg. H | 0.90 B.S. | Buff ware. Grit tempered. Buff slipped. Reddish brown paint. Late Middle Susiana |
| F | 4115 | Sdg. G | 0.55 B.S. | Buff ware. Grit tempered. Buff slipped. Red paint. Late Middle Susiana |
| G | 41078 | West Area | 1.30 B.S. | Buff ware. Grit tempered. Dense, gritty face. Buff slipped. Brown paint. Striations on the interior. Late Middle Susiana |
| H | 41043 | Tr. XIII | N/A | Buff ware. Grit tempered. Dense, gritty face. Buff slipped with a greenish tinge. Brown paint. Late Middle Susiana |

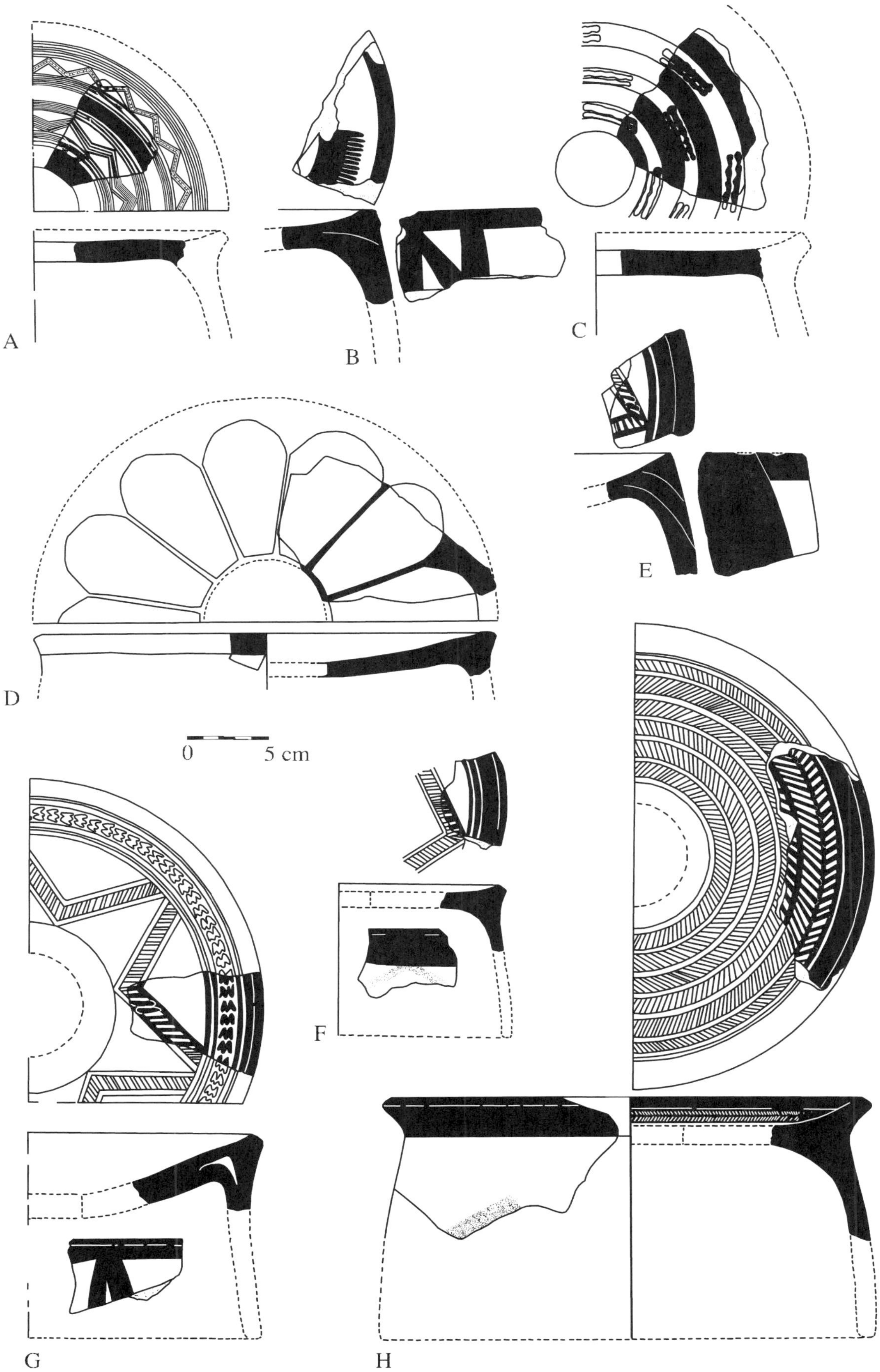


Figure 51. Middle Susiana Pottery "Stands"

Figure 52. Middle Susiana Tortoise Pottery Vessels

| | *Registration Number* | *Provenance* | *Elevation* | *Description* |
|---|---|---|---|---|
| A | 7070 | R27:702 | 77.63 | Standard buff. Sand tempered. Buff slipped. Black paint. Early Middle Susiana |
| B | 6409a | S20:609 West | 78.07 | Standard buff. Sand tempered. Buff slipped. Black paint |
| C | 7084 | R23:702 | 77.63 | Standard buff. Sand tempered with some chaff. Creamy buff slipped. Black paint |
| D | 7055 | G28:704 South | 75.54 | Standard buff. Small grit tempered with chaff. Buff slipped. Black paint |
| E | 6480 | P22:602 | 81.44 | Standard buff. Sand and grit tempered. Creamy buff slipped. Black paint. Early Middle Susiana |
| F | 8251 | Q25:802 West | 77.10 | Fine buff ware. Sand tempered. Creamy buff slipped. Plastic decoration of snake on neck. Dark paint |
| G | 6187 | Q23:601 | 81.40 | Buff ware. No visible inclusions. Yellowish buff slipped. Early Middle Susiana |
| H | 7130 | R23:702 | 77.78 | Buff ware. Grit tempered with some straw. Buff slipped. Black paint |
| I | 6409a | S20:609 West | 78.07 | Buff ware. Grit tempered. Yellowish buff slipped, smoothed. Black paint |
| J | 6301 | P23:603 | N/A | Buff ware. Sand tempered. Creamy buff slipped. Dark paint |

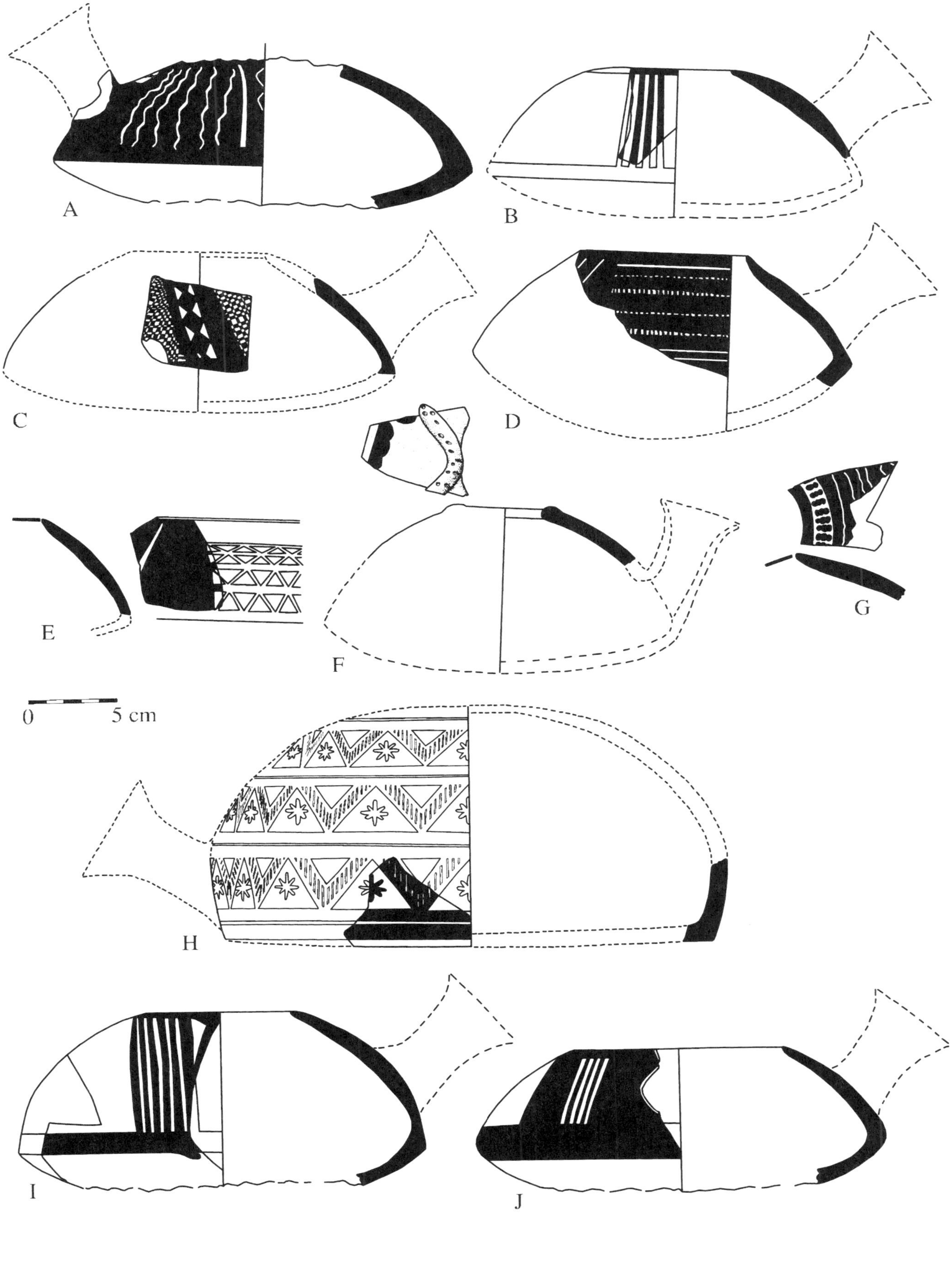


Figure 52. Middle Susiana Tortoise Pottery Vessels

Figure 53. Middle Susiana Plain Pottery Vessels

| | *Registration Number* | *Provenance* | *Elevation* | *Description* |
|---|---|---|---|---|
| A | 6858 | S20:620 | 78.20 | Standard buff ware. Sand tempered. Creamy buff slipped. Striations on lower body. Black band decoration on the lip. Late Middle Susiana |
| B | IX-56 | S18:907 | 81.45 | Red ware. Grayish core. Some sand. Red wash all over. Uneven lip. Late Middle Susiana |
| C | 9543 | R19:905 | 79.44 | Red ware. Red wash all over. Sand tempered. Smoothed. Late Middle Susiana |
| D | 81012 | S22:806 North | 76.93 | Standard buff. Sand tempered. Buff slipped. Sandy face lower part. Smoothed. Late Middle Susiana |
| E | VII-24 | G28:705 | N/A | Eggshell buff ware. No visible inclusions. Creamy buff slipped. Smoothed. Late Middle Susiana |
| F | IX-115 | R18:901 | 81.51 | Standard buff ware. Sand tempered. Buff slipped. Smoothed. Late Middle Susiana |
| G | IX-32 | R18:901 | 81.52 | Standard buff ware. Sand tempered. Buff slipped. Sandy face lower part. Late Middle Susiana |
| H | 9514 | P17:902 | 81.61 | Fine buff ware. No visible inclusions. Creamy buff slipped. Smoothed. Late Middle Susiana |
| I | 9205 | R18:902 | 81.22 | Fine buff ware. Some sand inclusions. Creamy buff slipped. Smoothed. Late Middle Susiana |
| J | 6046 | P23:606 | 82.05 | Standard buff ware. Sand tempered. Buff slipped. Late Middle Susiana |
| K | IX-48 | R18:901 | 80.46 | Standard buff ware. Sand tempered. Buff slipped. Inside smeared with bitumen. Early Middle Susiana |
| L | 8833 | Q25:802 | 75.70 | Red ware. Sand tempered with some calcite particles. Early Middle Susiana |
| M | IX-34 | R18:901 | 80.52 | Standard buff ware. Sand tempered. Buff slipped. Inside smeared with bitumen. Early Middle Susiana |
| N | 9150 | R18:908 South | 81.76 | Red ware. Sand inclusions. Red wash. Smoothed. Late Middle Susiana |
| O | 9123 | R18:901 | 81.33 | Red ware. Sand inclusions. Smoothed. Late Middle Susiana |
| P | 6183 | P22:606 North | 81.73 | Buff ware. Sand and grit tempered. Buff slipped. Early/ Middle Susiana transitional |
| Q | 7049 | G28:705 | 76.08 | Eggshell ware. No visible inclusions. Creamy buff slipped. Late Middle Susiana |
| R | 6134 | Tr. XXXV | 76.47 | Eggshell buff ware. No visible inclusions. Creamy buff slipped. Late Middle Susiana |
| S | 6114 | S20:620 | 78.20 | Buff ware. Grit tempered. Buff slipped. Smoothed. Late Middle Susiana |
| T | 6133 | Tr. XXXV | 76.13 | Fine buff ware. Some small grits included. Creamy buff slipped. Smoothed. Late Middle Susiana |
| U | IX-30 | S18:904 | 81.12 | Fine buff ware. No visible inclusions. Creamy buff slipped. Smoothed. Late Middle Susiana |
| V | 6859 | P23:606 | 82.05 | Standard buff ware. Sand tempered. Buff slipped. Smoothed. Late Middle Susiana |

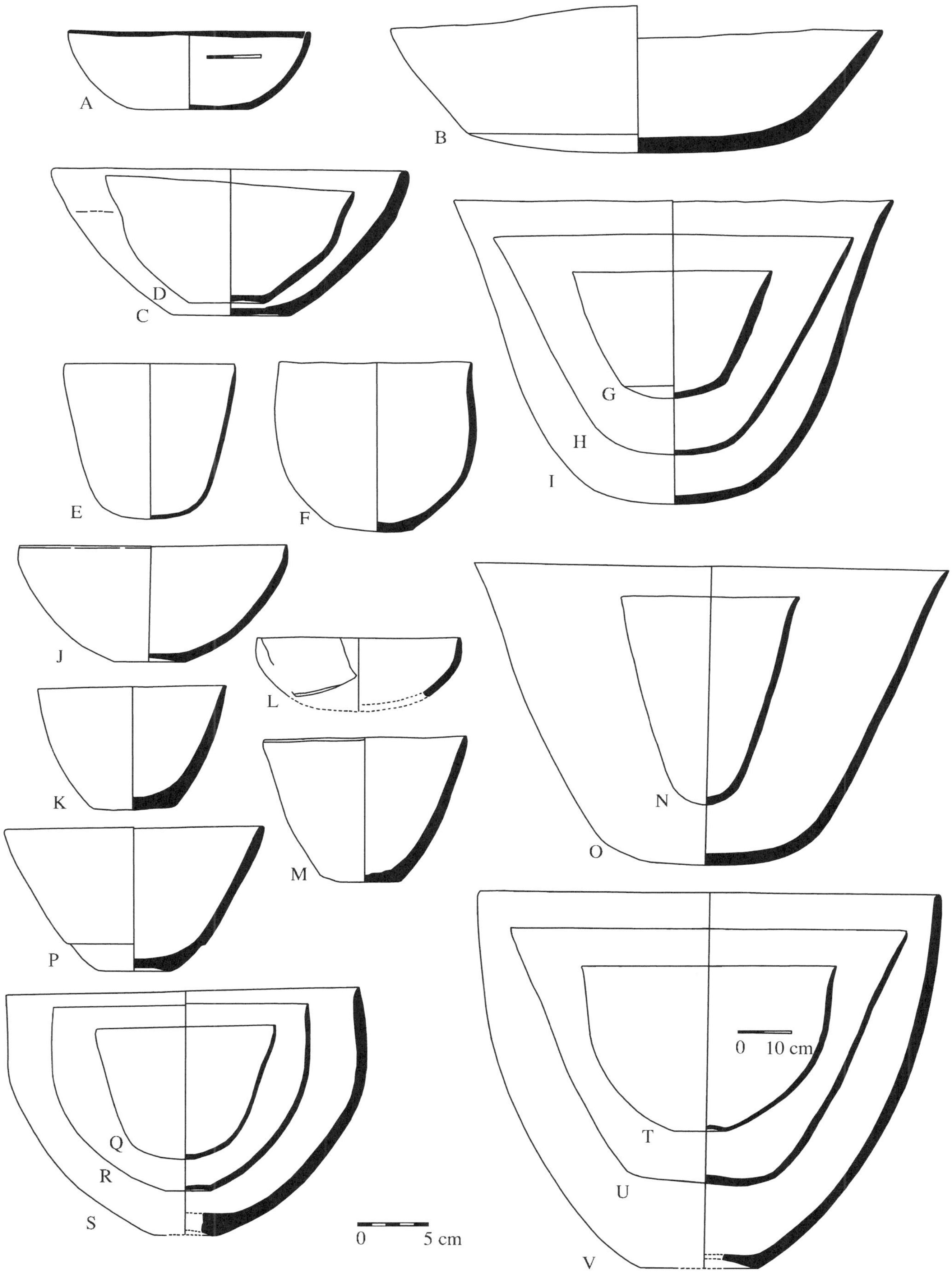


Figure 53. Middle Susiana Plain Pottery Vessels

Figure 54. Middle Susiana Plain Pottery Vessels

| | *Registration Number* | *Provenance* | *Elevation* | *Description* |
|---|---|---|---|---|
| A | IX-127 | S18:902 | 80.40 | Standard buff ware. Small dark grits tempered. Buff slipped, lower body gritty face. Smoothed. Early Middle Susiana |
| B | 6015 | S20:605 | 79.05 | Fine buff ware. Creamy buff slipped with a greenish tinge. Late Middle Susiana |
| C | 9178 | S18:915 | 81.69 | Red ware. Sand tempered. Dense. Smoothed. Late Middle Susiana |
| D | 8957 | Q25:802 | 77.00 | Fine buff ware. Light green buff surface. Buff slipped. Some scrape marks on lower body. Late Middle Susiana |
| E | 9176 | R18:901 | 80.52 | Fine buff ware. Sand tempered with few grits. Creamy buff slipped. Smoothed. Late Middle Susiana |
| F | 7184 | G28:705 | 74.86 | Fine buff ware. Sand tempered. Creamy buff slipped. Smoothed |
| G | IX-118 | R18:901 | 81.51 | Fine buff ware. Sand tempered. Smoothed. Light buff slipped. Late Middle Susiana |
| H | 6142 | Tr. XXV | 76.13 | Standard buff ware. Sand tempered. Creamy buff slipped. Smoothed. Late Middle Susiana |
| I | IX-128 | S18:906 | 81.50 | Standard buff ware. Sand tempered with few grits. Buff slipped |
| J | 9513 | R18:905 | 81.55 | Fine buff ware. Some sand included in paste. Creamy buff slipped. Smoothed. Late Middle Susiana |
| K | IX-31 | S18:902 | 80.97 | Fine buff ware. Some sand. Buff slipped. Smoothed. Late Middle Susiana |
| L | N/A | G28:705 | 79.60 | Fine red ware. Sand tempered. Orange buff paste. Red wash. Dark red paint on the neck. Late Middle Susiana |
| M | 9166 | R18:921 | 80.27 | Fine buff ware. Some sand included. Creamy buff slipped. Smoothed. Late Middle Susiana |
| N | 6224 | S20:605 | 79.05 | Fine red ware. Dense. Interior dark brown wash, white slip on the exterior. Late Middle Susiana |
| O | IX-20 | N/A | 1.0 B.S. | Buff ware. Sand tempered with some grits. Buff slipped. Late Middle Susiana |
| P | 7054 | G28:705 | 81.06 | Red ware. Gray core. White slipped. Smoothed. Late Middle Susiana |

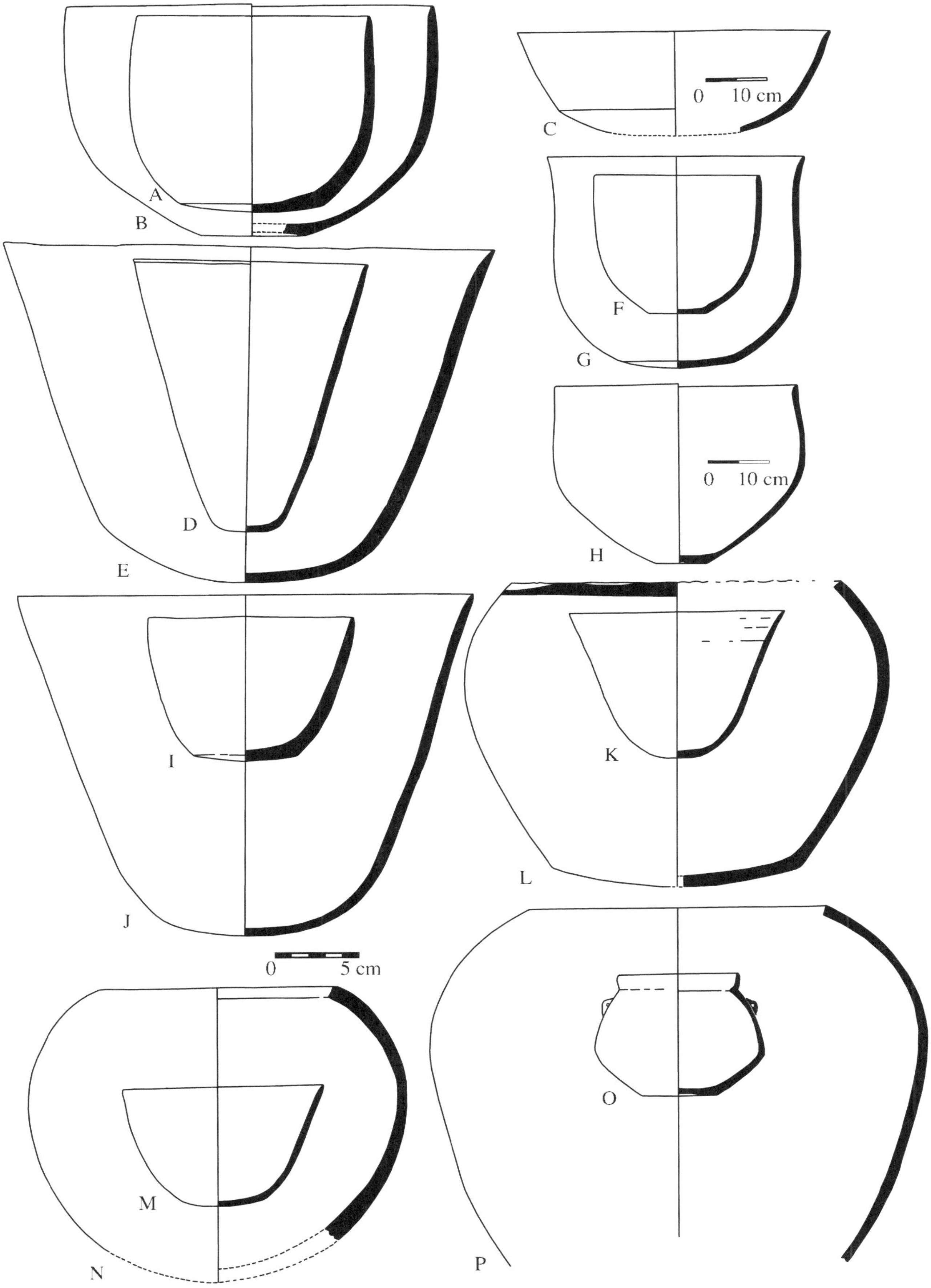


Figure 54. Middle Susiana Plain Pottery Vessels

Figure 55. Early Susiana Open Pottery Vessels

| | *Registration Number* | *Provenance* | *Elevation* | *Description* |
|---|---|---|---|---|
| A | 8062 | S22:808 | 75.67 | Buff ware. Grit tempered. Buff slipped. Black paint. Reserved wavy line below carination |
| B | 8128 | S22:826 | 75.49 | Buff ware. Grit tempered with some chaff. Buff slipped. Black paint |
| C | 8448 | S22:823 West | 74.24 | Buff ware. Grit and sand tempered. Creamy buff slipped. Black paint |
| D | 8427 | Gully Cut | Surface | Buff ware. Grit tempered with some chaff. Buff slipped. Black paint. Reserved wavy lines |
| E | 8184 | S22:808 | 75.55 | Buff ware. Dense with some grits. Buff slipped. Black paint. Reserved wavy lines |
| F | 6092 | S22:622 | 78.34 | Buff ware. Grit tempered. Smoothed. Buff slipped. Dark granulated matte paint. Early/ Middle Susiana |
| G | 8761 | S22:823 North | 75.03 | Buff ware. Dense with some grits. Buff slipped. Black paint |
| H | 8030 | S22:808 | 75.91 | Buff ware. Gritty. Buff slipped. Black paint. Reserved wavy lines |
| I | 8137 | S22:825 | 76.24 | Buff ware. Gritty. Buff slipped. Black paint. Reserved wavy lines |
| J | 6110 | P22:609 | 81.13 | Buff ware. Gritty. Buff slipped. Matte black paint. Reserved wavy lines |

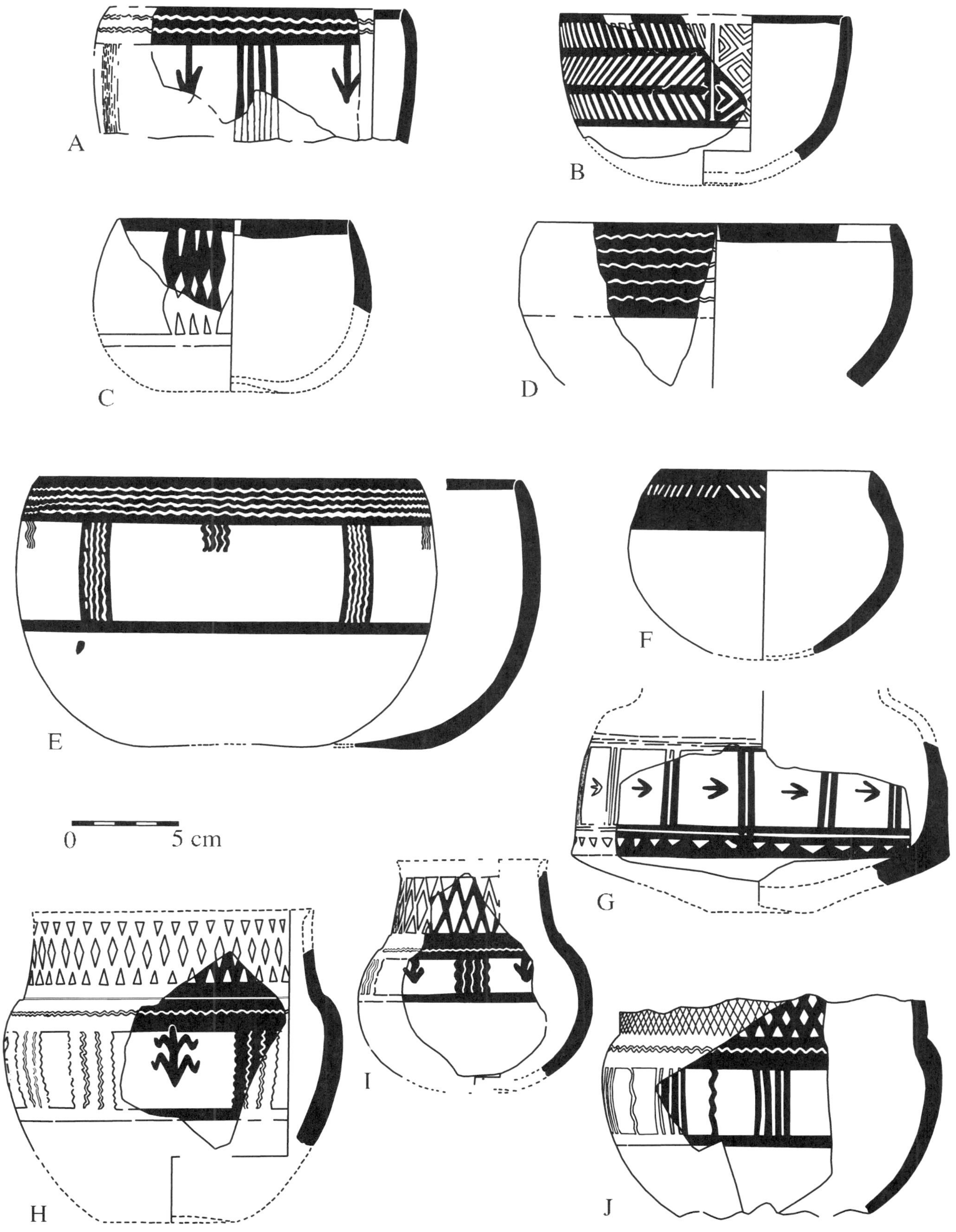


Figure 55. Early Susiana Open Pottery Vessels

Figure 56. Early Susiana Open Pottery Vessels

| | *Registration Number* | *Provenance* | *Elevation* | *Description* |
|---|---|---|---|---|
| A | 8260 | S22:823 | 75.90 | Buff ware. Grit tempered. Buff slipped. Slightly gritty face. Black paint |
| B | 7261 | Q23:702 | 79.08 | Buff ware. Grit tempered. Buff slipped. Slightly gritty face. Black paint |
| C | 6018 | P23:601 | 81.80 | Buff ware. Grit tempered. Buff slipped. Lip knob. Black paint |
| D | 8230 | S22:808 | 75.91 | Buff ware. Grit tempered with some straw. Buff slipped. Black paint |
| E | 8648 | S22:823 | 75.94 | Buff ware. Grit and sand tempered. Buff slipped with a greenish hue. Black paint |
| F | 8063 | S22:808 | 75.67 | Buff ware. Grit tempered. Buff slipped. Black paint |
| G | 8870 | S22:808 | 75.60 | Buff ware. Sand and grit tempered. Buff slipped. Black paint. Reserved wavy band below lip |
| H | 8248 | Q24:801 West | 77.22 | Buff ware. Grit and chaff tempered. Orange pink surface. Black paint. Probably intermediate between Archaic/Early Susiana |
| I | 8287 | S22:823 | 74.98 | Red ware. Sand and grit tempered. Pouring lip. Red slipped? Black paint |
| J | 6035 | P22:608 North | 81.32 | Buff ware. Grit tempered. Buff slipped with a greenish hue. Black matte paint. Reserved wavy lines below lip |
| K | 8490 | S22:823 | 75.43 | Buff ware. Grit tempered with some chaff. Buff slipped. Black paint |
| L | 6085 | P22:609 | 81.83 | Buff ware. Grit tempered. Over-fired greenish buff. Black matte paint |
| M | 6022 | P22:609 | 81.42 | Buff ware. Grit tempered. Over-fired greenish buff. Black matte paint |

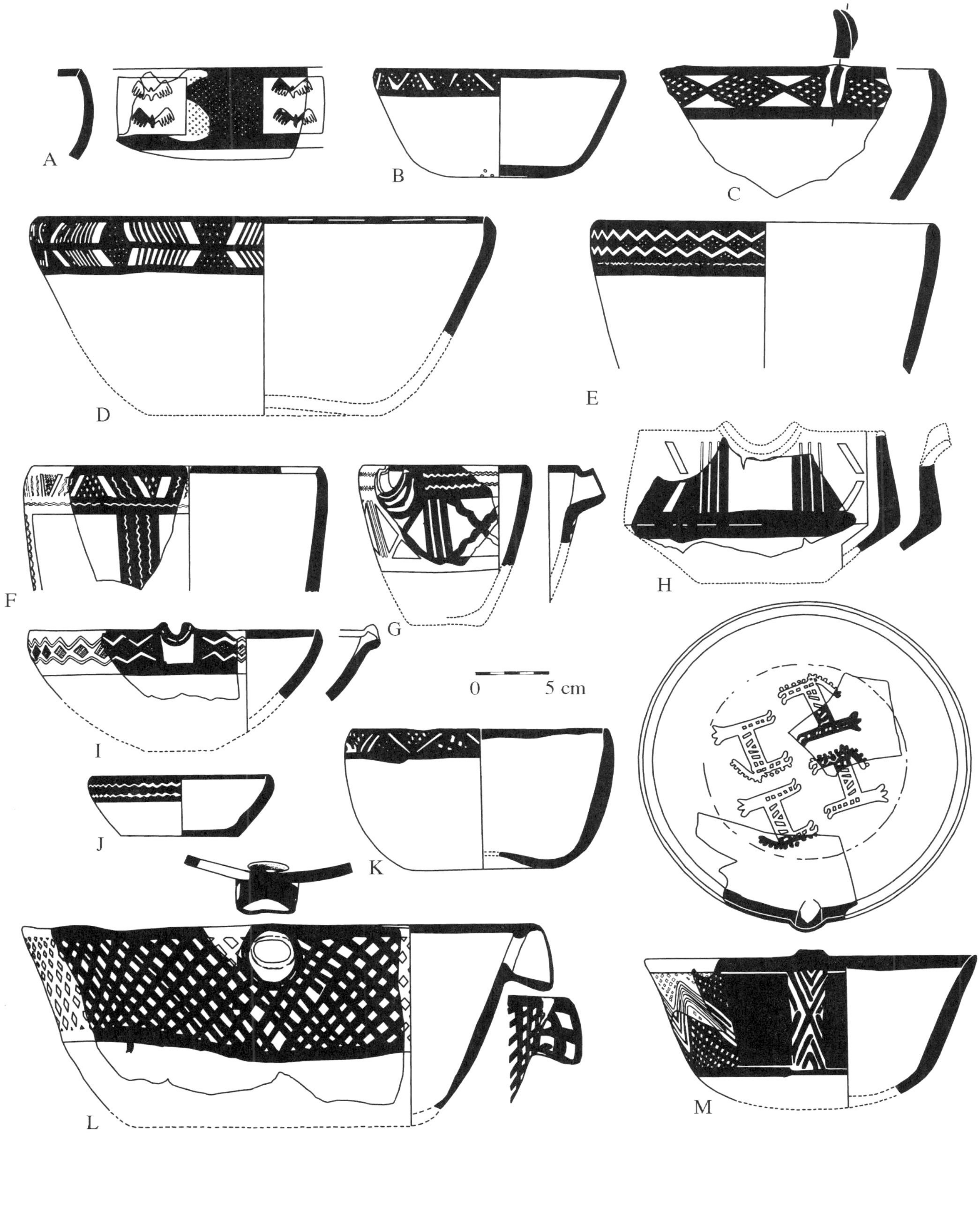


Figure 56. Early Susiana Open Pottery Vessels

Figure 57. Early Susiana Open Pottery Vessels

| | *Registration Number* | *Provenance* | *Elevation* | *Description* |
|---|---|---|---|---|
| A | 8064 | S22:808 | 75.67 | Buff ware. Grit tempered. Buff slipped. Black paint. Reserved wavy line below carination |
| B | N/A | P22:609 | 81.30 | Buff ware. Grit tempered. Buff slipped. Black paint |
| C | 8938 | S22:826 | 74.68 | Buff ware. Grit tempered. Buff slipped. Black paint |
| D | 8769 | S22:823 | 75.03 | Buff ware. Grit tempered. Buff slipped. Black paint |
| E | 6469 | S20:607 | 78.74 | Buff ware. Grit tempered. Buff slipped. Scraping marks on lower exterior |
| F | 8027 | Q24:802 East | 78.07 | Buff ware. Grit tempered with some chaff. Buff slipped. Black paint. Reserved wavy lines below lip |
| G | 6132 | P22:606 | 80.86 | Buff ware. Inverted rim with pouring lip. Grit tempered. Smoothed. Buff slipped. Black brown matte paint |
| H | 6144 | P23:603 | 82.22 | Buff ware. Grit tempered. Smoothed. Buff slipped. Black matte paint |
| I | 8239 | S22:808 | 75.94 | Buff ware. Inverted rim with pouring lip. Grit tempered. Smoothed. Buff slipped. Black matte paint |
| J | 6019 | P22:608 North | 81.13 | Buff ware. Inverted rim with pouring lip. Grit tempered. Smoothed. Buff slipped. Black matte paint |
| K | 5216 | Boneh Fazl Ali | N/A | Buff ware. Grit tempered. Gritty face, buff slipped. Black paint |

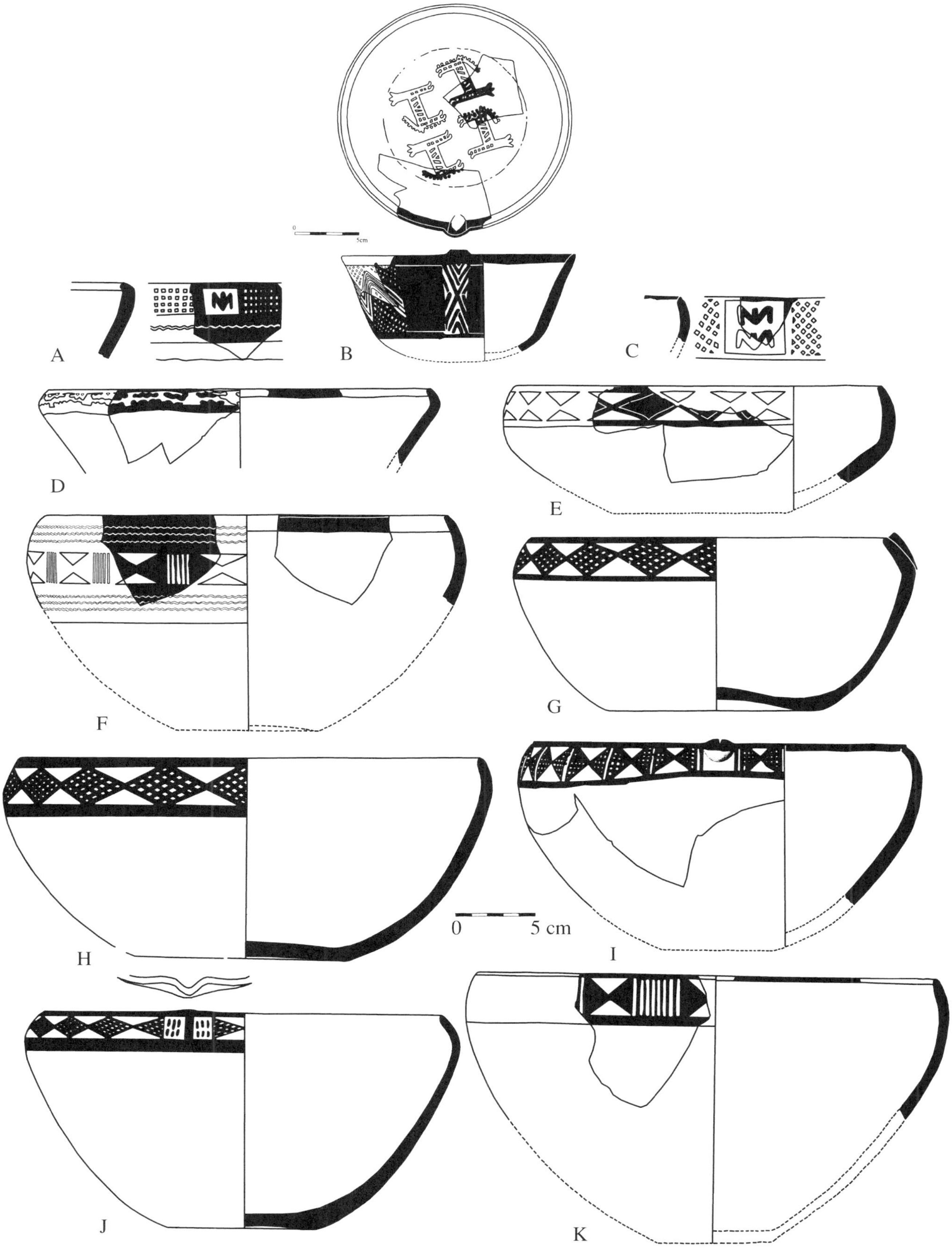


Figure 57. Early Susiana Open Pottery Vessels

Figure 58. Early Susiana Open Pottery Vessels

| | *Registration Number* | *Provenance* | *Elevation* | *Description* |
|---|---|---|---|---|
| A | 8114 | S22:822 | 76.18 | Buff ware. Sand and grit tempered, mostly sandy. Buff slipped. Smoothed. Black paint. Archaic/Early Susiana transitional |
| B | 8350 | S22:823 | 74.98 | Buff ware. Grit tempered. Probably buff slipped. Dark matte paint. Archaic/Early Susiana transitional |
| C | 8117 | S22:823 | 75.84 | Buff ware. Grit and straw tempered. Buff slipped. Black paint. Archaic/Early Susiana transitional |
| D | 6098 | P22:608 | 81.11 | Buff ware. Dense. Small grits. Buff slipped. Dark paint. Early/Middle Susiana transitional |
| E | 8104 | S22:823 | 75.98 | Buff ware. Grit and sand tempered with some chaff. Buff slipped. Black paint |
| F | 6863 | P22:606 | 81.14 | Buff ware. Grit tempered. Buff slipped. Dark paint. Early/Middle Susiana transitional |
| G | 8255 | S22:823 | 75.51 | Buff ware. Grit tempered. Gritty face. Buff slipped. Black paint |
| H | 8007 | S22:803 | 76.15 | Buff ware. Grit tempered with some straw. Buff slipped. Black paint |
| I | 6167 | P22:611 | 80.37 | Buff ware. Grit tempered. Buff slipped. Dark paint |
| J | 6048 | P22:606 | 80.86 | Buff ware. Sand and grit tempered. Buff slipped. Black paint. Early/Middle Susiana transitional |
| K | 6862 | P22:606 | 80.86 | Buff ware. Grit tempered. Buff slipped. Dark paint |

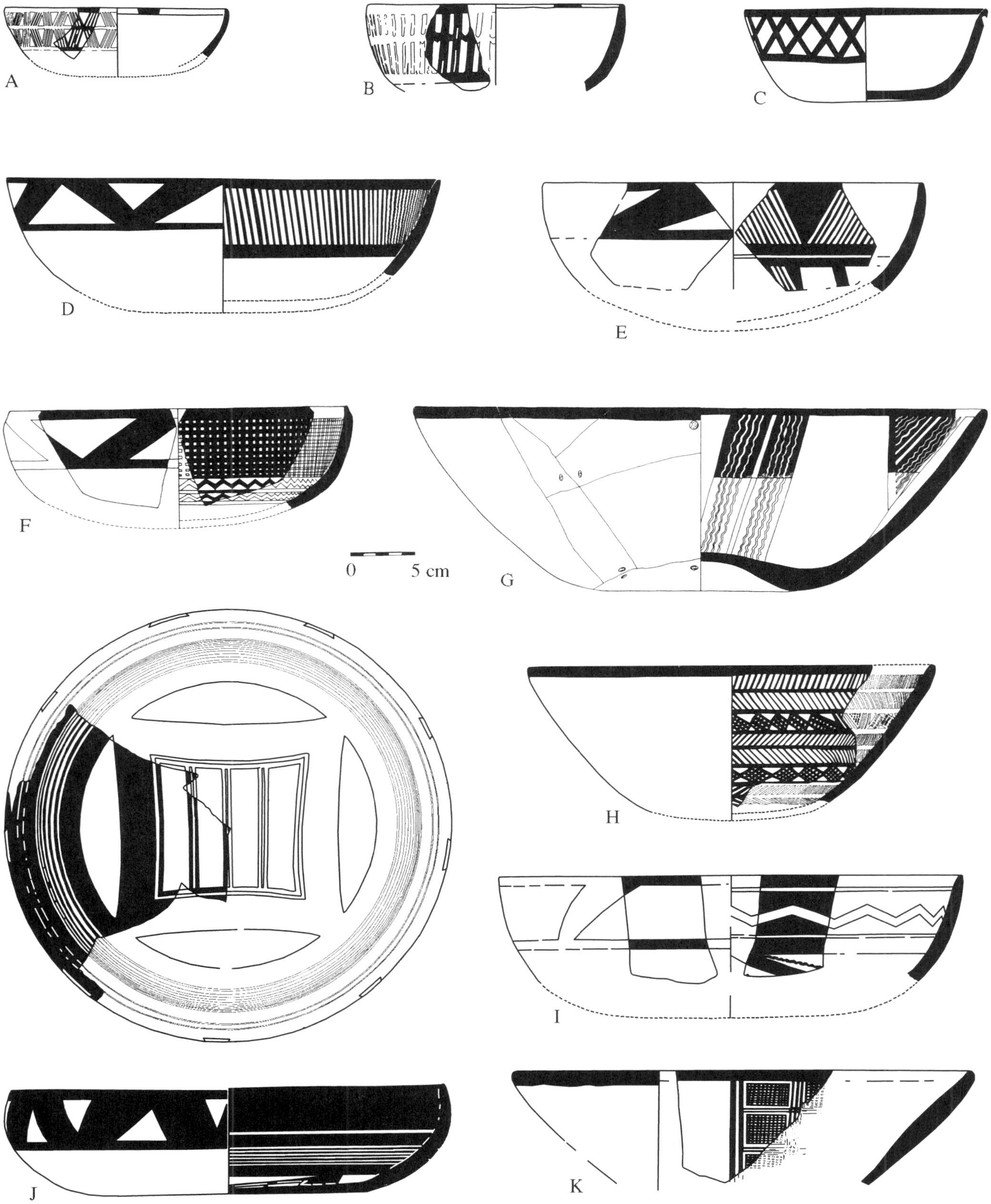


Figure 58. Early Susiana Open Pottery Vessels

Figure 59. Early Susiana Open Pottery Vessels

| | *Registration Number* | *Provenance* | *Elevation* | *Description* |
|---|---|---|---|---|
| A | 6533 | P22:606 | 81.52 | Buff ware. Grit tempered. Buff slipped. Black paint |
| B | 6082 | P22:611 | 80.37 | Buff ware. Grit tempered. Buff slipped. Black matte paint |
| C | 8254 | S22:823 | 75.94 | Buff ware. Grit tempered. Buff slipped. Black paint |
| D | 6178 | P22:606 | N/A | Buff ware. Grit tempered. Buff slipped. Black paint |

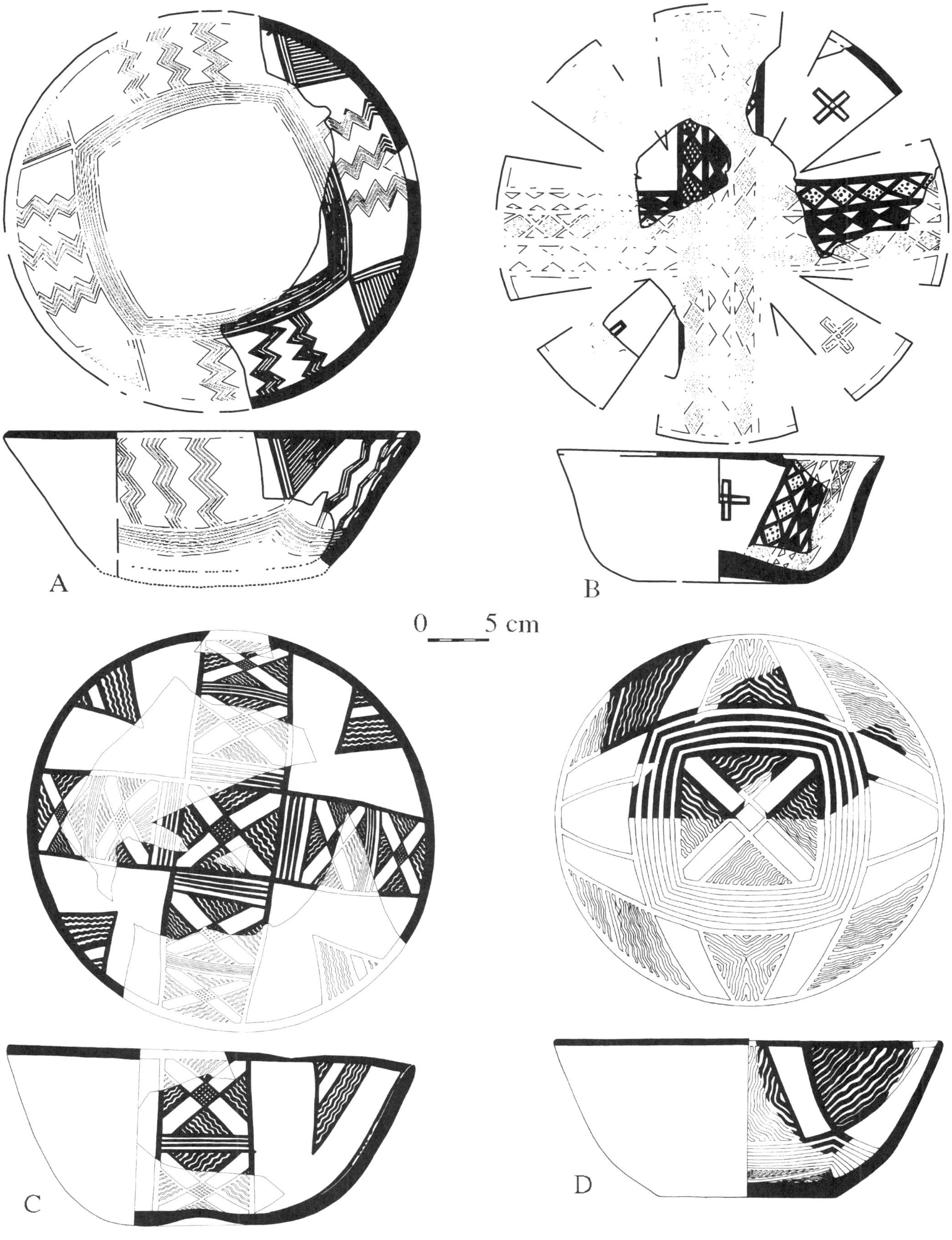


Figure 59. Early Susiana Open Pottery Vessels

Figure 60. Early Susiana Open Pottery Vessels

| | *Registration Number* | *Provenance* | *Elevation* | *Description* |
|---|---|---|---|---|
| A | 8001 | S22:803 | 75.91 | Buff ware. Grit tempered. Buff slipped. Black paint. Reserved wavy lines |
| B | 8738 | S22:808 | 75.46 | Buff ware. Grit tempered. Buff slipped. Black paint |
| C | 7075 | Q23:703 | 79.40 | Buff ware. Grit tempered. Buff slipped. Black paint |
| D | 6860 | P22:606 | N/A | Buff ware. Grit tempered. Buff slipped. Black paint |
| E | 7069 | R23:705 | 76.00 | Buff ware. Grit tempered. Buff slipped. Black paint |
| F | 7216 | Q23:713 | 77.59 | Buff ware. Grit tempered. Buff slipped. Black paint. Probably transitional Archaic/Early Susiana |
| G | 8099 | S22:825 | 76.35 | Buff ware. Grit tempered. Buff slipped. Black paint. Probably transitional Archaic/Early Susiana |

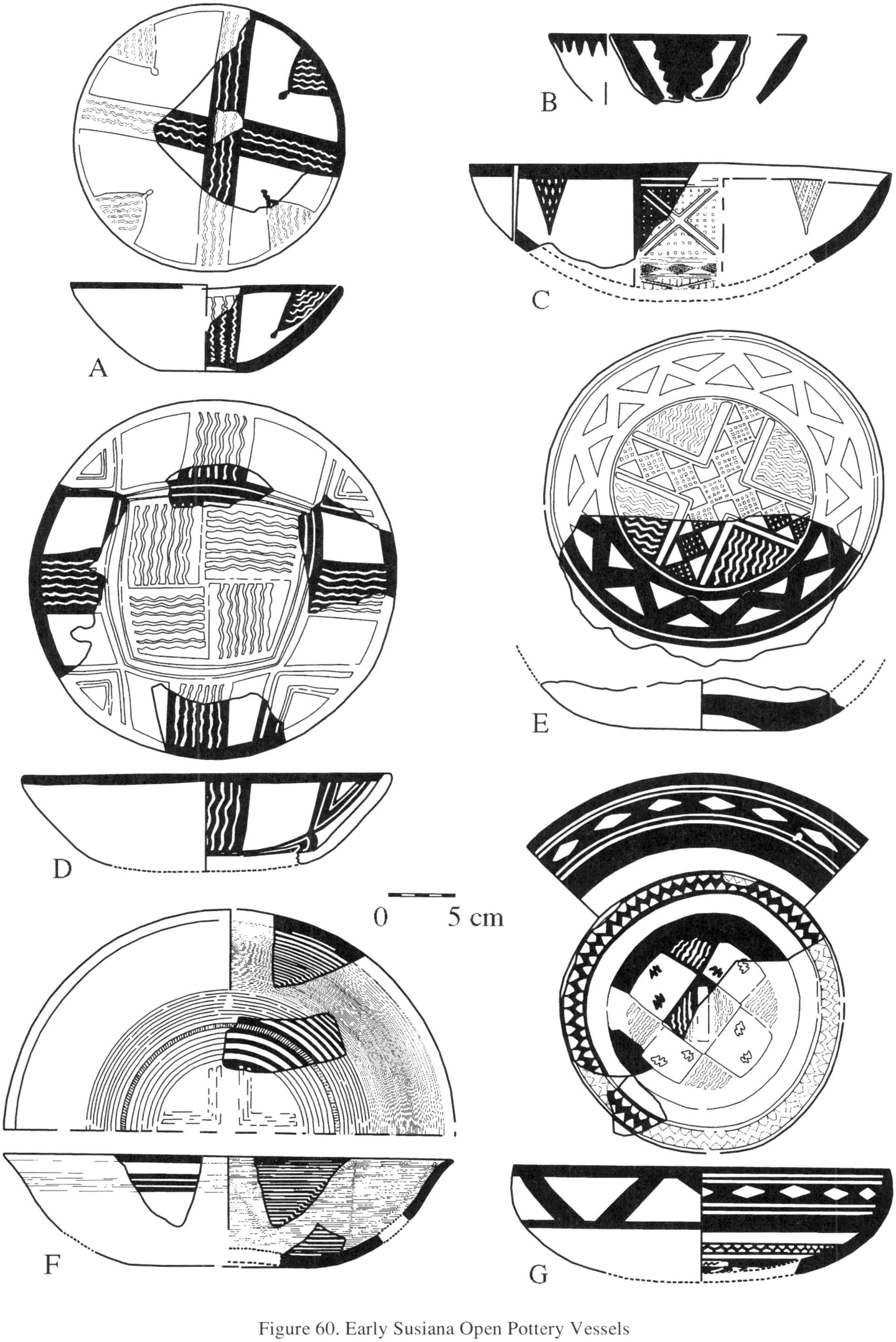


Figure 60. Early Susiana Open Pottery Vessels

Figure 61. Early Susiana Open and Closed Pottery Vessels

| | *Registration Number* | *Provenance* | *Elevation* | *Description* |
|---|---|---|---|---|
| A | VI-29 | Q22:602 | 80.47 | Gritty buff ware. Creamy buff slipped. Gritty face. Dark granular matte paint. Reserved wavy lines below lip |
| B | 8856 | S22:827 | 74.30 | Buff ware. Chaff tempered. Buff slipped. Black paint. Archaic/Early Susiana transitional |
| C | VI-30 | Q22:602 | 80.47 | Gritty buff ware. Creamy buff slipped. Gritty face. Dark granular matte paint. Reserved wavy lines below lip |
| D | 6861 | P22:611 | 80.81 | Gritty buff ware. Creamy buff slipped. Gritty face. Dark granular matte paint. Reserved wavy lines below lip |
| E | 8641 | S22:823 | 74.51 | Fine buff ware. Sand tempered. Buff slipped. Black paint. Reserved wavy lines |
| F | 8578 | S22:823 | 75.90 | Fine buff ware. Small grit tempered. White slipped on exterior and interior. Black paint. Reserved wavy lines |
| G | 8640 | S22:823 | 76.35 | Fine buff ware. Small grit tempered. Buff slipped. Black paint. Reserved wavy lines |
| H | 6111 | P22:609 | 80.74 | Fine buff ware. Small grit tempered. Buff slipped. Black paint. Reserved wavy lines |
| I | 8252 | S22:823 | 75.43 | Buff ware. Grit tempered. Friable. Buff slipped. Black paint |
| J | 8862 | S22:821 | 76.35 | Buff ware. Small grit tempered. Buff slipped. Black paint. Reserved wavy lines |
| K | 8758 | S22:823 | 75.43 | Gritty buff ware. Gritty face. Buff slipped. Uneven lip. Black paint |
| L | 8283 | S22:823 | 74.84 | Gritty buff ware. Gritty face lower body. Buff slipped. Black paint |
| M | 6248 | P22:611 | 80.50 | Gritty buff ware. Gritty face. Buff slipped with greenish hue. Over fired. Olive black paint, vitrified |
| N | 8308 | S22:823 | 74.98 | Gritty buff ware. Gritty face. Buff slipped. Black paint |
| O | 8360 | S22:823 | 75.44 | Buff ware. Grit tempered. Buff slipped. Black paint |

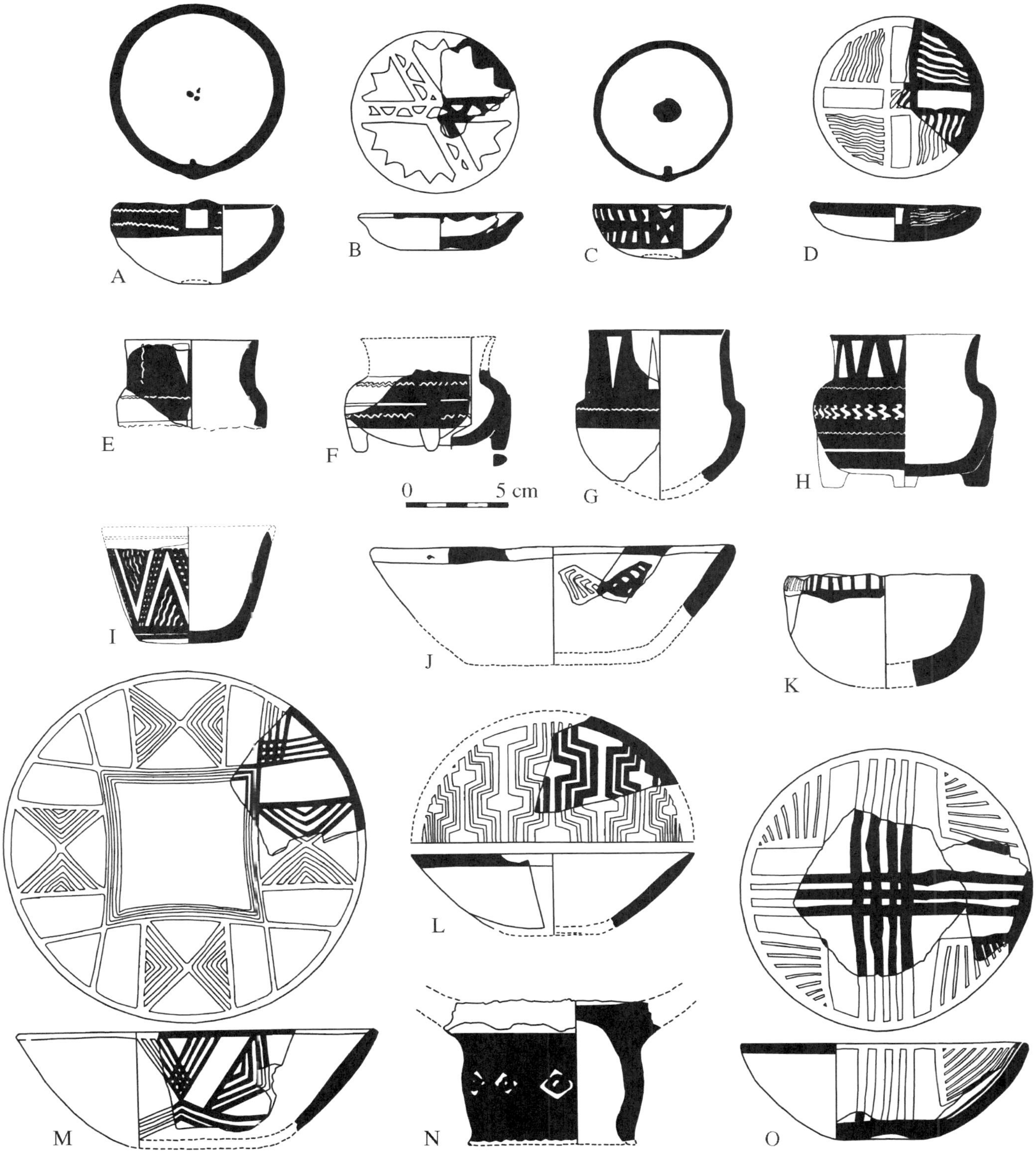


Figure 61. Early Susiana Open and Closed Pottery Vessels

Figure 62. Early Susiana Decorated Pottery Lids

| | *Registration Number* | *Provenance* | *Elevation* | *Description* |
|---|---|---|---|---|
| A | 6466 | S20:607 | 78.74 | Buff ware. Grit tempered. Gritty face. Buff slipped. Pinkish buff interior. Black paint |
| B | 6190 | Q22:603 | 81.42 | Buff ware. Grit tempered with chaff. Buff slipped. Black paint |
| C | 6864 | P22:606 | 81.77 | Buff ware. Grit tempered with chaff. Buff slipped. Black paint |
| D | 8065 | G28:802 East | 78.32 | Buff ware. Grit tempered. Buff slipped. Black paint |
| E | 6026 | Q22:601 | 80.89 | Gritty buff ware. Buff slipped with a greenish hue. Dark brown paint |
| F | 6865 | P22:606 | 80.85 | Buff ware. Grit tempered. Buff slipped. Black paint |
| G | VI-38 | P22:606 | 80.85 | Buff ware. Grit tempered. Buff slipped with a greenish hue. Olive black paint, somewhat sunken. See plate 20:C for photograph |
| H | 6175 | P22:606 | 80.85 | Buff ware. Grit tempered. Buff slipped with a greenish hue. Olive black paint, somewhat sunken |

Figure 62. Early Susiana Decorated Pottery Lids

Figure 63. Various Types of Early Susiana Pottery Vessels

| | *Registration Number* | *Provenance* | *Elevation* | *Description* |
|---|---|---|---|---|
| A | 6184 | P22:608 | 81.14 | Buff ware. Grit and sand tempered. Buff slipped. Black granular paint. Reserved wavy lines |
| B | 7140 | P23:704 | 75.44 | Buff ware. Grit tempered. Buff slipped. Black paint. Probably Archaic/Early Susiana transitional |
| C | 9267 | S22:914 | 74.77 | Buff ware. Grit and sand tempered. Buff slipped. Black paint. Archaic/Early Susiana transitional |
| D | 6021 | P22:607 | N/A | Ladle fragment. Buff ware. Grit tempered. Buff slipped. Reddish brown paint |
| E | 8802 | S22:808 | 75.46 | Buff ware. Chaff tempered with some grits. Buff slipped. Dark paint. Archaic/Early Susiana transitional |
| F | 8734 | S22:808 | 75.46 | Buff ware. Chaff tempered with some grits. Buff slipped. Black paint. Archaic/Early Susiana transitional |
| G | 8040 | G23:805 | 79.04 | Buff ware. Grit tempered. Buff slipped. Black paint. Archaic/Early Susiana transitional. (Another example [registration number 9305] comes from S22:913, at an elevation of 74.50) |
| H | 6033 | Tr. XXXIII | 77.21 | Ladle fragment. Buff ware. Grit tempered. Smoothed. Buff slipped. Reddish brown granulated matte paint |
| I | 6101 | P22:608 | 81.11 | Rectangular lid fragment. Buff ware. Grit tempered. Smoothed. Black matte paint |
| J | VI-102 | P22:611 | 80.57 | Box fragment. Greenish buff ware. Grit tempered. Gritty face. Probably slipped. Dark brown/black paint. Reserved wavy lines. See plate 20:B for photograph |
| L | 9134 | S22:903 | 75.39 | Box fragment. Buff ware. Grit tempered. Creamy buff slipped. Black paint |

Figure 63. Various Types of Early Susiana Pottery Vessels

Figure 64. Early Susiana Plain Pottery Vessels

| | *Registration Number* | *Provenance* | *Elevation* | *Description* |
|---|---|---|---|---|
| A | 6230 | P22:611 | 80.66 | Light reddish ware. Grit tempered. Buff slipped. Gritty face. Smoothed. "Potter's mark" on base |
| B | 6228 | P22:606 | 81.33 | Buff ware. Grit tempered with some chaff. Buff slipped. Gritty face lower body |
| C | 8399 | Q23:827 East | 78.82 | Red ware. Grit tempered. Very smoothed. Gritty face lower body. "Potter's mark" on base |
| D | VI-34 | P22:606 North | 81.75 | Buff ware. Grit tempered. Buff slipped. Smoothed. "Potter's mark" on base |
| E | VI-36 | P22:606 South | 81.06 | Buff ware. Grit tempered. Buff slipped. Smoothed |
| F | 6866 | S20:607 | 78.74 | Buff ware. Grit tempered with some chaff. Buff slipped. Gritty face lower body |
| G | 6241 | P22:611 | 80.50 | Buff ware. Grit and chaff tempered. Buff slipped. Smoothed |
| H | 6126 | P22:606 North | 81.73 | Buff ware. Grit tempered with some chaff. Buff slipped. Smoothed. Gritty face lower body. Bitumen stain on interior |
| I | 6867 | P22:611 West | 81.14 | Buff ware. Grit tempered. Buff slipped. Smoothed |
| J | 6123 | P22:606 | 80.86 | Buff ware. Grit tempered. Smoothed. Buff slipped |
| K | 6868 | P22:606 | 80.85 | Buff ware. Grit tempered. Buff slipped. Smoothed. "Potter's mark" on base |
| L | 6869 | P22:606 South | N/A | Buff ware. Grit tempered. Buff slipped. Smoothed |

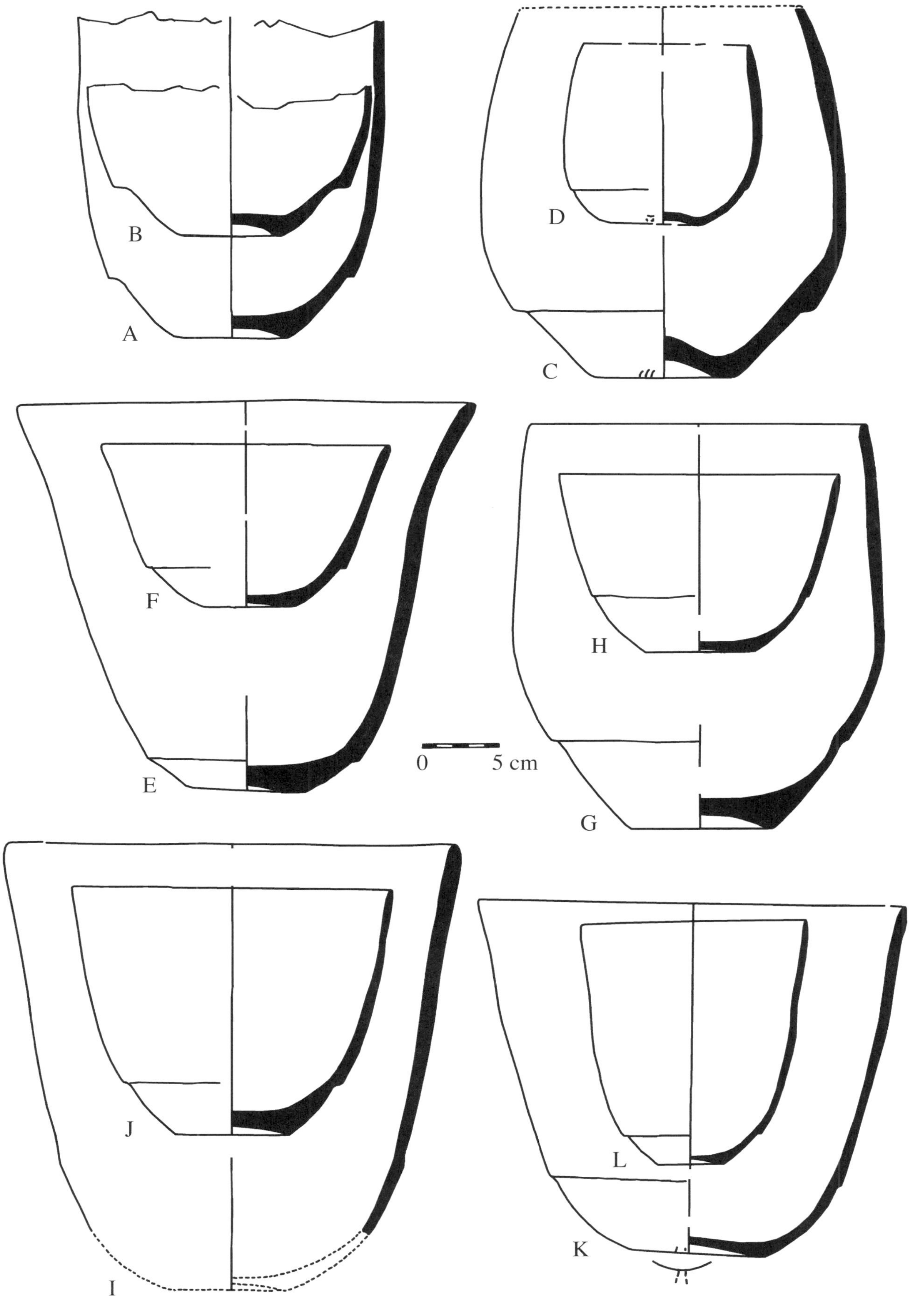


Figure 64. Early Susiana Plain Pottery Vessels

Figure 65. Early Susiana Plain Pottery Vessels

| | *Registration Number* | *Provenance* | *Elevation* | *Description* |
|---|---|---|---|---|
| A | 6845 | P22:606 | N/A | Standard buff ware. Grit tempered with mixture of crushed calcite or shells. Dark and red grits range from small to large. Mottled exterior ranging from light orange to creamy buff. Interior covered with bitumen. "Potter's mark" on base |
| B | 6231 | P22:611 | 80.38 | Standard buff ware. Grit tempered. Small to large grits. Probably buff slipped. Interior covered with bitumen. "Potter's mark" on base |
| C | 7152 | R23:701 | 77.59 | Buff ware. Grit tempered. Gritty face. Buff slipped. "Potter's mark" on base |
| D | 8762 | S22:823 | 75.84 | Standard buff ware. Grit tempered. Gritty face. Buff slipped with a greenish tinge. Smoothed |
| E | 6226 | P22:606 | 80.10 | Buff ware. Grit tempered with some chaff. Gritty face. Wall of the vessel made in three layers. Smoothed |
| F | 6229 | P22:606 | 80.12 | Red ware. Grit tempered. Tan-cream slipped. Very smoothed |
| G | 9277 | S22:909 South | 75.00 | Buff ware. Red wash all over. Straw tempered. Smoothed |
| H | 8298 | S22:823 West | 75.90 | Buff ware. Dark grit tempered with some chaff. Smoothed. Pouring lip |
| I | 8183 | S22:823 | 75.84 | Buff ware. Grit tempered with some chaff. "Potter's mark" on base |
| J | 6291 | P22:611 | 80.58 | Standard buff. Grit tempered. Gritty face. Light buff slipped. "Potter's mark" on base |
| K | N/A | Q22:602 | 80.47 | Buff ware. Grit tempered. Gritty face. Buff slipped. Bitumen-coated inside. "Potter's mark" on base |
| L | VI-23 | Q22:602 | 80.45 | Buff ware. Grit tempered. Gritty face. Buff slipped. "Potter's mark" on base |
| M | 6422 | P22:606 | 80.50 | Buff ware. Grit tempered. Gritty face. Buff slipped. "Potter's mark" on base |
| N | 6870 | P22:606 | 80.52 | Buff ware. Grit tempered. Gritty face. Buff slipped. "Potter's mark" on base |
| O | 8873 | Q24:801 East | 77.30 | Buff ware. Grit tempered. Smoothed |
| P | VI-40 | P22:614 | 80.30 | Buff ware. Chaff tempered with some grits. Buff slipped. Smoothed |
| Q | 8265 | Q23:805 | 78.80 | Buff ware. Grit tempered. Buff slipped. Smoothed |
| R | 6223 | P22:625 | 81.75 | Buff ware. Grit tempered. Gritty face. Smoothed |
| S | 6871 | S20:621 | 78.70 | Buff ware. Grit tempered. Gritty face. Smoothed |
| T | 6146 | P22:606 | 80.65 | Buff ware. Grit tempered. Gritty face. Smoothed |
| U | 7161 | R27:704 | 74.90 | Buff ware. Grit tempered. Pink orange slipped. Gray core |

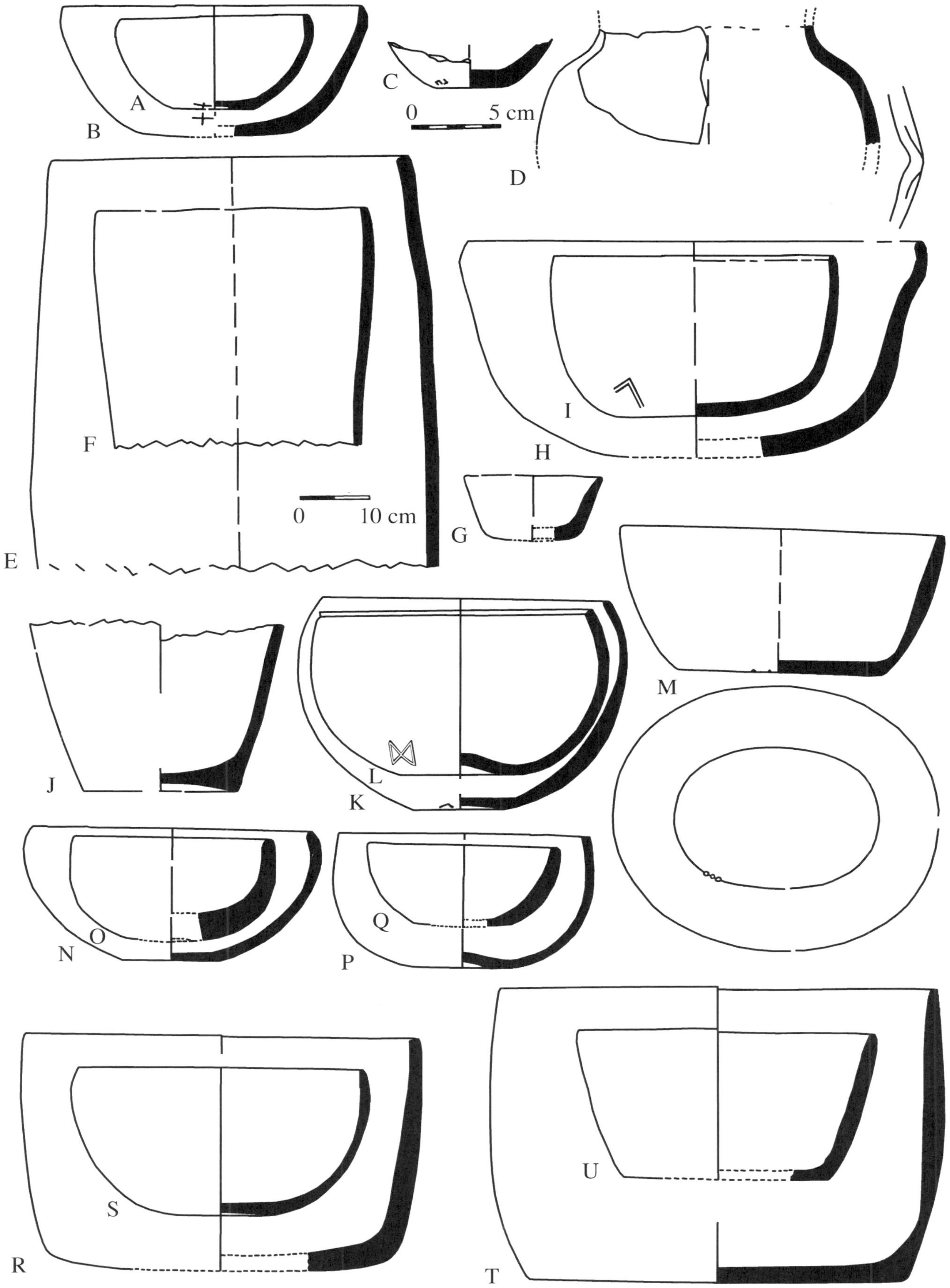


Figure 65. Early Susiana Plain Pottery Vessels

Figure 66. Archaic Susiana 3 Close-line Open Bowls

| | *Registration Number* | *Provenance* | *Elevation* | *Description* |
|---|---|---|---|---|
| A | 7251 | R23:710 | 77.82 | Buff ware. Small grit tempered. Buff slipped. Smoothed. Dark paint |
| B | 3083 | R21:301 South | B.S. | Buff ware. Small grit tempered. Buff slipped. Smoothed. Black paint |
| C | 8092 | Q23:810 | 77.90 | Buff ware. Grit and sand tempered with some fine chaff. Cream slipped. Black paint |
| D | 8110 | Q23:815 | 77.31 | Buff ware. Grit and sand tempered. Buff slipped. Black paint |
| E | 8775 | Q25:801 | 76.62 | Buff ware. Grit and sand tempered. Buff slipped. Black paint |
| F | 8238 | S22:824 | 75.08 | Buff ware. Sand tempered. Creamy buff slipped. Black paint |
| G | 6432 | S20:601 | 74.38 | Buff ware. Sand tempered. Buff slipped. Black paint. Interior coated with bitumen |
| H | BF-1 | H16:101 | N/A | Buff ware. Sand tempered. Warm buff slipped. Black paint |
| I | 7105 | R23:710 | 77.95 | Buff ware. Grit tempered. Creamy buff slipped. Scraping marks on the outside. Black paint |
| J | 81013 | Q23:810 | 77.69 | Buff ware. Sand tempered. Buff slipped. Black paint |
| K | 8227 | S22:808 | 75.55 | Buff ware. Grit tempered. Buff slipped. Brown paint |
| L | 8497 | S22:823 | 75.13 | Buff ware. Grit tempered with some chaff. Buff slipped. Black paint |
| M | 6058 | S20:619 | 75.20 | Buff ware. Sand tempered. Tan-buff slipped. Black paint |

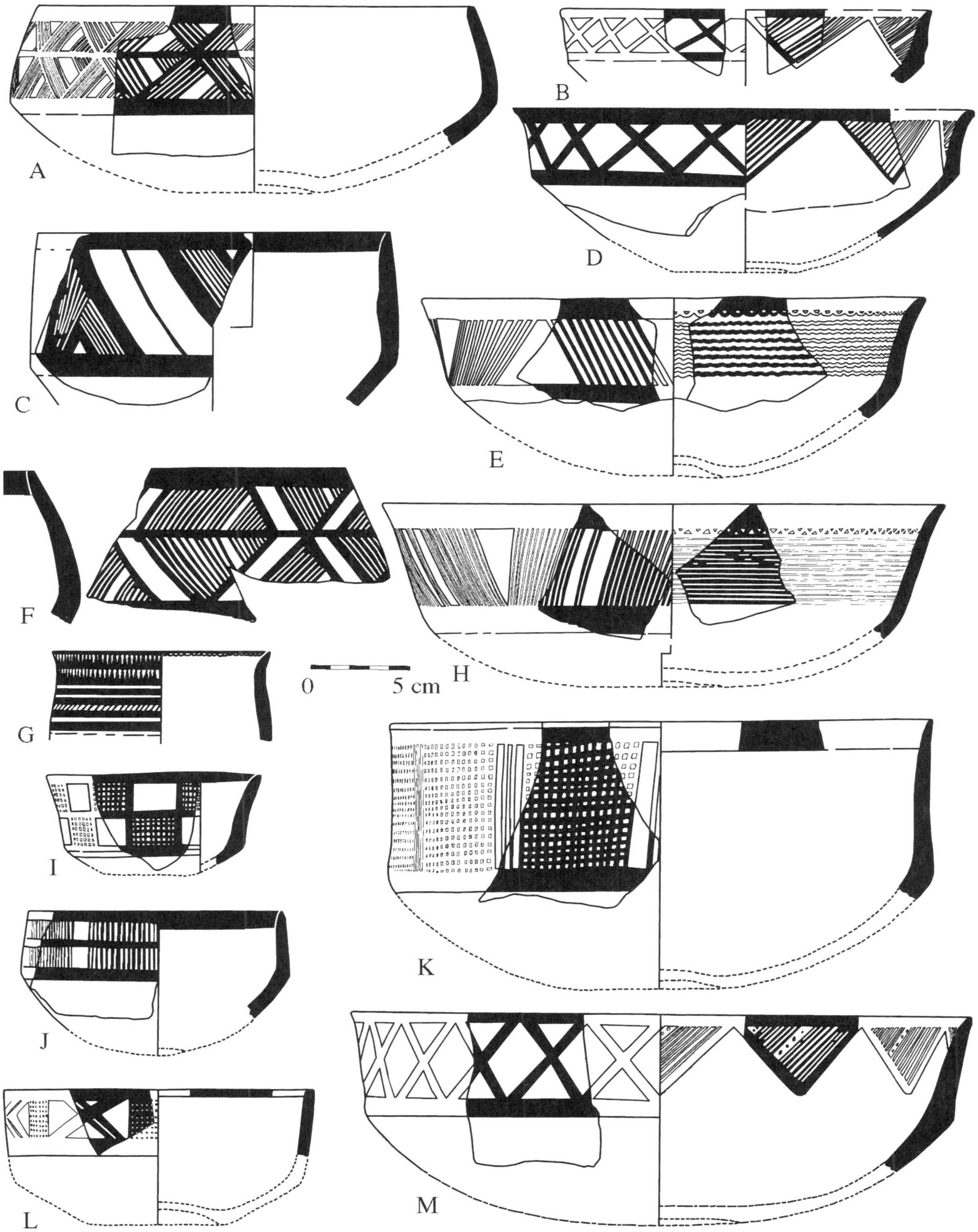


Figure 66. Archaic Susiana 3 Close-line Open Bowls

Figure 67. Archaic Susiana Pottery Vessels

| | *Registration Number* | *Provenance* | *Elevation* | *Description* |
|---|---|---|---|---|
| A | 9343 | S22:909 | 74.40 | Buff ware. Sand tempered. Buff slipped. Black paint. Archaic Susiana 3 |
| B | 6100 | P22:606 | 80.00 | Buff ware. Grit tempered with some straw. Buff slipped with a greenish hue. Smoothed. Archaic 3–Early Susiana transitional |
| C | 6872/VI-19 | P22:606 | 80.00 | Buff ware. Grit tempered with some straw. Light orange buff interior and exterior. Dark brown paint. Archaic 3–Early Susiana transitional |
| D | BF-2687 | N/A | N/A | Buff ware. Grit tempered with some straw. Light orange buff interior and exterior. Dark brown paint. Archaic 3–Early Susiana transitional. Compare with examples from Chogha Sefid (Hole 1977, fig. 42:a–b) |

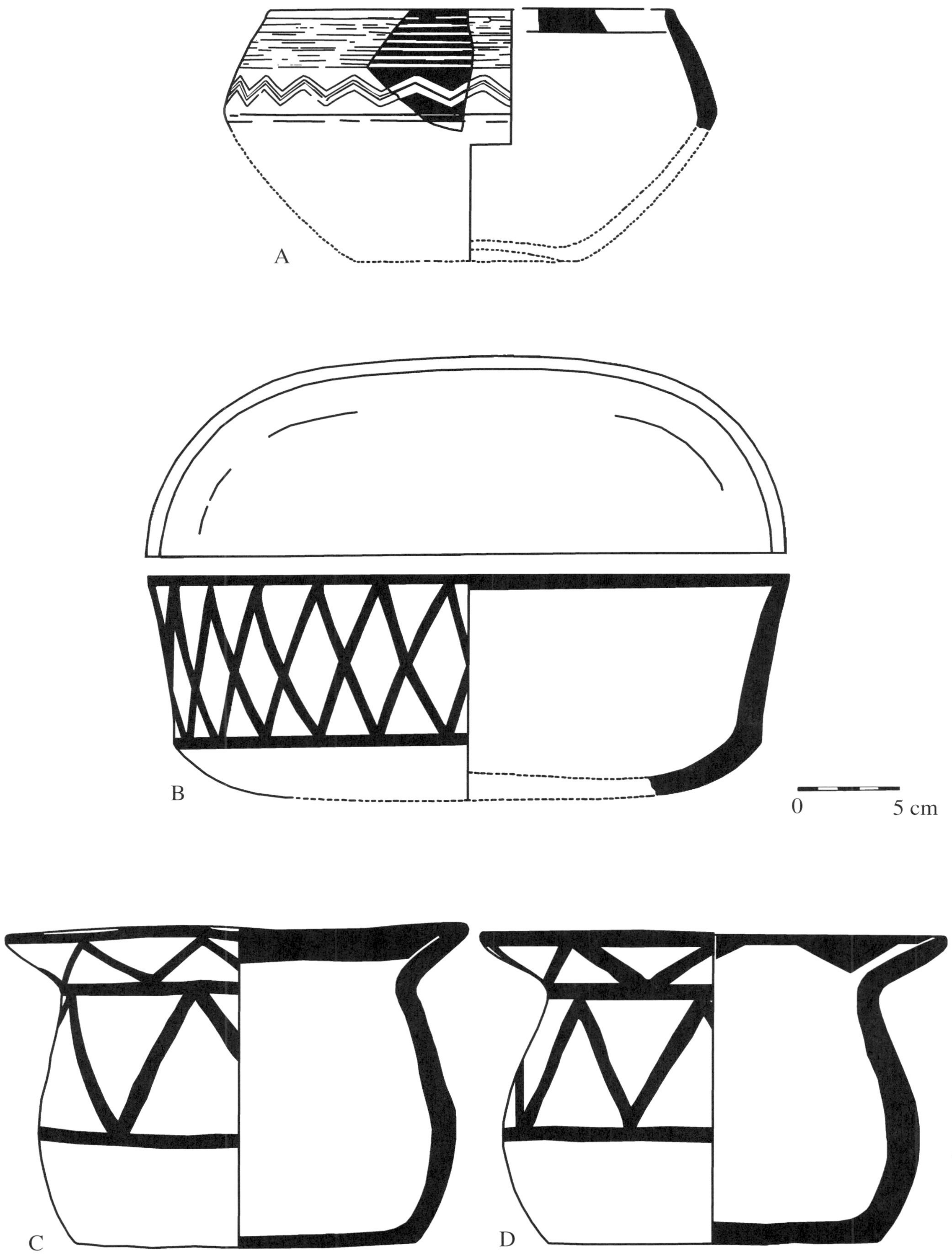


Figure 67. Archaic Susiana Pottery Vessels

Figure 68. Archaic Susiana Pottery Vessels

| | *Registration Number* | *Provenance* | *Elevation* | *Description* |
|---|---|---|---|---|
| A | 7253 | Q23:712 | 78.29 | Buff close-line ware. Sand tempered. Dense orange buff core. Buff slipped. Black paint. Archaic Susiana 3 |
| B | 9512/9370 | S22:912, S22:916 | 73.72, 73.70 | Buff ware. Sand tempered. Buff slipped. Smoothed. Brown paint. See plate 21:J–K for photographs. Archaic Susiana 3 |
| C | N/A | S22:601 | 73.67 | Painted-burnished variant. Buff ware. Gray core grading to buff. Sand tempered. Black paint. Archaic Susiana 1 |
| D | 8605 | S22:823 | 74.87 | Buff ware. Sand tempered with a few grits. Buff slipped. Black paint. Archaic Susiana 3 |
| E | 11158 | S22:1108 East | 72.27 | Painted-burnished variant. Sand and straw tempered. Pinkish buff surface. Dark maroon paint. Archaic Susiana 1 |

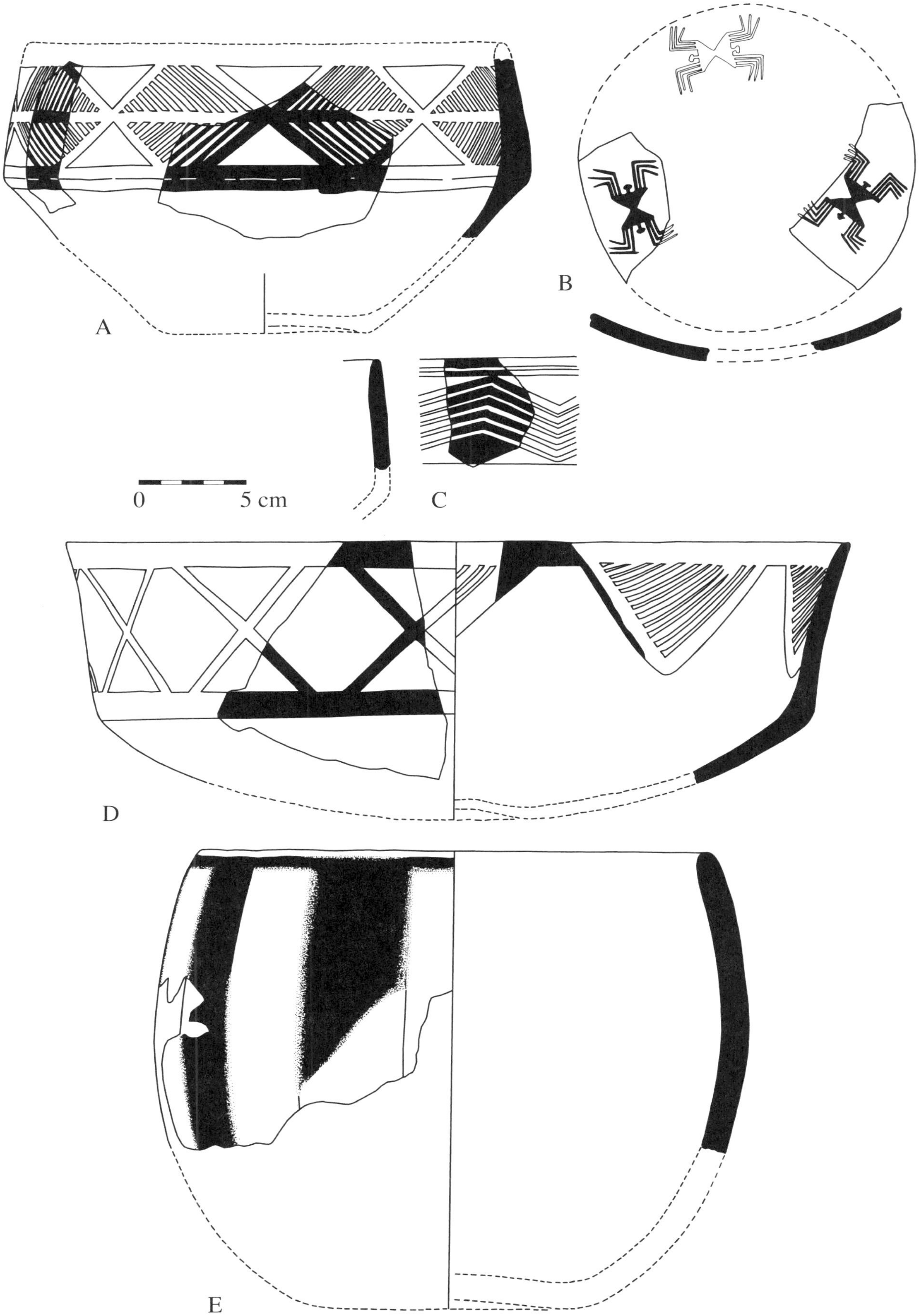


Figure 68. Archaic Susiana Pottery Vessels

Figure 69. Archaic Susiana 3 Pottery Vessels

| | *Registration Number* | *Provenance* | *Elevation* | *Description* |
|---|---|---|---|---|
| A | 8760 | S22:823 | 74.92 | Buff ware. Sand tempered. Dense. Creamy buff slipped. Black paint |
| B | 9269 | S22:911 | 74.00 | Buff ware. Sand tempered. Dense. Creamy buff slipped. Black paint |
| C | 6068 | S20:620 | 78.20 | Buff ware. Sand tempered. Smoothed. Buff slipped. Dark matte paint |
| D | 9237 | S22:912 | 74.57 | Buff ware. Sand tempered. Dense. Creamy buff slipped. Black paint |
| E | 7079 | S22:703 | 75.25 | Buff ware. Sand tempered. Dense. Creamy buff slipped. Black paint |
| F | 8289 | Q24:801 West | 77.22 | Buff ware. Grit tempered. Creamy buff slipped. Black paint |
| G | 6139 | P22:620 | 81.00 | Buff ware. Grit tempered. Creamy buff slipped. Brown paint |
| H | 3360 | Tr. XXV | 1.00 B.S. | Buff ware. Grit tempered. Creamy buff slipped. Black paint |
| I | 6009 | P23:604 | B.S. | Buff ware. Grit tempered. Creamy buff slipped. Black matte paint |
| J | BF-1010 | H10:102 | N/A | Buff ware. Grit tempered. Creamy buff slipped. Black paint. Compare Hole 1977, fig. 42, close to Early Susiana birds |
| K | 9364 | S22:912 | 74.52 | Buff ware. Grit tempered. Creamy buff slipped. Black paint |

Figure 69. Archaic Susiana 3 Pottery Vessels

Figure 70. Archaic Susiana 3 Matte-painted Pottery Vessels

| | *Registration Number* | *Provenance* | *Elevation* | *Description* |
|---|---|---|---|---|
| A | 9312 | S22:909 | 75.00 | Buff ware. Straw tempered. Buff slipped. Very smoothed. See plate 21:B for photograph. Black paint |
| B | 6422 | P22:606 | 80.00 | Buff ware. Grit tempered. Buff slipped. Smoothed, some shiny spots on exterior. Black paint |
| C | 6426 | S22:601 | 73.63 | Buff ware. Straw tempered. Buff slipped. Very smoothed. Black paint |
| D | 8348 | S22:823 | 75.08 | Buff ware. Grit and straw tempered. Probably buff slipped. Smoothed. Black paint |
| E | 5125 | S23:Steps | 75.46 | Buff ware. Straw tempered. Reddish buff surface (slip?). Black paint |
| F | VI-28/ A34802 | Q23:810 | 78.25 | Buff ware. Straw tempered. Yellowish buff slipped. Below painted panel, fugitive red wash. Black paint. See plate 20:F for photograph |
| G | 8070 | Q23:804 | 78.60 | Buff ware. Sand and chaff tempered. Buff slipped. Black matte paint |

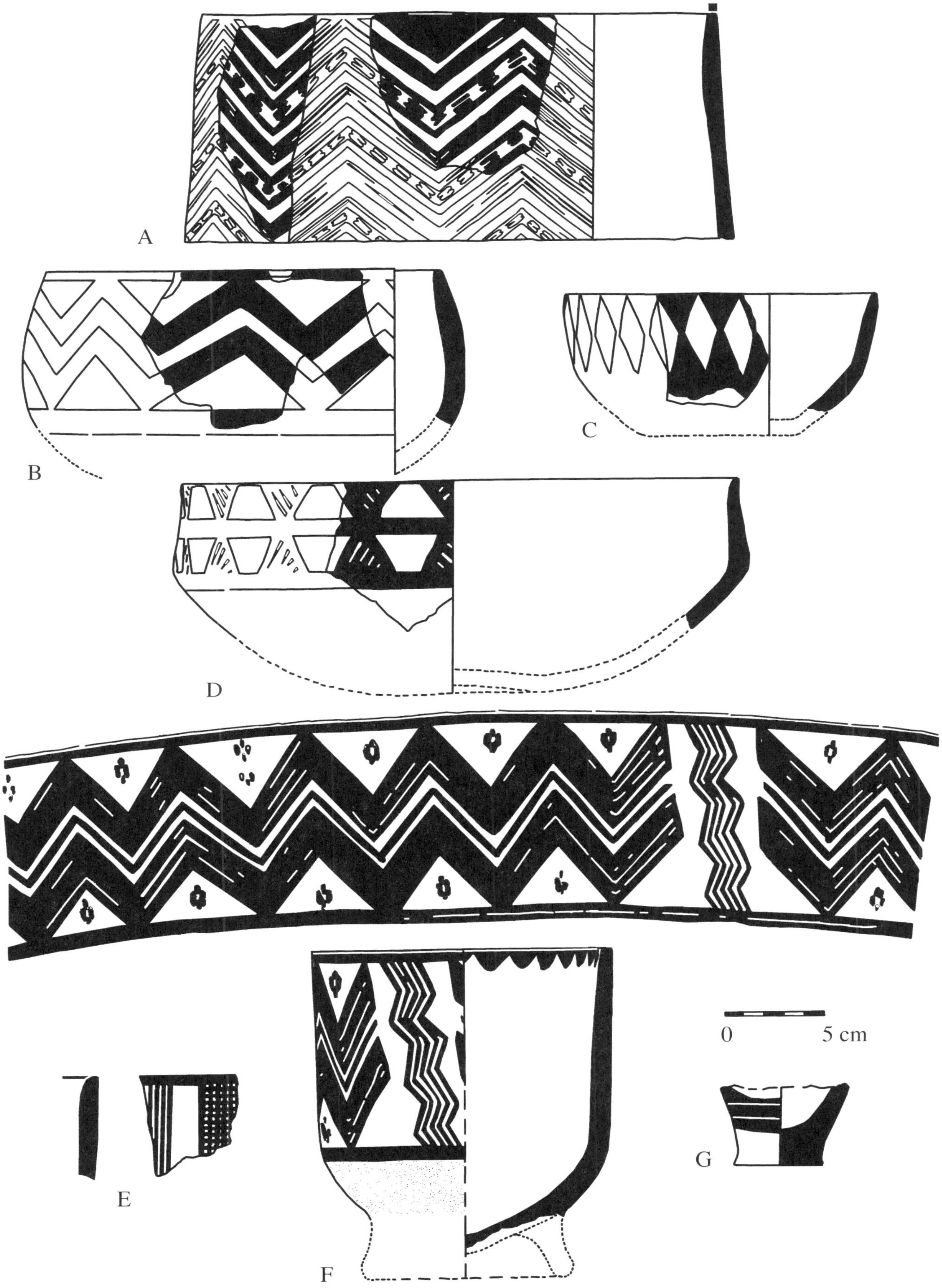


Figure 70. Archaic Susiana 3 Matte-painted Pottery Vessels

Figure 71. Archaic Susiana 3 Matte-painted Pottery Vessels

| | *Registration Number* | *Provenance* | *Elevation* | *Description* |
|---|---|---|---|---|
| A | 9268 | S22:911 | 74.00 | Buff ware. Straw tempered. Buff slipped. Black matte paint |
| B | N/A | P22:612 South | 79.25 | Buff ware. Straw tempered. Buff slipped. Black matte paint |
| C | N/A | Q23:804 | 78.50 | Buff ware. Straw tempered with some sand. Buff slipped. Black matte paint |
| D | 9511 | S22:914 | 74.02 | Buff ware. Chaff tempered. Buff slipped. Smoothed. Black matte paint |
| E | 9282 | S22:908 | 74.45 | Buff ware. Straw tempered. Buff slipped. Smoothed. Black matte paint |

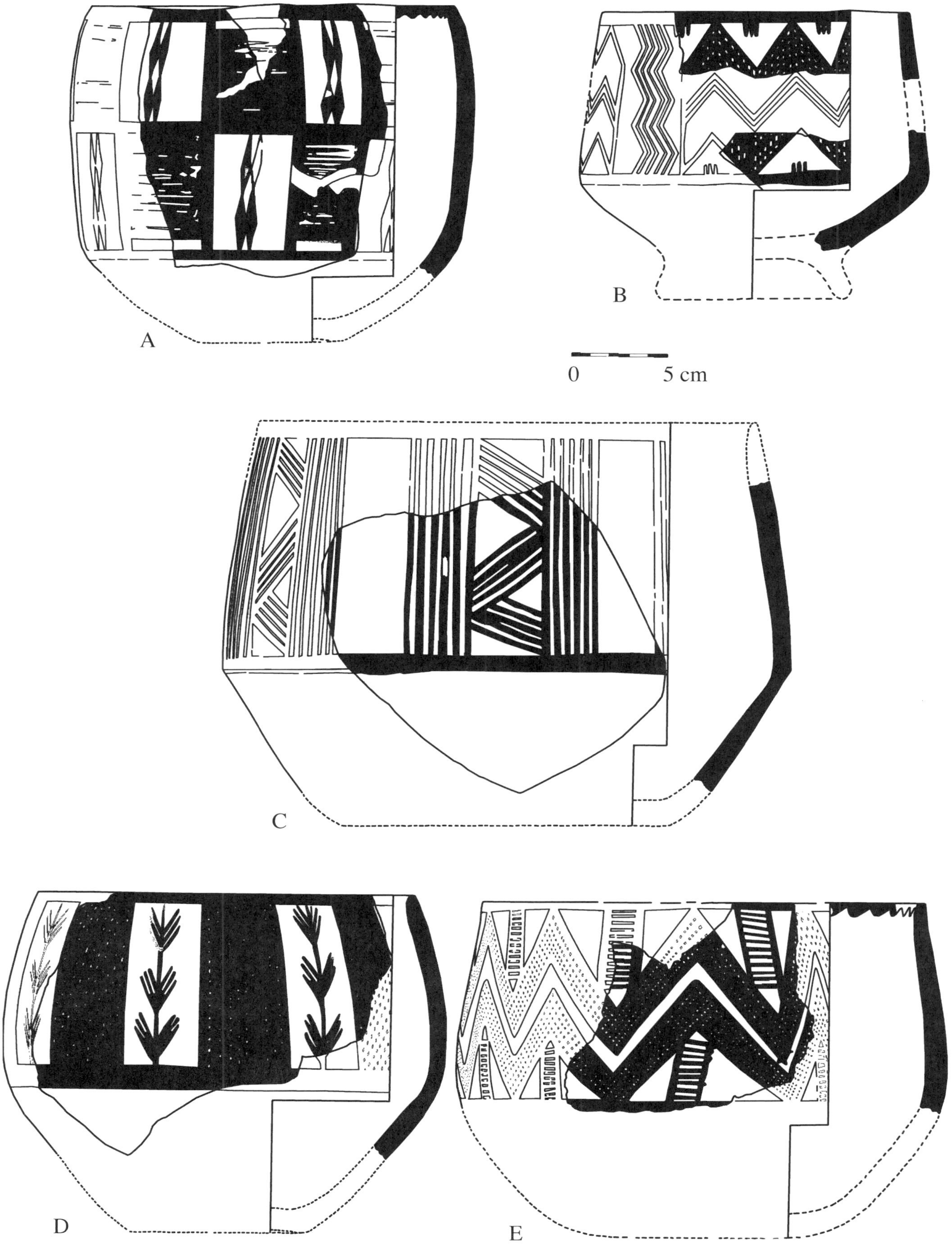


Figure 71. Archaic Susiana 3 Matte-painted Pottery Vessels

Figure 72. Archaic Susiana Pottery Vessels

| | *Registration Number* | *Provenance* | *Elevation* | *Description* |
|---|---|---|---|---|
| A | 8667 | Q22:804 North | 77.48 | Buff ware. Chaff tempered. Buff slipped. Smoothed. Black matte paint. Archaic Susiana 3 |
| B | 9328 | S22:912 | 74.74 | Buff ware, with slightly grayish core. Dense sandy. Chaff tempered. Red wash on exterior and interior. Black paint. Archaic Susiana 2 |
| C | 6370 | S20:601 | 74.38 | Buff ware. Dense sandy. Gray core. Some chaff included with a small amount of mica. Exterior creamy buff slipped. Pale red paint. Archaic Susiana 2 |
| D | 6427 | S22:601 | 73.63 | Red-line ware. Dense sandy. Dark buff paste. Sand tempered. Smoothed. Archaic Susiana 2 |
| E | 6433 | S22:601 | 73.46 | Red-line ware. Dense sandy. Some grits and chaff. Red slipped exterior and interior. Red paint. Archaic Susiana 2 |
| F | 6435 | S22:601 | 73.63 | Red-line ware. Dense sandy. Pinkish buff slipped. Fugitive red paint. Archaic Susiana 2 |
| G | 6372 | S20:601 | 73.63 | Red-line ware. Dense sandy, some chaff. Grayish buff core. Light orange, bright red glossy paint. Solid red wash below carination. Archaic Susiana 2 |
| H | 6841 | S22:601 | 73.67 | Red-line ware. Dense sandy with some chaff. Brownish buff core grades to orange buff toward surface. Red paint. Red wash below carination. Archaic Susiana 2 |
| I | 6232 | S22:601 | 73.60 | Red-line ware. Dense sandy with a lot of chaff. Light brown core grades to orange toward surface. Some burnish strokes on exterior. Matte fugitive paint. Red wash below carination. Archaic Susiana 2 |
| J | 6447 | Q22:602 | 79.57 | Straw-tempered, red wash ware. Red fugitive paint. Archaic Susiana 2 |
| K | N/A | S22:601 | 75.67 | Red-line ware. Dense sandy with chaff. Brownish core grades to orange buff toward surface. Red paint. Archaic Susiana 2 |

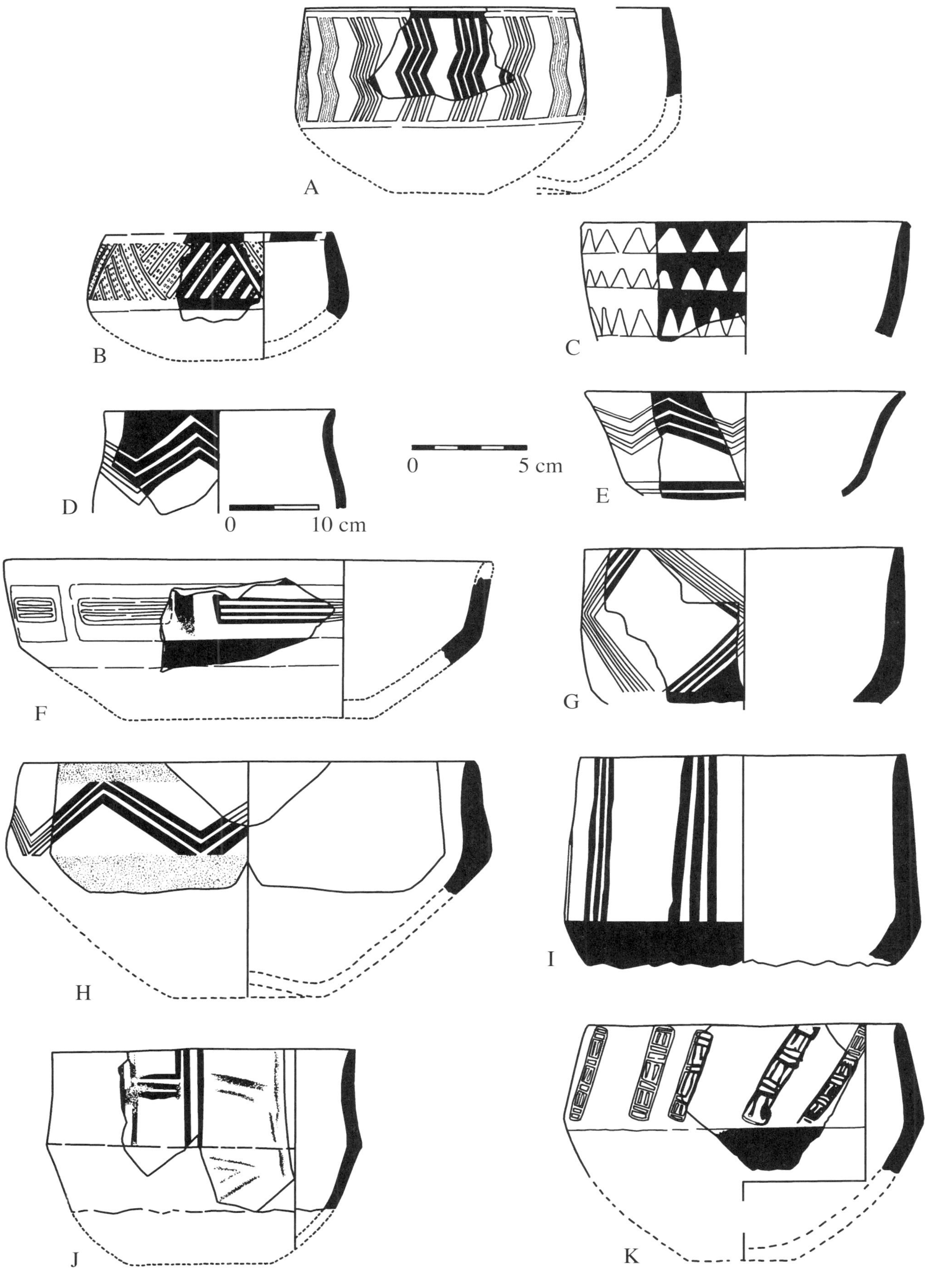


Figure 72. Archaic Susiana Pottery Vessels

Figure 73. Archaic Susiana 1 Painted-burnished Pottery Vessels

| | *Registration Number* | *Provenance* | *Elevation* | *Description* |
|---|---|---|---|---|
| A | 6164 | Q22:608 | 79.57 | Buff ware. Grayish core grades to pale orange buff toward surface. Dense straw tempered. Black paint, See plate 20:F for photograph |
| B | 41050 | R22:401 | 74.13 | Buff ware. Dense straw tempered. Gray core changes to orange buff toward surface. Yellowish buff slipped all over. Deep brown paint |
| C | 4520 | R22:401 | 74.15 | Buff ware. Dense straw tempered. Gray core changes to orange buff toward surface. Yellowish buff slipped all over. Deep brown paint |

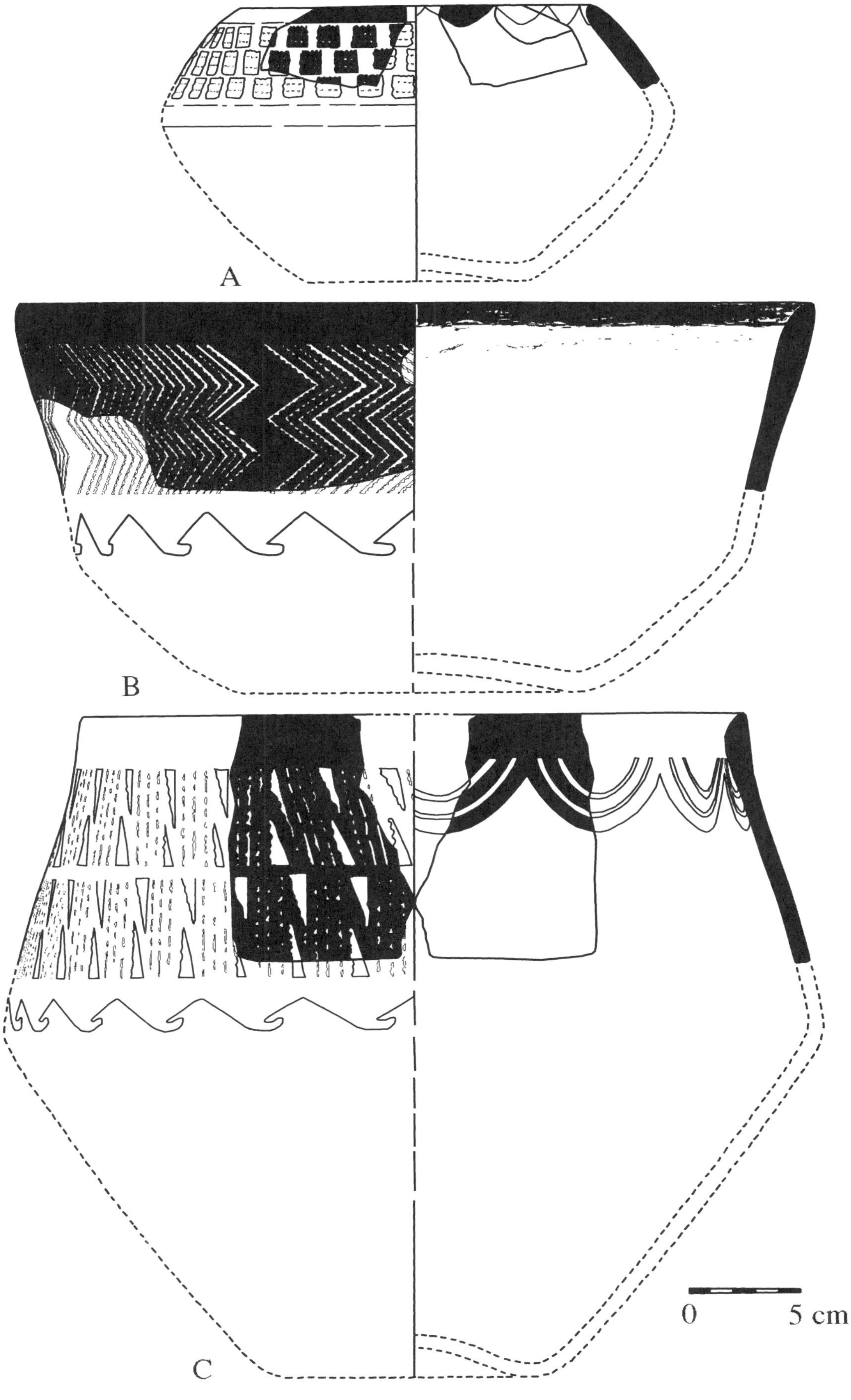


Figure 73. Archaic Susiana 1 Painted-burnished Pottery Vessels

Figure 74. Archaic Susiana Plain Pottery Vessels

| | *Registration Number* | *Provenance* | *Elevation* | *Description* |
|---|---|---|---|---|
| A | IX-102 | S22:923 | 74.54 | Straw-tempered smoothed ware. Dense. Archaic Susiana 3 |
| B | 6542 | S22:609 | 78.07(?) | Straw-tempered coarse ware. Buff paste, red washed. Uneven surface |
| C | 6025 | P22:608 Middle | 80.20 | Buff ware. Straw and grit tempered. Smoothed. Probably buff slipped. Archaic/Early Susiana |
| D | 8155 | Q23:802 | 78.30 | Straw-tempered buff ware. Buff slipped. Crudely made, lop-sided. Archaic Susiana 3 |
| E | 6180 | P22:606 | 79.50 | Straw-tempered buff ware. Some grits. Warm buff slipped. Archaic Susiana 3 |
| F | VI-39 | P22:606 | 80.55 | Red ware, grading to warm buff. Grit and chaff tempered. Wet smoothed. Archaic/Early Susiana |

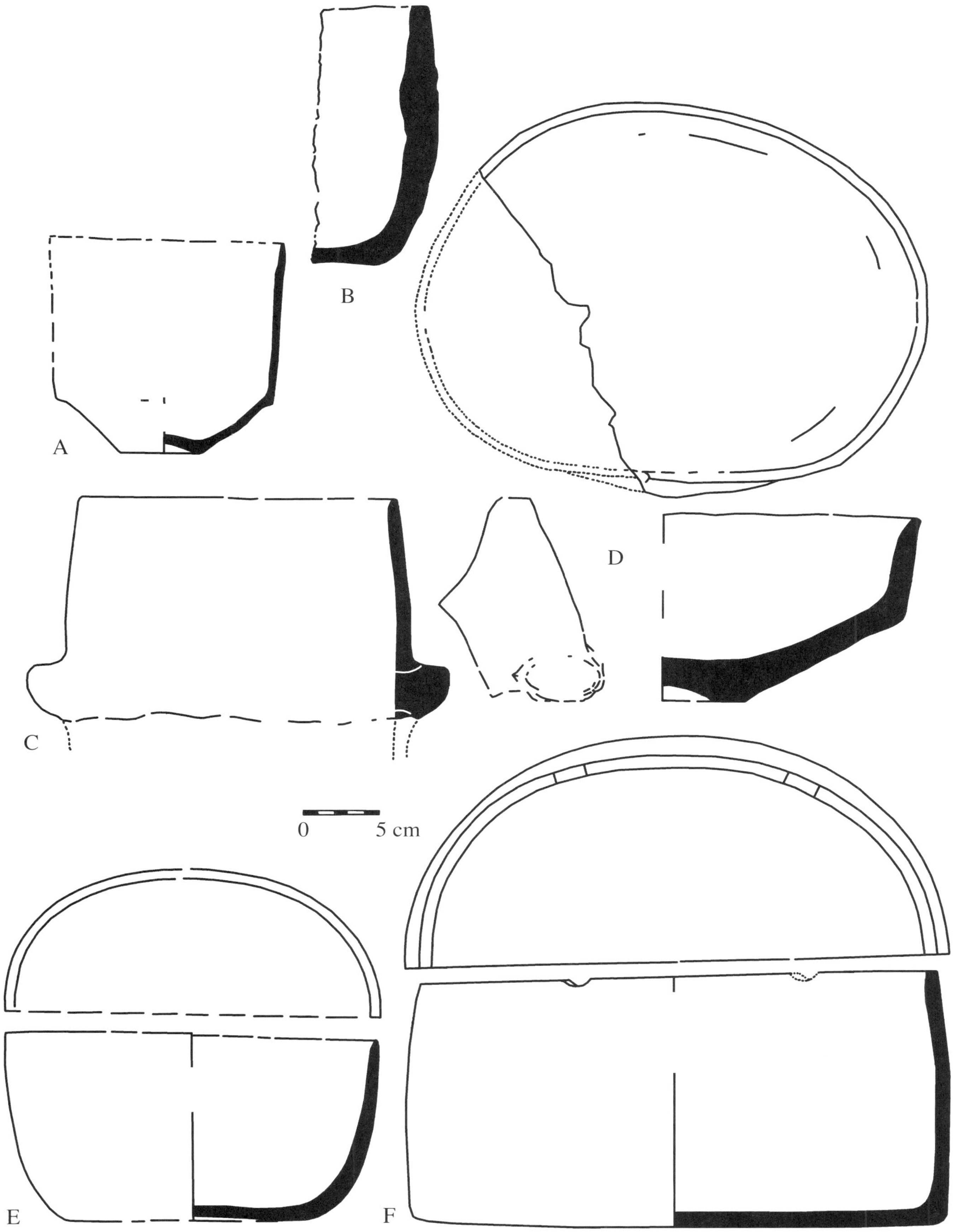


Figure 74. Archaic Susiana Plain Pottery Vessels

Figure 75. Archaic Susiana Plain Pottery Vessels

| | *Registration Number* | *Provenance* | *Elevation* | *Description* |
|---|---|---|---|---|
| A | 9107 | S22:909 | 74.57 | Buff ware. Grit and straw tempered. Coarse. Interior covered with bitumen. Archaic Susiana 2 |
| B | 8358 | S22:823 | 74.98 | Buff ware. Grit and straw tempered. Smoothed. Archaic Susiana 2 |
| C | 9225 | S22:914 | 73.70 | Straw-tempered smoothed ware. Mottled on the exterior. Archaic Susiana 2 |
| D | VI-25 | Q22:602 | 79.50 | Straw-tempered smoothed ware. Gray core, buff surface with pinkish spots. Traces of red wash on the exterior. Archaic Susiana 3 |
| E | 7178 | S22:703 | 74.86 | Straw-tempered smoothed ware. Probably buff slipped. Archaic Susiana 3 |
| F | 11068 | S22:904 | 74.72 | Straw-tempered smoothed ware. Gray core, pinkish buff exterior, mottled interior. Archaic Susiana 3 |
| G | VII-25 | Q22:708 | 79.40 | Straw-tempered smoothed ware. Gray core with reddish brown layers on exterior and interior surfaces. Made in two layers. Archaic Susiana 3 |
| H | 8292 | S22:831 North | 75.02 | Straw-tempered smoothed ware. Buff slipped, rough interior. Archaic Susiana 3 |
| I | N/A | S22:1101 | 78.95 | Straw-tempered smoothed ware. Gray core, buff slipped. Archaic Susiana 3 |
| J | 8440 | S22:823 | 75.30 | Straw-tempered ware. Light gray core grading to warm buff toward surface. Red wash exterior. Archaic Susiana 3 |
| K | 8249 | Q24:802 | 77.40 | Straw-tempered ware. Some grits included. Light gray core, pinkish buff surface. Archaic Susiana 3 |
| L | 11064 | S22:1103 | 73.20 | Straw-tempered smoothed ware. Light gray core. Mottled light orange surface. Archaic Susiana 3 |
| M | 11142 | S22:1108 | 72.68 | Dense sandy ware. Some chaff. Light gray core. Buff surface covered with red wash. Archaic Susiana 3 |
| N | 11179 | S22:1107 | 72.20 | Straw-tempered smoothed ware. Light gray core. Mottled light orange surface. Archaic Susiana 3 |
| O | 11006 | S22:1102 | 73.40 | Straw-tempered smoothed ware. Light gray core. Mottled light orange surface. Archaic Susiana 3 |
| P | 8660 | Q23:802 | 78.30 | Straw-tempered smoothed ware. Gray core grading to buff toward surface. Mottled gray, orange exterior. Archaic Susiana 3 |
| Q | 6239 | S22:601 | 73.21 | Straw-tempered smoothed ware. Gray core grading to buff toward surface. Mottled gray, orange exterior. Archaic Susiana 3 |
| R | 11186 | S22:1103 | 72.89 | Straw-tempered smoothed ware. Gray core grading to buff toward surface. Mottled gray, orange exterior. Archaic Susiana 2(?) |
| S | 11180 | S22:1103 | 72.74 | Straw-tempered smoothed ware. Gray core grading to buff toward surface. Mottled gray, orange exterior. Archaic Susiana 3 |
| T | 7091 | S22:703 | 75.25 | Straw-tempered smoothed ware. Gray core grading to buff toward surface. Red wash on exterior. Archaic Susiana 3 |
| U | 6439 | S22:601 | 73.46 | Coarse buff ware. Gray core abruptly changing to buff toward surface. Pinkish buff slipped. Smoothed. Archaic Susiana 3 |
| V | 6240 | S22:601 | 73.63 | Straw-tempered smoothed ware. Gray core grading to buff toward surface. Mottled gray, orange exterior. Archaic Susiana 3 |

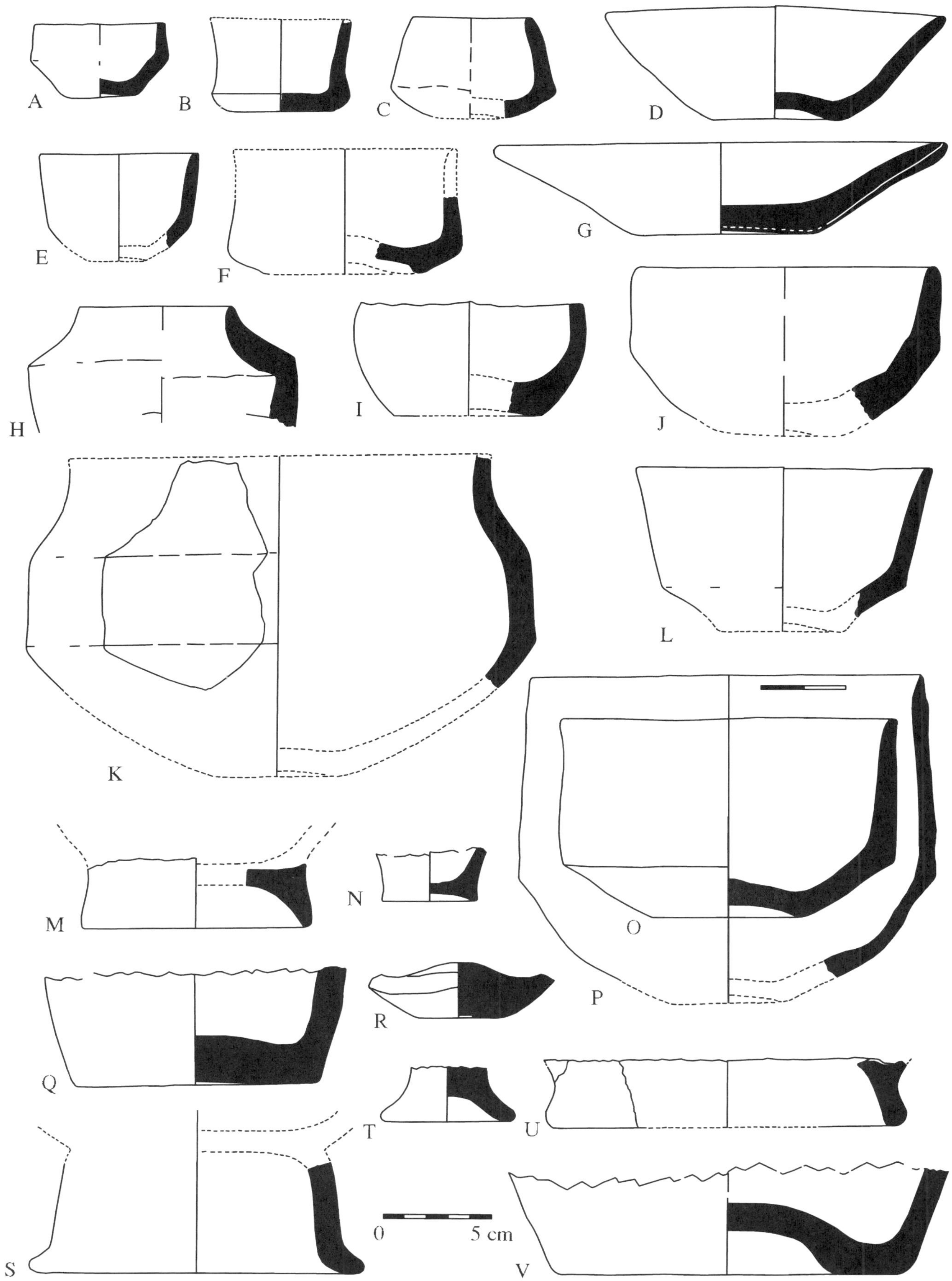


Figure 75. Archaic Susiana Plain Pottery Vessels

Figure 76. Seals and Sealings

| | *Registration Number* | *Provenance* | *Elevation* | *Description* |
|---|---|---|---|---|
| A | VIII-14 | High Mound | Surface | Stone stamp seal with perforated handle. Late Susiana(?) |
| B | 9906 | N/A | N/A | Baked-clay stamp seal. Drill hole in center. See plate 22:C. Late Susiana(?) |
| C | VIII-41 | High Mound | Surface | Baked-clay stamp seal. Incised design. Late Susiana(?) |
| D | VII-67 | R17:705 | 83.77 | White stone cylinder seal. Protoliterate |
| E | 9090 | R18:903 | 81.05 | Black stone stamp seal. Late Susiana(?) |
| F | II-202 | Tr. VI | N/A | Seal impression of a "lamb" on a clay ball. Protoliterate |
| G | II-241 | Tr. V | 1.50 B.S. | Impression of a female with butter-churning vessel on a jar sealing. Protoliterate |
| H | N/A | East Area | N/A | Seal impression on a bale sealing. Protoliterate |
| I | III-831 | Q18:314 | Sifting | Seal impression on a bale (flat) sealing. Protoliterate |
| J | II-213 | Tr. V | 1.20 B.S. | Seal impression of a female on a door sealing. Protoliterate |
| K | 9903 | R16:910 | 83.46 | Clay ball fragment with the impression of two rows of sacks of grain(?). Protoliterate |
| L | 7390b | R17:701 | 83.85 | Fragment of a bale sealing with a much eroded impression. Protoliterate |
| M | 9898 | R16:901 | 84.21 | Clay ball fragment with an impression of birds (chicken?). Protoliterate |
| N | 9873 | P17:902 | 81.15 | Bulla with impression of men working. See plate 24:D for photograph. Protoliterate |
| O | III-804 | R18:305 | 1.75 B.S. | Jar sealing with a much eroded impression probably of animals. Protoliterate |
| P | 7390a | R17:713 | 82.64 | Jar sealing with a much eroded impression. Protoliterate |
| Q | 9899 | R16:910 | 83.59 | Flat sealing with an impression of a building facade? Protoliterate |
| R | 9900 | R16:910 | 83.59 | Clay ball fragment with an impression of superimposed animals. Protoliterate |
| S | 7392 | G27:704 | N/A | Jar sealing fragment with an impression of hindquarters of a feline(?). Protoliterate |
| T | 9901 | R16:909 | 84.21 | Jar sealing fragment with an impression of a procession. Protoliterate |
| U | VII-2 | High Mound | Surface | Door sealing fragment with an impression of a stamp seal. Late Susiana(?) |
| V | 9874 | R18:908 | 80.91 | Door sealing fragment with a much eroded seal impression. Protoliterate |
| W | N/A | S20:608 East | 78.73 | Bale sealing fragment with an impression of top of "staff." Protoliterate |
| X | 8664 | R17:803 | 83.28 | Bottle stopper/sealing with the impression of cloth. Seal design completely eroded. Protoliterate |
| Y | 6836 | S20:601 | 0.40 B.S. | Door sealing with stamp seal impressions. Late Susiana(?) |
| Z | 9902 | R18:904 | 82.05 | Jar sealing fragment with an impression of a human, much eroded. Protoliterate |
| AA | 7387 | R17:714 | 82.65 | Clay ball with two different seal impressions of a procession and herding. See plate 24:F for photograph. Protoliterate |
| BB | 7389 | R17:704 West | 83.49 | Fragment of a bale sealing with stamp seal impression. See plate 23:B for photograph. Protoliterate |
| CC | 9904 | S18:902 | 81.14 | Sealing with four impressions of a decorated cylindrical object (cylinder seal?) tapering slightly at each end. For design, see FF. Highly unusual. See plate 22:J for photograph. Protoliterate |
| DD | 7388 | R17:714 | 82.65 | Clay ball with an impression of a battle scene. Protoliterate |
| EE | VI-100 | S22:601 | 74.38 | Clay tablet with impressed patterns of stippled triangles and bands. See plate 25:A for photograph. Probably Archaic Susiana |
| FF | 9905 | S18:902 | 81.14 | Sealing(?) with four impressions. See plate 22:K for photograph. Protoliterate |

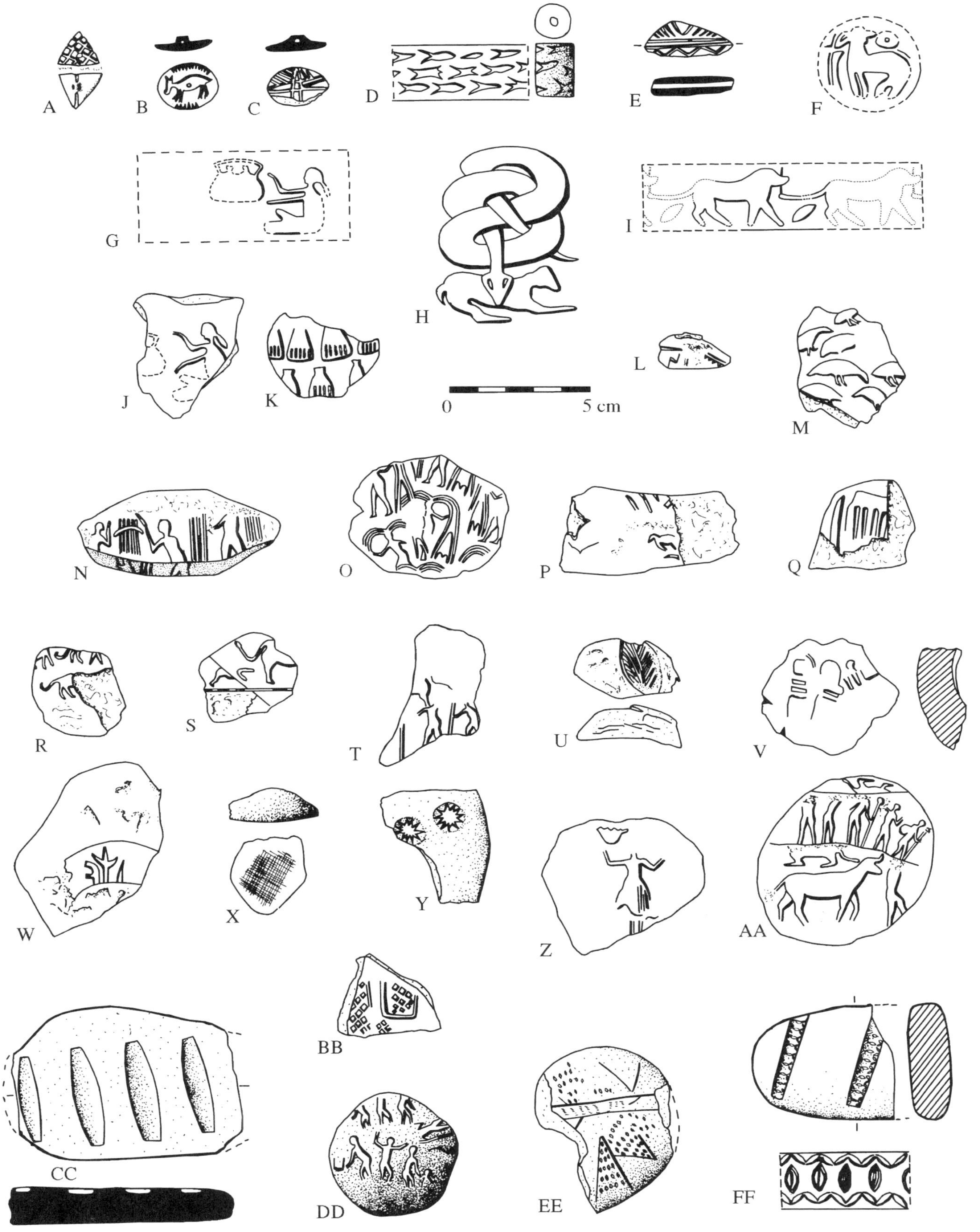


Figure 76. Seals and Sealings

Figure 77. Clay and Stone Tokens and Studs

| | *Registration Number* | *Provenance* | *Elevation* | *Description* |
|---|---|---|---|---|
| A | 9494 | S22:923 | 74.52 | Baked-clay token. No visible inclusions. Pinkish buff surface. Archaic Susiana |
| B | VIII-62 | S22:824 | 74.98 | Stone token. Polished white stone. Archaic Susiana |
| C | 9028 | S22:902 | 77.51 | Baked-clay token. No visible inclusions. Early Susiana |
| D | VII-6 | G27:702 | 82.43 | Baked-clay token. No visible inclusions. Orange buff surface. Smoothed. See plate 25:C for photograph. Early Susiana |
| E | VII-11 | Q22:704 | 79.34 | Stone token. Marble. Early Susiana |
| F | VII-7 | R23:702 | 77.82 | Baked-clay token or "thorn"-shaped figurine. Buff brown surface. See plate 25:C for photograph. Early Susiana(?) |
| G | 9495 | R16:903 | 83.26 | Stone token or pendant. White stone, perforated. Protoliterate |
| H | VIII-61 | Q23:821 | 78.59 | Stone token. Polished white stone. Early Susiana |
| I | VII-58 | S22:714 | 75.76 | Baked-clay token or figurine. No visible inclusions. Archaic Susiana |
| J | 7398 | G29:701 South | 77.47 | Bone token. Early Susiana(?) |
| K | VII-90 | Q23:713 | 76.98 | Baked-clay token(?). No visible inclusions. Dark brown paint. See plate 25:G for photograph. Early Susiana |
| L | VII-75 | R17:716 | 84.30 | Clay token. No visible inclusions. Buff. Protoliterate |
| M | VII-77 | R17:710 | 82.89 | Clay token. Buff, no visible inclusions. Protoliterate |
| N | VII-69 | R17:705 | 83.77 | Stone token or pendant. White speckled black stone. Perforated. Protoliterate |
| O | 9061 | S22:909 Middle | N/A | Unbaked clay token. Perforated. Archaic Susiana |
| P | 9064 | R18:913 | 80.23 | Clay token. No visible inclusions. Finger marks on both sides. Protoliterate |
| Q | 9110 | S18:918 | 81.12 | Clay token. No visible inclusions. Finger marks on both sides. Protoliterate |
| R | 9175 | East Area | Surface | Clay token. No visible inclusions. Finger marks on both sides. Protoliterate |
| S | VII-37 | Q22:703 | 79.28 | Clay token. Plano-convex. Buff ware with no visible inclusions. Excised groove on one side, perforated. Early Susiana(?) |

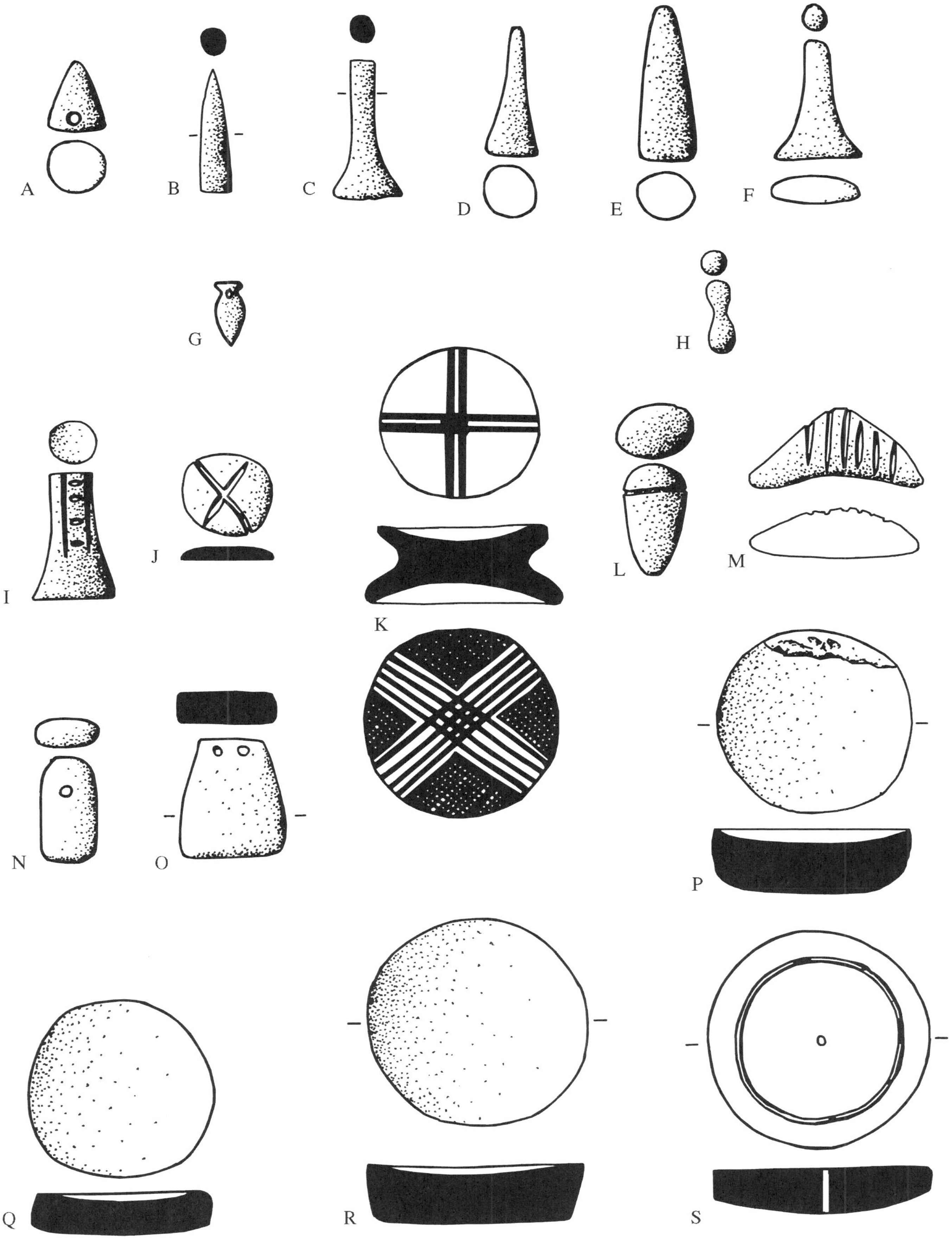


Figure 77. Clay and Stone Tokens and Studs. Scale 1:1

Figure 78. Clay Human Figurines

| | *Registration Number* | *Provenance* | *Elevation* | *Description* |
|---|---|---|---|---|
| A | VIII-84 | S22:823 North | 75.74 | Mid-section of a female figurine. Baked clay. Buff color, sand tempered. Smoothed. Black paint. Pubic area shown with excised lines. For possible reconstruction, see frontipiece; see plate 28:D for photograph. Early Susiana |
| B | V-100 | Q23:504 | 79.27 | Baked-clay figurine. Body broken. Yellowish buff clay, no visible inclusions. Early Susiana |
| C | VIII-85 | S22:826 | 74.66 | Baked-clay head of a human figurine. Buff clay, no visible inclusions. Dark paint. The eyes and the nose are molded. The head may have originally been elongated (representing elongated skull seen in actual skeletal evidence from Chogha Mish; see *Chogha Mish* I, pl. 69), but the upper part is broken. If the whole body was originally attached to the head, the height of the figurine may have reached over 30 cm. Black paint. Pubic area shown with excised lines. For possible reconstruction, see frontipiece; see plate 27:A for photograph. Early Susiana |
| D | 9039 | S22:913 | 74.54 | Head and torso of a highly stylized human figurine. Baked clay, buff ware, no visible inclusions. Black paint. See plate 28:K for photograph. Archaic Susiana 3 |
| E | 8695 | S22:808 North | 74.99 | Torso of a baked-clay female figurine. Reddish buff ware, no visible inclusions. Black paint. Unlike the majority of the Early Susiana figurines, this example is made in a naturalistic style. The painted strokes on the breasts may represent tattoos. See plate 28:A for photograph. Early Susiana |
| F | VI-3 | S22:601 | 74.93 | Baked-clay waist and lower body of a female figurine. Yellowish buff ware. Grit tempered. Black paint. See plate 28:J for photograph. Early Susiana |
| G | 8043 | S22:823 North | 75.74 | Baked-clay waist and lower body of a female figurine. Buff ware. Grit and sand tempered. Probably slipped. Black paint. See plate 28:C for photograph. Early Susiana |
| H | 8174 | S22:827 | 74.30 | Baked-clay waist and body of a female figurine. Buff ware, grit tempered. Black paint. See plate 28:B for photograph. Archaic/Early Susiana |

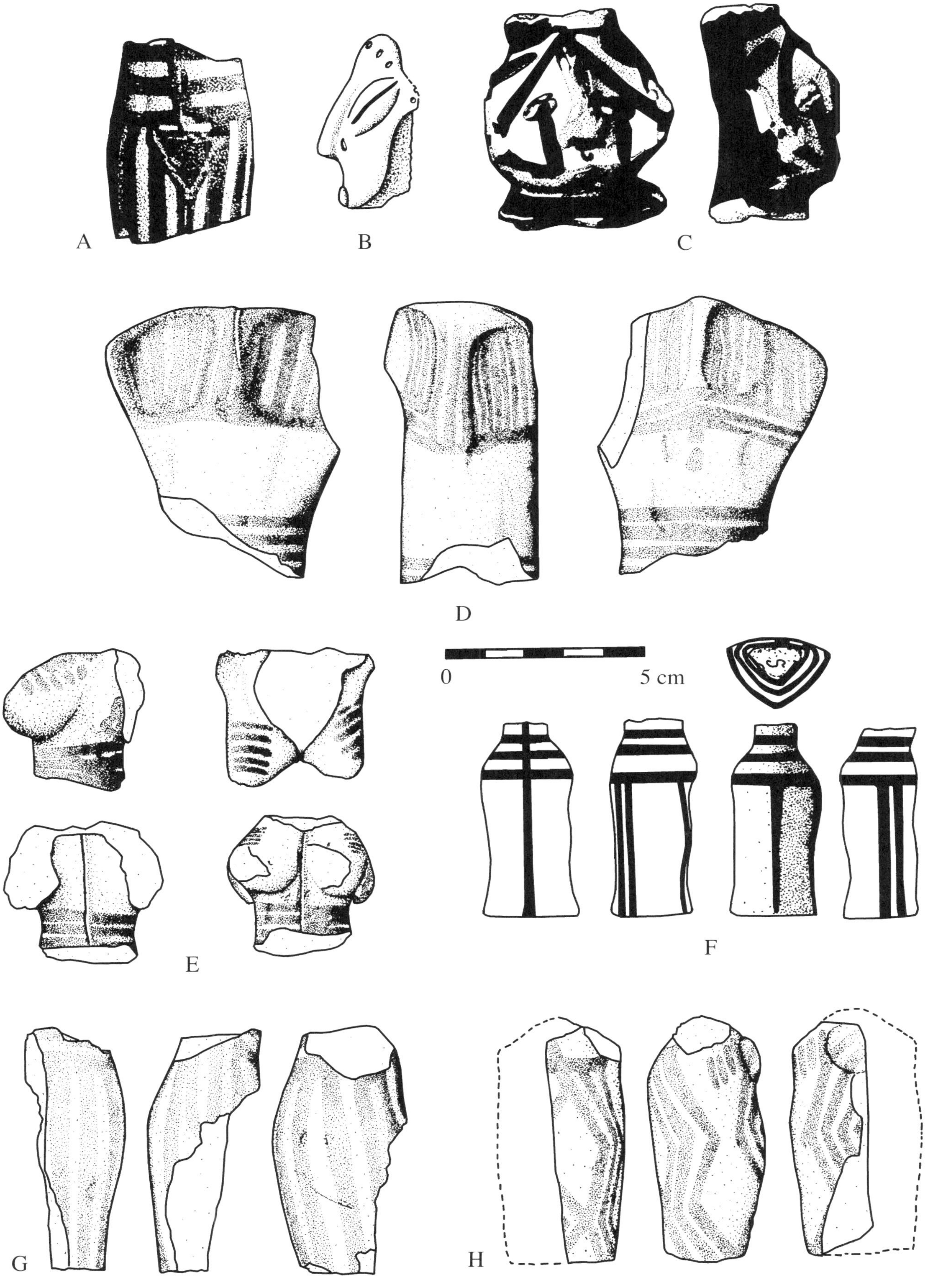


Figure 78. Clay Human Figurines

Figure 79. Clay Human Figurines

| | Registration Number | Provenance | Elevation | Description |
|---|---|---|---|---|
| A | 9127 | S22:916 | 77.19 | Baked-clay female figurine. Impressed dots perhaps represent tattoos on the breasts and back. Archaic Susiana 3 |
| B | VIII-1 | S22:808 | 75.77 | Baked-clay figurine of a seated female. The head is comparatively low. The head is triangular and a deep incision splits it in two equal parts. The whole face consists of three blobs of clay presumably representing the nose and cheeks. The breasts are highly exaggerated. See plate 27:F for photograph. Early Susiana |
| C | 9063 | S22:913 | 74.21 | Unbaked clay figurine, presumably of a female. The preserved buttocks are naturalistically rendered. Early Susiana |
| D | VIII-74 | S22:831 North | 75.02 | Baked-clay figurine of a female. Buff clay, sand tempered. Creamy buff slipped. The lower body is covered with a long skirt, the design of which is indicated by incision marks. Early Susiana |
| E | N/A | Tr. XXV | N/A | Baked-clay human female figurine. Buff ware, no visible inclusions. Probably Archaic Susiana 3 |
| F | 9040 | S22:912 East | 74.46 | Baked-clay human figurine. Buff ware, no visible inclusions. Upper part of the body is missing. The cloth on the lower part is decorated with four sunken panels and incisions. Traces of red paint on the raised parts of the lower body. See plate 28:F for photograph. Archaic Susiana 3 |
| G | VII-60 | R17:704 | 83.25 | Baked-clay figurine. Buff clay with no visible inclusions. Head and arms are missing. Protoliterate |
| H | N/A | S22:1103 | 74.20 | Baked-clay human figurine. Buff, no visible inclusions. Highly abstract figurine of a female. Archaic Susiana 3 |
| I | 9126 | S22:916 | 76.19 | Unbaked-clay chessman figurine. Impressed dots and the diagonally painted band probably represent some elements of clothing. Archaic/Early Susiana |
| J | 9008 | S22:909 South | 75.13 | Unbaked-clay chessman figurine. Impressed decoration on the lower body. See plate 28:I for photograph. Archaic Susiana 2 |
| K | 8471 | S22:831 | 75.41 | Unbaked-clay chessman figurine. Circular impressions decorate the body. Archaic Susiana 2 |
| L | N/A | Gully Cut | N/A | Archaic Susiana/Early Susiana |
| M | VII-59 | R23:706 | 76.64 | Unbaked-clay chessman figurine. Upper part is missing; lower part decorated with impressed motifs indicating pubic area. Archaic Susiana 2 |
| N | 9060 | S22:910 South | 74.68 | Unbaked-clay chessman figurine. Side perforation. Archaic Susiana 3 |

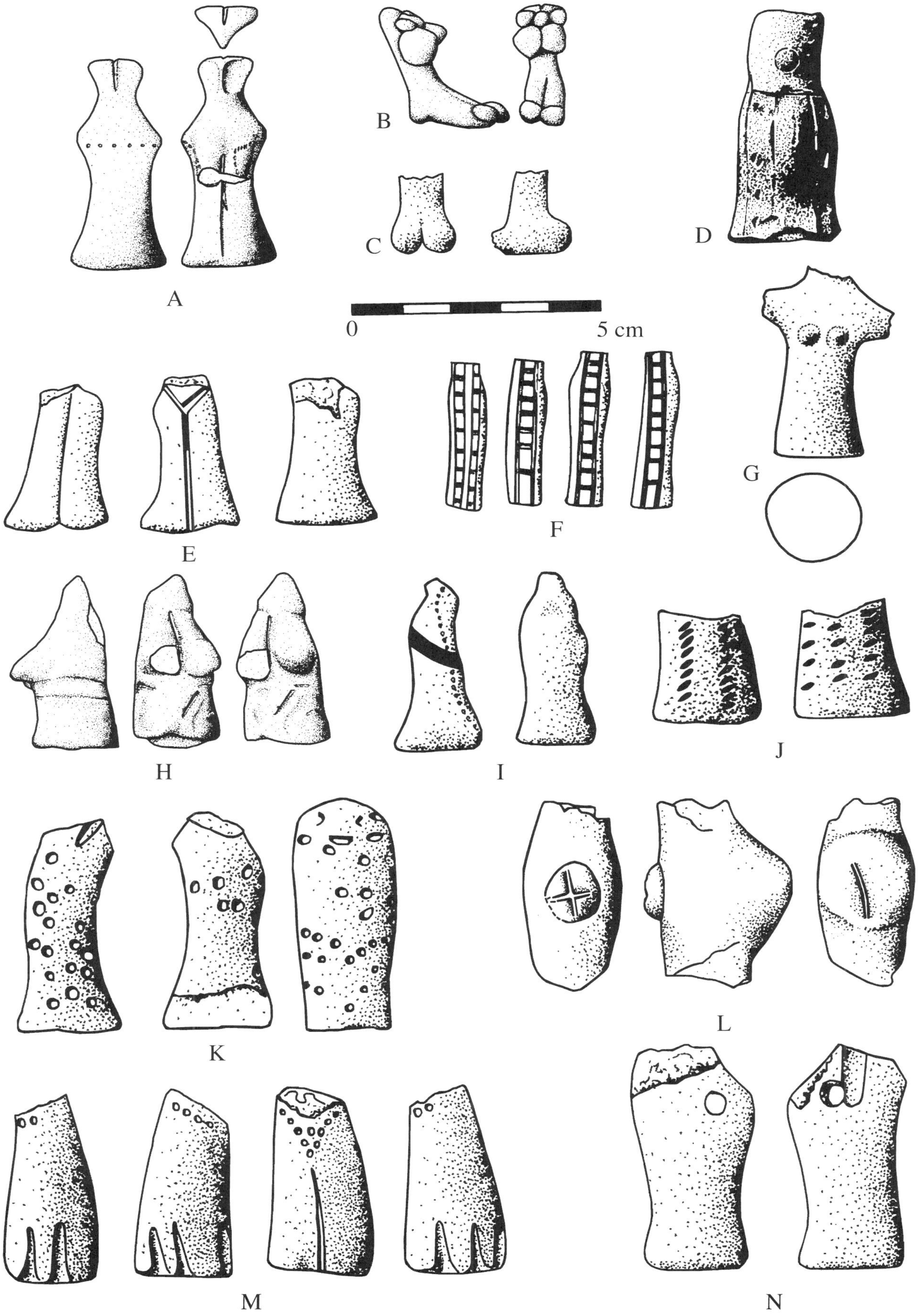


Figure 79. Clay Human Figurines

Figure 80. Clay and Stone Animal Figurines

| | *Registration Number* | *Provenance* | *Elevation* | *Description* |
|---|---|---|---|---|
| A | VIII-83 | R16:807 | 82.69 | Baked clay. Buff ware. No visible inclusions. Legs made separately. Faint traces of red paint. Protoliterate |
| B | VI-2 | P23:601 | B.S. | Baked-clay figurine of a bull or ram. Dense, sandy brownish buff clay. See plate 27:E for photograph. Middle Susiana |
| C | 9195 | P17:902 | 82.48 | Baked-clay figurine of a sheep(?). Red ware, no visible inclusions. Ears (or horns) are missing. Eyes are small lumps of clay added separately. Nostrils are indicated by two small depressions. Possibly plastic decoration of a vessel. Protoliterate context |
| D | VII-38 | G28:705 | 76.08 | Baked-clay figurine. Buff ware with no visible inclusions. Dark brown paint. Middle Susiana |
| E | 9093 | R18:904 | 81.78 | Baked clay. Buff ware. No visible inclusions. Dark paint. Middle Susiana |
| F | VIII-60 | S22:823 | 76.35 | Stone figurine of a boar. Light brown stone with white dots. Perforated rump suggests it may have been used as pendant. Archaic/Early Susiana |
| G | VI-1 | S20:601 | 0.20 B.S. | Baked-clay bull figurine/pendant. Buff ware, sand tempered, greenish black paint. Middle Susiana |
| H | 9128 | S22:916 | 77.19 | Baked-clay figurine of a dog(?). Buff ware mixed with some grits. Middle Susiana |
| I | 9561 | R18:903 | 81.38 | Baked-clay horn. Buff ware, no visible inclusions, buff slipped. Dark paint. Protoliterate context, but probably Middle or Late Susiana |
| J | 9253 | S22:912 East | 74.46 | Baked-clay horn. Buff ware, buff slipped. Black paint. Archaic Susiana/Early Susiana |
| K | 7185 | R23:710 West | 78.18 | Baked-clay animal figurine. Buff ware, grit tempered, black paint. Early Susiana |

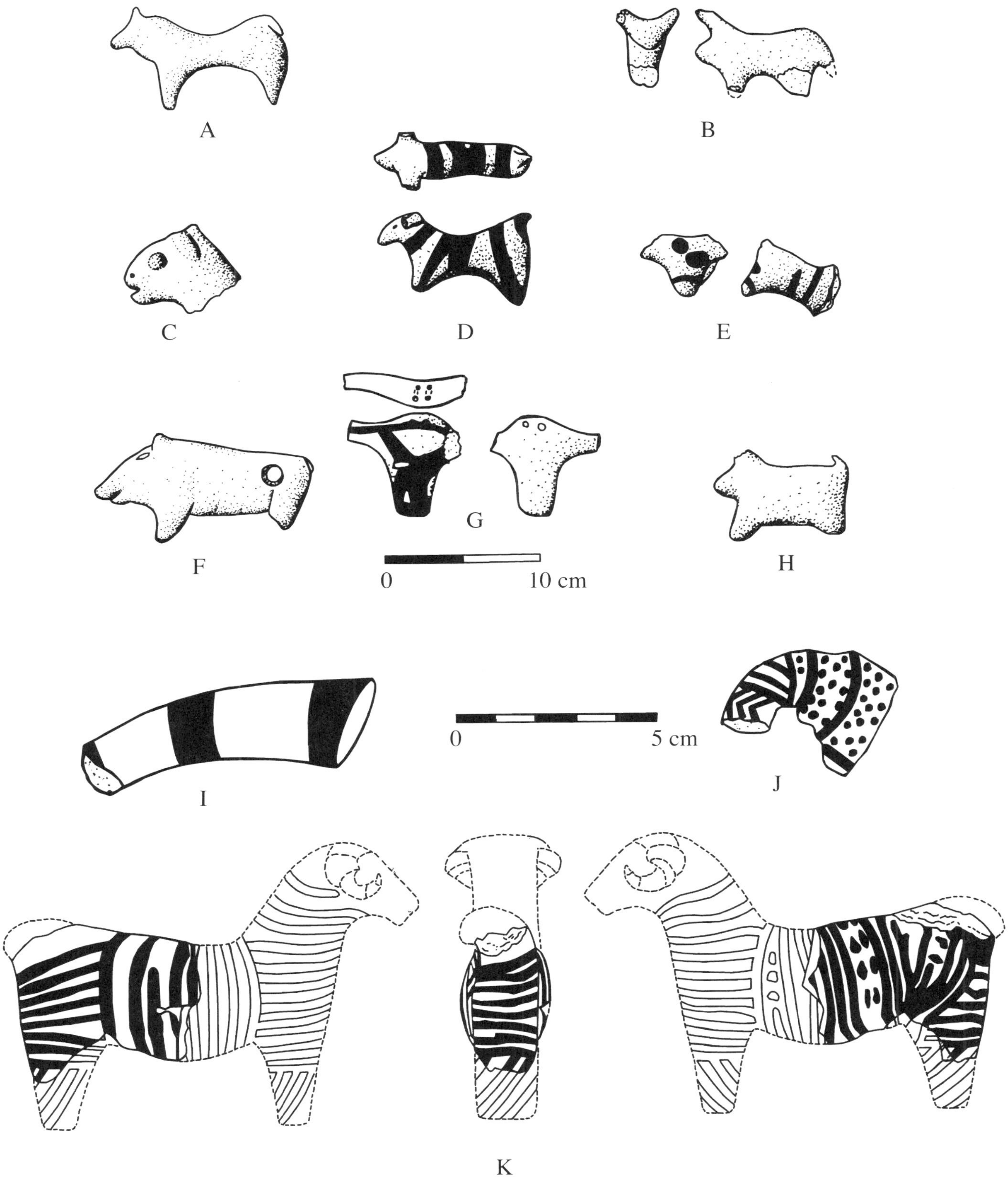


Figure 80. Clay and Stone Animal Figurines

Figure 81. Personal Ornaments

| | *Registration Number* | *Provenance* | *Elevation* | *Description* |
|---|---|---|---|---|
| A | VIII-42 | Q23:821 | 78.42 | White stone "plug" with two heads. Early Susiana |
| B | VIII-52 | S22:827 | 74.30 | White stone "plug." Archaic Susiana 3 |
| C | VIII-54 | S22:822 | 76.18 | White stone with dark veins. Early Susiana |
| D | VIII-67 | Q23:821 | 79.19 | Black-and-white stone "plug." Early Susiana |
| E | VIII-53 | Tr. XIII | Surface | Stone "plug." Yellowish white stone. Date(?) |
| F | VII-1 | Tr. XXXVI | N/A | White stone "plug" with dark vein used as the "eye" of the plug. See plate 25:C for photograph. Middle Susiana |
| G | VII-8 | R23:602 | 76.92 | Black stone "plug." See plate 25:C for photograph. Middle Susiana |
| H | VII-9 | G29:701 | 78.03 | Baked-clay "plug." No visible inclusions. See plate 25:C for photograph. Middle Susiana |
| I | VII-68 | R17:711 | 83.49 | Gray black stone pendant in the shape of a bird. Perforated. Protoliterate |
| J | VI-33 | P22:605 | 80.95 | Bitumen bracelet. See plate 25:E for photograph. Early Susiana |
| K | VI-32 | P22:605 | 80.95 | Bitumen bracelet. See plate 25:D for photograph. Early Susiana |
| L | 9468 | R18:921 | 81.13 | Yellowish white stone bead. Protoliterate |
| M | 9162 | Gully Cut | Dump | White stone bead |
| N | 9464 | S18:916 | 81.86 | Turquoise bead. Protoliterate |
| O | 9467 | R18:921 | 81.13 | Turquoise bead. Protoliterate |
| P | 9194 | S18:901 | 83.87 | Barrel-shaped baked-clay bead. Protoliterate |
| Q | VII-32 | S22:701 | 76.68 | Mother-of-pearl pendant. Early Susiana |
| R | VIII-63 | S22:823 | 74.79 | Mother-of-pearl pendant. Archaic Susiana |
| S | VII-34 | Q22:702 | 79.23 | Mother-of-pearl disc. Early Susiana |

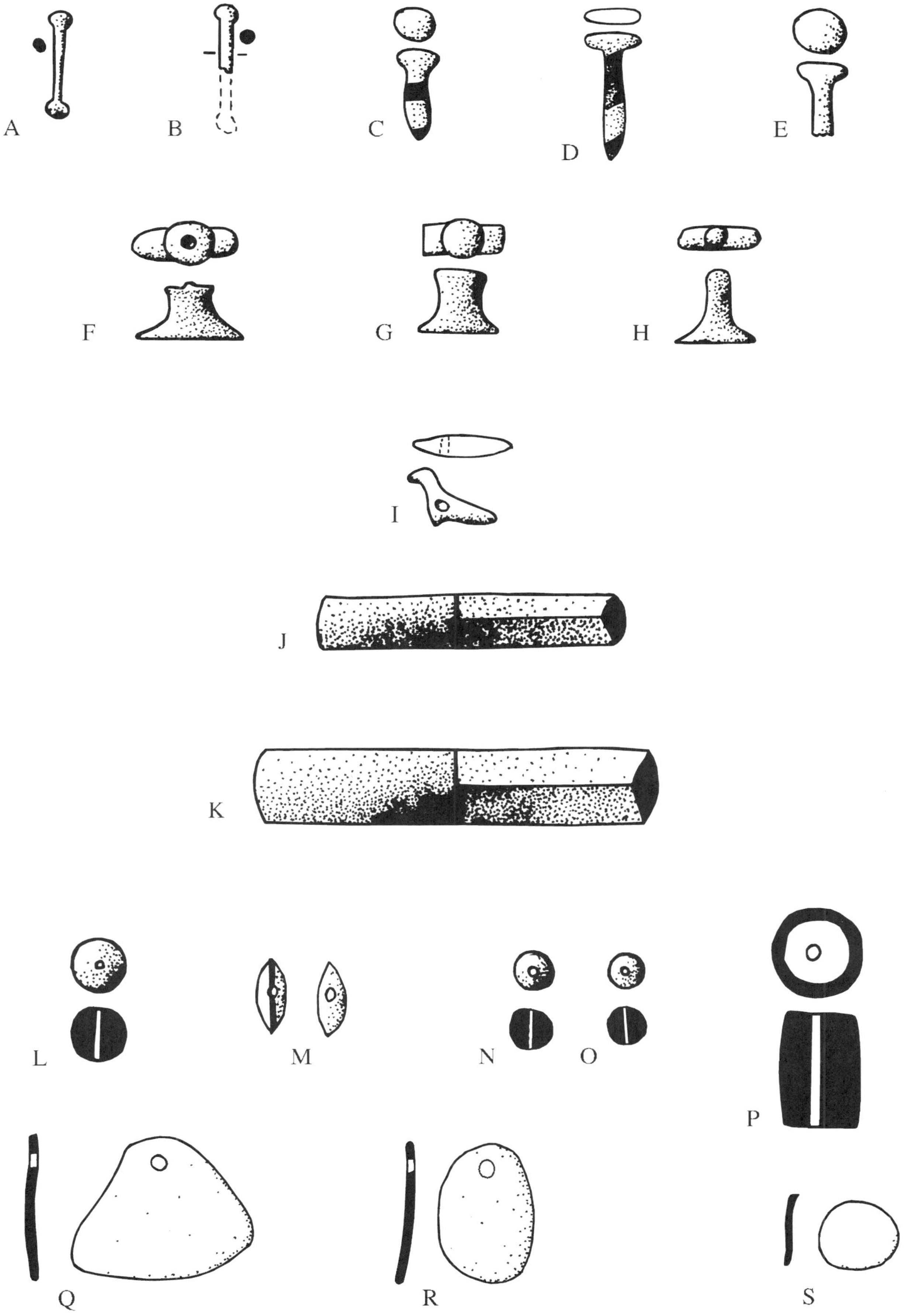


Figure 81. Personal Ornaments. Scale 1:1

Figure 82. Clay Objects and Tools

| | *Registration Number* | *Provenance* | *Elevation* | *Description* |
|---|---|---|---|---|
| A | 6300 | P22:624 | 80.85 | Lid(?) fragment. Buff ware. Dense sandy. Brown paint. Early Middle Susiana |
| B | 9033 | S22:908 | 76.90 | Stand/cup(?) fragment. Red ware. Grit and sand tempered. Protoliterate pit. See D and H |
| C | 9021 | Q17:903 West | 83.64 | Baked-clay spool. Protoliterate |
| D | 9215 | R16:907 | 83.13 | Red ware. Grit and sand tempered. Protoliterate |
| E | X-6 | Q17:1002 North | 83.58 | Baked-clay sinker/loom weight. Buff ware. Sand and grit tempered. Protoliterate |
| F | 9217 | Q17:907 Northeast | 83.60 | Baked-clay object. Buff ware. Sand tempered. Smoothed. Protoliterate |
| G | VII-22 | G28:701 | 78.87 | Baked-clay sinker/loom weight. Buff ware with sand. Protoliterate |
| H | 9215 | R16:905 | 83.13 | Red ware. Sand and grit tempered. Protoliterate |
| I | 7212 | R17:701 | 84.12 | Buff ware. Dense. Buff slipped. Red paint. Protoliterate |
| J | 7211 | R17:701 | 84.12 | Buff ware. Dense. Buff slipped. Red paint. Protoliterate |
| K | VIII-82 | R17:808 | 83.68 | Buff ware. Dense. Buff slipped. Polished. Red paint. Protoliterate |
| L | IX-59 | S22:904 | 76.22 | Strainer. Buff ware. Sand tempered. Smoothed. Protoliterate |
| M | VIII-92 | R17:704 | 82.50 | Left-handed sickle. Yellowish green buff. Sand and grit tempered. Protoliterate |
| N | VII-94 | R17:714 | 82.64 | Left-handed sickle. Yellowish green buff. Sand and grit tempered. Protoliterate |

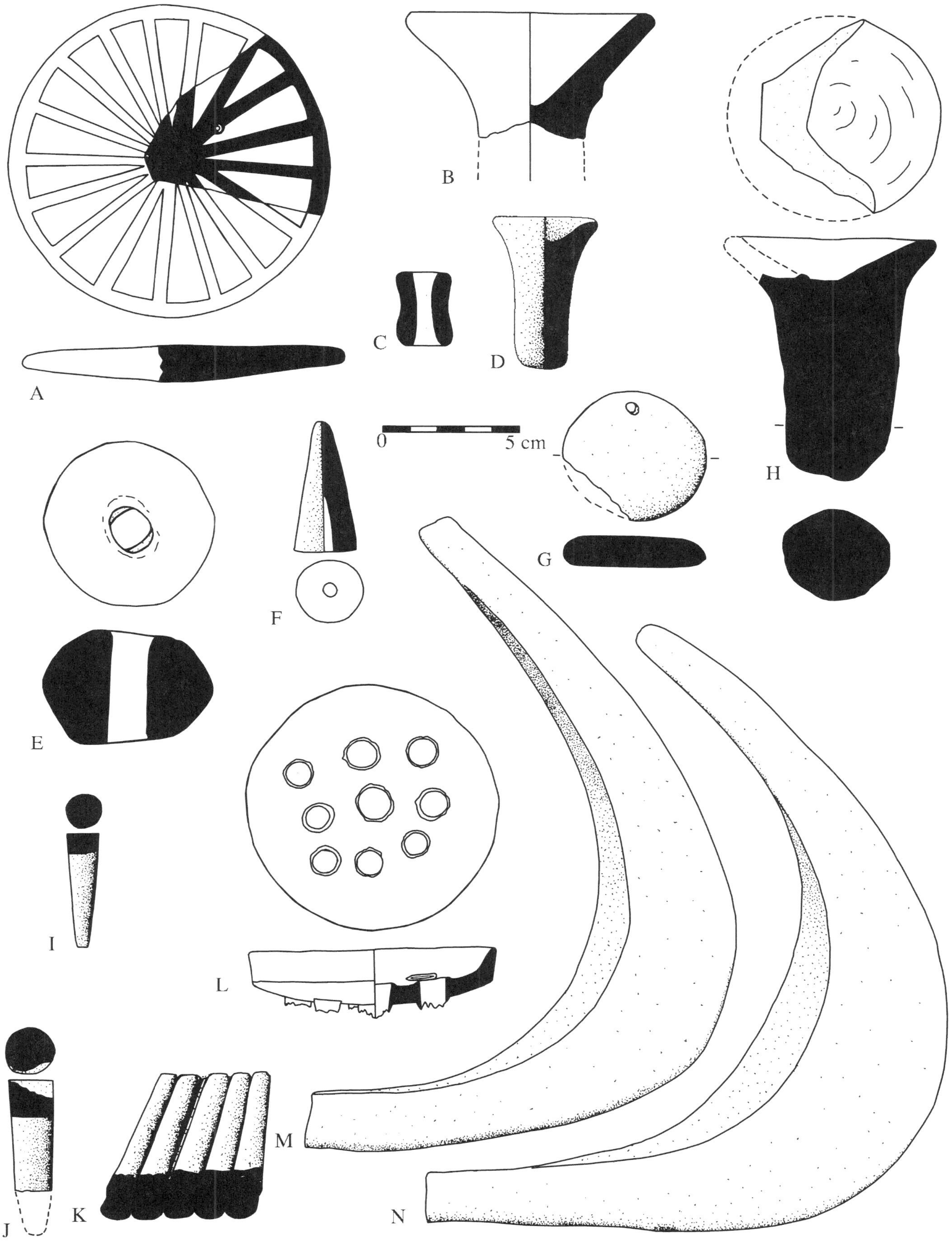


Figure 82. Clay Objects and Tools

Figure 83. Spindle Whorls

| | *Registration Number* | *Provenance* | *Elevation* | *Description* |
|---|---|---|---|---|
| A | 9135 | R18:921 | 81.13 | Buff ware. Sand tempered with some grits. Buff slipped. Black paint. Late Middle Susiana |
| B | 8923 | S22:819 | B.S. | Buff ware. Sand tempered. Creamy buff slipped. Black paint. Late Middle Susiana |
| C | 9044 | R18:908 South | 81.13 | Buff ware. Grit and sand tempered. Creamy buff slipped. Black paint. Late Middle Susiana |
| D | 8589 | S22:819 | 76.71 | Buff ware. Over-fired greenish buff. Sand and grit tempered. Greenish brown paint. Early Middle Susiana |
| E | VIII-38 | S22:823 North | 75.81 | Buff ware. Grit and sand tempered. Dark paint. Early Susiana |
| F | VIII-39 | Q23:803 | 78.72 | Buff ware. Grit tempered. Buff slipped. Red paint. Early Susiana |
| G | VI-8 | P22:601 | 82.55 | Buff ware. Grit tempered. Gritty face. See plate 25:H for photograph. Middle Susiana context, but is Early Susiana |
| H | 9036 | R18:912 | 81.22 | Pale red ware. Sand tempered. Red paint. Late Middle Susiana |
| I | B II-33 | Chogha Bonut/ M10:208 | 77.81 | Buff ware. Over-fired greenish buff. Grit tempered. Olive brown paint. Middle Susiana |

Figure 83. Spindle Whorls. Scale 1:1

Figure 84. Metal Objects

| | *Registration Number* | *Provenance* | *Elevation* | *Description* |
|---|---|---|---|---|
| A | VII-5 | G27:701 | 82.32 | Copper pin/nail. Protoliterate |
| B | 9137 | R18:920 | 81.97 | Copper pin. Protoliterate |
| C | VIII-56 | S22:819 North | 76.06 | Copper pin. Pit. Old Elamite(?) |
| D | VIII-58 | S22:823 | 74.79 | Copper. Edge of 808 pit. Protoliterate |
| E | VIII-15 | East Area | N/A | Bronze arrowhead. Achaemenid |
| F | VII-66 | R17:705 | 82.92 | Copper pin. Protoliterate |
| G | VIII-55 | Q17:804 South | 82.85 | Copper pin/nail. Protoliterate |
| H | VII-88 | R17:914 | 83.39 | Copper/bronze pin. Protoliterate |

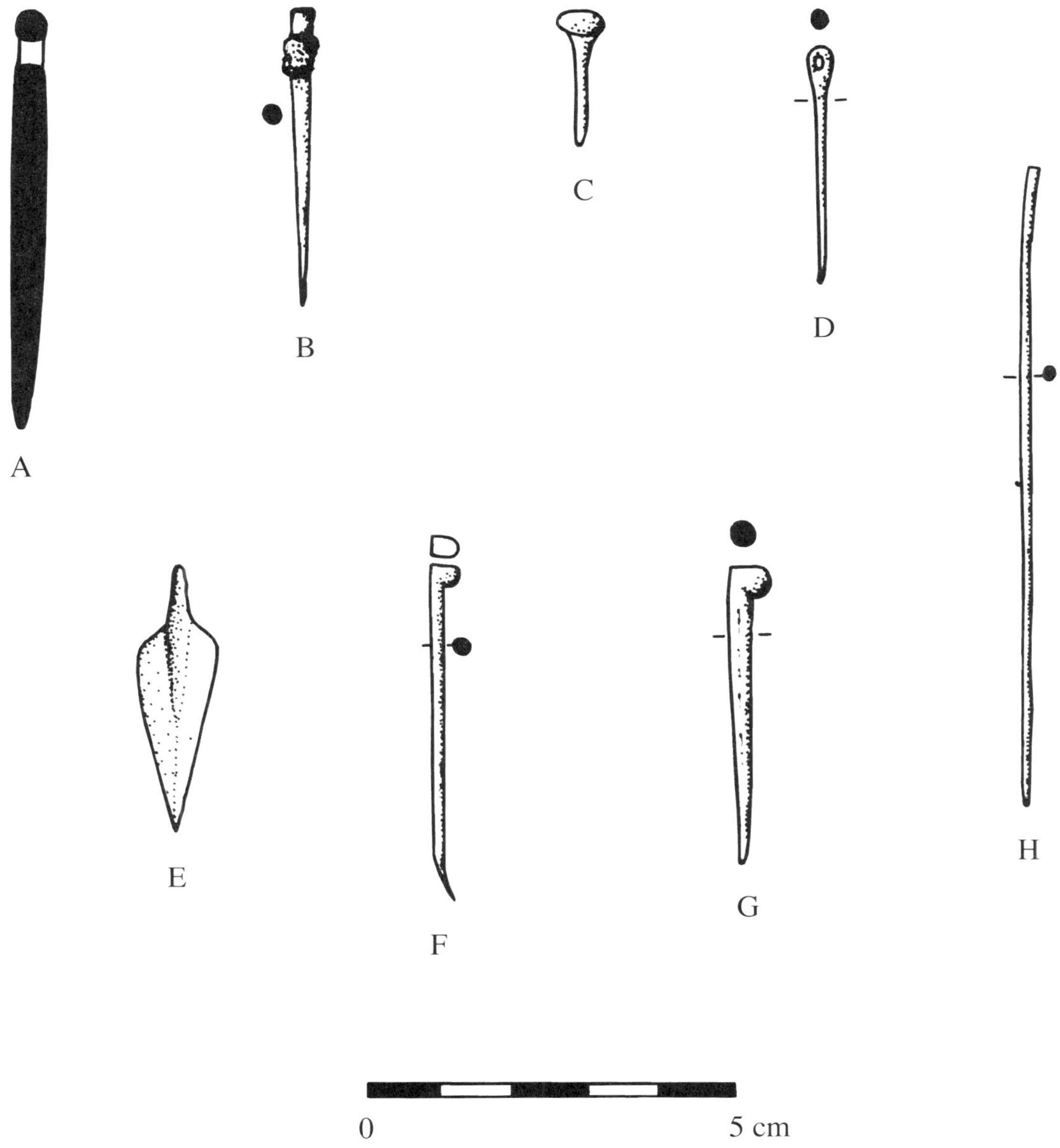


Figure 84. Metal Objects

Figure 85. Bone Objects

| | *Registration Number* | *Provenance* | *Elevation* | *Description* |
|---|---|---|---|---|
| A | VI-14 | P22:625 | 82.09 | Pin with stubby shaft. Middle Susiana |
| B | VI-13 | S20:609 | 77.05 | Pin or awl. Polished edges. See plate 25:B for photograph. Early Susiana |
| C | 9183 | S22:914 | 73.70 | Spatula fragment. Perforated handle. Archaic Susiana |
| D | VII-35 | Q23:709 | 79.99 | Awl. Polished with sheen. Early Susiana |
| E | 9454 | S22:926 | 77.09 | Awl. Smoothed but not highly polished. Tip broken. Middle Susiana |
| F | VIII-49 | S22:813 | 76.29 | Polished needle. Tip broken. Middle Susiana |
| G | 9080 | S22:902 | 76.83 | Bone tool. Some sheen on lower edge. Middle Susiana |
| H | VIII-57 | S22:823 | 75.94 | Awl with sheen on edges. Early Susiana |
| I | VIII-50 | S22:819 | 76.06 | Needle. Early Susiana |
| J | 9465 | S22:916 | 74.94 | Awl. Highly polished with sheen. Archaic Susiana |
| K | 9101 | S22:914 | 75.76 | Awl. Early Susiana |
| L | IV-24 | Tr. IX | 0.75 B.S. | Double-eyed needle. Archaic Susiana |
| M | 8468 | S22:823 | 76.35 | Awl. Smoothed and polished. Early Susiana |
| N | 9114 | R18:919 | 82.76 | Awl. Middle Susiana |
| O | 8465 | S22:823 North | 76.35 | Awl. Early Susiana |
| P | 8467 | S22:823 | 76.35 | Awl. Early Susiana |

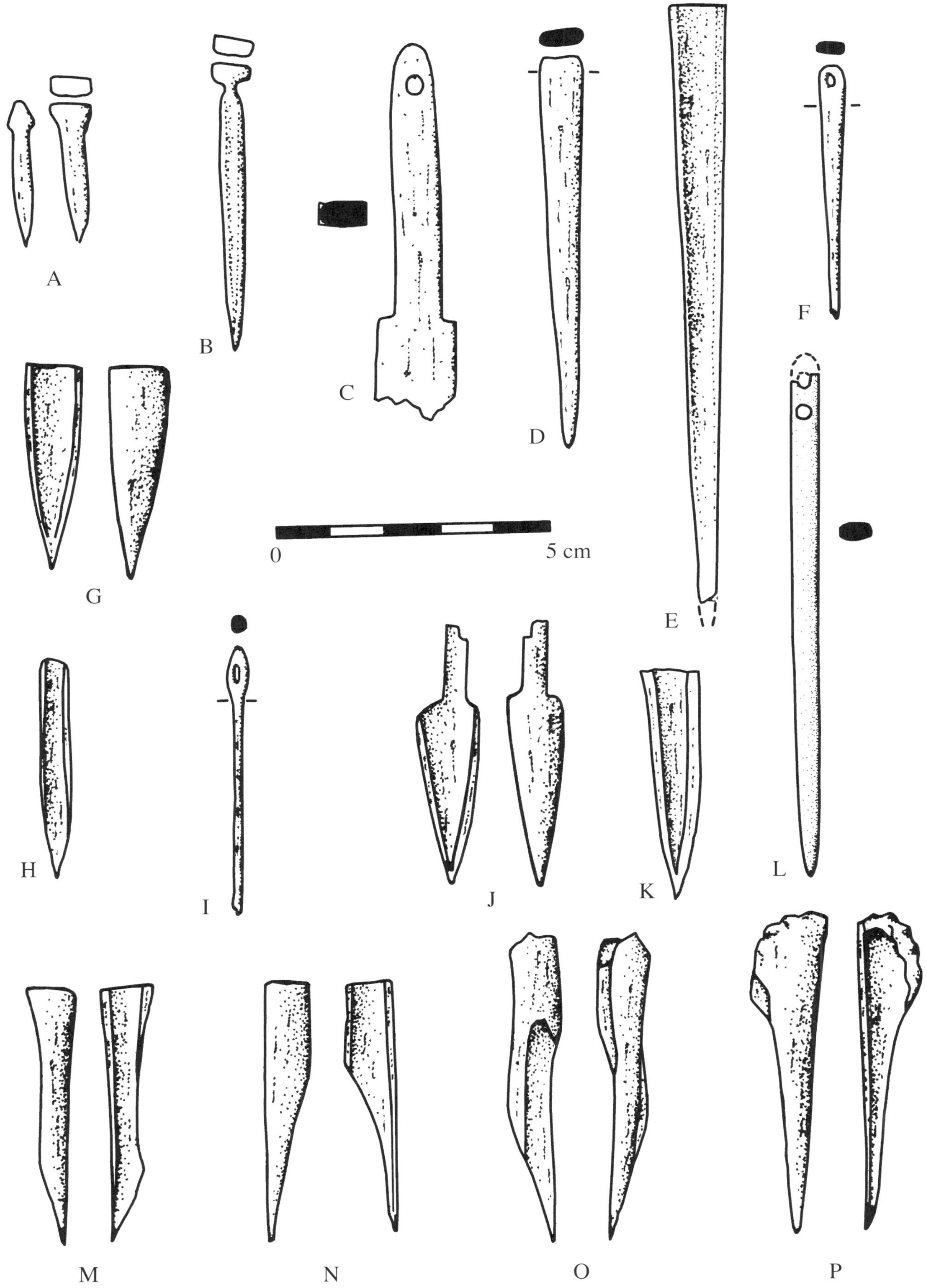


Figure 85. Bone Objects

Figure 86. Stone Vessels

| | *Registration Number* | *Provenance* | *Elevation* | *Description* |
|---|---|---|---|---|
| A | 9047 | S22:912 | 74.52 | White stone with horizontal gray veins in wavy lines alternating with pinkish veins and spots. Archaic Susiana 3 |
| B | N/A | R23:502 | 0.65 B.S. | Limestone. Early Susiana |
| C | N/A | R23:710 West | 78.18 | Bitumen vessel. Early Susiana |
| D | 7068 | R23:710 West | 78.18 | Bitumen vessel. Early Susiana |
| E | VIII-16 | Q22:804 South | 78.56 | Bowl of alabaster-like gypsum. Translucent white with a pinkish cast. Early Susiana |
| F | 7040 | G27:701 | 82.62 | Obsidian bowl fragment. Light gray. Archaic or Early Susiana |
| G | VII-84 | R17:704 | 82.90 | Black-and-white streaked stone. Smoothed. Protoliterate |
| H | N/A | Tr. XXXIII | 77.40 | Limestone. Early Middle Susiana(?) |
| I | 9043 | S22:909 Middle | 74.40 | Gray white transparent stone. Archaic Susiana 3 |
| J | 9502 | R18:906 | 81.66 | Gray sandstone. Protoliterate |
| K | VIII-18 | Q23:802 | 78.30 | Bitumen. Early Susiana |
| L | VIII-19 | Q23:802 | 78.30 | Bitumen. Early Susiana |
| M | 9026 | S18:916 | 81.71 | Black-and-white stone (marble?). Middle Susiana |
| N | N/A | R17:1115 | 83.00 | Black-and-white stone (marble?). Mending original. Protoliterate |
| O | VIII-21 | S22:809 | 76.77 | Yellow stone with white spots and a brown vein. Middle Susiana |
| P | 9051 | S18:918 | 81.12 | Black and white marble(?). Protoliterate |
| Q | VIII-20 | R17:808 | 83.15 | Buff colored stone. Protoliterate |
| R | 5510 | P27:502 | 79.14 | Cream color translucent stone. Middle Susiana |
| S | VIII-17 | R17:807 | 83.80 | Yellow translucent stone. See plate 29:B for photograph. Protoliterate |
| T | 9480 | R19:903 | 79.52 | Greenish gray sandstone. Protoliterate |
| U | IX-53 | S22:809 | 77.21 | Gray sandstone. Late Middle Susiana |
| V | 9141 | S22:816 | 77.19 | Bitumen. Late Middle Susiana |

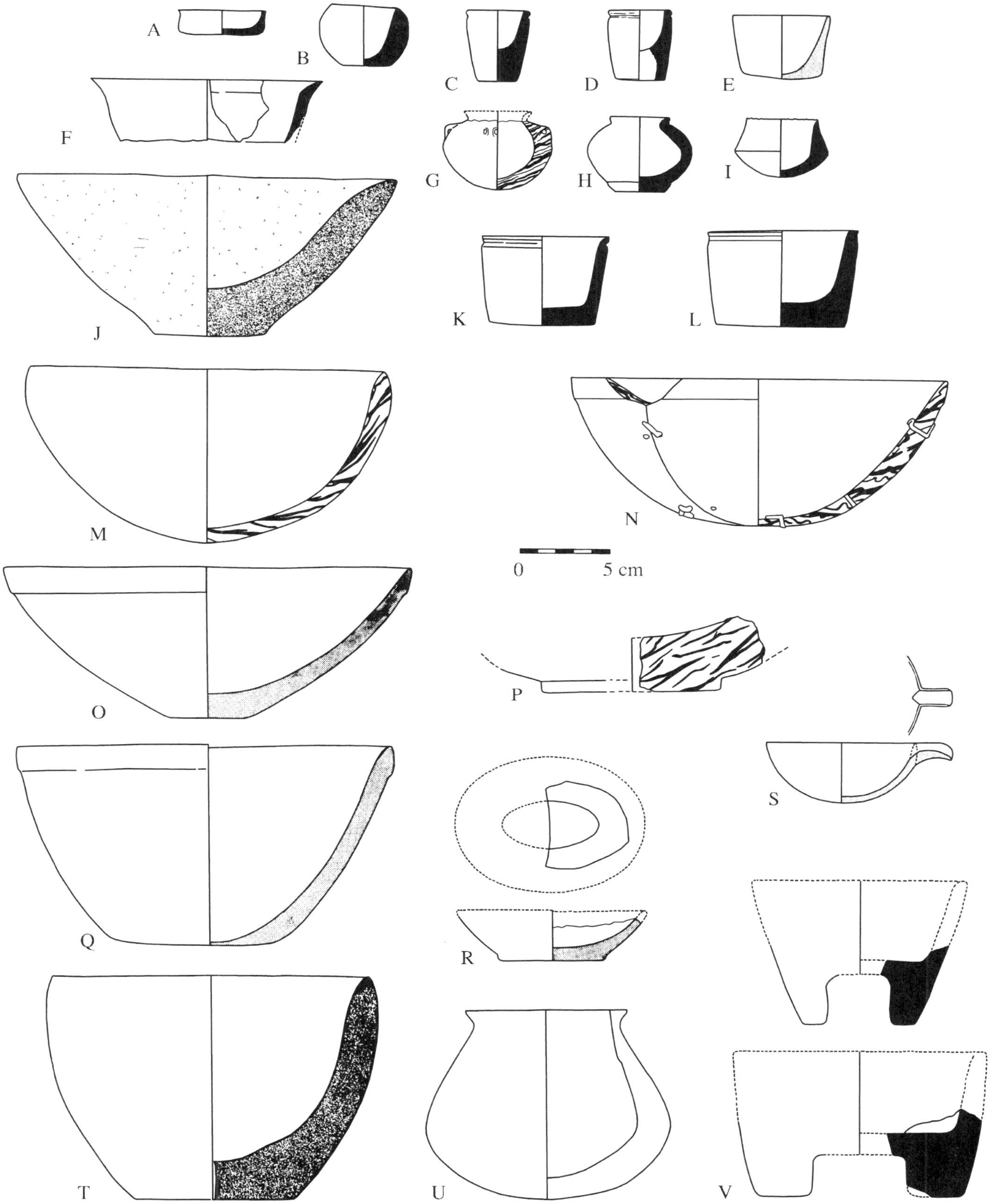


Figure 86. Stone Vessels

Figure 87. Stone Objects and Tools

| | *Registration Number* | *Provenance* | *Elevation* | *Description* |
|---|---|---|---|---|
| A | 9046 | R18:908 | 81.13 | Bitumen-hafted flint tool. Late Middle Susiana |
| B | 9045 | R18:908 | 81.13 | Bitumen-hafted flint tool. Late Middle Susiana |
| C | VI-16 | P22:623 | 80.50 | Stone hoe. Tang covered with bitumen bearing impressions of string. Early Susiana |
| D | VIII-4 | S22:823 | 75.08 | Brownish gray sandstone. Highly polished. Archaic Susiana 3 |
| E | VIII-5 | Q23:802 | 78.29 | Dark gray stone. Polished. Early Susiana |
| F | VIII-6 | Q23:801 | 78.47 | Whitish stone. Polished. Early Susiana |
| G | VIII-72 | Q17:816 | 82.59 | Alabaster miniature jar(?). Protoliterate |
| H | IX-26 | S22:813 | 76.30 | Sandstone mill. Early Susiana |
| I | 8665 | Q23:820 | 79.31 | Ball of bitumen stone. Early Susiana |
| J | VII-53 | Q22:701 | N/A | Stone hoe. Light gray. Smoothed on one side, rough surface on another. Rounded tang. See plate 30:F for photograph. Early Susiana |
| K | 9115 | S22:918 | 76.53 | Stone pestle fragment. Gray stone. Red pigment (ochre?) on the base and around the shaft. Early Susiana |
| L | VI-79 | P22:626 Southwest | 80.85 | Stone hoe. Greenish gray stone. Much secondary retouch. Early Susiana |
| M | VI-84 | Q22:605 | 80.11 | Stone celt. Dark bluish black stone. Polished. Retouched. Early Susiana |
| N | VI-83 | Q22:606 North | 80.35 | Stone celt. Grayish black stone. Pitted surface but smoothed. Early Susiana |
| O | VI-80 | Q22:614 | 80.77 | Stone hoe. Light gray stone. Retouched sides and tang. Early Susiana |

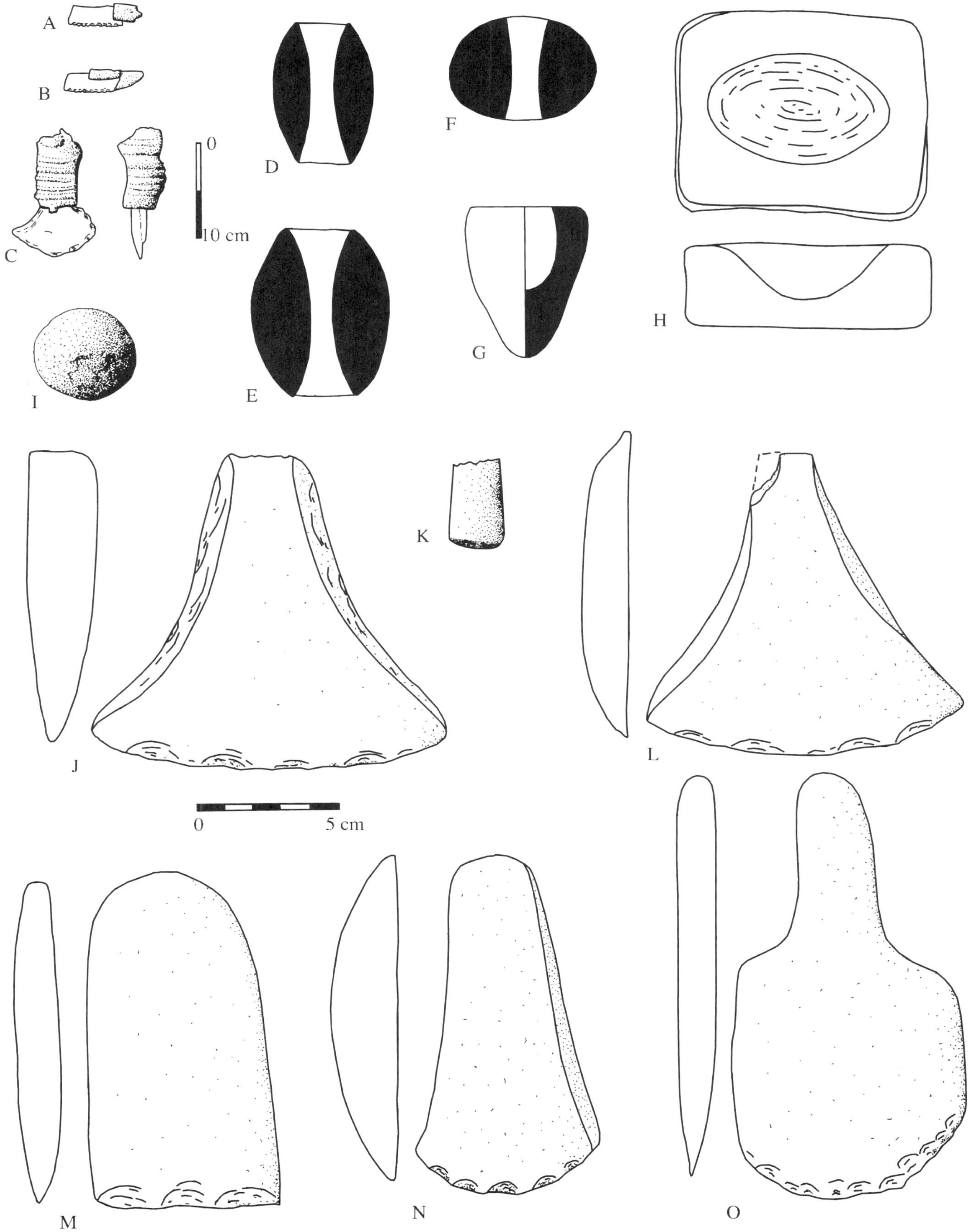


Figure 87. Stone Objects and Tools

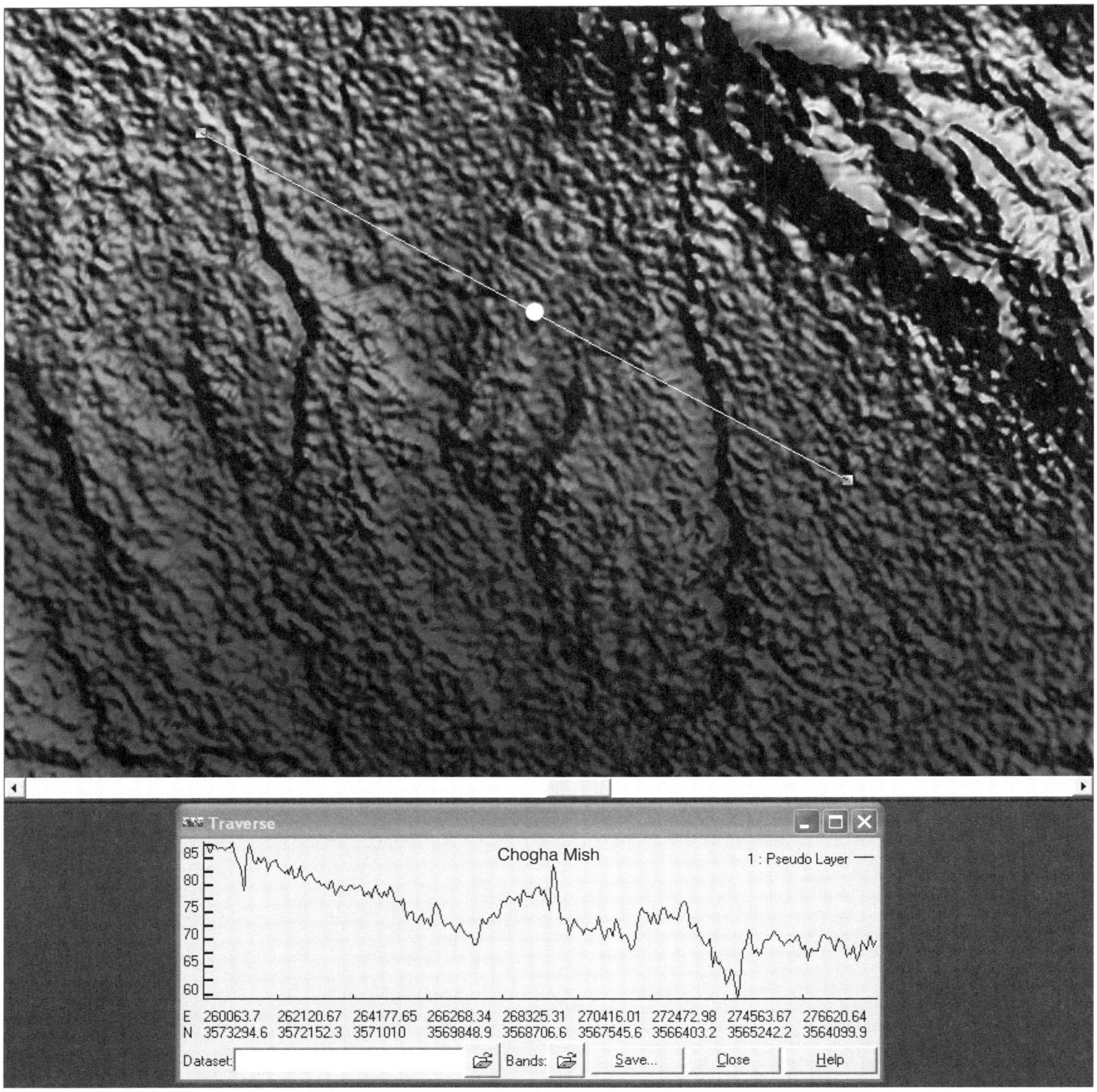


Figure 88. Composite Satellite Image of Central Khuzestan Showing the Elevation of Chogha Mish and Its Immediate Environs (courtesy of Nick Kouchoukos)

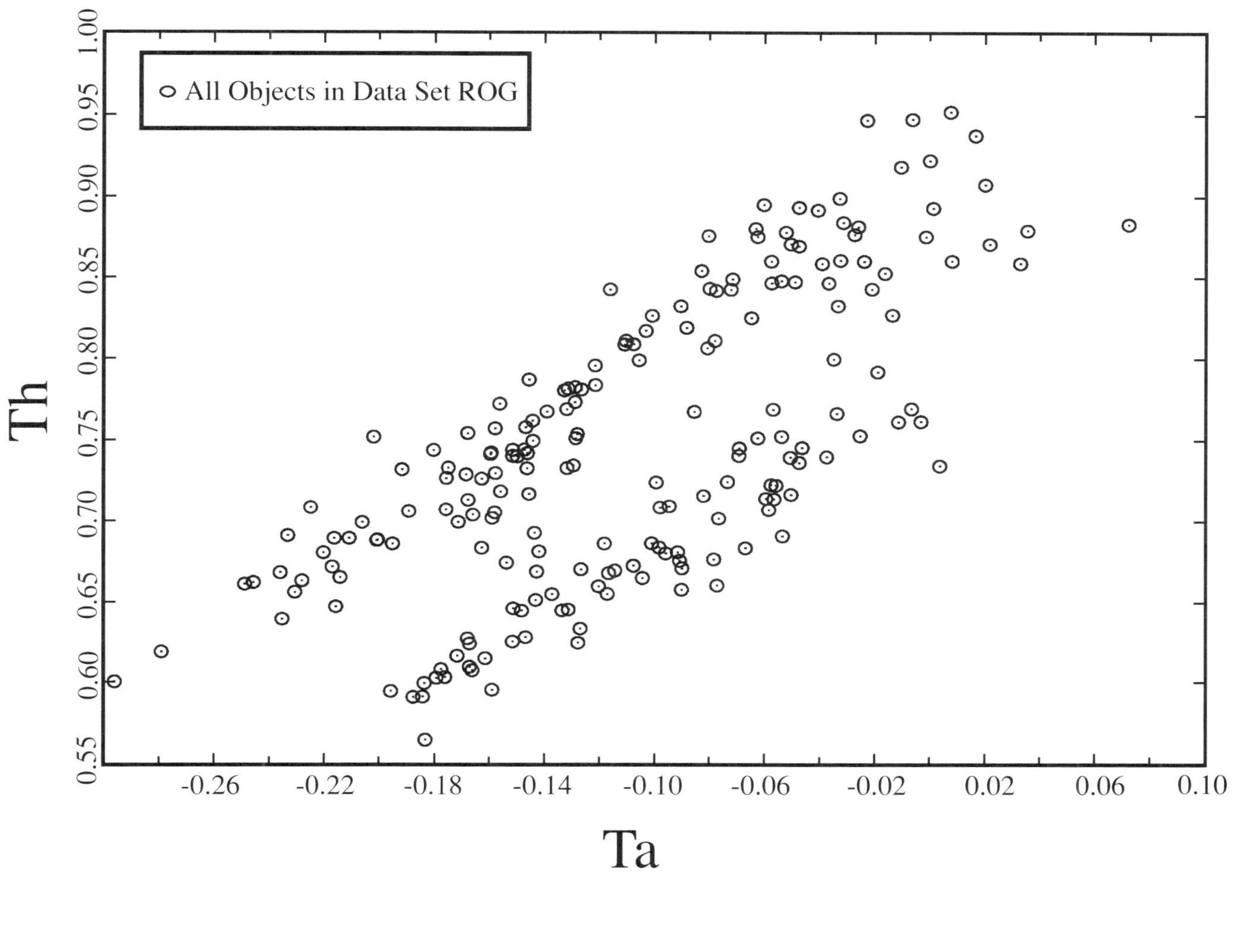


Figure 89. Bivariate Plot of Tantalum (Ta) and Thorium (Th) for All Specimens (200 in number) Studied in These Reports

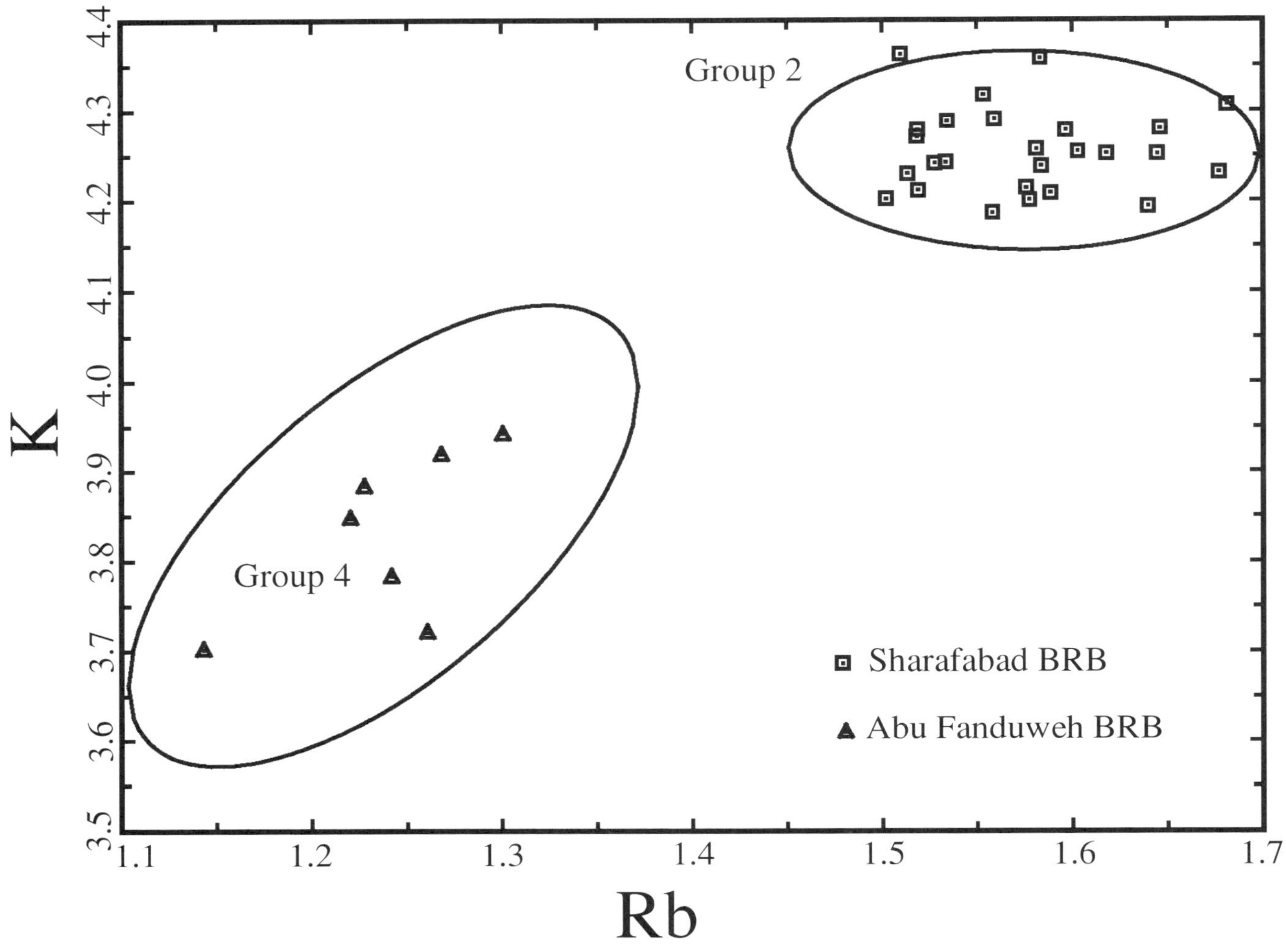


Figure 90. Log Base-10 Projection for Beveled-rim Bowls from Sharafabad (Group 2) and Abu Fanduweh (Group 4). Rubidium (Rb) and Potassium (K) Concentrations. Ellipses Represent a 90% Confidence Interval

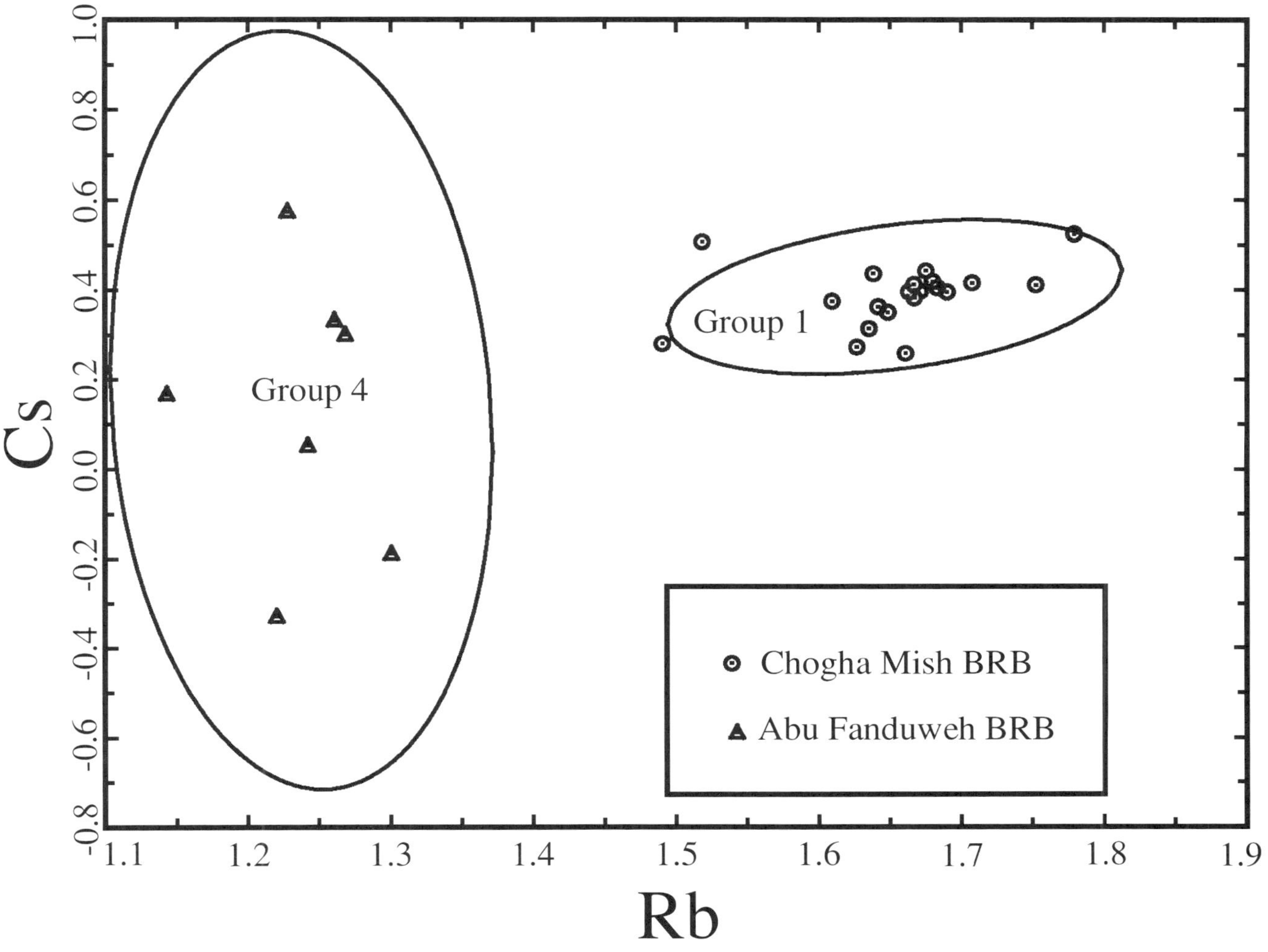


Figure 91. Log Base-10 Projection for Beveled-rim Bowls from Chogha Mish (Group 1) and Abu Fanduweh (Group 4). Rubidium (Rb) and Cesium (Cs) Concentrations. Ellipses Represent a 90% Confidence Interval

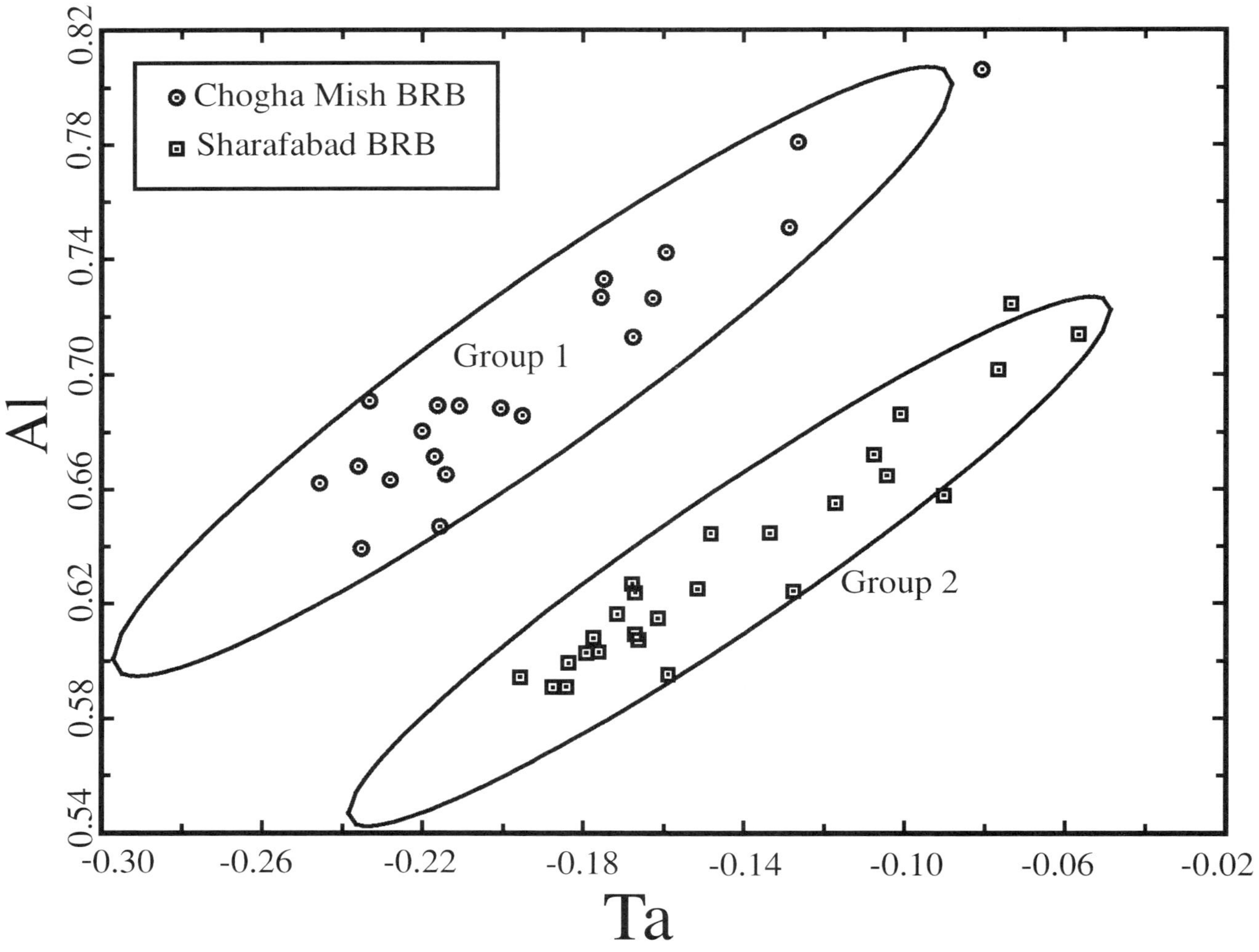


Figure 92. Log Base-10 Projection for Beveled-rim Bowls from Chogha Mish (Group 1) and Sharafabad (Group 2). Tantalum (Ta) and Aluminum (Al) Concentrations. Ellipses Represent a 90% Confidence Interval

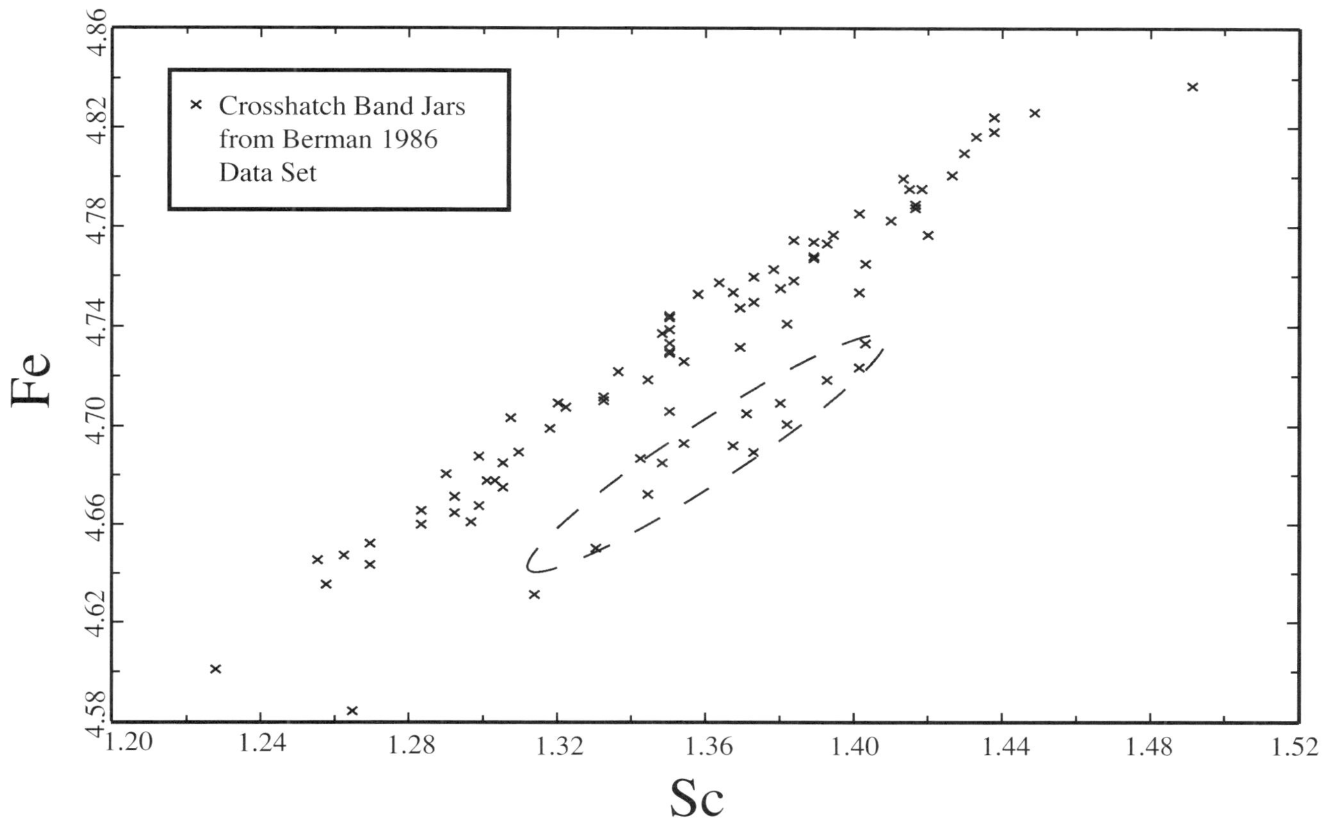


Figure 93. Bivariate Plot of Scandium (Sc) and Iron (Fe) Concentrations Produced for Eighty-seven Crosshatch Band Jars. Scatter-plot Reproduced from Berman (1986: 947). Dashed Ellipse Added by Author for Sake of Clarity (Note elements are not log transformed as in the original publication)

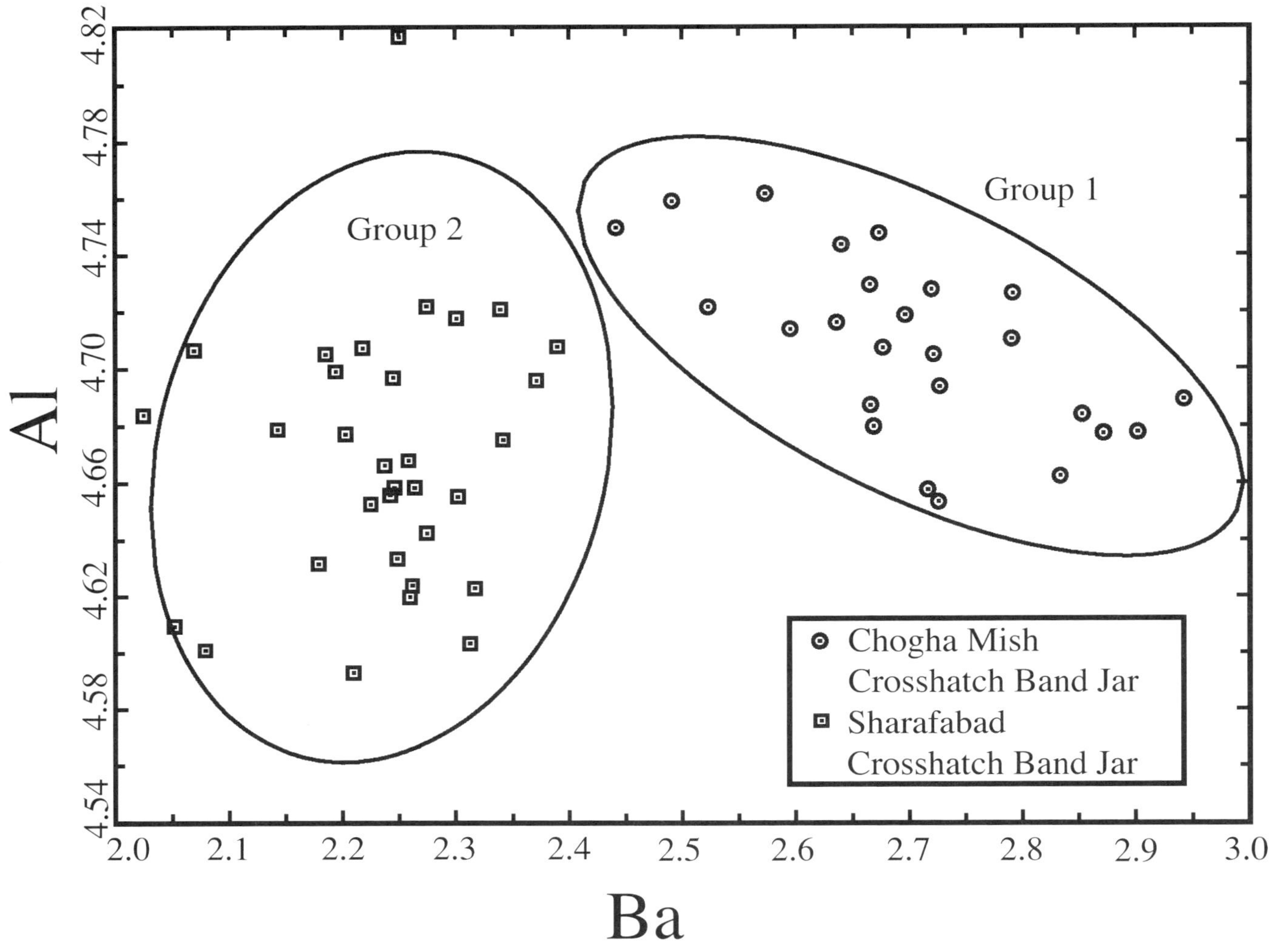


Figure 94. Log Base-10 Projection of Barium (Ba) and Aluminium (Al) Concentrations for Crosshatch Band Jars from Chogha Mish (Group 1) and Sharafabad (Group 2). Ellipses Represent a 90% Confidence Interval

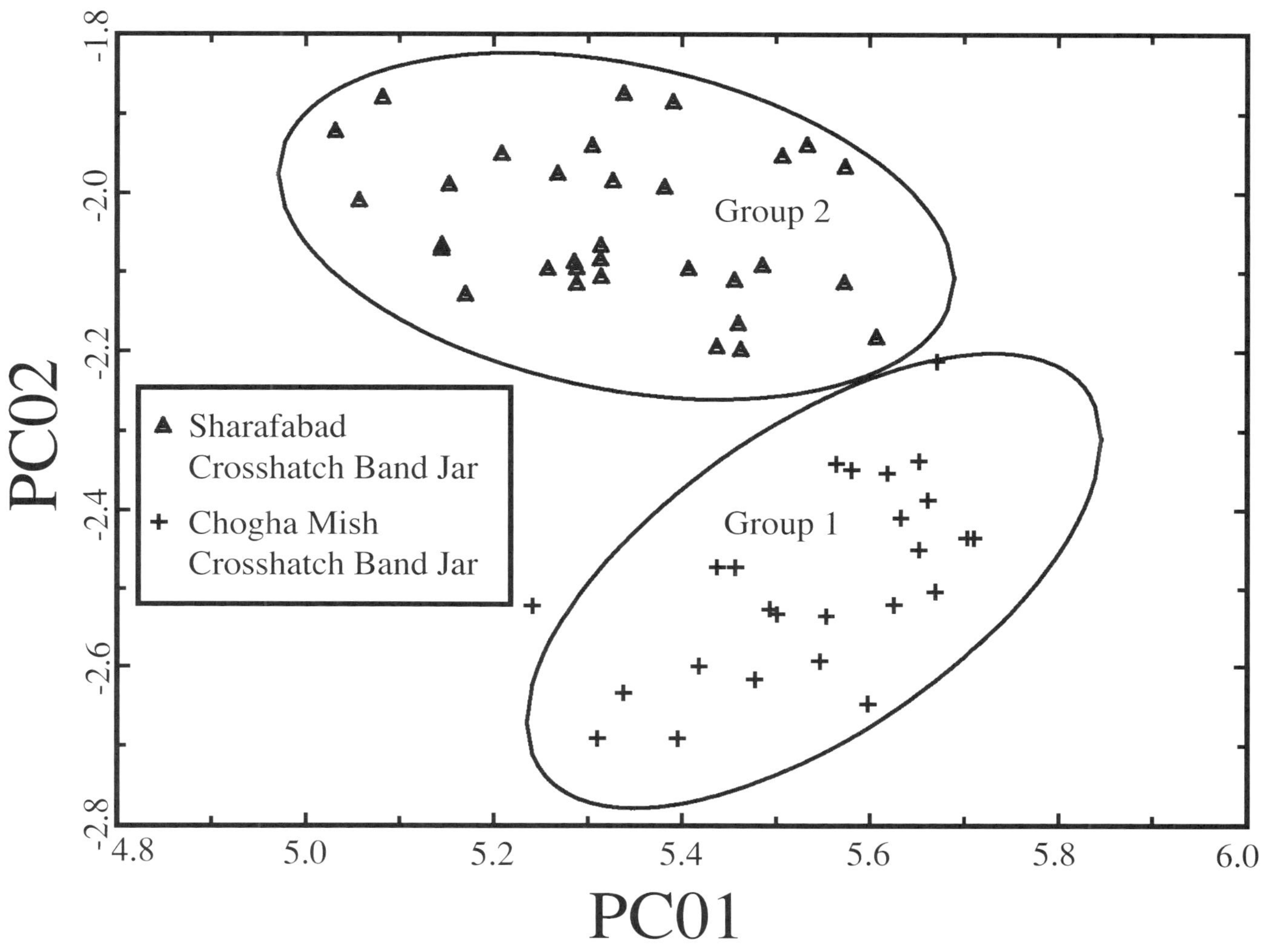


Figure 95. Principal Component Plot of First Two Components Comparing Crosshatch Band Jars from Sharafabad (Group 2) and Chogha Mish (Group 1). Ellipses Represent a 90% Confidence Interval

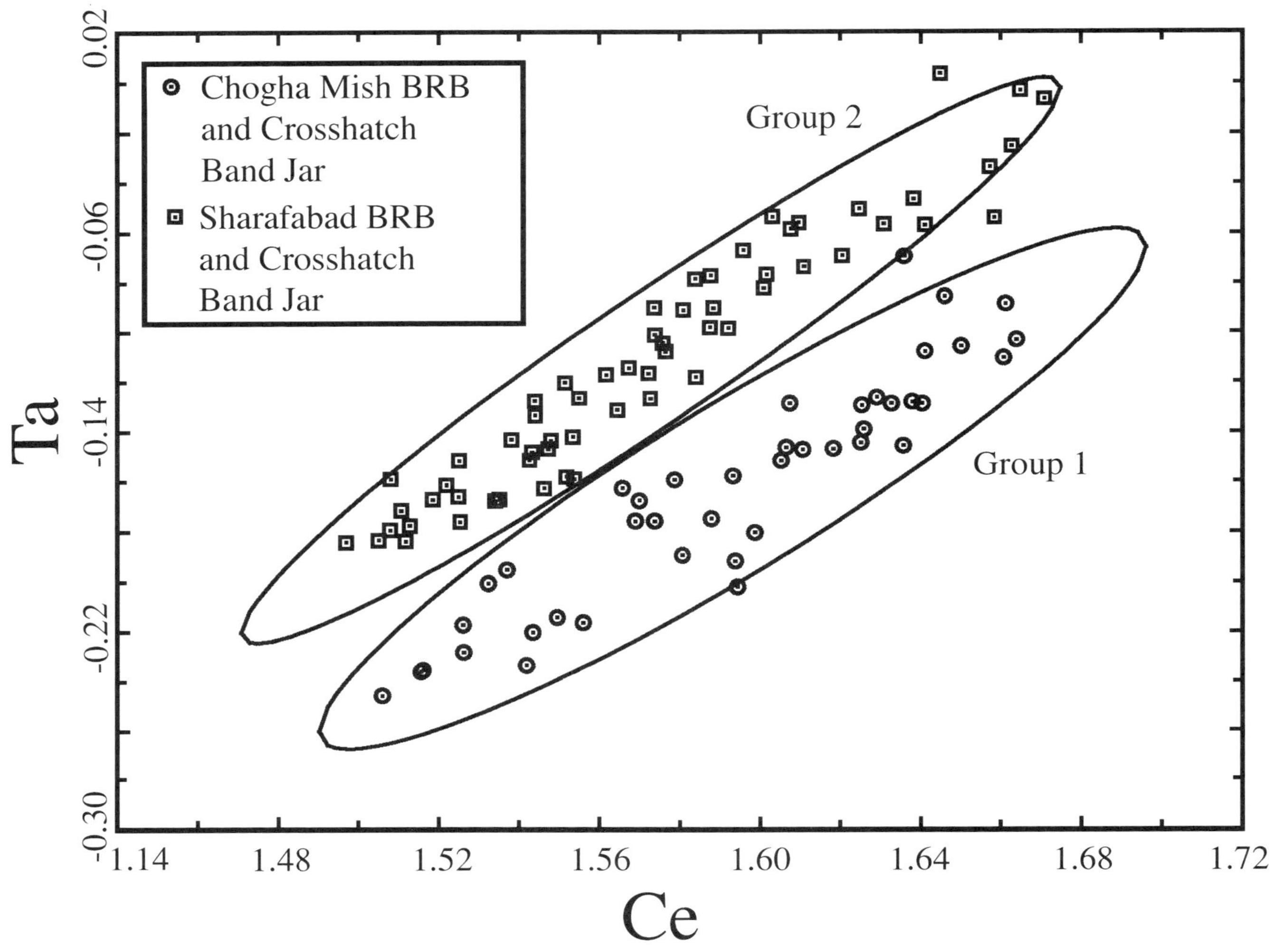


Figure 96. Bivariate Plot of Cesium (Cs) and Tantalum (Ts) for Both Beveled-rim Bowl and Crosshatch Band Jar Specimens from Chogha Mish (Group 1) and Sharafabad (Group 2). Ellipses Represent a 90% Confidence Interval

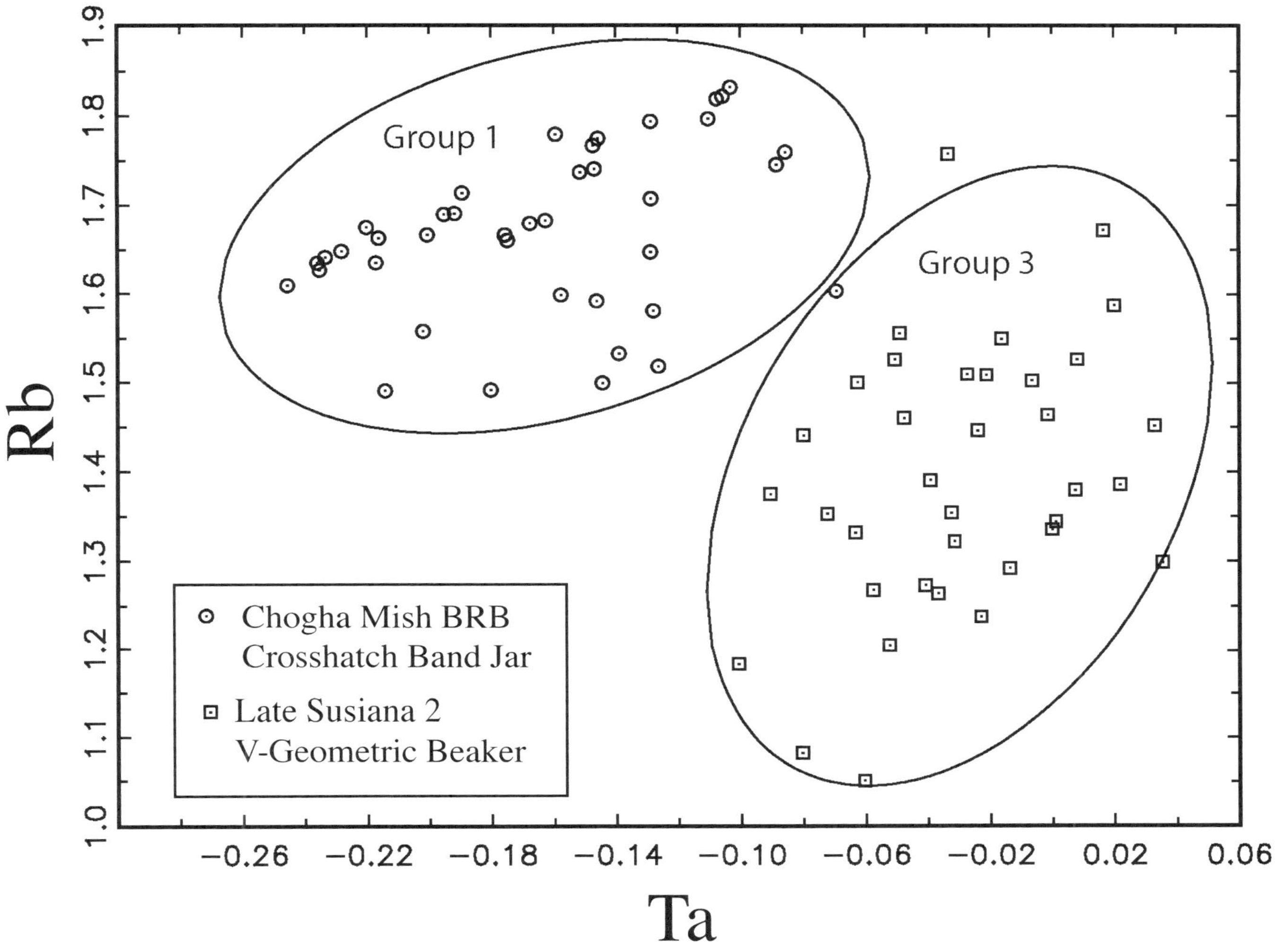


Figure 97. Bivariate Plot of Tantalum (Ta) and Rubidium (Rb) for Beveled-rim Bowl and Crosshatch Band Jar Aggregate Group from Chogha Mish (Group1) and the Combined Late Susiana 2 V-Geometric Beakers (Group 3). Ellipses Represent a 90% Confidence Interval

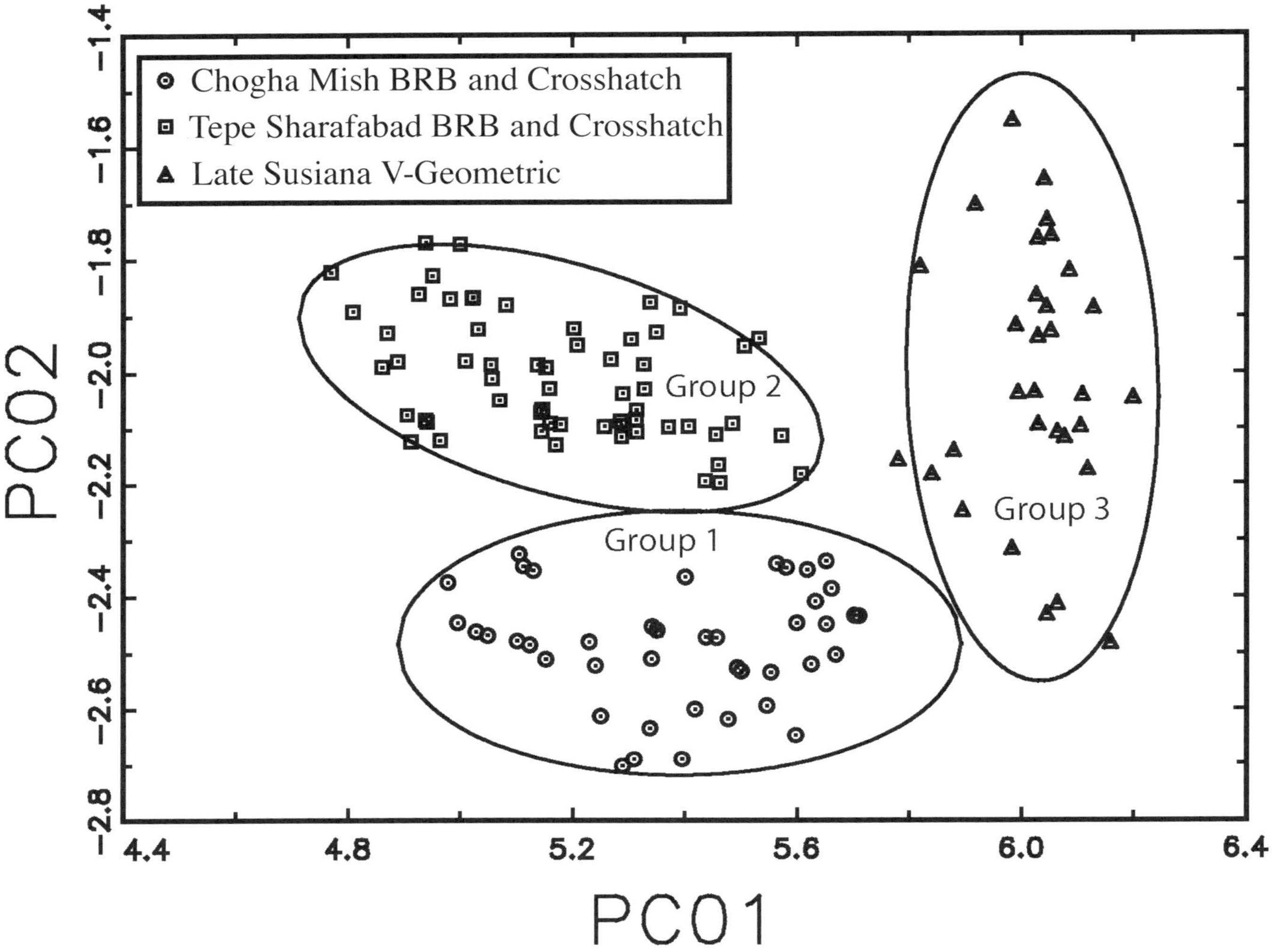


Figure 98. Principle Component Plot of Aggregate Groups Composed of Crosshatch Band Jars and Beveled-rim Bowls from Chogha Mish (Group 1) and Sharafabad (Group 2), as Well as V-Geometric Beakers (Group 3). Ellipses Represent a 90% Confidence Interval

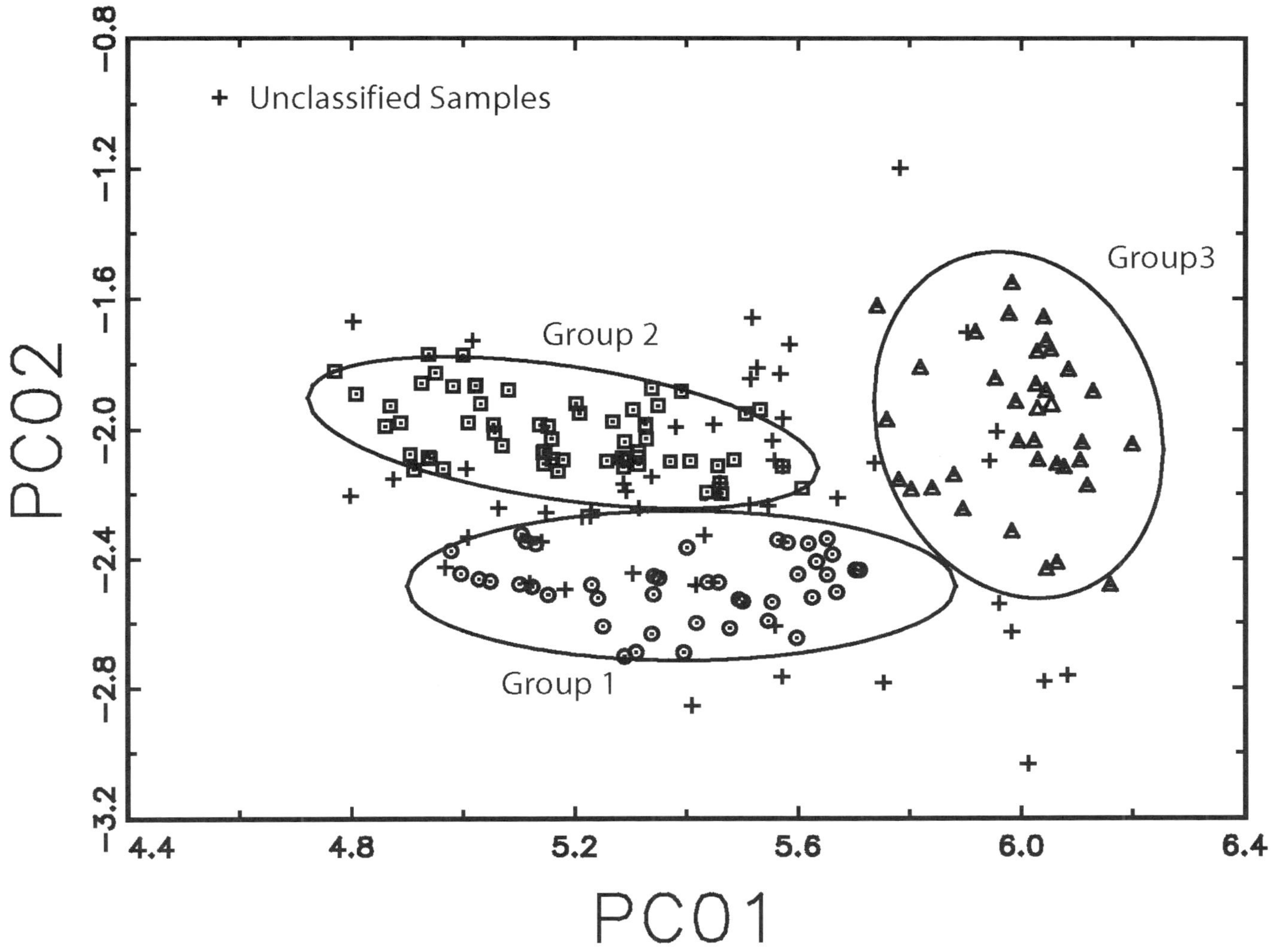


Figure 99. Principle Component Plot of Aggregate Groups Composed of Crosshatch Band Jars and Beveled-rim Bowls from Chogha Mish (Group 1) and Sharafabad (Group 2), as Well as V-Geometric Beakers (Group 3). Projected Against These Three Groups Are All the Unclassified Samples in the Present Data Analysis (fifty-two in number). Ellipses Represent a 90% Confidence Interval

A

B

A: Panoramic View of Chogha Mish, Zagros Mountains in the Background. Photo by Helene J. Kantor.
B: Eastern Face of Old Elamite Fortification Wall

Plate 2

A

B

A: Old Elamite Fortification Wall and Gate, Looking Northwest.
B: Detail of Fortification Wall, Looking Northwest. Photos by Diana Olson-Rasche

A

B

A: Old Elamite Trough in Square N8:1003, Looking East.
B: Old Elamite Pottery Pipes, Looking North (n.b., the sign marking the location is incorrect).
Photos by Diana Olson-Rasche

A

B

A: Old Elamite Water Cistern in Square N9:1003.
B: Inside View of Old Elamite Water Cistern. Photos by Diana Olson-Rasche

A

B

A: Old Elamite Brick Threshold in Square O8:1006, Looking North.
B: Protoliterate Drain in N9:1006, Looking Northwest. Photos by Diana Olson-Rasche

Plate 6

A

B

C

D

A: General View of Gully Cut, Looking Northeast.
B: Early Susiana Brick Pavement and a Circular Structure in Gully Cut, Looking Southeast.
C: Sample of an Early Susiana Impressed Mudbrick from Gully Cut.
D: Archaic Susiana 3 Pottery and Stone Objects in situ in Courtyard Q22:602, Looking North. Photos by Diana Olson-Rasche

A

B

C

D

E

A: Early Susiana Storage Magazines in P22:625, 621, 616S, and 621S, Looking West.
B: Archaic Susiana 3 Stone-filled Hearth in Q22:605, Looking North.
C: Details of Middle Susiana Mudbrick Wall in P22:602E, Looking East. D: Archaic Susiana 3 Long Magazine in Q22:604, Looking South. E: Early Susiana Courtyard in Q23:504/703. Photos by Diana Olson-Rasche

Plate 8

A

B

C

A: Early Susiana Brick Platform in Q23:811, Looking North.
B: Early Susiana Mudbrick Pavement in Q23:803/813, Looking Northwest.
C: Archaic Susiana 3 Pottery Vessels and Other Objects in situ in Q23:802, Looking West. Photos by Diana Olson-Rasche

A

B

C

D

A: Early Susiana Mudbrick-paved Room in Q23:813, Looking Northeast.
B: Details of Early Susiana Mudbrick Wall in Q23:502, Looking Northeast.
C: Archaic Susiana Stone Pavement in Q23:801N, Looking Northeast.
D: Archaic Susiana Circular Hearth in Q23:804, Looking Southwest. Photos by Diana Olson-Rasche

Eastern Wing of the Late Middle Susiana Burnt Building, Looking Northeast. Photo by Diana Olson-Rasche

A

B

A: Room S18:904 of the Late Middle Susiana Burnt Building, Looking South.
B: Top View of Mudbrick Platform in Room R18:901 in Late Middle Susiana Burnt Building.
Photos by Diana Olson-Rasche

A

B

A: Entrance to Courtyard of Protoliterate Tripartite Building, Q17:1111, Looking North.
B: Drain Pipes Leading from Courtyard of Protliterate Tripartite Building, Q16:1105. Looking Southwest.
Photos by Diana Olson-Rasche

A

B

A: Drain Pipes in Alley Q17:1106, South of Entrance to Protoliterate Tripartite Building, Looking Southwest.
B: Gazelle Femur Bones in situ in Vestibule Q17:1005 of Protoliterate Tripartite Building, Looking Southwest.
Photos by Diana Olson-Rasche

A

B

C

D

E

A: Protoliterate Pottery Vessels in situ in P17:1108. B: Cache of Beveled-rim Bowls in R18:920, Looking Northwest. C: Protoliterate Mudbrick Wall and Pottery Vessels in situ in Q17:806, Looking Northwest. D: Top View of Protoliterate Pit R19:903 Filled with Beveled-rim Bowls. E: Top View of Protoliterate Pit Filled with Pottery Vessels.
Photos by Helene J. Kantor

A

B

A: Old Elamite Cistern in N9:1002, Looking Southeast. B: Archaic Susiana 3 Stone-filled Hearth in Q22:605, Looking Northeast. Photos by Diana Olson-Rasche

A

B

C

D

E

A: Early Susiana Room S22:813 in Gully Cut, Looking South. B: Protoliterate, Phase 2, Architecture in Q17:815. C and E: Samples of Archaic Susiana Mudbricks. D: Rocks Mixed with Chipped Stone Blades and Pottery Sherds in Middle Susiana S22:909/919 in Gully Cut. Photos by Helene J. Kantor

A

B

C

D

E

A: Archaic Susiana 3 Grave 806 in Q23:801, Looking East. B: Archaic Susiana 3 Funerary Gifts from Grave 807 in Q23:807, Looking North. C: Archaic Susiana 3 Grave 812 in Q23:809, Looking North. D: Archaic Susiana 3 Grave 811 in S22:824. E: Early Susiana Grave 808 in Q23:802. Photos by Diana Olson-Rasche

A

B

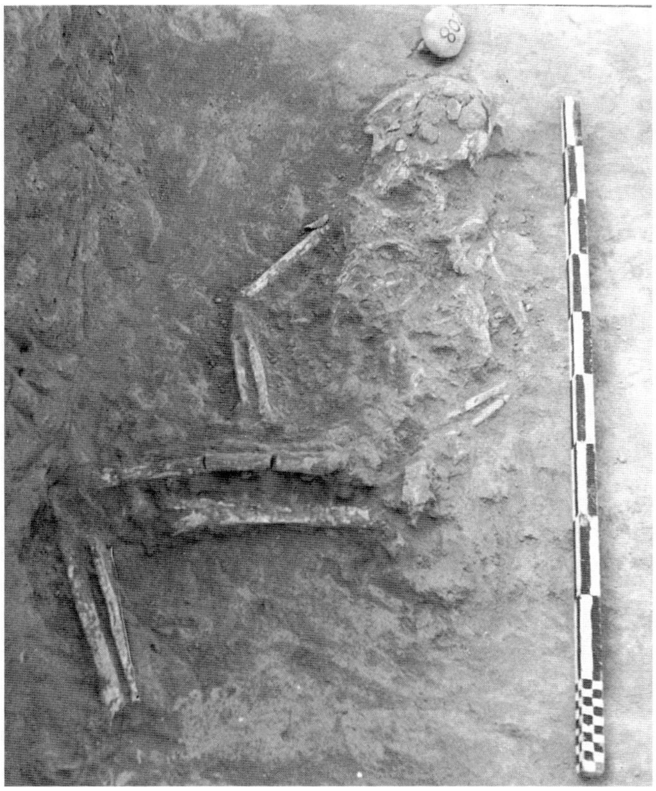

C

D

A: Archaic Susiana 3 Grave in Q23:803, Looking Southwest. B: Archaic Susiana 3 Grave in Q23:803, Looking Northwest.
C: Middle Susiana Grave 802 in P23:607, Looking Northwest. D: Archaic Susiana 3 Grave 804 in Q23:810S.
Photos by Diana Olson-Rasche

Plate 19. Late and Middle Susiana Pottery

| | *Registration Number* | *Provenance* | *Elevation* | *Description* |
|---|---|---|---|---|
| A | 6752 | N10 | High Mound | Buff ware. Sand tempered with scattered small grits. Buff slipped. Dark brown paint. Diameter ca. 30 cm, height 10 cm. Late Susiana 2 |
| B | 9631 | S17:901 | 81.20 | Creamy buff fine ware. No visible inclusions, black paint. See figure 35:A for drawing and scale. Late Susiana 2 |
| C | 6028 | Tr. XXXIII | 77.68 | Fine buff ware. No visible inclusions. Creamy buff slipped. Brown paint. See figure 42:S for drawing and scale. Late Middle Susiana |
| D | 6024 | Tr. XXXIII | 76.40 | Fine buff ware. No visible inclusions. Creamy buff slipped. Brown paint. See figure 42:R for drawing and scale. Late Middle Susiana |
| E | 6040 | S20:601 | 78.33 | Fine buff ware. No visible inclusions. Creamy buff slipped with a greenish tinge. Olive black matte paint. See figure 42:C for drawing and scale. Late Middle Susiana |
| F | 6050 | R20:602 | B.S. | Fine buff ware. No visible inclusions. Creamy buff slipped. Black matte paint. See figure 42:A for drawing and scale. Late Middle Susiana |
| G | N/A | R18:921 | 80.35 | Fine buff ware. No visible inclusions. Creamy buff slipped. Height 6.5 cm. Late Middle Susiana |
| H | 6036 | S20:601 | 0.40 B.S. | Buff ware. Small grit tempered. Smoothed. Light buff slipped. Dark brown paint. Base plate fragment. Height 7 cm. Late Middle Susiana |
| I | 6118 | Tr. XXXIII | 76.32 | Fine buff ware. No visible inclusions. Creamy buff slipped. Brown paint. Height 3 cm. Late Middle Susiana |
| J | 6051 | R20:602 | B.S. | Fine buff ware. No visible inclusions. Creamy buff slipped. Black matte paint. See figure 42:Q for drawing and scale. Late Middle Susiana |
| K | VI-41 | S20:620 | 77.86 | Fine buff ware. Dense. No visible inclusions. Creamy buff slipped. Somewhat shiny surface. Black granulated paint. See figure 41:E for drawing and scale. Late Middle Susiana |
| L | N/A | R18:921 | 80.40 | Fine buff ware. Dense. No visible inclusions. Yellowish buff slipped. Black paint. Height 11 cm. Late Middle Susiana |
| M | 6001 | Tr. XXV | 78.56 | Fine buff ware. No visible inclusions. Creamy buff slipped. Black paint. See figure 41:B for drawing and scale. Late Middle Susiana |
| N | 6751 | High Mound | N/A | Buff ware. Yellowish buff slipped. Very fine sand tempered, occasional small grits. Dark paint. Height 12.5 cm. Late Middle Susiana |

Late and Middle Susiana Pottery

Plate 20. Archaic–Middle Susiana Pottery

| | *Registration Number* | *Provenance* | *Elevation* | *Description* |
|---|---|---|---|---|
| A | VI-74 | P22:606 | B.S. | Buff ware. Greenish buff surface. Grit tempered. Paring marks on base. Thick, dark granular paint, almost vitrified. Wavy lines in reserve in broad wash. Height 9.2 cm. Early Middle Susiana |
| B | VI-102 | P22:611 | 80.57 | Box fragment. Greenish buff ware. Grit tempered. Gritty face. Probably slipped. Dark brown/black paint. Reserved wavy lines. See figure 63:J for drawing and scale. Early Susiana |
| C | VI-38 | P22:606 | 80.85 | Buff ware. Grit tempered. Buff slipped with a greenish hue. Olive black paint, somewhat sunken. See figure 62:G for drawing and scale. Early Susiana |
| D | VI-19/6872 | P22:606 | 80.00 | Buff ware. Grit tempered with some straw. Light orange buff interior and exterior. Dark brown paint. See figure 67:D for drawing and scale. Archaic 3–Early Susiana transitional |
| E | VI-28/A34802 | Q23:810 | 78.25 | Buff ware. Straw tempered. Yellowish buff slipped. Below painted panel, fugitive red wash. Black paint. See figure 70:F for drawing and scale. Matte-painted. Archaic Susiana 3 |
| F | 6164 | Q22:608 | 79.57 | Painted-burnished. Buff ware. Grayish core grades to pale orange buff toward surface. Dense straw tempered. Black paint. See figure 73:A for drawing and scale. Archaic Susiana 1 |
| G | VI-43 | P23:602 | 81.50 | Dense greenish buff ware. Sand and grit tempered. Matte, granular dark paint, mostly flaked off. Wavy lines incised into broad wash. See figure 44:P for drawing and scale. Early Middle Susiana |
| H | 7002 | G28:703 South | 76.98 | Standard buff ware. Sand tempered. Creamy buff slipped. Dark brown paint. See figure 39:B for drawing and scale. Early Middle Susiana |
| I | 7061 | G29:703 | B.S. | Standard buff ware. Sand tempered. Brown paint. See figure 50:F for drawing and scale. Early Middle Susiana |

Archaic–Middle Susiana Pottery

Plate 21. Archaic, Early, and Middle Susiana Pottery

| | *Registration Number* | *Provenance* | *Elevation* | *Description* |
|---|---|---|---|---|
| A | 9739 | S22:923 | 75.22 | Buff ware. Grit tempered. Buff slipped. Black paint. Reserved wavy lines. Height 11 cm. Early Susiana |
| B | 9783 | S22:919 | 76.61 | Buff ware. Grit tempered. Buff slipped. Black paint. Reserved wavy lines. Height 9.3 cm. Early Susiana |
| C | N/A | S22:825 | 76.30 | Buff ware. Grit tempered. Buff slipped. Black paint. Reserved wavy lines. Height 8.5 cm. Early Susiana |
| D | 9677 | R18:910 | 80.34 | Standard buff ware. Sand tempered with some grits. Buff slipped. Dark brown granulated paint. See figure 46:C for drawing and scale. Early Middle Susiana |
| E | 9312 | S22:909 | 75.00 | Matte-painted. Buff ware. Straw tempered. Buff slipped. Very smoothed. Black paint. See figure 70:A for drawing and scale. Archaic Susiana 3 |
| F | 6462 | P22:609 | 81.40 | Buff ware. Grit tempered. Buff slipped. Black paint. Reserved wavy lines. Height 6.8 cm. Early Susiana |
| G | 6462 | P22:609 | 81.40 | Interior of F |
| H | VIII-39 | P22:606 | 81.73 | Buff ware. Grit and chaff tempered. Gritty face, smoothed, light red core grading to buff toward surface. Height 16.4 cm, diameter ca. 30 cm. Early Susiana |
| I | 11212 | S22:929 | 74.90 | Yellowish buff ware. Straw tempered with some sand. Vessel made of vertical layers. Length 14 and 10 cm. Archaic Susiana 1 |
| J | 9512 | S22:912 | 73.72 | Buff ware. Sand tempered. Buff slipped. Smoothed. Brown paint. See figure 68:B for drawing and scale. Archaic Susiana 3 |
| K | 9370 | S22:916 | 73.70 | Buff ware. Sand tempered. Buff slipped. Smoothed. Brown paint. See figure 68:B for drawing and scale. Archaic Susiana 3 |

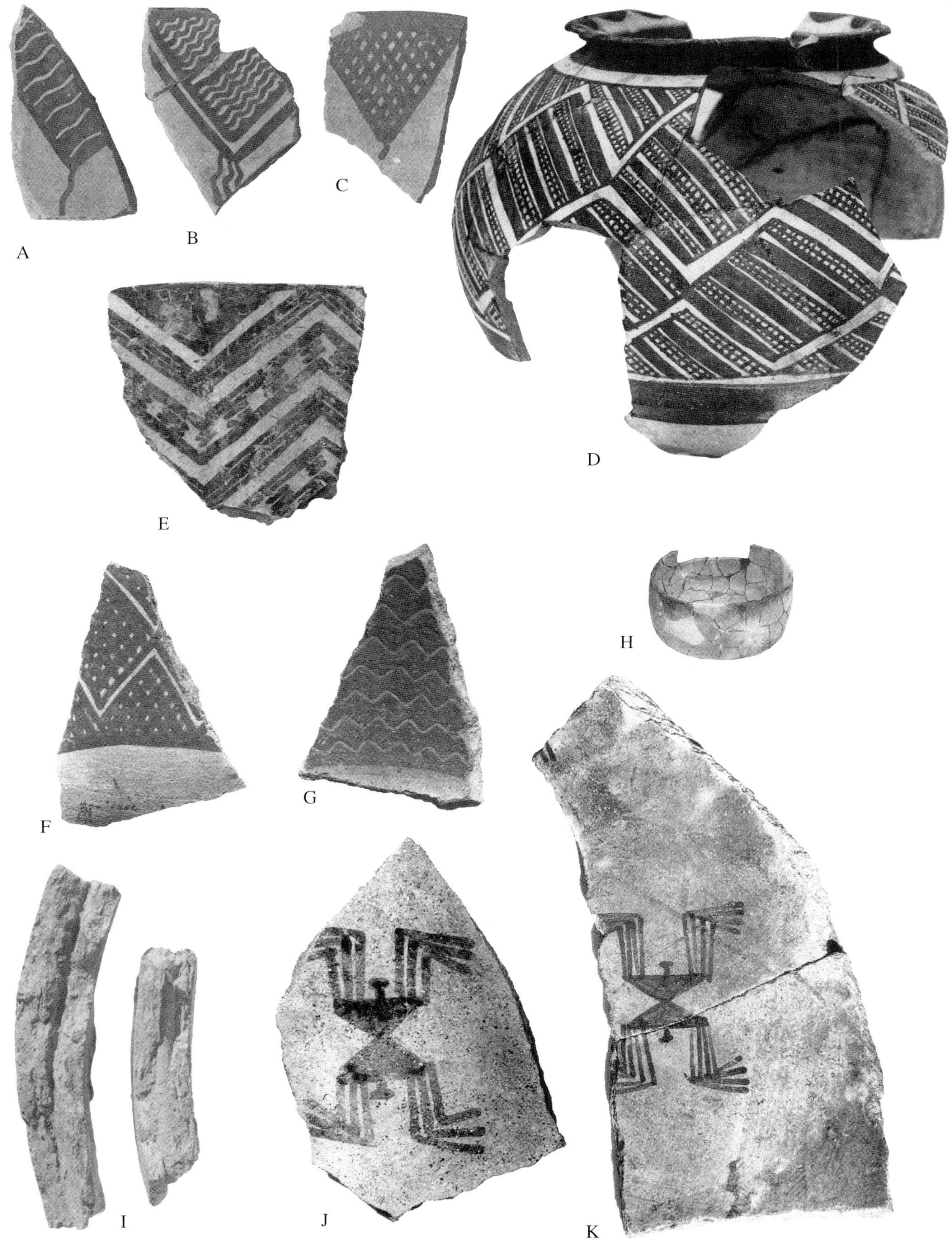


Archaic, Early, and Middle Susiana Pottery

Plate 22. Seals and Sealings

| | *Registration Number* | *Provenance* | *Elevation* | *Description* |
|---|---|---|---|---|
| A | IX-20 | High Mound | N/A | Pink stone stamp seal. Scale 1:1. Late Susiana 2 |
| B | IX-23 | P17:1102 | 81.08 | Gray stone button seal. Loop handled. Scale 1:1. Protoliterate |
| C | 9906 | N/A | N/A | Baked-clay stamp seal. Drill hole in the middle. Late Susiana(?). See figure 76:B for drawing and scale |
| D | IX-25 | P17:1102 | 81.08 | Black stone stamp seal with the impression of a foot drilled in. Scale 1:2. Protoliterate |
| E | N/A | P17:1102 | 81.60 | Unbaked clay "tablet" with one circular depression. 3.5 cm long. Protoliterate |
| F | IX-17 | P17:1102 | 81.64 | Slightly baked clay tablet or token with two large and one small depressions. Plain back. Scale 1:2. Protoliterate |
| G | N/A | P17:1102 | 81.60 | Unbaked clay "tablet" with at least two large oval and two small circular depressions. Length 5.5 cm. Protoliterate |
| H | IX-26 | P17:1102 | 81.90 | Unbaked numerical tablet. No seal impression on either side. Scale 1:2. Protoliterate |
| I | IX-24 | P17:1102 | 81.90 | Unbaked numerical tablet. No seal impression on either side. Scale 1:2. Protoliterate |
| J | 9904 | S18:902 | 81.14 | Sealing with four impressions of a decorated cylindrical object (cylinder seal?) tapering slightly at each end. Highly unusual. See figure 76:CC for drawing and scale. Protoliterate |
| K | 9905 | S18:902 | 81.14 | See above H and figure 76:FF for drawing and scale. Protoliterate |

Seals and Sealings

Plate 23. Sealings

| | *Registration Number* | *Provenance* | *Elevation* | *Description* |
|---|---|---|---|---|
| A | 10092 | R16:801 | 82.80 | Jar sealing fragment. Baked clay with no visible inclusions. Three impressions of a cylinder seal design with a quadruped, intertwined snakes, and a lion(?). Length 4.2 cm. Protoliterate |
| B | 7389 | R17:704 West | 83.49 | Bale sealing fragment. Unbaked clay with some sand. Two impressions of a cylinder seal with "net" design. Height 4.5 cm. See figure 76:BB for drawing. Protoliterate |
| C | 81186 | R16:801 | 82.80 | Jar sealing fragment. Baked clay with no visible inclusions. Cylinder seal impression of a crouching feline. Length 6.2 cm. Protoliterate |
| D | 81185 | R16:801 | 82.75 | Jar sealing fragment. Baked clay with no visible inclusions. Cylinder seal impression of a marching feline(?). Length 3.5 cm. Protoliterate |
| E | N/A | R16:801 | 82.75 | Jar sealing fragment. Baked clay with no visible inclusions. Cylinder seal impression of a walking animal. Height 5.2 cm. Protoliterate |
| F | 4658 | K22:402 | N/A | Jar sealing fragment. Baked clay. Stamp seal impression of a twelve-petaled rosette. Length 2.8 cm. Late Susiana/Protoliterate |
| G | 10093 | R16:803 | 82.45 | Door sealing fragment with rope and peg impressions. Baked clay with some sand inclusions. Length 3.2 cm. Protoliterate |
| H | 10916 | R16:803 | 82.45 | Door sealing fragment. Baked clay with no visible inclusions. Cylinder seal impression of a quadruped. Height 6.2 cm. Protoliterate |

Sealings

Plate 24. Sealings and Tokens

| | *Registration Number* | *Provenance* | *Elevation* | *Description* |
|---|---|---|---|---|
| A | 11243 | P17:806 | 83.28 | Crescent-shaped clay token. Width 1.5 cm. Protoliterate |
| B | 11245 | Q17:806 | 83.30 | Jar sealing fragment. Baked clay with no visible inclusions. Cylinder seal impression of a workshop. Length 5.2 cm. Protoliterate |
| C | 41030 | S17:404 | 82.28 | Horned conical clay token. Length 2.5 cm. Protoliterate |
| D | 9873 | P17:806 | 81.15 | Bulla with cylinder seal impression of workshop. Length 6.8 cm. See figure 76:N for drawing. Protoliterate |
| E | 81189 | Q17:806 | 83.28 | Conical clay token. Length 2 cm. Protoliterate |
| F | 7387 | R17:714 | 82.65 | Clay ball with equatorial and polar cylinder seal impressions of bearers and animal file. See figure 76:AA for drawing. Diameter 5 cm. Protoliterate |

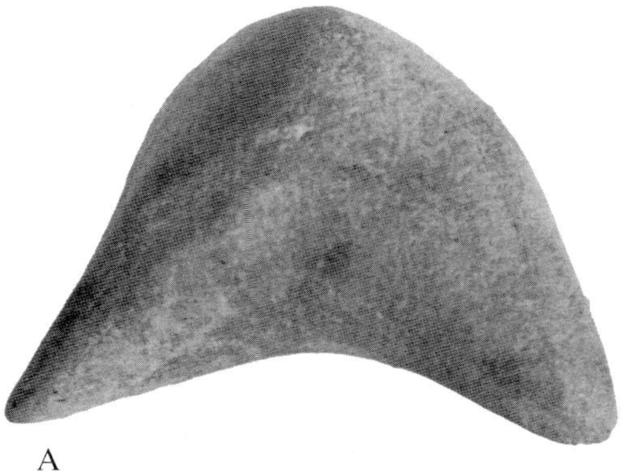

A

B

C

D

E

F

Sealings and Tokens

Plate 25. Miscellanea

| | *Registration Number* | *Provenance* | *Elevation* | *Description* |
|---|---|---|---|---|
| A | VI-100 | S22:601 | 74.38 | Baked-clay object (token?) with incised and impressed patterns. Length 5.9 cm, width 4.9 cm. See figure 76:EE for drawing and scale. Archaic Susiana |
| B | VI-13 | S20:609 | 75.05 | Bone needle. See figure 85:B for drawing and scale. Early Susiana |
| C | — | — | — | A group of tokens and labrets. Top row, left to right: VII-58, VII-33, VII-55, VII-6, VII-7, VII-9; middle row: VII-57, VII-1, VII-8, VII-11; bottom row: VII-10, VII-61, VII-65. Note VII-9 and VII-65 are chessman figurines. Scale not available |
| D | VI-32 | P22:605 | 80.95 | Bracelet made of bituminous stone. See figure 81:K for drawing and scale. Early Susiana |
| E | VI-33 | P22:605 | 80.95 | Bracelet made of bituminous stone. See figure 81:J for drawing and scale. Early Susiana |
| F | N/A | Q22:602 | 78.80 | Stone ball with incised mark. Scale 1:1. Early Susiana |
| G | VII-90 | Q23:713 | 76.98 | Baked-clay token(?). See figure 77:K for drawing and scale. Early Susiana |
| H | VI-8 | P22:601 | 82.55 | Baked-clay spindle whorl. See figure 83:G for drawing and scale. Early Susiana |
| I | VI-88 | L22:504 | 81.16 | Sinker/weight stone. Khakhi stone with natural hole. 10.4 × 9.1 cm. Middle Susiana |
| J | VI-86 | Tr. XIII | 82.24 | Stone socket/sinker. Light brown stone. Highly polished. Bored from both sides. Length 15.5 cm. Middle Susiana |
| K | VI-89 | R17:407 | 1.20 B.S. | Discoidal socket/weight. Light gray stone. Bored from both sides. 10.7 × 10.1 cm. Protoliterate |
| L | VI-87 | Tr. XIII | 0.95 B.S. | Stone sinker(?). Mottled buff gray stone with natural hole. Length 11.8 cm. Middle Susiana |

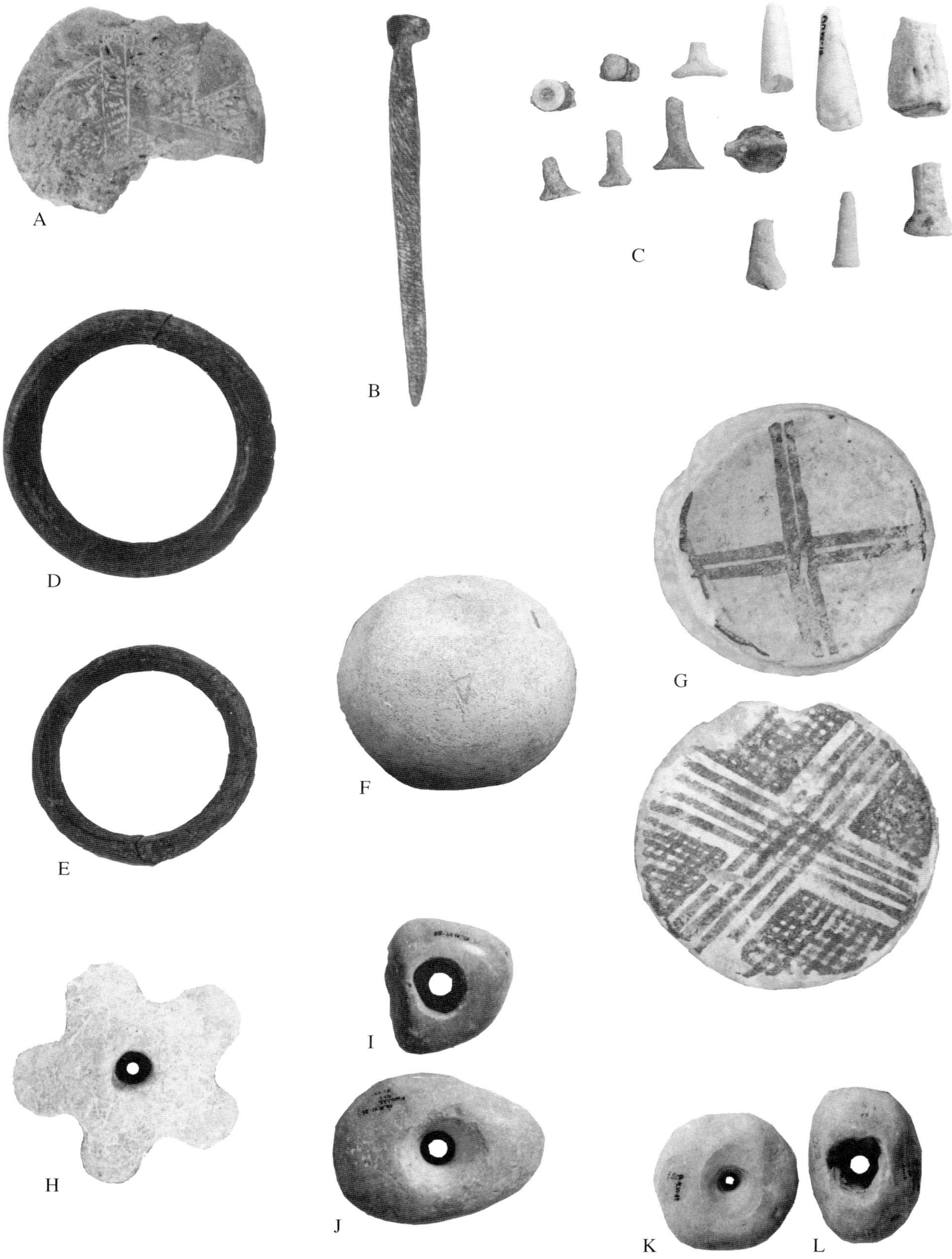


Miscellanea

A

B

C

A: Protoliterate Bone Female Figurine (IX-111) (height 3.5 cm). B and C: Old Elamite Goat-handled Cup (IX-112) of Bituminous Stone (height of goat handle, 16.80 cm; height of vessel, 14.25 cm; diameter at base, 7.30 cm). Photos by Helene J. Kantor

Plate 27. Archaic–Middle Susiana Figurines

| | *Registration Number* | *Provenance* | *Elevation* | *Description* |
|---|---|---|---|---|
| A | VIII-85 | S22:826 | 74.66 | Baked-clay head of a human figurine. Buff clay, no visible inclusions. Dark paint. The eyes and the nose are molded. The head may have originally been elongated (representing elongated skull seen in actual skeletal evidence from Chogha Mish; see *Chogha Mish* I, pl. 69), but the upper part is broken. If originally the whole body was attached to the head, the height of the figurine may have reached to over 30 cm. For a possible reconstruction, see frontispiece; see figure 78:C for drawing and scale. Early Susiana |
| B | VIII-60 | S22:823 | 76.35 | Stone figurine of a boar. Light brown stone with white dots. Perforated rump suggests it may have been used as pendant. See figure 80:F for drawing and scale. Archaic/ Early Susiana |
| C | VIII-68 | Q23:820 | 79.28 | T-shaped figurine. Black stone with white veins. Incised line around the base. Facial features indicated with incised lines. Height 2.6 cm, width 3.2 cm. Archaic Susiana 1–2 |
| D | VI-5 | P22:606 | 81.42 | Yellowish buff clay. Sand tempered. Red washed. See figure 78:B for drawing and scale. Early Susiana |
| E | VI-2 | P23:601 | B.S. | Baked-clay figurine of a bull or ram. Dense, sandy brownish buff clay. Height 4.2 cm, length 6.7 cm. Middle Susiana |
| F | VIII-1 | S22:808 | 75.77 | Baked clay figurine of a seated female. The head is comparatively low. The head is triangular and a deep incision splits it in two equal parts. The whole face consists of three blobs of clay presumably representing the nose and cheeks. The breasts are highly exaggerated. See figure 79:B for drawing and scale. Early Susiana |

Archaic–Middle Susiana Figurines

Plate 28. Archaic–Early Susiana Figurines

| | *Registration Number* | *Provenance* | *Elevation* | *Description* |
|---|---|---|---|---|
| A | 8695 | S22:808 North | 74.99 | Torso of a baked-clay female figurine. Reddish buff ware, no visible inclusions. Black paint. Unlike the majority of the Early Susiana figurines, this example is made with a naturalistic flavor. The painted strokes on the breasts may represent tattoos. For a possible reconstruction, see frontispiece; see figure 78:E for drawing and scale. Height 5 cm. Early Susiana |
| B | 8174 | S22:827 | 74.30 | Baked-clay waist and body of a female figurine. Buff ware, grit tempered. Black paint. See figure 78:H for drawing and scale. Height 9.2 cm. Archaic/Early Susiana |
| C | 8043 | S22:823 North | 75.74 | Baked-clay waist and lower body of a female figurine. Buff ware. Grit and sand tempered. Probably slipped. Black paint. See figure 78:G for drawing and scale. Early Susiana |
| D | VIII-84 | S22:823 North | 75.74 | Mid-section of a female figurine. Baked clay. Buff color, sand tempered. Smoothed. Black paint. Pubic area shown with excised lines. For a possible reconstruction, see frontispiece; see figure 78:A for drawing and scale. Early Susiana |
| E | N/A | S22:912 East | 75.55 | Baked-clay figurine. Sand and grit tempered. Black paint. Height 6 cm. Early Susiana |
| F | 9040 | S22:912 East | 74.46 | Baked-clay human figurine. Buff ware, no visible inclusions. Upper part of the body missing. The cloth on the lower part is decorated with four sunken panel and incisions. Traces of red paint on the raised parts of the lower body. Height 3.7 cm. See figure 78:F for drawing and scale. Archaic Susiana |
| G | 9138 | S22:909 | 73.70 | Buff ware, sand tempered. Head missing. Pleated skirt(?) with band holding pleats together. Height 2.8 cm. Archaic Susiana 2 |
| H | 9138 | S22:909 | 73.70 | Profile of G |
| I | 9008 | S22:909 South | 75.13 | Chessman figurine. Buff ware. Brownish buff surface. Some sand inclusions. See figure 79:J for drawing and scale. Archaic Susiana 2 |
| J | VI-3 | S22:601 | 74.93 | Baked-clay waist and lower body of a female figurine. Yellowish buff ware. Grit tempered. Black paint. See figure 78:F for drawing and scale. Early Susiana |
| K | 9039 | S22:913 | 74.54 | Head and torso of a highly stylized human figurine. Baked clay, buff ware, no visible inclusions. Black paint. See figure 78:D for drawing and scale. Archaic Susiana 3 |

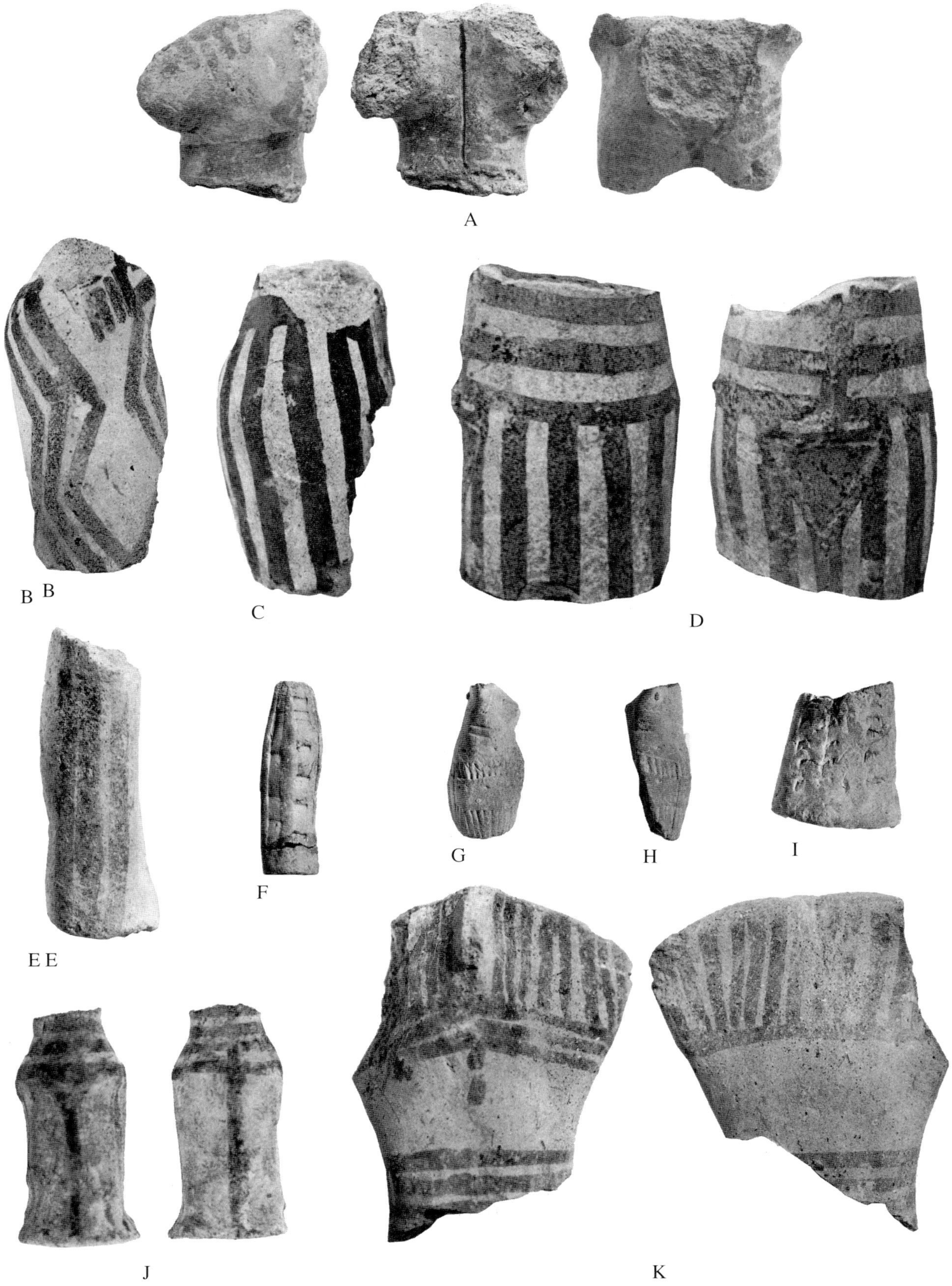


Archaic–Early Susiana Figurines

Plate 29. Miscellanea

| | *Registration Number* | *Provenance* | *Elevation* | *Description* |
|---|---|---|---|---|
| A | X-1 | Q17:1001 | 82.65 | Libation(?) vessel in the shape of a hedgehog. Bristles indicated with incised lines. See figure 34 for details and drawing. Protoliterate |
| B | VIII-17 | R17:807 | 83.80 | Trough-spouted bowl. Yellowish translucent stone. Diameter 9 cm, height 3.5 cm. Protoliterate |
| C | N/A | P17:1108 | 81.70 | Standard buff ware. Height 45 cm. Protoliterate |
| D | 6765 | P22:620 | 81.43 | Bitumen fragments with basket impression. Scale N/A. Early Susiana |
| E | 6765 | P22:620 | 81.43 | Fragment of a basket bitumen coating/shell. Width ca. 15 cm. See plate 30:C for another view. Early Susiana |

A

B

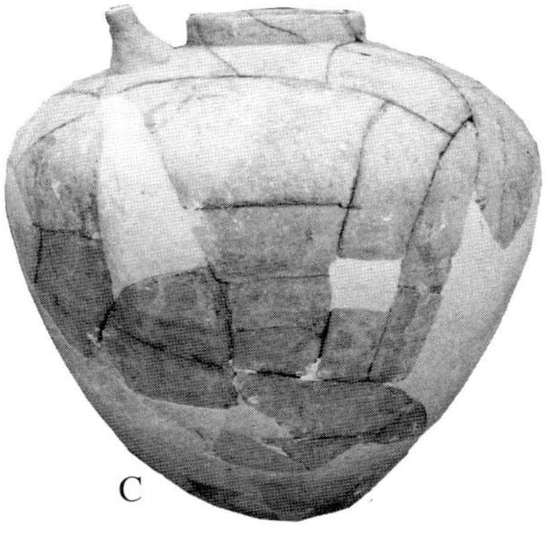

C

D

E

Miscellanea

Plate 30. Miscellanea

| | *Registration Number* | *Provenance* | *Elevation* | *Description* |
|---|---|---|---|---|
| A | VII-51 | P22:622 | 80.94 | Hafted flint hoe with bitumen and rope impressions. Height 11.8 cm. Early Susiana |
| B | VII-52 | Q22:702 | 79.11 | Hafted flint hoe with bitumen and rope impressions. Height 16 cm. Early Susiana |
| C | 6765 | P22:620 | 81.43 | Fragment of a basket bitumen coating/shell. Width ca. 15 cm. See plate 29:E for another view. Early Susiana |
| D | VI-27 | Q22:602 | 80.47 | Stone mill made of a medium- to large-grained sandstone. The other side, E, has a round depression. Length 37.6 cm, width 22.3 cm. Early Susiana |
| E | VI-27 | Q22:602 | 80.47 | Back view of D |
| F | VII-53 | Q22:701 | N/A | Stone hoe. Length 10.8 cm. Grayish flint. Back side rough. Early Susiana |
| G | VII-21 | G27:701 | 81.62 | Stone hoe. Length 16.5 cm. Grayish flint. Back side rough. Early Susiana |
| H | VII-50 | Q22:702 | 79.11 | Stone hoe with bitumen stain on handle. Rough back. Length 9.5 cm. Early Susiana |
| I | VI-26 | Q22:602 | 8047 | Stone pestle. Light brownish gray limestone. Length 20.5 cm. Early Susiana |
| J | VI-92 | R22:401 | 2.2 B.S. | Stone pestle. Greenish brown sandstone. Length 13.5 cm. Early Susiana |
| K | VI-90 | Tr. XIII | N/A | Stone pestle. Grayish green stone. Length 14 cm. Early Middle Susiana |
| L | VI-91 | Gully Cut | Surface | Stone pestle. Grayish green stone. Length 18.5 cm. Early Susiana |
| M | VI-93 | P22 | Surface | Stone pestle. Gray stone. Length 18.5 cm. Middle Susiana |
| N | VI-15 | Q22:602 North | 80.41 | Stone pestle. Dark gray stone. Length 24.5 cm. Early Susiana |

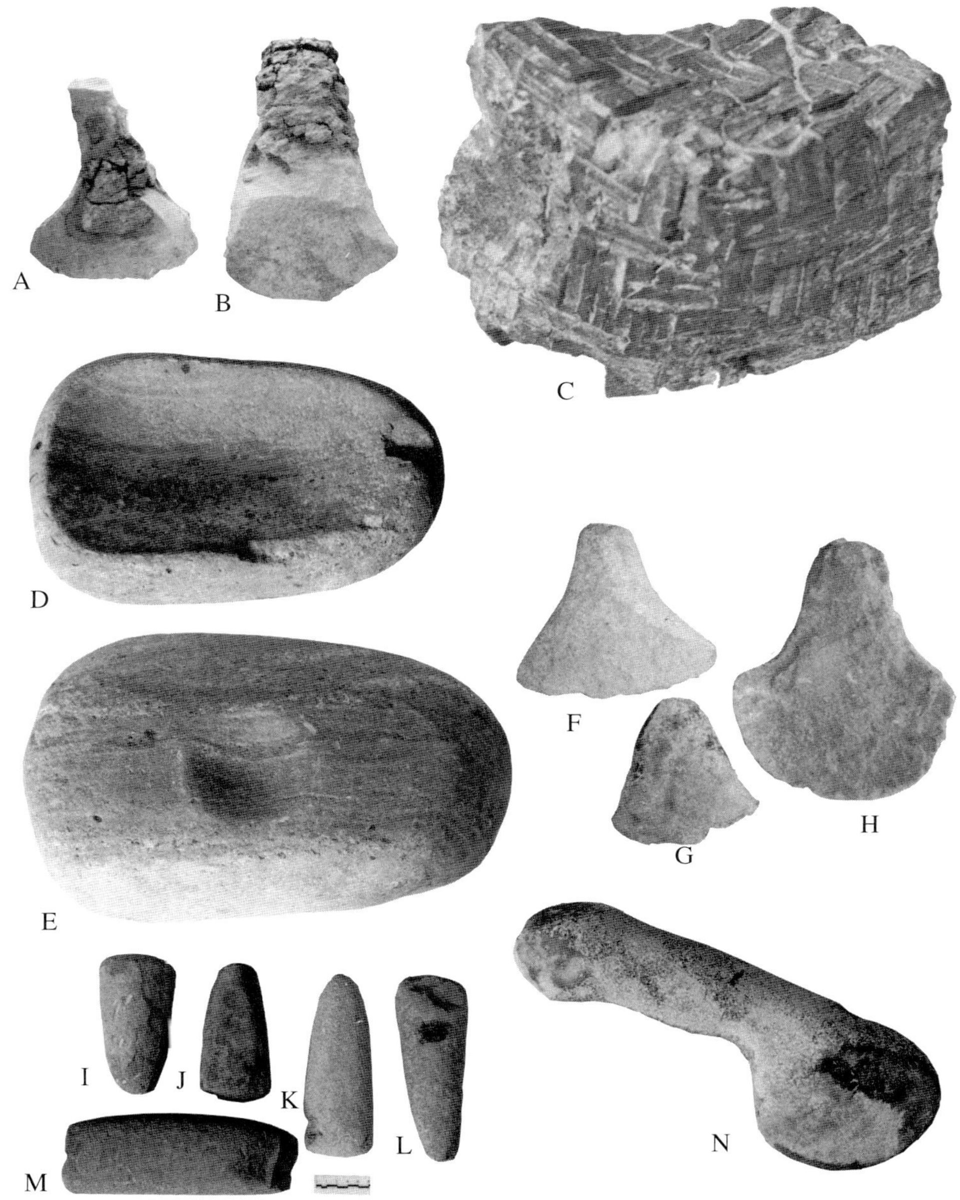


Miscellanea

Plate 31

Bakhtiyari Mobile Pastoralists Camping on East Area at Base of High Mound at Chogha Mish, Winter 2004